BIBLIOGRAPHY
OF
WILLIAM BLAKE

The Committee on Publications of The Grolier Club certifies that this copy of A Bibliography of William Blake, by Geoffrey Keynes, is one of an edition of two hundred and fifty copies printed on specially made paper at the Chiswick Press, London. The press-work was completed in the month of November in the year 1921.

[Colophon for the Original Edition]

GLAD DAY
Colour-print, about 1794

A BIBLIOGRAPHY

OF

WILLIAM BLAKE

BY

GEOFFREY KEYNES

M.A. M.D. F.R.C.S.

NEW YORK: THE GROLIER CLUB
OF NEW YORK
1921

L. C. Catalog Card Number 22-14055.

Reprinted with the permission of Geoffrey Keynes
KRAUS REPRINT CO.
A U.S. Division of Kraus-Thomson Organization Limited
New York
1969

Printed in U.S.A.

TO

WILLIAM BATESON F.R.S.

PREFACE

WILLIAM BLAKE has already, in the minds of many people, taken his place as one of the greatest figures in the history of English art. Some may consider this claim extravagant, but few will deny that his contributions to painting, poetry, and philosophy are of the first importance. This Bibliography, therefore, needs no further justification. It is not a mere catalogue of Blake's works and of books connected with him, but it is intended to serve as a foundation upon which future studies, whether biographical or critical, may be securely built. It records, wherever possible, ascertained fact, and seeks to avoid adding to the large amount of fiction and conjecture which has already collected around his life and personality.

The book was begun in December, 1908, when I was an undergraduate at Cambridge, and it represents therefore the slow accumulations of thirteen years. The greater part of the work had been done by August, 1914, so that during the four and a half years of war the task could be limited to noting new publications or fresh copies of Blake's works as they appeared. Since the armistice the work has been cast into its final shape, the prefaces have been written, and revisions made. It is difficult for an amateur bibliographer to arrive quickly at a standard form for his entries, particularly when, as in the present case, it has to be frequently changed to suit the varying nature of the material. Much of the work has been written and re-written three times, but even so it is to be feared that many imperfections still remain. No candid bibliographer will ever lay claim either to completeness or to absolute accuracy, and indulgence is therefore begged in advance for the omissions and mistakes which will surely be found here.

In the course of compiling this Bibliography, I have received so much valuable help from others, and have met with such uniform courtesy from the owners of Blake's works that I find it impossible to make individual acknowledgements. To a few friends, however, my obligations are so great that they must be specifically mentioned. At two different stages in its development the work has been submitted to Dr. John Sampson of Liverpool University, and his outspoken criticism has been of the very greatest value. Several fundamental modifications have been made at his suggestion, and, if the work does not even now reach the heights of scholarship which his greater experience would demand, he has at least saved it from remaining at a much lower level.

Miss Henrietta C. Bartlett is another friend without whose help one of the main sections of the book could never have been completed. In attempting to describe all the existing copies of the Illuminated Books it at once became evident that much work would have to be done in the United States of America, since so many of the books had already found their way to that country. This task was generously undertaken by Miss Bartlett and most competently carried out by her. She has made herself responsible for the descriptions of all the copies of these books in Mr. W. A. White's remarkable collection, and of many others in the H. E. Huntington Library and elsewhere. I cannot adequately thank her for what she has done. To Mr. White himself I owe a debt of gratitude for the great kindness with which he has always met my requests for information and help. He has contributed in many ways to the making of this volume, which I am glad to think forms in some measure a record of his deep interest in the subject.

Frequent mention will be found in these pages of the name of Mr. W. E. Moss of Hilfield Park, Hertfordshire. During the last ten years his wide knowledge of Blake and his large collection of books connected with him have afforded me much help.

Finally, I wish to acknowledge the assistance received during the last two years from Mr. S. Foster Damon, who has described for me a few of the Illuminated Books, and has supplied me with long lists of references gathered in the course of writing his own important work on Blake, soon to be published in America. He has also enabled me to make some corrections of detail. I can only hope that my work may be of as much use to him as his has been to me.

In choosing the illustrations I was necessarily limited by the kind of material with which I was dealing. I also wished to avoid reproducing those of Blake's works which are already very well known. In this I have been greatly assisted by the readiness with which many private owners have placed unpublished material at my disposal. Special thanks are due to General Archibald Stirling of Keir, and to Mr. T. H. Riches of Shenley, Hertfordshire, for having entrusted to the lithographers their unique copies of *Jerusalem* and *The Marriage of Heaven and Hell* for so long a period as three months in order that the reproductions in colour might be made.

My acknowledgements would not be complete without some reference to the work of the craftsmen to whose skill and patience the excellence of the press-work and the illustrations is due. To their representative, Mr. F. J. Newbery, General Manager to Messrs. Charles Whittingham and Griggs, Ltd., I wish to express my warm thanks for the unflagging care and attention that have been bestowed on the work.

The paper used for this book was specially made by Messrs. Hodgkinson and Co. at Wookey Hole in Somerset. Their factory has been established for more than a century at this spot, originally chosen on account of the exceptional purity of the water springing from the limestone of the Mendips.

The Members of the Publication Committee of The Grolier Club have left almost every detail to my own discretion, and no writer can ever have been subjected to less interference from those providing the means of printing his work. I cannot properly express my appreciation of the generous scale upon which they have authorized the production of this book.

GEOFFREY KEYNES.

London.
November, 1921.

ABBREVIATIONS

SWINBURNE: William Blake, A Critical Essay. By A. C. Swinburne. London. 1868. (No. 273.)

GILCHRIST: Life of William Blake. By Alexander Gilchrist. New Edition. London. 1880. 2 vols. (No. 285.)

RUSSELL, *LETTERS*: The Letters of William Blake. Edited by A. G. B. Russell. London. 1906. (No. 339.)

RUSSELL, *ENGRAVINGS*: The Engravings of William Blake. By A. G. B. Russell. London. 1912. (No. 369.)

SYMONS: William Blake. By Arthur Symons. London. 1907. (No. 348.)

WMR: The Poetical Works of William Blake. Edited by W. M. Rossetti. London. 1874. (No. 142.)

JS: The Poems of William Blake. [Edited by] Joseph Skipsey. London. 1885. (No. 145.)

EY: The Works of William Blake. Edited by E. J. Ellis and W. B. Yeats. London. 1893. 3 vols. (No. 150.)

LH: Selections from the Writings of William Blake. [Edited by] Laurence Housman. London. 1893. (No. 152.)

WBY: Poems of William Blake. Edited by W. B. Yeats. London. 1893. (No. 151.)

SAMPSON, 1905: The Poetical Works of William Blake. [Edited by] John Sampson. Oxford. 1905. (No. 166.)

SAMPSON, 1913: The Poetical Works of William Blake. Edited by John Sampson. Oxford. 1913. (No. 192.)

EJE: The Poetical Works of William Blake. Edited by E. J. Ellis. London. 1906. 2 vols. (No. 170.)

PIERCE, 1915: Selections from the Symbolic Poems of William Blake. [Edited by] F. E. Pierce. New Haven. 1915. (No. 196.)

GROLIER CAT.: Catalogue of Books, etc. Exhibited at the Grolier Club [New York]. 1905. (No. 674.)

NAT. GAL. CAT.: The National Gallery, British Art. Catalogue of Loan Exhibition of Works by William Blake. London. 1913. (No. 676.)

MANCHESTER CAT.: The Manchester Whitworth Institute. Catalogue of a Loan Exhibition of Works by William Blake. London. 1914. (No. 677.)

CONTENTS

ILLUSTRATIONS

Illustrations

FACING
PAGE

REPRODUCTIONS IN THE TEXT

I. BLAKE'S WORKS

BIBLIOGRAPHICAL PREFACE

A. *MANUSCRIPTS*

THE writings of Blake that still exist in manuscript are of peculiar interest in that they are for the most part works that were not issued by him in any other form, either typographical or etched. Those works which were actually published, such as the *Poetical Sketches*, the greater part of the *Descriptive Catalogue*, *The French Revolution*, *The Marriage of Heaven and Hell*, and most of the other illuminated books have not survived in manuscript. Frederick Tatham, a friend of Blake in his last years, obtained possession of his effects after Mrs. Blake's death,* and it is said that his scruples as an " Irvingite Angel " led him to destroy a large quantity of the unpublished works. This story has been readily believed, for the obscurity of some of Blake's published works has suggested to his would-be interpreters that there must have been other writings which would have supplied the key to the symbolism of those that have survived. There is, however, little or no evidence that such writings ever existed, and a study of the way in which Blake's mind worked leads to the belief that the key to the symbolism existed only in his own brain. A number of " Works lost or conjectural " are collected in an appendix to the present section, but the references to some of them are vague and inconclusive, and it is hardly justifiable to assume that we owe their loss to Tatham's alleged act of destruction.

Blake's circumstances were not such that he could amass a large bulk of manuscript material. As the years passed he became burdened with the growing accumulation of copper plates for his illuminated books, and it is probable that, at each of the several changes of house that he made, he destroyed the manuscripts of those works that were already printed or

* John Linnell denied that Mrs. Blake *bequeathed* her stock to Tatham; see Story's *Life of Linnell*, i, 241.

engraved, and, therefore, of no further use to him. Tatham admitted to Dr. Garnett that he had sold what he had of Blake's work, but denied that he had destroyed anything, and we possess no good evidence for disbelieving his word. It is clear that Blake himself did not readily destroy any writing which he had been unable to use in his published works. Thus the early manuscripts known as *The Passions* and *An Island in the Moon* have survived, and we should not be greatly the poorer had they been destroyed. The second of these is chiefly of interest in that it contains early drafts of some of the *Songs of Innocence*.

Of Blake's mystical works two exist in manuscript, and neither of these was published by him. The first, *Tiriel*, is probably the earliest of his so-called Prophetic Books; the second, *The Four Zoas*, is the most important of Blake's manuscripts known to exist. Unlike *Tiriel*, which has no drawings, it is illustrated on almost every page in the manner of the illuminated books. Blake kept this manuscript by him for many years, and seems to have abandoned any intention he may have had of engraving it, for long passages from it were incorporated in his later poems, *Milton* and *Jerusalem*. Both these manuscripts are now in the British Museum.

Next to *The Four Zoas* in order of importance comes the *Rossetti MS.*, which seems to have served Blake as a commonplace book during two periods of his life, first before 1793, and then again during the Felpham period, 1800-1803. It contains a large amount of poetry, including some of the best of the shorter poems, together with epigrams and topical pieces, which throw much light on Blake's mental life during the periods to which the manuscript belongs. There are also in it some prose pieces, including part of the *Descriptive Catalogue*, and sketches for many of the designs in the illuminated books are scattered through it.

The collection of ten poems known as the *Pickering MS.* is of obscure origin and purpose. The poems appear to have been copied out by Blake from his rough drafts which, with the exception of two in the *Rossetti MS.*, have now disappeared. Possibly these were all that Blake thought worth preserving out of an accumulation of manuscript material which he then destroyed. It may have been this collection that was lent by Crabb Robinson to Wordsworth.

The remaining manuscripts are of less importance, being fragments or short pieces. One of these, containing additional passages for the poem known as "The Everlasting Gospel," is certainly of interest, but it has not yet been printed, and I have been unable to obtain permission from the present owner to produce it here. The two fragments entitled *Genesis* are of widely different contents. The earlier is a valueless piece of blank verse, which is certainly not of Blake's composition, but may be a translation from Klopstock. The other is the beginning of an illustrated edition of the Bible, which Blake undertook towards the end of his life, and probably intended to execute in the same manner as the illuminated books. The lines to Mrs. Anna Flaxman in the lately re-discovered volume of illustrations by Blake for Gray's *Poems* have more biographical than literary interest, but a description of the volume is included here as it does not seem to fall naturally into place elsewhere. Finally, the manuscripts of the lines "A Fairy leapt upon my knee" and "On the Publication of Klopstock's Messiah" can only be imperfectly described; the present whereabouts of the originals is not known to me, but it is probable that they are still in existence.

B. *ANNOTATIONS IN BOOKS*

It is probable that Blake's limited means did not permit him to be at any time the owner of a very large number of books. Those, however, that he did possess he read with great care, and a considerable proportion of them bear the evidence of this in the notes he made on their pages. Blake's feelings, whether of approval or disapproval, were always strong, and he liked to record in a book as he read it the impressions he received, or the arguments with which he wished to refute opinions expressed by the author. A number of books with these annotations have survived to the present day, and they make a most valuable and interesting record of Blake's views on various aspects of art, ethics, philosophy, and religion. These annotations fall naturally into a class by themselves, and it is less artificial than at first sight appears to separate them from Blake's other writings; it is, in addition, bibliographically convenient to describe them all together.

Blake's books seem to have been dispersed among his friends, and they have only gradually come to light. Thus only four of the annotated volumes were known to Gilchrist, writing before 1863, namely, Lavater's

Aphorisms, Bacon's *Essays*, Reynolds's *Discourses*, and Wordsworth's *Poems*. Two of these, the Bacon and the Wordsworth, cannot now be traced, and, indeed, the latter was only known to Gilchrist owing to the fact that the annotations had been copied out in 1826 by Crabb Robinson. A later biographer, E. J. Ellis, was able to add in 1904 the notes to Swedenborg's *Wisdom of Angels concerning Divine Love and Divine Wisdom*, as well as those to Spurzheim's *Insanity*, Cennini's *Treatise on Painting*, and Dr. Thornton's pamphlet on the Lord's Prayer, though he did not print the latter in full. Other annotated volumes have appeared since that time, and through the courtesy of Mr. H. E. Huntington and Mr. W. E. Moss I am able to print for the first time in an appendix to the present work Blake's annotations to Bishop Watson's *Apology for the Bible*, written in 1798, and to Berkeley's *Siris*, written between 1804 and 1818. A complete transcript of the annotations to Dr. Thornton's pamphlet will appear in Mr. S. Foster Damon's forthcoming work on Blake. There only remain the annotations in a copy of Swedenborg's *Wisdom of Angels concerning the Divine Providence*, and these it is to be hoped will soon be made available. I have not been able to trace the history of all these annotated volumes. Three of them, however, were in the possession of Blake's friend, Samuel Palmer, one was vouched for by Frederick Tatham, and was presumably at one time in his keeping, and three others were in John Linnell's library. Blake did not annotate all the books that were in his possession; nevertheless, I have thought it worth while to record all the volumes that I could discover with evidence of his ownership, but those which merely contain his signature or inscription I have separated from the annotated volumes. Being of less importance, they will be found relegated to Section v.

C. *LETTERS*

Blake's biographers have not taken full advantage of his letters as a source of positive information concerning the details of his life and character. If read consecutively they will be found to bring out clearly his peculiar and unstable mentality; but at the same time it is clear that anyone who could deal so normally with the ordinary affairs of life as the writer of these letters cannot be regarded as a madman in the usual sense of the word, whatever view may be taken of the manifestations of his artistic genius.

Blake's letters cover a period of over thirty years, from 1795 to 1827, and, although the number of his correspondents was small, a relatively large number of letters has survived; but letters, once dispersed, are troublesome to gather together again, and several have for the present eluded my attempts to recapture them. Blake's earliest correspondent was George Cumberland, and he continued occasionally to address letters to him up to the last year of his life; several of these are preserved in the British Museum among the Cumberland papers, though they were not printed until 1903. Among his occasional correspondents were Dr. John Trusler, author of *Hogarth Moralized* and many other works, John Flaxman, Mrs. Anna Flaxman and her sister Miss Denman, Sir Richard Phillips, publisher, Ozias Humphrey, and Dawson Turner. He wrote also a number of letters to Thomas Butts during the years 1800 to 1803, when he was at Felpham, and these have all been printed by Gilchrist. Butts continued after this to be a constant patron, but their intercourse was no doubt carried on in person, and there are no letters to him after this date. An interesting record of their transactions remains, however, in the receipts given by Blake for various sums of money received from Butts in the years 1805-1810; a description of these is included here as they seemed to come more naturally among the letters than among Blake's other manuscripts. His letters to his family are not known to have survived except in one instance; this is a long and exceedingly interesting letter written from Felpham in 1803 to his brother, James Blake, describing his relations with Hayley and his intentions regarding his art. The letter has only recently come to light and is unpublished; by the courtesy of Mr. W. E. Moss it is printed in full in an appendix to the present work.

By far the most voluminous correspondent that Blake possessed, however, was William Hayley, and nearly half the total number of letters that have survived are addressed to him. A large number of these letters were not known to Gilchrist, and when, in 1878, they were dispersed with the Hayley papers at Sotheby's, no one seems to have thought it worth his while to make copies of those that were unpublished. A few of these have since come to light, and some of them I am able to print in an appendix to the present work, but the majority have not yet been traced; I am only able to indicate the nature of their contents by reprinting the extracts given in the sale catalogue, and it remains for a future editor to collect them as they appear, one by one, in the sale rooms or elsewhere. The correspondence with Hayley seems to have ceased after the year 1805, and very few letters exist to cast light on the years 1806 to 1818, the obscure period of Blake's life. After 1818 he began his friendship with John Linnell, who carefully preserved every piece of writing that he sent him, however trivial. The majority of the letters to Linnell were written during the last three years of Blake's life, when frequent illness prevented him from visiting his friend in person as often as he had previously done. Most of these letters were printed by Gilchrist, or by Story in his *Life of Linnell*; a few, however, remained unpublished, and are printed in the present work.

Mr. A. G. B. Russell edited in 1906 a volume containing all the letters that were then known to him. I am now able to add in an appendix twelve letters which are here collected and printed in full for the first time, including the one to James Blake already mentioned; of the others three were addressed to Hayley, one to George Cumberland, one to Ozias Humphrey, five to John Linnell, and one to Mr. Reveley, a publisher's agent. The total number of letters which I have been able to describe in greater or less detail is eighty-eight.

D. *PRINTED WORKS*

BLAKE did not care to have his works printed in ordinary typography, and there are only three books to be included under this heading. His earliest poems were privately printed for him by his friends in the volume called *Poetical Sketches*, 1783. These poems are now very well known, though the volume in which they originally appeared is rare. His next printed work was to have been issued in the ordinary way by a publisher; it was a long poem in seven books, entitled *The French Revolution*, but after the first part had been set up in type in 1791 and a specimen printed, the project was abandoned, and this specimen is the only copy that is now known to exist. Even this was lost for many years and was not reprinted until 1913, when it was made available in Dr. Sampson's edition of the poems. The third printed book is the *Descriptive Catalogue* of the exhibition of pictures held by Blake at his brother's house in 1809. This work is also very rare. The title-pages of all three books are here reproduced in facsimile. Blake's only other printed works consist of an advertisement of his exhibition of pictures and two prospectuses of his engraving of the Canterbury Pilgrims. The advertisement is mentioned by Gilchrist but it has never before been described or reprinted. It consists of a single leaf, and on the verso is an interesting manifesto by Blake on his method of "fresco painting." Both sides of the leaf are here reproduced in facsimile. The prospectuses are exceedingly rare, and I have never seen either of them; they have been reprinted by Mr. A. G. B. Russell in his work on the engravings.

E. *ILLUMINATED BOOKS*

Most of Blake's writings were published in a form which was invented and first used by him about the year 1788. He called the process " Illuminated Printing," and this name well indicates its character. The books are now commonly referred to as " the engraved books," but this is inaccurate, as the process is essentially one of relief etching. J. T. Smith relates that after Blake " had deeply perplexed himself as to the mode of accomplishing the " publication of his illustrated songs, without their being subject to the " expense of letter-press, his brother Robert stood before him in one of his " visionary imaginations, and so decidedly directed him in the way in which " he ought to proceed, that he immediately followed his advice, by writing " his poetry, and drawing his marginal subjects of embellishments in outline " upon the copper-plate with an impervious liquid, and then eating the " plain parts or lights away with aqua fortis considerably below them, so " that the outlines were left as a stereotype." * Robert Blake died in 1787; but Dr. Sampson has pointed out that the idea was in Blake's mind some years before this, for a passage in *An Island in the Moon*, written about 1784, evidently refers to the Illuminated Printing. The first part of the passage is unfortunately missing from the manuscript, and it begins abruptly as follows : " . . . ' thus illuminating the manuscript.'

* *Nollekens and his Times*, 1828, ii, 461.

c

" ' Ay,' said she, ' that would be excellent.'

" ' Then,' said he, ' I would have all the wording engraved instead of
" " printed, and at every other leaf a high-finished print,—all in three
" " volumes folio,—and sell them for a hundred pounds apiece. They would
" " print off two thousand.' "

It is, however, quite possible that the first idea was suggested to Blake
by someone else, and in this connexion it is of great interest to find that he
was to some extent anticipated by George Cumberland, who wrote to his
brother Richard early in 1784 as follows: " The occasion of my writing to
" you to-day is to send you the enclosed specimen of my new mode of
" Printing—it is the amusement of an evening and is capable of printing
" 2000 if I wanted them—you see here one page which is executed as easily
" as writing and the Cost is trifling for your Copper is worth at any rate
" near as much as it cost besides you are not obliged to print any more than
" you want at one time, so that if the Work don't take you have nothing to
" do but to cut the Copper to pieces or clean it—But if it does, you may print
" 4 editions, 2000, and then sell the Plates as well. All this would be [. . .]
" much if there was not some difficulty. A work thus printed can only be
" read with the help of a looking Glass as the letters are reversed . . .
" however we have a remedy for this defect also, for in printing 20 we can
" have 20 more right by only taking off the impression while wet—in fact
" this is only etching words instead of Landscapes, but nobody has yet
" thought of the utility of it that I know of; the expense of this page is
" 1/6 without reckoning time, wh. was never yet worth much to authors,
" and the Copper is worth 1/0 again when cut up. In my next I will tell
" you more and make you also an engraver of this sort, till when keep it to
" yourself." *

It is not known when Blake first made Cumberland's acquaintance, but
his earliest letter to him is dated Dec. 6, 1795, and the manner of address
in this letter makes it probable that they had met some time before this.
There is no evidence that either of the Cumberlands attended the *salons* in
Rathbone Place, at the house of Mrs. Mathews, whose guests are supposed
to have been satirized by Blake in *An Island in the Moon*, but it is within
the bounds of possibility; the passage from this work already quoted, with

* *The Cumberland Letters. Edited by Clementina Black. London. Secker. 1912*, pp. 317-318.
My attention was first drawn to this passage by Mr. W. E. Moss.

its reference to the engraved writing and the printing off of 2,000 copies, may well have been based on conversations concerning Cumberland's discovery heard by Blake at one of these gatherings. The manuscript is believed to belong to 1784, the same year as Cumberland's letter to his brother.

At whatever date it may have been that Blake first thought of his new method of book production, it is clear that he did not use it before 1788. For this we have the authority of his own statement in the colophon to *The Ghost of Abel*, issued in 1822: " Blake's original stereotype was 1788." It is still uncertain whether this refers to the first plates of the *Songs of Innocence* or to the plates of *There is No Natural Religion*. It is probable that Blake wrote out a full description of this and other technical processes invented by him, for he refers to " an account of my various inventions in Art, for which I " have procured a publisher" in a letter to George Cumberland, dated Dec. 19, 1808,* but the work seems never to have been completed and is not known to have survived in any form.

The essence of Blake's process was the reversal of the ordinary intaglio method, the whites being etched instead of the darks, so that the text and designs stood out on the plate in relief. The text was written out backwards on the metal, and the designs drawn on it by a brush with some medium impervious to acid. George Cumberland, according to his first description of the process already quoted, wrote out the text on the copper from left to right, so that it appeared backwards when the plate was printed. Blake, however, no doubt soon discovered that with the help of a mirror the writing can, with practice, be done backwards in the first place, so that the print is then the right way round. The exact composition of the fluid that Blake used is not known, but it was presumably some kind of stopping-out varnish. This method was used in the earliest books, including *There is No Natural Religion, Songs of Innocence and of Experience, Thel*, and *The Marriage of Heaven and Hell*. By 1793, however, Blake had evolved a modification of his original process which he himself called " wood-cutting on copper," and this he used in conjunction with the first method in most of the works issued after this date. The second method is best described in Blake's own words, taken from some memoranda written on page 10 of the *Rossetti MS.*:

* See letter no. 62.

" *Memorandum.*

" To wood-cut on pewter: Lay a ground on the plate, and smoke it
" as for etching. Then trace your outlines, and, beginning with the spots
" of light on each object, with an oval pointed needle scrape off the ground,
" as a direction for your graver. Then proceed to graving with the ground
" on the plate; being as careful as possible not to hurt the ground, because
" it, being black, will show perfectly what is wanted.

" *Memorandum.*

" To wood-cut on copper. Lay a ground as for etching; trace, etc.,
" and instead of etching the blacks, etch the whites, and bite it in."

This process differs from the first in that the plate was first covered
with a ground, and then the parts to be etched, that is to say the lines of
the designs, were scraped off with a pointed instrument; the area intended
for the text was then denuded of ground and the text written on the
metal as already described. Finally the whole plate was etched with acid.
The combination of the two methods was used in *America* and in *Europe*,
and also in the later books, *Milton* and *Jerusalem*. If the pages of an uncoloured copy of *Jerusalem* be closely examined it will be found quite easy
to distinguish by the quality of the outlines those designs that were drawn
with a brush from those that were done by the method of " wood-cutting
on copper." The process called by Blake " wood-cutting on pewter," which
depended on the use of a graver instead of on etching with an acid, is not
known to have been used in the illuminated books; it is believed, however, to have been used for the broadside, *Little Tom the Sailor*, described
in another section of the present work, and in the design known as
" The man sweeping the interpreter's parlour"; this occurs usually as a
separate print, but it was also used as a frontispiece for a copy of the
Poetical Sketches (see p. 78).

The plates of the illuminated books were printed in an ordinary press,
but it was no doubt a slow and laborious process, as was first pointed out
by John Jackson in his *Treatise on Wood Engraving*. " As it was difficult,"
he writes, " according to Blake's process, to corrode the large white parts
" to a depth sufficient to prevent their being touched by the dauber or ball
" in the process of inking, and thus presenting a soiled appearance in the
" impression, he was accustomed to wipe the ink out where it had touched

"in the hollows."* This was not, however, his invariable practice. It is quite evident, for instance, in some copies of *Jerusalem* that he obtained his high-lights by wiping out part only of the hollows, so that a granulated effect, giving a gradation of lights, was obtained from the remainder.

This conjectural reconstruction of Blake's methods will be more readily understood by reference to the two uncoloured pages of *Jerusalem* reproduced in the present work. The first is an example of "wood-cutting on copper"; the second illustrates the earlier method and is also an instance in which Blake practised the partial wiping out of the hollows. The relief etching was used in all the illuminated books with the exception of two, *The Book of Los* and *The Book of Ahania*; in these the text is executed by the ordinary process of etching.

The original copper plates have not survived to the present day. Sixteen of those for the *Songs of Innocence and of Experience* were still in existence in 1863, and electrotypes were made from them for the first edition of Gilchrist's *Life*, but even they have now disappeared. The whole number of etched plates that Blake accumulated must have been considerable, for the printing of the various books was done at intervals over a long period of years, and it is probable that almost the whole stock was in the possession of Blake's widow for several years after his death. Mrs. Blake does not seem to have made use of them, but when at her death Blake's stocks passed into the keeping of Frederick Tatham, several of the sets of plates were taken out and a few impressions made from them. Posthumous copies, as will be seen, of the *Songs of Innocence and of Experience*, *Europe*, *America*, and *Jerusalem* were all printed about 1832, and are recorded below. The plates are said then to have been stolen and sold as old metal, and their value from this point of view was no doubt considerable. The only relic of the original copper plates that I have seen is now in the possession of Mr. W. E. Moss. It is a fragment of plate *a* of *America*, the first of the three cancelled plates, of which the text is printed in an appendix to the present work. It was found in an old engraving cabinet once the property of young Butts,† to whom Blake had endeavoured to teach the elements of engraving.

* Jackson and Chatto's *Treatise on Wood Engraving*, 1839, p. 716. See no. 256.
† A school-fellow of Seymour Kirkup; see *Rossetti Papers*, 1903, p. 178, and an article in the *Connoisseur*, 1907 (no. 577), by a sister of Mrs. Butts.

It is of interest to notice that Blake reduced at once the bulk and expense of the plates by etching each on both sides. This is shown by the presence on a number of prints of the plate-maker's mark, which was presumably stamped on one side of the plate only. In the copies of the books issued by Blake himself this mark has usually been obliterated by the colouring, but in copies which were uncoloured, or were printed after his death, it is clearly seen, and can be deciphered as: *Jones and Pontifex, No.* 47 *Shoe Lane, London,* a firm represented at the present time by Messrs. H. Pontifex & Sons, Limited, Engineers, 43 Shoe Lane.

It has already been pointed out among the remarks on the manuscripts that the texts of none of the illuminated books have survived in manuscript, and we have therefore no means of judging to what extent Blake altered or re-wrote these poems. It has been stated that he never revised his work, but this is at once seen to be untrue if reference be made to the description of a manuscript such as *The Four Zoas* (no. 6). Further, I am able to record here for the first time three plates already mentioned, which Blake made for *America* and afterwards rejected. Two of these were not used at all; the third was included in the published book, but it was re-etched with various minor alterations in the text. It is evident, therefore, that Blake carefully revised his text, and sometimes even took the trouble to re-etch an entire plate for the sake of altering a few words which displeased him. He seems, however, always to have arrived at the final form of each plate before the book was printed, and I do not know of any instance of a plate being re-etched for the sake of incorporating textual variations in the later copies of any of the books. Nevertheless, there are many cases in which Blake varied the constitution of a book in different copies, plates being added or subtracted at different periods. Thus the *Songs of Innocence and of Experience* underwent a series of changes between 1789 and 1818, both in constitution and arrangement. Plate 4 of *The Book of Urizen* was included in only two of the copies known; five plates for *Milton* are found only in one of the three existing copies; plate iii of *Europe* is found only in two of the copies known. No doubt Blake had his reasons, sometimes no longer to be discovered, for thus altering his books, and it is well to remember, when considering whether a copy of an illuminated book is technically "perfect" or not, that other copies differing from it do not necessarily constitute a final criterion of this perfection. It need hardly be pointed out that the colouring of the books which was done at intervals, sometimes of many years, is never the same in any two copies, so that here again there is no definite standard of merit; the estimation of this must depend largely on the taste of the observer.

It follows from the foregoing remarks that, in attempting a bibliographical description of the illuminated books, it was useless merely to give details of each book from some one copy that happened to be readily available. Nothing less sufficed than a page-by-page description of an ideal copy supposed to contain all the plates, together with full details of every existing copy that could be traced, and in the following pages this plan has been pursued as far as possible. The inception of this task was due to a suggestion made to me some ten years ago by Dr. Sampson, who had himself made a beginning by describing in detail some of the copies of the *Songs of Innocence and of Experience* in his edition of the Poetical Works, published in 1905. Completion of such a task can hardly be considered feasible; always there will be some copies that have been temporarily lost to view, and others will only first come to light too late for inclusion in the work. The approximate completion of the task attained in this work has only been made possible by the willing help of friends in the United States of America, and by the invariable courtesy of the owners of the books both in Great Britain and America.

The gathering of these details concerning the illuminated books is not only of value to the collector and connoisseur, but becomes of considerable importance in elucidating the little known facts of Blake's life. It is probable that Blake's biographers have insisted too much on his poverty and hand-to-mouth existence. Since the facts were not available it was naturally forgotten that the illuminated books must have been a slow but steady source of income. In the following pages are collected details of nearly 150 copies of the various books, which were sold by him at prices varying from one to ten guineas; during the 130 years that have elapsed since Blake began to produce them some copies have no doubt been destroyed, and others have not yet come to light. The reward that Blake received for his books was certainly not proportionate to the genius and labour expended upon them, but they helped, nevertheless, to provide him with the means of subsistence and of carrying on his work. Three lists of Blake's works with their prices have come down to us, so that there is definite evidence as to the money he received for the books at different periods. These prices are quoted in the following pages among the notes on each book, so that the lists need not be reprinted here. They are to be found in the *Prospectus* of Oct. 10, 1793 (see no. 37), in a letter to Dawson Turner dated June 9, 1818 (letter 65), and in a letter to George Cumberland dated April 12, 1827 (letter 86). It appears from Blake's statements in the second of these letters that at that date he had disposed of his whole stock of books already printed with the exception of his coloured copy of *Jerusalem*, but that he was still ready to prepare copies when definitely ordered by a customer.

In summarizing the details gathered concerning each book certain generalizations can be made, which are sometimes of help in assigning a date to any particular copy. For these reference must be made to the notes printed in the pages following. In addition some still broader principles emerge. It is evident that Blake never printed more than a very small number of copies of any book at a time, for he varied the ground tint in which the plates were printed almost as much as he did the subsequent illumination. He used various shades of brown, yellow, sepia, green, blue, grey, or black; sometimes the colour may vary among the constituent plates of one copy. In almost every case the printing was done in monochrome; but some of the plates of the small dogmatic works on Natural Religion appear to have been printed in more than one colour. In the subsequent colouring of the books Blake used for the most part water-colours only, but in some copies done in the early years he used his peculiar opaque medium, the exact composition of which remains unknown. Occasionally he combined his opaque paints with water-colours, and in one book, *The Song of Los*, he confined himself entirely to the opaque medium. It is noticeable that as the years passed Blake's taste for elaboration grew, so that copies done after the period ending about 1800 are much more carefully finished than those done earlier. It was chiefly during the last ten years of his life that he heightened the effects of his water-colours by the use of gold.

In assigning dates to the various copies of the books it has been of great assistance to record carefully the watermarks found in the paper on which they are printed. In many copies no watermark can be seen, as it has been cut off with the marginal parts of the leaves, or rendered invisible by the colouring, especially if this were done with opaque pigments. In a great many copies, however, the watermarks, or, at any rate, parts of them, can be deciphered. The watermark most commonly found is that of *J Whatman*, with or without a date; it is evident that Blake bought this manufacturer's paper at intervals from 1794 to 1826, the following dates being found in the watermark: 1794, 1804, 1808, 1818, 1819, 1820, 1824, 1825, 1826. No watermark except that of *J Whatman* is found after 1815, and the same paper, dated 1831 or 1832, was used for those books of which copies were printed after Blake's death. Another watermark that is found with relative frequency is that of *I Taylor*; this usually has no date, but in three cases it is associated with other paper dated 1794 (*Songs of Innocence and of Experience*, copy A; *Urizen*, copy B; *Europe*, copy B), and in one case the date 1794 accompanies it (*Songs of Innocence and of Experience*, copy K) on the same leaf. It is probable, therefore, that all books with the watermark *I Taylor* are to be assigned to about the year 1794. In several books Blake has used paper made by *Edmead & Pine*, whose names appear in the watermark in two cases in full, together with the date 1802 (*Songs of Innocence*, copies O and P). More usually, their watermark appears as *E & P* without a date; but in one book (*Songs of Innocence and of Experience*, copy B) this watermark is found associated with leaves bearing the watermark *I Taylor* (*i.e.*, about 1794), and as there are other reasons for believing that this book belongs to 1794, I have thought it fair to assume that the watermark *E & P* also indicates the year 1794 (*e.g.*, *America*, copies C-F). The watermark of *Ruse & Turners* is found in seven books, together with the date 1815 (*Songs of Innocence and of Experience*, copies N and O, *The Marriage of Heaven and Hell*, copy G, etc.). The watermark of *T Stains*, with the date 1813, is found in four books (*America*, copies L and M, and *Europe*, copies G and H). Two watermarks that are found only once each are *Hayes & Wise* 1799 (*America*, copy K) and *Buttanshaw* 1802 (*Songs of Innocence and of Experience*, copy E). A few leaves of *There is No Natural Religion* (copies G and H) show part of the date 1811, but as this date does not occur in any other books the rest of the watermark cannot be supplied. The various indications supplied by the watermarks, the arrangement and constitution of the books, the character of their colouring, and their personal associations, have made it possible for me to assign an approximate date to almost every one of Blake's illuminated books of which I have been able to obtain a detailed description. It is probable that, as descriptions are obtained of books which are at present untraced, still greater accuracy in dating copies will be attained.

There is no record of the original ownership of a great many of the copies of the illuminated books, but such facts as have been gathered show that among Blake's best customers for them were Thomas Butts, Isaac D'Israeli, George Cumberland, and John Linnell. Of these, Butts, Cumberland, and Linnell, being among Blake's closest friends, would naturally buy copies of most of his works. The association with D'Israeli, however, is curious, for he made no reference to Blake in his writings although he felt enough interest in him about the year 1794 to buy six of his works. The *Songs of Innocence and of Experience* was evidently by far the most popular of Blake's books, and it seems to have attracted many customers who did not buy copies of Blake's other works. Soon after Blake's death, and about the middle of the nineteenth century, there were several eager collectors of Blake's books. William Beckford acquired many of them, including most of Cumberland's copies. Benjamin Disraeli inherited his father's copies and may have acquired others. Frederick Locker-Lampson bought a number of the books for the Rowfant Library. Francis Palgrave was the owner of several now in the British Museum, and a collection was formed by Thomas Gaisford. The most notable collection of all was that formed by Richard Monckton-Milnes, first Lord Houghton, who acquired among others several of the Butts copies when these were sold in 1852. Among the earliest American collectors to take an interest in Blake's books were Robert Hoe and Robert Balmanno, and between 1880 and 1890 a considerable collection was formed by E. W. Hooper of Harvard. He was followed in chronological order by Mr. W. A. White of New York, who from 1890 onwards has been forming the largest collection of Blake's works in existence. Mr. White took full advantage of the dispersal of the Monckton-Milnes books by the Earl of Crewe in 1903, and his collection is remarkable in containing more than one copy of several of the books, so that Blake's different periods are represented. During more recent years fine series have been formed by Mr. H. E. Huntington and by the Pierpont Morgan Library, and several are in the possession of Mr. A. E. Newton. There are no collections in England at the present time which can rival that of Mr. W. A. White. A good series, however, can be seen in the Reading Room and Print Room of the British Museum, and there are several in the Fitzwilliam Museum, Cambridge. All the D'Israeli copies, with some others, are in the possession of Mr. B. B. Macgeorge of Glasgow; the best of the Linnell copies belong to Mr. T. H. Riches of Shenley, Herts, whose wife is a granddaughter of John Linnell.

F. *WORKS EXECUTED IN LINE ENGRAVING*

MOST of Blake's works having been executed by the process of relief etching already described, there remain but few to be dealt with under the heading of line engravings. In 1793 he engraved a small work with the title, *For Children: The Gates of Paradise*, and about twelve years later he used most of the plates a second time in another distinct work called, *For the Sexes: The Gates of Paradise*. These two works have frequently been confused, but the differences between them are here made clear. Of the earlier work only four copies are known, and of the later work only seven, among which are found at least three different states of the plates.

Blake's other engraved works, as distinguished from the separate engravings which do not come within the scope of this Bibliography, include only three, the *Laocöon* [1818], the *Illustrations of the Book of Job*, 1826, and the *Illustrations to Dante* [1827]. Although the first of these is a single leaf, the text upon it is of more importance than the design, so that it may properly be included here. Both the other series of engravings were intended to be bound up as volumes, and were provided with a printed label to be pasted on the cover, so that these again could not be omitted from the present work. For all other engravings by Blake not to be found either here or in Section II, which deals with his book illustrations, reference must be made to Mr. A. G. B. Russell's work, *The Engravings of William Blake*, London, 1912.

G. *WORKS LOST OR CONJECTURAL*

THE question of Frederick Tatham's alleged responsibility for the disappearance of some of Blake's works has already been discussed in the remarks on the Manuscripts, and the conclusion was reached that there is but little evidence for the truth of the accusation. On the other hand it is possible that various works in manuscript may have been destroyed by Blake himself, or may have been lost to sight and will only appear again in the course of time. Under the present heading are gathered ten titles which may represent works yet to be discovered. They are only known at present from references to them scattered through Blake's writings. In four instances the references are definite, and no great surprise would be occasioned by the discovery of one or more copies of *The History of England*, a work resembling *The Gates of Paradise*, of *Outhoon*, a book in illuminated printing, of *Advertizement to Blake's Canterbury Pilgrims*, probably printed in ordinary typography, or of a " Work on Art," describing his technical processes, also in ordinary typography. It is further quite possible that a fifth, *The Book of Moonlight*, may have existed in manuscript. The references to the remaining five are less circumstantial, and it is probable that *The Bible of Hell*, *For Children: The Gates of Hell*, and *Barry, A Poem* were merely projected works and will never be discovered. It is improbable that *The Book of Enoch* or the *Vision of Genesis* ever existed.

A. *MANUSCRIPTS*

1   *Autograph Manuscript known as*: THE PASSIONS   [*about* 1777-1783]

Description*: 8° 19 × 12.5 cm. 4 leaves, without dated watermark, written in ink on both sides of the leaf; verso of last leaf blank. The leaves are now mounted on rather larger paper, and on the outer cover is written: 7 (*seven*) *Pages MS.*: *The handwriting of William Blake.*

> *Contents*: pp. [1]-[5]. A piece, beginning: 'then She bore Pale desire, father of
>   Curiosity, a Virgin ever young'. . .
>   p. [6]. A piece beginning: '"Woe," cried the muse, tears started at the
>   Sound . . .'
>   p. [7]. Two passages belonging to the first piece, marked for insertion
>   on p. [4].

Note: This early and incomplete MS. is written in much the same style as the prose pieces which were printed at the end of the *Poetical Sketches*, and on the strength of this evidence Dr. Sampson (1905, p. 329) assigns it to the period immediately preceding 1783. The two pieces are written as prose, the divisions into metrical lines having been marked in red ink by W. M. Rossetti, a former owner of the MS., to whom it was given about 1876 by John Deffett Francis; it is now in the possession of Signora Rossetti Angeli. The first piece was printed by W. M. Rossetti in *The Monthly Review*, 1903 (see no. 539), divided into metrical lines and entitled *The Passions*; the second piece has not been printed.

Printed: *The Monthly Review*, 1903; EJE.

2   *Autograph Manuscript known as* : AN ISLAND IN THE MOON

                                          [*about* 1784]

Description: Fcp. f° 31 × 18.5 cm. A single quire of 16 leaves, lacking two, or perhaps four, leaves from the centre. The MS., written in Blake's early hand, begins at the head of the first leaf, recto, and ends at line 19 of the ninth leaf, recto,

---

* These facts are derived from Sampson, 1905, p. 329, to whom the MS. was lent by its present owner.

that is on p. [17] (p. [21] or [25] when the MS. was complete), immediately following the gap in the text. The remaining 7 leaves are blank, with the exception of the
last leaf, verso, which is covered with rough pen and ink sketches of horses' heads,
a lion and a lamb, etc., with trials of signatures, one backwards, and with scattered
letters of the word 'Numeration,' which is written once in full. Dr. Sampson (1905,
p. 50) points out that this leaf is soiled, showing that it is the outer leaf of the MS.,
and, further, that the watermarks prove it to be the other half of the same sheet as the
first leaf, indicating that there never was any title-page. The MS. is now bound in
red morocco, lettered on the front: *Original Manuscript | William Blake | Island in
the Moon*. Four fly-leaves have been added at the beginning and two at the end; on
the third and fourth of these are mounted a letter from A. H. Palmer, and proof
impressions of four of Blake's woodcuts for Thornton's *Pastorals of Virgil*, signed
W. Blake fecit. Inside the cover is the label of C. Fairfax Murray.

Contents: [An Island in the Moon] Chapters 1-11, and a fragment of a subsequent
chapter.

Chap. 11 contains the first drafts of three of the *Songs of Innocence*:
1. Upon a Holy Thursday, their innocent faces clean [Holy Thursday]
2. When the tongues of the children are heard on the green [Nurse's Song]
3. O father, father where are you going [The Little Boy Lost]

The following poems are scattered through the text:
4. When old corruption first begun . . .   Chap. 6.
5. Phebe drest like beautie's Queen . . . [The Song of Phebe and Jellicoe *or*
     The Pilgrim] Chap. 8.
6. Hail Matrimony, made of Love . . .   Chap. 9.
7. To be or not to be . . .   Chap. 9.
8. This city & this country has brought forth many mayors . . . [Old English
     Hospitality] Chap. 9.
9. Leave O leave [me] to my sorrows . . . [A Song of Sorrows] Chap. 11.

Also the following pieces of doggerel:
10. Little Phebus came strutting in . . .   Chap. 3.
11. Honour & Genius is all I ask . . .   Chap. 3.
12. Hear then the pride & knowledge of a Sailor . . .   Chap. 8.
13. Lo the Bat with Leathern wing . . .   Chap. 9.
14. Want matches . . .   Chap. 9.
15. I cry my matches as far as Guildhall . . .   Chap. 9.
16. As I walk'd forth one may morning . . .   Chap. 9.
17. This frog he would a wooing ride . . .   Chap. 9.

Note: This unfinished and incomplete MS. is the least serious or valuable of Blake's works. It is usually supposed to be a somewhat incoherent satire on the distinguished personages whom Blake used to meet at the *salon* of Mrs. Mathews in Rathbone Place, and it was certainly never intended for publication. The title by which it is generally known is derived from the opening sentence: ' In the Moon is a certain Island, near by a mighty continent, which small island seems to have some affinity to England . . .' The chief importance of the MS. lies in the fact that it contains first drafts of three of the *Songs of Innocence* and that it concludes with a reference to Blake's method of ' illuminated printing,' which he did not actually use until some years later. The approximate date, 1784, at which it was written, has been satisfactorily indicated by Dr. Sampson (1905, p. 51).

The MS. is not mentioned by Gilchrist, but this omission was probably deliberate; it is evidently this MS. which was referred to in a letter from Mrs. Gilchrist to W. M. Rossetti, dated 1863, as "a long thing which I really believe even Mr. Swinburne will pronounce pure rubbish" (*Rossetti Papers*, p. 42), for Rossetti further explains (*ibid.*) that "' the long thing' . . . was a prose narrative of a domestic, and also fantastic, sort, clearly intended by its author to count as humouristic or funny, and somewhat in the Shandean vein. I read this performance, and heartily confirmed Mrs. Gilchrist in the conviction of its being rubbish; yet I was startled to learn soon afterwards that, on receiving my letter, she had burned the MS. The thing was stupid, but it was Blake's, and a curiosity." Rossetti seems, however, to have misunderstood Mrs. Gilchrist when he stated that she burned the whole MS., though the passage explains the fact noted above that two or more leaves, which may have contained some particularly offensive passages, are now missing. The MS. was transcribed by Dr. Sampson, but it has only once been printed in full (see below). It was for some time in the possession of the late Charles Fairfax Murray, but was presented by him about 1905 to the Fitzwilliam Museum, Cambridge.

Printed: In full by Ellis in *The Real Blake* (no. 346). Poems nos. 5, 8 (with title ' The Lawgiver's Song'), and 9 first printed in *The Light Blue*, 1867 (no. 440). EY, synopsis and copious extracts; LH, chaps. 1, 2, and 5, and poem no. 5; Sampson, 1905 and 1913, poems and doggerel except no. 18; EJE, poems and doggerel.

Facsimile Reproductions: Two pages, reduced, in *The Real Blake*.

3 *Autograph Manuscript:* TIRIEL   *[about* 1789*]*

Description: Fcp. 4° 21 × 16 cm. 8 leaves without dated watermark, written on both sides of the leaf; verso of last leaf blank. In the original blue-grey paper covers inscribed on the front: *Tiriel* in Blake's autograph; below this another hand has added: *MS by Mr. Blake.* The leaves and wrappers are now mounted on guards and bound in half morocco.

Contents: pp. [1]-[15] Tiriel, sections 1-8.
Each section, headed by an arabic numeral, begins at the top of a fresh page.

Note: It seems to be quite clear, as was first shown from internal evidence by Dr. Sampson (1905, p. 331), that this highly mystical work was written by Blake before *The Book of Thel*, engraved in 1789, and is therefore the earliest of the Prophetic Books. The MS., though containing many corrections and deletions, especially on pp. [11] and [14], is neatly written in Blake's earlier hand. W. M. Rossetti, owing to a change in the handwriting near the top of p. [14], thought that the greater part of section 8 was composed at a later date than the rest of the poem (see WMR, *p.* cxxiii), but Dr. Sampson points out that the change is merely such as might have been produced by the sharpening of a quill pen which had grown somewhat coarse. Rossetti in his Annotated Catalogue (Gilchrist, ii, 273) describes a set of twelve Indian ink drawings, which are believed to be illustrations of the poem. One is reproduced here by permission of Mr. Edward Marsh; this is said to be the best of the series, but I have not seen the others.

The earlier history of the MS. is not recorded. In 1863 it was the property of Mrs. Gilchrist and continued in her possession until after 1870. It was then lost sight of for a short time, but was consulted by W. M. Rossetti for his edition of the poems in 1874. The MS. then disappeared again for many years and was said to have been sent to America. In 1903, however, it was discovered in a box by Messrs. Bell and Son, the publishers of Rossetti's edition. It was subsequently sold at Sotheby's, and was acquired by Quaritch, from whom it was bought on February 13, 1909, by the British Museum authorities out of the Farnborough Fund; it is now in the Department of MSS. (EG 2876).

Printed: WMR; EY, iii; WBY; EJE; Sampson, 1913.

4 *Fragment*: 'A fairy leapt upon my knee.' *Autograph Manuscript*
                                             [about 1793*]*

Description: Sixteen lines of verse written on " a loose scrap of paper on the back of which is a pencilled sketch of Hercules throttling the serpents, . . . : an

DESIGN IN ILLUSTRATION OF "TIRIEL"
Sepia Drawing, about 1789

attendant, naked, falls back in terror . . .; Alcmena and Amphitryon watch the struggle . . ." (Swinburne, *Critical Essay*, pp. 143-144).

Note: Swinburne copied this fragment and described the original MS. as above ; the "scrap of paper" now seems not to be forthcoming, and Swinburne's text is therefore the only authority. The date given above is that assigned to it by Dr. Sampson, who points out that it resembles in theme and manner "The Fairy" (*Rossetti MS.*, I, 40), written about 1793, and the proem to *Europe*, executed in 1794.

Printed: Swinburne, pp. 143-144 ; Sampson, 1905, p. 311, and 1913, p. 127 ; EJE (entitled 'The Fairy '), i, 114.

5 *Autograph Manuscript known as*: THE ROSSETTI MS.; *also known as* The MS. Book, *or as* Ideas of Good and Evil   [*about* 1793-1811]

*Description** : Fcp. 4° 19.6 × 15.7 cm. 58 leaves, paginated consecutively 1-116 by the present owner, and made up of one gathering of 10 leaves and four gatherings of 16 and 18 leaves alternately. No watermark. A sheet, forming 2 leaves, of different and smaller paper is bound in at the end. Following this is a transcript made by D. G. Rossetti, consisting of 33 leaves of which 5 have been cut out; watermark 1844. Bound in half-calf and labelled *Blake MS.*

Contents : I. POEMS AND EPIGRAMS.
a. *Songs of Experience*, in the order in which they are found in the MS., written in the reversed book, pp. 115-103, about 1793. The titles, when given in brackets, are not in the MS.

1. [The Fly]
2. Holy Thursday (*fair copy*)
3. The Angel (*fair copy*)
4. The Little Vagabond (*fair copy*)
5. The Chimney Sweeper
6. [A Little Boy lost]
7. The Sick Rose (*fair copy*)
8. The Human Image [The Human Abstract]
9. The Tyger
10. [The Lilly]
11. [Nurse's Song] (*fair copy*)
12. London

* These facts are derived from Sampson, 1905, pp. 138-9, to whom they were supplied by Mr. W. A. White.

13. Earth's Answer
14. Infant Sorrow (8 *stanzas, of which only two were etched*)
15. Christian Forbearance [A Poison Tree] (*fair copy*)
16. [My Pretty Rose Tree]
17. [The Clod and the Pebble] (*fair copy*)
18. [The Garden of Love] (*fair copy*)

b. Miscellaneous Poems, written in the reversed book, pp. 115-98, about 1793. Where Blake provided no title the first line is given; titles subsequently used by his editors are given in square brackets.
19. I told my love, I told my love, . . . [Love's Secret]
20. I laid me down upon a bank, . . . [Thistles and Thorns; *also printed as the first two stanzas of no.* 18]
21. I saw a chapel all of gold . . . [The Defiled Sanctuary]
22. I asked a thief to steal me a peach: . . . [The Will and the Way]
23. I heard an Angel singing . . . [The Two Songs, *or* The Two Voices]
24. A Cradle Song (*usually included among the Songs of Experience*)
25. Silent, Silent Night, . . . [Night and Day]
26. O lapwing! thou fliest around the heath, . . .
27. I fear'd the fury of my wind . . . [Barren Blossom]
28. Why should I care for the men of Thames, . . . [Thames and Ohio]
29. Thou hast a lap full of seed, . . . [Seed Sowing]
30. In a Mirtle Shade (*first version*); To My Mirtle (*final version*)
31. To Nobodaddy [To Old Nobodaddy, *or* Father of Jealousy]
32. Are not the joys of morning sweeter . . . [Young Love]
33. They said this mystery shall never cease: . . . (*couplet*)
34. Love to faults is always blind; . . . [*printed, together with no.* 35, *as* Love and Deceit, *or* Freedom and Captivity, *or* The Chain of Deceit]
35. There souls of men are bought & sold, . . .
36. The Wild Flower's Song
37. Soft Snow
38. Merlin's Prophecy
39. Day
40. The Fairy [The Marriage Ring *del.*]
41. The sword sung on the barren heath, . . .
42. Abstinence sows sand all over . . .
43. In a wife I would desire . . .
44. If you trap the moment before it's ripe . . . [*printed as the second stanza of no.* 52. i, *with title* Opportunity]
45. The Kid (*first line only*)

46. Lacedemonian Instruction
47. Riches [*printed as stanza 2 of no. 145*]
48. An Answer to the Parson (*couplet*)
49. Motto to the Songs of Innocence and of Experience [A Motto]
50. Her Whole Life is an Epigram . . . (*couplet*)
51. An Old maid early e'er I knew . . .
52. Several Questions Answered
    i. He who bends to himself a joy . . . [Eternity; *printed as first stanza of no. 44 with title* Opportunity]
    ii. The look of love alarms, . . .
    iii. Soft decit & Idleness, . . . [*printed as last two lines of ii*]
    iv. What is it men in women require ? [The Question Answer'd]
    v. An ancient Proverb
53. 'Let the Brothels of Paris be openèd . . .' [*three versions; a mixture of the three is printed as* Lafayette]

c. Miscellaneous Poems, written on pp. 2-98, about 1810-1811.
54. My Spectre around me night & day . . . [My Spectre, Broken Love, *or* Spectre and Emanation]
55. When a Man has Married a Wife, he finds out whether . . . (*couplet*)
56. When Klopstock England defied, . . .
57. On the Virginity of the Virgin Mary & Johanna Southcott
58. Mock on, Mock on, Voltaire, Rousseau; . . . [Scoffers]
59. I saw a Monk of Charlemaine . . . (*first draft of* To the Deists *in* Jerusalem *and of* The Grey Monk *in the Pickering MS.*)
60. Morning [Daybreak]
61. Terror in the house does roar; . . . (*couplet*)
62. Each man is in his spectre's power . . . (*from* Jerusalem, *pl.* 41)
63. Three Virgins at the break of day, . . . (*earlier version of* The Golden Net *in the Pickering MS.*)
64. The Birds
65. No real Style of Colouring ever appears, . . . [Colour]
66. You don't believe—I won't attempt to make ye: . . . [Reason]
67. And in melodious accents I . . . (*couplet from the* Advertisement)
68. And his legs carried it like a long fork, . . .
69. Was I angry with Hayley who us'd me so ill, . . .
70. Anger & Wrath my bosom rends: . . . [Friends and Foes]
71. The Sussex Men are Noted Fools, . . . [On William Haines]
72. 'Madman,' I have been call'd: 'Fool,' they call thee . . . [On Flaxman] (*couplet*)

73. To H—— [To Hayley] (*couplet, probably addressed to Hunt*)
74. To F—— (*couplet*)
75. Can there be anything more mean, . . .
76. S—— in Childhood, on the nursery floor, . . .
77. To Nancy F—— (*couplet*)
78. Of H——'s birth this was the happy lot . . . [On Hayley] (*couplet*)
79. Sir Joshua praises Michael Angelo . . .
80. He's a Blockhead who wants a proof of what he can't Perceive; . . . [The Summing-up] (*couplet*)
81. Cr—— loves artists as he loves his Meat: . . . [On Cromek] (*couplet*)
82. A Petty Sneaking Knave I knew—— [Cromek] (*couplet*)
83. Sir Joshua praisèd Rubens with a smile, . . .
84. He is a Cock would . . . (*couplet*)
85. He has observ'd the Golden Rule, . . . (*couplet*)
86. To S——d
87. Mr Stothard to Mr Cromek
88. Mr Cromek to Mr Stothard
89. I am no Homer's Hero you all know; . . . [A Warning]
90. The Angel that presided o'er my birth . . .
91. Florentine Ingratitude
92. A Pitiful Case
93. To the Royal Academy
94. If it is true, what the Prophets write, . . . [Idolatry]
95. To F—— and S—— [On Certain Friends]
96. P—— lovèd me not as he lov'd his friends; . . . [On Thomas Phillips]
97. To forgive enemies H—— does pretend, . . . [On Hayley]
98. To F—— [To Flaxman]
99. On H——y's Friendship
100. Some men, created for destruction, come . . .
101. On S—— [On Stothard]
102. Imitation of Pope: a compliment to the Ladies
103. To H—— [On Hayley] (*couplet*)
104. Cosway, Frazer, & Baldwin of Egypt's Lake . . .
105. An Epitaph (*couplet*)
106. Another (*couplet*)
107. Another
108. My title as a Genius thus is prov'd: . . . [On Hayley] (*couplet*)
109. I, Rubens, am a Statesman and a Saint . . . [The Contrast] (*couplet*)
110. To English Connoisseurs
111. Swelled limbs, with no outline that you can descry, . . .

112. A Pretty Epigram for the encouragement of those Who have paid great sums in the Venetian and Flemish ooze [Raphael and Rubens]
113. These are the Idiots' chiefest arts : . . .
114. Rafael, Sublime, Majestic, Graceful, Wise——— . . . [The Sequel]
115. Learn the laborious stumble of a Fool! . . . (*couplet*)*
116. If I e'er Grow to Man's Estate, . . .
117. The cripple every step drudges & labours, . . .
118. On the great encouragement given by English Nobility & Gentry to Corregio, Rubens, Reynolds, Gainsborough, Catalani, Du Crow, and Dilbury Doodle
119. Give Pensions to the Learned Pig, . . .
120. All pictures that's painted with sense and with thought . . .
121. On H——— the Pickthank (*couplet*)
122. Cromek speaks
123. When you look at a picture, you always can see . . .
124. English Encouragement of Art : Cromek's opinions put into rhyme
125. You say their Pictures well Painted be . . .
126. The Washerwoman's Song (*couplet*)
127. When I see a Rubens, Rembrandt, Corregio . . .
128. I give you the end of a golden string . . . (*from Jerusalem, pl.* 77)
129. Great things are done when Men & Mountains meet ; . . . (*couplet*)
130. If you play a Game of Chance, Know, before you begin, . . . (*couplet*)
131. The only Man that e'er I knew . . . [Fuseli]
132. For this is being a Friend just in the nick, . . . [Blake's Friends]
133. I will tell you what Joseph of Arimathea . . .
134. Grown old in Love from Seven till Seven times Seven, . . . (*couplet*)
135. Why was Cupid a Boy, . . . [Cupid]
136. I askèd my Dear Friend Orator Prig : . . . [Orator Prig]
137. O dear Mother Outline ! of wisdom most sage, . . .
138. To Venetian Artists
139. Great Men and Fools do often me inspire ; . . . (*couplet*)
140. Having given great offence by writing in Prose, . . . [A Resolution]
141. If men will act like a maid smiling over a churn, . . .
142. Call that the Public Voice which is their Error? . . . [On Colourists, *or* Colour and Form]
143. Some people admire the work of a Fool, . . .
144. To God (*couplet*)

* Printed as a separate couplet in Sampson, 1905, but it was pointed out by W. M. Rossetti that these two lines, with a third omitted in Sampson, are really part of no. 114. Correctly printed in Sampson, 1913.

145. Since all the Riches of this World . . . [Riches, *or* The Two Kinds of Riches]
146. To Chloe's breast young Cupid slily stole, . . . (*couplet*)
147. 'Now Art has lost its mental Charms . . .'
148. Nail his neck to the Cross: nail it with a nail . . . (*couplet*)
149. The Caverns of the Grave I've seen, . . . [For a Picture of the Last Judgement : Dedication]
150. I rose up at the dawn of day— [Prayer, Mammon, *or* The Two Thrones]
151. Do what you will this life's a fiction, . . . (*couplet*)

d. Written in scattered fragments on pp. 33, 48-54, 98-101, and on the last leaf ; composed not earlier than 1810.
152. The Everlasting Gospel.

II. PROSE

153. Advertizement to Blake's Canterbury Pilgrims from Chaucer, containing anecdotes of Artists [Public Address] (*written in scattered fragments on pp. 1-67; another title on p. 65 is*: Chaucer's Canterbury Pilgrims. Being a complete Index of Human Characters as they exist age after age. *See no. 63*)
154. For the year 1810. Additions to Blake's Catalogue of Pictures, &c. (*written in scattered fragments on pp. 68-end, including the piece printed under the title*: A Vision of the Last Judgement)
155. *Fragment* : The Combats of Good & Evil . . . Knowledge of Good & Evil (*p.* 86)
156. Delicate Hands & Heads will never appear While Titian &c. as in the Book of Moonlight, p. 5 (*p.* 46 ; *see no.* 65)
157. *List of 22 subjects perhaps for a History of England* (*p.* 116 ; *see no.* 58)
158. *List of Plagues of Egypt* (*p.* 116)
159. *Sundry notes and memoranda* :
    i. Tuesday Jany 20, 1807, between Two & seven in the Evening Despair (*p.* 10)
    ii. I say I shan't live five years. And if I live one it will be a Wonder. June 1793. (*p.* 10)
    iii. To engrave on pewter. To woodcut on pewter. To woodcut on copper (*p.* 10)
    iv. I wonder who can say 'speak no ill of the dead' . . . (*p.* 17)
    v. Columbus discovered America . . . (*p.* 17)
    vi. Princes appear to me to be fools . . . (*p.* 18)
    vii. There is just the same science in Lebrun or Rubens . . . (*p.* 38)
    viii. Let a man who has made a drawing . . . (*p.* 44)

No Man of Sense can think that an Imitation of the Objects
of Nature in The Art of Painting or that such Imitation which
any one may easily perform is worthy of Notice much less
that such an Art should be the Glory & Pride of a
Nation ~~&~~ The Italians
laugh at English Connoisseurs who are ~~not~~ most of them such silly
Fellows as to believe this

ROSSETTI MS.
Page 67

III. SKETCHES in pencil, ink, sepia, or colour, scattered throughout the book. They include designs for all the illustrations in *The Gates of Paradise*, for most of those in *Visions of the Daughters of Albion*, for the figure of Nebuchadnezzar on pl. 24 of *The Marriage of Heaven and Hell*, and some for the *Songs of Experience*, *Urizen*, *Europe*, and *America*. There is also a profile portrait of Blake on p. 67.

Note: The dates assigned above to the contents of this MS. are given on the authority of Dr. Sampson, who considers that all those poems here included in sections I *a* and *b* were written before the end of the year 1793, and that after a lapse of several years Blake again began to use the book during the Felpham period, and wrote the poems in sections I *c* and *d* together with the prose pieces, these being some of the latest entries. The last dated entry is no. 161, i, above. The only authoritative text of the poetical contents is that printed by Dr. Sampson, the MS. having been transcribed for him by the present owner with elaborate care, and it is from his pages that the above description and list of contents have been compiled. In his Preface (1905, pp. 141-151) Dr. Sampson gives a full index to the MS. and to the Rossetti transcript, the contents being set out page by page; Ellis and Yeats (i, 202-232) also give a long description of the MS., in the course of which they print much of the text. Selections from the poems and prose pieces are given by most other editors. The contents have been classified and set out at length above for purposes of reference in the later parts of the present work.

The earlier history of this MS. is contained in a pencil note by D. G. Rossetti on the verso of the fly-leaf: " I purchased this original MS. of Palmer, an attendant " in the Antique Gallery at the British Museum, on the 30th April, '47. Palmer

"knew Blake personally, and it was from the artist's wife that he had the present
"MS. which he sold me for 10*s*. Among the sketches there are one or two profiles
"of Blake himself."—D.G.C.R. Rossetti made the partial transcript mentioned
above, which he considered contained "all that is of any value," and in 1861 lent the
MS. to Gilchrist, after whose death he printed many of the poems and much of the
prose in the selection given in the *Life*. The MS. was next in Swinburne's hands,
who gave further extracts in his *Critical Essay*. At the sale of Rossetti's library it
realized £110 and was presumably acquired by F. S. Ellis, with whose collection
it was again sold, at Sotheby's, Nov. 18, 1885 (Ellis and Scrutton, £85). Soon
afterwards it was acquired by Messrs. Dodd, Mead and Co., of New York, who
sold it on Jan. 26, 1887, to the present owner, Mr. W. A. White. A few years
later it was lent to Quaritch for use in the edition of the *Works* prepared by
Messrs. E. J. Ellis and W. B. Yeats, and a transcript was made for Mr. Ellis,
but this seems to have been not altogether accurate. For further details about this
MS. see Sampson, 1905, pp. 138-154.

Facsimile Reproductions: EY (3 pp. of sketches); Sampson, 1905 (pp. 52 and
109, reversed); E. L. Cary, *The Art of W. B.*, 1907 (seven pp.; see no. 343).

6 *Autograph Manuscript, illustrated*: VALA, *or*: THE FOUR ZOAS 1797
Title, first form: Vala / or / The Death and / Judgement / of the / Ancient
   Man / A Dream / of Nine Nights / by William Blake 1797
Title, second form: The Four Zoas / The Torments of Love & Jealousy in /
   The Death and / Judgement / of Albion the / Ancient Man / by William
   Blake 1797

Description: 70 separate leaves, about 41.5 × 32.5 cm., two small sheets, and
one torn fragment. The leaves are made up as follows: 21 sheets of drawing paper
with watermark *J Whatman* 1794, 47 sheets of the same paper with working proofs
of the engravings for Young's *Night Thoughts* on one side, and 2 sheets with parts
of an early engraving by Blake, *Edward and Elenor*, on one side. The title, on the
recto of the first leaf, was originally written in ink as above and afterwards altered in
pencil to the second form; on the verso is a pencil sketch. Of the other 69 leaves,
61 have the text written on both sides; the remainder have the text on one side and
on the other a full-page drawing or engraving. The great majority of the pages of
text have the margins, except where they are occupied by the engravings for Young's
Night Thoughts, decorated with pencil drawings, which are occasionally touched with
water-colour. Most of the text is written in ink, but a few leaves or added lines are

in pencil; some of the earlier leaves are in a formal copper-plate hand, but the rest are in Blake's ordinary writing. The text has undergone extensive erasures, alterations, and additions, so that the right arrangement of the leaves is in some cases doubtful. Only pp. 1-14 were numbered by Blake, but a pencilled foliation has been recently supplied. The leaves are now all mounted on guards, the small leaves being inlaid to a uniform size, and are bound up in half morocco.

Contents: 1*a*. Title as above. Below is a pencil sketch of a confused group of figures emerging from the ground. Down the right-hand margin sweeps a nude figure with a trumpet.

1*b*. No text. Pencil sketch of a nude figure, below which is written: *Rest before Labour.*

2*a*. Heading: *Vala. Night the First.* With quotation from Εφες. 5 κεφ. 12. Begins: *The Song of the Aged Mother which shook the heavens with wrath.* Below is a sketch in blue and sepia of a nude woman reclining on her back and gazing into the distance; her left leg, which is stiffly extended, is only lightly sketched.

2*b*. Begins: *In Eden; in the Auricular Nerves of Human Life.* Below is a sketch in ink and sepia of a nude man, who is shooting with a bow and arrow while kneeling on a coil of a huge worm, which rears its head up the left-hand side of the page.

3*a*. Begins: *She drew the Spectre forth from Tharmas in her shining loom.* Below is a pencil sketch of a winged figure lying asleep.

3*b*. Begins: *In Eden Females sleep the winter in soft silken veils.* Below is a water-colour sketch of a winged figure lying on his side with his face buried in his hands; he is surrounded by dark waters. The borders of the page are touched with blue.

4*a*. Begins: *Till with fierce pain she brought forth on the rocks her sorrow & woe.* Below is a pencil sketch of a woman reclining against a tree and suckling two infants.

4*b*. Begins: *I thought Tharmas a Sinner & I murderd his Emanation.* Below is a pencil sketch of a woman with flame-like hair and legs which merge into a coiling tail.

5*a*. Begins: *And then they wanderd far away she sought for them in vain.* Below is a pencil sketch of three figures; two children seem to scorn a woman who stumbles blindly after them.

5*b*. Begins: *But Enitharmon answerd with a dropping tear & frowning.* Below are figures lightly sketched.

6*a*. Begins: *I heard the sounding sea; I heard the voice weaker and weaker.* Below are figures lightly sketched.

6*b*. Begins: *Night darkend as she spoke, a shuddring ran from East to West*. Two lines have been added below in red chalk. At the bottom are the figures, lightly sketched, of a man striking a woman.

7*a*. Begins: *They listend to the Elemental Harps & Sphery Song*. Below is a slight sketch of a coiling serpent with a human head.

7*b*. Begins: *Stretch their immortal hands to smite the gold & silver Wires*. Below is a pencil sketch of a three-headed woman.

8*a*. Begins: *Enion blind & age-bent wept upon the desolate wind*. Below is a pencil sketch of a woman with her hands raised above her head.

8*b*. Begins: *Why is the Sheep given to the knife? the Lamb plays in the Sun*. Below: *End of The First Night*. A rough sketch of a figure sweeps across the page from left to right.

9*a*. Begins: *Jerusalem his Emanation is become a ruin*. Below: *End of The First Night*. At the bottom is a slight pencil sketch. The lower part of the leaf has been cut away.

9*b*. Written in pencil. Begins: *The Daughters of Beulah beheld the Emanation they pitied*. Below is a pencil sketch of a nude woman lying on her back; an infant's arm is protruding from her womb. [cf. *The Marriage of Heaven and Hell*, pl. 3.]

10*a*. Begins: *Then those in Great Eternity met in the Council of God*. No sketch.

10*b*. Begins: *Luvah replied Dictate to thy Equals. am not I*. Flames are sketched in along the left-hand margin.

11*a*. At the top: *Vala / Night the* [*First* del.]. Begins: *Rising upon his Couch of death Albion beheld his Sons*. Below is sketched the recumbent figure of an old man.

11*b*. Begins: *Mighty was the draught of Voidness to draw Existence in*. Below is a pencil sketch of a woman plunging downwards.

12*a*. Begins: *And the leopards coverd with skins of beasts tended the roaring fires*. Below is a pencil sketch of a kneeling figure struggling with bars of iron.

12*b*. Begins: *Vala incircle round the furna·es where Luvah was clos'd*. Below and in the left-hand margin are four dragons with wings and with womens' or birds' heads.

13*a*. Begins: *And I commanded the Great deep to hide her in his hand*. Below are sketched a young woman lying beside an old man with skeleton ribs.

13*b*. Begins: *These were the words of Luvah patient in afflictions*. Below is a pencil sketch of two figures; partly rubbed out.

14*a*. Begins: *That Luvah sent from the faint Heart of the Fallen Man*. Below is a pencil sketch of a man making a net.

14*b*. Begins: *Spread & many a Spirit caught, innumerable the nets*. On the left-hand margin is a sketch of a woman; partly rubbed out.

15*a*. Begins: *The King of Light beheld her mourning among the Brick kilns compelld*. Below is a sketch of a woman kneeling in an attitude of despair before a nude man; partly rubbed out.

And I commanded the Great deep to hide her in his hand

Till she became a little weeping Infant a span long

I carried her in my bosom as a man carries a lamb

I loved her I gave her all my soul & my delight

I hid her in soft gardens & in secret bowers of summer

Weaving mazes of delight along the sunny Paradise

Inextricable labyrinths, She bore me sons & daughters

And they have taken her away & hid her from my sight

They have surrounded me with walls of iron & brass, O Lamb

Of God clothed in Lavans garments little knowest thou

Of death Eternal that we all go to Eternal Death

To our Primeval Chaos in fortuitous concourse of incoherent

Discordant principles of love & hate I suffer affliction

Because I love for I was love but hatred awakes in me

And Urizen who was Faith & Certainty is changd to Doubt

The hand of Urizen is upon me because I blotted out

That Human delusion to deliver all the Sons of God

From bondage of the Human form. O first born Son of Light

O Urizen my enemy I weep for thy stern ambition

But weep in vain O when will you return Vala the Wanderer

THE FOUR ZOAS

Page 13a

15*b*. Begins: *Still she despised him, calling on his name & knowing him not.* Below is a sketch, partly rubbed out, of a group of women, standing and lying.

16*a*. Begins: *The seas & lakes they reard the mountains & the rocks & hills.* Below is an unintelligible sketch.

16*b*. Begins: *And Los & Enitharmon were drawn down by their desires.* No sketch.

17*a*. Begins: *I am made to sow the thistle for wheat, the nettle for a nourishing dainty.* Below is a sketch, partly rubbed out, of four or five nude women on their knees; to the right is a small girl, to the left a woman with a full basket on her head.

17*b*. Begins: *To listen to the hungry ravens cry in wintry season.* In the left-hand margin is a sketch of a woman plunging downwards.

18*a*. At the top: *Vala / Night The Third.* Begins: *Now sat the King of Light on high upon his starry throne.* Below is a rough sketch of a woman kneeling at a man's feet.

18*b*. Begins: *Infolded in thick clouds from whence his mighty voice burst forth.* Below is a sketch of a man embracing a woman; other figures have been rubbed out.

19*a*. Begins: *Raise then thy radiant eyes to him raise thy obedient hands.* A sketch below has been rubbed out.

19*b*. Begins: *In a soft cloud outstretch'd across, & Luvah dwelt in the cloud.* Below is a sketch of a man leaning over the prostrate body of a woman. On the man's back is seated a Cupid with spurs. Partly rubbed out.

20*a*. Begins: *In golden wreathes the sorrow of Man & the balmy drops fell down.* Below is a drawing of a nude woman lying on her back and grasping the male parts of a man who is standing at her head.

20*b*. Begins: *Saying, Go & die the Death of Man for Vala the sweet wanderer.* Below is a sketch, partly rubbed out, of a woman and two children. To the left a woman is pursuing a winged emblem of Priapus.

21*a*. Begins: *Then thunders rolld around & lightnings darted to & fro.* In the margins Young's *Night Thoughts*, pl. 30.

21*b*. Begins: *As when the thunderbolt down falleth on the appointed place.* On the left below is a sketch of a nude woman, on the right a man, lying on his back with right arm raised.

22*a*. Begins: *Have quite forsaken: O fool fool to lose my sweetest bliss.* In the margins Young's *Night Thoughts*, pl. 40.

22*b*. Begins: *Melting, a shower of falling tears, nothing but tears. Enion.* Below: *The End of the Third Night.* At the bottom a sketch of a nude man repelling a woman.

23*a*. Heading: *Vala / Night the Fourth.* Begins: *But Tharmas rode on the dark Abyss. The voice of Tharmas rolld.* In the margins, Young's *Night Thoughts*, pl. 26.

23*b*. Begins: *Deformd I see these lineaments of ungratified desire.* Below is a sketch of a seated figure gazing upwards.

24*a*. Begins: *What Sovereign Architect said Tharmas dare my will controll.* In the margins, Young's *Night Thoughts*, pl. 7.

24*b*. Begins: *I slumber here in weak repose. I well remember the day.* Below is a sketch of a woman lying in a wave with arms outstretched.

25*a*. Begins: *But my sweet Enion is vanishd & I never more.* In the margins, Young's *Night Thoughts*, pl. 19.

25*b*. Begins: *I will compell thee to rebuild by these my furious waves.* Below is a drawing of a kneeling man, and a woman holding him at arm's length.

26*a*. Begins: *The days & years in chains of iron round the limbs of Urizen.* In the margins, Young's *Night Thoughts*, pl. 4.

26*b*. Begins: *The Eternal Mind bounded began to roll eddies of wrath ceaseless.* Below is an unintelligible sketch.

27*a*. Begins: *And a fifth age passed & a state of dismal woe.* In the margins, Young's *Night Thoughts*, pl. 38.

27*b*. Begins: *Lord Saviour if thou hadst been here our brother had not died.* Below: *End of the Fourth Night.* At the bottom is a sketch of Christ drawing a youth towards him by his hands, and above this in faint pencil: *Christ's crucifixion shall be made an excuse for Executing Criminals.*

28*a*. Heading: *Vala | Night The Fifth.* Begins: *Infected Mad he dancd on his mountains high & dark as heaven.* In the margins, Young's *Night Thoughts*, pl. 32.

28*b*. Begins: *Her pale hands cling around her husband & over her weak head.* Below is a sketch of a recumbent woman, with a man standing at her head.

29*a*. Begins: *Where is sweet Vala gloomy prophet where the lovely form.* In the margins, Young's *Night Thoughts*, pl. 34.

29*b*. Begins: *And brass & silver & gold fourfold in dark prophetic fear.* Below is a drawing of a man and a woman embracing; at their feet kneels a figure with a cord round his body.

30*a*. Begins: *The hammer of Urthona smote the rivets in terror of brass.* In the margins, Young's *Night Thoughts*, pl. 37.

30*b*. Begins: *His loins inwove with silken fires, are like a furnace fierce.* Below is a sketch of Los, Orc, and Enitharmon, as in *America*, pl. 1.

31*a*. Begins: *Into the iron rock & grew a chain beneath the Earth.* In the margins, Young's *Night Thoughts*, pl. 13.

31*b*. Begins: *Once how I walked from my palace in gardens of delight.* Below is a sketch of a man and a woman kissing; beside them sits a figure with a net.

32*a*. Begins: *Thy pure feet stepd on the steps divine too pure for other feet.* Below: *End of the Fifth Night.* In the margins, Young's *Night Thoughts*, pl. 36.

And brass & silver & gold fourfold in dark prophetic fear
For now he feard Eternal Death & uttermost Extinction
He builded Golgonooza on the Lake of Udan Adan
Upon the Limit of Translucence then he builded Luban
Tharmas laid the Foundation & Los finishd it in howling woe

But when fourteen summers & winters had revolved over
Their solemn habitation Los beheld the ruddy boy
Embracing his bright mother & beheld malignant fires
In his young eyes discerning plain that Orc plotted his death
Grief rose upon his ruddy brows. a lightning girdle grew
Around his bosom like a bloody cord. in secret sobs
He burst it, but next morn another girdle succeeds
Around his bosom. Every day he viewd the fiery youth
With silent fear & his immortal cheeks grew deadly pale
Till many a morn & many a night passd over in dire woe
Forming a girdle in the day & bursting it at night
The girdle was formd by day by night was burst in twain
Falling down on the rock an iron chain link by link lockd

Enitharmon beheld the bloody chain of nights & days
Depending from the bosom of Los & how with dismal pain
He went each morning to his labours with the spectre dark
Calld it the chain of Jealousy. Now Los began to speak
His woes aloud to Enitharmon. since he could not hide
His uncouth plague. He siezd the boy in his immortal hands
While Enitharmon followd him weeping in dismal woe
Up to the iron mountains top & there the jealous chain
Fell from his bosom on the mountain. The spectre dark   100
Held the fierce boy Los naild him down binding around his limbs
The accursed chain O how bright Enitharmon howld & cried
Over her Son. Obdurate Los bound down her loved Joy

THE FOUR ZOAS
Page 29b

THE FOUR ZOAS
Page 32b

32*b*. No text. In the centre a pencil drawing of a nude man balancing a globe on his head; on either side of him two other figures, floating upwards or crouching.

33*a*. Heading: *Vala / Night the Sixth*. Begins: *So Urizen arose & leaning on his Spear explord his dens*. In the margins, Young's *Night Thoughts*, pl. 41.

33*b*. Begins: *And Urizen raisd his spear, they reard up a wall of rocks*. Below is a drawing of the head and shoulders of a woman drooping downwards, with loose, streaming hair.

34*a*. Begins: *Silent in ridges he beheld them stand round Urizen*. In the margins, Young's *Night Thoughts*, pl. 41.

34*b*. Begins: *Los brooded on the darkness nor saw Urizen with a globe of fire*. Below, a pencil drawing of a dragon with gaping crocodile-jaws.

35*a*. Begins: *He could not take their fetters off for they grew from the soul*. In the margins, Young's *Night Thoughts*, pl. 4.

35*b*. Begins: *The journey obstinate refuse to write time after time*. Below, pencil sketch of three women seated beside a blasted tree stump.

36*a*. Begins: *And laughter sat beneath the Oaks & innocence sported round*. In the margins, Young's *Night Thoughts*, pl. 24.

36*b*. Begins: *For every one opened within into Eternity at will*. Below, sketch of an old man striding along, with a globe hanging from his hand. [cf. *Urizen*, pl. 23.]

37*a*. Begins: *Redoubling his immortal efforts thro the narrow vales*. Below: *End of The Sixth Night*. In the margins, Young's *Night Thoughts*, pl. 35.

37*b*. No text. Pencil drawing of a nude woman with outstretched arms. [cf. the engraving known as *Glad Day*, Russell, *Engravings*, p. 54.]

38*a*. Heading: *Vala / Night the Seventh*. Begins: *Then Urizen arose The Spectre fled & Tharmas fled*. In the margins, Young's *Night Thoughts*, pl. 7.

38*b*. Begins: *For Urizen fixd in Envy sat brooding & coverd with Snow*. Below, pencil drawing of a nude man lying stiffly stretched out on his back.

39*a*. Begins: *I Rage in the deep for Lo my feet & hands are naild to the burning rock*. In the margins, Young's *Night Thoughts*, pl. 28. The lower part of the leaf is cut away.

39*b*. Begins: *And Urizen Read in his book of brass in sounding tones*. No drawing.

40*a*. Begins: *Of all his wandering Experiments in the horrible Abyss*. In the margins, Young's *Night Thoughts*, pl. 5.

40*b*. Begins: *Hid in a little silken veil scarce breathe & faintly shine*. Below, pencil drawing of a nude woman with striding legs holding a hoop set with stars.

41*a*. Begins: *His mother to the winds of heaven Intoxicated with . . . .* In the margins, Young's *Night Thoughts*, pl. 27.

41*b*. Begins: *The Spectre said Thou lovely Vision this delightful Tree*. Below, a rough sketch of a crouching figure with right arm raised.

42*a*. Begins: *Astonishd filld with tears the Spirit of Enitharmon beheld.*   In the margins, Young's *Night Thoughts*, pl. 42.

42*b*. Begins: *For me & thou annihilate evaporate & be no more.*   In the centre, pencil drawing of a nude woman on her knees and grasping her breasts with either hand.

43*a*. Begins: *But Enitharmon trembling fled & hid beneath Urizen's tree.*   No drawing.

43*b*. No text. The right-hand portion of a large engraving by Blake, *Edward & Elenor*, c. 1793 (see Russell, *Engravings*, p. 68). At the top is written in pencil: *The Christian Religion teaches that No Man is Indifferent to you but that every one is | Either your friend or your enemy; he must necessarily be either the one or the other | And that he will be equally profitable both ways if you treat him as he deserves.*

44*a*. Left-hand portion of *Edward & Elenor*.

44*b*. Begins: *So Enitharmon spoke trembling & in torrents of tears.*   No drawing.

45*a*. Heading: *Vala | Night the Seventh | This Night begins at line 153 the following comes at the end.* Begins: *Now in the Caverns of the Grave & Places of human seed.*   In the margins, Young's *Night Thoughts*, pl. 9.

45*b*. Begins: *Of death O northern drum awake O hand of iron sound.*   Below, sketch of two figures seated.

46*a*. Begins: *Lift up thy blue eyes Vala & put on thy sapphire shoes.*   In the margins, Young's *Night Thoughts*, pl. 29.

46*b*. Begins: *I wakend Enion in the morning & she turned away.*   Below, sketch of a figure lying in an attitude of despair and howling.

47*a*. Begins: *For far & wide she stretchd thro' all the worlds of Urizen's journey.*   In the margins, Young's *Night Thoughts*, pl. 20.

47*b*. Begins: *And in the inner part of the Temple wondrous workmanship.*   Below, a sketch of figures kneeling in worship before an immense emblem of Priapus.

48*a*. Begins: *My Waters like a flood around thee fear not trust in me.*   In the margins, Young's *Night Thoughts*, pl. 40.

48*b*. Begins: *And must not I obey the God thou Shadow of Jealousy.*   Below, a drawing of a human-headed serpent.

49*a*. Heading: *Vala | Night the Eighth.* Begins: *Then All in Great Eternity Met in the Council of God.*   In the margins, Young's *Night Thoughts*, pl. 14.

49*b*. Begins: *From out the War of Urizen & Tharmas receiving them.*   Below, a drawing of a human-headed bird with cloven feet.

50*a*. Begins: *To the four winds hopeless of future. All futurity.*   In the margins, Young's *Night Thoughts*, pl. 8.

50*b*. Begins: *The dire confusion till the battle faints those that remain.*   Below, a drawing of a nude youth lying on a bank.

THE FOUR ZOAS
Page 42b

51*a*. Begins: *The sorrower of Eternity in love with tears, submiss I rear.* In the margins, Young's *Night Thoughts*, pl. 17.

51*b*. Begins: *And Enitharmon namd the Female Jerusalem the holy.* Below, drawing of a woman on her knees striving against a wheel set with stars.

52*a*. Begins: *The Lamb of God stood before Satan opposite.* In the margins, Young's *Night Thoughts*, pl. 12.

52*b*. Begins: *Thus was the Lamb of God condemnd to Death.* Below, sketch of a recumbent man with two other figures standing.

53*a*. Begins: *The Elephant the Wolf the Bear the Lama the Satyr.* In the margins, Young's *Night Thoughts*, pl. 3.

53*b*. Begins: *Tharmas on high rode furious thro the afflicted worlds.* Below, sketch of a woman lying on her side, howling; a small figure with a bow is seated on her buttocks.

54*a*. Begins: *And the strong Eagle now with num[b]ing Cold blighted of feathers.* In the margins, Young's *Night Thoughts*, pl. 43.

54*b*. Begins: *The Lamb of God has rent the Veil of Mystery soon to return.* Below, sketch of a nude woman falling onto her face.

55*a*. Begins: *We behold with wonder Enitharmon's looms & Los's Forges.* No drawing.

55*b*. No text. Young's *Night Thoughts*, pl. 31.

56*a*. Begins: *And these are the Sons of Los & Enitharmon Rintrah Palamabron.* In the margins, Young's *Night Thoughts*, pl. 34.

56*b*. Begins: *Lo Enitharmon terrible & beautiful in Eternal youth.* Seven lines of text with full-page drawing of Christ parting the clouds. Similar to Young's *Night Thoughts*, pl. 31.

57*a*. Heading: *Vala | Night the Ninth | Being | The Last Judgment.* Begins: *And Los & Enitharmon builded Jerusalem weeping.* In the margins, Young's *Night Thoughts*, pl. 23.

57*b*. Begins: *Recievd her in the darkning South their bodies lost they stood.* Below, drawing of a group of three nude women struggling together.

58*a*. Begins: *In the fierce flames the limbs of Mystery lay consuming with howling.* In the margins, Young's *Night Thoughts*, pl. 37.

58*b*. Begins: *The voices of children in my tents to cries of helpless infants.* Below, sketch of a nude woman seated with her head buried in her arms.

59*a*. Begins: *Urizen wept in the dark deep anxious his scaly form.* In the margins, Young's *Night Thoughts*, pl. 22.

59*b*. Begins: *Behold Jerusalem in whose bosom the Lamb of God.* Below, sketch of a nude woman lying with her arms thrown back.

60*a*. Begins: *And all the marks remain of the slaves scourge & tyrants crown.* In the margins, Young's *Night Thoughts*, pl. 10.

60*b*. Begins: *Beheld the Vision of God & he arose up from the Rock*. Below, drawing of a young woman seated in a large flower; her right hand is stretched out to touch the forehead of an old man who is leaning on a staff before her.

61*a*. Begins: *He turned the horses loose & laid his Plow in the northern corner*. In the margins, Young's *Night Thoughts*, pl. 18.

61*b*. Begins: *And now fierce Orc had quite consumd himself in mental flames*. A confused sketch of various figures covers the greater part of the page.

62*a*. Begins: *Where dost thou dwell for it is thee I seek & but for thee*. In the margins, Young's *Night Thoughts*, pl. 15.

62*b*. Begins: *That sing & fly in the bright air but you do lick my feet*. Below, a drawing, touched with water-colours, of a semi-nude Persian woman, with a tambourine, lying on cushions. Above her is seated another woman with a flute, and to the left are two figures apparently treading grapes.

63*a*. Begins: *My Luvah smild I kneeld down he laid his hand on my head*. In the margins, Young's *Night Thoughts*, pl. 21.

63*b*. Begins: *And she arose out of the river & girded her golden girdle*. Below, a sketch of a figure recumbent, gazing upwards.

64*a*. Begins: *He said O Vala I am sick & all this garden of pleasure*. In the margins, Young's *Night Thoughts*, pl. 22.

64*b*. Begins: *The Universal Groan went up the Eternal Man was darkend*. Below, a sketch of a man bowing at the feet of a nude girl, who is standing in water. Other scribblings cover the page.

65*a*. Begins: *The Eternal Man arose he welcomd them to the Feast*. In the margins, Young's *Night Thoughts*, pl. 5.

65*b*. Begins: *And all Nations were threshed out & the Stars threshed from their husks*. Below, drawing of a bird with a woman's head and a long tail; on her back is seated a small figure with a stick in one hand and a wineglass in the other.

66*a*. Begins: *When in my fathers house I sat & heard his chearing voice*. In the margins, Young's *Night Thoughts*, pl. 16.

66*b*. Begins: *O terrible wine presses of Luvah O caverns of the Grave*. Below, drawing of a bearded head with wings.

67*a*. Begins: *They catch the Shrieks in cups of gold. They hand them to one another*. In the margins, Young's *Night Thoughts*, pl. 39.

67*b*. Begins: *Then dark Urthona took the corn out of the stores of Urizen*. Below, sketch of a nude woman recumbent, gazing upwards.

68*a*. Begins: *The Sun arises from his dewy bed & the fresh airs*. Below: *End of the Dream*. At the bottom, sketch of a nude figure springing up from a globe with arms outstretched.

68*b*. No text. Young's *Night Thoughts*, pl. 1.

Additional leaves and fragments.

69*a*. Begins: *The Horse is of more value than the Man. The Tyger fierce.* Below, pencil sketch touched with sepia of an old man, semi-recumbent, holding a rope, which passes up from left to right.

69*b*. Begins: *They melt the bones of Vala & the bones of Luvah into wedges.* Below, rough pencil sketch of two feet, and a small figure to the left.

70*a*. Begins: *Rahab triumphs over all she took Jerusalem.* In the margins, Young's *Night Thoughts*, pl. 34.

70*b*. No text. Pencil drawing of a nude man and woman; the man has his arm round the woman's middle, the woman's hands are raised above her head in an attitude of rage.

71*a*. Small sheet of thin paper. Begins, in ink: *Beneath the veil of Vala rose Tharmas from dewy tears.*

71*b*. Begins, in pencil: *The ocean calm the clouds fold round & fiery flames of love.*

72*a*. Torn fragment of drawing paper. Begins: *. . . mingling their bodies form in burning anguish.*

72*b* Begins: *That I should hide thee with my power . . .* Below is a sketch of a serpent coiling round a kneeling figure.

73*a*. Small sheet of thin paper. Begins: *The Lamb of God stood before Urizen opposite.*

73*b*. Blank.

Note: Blake seems to have kept this unfinished MS. by him for many years and finally, without completing it, to have presented it some time before his death to John Linnell (see Ellis, *The Real Blake*, pp. 410-411). Dr. Sampson describes it as " the longest as well as one of the most significant of his writings," and states that it " forms a valuable link between the earlier and the later Prophetic Books, indicating " as it does in his successive revisions and additions the beginning of a new set of " mystical ideas and symbols which we find fully developed in *Milton* and *Jerusalem.* ". . . The date on the title-page, 1797, doubtless denotes the year in which Blake " began his fair transcript of a poem probably composed a twelvemonth earlier. This " work was rehandled at Felpham, and in that period of new spiritual illumination " (*circa* 1800-3) was subjected to many changes, long passages being erased with the " knife and laboriously rewritten, while the whole of Night VII was entirely recast in " the light of his later tenets. . . . There is no evidence that Blake at any time con- " templated engraving and publishing this work in the same manner as the other " prophetic writings. Indeed, the extreme care and finish with which the greater part " of the book is written point rather to an intention to produce a single perfect copy " only in MS. form. This conjecture is supported by the fact that Blake afterwards " excerpted long passages from the poem and engraved them as part of *Milton* and " *Jerusalem.*" (Sampson, 1913, pp. xxxviii-ix.)

The MS. remained in the possession of Linnell's descendants until his collection was sold at Christie's on March 15, 1918 (lot 206, Parsons, £420); the purchaser, who has remained anonymous, soon afterwards presented it to the British Museum, and it is now in the Dept. of MSS. (Add. 39764). The MS. was transcribed and printed in full by Ellis and Yeats in their edition of Blake's *Works*, 1893, and this text was revised by EJE, but both texts are exceedingly inaccurate. It was also consulted by Dr. Sampson when preparing his edition of 1913, which includes a selection of passages from the poem. Dr. Sampson (1913, p. xxxix) stated that the MS. consists of 70 separate leaves and 4 smaller fragments, but this seems to have been an error, since no part of the text is missing at the present time. This may have arisen from the fact that the lower half of leaf 55 has been cut away so that it was counted both among the leaves and the fragments; or possibly a fragment of paper with a note by Blake on Spurzheim (see no. 19A), which was formerly placed among the leaves of *The Four Zoas*, was reckoned as belonging to it. In several of the drawings Blake has used a frankly sexual symbolism, and some of them were rubbed out or obliterated by John Linnell after the MS. came into his possession (Ellis, *The Real Blake*, p. 411). Since it is desirable to have a permanent record of the constitution of the MS. a page-by-page description is given here.

Printed: EY, iii, 1-174; Sampson, 1905 (extracts); EJE, ii, 1-240; Sampson, 1913 (selections); F. E. Pierce, 1915 (selections). Extracts translated into German by Knoblauch, 1907 (no. 175), and von Taube, 1907 (no. 176).

Facsimile Reproductions: EY, iii (19 pp., lithographic, reduced).

7 *Autograph Manuscript*: GENESIS [*not earlier than* 1797]

Title: Genesis / The Seven Days / of the Created World

Description: 28 leaves of handmade paper, 20.5 × 16.5 cm., with watermark 1797; text written in ink on one side only of the first 8 leaves. In contemporary blue paper covers without label.

Contents: About 200 lines of blank verse, headed as above and beginning:

> " Thou Sire of Heaven & of the Eternal Sire
> " Eternal Son & Offspring Increate . . ."

The first 150 lines are numbered by tens in the margins; over 50 unnumbered lines follow and end suddenly without a stop.

Note: The origin and purpose of this MS. are obscure. The handwriting is certainly Blake's, but Symons points out (pp. 140-143) that, although at first large and careful, it becomes smaller and more hurried, as if it had all been written at a single sitting. In the later part of the MS. there are corrections, sometimes as much

WILLIAM BLAKE
Pencil drawing by John Flaxman, 1804

as a line and a half being crossed out and rewritten. The poem consists of an argument or statement written in a formal manner with pious invocations, and, according to Symons, "nowhere is there any characteristic felicity or any recognisable sign of Blake." It differs from any of Blake's early attempts at blank verse in the absolute regularity of the metre. Symons suggests that it may be a translation of Klopstock, dictated by Hayley, or that it may be a copy of a very early work made at Hayley's instigation. If it is a translation from Klopstock, it is no doubt the piece that called forth from Blake the scurrilous lines recorded under no. 10. The manner and matter resemble Klopstock's in their empty verbosity, but I have not been able to identify the poem with any passage in the *Messiah*. It seems very improbable that this work, which is certainly not Blake's own composition, is the same as that referred to by Crabb Robinson as a *Vision* (or *Version*) *of Genesis* (see no. 64). The MS. was formerly in the possession of the late H. Buxton Forman, C.B., who kindly supplied me with the descriptive details given above. It was sold with his library at the Anderson Galleries, New York, on March 15, 1920 (Rosenbach Co., $1,350). The first page of the MS. is reproduced in facsimile in the sale catalogue, but the rest of the poem has never been printed.

8 *Blake's designs for Gray's Poems, containing the lines* "To Mrs Anna Flaxman" (A little Flower grew in a lovely vale)   [*about* 1801]

Description: 67 leaves of drawing paper, about 42 × 32 cm., bound in contemporary half-calf. In the centre of each leaf is inserted a leaf of Gray's *Poems*, London, Murray, 1790, measuring about 15 × 8 cm. In the margins of the pages thus formed are 114 water-colour designs by Blake in illustration of the following poems:

Ode on the Spring	6 designs
Ode on the Death of a Favourite Cat	6 ,,
Ode on a Distant Prospect of Eton College	10 ,,
A Long Story	12 ,,
Hymn to Adversity	6 ,,
The Progress of Poesy	12 ,,
The Bard	14 ,,
The Fatal Sisters	10 ,,
The Descent of Odin	10 ,,
The Triumphs of Owen	6 ,,
Installation Ode	10 ,,
Epitaph on Mrs. Jane Clerke	2 ,,
Elegy written in a Country Church-yard	12 ,,

Before each poem is a list of the designs in Blake's hand; below the list for the "Ode on the Spring" he has added the couplet:

> "Around the Springs of Gray my wild root weaves
> "Traveller repose and dream among my leaves.
>
> "WILL BLAKE."

On the last leaf Blake has written the lines:

> "To MRS ANNA FLAXMAN
>
> "A little Flower grew in a lovely vale
> "Its form was lovely but its colours pale.
> "One standing in the Porches of the Sun
> "When his Meridian Glories were begun,
> "Leap'd from the steps of fire and on the grass
> "Alighted where the little flower was.
> "With haste divine he mov'd the gentle sod,
> "And took the Flower up in its native clod.
> "Then planting it upon a Mountain brow,
> "'Tis your own fault if you don't flourish now.
>
> "WILLIAM BLAKE."

On the front fly-leaf is a pencil drawing of Blake's head in profile by Flaxman, resembling the full face drawing reproduced in the present work.

Note: This volume, as may be inferred from the lines written at the end, was given by Blake to Mrs. Flaxman, but there is no indication of the exact year in which he made it. I have given the conjectural date of 1801 to the designs on the assumption that the lines to Mrs. Flaxman express Blake's gratitude to Flaxman ("One standing in the Porches of the Sun")* for having been instrumental in transplanting him to Felpham, where he lived from September 1800 to September 1803. The general style of the designs is similar to that of the illustrations to Young's *Night Thoughts*, 1797 (no. 70).

The book was sold with Flaxman's effects at Christie's on July 1, 1828, and was bought by "Clarke" for eight guineas. It is probable that the buyer was William Clarke of New Bond Street, and that the book was sold by him to William Beckford, who possessed a considerable number of Blake's illuminated books. The designs are not mentioned by Gilchrist and were not seen by him, being only recorded in W. M. Rossetti's list of "Works of Unascertained Method" (Gilchrist, ii, 275), where they are described as "One hundred and fourteen Designs to Gray's Poems (The Duke of Hamilton) Reputed to be among the very finest works

---

* *Cf.* "You, O dear Flaxman, are a sublime archangel, my friend and companion from eternity" (Sept. 21, 1800, Russell, *Letters*, p. 76).

Thy Brother has arrind himself in Steel
To avenge the wrongs thy Children feel

But vain the Sword & vain the Bow
They never can work Wars overthrow
The Hermits Prayer & the Widows tear
Alone can free the World from fear

For a Tear is an Intellectual Thing
And a Sigh is the Sword of an Angel King
And the bitter groan of the Martyrs woe
Is an Arrow from the Almighties Bow

The hand of Vengeance found the Bed
To which the Purple Tyrant fled
The iron hand crushd the Tyrants head
And became a Tyrant in his Stead

Auguries of Innocence

To see a World in a Grain of Sand
And a Heaven in a Wild Flower
Hold Infinity in the palm of your hand
And Eternity in an hour
A Robin Red breast in a Cage
Puts all Heaven in a Rage
A Dove house filld with Doves & Pigeons

14 Shudders Hell thro all its regions
A dog starvd at his Masters Gate
Predicts the ruin of the State
A Horse misusd upon the Road
Calls to Heaven for Human blood
Each outcry of the hunted Hare
A fibre from the Brain does tear
A Skylark wounded in the wing
A Cherubim does cease to sing
The Game Cock clipd & armd for fight
Does the Rising Sun affright
Every Wolfs & Lions howl
Raises from Hell a Human Soul
The wild deer wandring here & there
Keeps the Human Soul from Care
The Lamb misusd breeds Public strife
And yet forgives the Butchers Knife
The Bat that flits at close of Eve
Has left the Brain that wont Believe
The Owl that calls upon the Night
Speaks the Unbelievers fright
He who shall hurt the little Wren
-Shall never be belovd by Men

executed by Blake." The book was not included in the sales of the Beckford or the Hamilton Libraries, having probably been overlooked, and it remained lost to sight in Hamilton Palace until 1919, when it was described by Professor H. J. C. Grierson in the *Times* of November 4, the details given above as to its sale in 1828 being added by an anonymous correspondent in the issue of November 5. By the kindness of the Duchess of Hamilton I was allowed to examine the volume soon afterwards. Professor Grierson has announced that a reproduction of the volume under his editorship is contemplated. The lines of poetry by Blake were unpublished until they were printed in the *Times* by Professor Grierson, who suggested the interpretation of them given above.

9 *Autograph Manuscript known as*: THE PICKERING MS. [*about* 1801-1803]

*Description**: Fcp. 4°; 11 leaves, 20.5 × 15 cm., without watermark, paginated consecutively by Blake 1-22. According to W. M. Rossetti, the volume was originally "stitched into a darkish, olive-tinted cover"; later it was bound for B. M. Pickering by F. Bedford, and the pages were somewhat trimmed down, the top and bottom lines of pp. 17 and 18 being grazed in the process. Inside the cover is the armorial bookplate of William Mitchell.

Contents:

	PAGE
1. The Smile [Smile and Frown, *some editors*]	1
2. The Golden Net	2
3. The Mental Traveller	3
4. The Land of Dreams	7
5. Mary	8
6. The Crystal Cabinet	10
7. The Grey Monk	12
8. Auguries of Innocence	13
9. Long John Brown & Little Mary Bell	19
10. William Bond	20

Note: The date of this MS. given above is that deduced by Dr. Sampson from internal evidence; he states (1905, p. 267) that it may confidently be referred to Blake's Felpham period. The poems seem to be fair copies of pieces, the form of which had already been approved, and the few corrections that occur are mostly in the use of capitals; there is, however, no title-page and no indication of the purpose for which the collection was transcribed. Rough drafts of two of the poems, nos. 2 and 7 above, are found in the *Rossetti MS.* (I, 63 and 59), but for the rest the *Pickering*

* These facts are derived from Sampson, 1905, p. 265, to whom they were supplied by Mr. W. A. White.

MS. is the only authority. At whatever period the poems were composed it is at least possible that they were copied out at a much later date, and in connection with this the following statement made by Crabb Robinson in a letter to Dorothy Wordsworth, dated Feb. 20, 1826, is suggestive—" I gave your brother some poems " in MS. by him [Blake], and they interested him—as well they might, for there is an " affinity between them, as there is between the regulated imagination of a wise poet " and the incoherent dreams of a poet." (Symons, p. 273.)

Except for the above suggestion the history of this volume is unknown before 1863, when it was, at any rate temporarily, in the hands of D. G. Rossetti; in 1866 it was bought by B. M. Pickering. About the time of the latter's death in 1878 it was lost sight of, but seems to have passed into the possession of William Mitchell, whose bookplate is inside the cover. It was next acquired by Locker-Lampson and remained in the Rowfant Library until, in 1905, the collection was sold to Messrs. Dodd, Mead and Co. of New York, from whom this volume was bought, together with other Blake originals, by Mr. W. A. White.

These poems were first printed in 1863 by D. G. Rossetti in the selection given in Gilchrist, vol. ii; in 1866 and 1868 they were included by R. H. Shepherd in Pickering's editions of the *Songs of Innocence and of Experience* (nos. 138 and 139). Later editors could only follow these two texts owing to the disappearance of the original MS., but its recovery in 1905 made it possible for an accurate text to be given by Dr. Sampson (1905, pp. 269-298, and 1913, pp. 161-180). Except for the two pages given in the present work, the MS. has never been reproduced in facsimile.

10   *Manuscript*: ON THE PUBLICATION OF KLOPSTOCK'S MESSIAH
[*about* 1803]

Description: From an article on "Lord Crewe's Blake Collection," by Thomas Nutt in *The Critic*, New York, 1903 (see no. 538): "On looking through the " padlocked box containing these treasures some time before the sale I found inside " one of the volumes a small note-head containing thirty-four lines of verse, written on " both sides of the sheet, and signed 'W. Blake—on the publication of Klopstock's " Messiah.' Some of these verses are unspeakably coarse, yet there is no reason, so far " as I know, to question their authenticity. Curiously enough the catalogue ignores " them."

Note: These verses have not, as far as I know, been printed, nor are they mentioned anywhere else; possibly they are a transcript of the piece in the *Rossetti MS.* beginning "When Klopstock England defied" (Sampson, 1905, pp. 192-3), but this consists of 32 lines. Hayley has recorded in his diary, under the date 26-27 March, 1803: "Read the death of Klopstock in the newspaper of the day,

" and looked into his Messiah, both the original and the translation. Read Klopstock
" into English to Blake; and translated the opening of his third canto, where he speaks
" of his own death." * It was perhaps after this incident that Blake wrote the lines
in question. A poem written in his hand, which may be a translation from Klopstock,
is described under no. 7.

11   *Autograph Manuscript*: [THE EVERLASTING GOSPEL, *additional
fragment*]   [*about* 1818]

Description: 13.7 × 9.5 cm. A small folded leaf of 4 pp. Watermark 1818.
Blake has written in ink on the first three pages and in pencil on the fourth; he has
made some corrections and marginal additions.
   Contents: No title, but Blake has written at the top: *This is to come first.*
   pp. [1]-[3]. 56 lines of rhymed verse written by Blake in ink without punctuation and beginning:

> " If moral virtue was Christianity
> " Christ's pretensions were all vanity
> " And Cai[a]phas and Pilate men
> " Praiseworthy and the lion's den
> " And not the sheepfold allegories
> " Of God and heaven and their glories "

   p. [4]. 16 lines of prose, written by Blake in pencil and beginning:

" There is not one moral virtue Jesus inculcated but Plato and Cicero inculcated
" before Him."

   Note: This MS. consists of passages supplementary to *The Everlasting Gospel*
(*Rossetti MS.*, I, 152). It has not yet been printed. The fact that it cannot have
been written earlier than 1818 may throw some light on the date of *The Everlasting
Gospel* itself, which is considered by Dr. Sampson (1913, p. 146) to have been written
not earlier than 1810. The poem is referred to by Swinburne in a footnote on
pp. 175-6 of his *Critical Essay*, where he summarizes the meaning of the passages
and quotes six lines, but this reference seems to have escaped the notice of
Dr. Sampson and other editors. Except for the fact that the MS. was seen by
Swinburne, I do not know anything of its history. It is now in the possession of
Mr. E. J. Shaw of Walsall, by whose courtesy I am able to publish this description.

* *Memoirs of William Hayley*, 1823, ii, 42. See no. 245.

12 *Autograph Manuscript, illustrated*: GENESIS [*about* 1826]

Description: 13 leaves, 38 × 28 cm., consisting of two designs for title-pages and eleven pages of text with illustrations. The title-pages and some of the following leaves are in colours, and the text on the latter has been carefully illuminated in green; on the last pages the text is in pencil and is accompanied by rough pencil sketches. The watermark is dated 1826.

Contents: The headings of the chapters are as follows:

Chap. I. The Creation of the Natural Man.

Chap. II. The Natural Man divided into Male & Female, & of the Tree of Life, & of the tree of Good and Evil.

Chap. III. Of Sexual Nature, & its Fall into Generation and Death.

Chap. IV. How Generation and Death took Possession of the Natural Man & Of the Forgiveness of Sins written on the Murderer's Forehead.

Note: This fragment, the beginning of an illustrated MS. copy of Genesis or of the Bible, was done for John Linnell, and was in the possession of his descendants until March, 1918, when it was sold at Christie's with the Linnell collection (lot 192, G. D. Smith, 150 gns.); it is now in the library of Mr. H. E. Huntington. It ends at Chap. IV, verse 15, and seems to be distinct from the *Vision* or *Version of Genesis* (no. 64) referred to by Crabb Robinson, since the latter was an original composition "in a style resembling the Bible" instead of a MS. copy.

B. *ANNOTATIONS IN BOOKS*

13 APHORISMS ON MAN: Translated from the Original Manuscript of the Rev. John Caspar Lavater, . . . MDCCLXXXVIII. 8° pp. vi + [ii] + 224.

Frontispiece: See no. 101.

Annotations: In his own copy of this book, for which he engraved the frontispiece, Blake has written many comments. On the title-page, below the name Lavater, he has written *Will. Blake*, and round the two names he has drawn the outline of a heart. Of the aphorisms 200 are either underlined or have marginal annotations, and on the fly-leaves at the end are three pages of his writing, which begins as follows:

" I hope no one will call what I have written cavilling, because he may think my " remarks of small consequence, for I write from the warmth of my heart, and cannot " resist the impulse I feel to rectify what I think false in a book I love so much, and " approve so generally."

Note: This volume formerly belonged to Samuel Palmer, and remained for some time in the possession of his descendants. Eventually, it came into the possession of the late Robert Hoe, and was sold with his library at the Anderson Galleries, New York, on April 25, 1911 (lot 396, $1,525.00). It is now in the collection of Mr. H. E. Huntington.

Printed: Gilchrist, i, 62-67 (extracts); Ellis, *The Real Blake*, pp. 122-151 (in full).

14 THE WISDOM OF ANGELS, CONCERNING DIVINE LOVE AND DIVINE WISDOM. Translated from the Original Latin of the Hon. Emmanuel Swedenborg. London: Printed and Sold by W. Chalklen, Grocers Court, Poultry. M.DCC.LXXXVIII. 8° pp. [iv] + 4 + v-xxii + [ii] + 461 + [3]

Annotations: Blake's copy contains numerous pencil notes in his handwriting in the margins. The front fly-leaf was also covered with pencil writing, beginning: " There " can be no Good Will. Will is always Evil & experience to others or suffering. If "it is anything it is understanding . . .", but this has been rubbed out and is now mostly illegible.

Note: At the top of the half-title is a note in ink: "The MS. notes by Blake "the Artist, acc^g to Mr Tatham (an architect) a friend of Blake, from whose posses-"sion the volume came. Jan. 1, 1839." The volume was generally unknown until it was lent to the Burlington Club for exhibition in 1876 by Mr. J. R. P. Kirby. It is now in the B.M. Reading Room, bound in green morocco, uncut, and enclosed in a green morocco case (pressmark, c. 45, e. 1).

Blake's relation to Swedenborg and his writings has recently attracted much attention, and there can be no doubt that he was greatly influenced by Swedenborg from an early period of his life. He was born in 1757, and in the same year Swedenborg established the New Church, of which Blake's father became a member. Blake himself and his wife were members of the New Church in 1789 (see no. 292). Blake also annotated Swedenborg's *Wisdom of Angels concerning the Divine Providence* (see next entry) and makes several references to him in *The Marriage of Heaven and Hell*.

Printed: Ellis, *The Real Blake*, pp. 109-115; Berger, *William Blake*, Paris, 1907, pp. 468-477.

15 THE WISDOM OF ANGELS CONCERNING THE DIVINE PROVIDENCE. Translated from the Latin of the Hon. Emmanuel Swedenborg. Originally published at Amsterdam, anno 1764. London: printed and sold by R. Hindmarsh, . . . 1790. 8° pp. xl + 600.

Annotations: Blake's copy has his signature in ink on the half-title and annotations by him in pencil in the margins of the pages.

Note: The early history of this volume is unknown. It was first recorded in Hyde's *Bibliography of the Works of Swedenborg*, London, 1906, 8°, p. 439, and was then in the library of the late James Spiers, publisher to the Swedenborg Society. It is now in the possession of Mr. C. H. Whittington. The book was described by Mr. Stanley Redgrove at a meeting of the Blake Society in 1915, and the annotations, which are at present unpublished, are to be printed in a projected work by Mr. Redgrove on Blake and Swedenborg.

16 AN APOLOGY FOR THE BIBLE, in a series of letters addressed to Thomas Paine. By R. Watson, D.D., F.R.S., Lord Bishop of Landaff; and Regius Professor of Divinity in the University of Cambridge. Eighth

Edition. London: Printed for T. Evans in Paternoster Row. 1797 . . .
12° pp. [iv] + 120.

Annotations: Copious annotations in Blake's hand are written in ink and pencil
on the back of the title-page and in the margins of the succeeding pages. The back
of the title-page is headed:
"Notes on the B. of L's Apology for the Bible by William Blake
"To defend the Bible in this year 1798 would cost a man his life."

Note: These annotations, which throw much light on Blake's attitude towards
the Bible and Christianity, have not been previously recorded. On the title-page is
the signature of Samuel Palmer. The book, which is bound in blue morocco by
F. Bedford, was for many years in the possession of the late T. G. Arthur, of Carrick
House, Ayr, with whose library it was sold at Sotheby's on July 15, 1914 (lot 44,
G. D. Smith, £47). It is now in the library of Mr. H. E. Huntington, by whose
courtesy the annotations are printed in full in an appendix to the present work, together with the passages to which they refer. I am indebted to the late G. D. Smith
for permission to copy them, and to Mr. Wilfred Merton for help in doing so.

17 BACON'S ESSAYS. London. Edwards. 1798. 12°

Annotations: Blake's copy of this edition of the *Essays* has been annotated by
him in pencil. On the title-page he has written: "Good advice for Satan's Kingdom";
there are frequent notes and abusive epithets in the margins.

Note: This volume was seen by Gilchrist, who printed some of Blake's annotations, but it has not been consulted by any other authority. I have been informed by
Mr. A. G. B. Russell that it was in the possession of Mr. Lionel Isaacs of the
Haymarket about 1900, but I have not been able to trace it any farther. The notes
that have been printed show Blake in the same mood as when he was annotating
Watson's *Apology for the Bible*, and it is probable that they belong to about the same
year, 1798.

Printed: Extracts in Gilchrist, i, 315-316; Ellis, *The Real Blake*, pp. 362-363.

18 THE WORKS OF SIR JOSHUA REYNOLDS, KNIGHT; . . .
In Three Volumes. To which is prefixed an Account of the Life &
Writings of the Author, By Edward Malone, Esq. . . . The Second Edition

Corrected . . . London: . . . 1798. [*annotations about* 1808] 8° Vol. I, pp. viii + cxxiv + iv + 287 + [1]. Vol. II, pp. [vi] + 427 + [1]. Vol. III, pp. [vi] + 370.

Annotations: Vol. I of Blake's copy, containing the Discourses, has been annotated throughout by him in pen and pencil. At the top of the title-page he has written:

"This Man was Hired to Deprefs Art. This is the Opinion of Will Blake my " Proofs of this Opinion are given in the following Notes."

The annotations include the following verses and epigrams:
1. Advice of the Popes who succeeded the Age of Rafael (title-page)
2. Some look to see the sweet Outlines . . . (p. xv) [On Sir Joshua Reynolds' disappointment at his first impressions of Raphael]
3. When France got free, Europe, 'twixt fools & knaves . . . (p. ciii)
4. When Sʳ Joshua Reynolds died . . . (p. cix)
5. When Nations grow Old, The Arts grow Cold . . . (p. iv) [On the Foundation of the Royal Academy]
6. On the Venetian Painter (p. 98)
7. A Pair of Stays to mend the Shape . . . (p. 99)
8. Venetian! all thy Colouring is no more . . . (p. 100)
9. O Reader, behold the Philosopher's Grave! . . . (p. 147) [On Sir Joshua Reynolds]

Note: Gilchrist, i, 305, assigns the annotations to 1820, evidently on the strength of the last line of Epigram 5: "For all are Born Poor. Aged Sixty-three.", but this is probably incorrect. Dr. Sampson points out (1905, p. 318) that "the " annotations in Blake's Reynolds all refer to the first eight Discourses contained in " the first volume of the *Works*, while those on the following Discourses are jotted " down in the MS. Book. As the latter are mixed with verses referring to his quarrel " with Cromek and Stothard the whole of the epigrams may be dated *circa* 1808, those " written in the copy of Reynolds being probably rather the earlier of the two."

These volumes are now in the B.M. Reading Room (pressmark, c. 45. e. 18-20).

Printed: Gilchrist, i, 305-314 (extracts); EY, ii, 318-344; Ellis, *The Real Blake*, pp. 371-396; Sampson, 1905, pp. 320-323 (verses and epigrams only); Sampson, 1913 (ditto).

19 SIRIS: A Chain of Philosophical Reflexions and Inquiries Concerning the Virtues of Tar Water, And divers other Subjects connected together and arising one from another. By G.L.B.O.C. . . . Dublin: Printed by Marg^t Rhames, For R. Gunne, . . . MDCCXLIX. [annotations 1804-1818] 8° pp. 261 + [3]

Annotations: On pp. 203-205, 212-215, 217-219, and 241, are marginal annotations in Blake's autograph in pencil, chiefly concerning the imagination and the senses.

Note: This copy of the first edition of Bishop Berkeley's treatise has on the fly-leaf the inscription, "From the author." Inside the cover is written, "Samuel Palmer, 1833." The book, which is bound in old calf, was acquired by Mr. W. E. Moss about 1909 from Mr. Tregaskis. The annotations, except for the few sentences given by Mr. Tregaskis in his catalogue have not hitherto been printed, but they will be found, together with the passages from *Siris* to which they refer, in an appendix to the present work. It is evident from the similarity of the opinions expressed that these annotations belong to the same period as *Jerusalem*, 1804-1818.

19A OBSERVATIONS ON THE DERANGED MANIFESTATIONS OF THE MIND, OR INSANITY. By J. G. Spurzheim, M.D. . . . London: . . . 1817. 8° pp. viii + 312.

Annotation: On a torn fragment of paper is a note in Blake's hand beginning, "Cowper came to me and said," with a reference to Spurzheim, p. 154.

Note: This fragment was formerly (1914) among the leaves of *The Four Zoas* (no. 6), but it is no longer to be found there, and seems to have been lost. Another reference to Spurzheim is written by Blake on a drawing of a "Visionary Head," which is in the possession of Mr. W. Graham Robertson.

Printed: The note and the passage referred to are given by Symons, pp. 17-18; the note alone in EY, i, 155.

20 DI CENNINO CENNINI, TRATTATO DELLA PITTURA messo in luce la prima volta con annotazioni dal Cavaliere Giuseppe Tambroni. Roma: Coi Torchj di Paolo Sabriucci, 1821. 8° pp. lii + 171 + [1]

Annotation: See Ellis, *The Real Blake*, p. 420, where it is stated that "in the "margin of a copy of Cennini's book on fresco painting that Linnell lent to Blake "we read—

" 'The Pope supposes Nature and the Virgin Mary to be the same allegorical
" 'personages, but the Protestant considers Nature as incapable of bearing a Child.' "

Note: Gilchrist, i, 414, gives an extract from a letter to him from Linnell, who
wrote: " I believe that the first copy of Cennino Cennini's book seen in England was
" the one I obtained from Italy, and gave to Blake, who soon made it out, and was
" gratified to find that he had been using the same materials and methods in painting
" as Cennini describes, particularly the carpenter's glue." The volume was no doubt
seen by E. J. Ellis among the Linnell collection, but it is not known to the present
representatives of the family, and has not been seen by me.

An extract from Cennini's work written in Blake's hand is to be found in a
sketch book * which belonged formerly to George Richmond, R.A.,† and, according
to the date of the watermark in the leaves, was used after 1824.

21 POEMS BY WILLIAM WORDSWORTH: Including Lyrical Ballads,
and the Miscellaneous Pieces of the Author. With Additional Poems, A
New Preface, and a Supplementary Essay. In Two Volumes. . . .
London: . . . 1815 [annotations 1826]. 8° Vol. i, pp. lii + 375 + [1].
Vol. ii, pp. [ii] + 440.

Annotations: A copy of this book which was lent to Blake was annotated by him
in pencil in the margins.

Note: Crabb Robinson in his *Reminiscences* writes under the date 1826:
" I lent him [Blake] the 8vo edition, two vols., of Wordsworth's poems, which
" he had in his possession at the time of his death. They were sent me then. I did
" not recognise the pencil notes he made in them to be his for some time, and was on
" the point of rubbing them out under that impression, when I made the discovery "
(Symons, p. 299).

In the same place he records the marginalia, and, since the present whereabouts
of the volumes are unknown, this remains the only authority for them. He also
states (Symons, p. 266) that Blake copied out Wordsworth's preface to *The Excursion*, and added at the end a note of his own, beginning: " Solomon, when he
married Pharaoh's daughter." This MS. was given to him by Blake, but it too has
disappeared. Crabb Robinson also records other opinions of Blake concerning
Wordsworth, and Wordsworth's estimate of Blake's poetry.‡

---

* Sold at Sotheby's, July 28, 1920, lot 162.
† For an account of Richmond's relations with Blake see Gilchrist, i, 342.
‡ *Diary and Reminiscences*, i, 385; Symons, p. 281: " There is no doubt this poor man was mad, but
there is something in the madness of this man which interests me more than the sanity of Lord Byron
and Walter Scott."

Printed: Crabb Robinson, *Diary and Reminiscences*, 1869, ii, 381-382; Gilchrist, i, 387-390; Symons, pp. 296-301; Ellis, *The Real Blake*, pp. 415-419.

22 THE LORD'S PRAYER Newly Translated from the Original Greek, with Critical and Explanatory Notes, by Robert John Thornton, M.D. of Trinity College Cambridge and Member of the Royal London College of Physicians. . . . Published by Sherwood and Co. . . . and Dr. Thornton, . . . Price, 1*s.* 6*d.* . . . 1827 4° pp. [iv] + 8 + [2]

Frontispiece: The woman with an issue of blood touching Christ's garment; engraved by Cook after Harlow. Lettered: . . . *London Published* . . . *March* 31, 1827, *by Dr Thornton*.

Annotations: Blake's copy has been extensively annotated by him in pen and pencil. On the title-page he has written:

" I look upon this as a Most Malignant & Artful attack upon the Kingdom of
" Jesus By the Clafsical Learned, thro the Instrumentality of Dr. Thornton. The
" Greek & Roman Clafsics is the Antichrist. I say Is & not Are, as most exprefsive,
" & correct too."

Note: Dr. Thornton, for whose *Pastorals of Virgil* (no. 77) Blake had made some woodcuts in 1821, was the author of many works, chiefly medical and botanical. He died in 1837 at the age of about sixty-nine. Blake's copy of his pamphlet, in its original blue paper covers, was formerly in the Linnell collection, and was sold at Christie's March 15, 1918 (lot 204, G. D. Smith, 48 gns.); it is now in the library of Mr. H. E. Huntington. The annotations, which have never been printed in full, will be given in a forthcoming book by Mr. S. Foster Damon.

Printed: Ellis, *The Real Blake*, pp. 365-7 (inaccurate and incomplete).

C. *LETTERS*

23 LETTERS, 1-88. *December, 1795, to July, 1827.*

1. TO GEORGE CUMBERLAND   6 December 1795
Addressed to: G. Cumberland Esq., Bishopsgate, near Egham, Surrey. Dated: Lambeth 6 December 1795. A single leaf, written on one side. No watermark. Size 37.5 × 23 cm.
> Now in the B.M. among the Cumberland Correspondence (MSS. 36498, f. 51).
> Printed: *Hampstead Annual*, 1903; Russell, *Letters*, p. 53.

2. TO GEORGE CUMBERLAND   23 December 1795
Addressed as above. Dated: Lambeth 23 December 1795. A single leaf written on one side. No dated watermark. Size 31 × 19 cm.
> Now in the B.M. among the Cumberland Correspondence (MSS. 36498, f. 155).
> Printed: *Hampstead Annual*, 1903; Russell, *Letters*, p. 56.

3. TO DR. TRUSLER   16 August 1799
Addressed: To the Revd. Dr. Trusler. Dated: Hercules Buildings, Lambeth, August 16, 1799. A double leaf, written on three sides. No dated watermark. Size 19 × 15.5 cm.
> Now in the B.M. among the Cumberland Correspondence (MSS. 36498, f. 324).
> Printed: *Hampstead Annual*, 1903; Russell, *Letters*, p. 57.

4. TO DR. TRUSLER   23 August 1799
Addressed: To the Rev^d Dr. Trusler, Englefield Green, Egham, Surrey. Dated: 13 Hercules Buildings, Lambeth, August 23, 1799. A double leaf written on three sides. Watermark dated 1795. Size 19 × 15.5 cm.
> Now in the B.M. among the Cumberland Correspondence (MSS. 36498, f. 328).
> Printed: *Hampstead Annual*, 1903; Russell, *Letters*, p. 60.

5. TO GEORGE CUMBERLAND   26 August 1799
Addressed to: Mr Cumberland, Bishopsgate, Windsor Great Park. Dated: Hercules Buildings, Lambeth, August 26, 1799. A double leaf, written on three sides. Watermark dated 1795. Size 19 × 15.5 cm.
> Now in the B.M. among the Cumberland Correspondence (MSS. 36498, f. 330).
> Printed: *Hampstead Annual*, 1903; Russell, *Letters*, p. 64.

6. TO WILLIAM HAYLEY   1 April 1800

Addressed to: William Hayley Esqr., Eartham, near Chichester, Sussex. Dated: Hercules Buildings, Lambeth, 1 April, 1800. A double leaf, 4°, written on the first leaf; with a part of the seal.

Sold at Sotheby's, May 20, 1878 (lot 2, Naylor, 25*s*.). Offered for sale in several catalogues of the stock of Mr. James Tregaskis about 1910. Sold at the Anderson Galleries, New York, Jan. 10, 1908 ($50.00), and at Sotheby's, June 2, 1919 (lot 113).

Printed in several of Mr. Tregaskis's catalogues, but otherwise unpublished. Reprinted in an appendix to the present work.

7. TO WILLIAM HAYLEY   6 May 1800

Addressed as above. Dated: Lambeth, 6 May, 1800. A single leaf, 4°.

Sold at Sotheby's, May 20, 1878 (lot 1, Naylor, 3 gns.). In the Rowfant Library in 1886. Not traced farther, but probably now in America.

Printed: Gilchrist, i, 144; Russell, *Letters*, p. 68.

8. TO GEORGE CUMBERLAND   2 July 1800

Addressed: To Mr Cumberland, Bishopsgate, Windsor Great Park. Dated: 13 Hercules Buildings, Lambeth, 2 July, 1800. A double leaf, written on three sides. No dated watermark. Size 20 × 16 cm.

Sold at Sotheby's, April 11, 1893. Subsequently in the collection of the late Charles Fairfax Murray, which was sold *en bloc* at Sotheby's, Feb. 5, 1920 (lot 18, Morton).

Printed: Extracts were given in the sale catalogue of 1893, and these were reprinted in Russell, *Letters*, pp. 69-70. Printed in full by Ellis in *The Real Blake*, p. 206. Reprinted in an appendix to the present work, having been copied by the present writer in 1912 by permission of the late owner.

9. TO JOHN FLAXMAN   12 September 1800

Addressed to: Mr Flaxman, Buckingham Street, Fitzroy Square. Postmark dated: 12 o'clock 12 Sp. 1800. Watermark dated 1798. A double leaf, written on both sides of the first leaf. Size 19.5 × 16 cm. Contains the poem: "To my Dearest Friend John Flaxman these lines."

In the collection of Mr. B. B. Macgeorge of Glasgow.

Printed in full: Russell, *Letters*, p. 70. The poem only: Sampson, 1905, p. 218; Ellis, *The Real Blake*, p. ix; Sampson, 1913, p. 183.

10. TO MRS. ANNA FLAXMAN   14 September 1800

From Mrs. Blake to Mrs. Flaxman. Dated: H. B., Lambeth, 14 Sept. 1800.

Contains the poem of four stanzas by Blake: "To my dear Friend, Mrs Anna Flaxman."

Formerly in the possession of Mrs. Flaxman's sister, Miss Denman, from whom Gilchrist obtained a copy. Now in the Pierpont Morgan Library.

Printed in full: Gilchrist, i, 147; Russell, *Letters*, p. 72; E. V. Lucas, *The Second Post* [1910], p. 97. The poem only: WMR; WBY; Sampson, 1905, p. 301; EJE; Sampson, 1913, p. 184.

11. TO WILLIAM HAYLEY   16 September 1800

A single leaf, 4°, with portrait, both inlaid.

Sold at Sotheby's, May 20, 1878 (lot 3, Webster, £2 17*s*.). Sold again with the collection of Louis J. Haber, Part III, at the Anderson Galleries, New York, Dec. 9, 1909 (lot 47, G. H. Richmond, $55.00). Not traced any farther.

A description and extracts were printed in the second sale catalogue as follows: "To William Hayley in answer to his invitation to take up his residence at Felpham "while engraving the illustrations for the *Life of Cowper*, addressing him as 'Leader "'of My Angels'—'I invoke the Good Genii that surround Miss Poole's Villa to "'shine upon my journey—whether I come on Wednesday or Thursday that Day shall "'be marked in my calendar with a star of first magnitude. Eartham will be my first "'temple & altar—My Wife is like a flame of many colours of precious jewels whenever "'she hears it named—My fingers emit sparks of fire with Expectation of my future "'labour.'"

Two sentences are quoted by Gilchrist, i, 148. Otherwise unpublished.

12. TO JOHN FLAXMAN   21 September 1800

Addressed to: Mr. Flaxman, Buckingham Street, Fitzroy Square, London. Dated: Felpham, Sepr 21, 1800, Sunday Morning. A double leaf, written on three sides. No dated watermark. Size 18.5 × 15.5 cm.

Formerly in the collection of the late Charles Fairfax Murray, which was sold *en bloc* at Sotheby's, Feb. 5, 1920 (lot 19, Morton).

Printed: *Nollekens and his Times*, ii, 464; Gilchrist, i, 149; Russell, *Letters*, p. 74.

13. TO THOMAS BUTTS   23 September 1800

Addressed to: Mr Butts, G^r Marlborough Street, near Oxford Street, London. Postmark dated: Sep. 23, 1800. A double leaf, written on three sides. Size 19 × 15.5 cm.

From the Butts collection. Now in the possession of Mr. W. Graham Robertson.

Printed: Gilchrist, i, 151 (second half only); Russell, *Letters*, p. 77.

14. TO THOMAS BUTTS   2 October 1800
Addressed to: Mr Butts, Great Marlborough Street. Dated: Felpham, Oᶜᵗʳ 2ᵈ 1800. A double leaf, written on three sides. Watermark: A Blackwell 1798. Size 19 × 15.5 cm.
Contains the poems: "To my Friend Butts I write," and "To Mrs Butts."
From the Butts collection. Now in the possession of Mr. W. Graham Robertson.
Printed in full: Gilchrist, i, 152; Russell, *Letters*, p. 81. Poems only: WMR; Sampson, 1905, pp. 302, 304; EJE; Sampson, 1913, pp. 184, 187.

15. TO WILLIAM HAYLEY   26 November 1800
Dated: Felpham, 26 November, 1800.
Sold at Sotheby's, May 20, 1878 (lot 33, Quaritch, £3 14*s*.). Not traced.
Printed: Gilchrist, i, 163; *Century Guild Hobby Horse*, 1886; Russell, *Letters*, p. 85.

16. [? TO JOHN FLAXMAN]   [? *c.* 1800]
Apparently not dated or addressed. A single leaf, 8°.
Sold with the collection of H. V. Morten at Sotheby's, May 5, 1890 (lot 22, Elliston, 2 gns.). Not traced.
Extracts in the sale catalogue as follows: "Sending all the sketches he has ever "produced; has studied 'The Presentation' but not yet put it on paper; is full of "business, and feels perfectly happy, thanks to his correspondents and Mr Flaxman." Otherwise unpublished.

17. TO THOMAS BUTTS   10 May 1801
Dated: Felpham, May 10, 1801. A single leaf, written on both sides; the other half missing. Size 19 × 15.5 cm.
From the Butts collection. Now in the possession of Mr. W. Graham Robertson.
Printed: Gilchrist, i, 164; Russell, *Letters*, p. 88.

18. TO THOMAS BUTTS   11 September 1801
Addressed to: Mr Butts, Great Marlborough Street, London.
Dated: Felpham Cottage of Cottages the prettiest, September 11, 1801. A double leaf, 31 × 19 cm., with postscript.
From the Butts collection. Now in the possession of Mr. W. Graham Robertson.
Printed: Gilchrist, i, 167; Russell, *Letters*, p. 90 (printed as two letters).

19. TO JOHN FLAXMAN   19 October 1801
Presumably addressed and dated as above. Not traced.
Printed: Russell, *Letters*, p. 95.

20. TO THOMAS BUTTS   10 January 1802

Addressed to: Mr. Butts, Great Marlborough Street, Oxford Street, London. Dated: Felpham, Jany 10, 1802. A double leaf, written on four sides. Watermark: A Blackwell 1798. Size 19 × 15.5 cm.

From the Butts collection. Now in the possession of Mr. W. Graham Robertson. Printed: Gilchrist, i, 172; Russell, *Letters*, p. 96.

21. TO THOMAS BUTTS   22 November 1802

Addressed to: Mr Butts, Gr. Marlborough Street. Dated: Felpham, Novr 22: 1802. A double leaf, size 19 × 15.5 cm.

From the Butts collection. Now in the possession of Mr. W. Graham Robertson. Printed: Gilchrist, i, 178; Russell, *Letters*, p. 102.

22. TO THOMAS BUTTS   22 November 1802

A single leaf, written on both sides; the other half missing. Size 19 × 15.5 cm. Contains the poem beginning: " With happiness stretched across the hills."

From the Butts collection. Now in the possession of Mr. W. Graham Robertson. Printed: Gilchrist, i, 181; Russell, *Letters*, p. 107. The poem only: WMR; WBY; Sampson, 1905, p. 305; EJE; Sampson, 1913, p. 187.

23. TO JAMES BLAKE   30 January 1803

Dated: Felpham, January 30, 1803. A double leaf, 24 × 15.5 cm., written on four sides. Each half of the leaf is now mounted on a guard and bound together in a morocco volume, gilt, by Sangorski and Sutcliffe, with a manuscript title-page and a type-transcript of the letter at the end.

From the Morrison collection. Sold at Hodgson's, March 21, 1917 (lot 168, Dobell, £31). Afterwards acquired by Messrs. Maggs, and sold by them to Mr. W. E. Moss.

Unpublished. Printed in full in an appendix to the present work.

24. TO THOMAS BUTTS   25 April 1803

Addressed to: Mr Butts, Gr^t Marlborough Street. Dated: Felpham. April 25, 1803. A double leaf, 19 × 15.5 cm. Watermark: A Blackwell 1798.

From the Butts collection. Now in the possession of Mr. W. Graham Robertson. Printed: Gilchrist, i, 184; Russell, *Letters*, p. 113.

25. TO THOMAS BUTTS   6 July 1803

Dated: Felpham July 6 1803. A double leaf, 19 × 15.5 cm. Watermark: A Blackwell 1798.

From the Butts collection. Now in the possession of Mr. W. Graham Robertson. Printed: Gilchrist, i, 186; Russell, *Letters*, p. 117.

26. TO THOMAS BUTTS   16 August 1803

Addressed to: Mr Butts, Gr Marlborough St, London. Dated: Felpham August 16 1803. A double leaf, 19 × 15.5 cm. Watermark: A Blackwell 1798. Contains the poem beginning: "O why was I born with a different face?"

From the Butts collection. Now in the possession of Mr. W. Graham Robertson.

Printed: Gilchrist, i, 190; Russell, *Letters*, p. 124. The poem only: WMR; Sampson, 1905, p. 310; EJE; Sampson, 1913, p. 190.

27. TO WILLIAM HAYLEY   19 September 1803

Presumably addressed and dated as above.

Sold at Sotheby's, May 20, 1878 (lot 4, Naylor, £2 12s.). Not traced. An extract was given in the sale catalogue as follows: "'My admiration of Flaxman's genius is "'more and more—his industry is equal to his other great powers.' Speaks of his "works in progress in his studio, and of various matters connected with art." Otherwise unpublished.

28. TO WILLIAM HAYLEY   7 October 1803

Presumably addressed and dated as above. A double leaf, 4°.

Sold at Sotheby's, May 20, 1878 (lot 5, Webster, 4 gns.). Not traced. Extracts were given in the sale catalogue as follows: "Speaks of his arrival in London, calling "himself 'your devoted rebel.' Says farther on, 'I lose no moment to complete Romney "'to satisfaction.' Philosophical remarks follow in his peculiar style. 'Some say that "'Happiness is not good for Mortals, and they ought to be answered that sorrow is "'not good for Immortals; a blight never does good to a tree, and if a blight kill not a "'tree, but it shall bear fruit, let none say that the fruit was in consequence of the "'blight.' A curious allusion to a good-natured Devil in him occurs." Otherwise unpublished.

29. TO WILLIAM HAYLEY   26 October 1803

Dated: South Molton Street, 26 October, 1803. Signed: W. and C. Blake.

Sold at Sotheby's together with letter no. 46, May 20, 1878 (lot 32, Quaritch, £3). Not traced.

Printed: Gilchrist, i, 194; Russell, *Letters*, p. 130.

30. TO WILLIAM HAYLEY   13 December 1803

Presumably addressed and dated as above. A double leaf, 4°, written on three sides.

Sold at Sotheby's, May 20, 1878 (lot 8, Naylor, £2 7s.). Not traced. An extract was given in the sale catalogue as follows: "Speaks of his success. 'Business "'comes in, and I shall be at ease if this infernal business of the soldier can be got "'over.' He then alludes to Romney and Flaxman, giving some interesting details." Otherwise unpublished.

31. **TO WILLIAM HAYLEY** 14 January 1804
Dated: London January 14 1804. A double leaf, 4°, written on three sides.
Sold at Sotheby's, May 20, 1878 (lot 9, Naylor, £2 15s.). It was in the Rowfant Library in 1886, and is presumably now in America.
Printed: Gilchrist, i, 199; Russell, *Letters*, p. 137.

32. **TO WILLIAM HAYLEY** 27 January 1804
Dated: South Molton Street 27 January 1804. A double leaf, 4°, written on three sides.
Sold at Sotheby's, May 20, 1878 (lot 10, Naylor, £5). It was in the Rowfant Library in 1886, and is presumably now in America.
Printed: Gilchrist, i, 201; Russell, *Letters*, p. 139.

33. **TO WILLIAM HAYLEY** 23 February 1804
Addressed to: William Hayley Esqre. Dated: Sth Molton Street, 23 February, 1804. A double leaf, written on three sides. Size 23 × 18.5 cm.
Sold at Sotheby's, May 20, 1878 (lot 11, Quaritch, 4 gns.).
Purchased from Quaritch for the B.M., June 15, 1878. Now in the Dept. of MSS. (30262, f. 86).
Printed: Gilchrist, i, 203; Russell, *Letters*, p. 142.

34. **TO WILLIAM HAYLEY** 12 March 1804
Addressed: To William Hayley Esqre, Felpham, near Chichester, Sussex. Dated: March 12, 1804. A single leaf, 4°.
Sold at Sotheby's, May 20, 1878 (lot 7, Waller, £2 15s.). Afterwards in the collection of the late H. Buxton Forman and sold with his library at the Anderson Galleries, New York, March 15, 1920 (lot 69).
Printed: Gilchrist, i, 205; Russell, *Letters*, p. 146.

35. **TO WILLIAM HAYLEY** 16 March 1804
Addressed: To William Hayley Esq. Dated: 16 March, 1804. A double leaf, written on three sides. Size 23 × 18.5 cm.
Sold at Sotheby's, May 20, 1878 (lot 12, Naylor, 3 gns.). In 1886 in the possession of "Mr Shepherd, 46 Pall Mall," by whom it was lent to Mr. Muir. Afterwards in the collection of the late Charles Fairfax Murray, which was sold *en bloc* at Sotheby's, Feb. 5, 1920 (lot 20, Morton).
A lithographic facsimile of this letter was appended by Mr. William Muir to his edition of *The Marriage of Heaven and Hell* (see no. 217, f), but it is otherwise unpublished.
Printed in full in an appendix to the present work.

36. TO WILLIAM HAYLEY 21 March 1804

Presumably addressed and dated as above. A single leaf, 4°.

Sold at Sotheby's, May 20, 1878 (lot 13, Naylor, £3 5s.). Not traced.

Described in the sale catalogue as follows: "Sends the proofs of each of the "Monumental Plates, and speaks of various subjects connected with art and design "in special allusion to Flaxman." Unpublished.

37. TO WILLIAM HAYLEY 31 March 1804

Addressed: To William Hayley Esqre, Felpham, near Chichester, Sussex. Dated: Sᵗʰ Molton St, March 31, 1804. A single leaf, 4°.

Sold at Sotheby's, May 20, 1878, together with letter no. 38 (lot 14, Waller, £4). Afterwards in the collection of the late H. Buxton Forman and sold with his library at the Anderson Galleries, New York, March 15, 1920 (lot 70).

Printed: Russell, *Letters*, p. 320.

38. TO WILLIAM HAYLEY 2 April 1804

Presumably addressed and dated as above.

Sold at Sotheby's, May 20, 1878, together with letter no. 37 (lot 14, Waller, £4). Not traced.

Printed, without the beginning: Gilchrist, i, 205; Russell, *Letters*, p. 147. Not yet printed in full.

39. TO WILLIAM HAYLEY 7 April 1804

Dated: Sth Molton Street, 7 April, 1804. A double leaf, 4°, written on three sides.

Sold at Sotheby's, May 20, 1878 (lot 15, Naylor, £2 19s.). It was in the Rowfant Library in 1886, and is presumably now in America.

Printed: Gilchrist, i, 207; Russell, *Letters*, p. 148.

40. TO WILLIAM HAYLEY 27 April 1804

Addressed to: William Hayley Esqre, Felpham, near Chichester, Sussex. A double leaf, 4°, written on three sides.

Sold at Sotheby's, May 20, 1878 (lot 16, Waller, £2 10s.). Afterwards in the collection of the late H. Buxton Forman, and sold with his library at the Anderson Galleries, New York, March 15, 1920 (lot 71).

Printed: Gilchrist, i, 207; Russell, *Letters*, p. 150.

41. TO WILLIAM HAYLEY 4 May 1804

Presumably addressed and dated as above. A double leaf, 4°, written on three sides.

Sold at Sotheby's, May 20, 1878 (lot 17, Quaritch, £4). Not traced.

Printed: Gilchrist, i, 209; Russell, *Letters*, p. 152.

42. TO WILLIAM HAYLEY 28 May 1804

Presumably addressed and dated as above. A double leaf, 4°, written on four sides.

Sold at Sotheby's, May 20, 1878 (lot 18, Quaritch, £5 10s.). Not traced.

Printed: Gilchrist, i, 210; Russell, *Letters*, p. 156.

43. TO WILLIAM HAYLEY 22 June 1804

Dated: South Molton Street, 22 June, 1804. A double leaf, 4°, written on three sides.

Sold at Sotheby's, May 20, 1878 (lot 20, Weston, 4 gns.). Now in the Pierpont Morgan Library.

Printed: Russell, *Letters*, p. 162.

44. TO WILLIAM HAYLEY 16 July 1804

Presumably addressed and dated as above. A double leaf, 4°, written on three sides.

Sold at Sotheby's, May 20, 1878 (lot 21, Naylor, £3 1s.). Not traced.

Described in the sale catalogue as follows: " Speaks in high praise of Mrs. " Klopstock's Letters, and says that Richardson has won his heart. The letter opens " with allusions to professional and other matters." Unpublished.

45. TO WILLIAM HAYLEY 7 August 1804

Presumably addressed and dated as above. A double leaf, 4°, written on three sides.

Sold at Sotheby's, May 20, 1878 (lot 22, Naylor, £3 10s.). Not traced.

Extracts given in the sale catalogue as follows: " ' It is certainly necessary that " ' the best artists that can be engaged should be employed on the work of Romney's " ' Life.' The following is characteristic, ' Money flies from me. Profit never ventures " ' upon my Threshold, tho' every other man's doorstone is worn down into the **very** " ' Earth by the footsteps of the fiends of commerce.' " Unpublished.

46. TO WILLIAM HAYLEY 9 August 1804

Presumably addressed and dated as above. Signed: W. and C. Blake.

Sold at Sotheby's, May 20, 1878, together with letter no. 29 (lot 32, Quaritch, £3). Not traced.

Unpublished.

47. TO WILLIAM HAYLEY 28 September 1804

Addressed to: William Hayley Esqre, Felpham. Dated: S^th Molton St, 28 Sept^r, 1804. One and a quarter pp., 4°.

Sold at Sotheby's, May 20, 1878 (lot 24, Waller, £2 13s.). Afterwards in the collection of the late H. Buxton Forman, and sold with his library at the Anderson Galleries, New York, March 15, 1920 (lot 72).

Printed: Gilchrist, i, 214; Russell, *Letters*, p. 166 (both under the erroneous date Sept. 20, 1804).

48. TO WILLIAM HAYLEY   23 October 1804

Presumably addressed and dated as above. A double leaf, 4°, written on three sides.

Sold at Sotheby's, May 20, 1878 (lot 23, Quaritch, £6 14s.). Not traced.

Printed: Gilchrist, i, 215; Russell, *Letters*, p. 168.

49. TO WILLIAM HAYLEY   4 December 1804

Dated: London, Dec. 4, 1804. A double leaf, 4°, written on three sides.

Sold at Sotheby's, May 20, 1878 (lot 26, Naylor, £4), and at the Anderson Galleries, New York, May 16, 1914 ($275.00). Not traced.

Extracts given in the sale catalogue as follows: " ' Proofs of my plates will wait " ' on you in a few days. I have mentioned your proposals to our noble Flaxman, " ' whose high & generous spirit relinquishes the whole to me—but that he will " ' overlook and advise.' The letter closes, ' I have indeed fought thro' a Hell of " ' terrors and horrors (which none could know but myself) in a divided existence; " ' now no longer divided nor at war with myself, I shall travel on in the strength of " ' the Lord God, as Poor Pilgrim says.' " Otherwise unpublished.

50. TO WILLIAM HAYLEY   18 December 1804

Presumably addressed and dated as above. A double leaf, 4°, written on three sides.

Sold at Sotheby's, May 20, 1878 (lot 27, Quaritch, £5 10s.). Not traced.

Printed: Gilchrist, i, 218; Russell, *Letters*, p. 172.

51. TO WILLIAM HAYLEY   28 December 1804

Addressed to: William Hayley Esqre, Felpham, near Chichester, Sussex. Dated: Sth Molton Street, 28 Dec^r, 1804. A double leaf, 4°, written on four sides.

Sold at Sotheby's, May 20, 1878 (lot 28, Naylor, £7 10s.). In 1891 in the possession of Mr. Ferdinand J. Dreer, Philadelphia.

Printed: Boston Museum Catalogue, 1891, pp. 43-45; Russell, *Letters*, p. 174.

52. TO WILLIAM HAYLEY   19 January 1805

Presumably addressed and dated as above. A double leaf, 4°, written on three sides.

Sold at Sotheby's, May 20, 1878 (lot 29, Naylor, £3 16s.). Not traced.

Described in the sale catalogue as follows: "Relates to the appointment of a "publisher of Mr Hayley's Poems and various matters of kindred nature."
Unpublished.

53. TO WILLIAM HAYLEY   22 January 1805
Presumably addressed and dated as above. A double leaf, 4°, written on three sides.

Sold at Sotheby's, May 20, 1878 (lot 30, Quaritch, £4 8s.). Not traced.
Printed: Gilchrist, i, 219; Russell, *Letters*, p. 178.

54. TO WILLIAM HAYLEY   25 April 1805
Presumably addressed and dated as above.

Sold at Sotheby's, May 20, 1878 (lot 6, Naylor, £3 5s.). It was in the Rowfant Library in 1886, and is probably now in America.
Printed: Gilchrist, i, 220; Russell, *Letters*, p. 180.

55. TO WILLIAM HAYLEY   17 May 1805
Presumably addressed and dated as above. A double leaf, written on three sides.

Sold at Sotheby's, May 20, 1878 (lot 25, Quaritch, 5 gns.). Not traced.
Described in the sale catalogue as follows: "Opens thus: 'Reading in the Bible "'of the Eyes of the Almighty, I could not help putting up a petition for yours.' "Speaks of his rough sketch of an advertisement (the direction of which has been "improved) and says, 'that if any of my writings should hereafter appear before the "'Public, they will fall far short of this first specimen.'"
Unpublished.

56. TO WILLIAM HAYLEY   4 June 1805
Presumably addressed and dated as above. A single leaf, folio, written on both sides.

Sold at Sotheby's, May 20, 1878 (lot 31, Quaritch, £3 15s.). Not traced.
Printed: Gilchrist, i, 222; Russell, *Letters*, p. 184.

57. TO WILLIAM HAYLEY   27 November 1805
Addressed to: Mr Hayley. Dated as above. A double leaf, 4°, written on three sides.

Formerly in the collection of Robert Hoe, and sold with his library at the Anderson Galleries, New York, April 25, 1911 (lot 397, $180.00). Now in the possession of Miss Amy Lowell.
Unpublished. Printed in full in an appendix to the present work.

58. **TO WILLIAM HAYLEY** 11 December 1805

Addressed : To William Hayley Esq, Felpham, near Chichester, Sussex. Dated : S^th Molton Street, Decemb^r 11, 1805. Signed : Will. Blake and his Wife Catherine Blake.

In 1893 in the possession of Mr. Daniel, London, who lent it for printing to Messrs. Ellis and Yeats. Present owner not traced.

Printed : EY, i, 172 ; Russell, *Letters*, p. 187.

59. **TO RICHARD PHILIPS** June 1806

Addressed : To the Editor of the Monthly Magazine. Printed in *The Monthly Magazine ; or, British Register*. Vol. XXI. Part I for 1806. London : Richard Philips. 8°. (see no. 396). It is in the number for July 1, p. 520. First discovered and reprinted by Swinburne. The original is not known to have survived.

Reprinted : Swinburne, *Critical Essay*, p. 62 ; Gilchrist, i, 258 (not in 1st ed.) ; Russell, *Letters*, p. 90.

60. **TO RICHARD PHILIPS** 14 October 1807

Dated : 17 South Molton Street, 14 October, 1807. Marked by the recipient : " Recd. 27th October 1807, with no p." It was not printed in *The Monthly Magazine*. Original not traced.

Printed : Russell, *Letters*, p. 197.

61. **TO OZIAS HUMPHREY** 18 January 1808

Addressed : To Ozias Humphrey, Esqre. Dated : 18 January, 1808. A double leaf, 22 × 18.4 cm., written on four sides.

Formerly in the possession of Major C. H. Simpson of Bath ; sold with his collection at Sotheby's, March 15, 1916 (lot 33, G. D. Smith, £51). Now in the possession of Mr. H. E. Huntington. It was first printed by J. T. Smith, who appears to have obtained the letter from William Upcott, son of Ozias Humphrey, but his text contains some inaccuracies. Reprinted by Gilchrist, who gives the date wrongly as February 18, and states that the letter was then (1863) " in the possession " of Mr Anderdon."

Printed : *Nollekens and his Times*, ii, 482 ; Gilchrist, i, 260 ; Russell, *Letters*, p. 198.

62. **TO GEORGE CUMBERLAND** 19 December 1808

Addressed and dated as above. A single leaf, written on both sides. Size 24 × 19 cm.

Now in the B.M. among the Cumberland Correspondence (MSS. 36501, f. 314), following a letter from George Cumberland to Blake.

Printed : *Hampstead Annual*, 1903 ; Russell, *Letters*, p. 205.

63. TO OZIAS HUMPHREY　　　　　　　　　　　　　　　　　　[c. 1809]

Addressed to: Ozias Humphrey Esqre. Not dated. A double leaf, 20 × 16 cm., written on both sides of the first leaf.

Formerly in the collection of C. J. Toovey. Sold at Sotheby's, April 25, 1912 (lot 10); offered for sale by Messrs. Maggs Bros. in July, 1912 (cat. 293, £35).

An extract is given by Messrs. Maggs in their catalogue with a facsimile. Otherwise unpublished. Printed in full in an appendix to the present work.

64. TO MR. REVELEY　　　　　　　　　　　　　　　　　　　[c. 1818]

Addressed on the outside to: Mr Blake, Engraver. A small folded sheet bearing a note in the third person addressed to Blake with his answer. The communications evidently refer to the engravings for vol. ii of Rees' *Cyclopædia*, which were executed in 1818 (see no. 132).

Formerly in the Linnell collection. Sold at Christie's, March 15, 1918, with twelve others (lot 214, G. D. Smith, 80 gns.). Now in the collection of Mr. H. E. Huntington.

Unpublished. Printed in full in an appendix to the present work.

65. TO DAWSON TURNER　　　　　　　　　　　　　　　　9 June 1818

Addressed to: Dawson Turner Esqre, Yarmouth, Norfolk. Dated: 17 South Molton Street. A double leaf, 21 × 16.5 cm., written on three sides. Contains a list of works offered for sale with their prices.

Sold with the Dawson Turner collection of MSS. at Puttick and Simpson's, June 6, 1859. Now in the possession of Mr. W. A. White.

Printed: Grolier Cat., 1905, p. 136; Russell, *Letters*, p. 207.

66. TO JOHN LINNELL [?]　　　　　　　　　　　　　　　11 October 1819

Not addressed. Dated: 11 October, 1819. Monday Evening. Not traced.

Printed: Russell, *Letters*, p. 208.

67. TO MRS. LINNELL　　　　　　　　　　　　　　　　11 October 1825

Addressed to: Mrs Linnell, Collins's Farm, North End, Hampstead. A double leaf, 4°, written on the first page.

Formerly in the Linnell collection. Sold at Christie's, March 15, 1918, with twelve others (lot 214, G. D. Smith, 80 gns.). Now in the collection of Mr. H. E. Huntington.

Printed: Gilchrist, i, 337; Story's *Life of Linnell*, i, 171; Russell, *Letters*, p. 209.

68. TO JOHN LINNELL　　　　　　　　　　　　　　　　　　[1825]

Addressed to: J. Linnell Esqr, Cirencester Place, Fitzroy Square. Marked: 12 o'clock Wednesday; but not dated. A single leaf, 4°, written on one side.

Formerly in the Linnell collection. Sold at Christie's, March 15, 1918, with twelve others (lot 214, G. D. Smith, 80 gns.). Now in the collection of Mr. H. E. Huntington.

Unpublished. Printed in full in an appendix to the present work.

69. TO JOHN LINNELL   10 November 1825

Addressed to: John Linnell Esqr, Cirencester Place, Fitzroy Square. Dated: Thursday Evening, 10 Nov^r, 1825, Fountain Court, Strand. A single sheet, 4°, written on one side.

Formerly in the Linnell collection. Sold at Christie's, March 15, 1918, with twelve others (lot 214, G. D. Smith, 80 gns.). Now in the collection of Mr. H. E. Huntington.

Printed: Gilchrist, i, 378; Story's *Life of Linnell*, i, 232; Russell, *Letters*, p. 210.

70. TO MRS. LINNELL   [? 1825]

Not addressed. Marked: London, Sunday Morning; but not dated. A single leaf, 4°, written on one side.

Formerly in the Linnell collection. Sold at Christie's, March 15, 1918, with twelve others (lot 214, G. D. Smith, 80 gns.). Now in the collection of Mr. H. E. Huntington.

Unpublished. Printed in full in an appendix to the present work.

71. TO JOHN LINNELL   1 February 1826

Addressed: To John Linnell Esqr, N 6 Cirencester Place, Fitzroy Square. Dated: Feb. 1, 1826. Postmark dated: Jan. 31. A double leaf, 4°, written on two sides. Watermark, *Ruse & Turner* 1810.

Formerly in the Linnell collection. Sold at Christie's, March 15, 1918 (lot 208, G. D. Smith, 30 gns.). Now in the collection of Mr. H. E. Huntington.

Printed: Gilchrist, i, 390; Story's *Life of Linnell*, i, 232; Russell, *Letters*, p. 211.

72. TO JOHN LINNELL   [1825 or 1826]

Addressed to: Mr Linnell, 6 Cirencester Place, Fitzroy Square. Marked: Tuesday Night; but not dated. A single leaf, 8°, written on one side.

Formerly in the Linnell collection. Sold at Christie's, March 15, 1918 (lot 209, G. D. Smith, 24 gns.). Now in the collection of Mr. H. E. Huntington.

Printed: Story's *Life of Linnell*, i, 234; Russell, *Letters*, p. 213.

73. TO JOHN LINNELL   19 May 1826

Addressed: To John Linnell Esqre, N 6 Cirencester Place, Fitzroy Square. Dated: Tuesday Evening, May 19, 1826. A single leaf, 4°, written on one side.

Formerly in the Linnell collection. Sold at Christie's, March 15, 1918, with twelve others (lot 214, G. D. Smith, 80 gns.). Now in the collection of Mr. H. E. Huntington.

Printed: Gilchrist, i, 392; Russell, *Letters*, p. 214.

74. TO JOHN LINNELL   2 July 1826

Addressed: To John Linnell Esqre, N 6 Cirencester Place, Fitzroy Square. Postmark dated: 2 July 1826. A single leaf, 4°, written on one side.

Formerly in the Linnell collection. Sold at Christie's, March 15, 1918 (lot 210, Dobell, 29 gns.).

Printed: Gilchrist, i, 393; Story's *Life of Linnell*, i, 235; Russell, *Letters*, p. 215.

75. TO JOHN LINNELL   5 July 1826

Addressed to: John Linnell Esqr, Cirencester Place. Dated: 5 July, 1826. A single leaf, 4°, written on one side.

Formerly in the Linnell collection. Sold at Christie's, March 15, 1918, with twelve others (lot 214, G. D. Smith, 80 gns.). Now in the collection of Mr. H. E. Huntington.

Printed: Gilchrist, i, 394; Story's *Life of Linnell*, i, 236; Russell, *Letters*, p. 216.

76. TO JOHN LINNELL   16 July 1826

Addressed: To J. Linnell Esqre, Cirencester Place, Fitzroy Square. Dated: Sunday Afternoon, July 16, 1826. A single leaf, 4°, written on one side.

Formerly in the Linnell collection. Sold at Christie's, March 15, 1918, with twelve others (lot 214, G. D. Smith, 80 gns.). Now in the collection of Mr. H. E. Huntington.

Printed: Gilchrist, i, 394; Story's *Life of Linnell*, i, 236; Russell, *Letters*, p. 217.

77. TO JOHN LINNELL   29 July 1826

Addressed to: Mr Linnell, 6 Cirencester Place, Fitzroy Square. Dated: 29 July, 1826. A single leaf, 4°, written on one side.

Formerly in the Linnell collection. Sold at Christie's, March 15, 1918, with twelve others (lot 214, G. D. Smith, 80 gns.). Now in the collection of Mr. H. E. Huntington.

Unpublished. Printed in full in an appendix to the present work.

78. TO JOHN LINNELL   1 August 1826
    Addressed: To Mr Linnell, Cirencester Place, Fitzroy Square. Dated: Aug^st 1, 1826. A single leaf, 4°, written on one side.
    Formerly in the Linnell collection. Sold at Christie's, March 15, 1918, with twelve others (lot 214, G. D. Smith, 80 gns.). Now in the collection of Mr. H. E. Huntington.
    Printed: Gilchrist, i, 395; Story's *Life of Linnell*, i, 237; Russell, *Letters*, p. 218.

79. TO JOHN LINNELL   27 January 1827
    Addressed to: Mr Linnell, 6 Cirencester Place, Fitzroy Square. Dated: Saturday Night, Jany 27, 1827. A single leaf, 4°, written on one side.
    Formerly in the Linnell collection. Sold at Christie's, March 15, 1918, with twelve others (lot 214, G. D. Smith, 80 gns.). Now in the collection of Mr. H. E. Huntington.
    Unpublished. Printed in full in an appendix to the present work.

80. TO JOHN LINNELL   [? February 1827]
    Addressed to: Mr Linnell, Cirencester Place, Fitzroy Square. Not dated. A single leaf, 4°, written on one side.
    Formerly in the Linnell collection. Sold at Christie's, March 15, 1918 (lot 211, Dobell, 29 gns.).
    Printed: Gilchrist, i, 398; Story's *Life of Linnell*, i, 238; Russell, *Letters*, p. 218.

81. TO JOHN LINNELL   [? February 1827]
    Addressed to: J. Linnell Esqr. Not dated. Written on a slip of paper, which was evidently left by Blake at Linnell's house.
    Formerly in the Linnell collection. Sold at Christie's, March 15, 1918, with twelve others (lot 214, G. D. Smith, 80 gns.). Now in the collection of Mr. H. E. Huntington.
    Unpublished. Printed in full in an appendix to the present work.

82. TO JOHN LINNELL   15 March 1827
    Addressed to: Mr Linnell, Cirencester Place, Fitzroy Square. Dated: 15 March, 1827. A single leaf, 4°, written on one side.
    Formerly in the Linnell collection. Sold at Christie's, March 15, 1918 (lot 212, Carfax, 30 gns.). Now in the possession of Mr. T. H. Riches.
    Printed: Gilchrist, i, 398; Russell, *Letters*, p. 220.

83. TO MISS DENMAN 16 March 1827

Addressed and dated as above. A single leaf, 20 × 13 cm., written on one side. A note in the third person concerning Blake's engravings after Flaxman's designs for the Hesiod.

In 1913 in the possession of Mr. W. T. Spencer, London.

Unpublished.

84. [? TO MISS DENMAN] 18 March 1827

Dated as above. A single leaf, 4°. A note in the third person.

Sold at Henckel's Auction Rooms, New York, Nov. 8, 1912 (lot 554, $30.00). Not traced.

Unpublished.

85. TO JOHN LINNELL [1827]

Addressed to: John Linnell Esqr, Cirencester Place, Fitzroy Square. Not dated. A single leaf, 8°.

In the possession of Mr. W. A. White, having been formerly inserted in copy P of the *Songs of Innocence*.

Printed: Grolier Cat., 1905, p. 138; Russell, *Letters*, p. 221.

86. TO GEORGE CUMBERLAND 12 April 1827

Addressed to: George Cumberland Esqr, Culver Street, Bristol. Dated: April 12, 1827. A double leaf, 21 × 16.5 cm., written on two sides. On the recto of the second leaf are notes by Cumberland concerning Blake's death and burial and his card-plate, a print from which is pasted on below. The letter contains a priced list of the illuminated books.

In the Charles Fairfax Murray collection, which was sold *en bloc* at Sotheby's Feb. 5, 1920 (lot 21, Morton).

Printed: EY, i, 162; Ellis, *The Real Blake*, p. 433; Russell, *Letters*, p. 221. The sale catalogue contains a facsimile of the second page.

87. TO JOHN LINNELL 25 April 1827

Addressed to: Mr Linnell, 6 Cirencester Place, Fitzroy Square. Dated: 25 April, 1827. A single leaf, 4°, written on one side.

Formerly in the Linnell collection. Sold at Sotheby's, March 15, 1918 (lot 213, G. D. Smith, 25 gns.). Now in the collection of Mr. H. E. Huntington.

Printed: Gilchrist, i, 400; Story's *Life of Linnell*, i, 239; Russell, *Letters*, p. 224.

88. TO JOHN LINNELL   3 July 1827

Addressed to: Mr Linnell, 6 Cirencester Place, Fitzroy Square. Dated: 3 July, 1827. A double leaf, 4°.

Formerly in the Linnell collection. Sold at Christie's, March 15, 1918, with twelve others (lot 214, G. D. Smith, 80 gns.). Now in the collection of Mr. H. E. Huntington.

Printed: Gilchrist, i, 403; Story's *Life of Linnell*, i, 240; Russell, *Letters*, p. 225.

APPENDIX TO LETTERS

24 TO THOMAS BUTTS. RECEIPTS FOR MONEY RECEIVED

January 1805—December 1810

The majority of the receipts take the following form:

7 *Dec^r* 1808

Received of Mr. Butts five Guineas on further account
£5 5s.   *William Blake*

They are written in a formal hand on slips of paper, measuring about 8 × 20 cm., and all but one are signed by Blake. The paper bears various watermarks, and some of the slips have a revenue stamp at one end. One of the receipts (no. x) is signed by Mrs. Blake, and one (no. vi) is entirely in Blake's autograph.

i. 22 January 1805, £12 12s.
ii. 5 July 1805, £5 7s.
iii. 7 September 1805, £4 4s.
iv. 30 June 1806, £21 10s.
v. 15 October 1806, £5 5s.
vi. March 1807, £28 6s.
vii. 2 June 1807, £12 1s. 6d.
viii. 13 July 1807, £15 15s.
ix. 6 October 1807, £10 10s.
x. 14 January 1808, £26 5s.
xi. 29 February 1808, £10.
xii. 29 July 1808, £10.
xiii. 3 November 1808, £5 5s.
xiv. 7 December 1808, £5 5s.
xv. 7 April 1809, £21.
xvi. 10 July 1809, £10 10s.
xvii. 10 August 1809, £10 10s.
xviii. 4 October 1809, £10 10s.
xix. 25 November 1809, £20.
xx. 16 January 1810, £21.
xxi. 3 March 1810, £10 10s.
xxii. 14 April 1810, £21.
xxiii. 30 June 1810, £5 5s.
xxiv. 14 July 1810, £15 15s.

xxv. 20 September 1810, £10 10s.
xxvi. 18 December 1810, £10 10s.
From the Butts collection and now in the possession of Mr. W. Graham Robertson. The whole sum for the six years represented here amounts to £339 5s. 6d.

25 TO THOMAS BUTTS ACCOUNT JAN. TO DEC. 1805 WITH RECEIPT DATED 3 March 1806

The account is written in Blake's autograph in two columns on a sheet of paper 19 × 15.5 cm. It dates from January to December, 1805. Attached to one corner by a wafer is the receipt, also in Blake's autograph, written on a slip of paper similar to those described in no. 24, with a revenue stamp at one end. The receipt runs as follows:

Receivd of Mr Butts, March 3, 1806 the Sum of Sixteen Pounds Seven & Fourpence Balance to this day as per annexed Account
£16 7s. 4d. *William Blake*

From the Butts collection, and now in the possession of Mr. W. Graham Robertson. It is of importance as it specifies the prints and pictures done for Butts during 1805, and the prices received for them. Receipts for the first three amounts mentioned on the credit side of the account are found among those described under no. 24.
Printed: Gilchrist, ii, 278.

POETICAL

SKETCHES.

By W. B.

LONDON:

Printed in the Year M DCC LXXXIII.

D. *WORKS PRINTED IN ORDINARY TYPE*

26 POETICAL / SKETCHES. / By W. B. / London: / Printed in the Year
M DCC LXXXIII.

Collation: [A]², B-K⁴; 38 leaves, 23 × 14 cm., uncut. A1*a* title; A1*b* blank;
A2*a* *Advertisement*; A2*b* blank; B1*a*-K3*b* (pp. 1-70) text; K4 blank. The pagination,
though typographically erratic, is numerically correct. There is no index, or table
of contents.

Contents:

Note: This volume is the earliest of Blake's poetical works, and is the only one besides the first book of *The French Revolution* (no. 27) which was printed in ordinary type. It contains no publisher's or printer's name, and the following account of its origin is given by J. T. Smith (*Nollekens and his Times*, 1828, ii, 455-6): " This lady [Mrs. Mathew] . . . was so extremely zealous in promoting the celebrity " of Blake, that upon hearing him read some of his early efforts in poetry, she thought " so well of them, as to request the Rev. Henry Mathew, her husband, to join " Mr. Flaxman in his truly kind offer of defraying the expense of printing them; in " which he not only acquiesced, but, with his usual urbanity, wrote the following " advertisement, which precedes the poems. . . . The whole copy of this little work . . . " was given to Blake to sell to friends, or publish, as he might think proper."

Blake does not seem, however, to have distributed many copies, and the book is now exceedingly rare. Among the fourteen copies recorded below is one with the inscription, "To Charles Tulk Esq.—from William Blake"; another bears the signature of George Cumberland. Others belonged to John Flaxman, Mrs. Anna Flaxman, Samuel Palmer, and Thomas Butts. The *Advertisement*, beginning: " The " following Sketches were the production of untutored youth, commenced in his " twelfth, and occasionally resumed by the author till his twentieth year," is well known, and need not be given here in full. With regard to the text Dr. Sampson (1905, p. 3) writes: " While the book contains a few obvious misprints, such as " ' cares' for ' ears' in ' An Imitation of Spencer,' and ' her' for ' his' in the fourth " stanza of the ' Song' on p. 12; yet its general inaccuracy is far less than has been " represented, and by no means warrants such violent changes as D. G. Rossetti's " ' rustling birds of dawn' for ' rustling beds of dawn' in the ' Mad Song.' The " printer, while generally respecting Blake's use of 'd or ed where the latter is to be " pronounced as a separate syllable, has evidently corrected Blake's spelling, omitted " capitals, and supplied his own punctuation, frequently a faulty one."

Rossetti's emendation in the " Mad Song," which had been previously made by Southey (see no. 260), is, as a matter of fact, correct, and has the authority of Blake himself, who, in at least two copies, has carefully altered " beds " to " birds." One of these copies (B) which still remains exactly as issued by Blake, is stitched into blue-grey paper wrappers and measures, uncut, 22.5 × 14.5 cm.; it was formerly in the Butts collection, and now belongs to Mr. T. J. Wise. The other copy (E) has on the

WILLIAM BLAKE AT THE AGE OF 28

Pencil Drawing by Mrs. Blake, 1785

title-page the inscription, "To Mr Long from J. Flaxman," and is evidently the book referred to by Flaxman in a letter to William Hayley, 26 April [1783]: "I have left "a pamphlet of poems with Mr Long,* which he will transmit to Eartham; they are "the writings of a Mr Blake you have heard me mention: his education will plead "sufficient excuse to your liberal mind for the defects of his work.† . . ." In both of these copies Blake has made another alteration, which has not been suggested by any of his editors; on page 4 in line 3, stanza 3, of "To Winter,"

> "He withers all in silence, and *in* his hand
> "Unclothes the earth, and freezes up frail life."

he has deleted the word here printed in italics with evident advantage to the metre.‡

Dr. Malkin was the first to give extracts from the *Poetical Sketches*; he prints the two songs, "How sweet I roam'd from field to field," and "I love the jocund dance," stating that the former was written before the age of fourteen. Extracts were afterwards printed elsewhere, but it was not until 1868 that the book was reprinted in full under the editorship of R. H. Shepherd, whose text has been followed by later editors, though with individual variations. Dr. Sampson gives an absolutely accurate text, though he amends the punctuation.

There is one copy (F) of the *Poetical Sketches* which is of special importance, as it contains three additional songs written on the fly-leaves. These songs are not in Blake's autograph, though it is possible that they were copied in by Mrs. Blake. They are headed "Songs by Mr. Blake," and are as follows:

> Song 1st by a Shepherd
> Song 2nd by a young Shepherd
> Song 3rd by an old Shepherd.

The first and third of these were first printed by R. H. Shepherd in 1868 in his second edition of the *Songs of Innocence and of Experience* (no. 139). For some time after this the volume was lost sight of, but it appeared again in 1910, being sold on March 22 at Sotheby's. For further information concerning this volume see *Notes and Queries* for Sept. 24, 1910 (no. 609), where it has been described in detail by the present writer; the article includes the text of the second song, which is an earlier version of the "Laughing Song," afterwards engraved among the *Songs of Innocence*.

Facsimile Reprint: Lithographed by W. Griggs, 1890 (no. 220).

Reprints: Nos. 8 and 11 first reprinted in Malkin's *Father's Memoirs of his Child*, 1806 (no. 80); no. 16 first reprinted and translated into German in the *Vaterländisches Museum*, 1811 (no. 401); no. 8 reprinted in Smith's *Nollekens and*

---

* William Long (1747-1818), Surgeon.   † Russell, *Letters*, p. 51.
‡ For a correspondence in the *Times* on these emendations see nos. 662 and 666.

his Times, 1828 (no. 247); no. 16 and 29 lines from no. 20 reprinted in Cunningham's *Lives of the British Painters*, 1830 (no. 249); part of no. 17 first reprinted together with no. 11 in Cunningham's *Lives*, ed. 2, 1830; no. 13, first reprinted in Southey's *Doctor*, 1847 (no. 260). Nos. 1, 2, 5, 8-13, 16, and extracts from no. 20 reprinted by D. G. Rossetti in Gilchrist's *Life*, 1863 (no. 270). The *Poetical Sketches* first reprinted in full by R. H. Shepherd, 1868 (no. 140), and in full or in part by all subsequent editors.

Copies:

A. British Museum Reading Room; pressmark C. 59, c. 30. In whole calf, uncut. Possibly one of Samuel Palmer's copies; see copy G below.

B. Butts copy (see above). Sold at Sotheby's, May 2, 1906 (£60). Now in the library of Mr. T. J. Wise. In original wrappers, uncut. Contains alterations in Blake's hand.

C. Charles Tulk copy (see above). Sold in 1906 (B. F. Stevens, £109). Resold with part I of the Hoe library at the Anderson Galleries, New York, April 26, 1911 (lot 389, $725). Now in the library of Mr. H. E. Huntington. In citron morocco, gilt, by the Club Bindery.

D. George Cumberland copy (see above), with an engraving * by Blake added as a frontispiece. Given by Cumberland to Linnell, and sold at Sotheby's with Linnell's books, June 3, 1918 (lot 3, Pickering, £60). Now in the library of Mr. Beverly Chew. In half-calf.

E. Copy given by John Flaxman to William Long (see above). Offered for sale by Mr. T. Thorp of Guildford, Dec. 1919. Bound with several dramatic works in half-calf. Contains alterations in Blake's hand.

F. Mrs. Anna Flaxman copy, with additional poems written on the fly-leaves (see above). From the Reed sale, 1807; sold with the Heber library, Dec. 9, 1834; sold at Sotheby's, March 22, 1910 (lot 448, Edwards, £52). In contemporary red morocco, yellow edges.

G. Samuel Palmer copy, containing pencil note by John Linnell, stating that it was one of three copies found by him at Palmer's house. It was then unbound. Now bound in half morocco, trimmed. Sold at Hodgson's in 1906 (Maggs, £16 5s.).

H. Pearson copy. Sold at Sotheby's, Nov. 7, 1916 (Dobell, £51); sold with Herschel V. Jones library, Anderson Galleries, New York, Dec. 2, 1918 (lot 181, G. D. Smith, $445). In green morocco, gilt, uncut, by F. Bedford.

I. T. G. Arthur copy. Sold at Sotheby's, July 15, 1914 (lot 46, G. D. Smith, £56). In red morocco, gilt, uncut, by Lortic *frères*.

* "The man sweeping the interpreter's parlour"; it is here inscribed by Blake: "The parable of the relapsed sinner & her 7 Devils." (Russell, *Engravings*, p. 102.)

K. R. A. Potts copy. Sold at Sotheby's, Feb. 20, 1913 (lot 71, £8 5s.). In calf, gilt. Pp. 49-70 in facsimile.

L. A copy sold at Sotheby's, May 2, 1911 (lot 321, Quaritch, £49). In contemporary red morocco, g.e.

M. Buxton Forman copy. Sold at the Anderson Galleries, New York, March 15, 1920. In blue morocco, gilt, by Roger de Coverly. Contains a sonnet by Buxton Forman in his autograph on the fly-leaf, and corrections copied by him from B above.

N. Gaisford copy. Sold at Sotheby's, April 23, 1890 (lot 184, Quaritch, £48). Now in the library of Mr. B. B. Macgeorge of Glasgow. Bound in blue morocco by Bedford.

O. Copy in the library of Mr. W. E. Moss. Bound in red morocco, gilt, edges cut.

27 THE / FRENCH REVOLUTION. / A Poem, / in Seven Books. / Book the First. / London: / Printed for J. Johnson, Nº 72, St Paul's Church-Yard. / MDCCXCI. / [Price One Shilling.]
Colophon: End of the First Book.

Collation: [A]², B-C⁴; 10 leaves, 28.5 × 23 cm., uncut. [A]1*a* title; [A]1*b* blank; [A]2*a* *Advertisement*; [A]2*b* blank; B1*a*-C4*b* (pp. 1-16) text.

Note: Only one copy of this work is known to exist. It is a quarto volume, stitched into plain blue-grey paper wrappers, and the text is on thin paper which bears no watermark. It was printed anonymously, but in the copy here described the words *By Wᵐ Blake* have been added in ink on the title-page below *A Poem*. On the top left-hand corner of the title-page is the autograph in ink of " John Linnell, Red Hill, 1860." The book was seen by Gilchrist, who refers to it (i, 89) as follows:

" These were prolific years [1791-2] with Blake, both in poetry and design. In
" 1791 he even found a publisher, for the first and last time in his life, in Johnson of
" St. Paul's Churchyard, to whom Fuseli had originally introduced him, and for
" whom he had already engraved. Johnson in this year—the same in which he
" published Mary Wollstonecraft's *Rights of Women*—issued, without Blake's name,
" and unillustrated, a thin quarto, entitled *The French Revolution, a Poem in Seven*
" *Books. Book the First. One Shilling*. Of the Revolution itself, only the first book,
" ending with the taking of the Bastille, had as yet been enacted. In due time the
" remainder followed. Those of Blake's epic already written were never printed,
" events taking a different turn from the anticipated one. *The French Revolution*,
" though ushered into the world by a regular publisher, was no more successful than
" the privately printed *Poetical Sketches*, or the privately engraved *Songs of Innocence*,
" in reaching the public, or even in getting noticed by the monthly reviewers. It finds
" no place in their indices, nor in the catalogue of the Museum Library."

THE

FRENCH REVOLUTION.

A POEM,

IN SEVEN BOOKS.

BOOK THE FIRST.

LONDON:

PRINTED FOR J. JOHNSON, N⁰ 72, ST PAUL'S CHURCH-YARD.

MDCCXCI.

[PRICE ONE SHILLING.]

In 1863 Mrs. Gilchrist possessed a transcript of the text, but later neither this nor the original volume could be traced. In 1912, however, a copy was discovered among the Linnell collection of Blake's works by Mr. Herbert Linnell, one of the trustees, who then permitted me to make this description.

The *Advertisement* on the second leaf is very short; it merely states that " The " remaining Books of this Poem are finished, and will be published in their Order," but it seems unlikely that even this book can have been issued to the public, and certainly no more were printed. Dr. Sampson has demonstrated that the copy here described is merely a page proof, " preserved perhaps by Blake in lieu of the original MS." He adduces as evidence the defective register of the pages, the excessive impression of the press, and other typographical details, and points out that there is " more than one misprint which could hardly have escaped the eye of the proof-reader: " *e.g.* ' Eeternally ' at the beginning of line 15 of p. 3, ' were away ' for ' wear away ' " on p. 5, l. 5, and an inverted 8 in the page number, etc." (Sampson, 1913, pp. xxxi-xxxii). None of the MS. has survived; perhaps it was among the writings believed to have been destroyed by Tatham.

The First Book of *The French Revolution* is printed in 296 lines, which vary from 16 to 21 syllables in length. Professor Saintsbury writes of its prosodical qualities: " The metrical norm is a seven-foot anapaest, sometimes cut short, some-" times extended, and undergoing substitution of the most unlimited kind " (see no. 363). Gilchrist makes no comments on the poem, and gives no extracts. W. M. Rossetti in a letter to Dr. Sampson, dated June 21, 1905, related what he remembered of the book and stated that D. G. Rossetti, Swinburne, and he himself, read the poem, but that they all " held it in no esteem " (Sampson, 1905, p. 333). Swinburne's own opinion is to be found on p. 15 of his *Critical Essay* (no. 273):

" His poem, or apology for a poem, called ' The French Revolution ' (the first " of seven projected books), is, as far as I know, the only original work of its author " worth little or even nothing; consisting mainly of mere wind and splutter. The six " other books, if extant, ought nevertheless to be looked up, as they can hardly be " without some personal interest or empirical value, even if no better in workmanship " than this first book."

On the other hand, at the present day, Professor Saintsbury is utterly at a loss to understand how Swinburne could have thought it " mere wind and splutter."

Reprinted: 13 lines in Saintsbury's *History of English Prosody*, vol. iii, pp. 24-25 (no. 363); in full in Sampson, 1913, pp. 263-280; 27 lines in Berger's *William Blake*, 1914, pp. 334-336 (no. 379).

Copy: Formerly in the Linnell collection. Sold at Christie's, March 15, 1918 (lot 191, G. D. Smith, 125 gns.). Now in the library of Mr. H. E. Huntington.

28 EXHIBITION / OF / PAINTINGS IN FRESCO, / POETICAL AND HISTORICAL INVENTIONS, / By Wm. Blake. / [rule] / The Ancient Britons— . . . / The Canterbury Pilgrims from *Chaucer*— . . . / Two Pictures, representing grand Apotheoses of Nelson and Pitt, / with variety of cabinet Pictures, unchangeable and permanent in / Fresco, and Drawings for Public Inspection and for Sale by Private / Contract, at / No. 28, Corner of Broad Street, Golden-Square. / [rule]

" *Fit Audience find tho' few* " MILTON

[rule] Admittance 2*s.* 6*d.* each Person, a descriptive Catalogue included. / [rule] / Watts & Co. Printers, Southmolton St. [May, 1809] (See facsimile)

Description : A single leaf, 24 × 18.5 cm., printed on both sides.

Contents : Recto : Title-page as above. Verso : headed *The Invention of a portable Fresco*, signed at the bottom *William Blake.*

Note : A copy of this very rare advertisement of Blake's exhibition is in the Bodleian Library (acquired December 6, 1893). On the recto, at the bottom, Blake has written after the word " included " *Containing Ample Illustrations on Art* ; on the verso, at the bottom, is the date *May* 15, 1809, also in Blake's autograph. Gilchrist, who only prints the six lines about " The Ancient Britons " (i, 276), mentions another copy, which was then (1863) in the possession of Mr. Alex. C. Weston ; this copy bore the same date in Blake's autograph and was directed to Ozias Humphrey. Another, or perhaps the same, copy is now among the Upcott papers in the library of the Royal Academy.

A manuscript copy of part of the last paragraph of Blake's manifesto was found by Mr. K. A. Esdaile among Crabb Robinson's papers, and was printed by him in an article in *The Library*, 1914 (see no. 631). With the exceptions of this passage and the lines quoted by Gilchrist the leaf has not been reprinted or described. Facsimile reproductions of both sides of the leaf are given here.

29 BLAKE'S CHAUCER, / THE CANTERBURY PILGRIMS. / The Fresco Picture, / Representing Chaucer's Characters, painted by / William Blake, / As it is now submitted to the Public.

. . . The price to Subscribers, Four Guineas ; two to be paid at the time of subscribing, the other two on delivery of the print.

Subscriptions received at No. 28, corner of Broad Street, Golden Square,

EXHIBITION

OF

𝕻𝖆𝖎𝖓𝖙𝖎𝖓𝖌𝖘 𝖎𝖓 𝕱𝖗𝖊𝖘𝖈𝖔,

Poetical and Historical Inventions,

By. Wm. BLAKE.

The Ancient Britons—Three Ancient Britons overthrowing the Army of armed Romans; the Figures full as large as Life—From the Welch Triades.

In the last Battle that Arthur fought, the most Beautiful was one
That return'd, and the most Strong another: with them also return'd
The most Ugly, and no other beside return'd from the bloody Field.

The most Beautiful, the Roman Warriors trembled before and worshipped:
The most Strong, they melted before him and dissolved in his presence:
The most Ugly they fled with outcries and contortion of their Limbs.

The Canterbury Pilgrims from *Chaucer*—a cabinet Picture in Fresco—Thirty Figures on Horse-back, in a brilliant Morning Scene.

Two Pictures, representing grand Apotheoses of Nelson and Pitt, with variety of cabinet Pictures, unchangeable and permanent in Fresco, and Drawings for Public Inspection and for Sale by Private Contract, at

No. 28, Corner of BROADSTREET, Golden-Square.

"Fit Audience find tho' few" MILTON.

Admittance 2s. 6d. each Person, a discriptive Catalogue included. *Containing*

Watts & Co. Printers, Southmolton St.

Ample Illustration on Art

The Invention of a portable Fresco.

A Wall on Canvas or Wood, or any other portable thing, of dimensions ever so large, or ever so small, which may be removed with the same convenience as so many easel Pictures; is worthy the consideration of the Rich and those who have the direction of public Works. If the Frescos of APELLES, of PROTOGENES, of RAPHAEL, or MICHAEL ANGELO could have been removed, we might, perhaps, have them now in England. I could divide Westminster Hall, or the walls of any other great Building, into compartments and ornament them with Frescos, which would be removable at pleasure.

Oil will not drink or absorb Colour enough to stand the test of very little Time and of the Air; it grows yellow, and at length brown. It was never generally used till after VANDYKE's time. All the little old Pictures, called cabinet Pictures, are in Fresco, and not in Oil.

Fresco Painting is properly Miniature, or Enamel Painting; every thing in Fresco is as high finished as Miniature or Enamel, although in Works larger than Life. The Art has been lost: I have recovered it. How this was done, will be told, together with the whole Process, in a Work on Art, now in the Press. The ignorant Insults of Individuals will not hinder me from doing my duty to my Art. Fresco Painting, as it is now practised, is like most other things, the contrary of what it pretends to be.

The execution of my Designs, being all in Water-colours, (that is in Fresco) are regularly refused to be exhibited by the *Royal Academy*, and the *British Institution* has, this year, followed its example, and has effectually excluded me by this Resolution; I therefore invite those Noblemen and Gentleman, who are its Subscribers, to inspect what they have excluded: and those who have been told that my Works are but an unscientific and irregular Eccentricity, a Madman's Scrawls, I demand of them to do me the justice to examine before they decide.

There cannot be more than two or three great Painters or Poets in any Age or Country; and these, in a corrupt state of Society, are easily excluded, but not so easily obstructed. They have exluded Water-colours; it is therefore become necessary that I should exhibit to the Public, in an Exhibition of my own, my Designs, Painted in Water-colours. If Italy is enriched and made great by RAPHAEL, if MICHAEL ANGELO is its supreme glory, if Art is the glory of a Nation, if Genius and Inspiration are the great Origin and Bond of Society, the distinction my Works have obtained from those who best understand such things, calls for my Exhibition as the greatest of Duties to my Country.

May 15. 1809   WILLIAM BLAKE.

where the Picture is now exhibiting, among other works, by the same artist. The price will be considerably raised to non-subscribers. [*Dated May* 15th. 1809]

Note: A copy of this prospectus was seen by Gilchrist, by whom it was reprinted, but he gives no description of it, and no indication of where it was to be found. Another prospectus was issued later (see no. 31), and Blake also wrote an *Advertizement to Blake's Canterbury Pilgrims from Chaucer, containing anecdotes of Artists* (no. 63), which may not have been actually published.

Reprinted: Gilchrist, i, 277 ; Russell, *Engravings*, p. 212.

30   A / DESCRIPTIVE CATALOGUE / OF / PICTURES, / Poetical and Historical Inventions, / Painted by / William Blake / in / Water Colours, / being the Ancient Method of / Fresco Painting Restored : / and / Drawings, / for Public Inspection, / and for / Sale by Private Contract, / [rule] / London : / Printed by D. N. Shury, 7, Berwick-Street, Soho, / for J. Blake, 28, Broad-Street, Golden-Square. / 1809.

Collation: [A]⁴, B-F⁶, G⁴ ; 38 leaves, 19 × 11.5 cm., uncut. [A]1 blank ; [A]2*a* title ; [A]2*b Conditions of Sale* ; [A]3 (pp. iii-iv) *Preface* ; [A]4 index to the Catalogue ; B1-G3 (pp. 1-66) text ; G4 blank.

Contents: In this list the titles are printed as given in the index, the alterations or additions given in the headings to the text being printed in square brackets.

A

DESCRIPTIVE CATALOGUE

OF

PICTURES,

Poetical and Historical Inventions,

PAINTED BY

WILLIAM BLAKE,

IN

WATER COLOURS,

BEING THE ANCIENT METHOD OF

FRESCO PAINTING RESTORED:

AND

DRAWINGS,

FOR PUBLIC INSPECTION,

AND FOR

Sale by Private Contract,

LONDON:

Printed by D. N. Shury, 7, Berwick-Street, Soho,
for J. BLAKE, 28, Broad-Street, Golden-Square.

1809.

THE SPIRITUAL FORM OF NELSON GUIDING LEVIATHAN
Tempera, about 1809

and the Sun of Britain set, but shall rise again with tenfold splendor when Arthur shall awake from sleep, and resume his dominion over earth and ocean.]   39 [30]

Note: The *Descriptive Catalogue*, issued in blue-grey wrappers at half a crown, is now rare, but it has been many times reprinted in part or in full and has become one of the best known of Blake's writings. It seems on the whole to have been accurately printed, but the pagination is faulty, and in several copies seen by the present writer the words "the idea of want in the artist's mind" on p. 65 have been altered in Blake's hand to "the want of idea in the artist's mind," which is clearly the better reading. Blake has in several copies also written above the rule on the title-page "At N 28 Corner of Broad Street Golden Square." A continuation of the *Catalogue* is found written in the *Rossetti MS.* (II, 154) with the title—*For the year* 1810. *Additions to Blake's Catalogue of Pictures &c.*; it consists of scattered fragments and includes the piece generally printed under the title *A Vision of the Last Judgement*. On the last two leaves of the same MS. (II, 160) is written the description of the picture of the Canterbury Pilgrims, which is printed in the *Catalogue*.

The exhibition was opened during May, 1809, as appears from a shorter programme of it, and from a prospectus of the engraving of the Canterbury Pilgrims, both of which are dated May 15, 1809 (see nos. 28 and 29), and Blake announced in his Conditions of Sale (p. ii of the *Catalogue*) that it would close on September 29 of the same year. It probably did not attract many visitors, but these included Seymour

Kirkup, who considered "The Ancient Britons" to be Blake's finest work (see Swinburne's *Critical Essay*, pp. 58, 80, and the *Rossetti Papers*, no. 332), and Crabb Robinson. Southey had a copy of the *Catalogue* (see no. 260) and may have been to the exhibition, but it is more likely that the book was given to him by Crabb Robinson, who wrote the following account of his visit (Symons, pp. 283-4):

"I went to see an exhibition of Blake's original paintings in Carnaby Market,
"at a hosier's, Blake's brother. These paintings filled several rooms of an ordinary
"dwelling-house, and for the sight a half-crown was demanded of the visitor, for
"which he had a catalogue. This catalogue I possess and it is a very curious
"exposure of the state of the artist's mind. I wished to send it to Germany and to
"give a copy to Lamb and others, so I took four, and giving 10s., bargained that I
"should be at liberty to go again. 'Free! as long as you live,' said the brother,
"astonished at such a liberality, which he had never experienced before, nor I dare
"say did afterwards. *Lamb* was delighted with the catalogue, especially with the
"description of a painting afterwards engraved [the Canterbury Pilgrims]. . . .
"Lamb preferred it greatly to Stodart's, and declared that Blake's description was
"the finest criticism he had ever read of Chaucer's poem. . . . There were about
"thirty oil-paintings, the colouring excessively dark and high, the veins black, and
"the colour of the primitive men very like that of the Red Indians. . . . Many of
"his designs were unconscious imitations."

Blake also sent the *Catalogue*, the announcement of the exhibition, and a ticket of admission (see Letter 63) to Ozias Humphrey, who may therefore have seen the exhibition. Only one contemporary notice of the exhibition has hitherto been discovered; this appeared in the *Examiner* for September, 1809 (see no. 400), and was made the occasion for a violent attack on Blake and his work. Most of the works exhibited are still extant, but the large picture of "The Ancient Britons" seems to have disappeared.

The first picture in the *Catalogue*, "The Spiritual Form of Nelson," which is reproduced here, is now in the National Gallery of British Art.

Reprints: Gilchrist, ii, 139-163 (without the *Preface*); Ellis, *The Real Blake*, pp. 274-292. Extracts first given in the *Examiner*, 1809 (no. 400), in Southey's *Doctor*, 1847 (no. 260), and, translated into German, in the *Vaterländisches Museum*, 1811 (no. 401); also in LH, WY, JS, Sampson, 1913, and in *English Critical Essays*, ed. E. D. Jones, Oxford, 1920.

Copies:
A. British Museum Reading Room. Acquired March 29, 1864. Pressmark, C. 31.h.21. Bound in morocco, gilt, 18 × 11 cm. There are no additions on the title-page.
B. British Museum Print Room. With inscription: "Presented by William Smith

Esq., 1856." 18 × 10.5 cm. Bound in cloth, morocco back. Has the MS. addition on the title-page.

C. Copy offered for sale in a catalogue by Messrs. Lowe Brothers, Birmingham, at 7s. 6d. in Feb. 1915. Probably to be identified with the copy now in the possession of Mr. W. Bateson, F.R.S., who obtained it from Messrs. Maggs in 1916. In original blue wrappers, 19 × 11.5 cm., uncut.

D. T. G. Arthur copy. Sold at Sotheby's, July 15, 1914 (lot 45, G. D. Smith, £24 10s.). Probably the copy now in the library of Mr. H. E. Huntington. In brown morocco, g.e., by Bedford.

E. William Cowan copy. Sold at Sotheby's, Dec. 4, 1912 (lot 849, Quaritch, £4). Probably the copy now in the library of Mr. W. E. Moss. 19 × 11 cm. In morocco, gilt. Has the MS. addition on the title-page.

F. Beckford-Hamilton Palace copy. Sold at Sotheby's, July 4, 1882 (Quaritch, £9). In green morocco, g.e.

G. Copy from the library of Charles Fairfax Murray, by whom it was presented to the Fitzwilliam Museum, Cambridge. 19 × 11.5 cm. Bound with the original wrappers in blue morocco, gilt. Has the MS. addition on the title-page.

H. Bodleian Library, Oxford. Bequeathed by Francis Douce in 1835. 18 × 11 cm. Bound in half-calf. Has the MS. addition on the title-page and correction on p. 65.

I. Balmanno copy. Bound up with an uncoloured copy of the *Songs of Innocence* (see copy U) and the *Canterbury Pilgrims*, 1812.

31 BLAKE'S CHAUCER: an Original Engraving by him from his Frescoe Painting of Sir Jeffery Chaucer and his nine and twenty Pilgrims setting forth from Southwark on their Journey to Canterbury. Three feet 1 inch long, and 1 foot high; price Three Guineas. . . .

Subscriptions received at No. 28, Corner of Broad Street, Golden Square. G. Smeeton, Printer, 17, St Martin's Lane, London. [c. 1810]

Note: A copy of this prospectus was seen by Mr. Russell, but it is not recorded by any other authority. The text consists of a detailed description of the subject of the engraving.

Reprinted: Russell, *Engravings*, p. 213.

E. ILLUMINATED BOOKS

32 THERE is NO NATURAL RELIGION, series a and b. [about 1788-1794]

a. There / is No / Natural / Religion

Description: Title, frontispiece, Argument, 3 pl., Propositions I-VI, 6 pl., Conclusion, 1 pl. = 10 plates, about 5 × 4 cm., relief-etching, printed in three colours, some plates touched with water-colour.

Contents:
1. Title-page. *There is No Natural Religion*, within a Gothic archway; small figures above and at the sides. 5.3 × 4.1 cm.
2. Frontispiece. An old man and a woman are seated beneath a tree; two nude youths stand in front of them. Lettered below, in reversed writing: *The Author & Printer W. Blake*. 5.4 × 4.5 cm.
3. *The Argument. Man has no notion of moral fitneſs but from Education. Naturally he is only a natu-ral organ subjeƈt to Sense.* A figure with a book is seated among trees. A child stands at one side; another reclines on the ground at the other side. 5.2 × 4.3 cm.
4. *I. Man cannot naturally Per-ceive but through his natural or bodily organs.* An aged man is leaning on a staff beneath a tree; his dog is at his feet. 5.2 × 4.3 cm.
5. *II. Man by his reason-ing power can only compare & judge of what he has already perceiv'd.* A kneeling woman holds a child, which stretches out its arms after a bird (cf. Young's *Night Thoughts*, pl. 7). 5 × 4.1 cm.
6. *III. From a perception of only 3 senses or 3 ele-ments none could de-duce a fourth or fifth.* A nude man is seated on the ground; a winged boy stands at his side. 5 × 3.8 cm.
7. *IV. None could have other than natural or organic thoughts if he had none but organic perceptions.* A shepherd is seated on the ground piping; sheep in the background. 4.8 × 4 cm.
8. *V. Mans desires are limited by his percepti-ons, none can de-sire what he has not perceivd.* A boy stretches out his hands towards a duck on the water. 4.8 × 3.5 cm.
9. *VI. The desires & percepti-ons of man untaught by anything but organs of sense*

must be limited to objects of sense. An old man reclines among grass reading a book (cf. *All Religions are One*, pl. 3). 3.6 × 4.4 cm.

10. *Conclusion. If it were not for the Poetic or Prophetic character the Philo-sophic & Experimen-tal would soon be at the ratio of all things, & stand still unable to do other than repeat the same dull round over a-gain.* 5.5 × 4.2 cm.

Note, copies, facsimiles, typ. reprints: See under series b.

b. [There / is No / Natural / Religion]

Description: Title, frontispiece, 2 pl., Propositions I-VII, 7 pl., Application, 2 pl. = 11 plates, about 6 × 4 cm., relief-etching, printed in three colours, one or more plates touched with water-colour.

Contents:
1. [Title-page not known. Presumably the same as for series a.]
2. Frontispiece. A robed figure stands with his left arm outstretched over a nude man, who is half reclining on the ground (cf. Young's *Night Thoughts*, pl. 40). 5.3 × 3.9 cm.
3. *I. Mans percepti-ons are not bound-ed by organs of perception he per-ceives more than sense (tho' ever so acute) can discover.* An old man is reclining on the ground. 5.9 × 4.4 cm.
4. *II. Reason or the ra-tio of all we have already known is not the same that it shall be when we know more.* A figure lying prone on the ground. 5.6 × 4 cm.
5. [No copy of Proposition III appears to have survived.]
6. *IV. The bounded is loathed by its pof-sefsor. The same dull round even of a univer[s]e would soon become a mill with complica-ted wheels.* 6.4 × 4.3 cm.
7. *V. If the many be-come the same as the few, when pof-sefs'd, More! More! is the cry of a mista-ken soul, lefs than All cannot satisfy Man.* 5.8 × 4 cm.
8. *VI. If any could de-sire what he is incapable of pofsef-sing, despair must be his eternal lot.* A nude figure is seated on the ground in an attitude of despair (cf. *Urizen*, pl. 4). 5.5 × 4.2 cm.
9. *VII. The desire of Man being Infi-nite the pofsefsion is Infinite & him-self Infinite.* A nude figure with outstretched arms rises out of clouds. 6 × 4.2 cm.
10. *Application. He who sees the In-finite in all things sees God. He who sees the Ratio only sees himself only.* An old man is kneeling on the ground and drawing with a pair of compasses.* 5 × 4.1 cm.
11. *Therefore God becomes as we are that we may be as he is.* A nude figure with a halo is lying supine on the ground. 6.1 × 4.6 cm.

* A large pencil drawing of this subject is in the possession of Miss A. M. Butterworth.

Note: Very little is definitely known about these brief philosophical treatises, but it will be noticed that none of the existing copies corresponds in constitution or arrangement with either of the two series, a or b, described above. Thus copies A and B consist of eight plates from series a and three from series b; copy C consisted originally of only eight plates altogether, and copy D has only nine. Nevertheless there can be little doubt that Blake originally intended them to take the forms in which they are set out above. Until 1886 the two copies, A and C, were the only ones that were at all generally known, and the sentences have usually been printed as they are found in copy A. About that time, however, Mr. William Muir obtained rough proofs of six additional plates, and, with these to fill in the gaps, Blake's original intention became evident, since the different styles of lettering made it possible to separate the plates into two series. Mr. Muir took advantage of this, and incorporated the new plates in his admirable facsimile of 1886, arranging the plates almost exactly as given above, though pl. 5 of series b was still missing, and has, indeed, not yet come to light. Mr. Muir remembers that these six proofs were irregularly arranged, several together, on scraps of paper, but he gave them away many years ago, and they have not been seen by the present writer. Accompanying these was a proof of another plate, which Mr. Muir used as a title-page for version b, but was more probably intended by Blake to be the title-page of another companion work described under no. 33. It is impossible to explain why Blake omitted eight of the plates which he had made for series b from the few sets which he printed.

The plates, some of which have the appearance of having been printed in three different inks, olive-green, brown, and black, are in some cases lightly touched with water-colours. The sets known to me are all on paper of almost exactly one size, about 14 × 11 cm., and are very similar in character, so that it is possible that they were all executed about the same time. The actual date, however, of these treatises has never been accurately determined. The opinions expressed in them show that they were early compositions, and it has been suggested* that they may have been called forth by Hume's *Dialogues Concerning Natural Religion*, published in 1779. Russell further suggests † that they should be dated 1788, since, in the colophon to *The Ghost of Abel*, 1822, it is stated that *W Blake's Original Stereotype was* 1788, and "the somewhat "tentative and experimental aspect of the books themselves" lends colour to the idea that they were the first fruits of Blake's newly invented process. Dr. Sampson is of the same opinion.‡ There are no contemporary references to the works, and I do not know the early history of any of the sets of plates described below. They can at any rate be assigned with certainty to the period 1788-1794 for several reasons: (i) The text on the majority of the plates is etched in minuscule roman, a style of lettering which is only found in the *Songs of Innocence*, 1789, and on three plates of *The Marriage of Heaven*

* *Milton*, ed. Russell and Maclagan, p. x (no. 171).　　　† *Engravings*, p. 205.
‡ Sampson, 1913, p. xxviii.

and Hell, 1790. (ii) Several of the designs (pl. a5, b2, b8) closely resemble others found elsewhere which certainly belong to about the year 1794. (iii) The watermark, *Taylor*, which occurs in set B, strongly suggests that some of them were printed in 1794.* The date 1811, parts of which are found in the watermark of sets G and H, is not of value as evidence of the original date of composition, since the pile of leaves forming sets E-H may have been printed together at a later date than the others. A third series of similar plates, apparently produced at the same time, is described under the next entry.

Copies:

A. 11 plates on 11 leaves. No watermark. Printed in olive-green, brown, and black. The first and last plates are touched with water-colours. Arrangement: a3, b3, a5-9, a4, b4, b11, a2. Size of original leaf 13.5 × 11 cm.; now mounted on leaves 24 × 17.5 cm. Bound in morocco, g.e.
Copy in the B.M. Print Room; presented by F. T. Palgrave in 1878.

B. 11 plates on 11 leaves. Watermark *Taylor* on one plate. Printed in varying depths of brownish-grey. Frontispiece painted with water-colours; the other plates slightly touched with colour. Arrangement: a2-9, b11, b3, b4. No foliation. Size 13.5 × 10.5 cm. Bound in russia, g.e., with crest of Milnes family on front cover.
Copy formerly in the possession of the Earl of Crewe, having been bought at Sotheby's on April 29, 1862 (R. Monckton Milnes, 16s.); sold with his collection at Sotheby's on March 30, 1903 (lot 10, Quaritch, £53), and acquired by Mr. W. A. White (Grolier Cat., no. 40).

C. 11 plates on 11 leaves. No watermark. Printed in greyish black, except the fifth and ninth plates which are in green. The frontispiece elaborately painted with water-colours, the other plates slightly coloured. Arrangement: a1-5, b4, b11, b3, a6, a8-9. Foliated in pencil. Size 13.5 × 10.5 cm. Title-page inlaid. Bound in morocco, g.e., by Bedford.
Frederick Locker's copy with his bookplate. Pencil notes by Locker on the fly-leaves state that the title-page and the last two plates were added by him, July 26, 1878. In the corner of a fly-leaf is stamped *B. M. Pickering*. Now in the possession of Mr. W. A. White, who bought it from Messrs. Dodd, Mead and Co. (Burlington Cat., 1876, item 310).

D. 9 plates on 9 leaves. No watermark. Title-page and frontispiece printed in black, the other plates in several colours. The frontispiece is lightly painted with water-colours. Size 14 × 11 cm. Bound in boards.
Formerly in the E. W. Hooper collection, and now in the possession of the family of Mrs. R. S. Warner, Boston, Mass. (Boston Mus. Cat., 1891, no. 9).

* See p. 17 of present work.

[E-H. A pile of leaves of *There is No Natural Religion* was bought many years ago in a shop in Edinburgh by the late H. Stopford Brooke and R. A. Potts; these were afterwards divided up into the four copies next described.]

E. 8 plates on 8 leaves. No watermark. Printed in light brown. Lightly painted with water-colours, pl. a2 and a4 more elaborately than the rest. Consists of plates: a2-4, a8-9, b3-4, b11. Size 14 × 11.5 cm., uncut. Wrappers; unbound.

Formerly in the possession of the late H. Stopford Brooke. Sold with his library at Sotheby's, July 27, 1917 (lot 791, Tregaskis, £38).

F. 8 plates on 8 leaves. No watermark. Printed in various shades of brown. Painted with water-colours, the frontispiece more elaborately than the rest. Consists of plates: a2-4, a8-9, b3-4, b11. Size 14 × 11.5 cm., uncut. Stitched in wrappers.

Formerly in the collection of R. A. Potts, and sold with his library at Sotheby's on Feb. 20, 1913 (lot 65, Tregaskis, £13). Now the property of Mr. Frank Rinder.

G. 8 plates on 8 leaves. Watermark . . . 11 on one leaf; probably part of date, 1811. Printed in various shades of brown. Lightly painted with water-colours, the frontispiece more elaborately than the rest. Consists of plates: a2-4, a8-9, b3-4, b11. Size 14 × 11.5 cm., uncut. Bound in brown morocco, inlaid, by Rivière.

In the possession of Mr. T. J. Wise.

H. 10 plates on 10 leaves. Watermark with figures 811 visible; probably part of date, 1811. Printed in various shades of brown. Painted with water-colours. Consists of plates: a2-4, a8-9, b3-4, b11, with duplicates of a9 and b11. Unbound, in slip case. Size 14 × 11.5 cm.

Formerly in the collection of H. Buxton Forman. Sold with his library at the Anderson Galleries, New York, March 15, 1920 (lot 48).

[I. "Eleven small stamped and water-coloured designs, with maxims on religion, etc." In three frames. Lent to the Burlington Club exhibition in 1876 by Mrs. Tulk (nos. 304-306 in cat.). Possibly to be identified with copy A above.]

Facsimile Reproductions: Pickering, 1886, 11 plates, coloured (no. 218); W. Muir, 1886, coloured (no. 217, g); EY, iii, 11 plates.

Typ. Reprints: WBY, LH (as in copy A); EJE, Sampson, 1913 (complete); translated into German by von Taube, 1907 (no. 176).

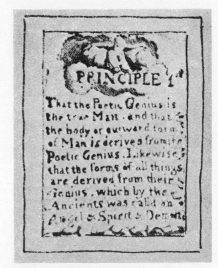

ALL RELIGIONS ARE ONE

Plates 1-4

PRINCIPLE 2.
As all men are alike in
outward form, So (and
with the same infinite
variety) all are alike in
the Poetic Genius

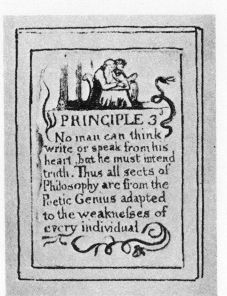

PRINCIPLE 3.
No man can think
write or speak from his
heart, but he must intend
truth. Thus all sects of
Philosophy are from the
Poetic Genius adapted
to the weaknesses of
every individual

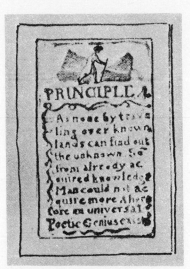

PRINCIPLE 4.
As none by travel-
ling over known
lands can find out
the unknown. So
from already ac-
quired knowledge
Man could not ac-
quire more. There-
fore an universal
Poetic Genius exists

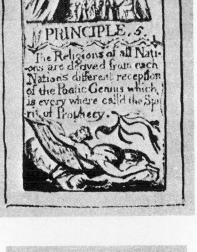

PRINCIPLE. 5.
The Religions of all Nations are derived from each
Nations different reception
of the Poetic Genius which
is every where call'd the Spirit of Prophecy.

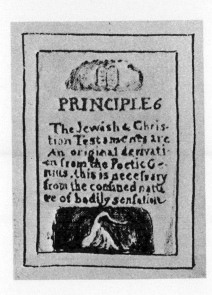

PRINCIPLE 6
The Jewish & Chris-
tian Testaments are
An original derivati-
on from the Poetic G-
enius, this is necessary
from the confined natu-
re of bodily sensation

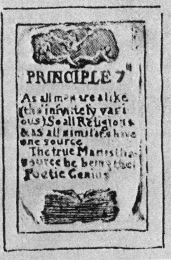

PRINCIPLE 7ᵗʰ
As all men are alike
(tho' infinitely vari-
ous) So all Religions
& as all similars have
one source
The true Man is the
source he being the
Poetic Genius

ALL RELIGIONS ARE ONE

Plates 5-10

33 ALL / RELIGIONS / are / ONE [about 1788-1794]

Description: Title, frontispiece, *Argument*, 3 pl., *Principles* 1-7, 7 pl. = 10 plates, unnumbered, about 5.5 × 4 cm.; relief etching with text and small pictorial designs.

Contents:

1. Title-page. *All Religions are One*, inscribed on a stone tablet, beside which is seated an aged man with an open book on his knee; a winged figure stands behind. 5.2 × 3.4 cm.

2. Frontispiece. A youthful figure, nude except for a cloak over one knee, is seated on a rock beneath trees; he is pointing with both hands to the right. Below is inscribed: *The Voice of one crying in the Wilderneſs.* 4.6 × 4.2 cm.

3. *The Argument.* *As the true method of knowledge is experiment the true faculty of knowing must be the faculty which experiences. This faculty I treat of.* Below is a figure full-length on the ground, supporting his head on one hand (cf. *There is No Natural Religion*, pl. 9). 4.8 × 3 cm.

4. *PRINCIPLE 1ˢᵗ. That the Poetic Genius is the true Man, and that the body or outward form of Man is derived from the Poetic Genius. Likewise that the forms of all things are derived from their Genius, which by the Ancients was call'd an Angel & Spirit & Demon.* Above is a seated figure of Jehovah with his arms stretched out upon clouds (exactly as in *America*, pl. 8). 5.4 × 3.8 cm.

5. *PRINCIPLE 2ᵈ. As all men are alike in outward form, So (and with the same infinite variety) all are alike in the Poetic Genius.* Above are two figures reclining on the ground and gazing upwards; below, a flock of sheep, grazing. 5 × 4.5 cm.

6. *PRINCIPLE 3ᵈ. No man can think write or speak from his heart, but he must intend truth. Thus all sects of Philosophy are from the Poetic Genius adapted to the weakneſses of every individual.* Above are the seated figures of two old men, one writing in a book, the other reading. 5.8 × 4 cm.

7. *PRINCIPLE 4. As none by traveling over known lands can find out the unknown. So from already acquired knowledge Man could not acquire more. therefore an universal Poetic Genius exists.* Above, a traveller with his staff (cf. *Gates of Paradise*, pl. 14). 5.2 × 3 cm.

8. *PRINCIPLE 5. The Religions of all Nations are derived from each Nations different reception of the Poetic Genius which is everywhere call'd the Spirit of Prophecy.* Above is a seated figure instructing a group of children. Below is the nude figure of a man running with long strides from right to left; in his hands he holds what appears to be a lyre. 5.7 × 4.2 cm.

9. *PRINCIPLE 6. The Jewish & Christian Testaments are An original derivation from the Poetic Genius. this is neceſsary from the confined nature of bodily*

senſation. Above is an open book ; below, a draped figure groping with outstretched arms in darkness.   5.5 × 3.7 cm.

10. *PRINCIPLE 7ᵗʰ. As all men are alike (tho' infinitely various) So all Religions & as all similars have one source. The true Man is the source he being the Poetic Genius.* Above, two figures recline on the ground on either side, and a third appears to them in the centre with outstretched arms ; below, a bird flying over dark waters.   5.5 × 3.4 cm.

Note : This work is similar in character to the two series of plates with the title *There is No Natural Religion* already dealt with, but it is known only by the single copy described below. It is to be assigned to the period 1788-1794 for the same reasons as have already been mentioned in the case of *There is No Natural Religion* ; the only copy known to exist has the same title-page as this work, but it is evident, as was first pointed out by Dr. Sampson (1913, p. xxviii), that the plate reproduced by Mr. Muir as the title-page of series b of *There is No Natural Religion*, bearing the words *All Religions are One*, was in reality intended by Blake to be the title-page of the present work, and I have accordingly restored it to this position. Dr. Sampson further suggests that the copy here described was printed by Tatham after Blake's death, but the fact that it is printed on paper which was not used by Blake after 1794, makes this suggestion improbable.

Copy : 10 plates on 10 leaves. Watermark, *I Taylor* on one leaf. The title-page [*There is No Natural Religion*] printed in black ; pl. 2-10 printed in shades of green. Uncoloured. Plates 2-10 with four or five framing lines. Unbound. Size 38 × 25 cm., uncut.

John Linnell's copy. Sold with his collection at Christie's, March 15, 1918 (lot 203, G. D. Smith, £84). It is now in the library of Mr. H. E. Huntington.

The title-page, as is explained above, does not belong to this work ; it is printed more roughly than the other plates and in a different colour.   It is therefore possible that it was supplied later.

Facsimile Reproduction : In the present work.

Typ. Reprints : EY, iii ; WBY ; EJE ; Sampson, 1913 ; translated into German by von Taube, 1907 (no. 176).

34 SONGS / of / Innocence / 1789 / The Author & Printer W Blake

Description: Frontispiece, title, 2 pl., *Songs*, 29 pl. = 31 plates, about 11 × 7 cm., relief etching, usually painted with water-colours.

Contents: As arranged in copy A—

1. [Frontispiece. The Piper.]	16-17. Night.
2. [Title-page] Songs etc.	18-19. A Cradle Song.
3. Introduction.	20. The Little Boy lost.
4. A Dream.	21. The Little Boy found.
5-7. The Little Girl Lost [and] The Little Girl Found.	22. Nurse's Song.
	23. Holy Thursday.
8. The Lamb.	24. On Another's Sorrow.
9. The Blossom.	25-26. Spring.
10-11. The Ecchoing Green.	27. The School Boy.
12. The Divine Image.	28. Laughing Song.
13. The Chimney Sweeper.	29-30. The Little Black Boy.
14. Infant Joy.	31. The Voice of the Ancient Bard.
15. The Shepherd.	

Note: The *Songs of Innocence* formed, with the doubtful exception of *There is No Natural Religion*, the first book executed by Blake by the method of illuminated printing described in the introduction to this section. All the copies known to me are octavo volumes, measuring about 19 × 13 cm., and copy A, which seems to be in a more original condition than any other, shows that the leaves were stitched into blue-grey paper covers. The earlier copies, when complete, consist of 31 plates, printed, with the exception of the first three, on both sides of the leaf. The later copies are printed on one side of the leaf only, and usually contain fewer plates; nos. 5-7 are the plates which are most constantly missing, owing to the fact that they were transferred by Blake after 1794 to the *Songs of Experience*. In cases where other plates are also missing it is difficult to say whether these copies are as issued by Blake or not; the order of the plates varies so much that there is no reason to suppose that Blake was any more consistent in the precise number of plates, which he included, than he was in their arrangement. Very few of the copies were paginated by Blake, and, for lack of any more definite guide, I have followed Dr. Sampson in adopting as an arbitrary standard the arrangement found in copy A, this being the only one which certainly remains exactly as it was when issued.

The plates in the majority of the copies are printed in golden brown, though green or blue has been used in a few instances (copies F, H, M); one copy (U), uncoloured and probably a late one, is printed in black. The colouring in all the copies is done in water-colours, and in most of them it is characterized by great simplicity; its quality varies considerably, and in one case at least (copy O) it is probable that it was partly done by Mrs. Blake. The text of the *Songs of Innocence* " is " engraved in minuscule roman with the exception of The Voice of the Ancient " Bard, which is in italic " (Sampson, 1905, p. 69). The designs on the plates have not been described above, under the heading *Contents*, as in the later illuminated books, partly because they are too well known to need it, but also because each plate is sufficiently well distinguished by the title of the poem engraved on it, and because the designs in most cases bear a much more direct and obvious relation to the text than do those in the other books.

Dr. Sampson writing in 1905 described five copies of the separate issue of the *Songs of Innocence*. The number is here increased to twenty-one, though some are fragmentary copies, and I have not been able to trace all of them and obtain detailed descriptions. There is no contemporary reference to the *Songs of Innocence* before the completion of the companion volume, the *Songs of Experience*, but in the *Prospectus* of 1793 these two volumes are advertised at 5 shillings each, and are stated each to contain 25 plates. In 1818 Blake offered the *Songs of Innocence*, containing 28 plates, at 3 guineas, but there is no evidence to show that any copy of the book by itself was issued as late as this. The latest copy (Q), to which a definite date can be assigned, was issued not earlier than 1808.

Nearly all Blake's original designs for the plates seem to have disappeared. In Quaritch's *General Catalogue*, 1887, p. 935, two designs resembling the frontispiece and the Introduction are described, and these may have been done before the plates were made. Manuscript sources of the text are almost equally rare, and versions of only three of the poems (nos. 20, 22, and 23) are to be found in Blake's autograph in the MS. known as *An Island in the Moon* (no. 2). A different version of the Laughing Song,* probably earlier, is to be found in MS., though not in Blake's autograph, on the fly-leaf of a copy of the *Poetical Sketches* (see no. 26, note).

This account of the *Songs of Innocence* is necessarily incomplete without the further account of the combined issue of the *Songs of Innocence and of Experience* (see no. 38, note), and the two should be read in conjunction.

Copies: [A-I, 1790-1794]

A. 31 plates on 17 leaves. Watermark *Whatman*; no date. Printed in golden brown. Painted with water-colours; tints simple, blue predominating. No pagination. Arrangement as above. Stitched into the original blue-grey paper covers. Size 19 × 13.5 cm., uncut.

A copy sold at Sotheby's, July 1, 1895 (lot 501, Quaritch, £20). Acquired in

---

* For the text of this see *Notes and Queries*, Sept. 24, 1910, and Sampson, 1913, p. 69.

that year by Mr. W. A. White, and given by him to his daughter, Mrs. William Emerson, Cambridge, Mass. (Sampson, 1905, copy A; Grolier Cat., no. 2.)

B. 31 plates on 17 leaves. No watermark. Printed in brown. Painted with water-colours in a predominating tone of yellow-brown. No pagination. Arrangement: 1-3, 15, 14, 18-19, 28-31, 10-11, 22-27, 4-7, 9, 8, 20, 21, 16-17, 13, 12. Originally in worn red leather binding; recently re-bound in citron morocco, inlaid, gilt over rough edges by the Club Bindery. Size 19 × 13 cm.

Stated to have been the copy given by Blake to his physician, and to have been originally stitched into account-book covers. Sold at Sotheby's, Feb. 22, 1897 (Stevens, £42); acquired by the late Robert Hoe of New York, and sold with part 11 of his library, Jan. 8, 1912 ($665.00). Now in the library of Mr. H. E. Huntington. (Sampson, 1905, copy B; Grolier Cat., no. 3.)

C. 31 plates on 17 leaves. No watermark. Printed in yellow-brown. Coloured with extreme finish in water-colours. Arrangement: 1-3, 10-11, 28-31, 9, 8, 4-7, 22, 23, 14-17, 20, 21, 12, 13, 18, 19, 24-27. Bound in citron morocco by Bedford. Size 16.5 × 12.5 cm.

Flaxman's copy with the autograph of his wife, Mrs. Anna Flaxman. Sold at Christie's with the first portion of Flaxman's effects, June, 1875; acquired by Mr. John Pearson of Worthing (formerly of Sydenham) and sold with his library at Sotheby's, Nov. 7, 1916 (lot 41, Sawyer, £205). (Sampson, 1905, copy C.)

D. 31 plates on 17 leaves. Watermark *Whatman* on one page. Printed in sepia. Painted with water-colours; predominating tones yellow, blue-green, and dark violet. No pagination. Arrangement: 1-3, 18-21, 12-13, 24-27, 8-9, 4-7, 28-31, 23, 22, 10-11, 16-17, 14-15. Bound in green levant morocco, inlaid, by Bedford; t.e.g., otherwise uncut. Size 19 × 12.5 cm.

This copy is stated to have been done for Samuel Rogers, and to be of great beauty. It was seen by R. H. Shepherd in 1875 and was described by him in the *Academy* for June of that year (see no. 453); it was then the property of Mr. John Pearson. In 1915 it was acquired privately by Messrs. Quaritch, by whom it was offered in a catalogue (March, 1915, £220), being sold shortly afterwards. It is now in the possession of Prof. G. H. Palmer of Newton, Mass., and will eventually go to Wellesley College.

E. 31 plates on 17 leaves. No watermark. Printed in brown. Painted in a simple manner with water-colour washes. No pagination. Arrangement: 1-3, 15, 14, 24, 27, 23, 22, 28-31, 10-11, 13, 12, 4-7, 20, 21, 18-19, 25-26, 9, 8, 16-17. Bound in stamped russia, rebacked. Fly-leaf with watermark dated 1825. Size 17.8 × 12.5 cm.

On the fly-leaf is the signature "R. H. Clarke." This copy was sold at Sotheby's,

May 25, 1906 (Robson, £83). It is now in the possession of Mr. W. E. Moss. (Manchester Cat., 1914, no. 148.)

F. 31 plates on 17 leaves. Watermark *E & P* (*i.e.*, c. 1794). Printed in green and blue. Painted with water-colours, green and blue predominating. Paginated in pencil. Arrangement: 1-3, 15, 29-31, 18-19, 9, 5-8, 22, 14, 24, 20, 21, 13, 25-28, 4, 23, 12, 10-11, 16-17. Bound in contemporary mottled calf, with central ornament on each cover; in case. Size 18 × 12.5 cm.
Formerly in the possession of John Linnell; later in the collection of Robert Hoe of New York, who wrote in it: "I paid £4.4.0 for this book. R.H." It was sold with part 1 of the Hoe Library, April 25, 1911 (lot 390, $700.00)· (Sampson, 1905, copy D; Grolier Cat., no. 4. History wrongly given in both.)

G. 27 plates on 15 leaves. Watermark *E & P* (*i.e.*, c. 1794) on two leaves. Printed in light sepia, the outlines touched up with black. Painted with water-colours, the tints bright but delicate. Paginated by Blake in black, 1-27. Arrangement: 1-3, 15, 14, 8, 9, 28-31, 20-21, 12-13, 18-19, 16-17, 24-27, 4-7. Lacks 10, 11, 22, 23. The leaves show the original stitch holes, but are now interleaved and bound in brown morocco, gilt, g.e. Size 18.5 × 13.5 cm. Bought by Miss Amy Lowell from Quaritch in 1898, and still in her possession.

H. 21 plates on 12 leaves. Watermark *E & P* (*i.e.*, c. 1794). Printed in green. Delicately painted with water-colours, green predominating. No pagination. Arrangement: 1-3, 15, 29-31, 12, 4, 10, 11, 24, 14, 8, 25, 26, 9, 22, 13, 18, 19. Bound in old half leather, gilt, now enclosed in a modern embroidered cover. Size 16 × 11.5 cm.
An incomplete copy, sold at Sotheby's, Nov. 20, 1900 (Quaritch). Now the property of Mr. E. J. Shaw of Walsall. (Sampson, 1905, copy E.)

I. 29 plates on 29 leaves. Watermark, portions of *J. Whatman*; the date is not visible. Printed in dark grey. Painted with water-colours; tints rich but simple. The text is tinted. General effect fine. No foliation. Arrangement: 1-3, 15, 14, 24, 23, 22, 29-31, 10-11, 13, 12, 4-7, 20, 21, 18-19, 25-26, 9, 8, 16-17. Lacks 27, 28. Bound in whole russia, blind tooled. Size 18.5 × 14 cm. A copy sold at Hodgson's, April, 1910 (Edwards, £47). Offered for sale by Messrs. Maggs in 1911 (cat. 268, no. 35, £110). Now in the possession of Miss Catherine Bullard, Boston, Mass.

[K-Q, 1795-1808.]

K. 28 plates on 16 leaves. No watermark. Printed in brown. Delicately painted with water-colours; colours dull. On some of the earlier pages the letters of the text have been carefully illuminated in red or green. No pagination.

Arrangement: 1-3, 10-11, 28, 29-30, 31, 9, 8, 4, 25-27, 14, 15, 18-19, 22, 23, 13, 12, 20, 21, 16-17, 24. Lacks 5-7. Bound in straight-grained black morocco by C. Murdon. Size 17 × 11.5 cm.

Copy from the library of the late Sir Charles Dilke, with his autograph on the fly-leaf. Offered for sale at Christie's, May 9, 1911, but withdrawn at £250. Now in the possession of Mr. Carl H. Pforzheimer, New York.

L. 27 plates on 15 leaves. No watermark. Printed in brown. Painted with water-colours. No pagination. Arrangement: 1-3, 15, 14, 22-31, 10-11, 18-21, 8, 9, 12, 13, 16, 17. Lacks 4-7. Stitch holes at back of leaves. Now bound in plain brown morocco by Zaehnsdorf. Size 19 × 13.5 cm.

This copy was sold at Sotheby's, July 21, 1902 (Parsons, £19 10s.). Now in the possession of Miss A. G. E. Carthew.

M. 9 plates on 9 leaves. No watermark. Printed in blue or brown. Painted with water-colours. Foliated by Blake. Arranged as follows, Blake's numbers being given in brackets: 1[1], 23[18], 16[19], 25-26[22-23], 22[24], 14[25], 4[27], 24[28]. The leaves are mounted on larger paper and recently bound in straight-grained morocco by Cockerell. Size of original leaf about 20 × 15 cm., though some of the leaves are charred and irregularly cut down.

An incomplete copy in the possession of Baron Dimsdale. It is probable that the series was originally complete, these nine leaves having been rescued by their owner from a bonfire. The book was acquired by the first Baron Dimsdale during Blake's lifetime.

N. 29 plates on 29 leaves. No watermark. Printed in golden brown. Uncoloured. Foliated by Blake. Leaves now unbound. Size about 18.5 × 13.5 cm.

Formerly in the E. W. Hooper collection and probably still in the possession of his family, but it cannot now be traced. A leaf from another copy, printed in green on both sides, with the plates of the Ecchoing Green, and painted with water-colours, has been added to this copy.

O. 26 plates on 26 leaves. Watermarks *J Whatman* and *Edmead & [Pine]* 1802. Printed in golden brown. Very lightly painted with water-colours, the tints being for the most part rather pale. Probably executed in part by Mrs. Blake. No foliation. Arrangement: 1-3, 14, 10-11, 25-26, 12, 23, 27, 20, 21, 24, 4, 28, 9, 16-17, 8, 15, 31, 13, 22, 29, 18. Lacks 5-7, 19, 30. Bound in contemporary straight-grained morocco, with velvet panels and arms stamped in the centre; g.e. Size 18 × 12.5 cm.

On the recto of the first leaf is written: "The gift of Mr Malkin—1805," so that this volume evidently belonged to the author of *A Father's Memoirs of his Child*, 1806 (see no. 80). More recently it was the property of L. W. Hodson of Compton Hall, Wolverhampton, whose label is inside the cover, and it was sold with his library at Sotheby's, Dec. 3, 1906 (Tregaskis, £107). It was in the possession of Dr. Greville MacDonald until 1920, when it was sold by him to Mr. Francis Edwards. (Manchester Cat., 1914, no. 149.)

P. 28 plates on 28 leaves. Watermarks, *Edmead & Pine* 1802 and *J Whatman* 1804. Painted in golden brown. Very beautifully painted with water-colours. Foliated 1-28 by Blake. Arrangement: 1-3, 10, 11, 9, 25, 26, 14, 31, 15, 29, 30, 24, 18-19, 12, 23, 8, 13, 4, 27, 28, 22, 20, 21, 16-17. Lacks 5-7. Bound in olive-green calf. Size 17.5 × 12 cm.

Erroneously stated to have been John Linnell's copy, probably because a pen-and-ink portrait of Blake by Linnell and an autograph letter from Blake to him were at one time inserted.

Sold at Sotheby's, July 27, 1893 (Heath, £49 10s.). In 1900 it was sold by Quaritch to Mr. Marsden J. Perry of Providence. Later it was bought by Mr. W. A. White, and was given by him to Mr. A. T. White. (Sampson, 1905, copy G; Grolier Cat., nos. 5-6.) A sketch by Blake of a woman holding a nude boy is pasted in at the end.

Q. 27 plates on 27 leaves. Watermark *J Whatman* 1808. Printed in grey. Painted with water-colours; colouring subdued but carefully finished. Foliated by Blake 2-28. Arrangement: 2, 3, 15, 10-11, 8, 29-30, 9, 13, 20, 21, 28, 18-19, 12, 23, 16-17, 27, 25-26, 22, 14, 31, 4, 24. Lacks 1, 5-7; Blake's foliation shows that the frontispiece was originally included. The leaves measure about 20.5 × 14.5 cm.; they are untrimmed and show the original stitch-holes. They have been recently hinged on sunk mounts and bound in brown morocco, gilt, by Rivière.

This copy has but recently come to light; it was bought by Messrs. Quaritch from a private source, and was offered in their catalogue no. 361, Dec. 1920, for £350.

[R-U, date uncertain.]

R. 30 plates on 30 leaves. Coloured. Lacks title-page. Bound in half-leather. Size given as 8°.

Copy from the library of W. H. Crawford of Lakelands, co. Cork. Sold at Sotheby's, March 12, 1891 (lot 350, Tregaskis, £8, w.a.f.).

S. 21 plates. Coloured. Lacks 10-11, 22, 23, and others. Bound in whole morocco, gauffred edges, gilt, by C. Lewis. Size given as sm. 4° or 8°.

An imperfect copy from the library of E. H. Lawrence, F.S.A., sold at Sotheby's, May 9, 1892 (Pearson, £52); it was again sold at Sotheby's with the library of J. B. Ditchfield, M.D., April 24, 1893 (Pearson, £18). It was then acquired by Mr. T. J. Wise, but was resold by him in 1899. (Mentioned in Sampson, 1905, p. 70.)

T. 31 plates. Coloured. Unnumbered. Bound in green morocco, g.e., by J. Smith. Size given as sm. 4°.

Gaisford copy. Sold at Sotheby's, April 23, 1890 (Quaritch, £41). Not traced.

U. 31 plates on 31 leaves. No watermark. Printed in black. Uncoloured. Consists of: 2, 1, 3, 10-11, 29-30, 9, 22, 28, 13, 14, 8, 20, 21, 16-17, 27, 24, 18-19, 12, 23, 25-26, 31, 4, 15, 5-7. Bound up with the *Descriptive Catalogue*, 1809, and the *Canterbury Pilgrims*, 1812; fly-leaf with watermark dated 1818. Size 19 × 11.5 cm.

From the collection of Robert Balmanno, New York. Afterwards in the E. W. Hooper collection, and now in the possession of Mrs. Greely S. Curtis, Jr., Boston, Mass.

Reproduced by Little, Brown, and Co., Boston, 1883 (see no. 216).

[V. A series of the coloured prints was lent to the Burlington Fine Arts Club Exhibition in 1876 by Miss E. J. Carey (items 273-274). This is probably to be identified with a copy already described.]

Facsimile Reproductions, Typ. Reprints: See under no. 38.

35 THE / BOOK / of / THEL / The Author & Printer Willm Blake. 1789.

Description: *Thel's Motto*, title, 2 pl., *Thel* ch. i-iv, 6 pl. = 8 plates, 15.5 × 11 cm. (except pl. i), relief etching, painted with water-colours. Plates 1-6 are numbered at the top right-hand corner.

Contents: [i] *Thel's Motto*, 4 lines on a small plate, 6 × 10 cm.

[ii] Title-page, *The Book of Thel*, etc. A slender tree extends up the left-hand side and droops over to the right; Thel stands beside it gazing at a plant, from the flowers of which spring two small figures.

1. *Thel I.* Begins: *The daughters of Mne Seraphim led round their sunny flocks.* The heading is surrounded by an eagle and various small figures.

2 [*I*, cont.] Begins: *Why should the mistrefs of the vales of Har, utter a sigh.* Below, on the right, is a tree the branches of which droop over Thel and the Lily bowing before her.

3. *II.* Begins: *O little Cloud the virgin said, I charge thee tell to me.*

4. *III.* Begins: *Then Thel astonish'd view'd the Worm upon its dewy bed.* Above, Thel standing beside an infant on a lily (the Worm); a small figure is floating in the air (the Cloud).

5. [*III*, cont.] Begins: *But he that loves the lowly, pours his oil upon my head.*

Below, Thel seated, weeping with her head bowed on her knees; at her feet are a nude woman and an infant (the matron Clay and the Worm).

6. *IV.* Begins: *The eternal gates terrific porter lifted the northern bar.* Below, three children astride a serpent (cf. *America*, pl. 11).

Note: *The Book of Thel* was probably the second work executed by Blake in illuminated printing. I have obtained full descriptions of twelve copies; three more are to be found among the sale records, but these should perhaps be identified with some of the first twelve. It is a volume of large quarto size, measuring usually about 30 × 23 cm., and consists of eight plates, which are always printed on one side of the leaf only. The arrangement and constitution of the plates found in the copies described below do not vary, except in copy K, which has only seven plates, and in copy M, in which plate i is placed at the end. In copies A-L the plates are printed in yellow-brown or green ink, and are coloured with transparent water-colour washes; the character of the colouring is simple and of great beauty, and it does not vary so much as in some of the other illuminated books. The Beaconsfield copy (K) is printed on larger paper than the rest, with watermark *I Taylor*; it probably belongs to the year 1794, having been executed for Isaac D'Israeli at the same time as the other books from that collection. All the other copies of which I have obtained details except one are printed on paper which bears no watermark; this fact and the uniformity of the colouring make it seem probable that they were all printed and illuminated by Blake at about the same time, perhaps in the years 1789-1793. The exception, copy M, has a watermark dated 1815, and it is more elaborately coloured than the other copies. The text, which is etched throughout in italic, as in the later books, does not vary, except that in copies G, H, and M Blake has erased the last two lines but two. The first line of the poem, which reads:

"The daughters of Mne Seraphim led round their sunny flocks"

has given rise to some conjecture. Mr. W. B. Yeats has suggested that Blake first intended to write "The daughters of Mnetha," but afterwards adopted the above reading and omitted to alter "Mne" into "the." Recently Mr. Perugini has made the alternative and more probable suggestion that "Mne Seraphim" is a mystical name, which is correct as it stands (for his evidence see no. 593).

In the *Prospectus* of 1793 *Thel* was advertised as "The Book of Thel, a Poem in Illuminated Printing. Quarto with 6 designs price 3*s.*" Evidently Blake reckoned as "designs" only the six plates of text, which he had numbered on the copper 1-6. In 1818 the book was offered as "Thel 6 prints quarto £2.2.0," and in 1827 the price was increased to £3 3*s.*

Copies:

A. 8 plates on 8 leaves. No watermark. Printed in light brown. Delicately painted with water-colour washes. Size 26.5 × 18.5 cm. Formerly bound in half-calf, together with *Urizen*, copy D, and *The Marriage of Heaven and Hell*, copy A; now unbound. The volume was marked "Cumberland's Sale," *i.e.*, this is George Cumberland's copy. Later in Beckford's. library, and sold at Sotheby's on Nov. 29, 1883, in the Hamilton Palace sale (pt. 4, lot 764, Quaritch, £121). Then in the collection of E. W. Hooper of Harvard. After his death the volume was divided up, and the *Thel* is now in the possession of Mrs. John B. Potter, Boston, Mass. (Boston Mus. Cat., 1891, no. 2.)

B. 8 plates on 8 leaves. No watermark. Printed in golden brown. Delicately painted with water-colour washes. In olive morocco binding by Cockerell, 1904. Size 29 × 23 cm.
Formerly in the collection of the Earl of Crewe. Sold at Sotheby's on March 30, 1903 (lot 2, Edwards, £77); now the property of Mr. A. M. S. Methuen. This copy is said to have been originally in the Butts collection, but see copy H. (Nat. Gal. Cat., 1913, no. 89.)

C. 8 plates on 8 leaves. No watermark. Printed in light brown; pl. 1 has several letters touched up with black ink. Delicately painted with water-colours. Size 28.5 × 22 cm. Bound in red morocco, g.e., by Rivière.
Formerly Thomas Gaisford's copy, and contains his bookplate; sold with his library at Sotheby's on April 23, 1890 (lot 185, Quaritch, £29). Acquired by Mr. W. A. White in 1891. (Grolier Cat., no. 10.)

D. 8 plates on 8 leaves. No watermark. Printed in yellow. Lightly touched with water-colours; prevailing tint blue. Size 29 × 22 cm. Bound in half-morocco, g.e., interleaved.
Now in the B.M. Print Room, having been purchased from Messrs. Evans in 1856.

E. 8 plates on 8 leaves. No watermark. Printed in blue-green. Delicately painted with water-colours. Size 30 × 24 cm. Recently bound in morocco, gilt.
Formerly in the possession of Charles Fairfax Murray, whose label is inside the cover, but presented by him in 1912 to the Fitzwilliam Museum, Cambridge.

F. 8 plates on 8 leaves. No watermark. Printed in green. Delicately painted with water-colour washes. Size 31 × 23.5 cm., uncut. Bound in blue morocco by Rivière.
Formerly in the possession of Mr. F. P. Osmaston. It was sold at Sotheby's on June 1, 1905 (Dobell, £69); Mr. Dobell believes that he sold it to another bookseller. It was bought from Mr. Tregaskis in 1906 by Dr. Greville MacDonald, by whom it was sold in March, 1920, to Mr. Francis Edwards. (Manchester Cat., 1914, no. 158.)

G. 8 plates on 8 leaves. No watermark. Printed in green. Delicately painted

with water-colours; prevailing tints blue, yellow, and pink. Size 29.5 × 23 cm.
Bound in half-calf. The last two lines of the text but two have been erased,
and some decorations painted over them.
Formerly in the library of Francis Douce, whose bookplate is inside the cover.
Bequeathed by him to the Bodleian Library, Oxford, in 1835.

H. 8 plates on 8 leaves. No watermark. Printed in green. Delicately painted
with water-colour washes. The last two lines of the text but two have been
erased and tinted over by Blake as in copy G. Size 29.5 × 15.5 cm. Bound,
together with *Visions of the Daughters of Albion*, copy I, in worn straight-
grained olive morocco by Hering, lettered: *The Book of Thel by Blake* 1789.
Interleaved with tissue paper, most of which is watermarked 1811. Two of the
fly-leaves have a watermark dated 1816.
Sold at Christie's in 1881. Bought about 1900 from Quaritch by Miss Amy
Lowell, and still in her possession.

I. 8 plates on 8 leaves. No watermark. Printed in green. Painted with water-
colours. Size 30 × 24 cm. Bound in green morocco, g.e., by Bedford.
Originally in the possession of Thomas Butts, and sold with his collection at
Sotheby's on March 26, 1852 (F. T. Palgrave, £2 15s.). From Francis
Palgrave it passed to Locker-Lampson, and was for some years in the Rowfant
Library. When this was sold it passed into the collection of the late E. D. Church,
and is now in the possession of Mr. H. E. Huntington.

K. 7 plates on 7 leaves. No watermark. Printed in brown. Delicately painted
with water-colours. Size 30 × 23.5 cm. In original wrappers, edges frayed,
sewn. In morocco case. Lacks pl. [i].
On the wrapper is written: "Stothard's Copy. Preserve." This copy was seen
by Gilchrist who wrote (i, 78): "I may mention in corroboration of a previous
"assertion of Stothard's obligation as a designer to Blake, that the copy of
"*Thel*, formerly Stothard's, bears evidence of familiar use on his part, in broken
"edges, and the marks of a painter's oily fingers." These marks are, however,
stated to be now extremely faint. This copy is probably to be identified with
one from the library of Sir Robert Comyn, which was sold at Sotheby's on
March 13, 1893 (Robson, £14 10s.). It was shortly afterwards acquired by
Mr. T. J. Wise, but was resold by him in 1899. It eventually came into the
possession of Mr. Herschel V. Jones, and was sold with his library at the
Anderson Galleries, New York, Dec. 2, 1918 (lot 182, Rosenbach, $793). It
is now in the collection of Mr. A. E. Newton.

L. 8 plates on 8 leaves. Watermark *I Taylor*. Printed in golden brown.
Delicately painted with water-colours. The leaves, which show Blake's stitch-
holes, are now mounted on hinges in a volume bound in modern boards with
leather back. Size 37.5 × 27 cm., uncut.

The Beaconsfield copy, probably bought from Blake by Isaac D'Israeli. Sold with the Beaconsfield library at Sotheby's on March 20, 1882 (Ellis and White, £23), and acquired by Mr. B. B. Macgeorge of Glasgow. (Nat. Gal. Cat., 1913, no. 88 ; Manchester Cat., 1914, no. 157.)

M. 8 plates on 8 leaves. Watermark *Ruse & Turners*, 1815. Printed in red-brown. Very beautifully painted with water-colours. Arrangement: ii, 1-6, i. Numbered by Blake on pl. 2 and 6-8. The last two lines but two of the text have been erased. Bound in red straight-grained morocco, g.e. Size 28 × 23 cm.

Formerly bound in calf, together with *The Marriage of Heaven and Hell*, copy G, and *Visions of the Daughters of Albion*, copy N. This volume was sold at Sotheby's, Feb. 17, 1890 (lot 301, Robson). It was then divided up, and *Thel* was sold to the late Alexander Mackay for £32. After the decease of his widow, the book was resold at Christie's, April 26, 1921 (lot 1, " Shoebridge," £205).

N. 8 plates on 8 leaves. Coloured. Size given as 4°. Sewn.
A copy sold at Sotheby's on July 1, 1895 (lot 502, Ellis, £14). Perhaps to be identified with one of the copies above.

O. 8 plates on 8 leaves. Coloured. Sewn. Size given as folio, uncut.
A copy sold at Sotheby's on Feb. 22, 1897 (Gerrard, £18 5s.). Perhaps to be identified with one of the copies above.

P. 8 plates on 8 leaves. Coloured. Size given as folio, uncut. Wrappers.
A copy sold at Puttick and Simpson's on Nov. 19, 1900 (Quaritch, £46). Perhaps to be identified with one of the copies above.

Facsimile Reproductions: In *Works by William Blake*, 1876 (no. 212); W. Muir, 1884, coloured (no. 217, b); EY, iii; W. Muir, 1920, coloured (no. 240).

Typ. Reprints: Extracts (37 lines) first printed in the *London University Magazine*, 1830 (no. 408). First printed in full by Gilchrist, 1863; later by WMR, WBY, LH, EJE, Sampson, 1913.

36 THE / MARRIAGE / of / HEAVEN / and / HELL [*including*] A Song of Liberty [*about* 1790]

Description: Title, 1 pl., *The Marriage of Heaven and Hell*, 23 pl., *A Song of Liberty*, 3 pl. = 27 plates, 16 × 11 cm., relief etching, usually coloured.

Contents:

1. Title-page, *The Marriage*, etc. Above are leafless trees, with four small figures. Below, two nude figures meet and kiss; the left-hand figure is borne on flames, the right-hand figure on clouds. In the centre float various small figures.

2. *The Argument*. Begins: *Rintrah roars & shakes his fires in the burdend air.*

A tree extends up the right-hand margin of the plate; among the branches is a youth, who is reaching fruit down to a woman standing below.

3. Begins: *As a new heaven is begun.*   Above, a naked woman lying among flames; below, a woman with an infant's arm protruding from her womb, and two children running away (cf. *The Four Zoas*, p. 9*b*).

4. *The voice of the Devil.*   Begins: *All Bibles or sacred codes.*   Below, on the left a naked figure clasping a child strides across the sea; on the right a youth, fettered by one ankle, dashes out of flames towards him.   Behind is a rising sun.

5. Begins: *Those who restrain desire.*   Above, a naked man and a horse falling headlong into flames.

6. Begins: *[Messi]-ah fell, & formed a heaven.*   In the centre: *A Memorable Fancy*, beginning: *As I was walking among the fires of hell.*

7. Begins: *[cor]-roding fires he wrote the following sentence.*   Near the top: *Proverbs of Hell*, beginning: *In seed time learn.*

8. *Proverbs of Hell.*   Begins: *Prisons are built with stones of Law.*

9. *Proverbs of Hell.*   Begins: *The fox provides for himself.*

10. *Proverbs of Hell.*   Begins: *The head Sublime.*   Below, an angel of the Devil kneels in the centre with a long scroll unrolled across his knees.   A woman is seated on each side of him, making notes in a book.

11. Begins: *The ancient Poets animated all sensible objects.*   Above is a naked woman with an infant on a lily; a figure with flaming hair and arms upraised is rising out of the ground.

12. *A Memorable Fancy.*   Begins: *The Prophets Isaiah and Ezekiel dined with me.*

13. Begins: *. . . would at last be proved to originate in ours.*

14. Begins: *The ancient tradition that the world will be consumed in fire.*   Above, a naked man is lying on his back; flames rise round him, and over him floats a woman with outstretched arms.

15. *A Memorable Fancy.*   Begins: *I was in a Printing house in Hell.*   Below, an eagle with a snake in its talons.

16. Begins: *The Giants who formed this world.*   Above are five figures squatting in a huddled group with their knees drawn up to their chins.

17. Begins: *. . . to reconcile them seeks to destroy existence.*   Near the top: *A Memorable Fancy*, beginning: *An Angel came to me and said.*

18. Begins: *. . . root of an oak, he was suspended in a fungus.*

19. Begins: *. . . us with all the fury of a spiritual existence.*

20. Begins: *. . . number of monkeys, baboons, & all of that species.*   Below, a serpent writhing in huge coils in the sea, beneath which is inscribed: *Opposition is true Friendship* (legible only in copies D, F, and G *).

* In the first two the last word is very indistinct; in the third it is quite clear.

number of monkeys, baboons, & all of that species
chaind by the middle, grinning and snatching at
one another, but witheld by the shortness of their
chains; however I saw that they sometimes grew nu
merous, and then the weak were caught by the strong
and with a grinning aspect, first coupled with & then
devourd, by plucking off first one limb and then another till the body was left a helpless trunk. thus after
grinning & kissing it with seeming fondness they devourd too; and here & there I saw one savourily picking the flesh off of his own tail; as the stench ter-
ribly annoyd us both we went into the mill, & I in
my hand brought the skeleton of a body, which in
the mill was Aristotles Analytics.

So the Angel said: thy phantasy has imposed
upon me & thou oughtest to be ashamed.

I answerd: we impose on one another, & it is
but lost time to converse with you whose works
are only Analytics

THE MARRIAGE OF HEAVEN AND HELL
Plate 20

21. Begins: *I have always found that Angels have the vanity*. Above, a naked youth is seated on the ground and gazing upwards; his left knee rests on a skull (cf. *America*, pl. 6, and illustrations to Blair's *Grave*, pl. 13).

22. Begins: . . . *one on earth that ever broke a net*. Near the bottom: *A Memorable Fancy*, beginning: *Once I saw a Devil in a flame of fire*.

23. Begins: . . . *greatest men best, those who envy or calumniate*.

24. Begins: . . . *[im]-pulse not from rules*. Below, a bearded man crawling on hands and knees (Nebuchadnezzar). At the bottom is inscribed: *One Law for the Lion & Ox is Oppression*.

25. *A Song of Liberty*, 1-10, beginning: *The Eternal Female groand!*

26. Ditto, [10]-18, beginning: . . . *hurl'd the new born wonder*.

27. Ditto, [18]-20, beginning: . . . *he promulgates his ten commands*. Near the centre, *Chorus*, beginning: *Let the Priests of the Raven of dawn*.

Note: The title-page of *The Marriage of Heaven and Hell* is not dated, but the book is probably to be assigned to the year 1790. As has been pointed out by Ellis,* the opening passage, "As a new heaven is begun and it is now thirty-three years "since its advent," may refer to the year of Blake's birth; he was born in 1757, and was therefore thirty-three years old in 1790. On the other hand Dr. Sampson (1913, p. xxx) considers that this sentence "can only refer to the new era of the "dispensation of the Spirit, predicted by [Swedenborg] for 1757." The whole work is in the manner of Swedenborg, and it was about this period that Blake was reading and annotating his works.

Eight complete copies of the book are known to me, and three fragments in addition are described below. The volume varies in size from octavo (18.5 × 9.5 cm.) up to folio (about 38 × 27 cm.). A complete copy, including the *Song of Liberty*, consists of twenty-seven plates, which are printed sometimes on both sides of the leaf, sometimes on one side only. One copy (D), probably an early one, has the engraving known as "The Three Accusers" added as a frontispiece. The last three plates, with the text of *A Song of Liberty*, occur separately, and Dr. Sampson (1913, p. xxx) considers this to be "certainly a separate and later Prophecy, nearer in style and symbolism to *America*"; but I have no evidence that the book was ever issued by Blake without these plates. Gilchrist, i, 88, describes the book as consisting of only twenty-four plates, but this was evidently an error, for two copies which he afterwards mentions both contain the *Song of Liberty*. All the copies known to me are coloured except one (D). The earlier examples are printed in various shades of brown or green ink, and are painted with a combination of water-colours and opaque pigment; the four latest ones, three of which are printed in red, are painted with water-colours only. Some

* EJE, i, 254.

gold has been used in two of these (H and I), and in the copy which formerly belonged to John Linnell (I), a book of extraordinary beauty, the text has been illuminated with various bright colours. Some of the designs vary slightly in different copies, but the text does not vary. A sentence inscribed below the design on pl. 20 is legible only in three copies, and has not previously been noticed. The text of "The Argument" and of the "Proverbs of Hell" is etched in minuscule roman lettering as in the *Songs of Innocence* and *There is No Natural Religion*; the rest is in italic as in the later books. There is no MS. authority for any of the text, but two of the designs (pl. 4 and 24) were also used by Blake in his large colour prints known as "The Good and Evil Angels" and "Nebuchadnezzar," and a sketch for the second of these is to be found in the *Rossetti MS.*

Mr. William Muir has recently supplied me with a list of titles for the designs, which he copied from pencil writing on a fly-leaf of the Cumberland-Beckford copy (A) of the original. These may have been invented by Cumberland or Beckford; it is, on the other hand, quite possible that they were obtained by Cumberland from Blake himself. The titles are as follows: Pl. 1. The Union of the Elements. 2. Earth. 3. Fire. 4. Water. 5. Air. 11. The Dawn. 14. The Body of Hector. 15. Genius. 16. Ugolino. 20. A Dream. 21. Satan addressing the Sun. 24. Arbitrary Power.

In the *Prospectus* of 1793 Blake advertised this book as "The Marriage of "Heaven and Hell, in Illuminated Printing. Quarto with fourteen designs, 7*s*. 6*d*." He has evidently reckoned among these fourteen designs the title-page and both the designs on pl. 3. The book was not included in the lists of 1818 and 1827.

Copies:

A. 27 plates on 15 leaves. Printed in brown. Heavily painted with water-colours (? and opaque pigment). Size 26.5 × 18.5 cm.

Formerly bound in half-calf together with *Urizen*, copy D, and *Thel*, copy A; now unbound. The volume belonged to George Cumberland, and was later in Beckford's library, being sold at Sotheby's, Nov. 29, 1883, in the Hamilton Palace sale (pt. 4, lot 764, Quaritch, £121). Then in the collection of E. W. Hooper of Harvard. After his death the volume was divided up, and *The Marriage of Heaven and Hell* is now in the possession of Mrs. Bancel Lafarge, Mount Carmel, Connecticutt.

B. 27 plates on 27 leaves. No watermark. Printed in shades of brown. The larger designs are painted with opaque pigment, the small illuminations sometimes with water-colours. Plate 16 is uncoloured. Arrangement: 1-3, 5-10, 4, 11, 14, 12, 13, 16-27, 15. Foliated in pencil, but not by Blake. Size 26.5 × 20 cm. Bound in half-morocco.

Purchased from Quaritch by Mr. W. A. White in 1896 (Grolier Cat., no. 11).

The pigments on some of the designs were much darkened, but were restored at the B.M. in 1912.

C. 27 plates on 27 leaves. No watermarks. Printed in greenish grey. Painted with a combination of water-colours and opaque pigment. No foliation. Arranged as above. Size 26 × 19 cm. Bound in red morocco, with the Milnes crest on the sides.

Originally in the possession of Thomas Butts, and sold with his collection at Sotheby's on March 26, 1852 (R. Monckton Milnes, £5 5s.). Resold with the Crewe collection at Sotheby's on March 30, 1903 (lot 12, Osmaston, £260). Offered at Sotheby's, June 1, 1905, but apparently withdrawn at £150. On the front fly-leaf is the signature of Mr. F. P. Osmaston, by whom it was presented to the Red Cross sale at Christie's, April 5, 1917 (Stevens and Brown, £350). It is now in the collection of Mr. A. E. Newton.

D. 28 plates on 16 leaves. No watermark. Printed in various shades of green and brown. Uncoloured except for slight water-colour washes on pl. 1-4. Arranged as above with the addition of the plate known as "The Three Accusers" as frontispiece, which is printed in green and lettered: *Our End is come | Publishd June 5 1793 by W. Blake Lambeth.** No pagination. Size 23.5 × 15 cm. Bound in half-morocco.

Copy from the library of Francis Douce, whose bookplate is inside the cover; it was bequeathed by him to the Bodleian Library, Oxford, in 1835.

E. 27 plates on 27 leaves. Watermark *I Taylor* (*i.e.*, about 1794). Printed in blue-green. Painted with water-colours in a simple style, occasionally with some opaque pigment. The design on pl. 21 has two pyramids added in the background. Arranged as above and foliated by Blake 1-27. Size 38 × 27 cm., uncut. The leaves, which show Blake's stitch-holes, are mounted on hinges in a volume bound in boards with leather back.

The Beaconsfield copy, probably bought from Blake by Isaac D'Israeli about 1794. Sold with the Beaconsfield library at Sotheby's on March 20, 1882 (Bain, £50), and acquired by Mr. B. B. Macgeorge of Glasgow.

F. 27 plates on 15 leaves. Watermark *J Whatman* without date. Printed in green. Delicately painted with water-colours, blue and green predominating. Arranged as above. The legend below the design in pl. 20 can be deciphered in this copy. Size 26.5 × 17 cm. Bound in contemporary tree calf, gilt.

Sold at Sotheby's on May 13, 1892 (Bain, £50). Afterwards in the possession of the late Robert Hoe, and sold with his library on April 25, 1911 (lot 391, $3,500.00).

Now in the Pierpont Morgan Library. (Grolier Cat., no. 12.)

---

* See Russell, *Engravings*, p. 66.

G. 27 plates on 27 leaves. Watermark *Ruse & Turners* 1815. Printed in red-brown. Delicately painted with water-colour washes. Each plate has a single framing line. Arranged as above. Numbered by Blake 1-27. The legend at the bottom of pl. 20 is clearly read. Bound in blue straight-grained morocco, g.e. Size 28 × 23 cm.

Formerly bound in calf, together with *Thel*, copy M, and *Visions of the Daughters of Albion*, copy N. This volume was sold at Sotheby's, Feb. 17, 1890 (lot 301, Robson). It was then divided up, and *The Marriage of Heaven and Hell* was sold to the late Alexander Mackay for £63. After the decease of his widow it was resold at Christie's, April 26, 1921 (lot 3, "Shoebridge," £460).

H. 27 plates on 27 leaves. Watermark *J Whatman* 1825. Printed in brick-red. Richly painted with water-colours and gold. Each plate is surrounded by a single painted line. Arranged as above. Foliated by Blake 1-27. Size 30 × 23 cm. The leaves are mounted on guards, and are in a cloth binding with leather back.

Formerly in the possession of Richard Edward Kenrick, Cambridge University Librarian, whose autograph is on the fly-leaf dated 1856; bequeathed by him to the Fitzwilliam Museum, Cambridge.

I. 27 plates on 15 leaves. No watermarks. Printed in red. Richly painted with water-colours and gold; in addition to the usual colouring, parts of the text have been illuminated with various bright tints. Paginated by Blake 1-27. Size 20.5 × 13.5 cm. Bound in vellum, gilt.

John Linnell's copy; sold with his collection at Christie's, March 15, 1918 (lot 195, Carfax, £756). Now in the possession of Mr. T. H. Riches. (Nat. Gal. Cat., 1913, no. 90; Manchester Cat., no. 146.)

K. A fragment, 4 plates on 2 leaves. No watermark. Printed in black. Uncoloured. Consists of pl. 21-24; the design is omitted from pl. 24. Size 24 × 14.5 cm. Recently bound in morocco by Rivière.

These leaves were found loose by C. Fairfax Murray in the copy (S) of the *Songs of Innocence and of Experience* bequeathed to him by Sir F. Burton. They were given in 1912 to the Fitzwilliam Museum, Cambridge.

L. A fragment, 3 plates on a double leaf. Watermark *J Whatman* without date. Printed in greenish grey. Uncoloured. Consists of the *Song of Liberty*, pl. 25-27. Unbound.

Formerly belonged to John Linnell; sold with his collection at Christie's, March 15, 1918 (lot 197, Tregaskis, 11 gns.).

M. Similar to L; also in the Linnell collection.

Sold at Christie's, March 15, 1918 (lot 198, Tregaskis, £8 18*s*. 6*d*.).

N. Mr. A. G. B. Russell informs me that a copy of *The Marriage of Heaven and Hell* was in the possession of Mrs. Crawfurd, widow of the late Oswald

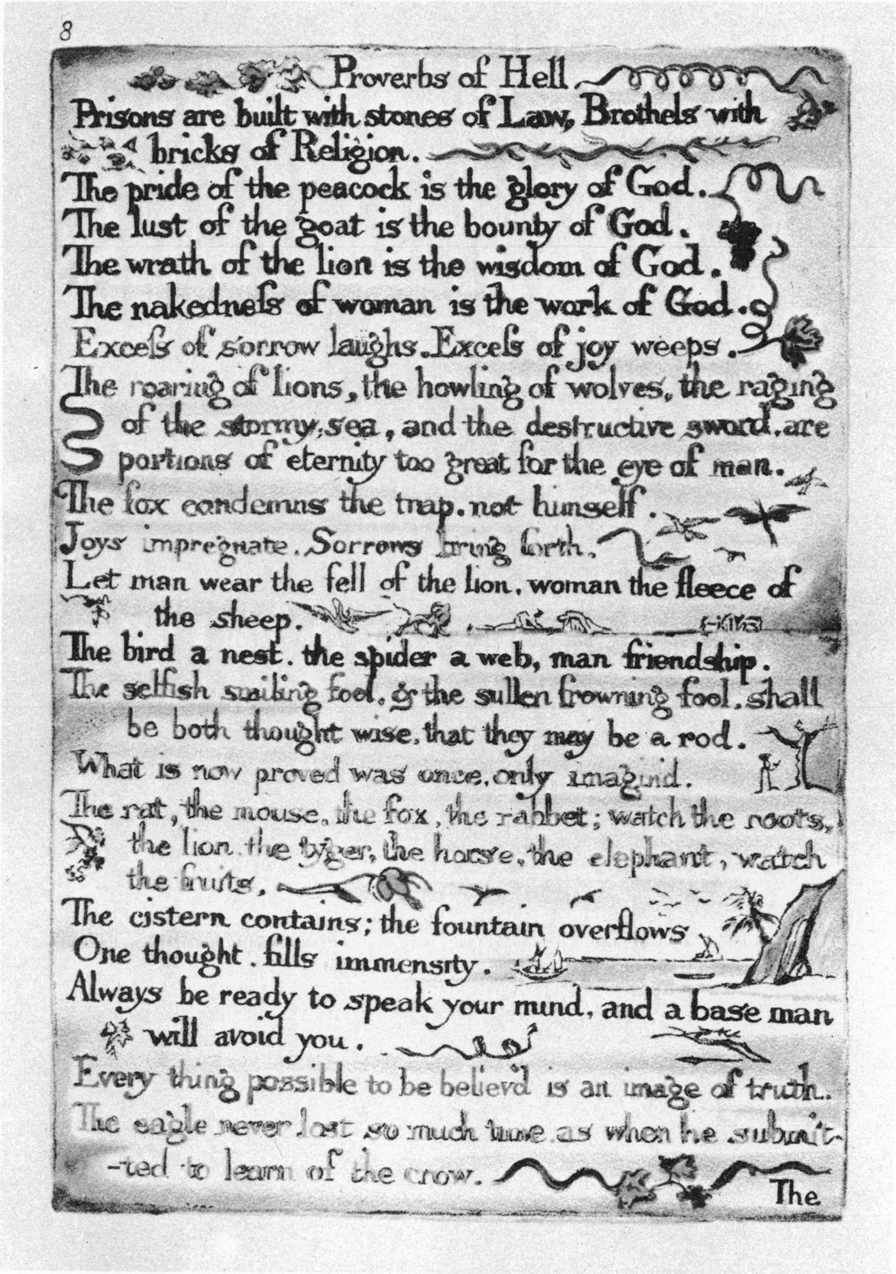

Proverbs of Hell

Prisons are built with stones of Law, Brothels with
    bricks of Religion.

The pride of the peacock is the glory of God.

The lust of the goat is the bounty of God.

The wrath of the lion is the wisdom of God.

The nakedness of woman is the work of God.

Excess of sorrow laughs. Excess of joy weeps.

The roaring of lions, the howling of wolves, the raging
    of the stormy sea, and the destructive sword, are
    portions of eternity too great for the eye of man.

The fox condemns the trap, not himself.

Joys impregnate. Sorrows bring forth.

Let man wear the fell of the lion, woman the fleece of
    the sheep.

The bird a nest, the spider a web, man friendship.

The selfish smiling fool, & the sullen frowning fool, shall
    be both thought wise, that they may be a rod.

What is now proved was once, only imagin'd.

The rat, the mouse, the fox, the rabbet; watch the roots,
    the lion, the tyger, the horse, the elephant, watch
    the fruits.

The cistern contains; the fountain overflows

One thought, fills immensity.

Always be ready to speak your mind, and a base man
    will avoid you.

Every thing possible to be believ'd is an image of truth.

The eagle never lost so much time, as when he submit-
    -ted to learn of the crow.   The

THE MARRIAGE OF HEAVEN AND HELL

Plate 8

Crawfurd, C.M.G., who acquired it many years ago; but at the present time the volume cannot be found.

Facsimile Reproductions: Swinburne, pl. 1, 8, and 20, coloured; Camden Hotten, 1868, coloured (no. 210); W. Muir, 1885, coloured (no. 217, e); EY, iii.

Typ. Reprints: Extracts first printed by Gilchrist, i, 78, and Swinburne, p. 208. Printed in full in the *Century Guild Hobby Horse*, 1887 (no. 492), and by WBY, LH, EJE, Sampson, 1913. Separate reprints by Grant Richards, 1906 (no. 169), J. P. Raverat, 1910 (no. 178), Florence Press, 1911 (no. 180). Translated into German by Knoblauch, 1907 (no. 175; extracts), and von Taube, 1907 (no. 176; almost in full).

37 TO THE PUBLIC.   October 10, 1793.

Description: A single plate, relief etching.

Contents: Begins: *The Labours of the Artist, the Poet, the Musician, have been proverbially attended by poverty and obscurity.* Blake draws attention to his new method of book-production, and after a eulogy of himself gives a list of the works on sale at Mr. Blake's, No. 13 Hercules Buildings, Lambeth, as follows:

1. Job, a Historical Engraving. Size 1 ft. 7½ in. by 1 ft. 2 in.: price 12s.
2. Edward and Elinor, a Historical Engraving. Size 1 ft. 6½ in. by 1 ft.: price 10s. 6d.
3. America, a Prophecy, in Illuminated Printing. Folio, with 18 designs, price 10s. 6d.
4. Visions of the Daughters of Albion, in Illuminated Printing. Folio, with 8 designs, price 7s. 6d.
5. The Book of Thel, a Poem in Illuminated Printing. Quarto, with 6 designs, price 3s.
6. The Marriage of Heaven and Hell, in Illuminated Printing. Quarto, with 14 designs, price 7s. 6d.
7. Songs of Innocence, in Illuminated Printing. Octavo, with 25 designs, price 5s.
8. Songs of Experience, in Illuminated Printing. Octavo, with 25 designs, price 5s.
9. The History of England, a small book of Engravings. Price 3s.
10. The Gates of Paradise, a small book of Engravings. Price 3s.

Note: This characteristic prospectus is exceedingly rare, and I have not yet seen a copy. The details below are derived from Gilchrist, ii, 285.

Copy: A single leaf. Plate printed in blue. Size about 28 × 19 cm. This copy was seen by Gilchrist, who obtained it through the late W. E. Frost, A.R.A., but it is not recorded to whom it belonged.

Typ. Reprints: Gilchrist, ii, 285; Ellis, *The Real Blake*, p. 181; Russell, *Engravings*, p. 210.

38 SONGS / Of / INNOCENCE / and Of / EXPERIENCE / Shewing the Two Contrary States / of the Human Soul

Sub-title a: SONGS / of / INNOCENCE / 1789 / The Author & Printer W Blake

Sub-title b: SONGS / of / EXPERIENCE / 1794 / The Author & Printer W Blake

Description: General title, Frontispiece, and sub-title a, 3 pl., *Songs of Innocence*, 24 pl., Frontispiece and sub-title b, 2 pl., *Songs of Experience*, 25 pl. = 54 plates, about 11 × 7 cm., relief etching, painted with water-colours.

Contents:

1. [General title-page], Songs, etc.	22-23. Spring.
2. [Frontispiece. The Piper.]	24. Nurse's Song.
3. [Sub-title a], Songs, etc.	25. Infant Joy.
4. Introduction.	26. A Dream.
5. The Shepherd.	27. On Another's Sorrow.
6-7. The Ecchoing Green.	28. [Frontispiece. Cherub on shepherd's head.]
8. The Lamb.	
9-10. The Little Black Boy.	29. [Sub-title b], Songs, etc.
11. The Blossom.	30. Introduction.
12. The Chimney Sweeper.	31. Earth's Answer.
13. The Little Boy lost.	32. The Clod & the Pebble.
14. The Little Boy found.	33. Holy Thursday.
15. Laughing Song.	34-36. The Little Girl Lost [and] The Little Girl Found.
16-17. A Cradle Song.	
18. The Divine Image.	37. The Chimney Sweeper.
19. Holy Thursday.	38. Nurse's Song.
20-21. Night.	39. The Sick Rose.

Cancelled plates: a. A nude male figure borne upwards by five cherubs; no text. 6.5 × 5.5 cm.*

b. A Divine Image.

Note: In Blake's prospectus of 1793 the *Songs of Innocence* and *Songs of Experience* are advertised as separate works, containing 25 illuminated plates, at 5 shillings each; no authentic copy, however, of the *Songs of Experience* in this form is known, the only separate examples of this work described below having originally belonged, as is shown by their foliation, to copies of the combined issue. The *Songs of Experience* are therefore not described here separately.

The title-page of the *Songs of Experience* is dated 1794, and the earliest copy of the *Songs of Innocence and of Experience* known to me belongs to this year. This consists of 50 plates, and therefore agrees as regards the number of plates with the advertisement of 1793, though they are not distributed quite in the same way, the *Songs of Innocence* consisting of 28 plates, and the *Songs of Experience* of 22; this is evidently due to the fact that in 1793 Blake was still counting the three plates of The Little Girl Lost and The Little Girl Found (34-36) among the *Songs of Innocence*, but when the two series were actually issued together in 1794 these plates were transferred to the *Songs of Experience*, where they remained in all copies issued after that date. When this copy was issued, four plates, namely, the general title-page, A Little Boy Lost, A Little Girl Lost, and To Tirzah had not yet been engraved. All later copies consist of 54 plates, though one of the four extra plates did not reach its final form at once; for two copies (B and C), also issued about the year 1794, contain, instead of the plate To Tirzah, a design without text (a) representing a nude figure borne aloft by cherubs. This plate has the appearance of being one of Blake's so-called "woodcuts on pewter"; it is not found in any other book.† Copies B and C are also peculiar in that A Dream is placed among the *Songs of Experience*.

* See Russell, *Engravings*, p. 71, where it is described as "Subject resembling the Ecstasy of St. Mary Magdalene," but the figure is undoubtedly that of a man.

† A separate print of this plate, which belonged formerly to the late H. Stopford Brooke, was recently offered by Mr. Tregaskis (Cat. 810, Jan. 20, 1919, £23).

A complete copy, therefore, issued after 1794, consists of 54 plates distributed in the earlier copies as follows: General title-page, 1 plate, *Songs of Innocence*, 28 plates, *Songs of Experience*, 25 plates; this system was followed until about 1814. After that date two plates, The Schoolboy and The Voice of the Ancient Bard, were transferred from the *Songs of Innocence* to the *Songs of Experience*, so that the two works then consisted of 26 plates and 27 plates respectively. This distribution is found in all the later copies, with two exceptions (L and M), in which The Voice of the Ancient Bard was included among the *Songs of Innocence*; this may be an intermediate condition, and I have therefore assigned it conjecturally to the date 1814, or it is possible that these copies belong to the year 1818, when Blake offered the two works containing 28 plates (*i.e.*, general title-page and 27 plates) and 26 plates respectively, numbers which correspond with this aberrant constitution.

The order in which Blake arranged the plates shows in the earlier copies the same lack of uniformity as is found in the separate issues of the *Songs of Innocence*. About 1808, however, he began to adopt the order given above, at any rate for the *Songs of Innocence*. In 1815 he used this order for the whole book and, with one exception, kept to it in all copies issued after this date. This exception (copy U) is peculiar in that Blake seems to have taken the trouble to write out a MS. index, but only to reject it after having used it in this single copy, the paper of which bears the date 1818. I have not followed Dr. Sampson in using the arrangement found in this index as a standard, as it does not seem to me to constitute so weighty an authority as the arrangement found in seven of the latest copies issued by Blake, all of which bear his own foliation. The plates were usually printed in some shade of brown, but Blake occasionally used olive-green or sepia. All the copies except one are printed, as in the later copies of the *Songs of Innocence*, on one side of the leaf only. The book is usually on paper measuring about 20 × 14 cm.; those copies which are smaller have probably been cut down. The lettering used in the *Songs of Innocence* has already been referred to. In the *Songs of Experience* " Blake substituted for roman " the more easily formed italic characters which he first adopted in the *Book of Thel* " (1789) and used in all his subsequent works; only four songs, The Tyger, Ah ! " Sunflower, London, and A Poison Tree, with the introductory stanza to A Little Girl " Lost, being written in the former style of lettering " (Sampson, 1905, p. 69). In the earliest copies of the *Songs of Innocence and of Experience* Blake's water-colour illuminating is almost as simple in character as that which he used in the earlier copies of the *Songs of Innocence*. Later his method became more elaborate, and in most of the copies issued from 1814 onwards he heightened the effect by the use of gold. In two instances (copies B and H) he used opaque pigments as well as water-colours, and another copy (N) contains twelve plates coloured with opaque pigments only, but

SONGS OF EXPERIENCE

Plate a

these were probably executed much earlier than the other plates in the volume, which belong to the year 1815.

Dr. Sampson, writing in 1905, described twelve copies of the *Songs of Innocence and of Experience* and one copy of the *Songs of Experience*, and was led to make several wrong conclusions by inaccuracies in the facts at his disposal. These numbers are here increased to twenty-three copies of the former and four of the latter, and the data have, for the most part, been thoroughly revised. I have also included eight series of the plates printed after Blake's death, one of which was described by Dr. Sampson; these naturally have little bibliographical value, but two of them contain pl. b, A Divine Image, which is not found in any copy issued by Blake himself.* Eighteen of the *Songs of Experience* are found in Blake's autograph in the *Rossetti MS.*, and several of these appear to be fair copies, but there are no other manuscript sources of the text. In the same MS. are found the original sketches for The Angel and The Sick Rose. In 1863 ten of the original copper-plates, six of them engraved on both sides, were in existence. Electrotypes were made of these sixteen designs and were used by Messrs. Macmillan in the first and second editions of Gilchrist's *Life*. These ten plates seem now to have disappeared.

As already mentioned, the *Songs of Innocence* and *Songs of Experience* were advertised by Blake in 1793 at 5 shillings each, containing altogether 50 plates. In 1818 the whole 54 plates were offered at 6 guineas, and we know that Mr. Aders (copy R) and Crabb Robinson (copy S) each paid 5 guineas for a copy in 1826. In 1827 Blake offered the book for 10 guineas, and after his death Mrs. Blake sent a copy (Q) in return for a present of 20 guineas. These facts are established and show that Blake received a steadily increasing price for his work. Gilchrist (i, 121) writes as follows: " The illustrated *Songs of Innocence and Experience* was issued to Blake's " public at the modest price of thirty shillings or two guineas. . . . Later in Blake's " life . . . five guineas were given him, and in some cases when intended as a delicate " means of helping the artist larger sums. Flaxman recommended more than one " friend to take copies, a Mr. Thomas among them, who wishing to give the artist a " present made the price ten guineas. . . . In the last years of his life Sir Thomas " Lawrence, Sir Francis Chantrey, and others paid as much as twelve and twenty " guineas." No authority is given for these facts and no reliance can be placed upon some of them. The former owners of the copies described below include Charles Augustus Tulk, Isaac D'Israeli, Thomas Butts, John Linnell, Richard Edwards, T. G. Wainewright, Dr. Jebb, Richard Calvert, and John Flaxman.

This account of the *Songs of Innocence and of Experience* should be read in conjunction with the separate account of the *Songs of Innocence* on pp. 97-8 of the present work.

---

* Another example of this rare plate is to be found among a miscellaneous collection of leaves from Blake's works which is now in the Pierpont Morgan Library.

Copies : The copies described below may be tabulated as follows :

DATE	CHARACTERISTICS	COPIES
1794	50 plates. Pl. 53, 54, among *Songs of Innocence*. Pl. 1, 50-52 not yet engraved.	A
1794	54 plates. Pl. 53, 54, among *Songs of Innocence*. Pl. 26 among the *Songs of Experience*. Pl. 52 not yet engraved; replaced by plate without text.	B, C
c. 1795-1807	54 plates. Pl. 53, 54, among *Songs of Innocence*. Arrangement irregular. Colouring simple.	D, E, F, G, H, I
c. 1808	54 plates. Pl. 53, 54, among *Songs of Innocence*. Arrangement of *Songs of Innocence* or of whole book approximates to that given above. Colouring simple.	J, K
?*c.* 1814	54 plates. Pl. 54 among *Songs of Innocence*, Pl. 53 among *Songs of Experience*.	L, M
1815-1827	54 plates. Pl. 53, 54, among *Songs of Experience*. Arrangement as above. Colouring more elaborate. Gold used.	N, O, P, Q, R, S, T
1818	54 plates. Pl. 53, 54, among *Songs of Experience*. Arrangement according to MS. index.	U
Date not assigned	*Songs of Experience* only.	V
	Description not obtained.	W, X, Y, Z
Posthumous 1831-1832		a, b, c, d, e, f, g, h

A. 50 plates on 50 leaves. Watermark *I Taylor*, and, on one plate of the *Songs of Experience*, 1794. Printed in olive-brown. Painted with water-colours; tints very simple. The *Songs of Innocence* and *Songs of Experience* are foliated by

Blake separately. In each case the title-page and frontispiece are unnumbered, the other plates being numbered 1-26 and 1-20 respectively. Arrangement: 2-4, 22-23, 6-7, 9-10, 13, 20-21, 11, 24, 27, 54, 15, 18, 12, 19, 53, 14, 8, 5, 16-17, 26, 25, 29, 28, 30, 31, 40, 32, 41, 37, 42, 48, 45, 38, 47, 34-36, 44, 49, 46, 39, 33, 43. Lacks 1, 50-52. Inserted are uncoloured facsimiles of 50-52 and A Divine Image. The leaves show the original stitch-holes; they are now inserted in slide mounts bound in two large vellum volumes. Size of leaf 38 × 27 cm., uncut.

The Beaconsfield copy, probably bought from Blake by Isaac D'Israeli. Sold at Sotheby's at the Beaconsfield sale, March 20, 1882 (Dowdeswell, £85), and acquired about 1885 by Mr. B. B. Macgeorge of Glasgow. Although the *Songs of Innocence* and *Songs of Experience* are foliated separately, the similarity of the styles of colouring show that they were executed at the same time and form a copy of the combined issue.

B. 54 plates on 30 leaves. Watermarks *E & P*, *I Taylor*, and *Whatman*; no date. Printed in shades of brown or orange except pl. 47, which is in green. Painted with water-colour washes, with opaque pigments, or with a combination of the two. The colouring is simple, and in some cases very beautiful. No pagination. Arrangement: 2, 1, 3, 4, 25, 5, 16-17, 8, 11, 24, 19, 6-7, 27, 22-23, 53, 18, 12, 15, 9-10, 54, 20-21, 13, 14; 28-31, 48, 51, 38, 41, 39, 44, 45, 47, 26, 34-36, 50, 37, 40, 49, 46, 42, 43, 33, 32, a. Lacks 52, but contains a, which is found in no other copy except C; this plate appears to have been printed in more than one colour as in the case of *There is No Natural Religion* (no. 32). Plate 26 is among the *Songs of Experience* as in copy C. Bound in contemporary citron morocco, gilt, the sides covered with small stars in diamond-shaped compartments. Size 18 × 12.5 cm.

Nothing is known of the early history of this volume. It was sold at Sotheby's on March 16, 1909 (lot 172, Dobell, £166), and was afterwards offered by Mr. Tregaskis in one of his catalogues (245 guineas). It is now in the possession of Mr. W. E. Moss. (Manchester Cat., 1914, no. 147.)

C. 54 plates on 30 leaves. No watermarks. Printed in shades of brown. Delicately painted with water-colours. No pagination. Arrangement: 2, 1, 3-4, 15, 9-10, 54, 27, 22-23, 53, 6-7, 16-17, 20-21, 5, 25, 24, 19, 8, 11, 18, 12-14, 28-31, 40, 49, 46, 42, 39, 44, 26, 34-36, 48, 51, 47, 45, 50, 37, 41, 38, 33, 43, 32, a. Lacks 52, but contains a as in copy B. Plate 26 among the *Songs of Experience*, as in copy B. Bound in contemporary straight-grained morocco. Size 17.5 × 12 cm.

On the front fly-leaf are the signatures " C. L. Shipley " and " Fanny F. S. Milner," but nothing further is known of its early history. It was in the hands of Messrs. Quaritch in March, 1916, and now belongs to Mr. A. E. Newton.

D. 54 plates on 31 leaves. Watermark *Whatman*; no date. The majority of the plates are printed in brown, but a few are in yellow, green, or red. Painted with water-colours. Paginated 1-54. Arrangement: 1-5, 25, 11, 8, 15, 9-10, 54, 18, 12, 16-17, 6-7, 27, 22-23, 53, 24, 19; 13, 14, 20-21, 26; 28-31, 15, 34-36, 50, 37, 42, 46, 44, 39, 38, 41, 45, 47, 40, 49, 48, 51, 33, 43, 52. Lacks 32, which is replaced by a duplicate of 15. Bound in whole morocco, g.e., by Bedford. Size 18.5 × 11.5 cm.

Originally in the possession of Thomas Butts, and sold with his collection at Sotheby's, March 26, 1852 (Hartington, £12 12s.); it is described in the sale catalogue as " 3 vols. 8°." The leaves were bound by a later owner in the covers of an old washing book. In this condition it came into the possession of Frederick Locker, and was incorporated in the Rowfant Library. It was next in the possession of Mr. Beverly Chew, but was sold with his library in 1912 to Mr. H. E. Huntington. (Sampson, 1905, copy F; wrongly described.)

[Locker's bookplate is inside the cover, and his autograph is in pencil on the frontispiece and in ink on the first title; two pages copied in his autograph from Swinburne are laid in. Inserted at the end are an extra copy of pl. 32 obtained by Locker, two MS. parodies of pl. 4, and three pages in the writing of Alexander Gilchrist.]

E. 54 plates in two vols. as follows:

a. *Songs of Innocence.* 28 plates on 28 leaves. Watermark [*Wh*]atman [18]04. Printed in orange-brown. Uncoloured, but the details on most of the plates have been delicately outlined in sepia; a light brown wash has been added on a few plates. Foliated by Blake 1-28. Arrangement: 2-4, 6-7, 5, 11, 22-23, 12, 54, 53, 25, 15, 26, 8-10, 16-17, 19, 24, 27, 18, 13, 14, 20-21. Bound in contemporary quarter-calf; fly-leaf with watermark 1801. Size 18.5 × 12.5 cm.

b. *Songs of Experience.* 26 plates on 26 leaves. Watermark *Buttanshaw* 1802. Printed in dark brown. The plates are coloured only with water-colour washes, chiefly brown and sepia, and in a few cases blue. Very strong effect. Foliated by Blake 1-26. Arrangement: 28, 1, 29-31, 48, 42, 37, 34-36, 38, 32, 40, 50, 47, 52, 39, 44, 46, 51, 41, 49, 45, 33, 43. Bound in contemporary quarter-calf. Size 18 × 12.5 cm.

These volumes were formerly in the possession of Principal Chase of St. Mary Hall, Oxford, and were given by him about 1863 to the late Alexander Macmillan, whose autograph is on the fly-leaf of each volume. They are now the property of his daughter, Mrs. Lewis Dyer. I was permitted to see them by the courtesy of Mr. George Macmillan.

F. 54 plates on 54 leaves. No dated watermark. Printed in sepia. Simply and brightly painted with water-colours; predominating tones, blue, yellow, and pink. Some tinting of the text. Foliated by Blake 1-54. Arrangement: 2, 1,

3-5, 11, 9-10, 22-23, 19, 6-7, 25, 8, 24, 15, 12, 18, 26, 27, 53, 54, 16-17, 20-21, 13, 14; 28-33, 48, 41, 39, 40, 50, 51, 43, 37, 45, 49, 44, 46, 47, 38, 42, 34-36, 52. Bound in purple cloth with leather label, *c.* 1830. Size given as 8°.

This copy bears the autographs of H. W. Phillips, the painter, to whom it is said to have been given by Blake, and of Gerald Massey, the poet. Sold at Sotheby's, June 3, 1902 (lot 140, Quaritch, £216). In 1905 it was still in the possession of Mr. Bernard Quaritch, who subsequently sold it to the late George C. Thomas of Philadelphia. It is now in the Harry Elkins Widener Memorial Library of Harvard University. (Sampson, 1905, copy H.)

G. 11 plates on 11 leaves. No watermark visible. Printed in brown. Uncoloured. Foliated by Blake. Arranged as follows, Blake's numbers being given in square brackets: 28[30], 29[31], 38[35], 48[36], 42[37], 40[41], 34-36[47-49], 49[51], 43[52]. An incomplete copy, but Blake's foliation shows that it was originally complete, and that the *Songs of Innocence* included pl. 53 and 54. Leaves mounted to a large size and bound in half-morocco. Size 18 × 14 cm. From the Toovey collection with bookplate. Now in the Pierpont Morgan Library.

H. 53 plates on 53 leaves. Watermark *J. Whatman*; no date. Printed in brown. Brightly painted with water-colours and opaque pigment. 12 leaves with Blake's foliation. Arranged as follows, Blake's numbers being given in square brackets: 1-27, 54; 28, 29, 30-32[32-34], 33[38], 34-36, 37[35], 39, 38, 40, 41[39], 42, 43, 44[46], 45[43], 46[40], 47[42], 48, 49, 50[44], 51[45], 52. Lacks 53, which appears to have been originally included among the *Songs of Innocence.*

Probably a copy sold at Sotheby's on April 28, 1862 (Toovey, £4 6s.). Later in the Toovey collection, with bookplate. Now in the Pierpont Morgan Library.

I. 54 plates. Coloured. Arrangement: 1-5, 22-23, 19, 15, 24, 18, 8-10, 25, 6-7, 16-17, 53, 20-21, 27, 26, 13, 14, 11, 12, 54; 30, 31, 48, 32, 44, 40, 42, 50, 33, 43, 41, 38, 34-36, 47, 37, 52, 49, 51, 46, 39, 45. The leaves were originally of 8° size, but have been inlaid to 4° size.

This copy belonged to Charles Augustus Tulk, a friend of Blake, from whom it was no doubt obtained direct. I have not actually seen the book, but its arrangement and therefore its approximate date, 1795-1807, may be inferred from the facts that Tulk is known to have lent his copy of the *Songs* to Coleridge in 1818 (see no. 316), and to Garth Wilkinson in 1838 (see no. 134), and that the list of the poems given by Coleridge in his letter to Tulk agrees precisely in arrangement with that adopted by Wilkinson in his edition of the *Songs* issued in 1839. The book was bought by Mr. Bain, the bookseller, about

R

1870, from a member of Tulk's family, who was then resident in Australia, and it was next in the possession of Mr. Dew-Smith of Cambridge. It was again bought by Mr. Bain towards the year 1900, and was soon afterwards sold to the late Lord Rothschild, who left it, however, in Mr. Bain's hands for nearly twenty years. At its owner's death the book was delivered to his executors, and is presumably now in the possession of the present Lord Rothschild.

Coleridge's original letter to Tulk, recorded under no. 316, accompanies the volume. The details of the recent history of this copy have been supplied by Mr. Bain.

J. 54 plates on 54 leaves. Watermark *Whatman* 1808. Very beautifully coloured. Each book is separately foliated, the general title-page being without foliation. Arrangement: 1-21, 53, 22-25, 54, 26, 27; 28-32, 38, 42, 37, 49, 45, 33, 43, 47, 50, 41, 48, 34-36, 46, 44, 39, 40, 51, 52. Bound in old calf, *c.* 1830. A sheet of brown paper, possibly part of the original wrappers, is inserted between the two series. [By an error of the binder, the *Songs of Experience* are placed after the general title-page before the *Songs of Innocence*.] Size 19 × 12.5 cm.

Probably a copy sold at Sotheby's in August, 1890 (Maggs, £48). In 1905 in the possession of Mrs. John R. Wade of New York; now in the library of Mr. Beverly Chew. (Sampson, 1905, copy K.)

K. 54 plates on 54 leaves. Watermarks *I Taylor* 1794, and, on one leaf, *J Whatman* 1808. Printed in various shades of grey-green, with three or more framing lines in sepia. General title-page unnumbered. The other plates foliated by Blake 1-28 and 1-25. Arrangement: 1-21, 53, 22-25, 54, 26, 27; 28-49, 52, 51, 50. In white vellum binding; fly-leaf with watermark dated 1824. Size 30 × 21.5 cm. Brightly painted with water-colours. The earlier plates of the *Songs of Innocence* were certainly coloured by Blake, and possibly most of them; but the *Songs of Experience* are of inferior quality and were probably coloured by Mrs. Blake.

Bought from Blake on August 27, 1819, by John Linnell, sen., and given by him to his son William on April 28, 1863. From William Linnell it passed to his daughter, Mrs. T. H. Riches, and is still in her possession. (Sampson, 1905, copy L.)

L. 54 plates on 54 leaves. No watermark. Printed in dark brown. Crudely painted with water-colour washes; probably not done by Blake himself. Foliated 1-54. Arrangement: 1, 3, 2, 4, 8, 6-7, 15, 20-21, 19, 18, 13, 14, 27, 9-10, 26, 11, 54, 5, 22-23, 24, 25, 16-17, 12; 28-32, 49, 42, 41, 39, 52, 44, 50, 51, 37, 47, 34-36, 38, 48, 45, 40, 46, 53, 43, 33. Bound in red morocco, g.e., by Rivière. Size 19 × 13 cm.

Probably Sir William Tite's copy, sold at Sotheby's, May 19, 1874 (lot 292, Pearson, £61). Later in Thomas Gaisford's collection, and contains his bookplate; resold with his library at Sotheby's, April 23, 1890 (lot 187, Robson, £87). Then acquired by the late Alexander Mackay, and, after the decease of his widow, again sold at Christie's, April 26, 1921 (lot 4, "Shoebridge," £470).

M. 25 plates on 25 leaves. No watermark. Richly painted with water-colours and gold. *Songs of Experience* only, foliated 30-54 by Blake. Arrangement: 29-32, 37, 49, 48, 42, 40, 39, 47, 51, 34-36, 44, 41, 43, 50, 52, 46, 45, 33, 38, 53. Lacks 28, 54. Bound in modern English maroon morocco, g.e. Size 19.5 × 13.5 cm.

Sold at Sotheby's in July, 1894, with books from the library of Howell Wills of Florence (Quaritch, £40). Later in the possession of Robert Hoe, and sold with part 1 of his library, April 25, 1911 ($700.00). Now in the library of Mr. H. E. Huntington. (Sampson, 1905, copy V, arrangement given inaccurately; Grolier Cat., no. 9.)

N. 38 plates on 38 leaves, forming part of a copy with watermark *Ruse & Turners* [181]5.* Printed in reddish-brown, with two framing lines. Painted with water-colours. Foliated by Blake 1-54. Arranged as above, but lacking pl. 6, 7, 19, 24, 28, 32, 33, 38, 40-43, 47, 49-51, which have been replaced as follows:

i. 4 plates on 2 leaves. No watermark. Printed in sepia. Painted with water-colours with extreme simplicity. Unnumbered, consisting of pl. 6, 7, 19, 24.

ii. 12 plates on 12 leaves. No watermark. Printed in several tints. Painted, rather poorly, with opaque pigments. Unnumbered, consisting of pl. 28, 32, 33, 38, 40-43, 47, 49-51. Probably executed *c.* 1795.

The volume is bound in morocco. Size 18.5 × 12 cm.

Acquired by the B.M. Print Room in 1856. (Sampson, 1905, copy S.)

O. 54 plates on 54 leaves. Watermark *Ruse & Turners* 1815. Printed in red-brown. Elaborately and brilliantly coloured with water-colours and gold. Foliated by Blake 1-54. Arranged as above. Bound in morocco by C. Lewis. Size 22 × 14 cm.

This copy is marked in pencil "Edwards May 1828," and probably belonged to Richard Edwards, the publisher. It was later in Beckford's collection, and was sold at the Hamilton Palace sale, July 4, 1882 (Quaritch, £146). It was acquired by Mr. W. A. White in 1895. (Sampson, 1905, copy N; Grolier Cat., no. 7.) This copy was used by Quaritch for his facsimile; see no. 222.

P. 54 plates on 54 leaves. Watermark *J Whatman* 1825. Printed in dull orange-red, with border lines of the same colour. Elaborately and very beautifully painted

---

* Only the last figure of the date is visible, but the rest may be supplied with some certainty, as 1815 is the only date with which the watermark of *Ruse & Turners* occurs. See p. 17.

with water-colours and gold. Foliated by Blake 1-54. Arranged as above. Printed on leaves 26.5 × 19.5 cm., which were originally bound in green calico. Later mounted on larger sheets, bound in half-morocco. Recently rebound in red morocco, and enclosed in morocco case, by Rivière.

Bought from Blake by T. G. Wainewright *c.* 1820-1824. Later in the library of James Weale, who has inserted a pencil note dated May, 1835, concerning its history. Obtained by John Linnell, sen., on Dec. 13, 1842, from a Mr. White. Linnell later gave it to his son, as appears from the inscription inside the cover—"Given to John Linnell, Jnr. by John Linnell, Senr. April 28th, 1863." It remained in the Linnell collection until this was sold at Christie's, March 15, 1918 (lot 201, Deighton, £735). Resold at Sotheby's from an anonymous source, on June 9, 1921 (lot 3, Sabin, £510). (Sampson, 1905, copy O.)

Q. 54 plates on 54 leaves. Watermark *J Whatman* 1825 (one leaf is dated 1818). Printed in red-brown. Elaborately painted with water-colours and gold. A simple water-colour border has been added to each plate, possibly by Mrs. Blake. No framing lines. Foliated by Blake 1-54. Arranged as above.* Bound in morocco, g.e., by Bedford. Size 28.5 × 22 cm.

It is stated by Gilchrist (i, 409) that this copy was sent by Mrs. Blake to Dr. Jebb, Bishop of Limerick, in return for a present of 20 guineas, sent through Mr. Haviland Burke. I am assured by Miss L. M. Forster, a former owner of the book, that this is a true account of the transaction. On the other hand, this is denied by Mr. Story (see his *Life of Linnell*, i, 243), who states that the book was bought by the Bishop together with the large engravings of *Job* and *Ezekiel*, and two drawings, as an ordinary business transaction, the money being sent after the works had been received by the Bishop. The volume was left in 1833 by Dr. Jebb to his chaplain, the Rev. Charles Forster; at the latter's death it passed to his daughter, Miss L. M. Forster, by whom it was given in 1904 to her nephew, Mr. E. M. Forster. At the beginning of the volume is Miss Forster's bookplate, and laid in, loose, is an early MS. copy of a nonsense rhyme as follows :

MR. BLAKE'S NURSERY RHYME

" The sow came in with the saddle,
" The little pig rocked the cradle,

---

* Sampson, 1905, pp. 82-83, classifies this as a copy in which pl. 54 has been " retransferred to the end of the *Songs of Innocence.*" This, however, is not the case, pl. 53 and 54 being the last two plates in the *Songs of Experience.* This mistake is evidently due to the fact that Dr. Sampson, without seeing this copy of the *Songs*, accepted Gilchrist's statement (i, 410) that he had adopted the arrangement found in it. As a matter of fact Gilchrist's arrangement does not correspond with that found in any copy known to me.

" The dish jumped o' top of the table
" To see the brass pot swallow the ladle.
" The old pot behind the door
" Called the kettle a blackamoor.
" ' Odd bobbs ' said the gridiron, ' can't you agree?
" ' I'm the head constable, bring them to me.' "

There does not seem to be any reason for doubting that this rhyme was at some time recited by Blake for the amusement of children of his acquaintance; possibly these were the young Linnells. (Sampson, 1905, copy T.)

R. 54 plates on 54 leaves. Watermark not visible (probably *c.* 1825). Printed in orange-red, with framing lines of the same colour. Elaborately and splendidly painted with water-colours. Foliated by Blake 1-54. Arranged as above. Size of original leaves 16 × 11.5 cm.; now mounted on larger leaves, and bound in red cloth. Bought from Blake, through John Linnell, by Mr. Aders, July, 1826, for 5 guineas. Afterwards bought by Linnell from Mr. or Mrs. Aders, and subsequently given by him to his son James as appears from the inscription on the fly-leaf: "Given to James Thomas Linnell, by John Linnell, Senr., April 28, 1863." It remained in the Linnell collection until this was sold at Christie's, March 15, 1918 (lot 215, Carfax, £735). It is now in the possession of Mr. T. H. Riches. (Sampson, 1905, copy P.)

S. 54 plates on 54 leaves. Watermark *J Whatman* 182[5]. Printed in orange-brown. Richly painted with water-colours and gold; each plate has one framing line. Foliated by Blake 1-54 in red. Arranged as above. Bound in russia, g.e., fly-leaves with watermark dated 1826. Size 21.5 × 13 cm.
Crabb Robinson's copy, with his bookplate; it is referred to in his *Diary* under the date Feb. 18, 1826, as follows: "He told me my copy of his songs would " be 5 guineas, and was pleased by my manner of receiving the information " (Symons, p. 268). On one fly-leaf is a MS. note: "This copy I received from " Blake himself and coloured by his own hand, which I present with great " pleasure to Edwin W. Field. H. C. Robinson. March 11th 1863." Other notes are as follows: "Given to F. W. Burton by Mrs. Edwin Field in memory " of her husband. Oct. 6, 1871." "Directed by my uncle, Sir Frederic Burton " (when dying) to be given to Chas. Fairfax Murray Esq. 20. 6. 1900. H. B. " Burton." Sold with part of the Fairfax Murray Library at Sotheby's, July 7, 1919 (lot 8, Sabin, £600). (Sampson, 1905, copy Q.)

T. 54 plates on 54 leaves. Watermark *Whatman* 1825. Printed in yellow-brown. Elaborately and brilliantly coloured with water-colours and gold. In addition each plate has a delicate border of floral tracery about .5 cm. wide. Foliated by Blake 1-54 in red. Arranged as above. Leaves on hinged mounts, enclosed in two brown morocco boxes. Size 15.5 × 14 cm.

Originally in the possession of Edward Calvert. Sold at Sotheby's on Nov. 4, 1901, from the library of F. S. Ellis (lot 5, Jackson, £700). Then for several years it was the property of Mr. Marsden J. Perry of Providence, R.I., but about 1906 it was bought from him by Mr. W. A. White. Finally acquired by the Metropolitan Museum, New York, in 1917. (Sampson, 1905, copy R ; Grolier Cat., no. 8.)

U. 54 plates on 54 leaves. Watermark *J Whatman* 1818. Printed in golden-brown. Brightly painted with water-colours, and with wide wash borders. Foliated by Blake 1-54 in black. Arranged in accordance with the MS. index * as follows : 1-4, 6-8, 5, 25, 9-10, 15, 22-23, 16-17, 24, 19, 11, 12, 18, 20-21, 26, 27, 13-14 ; 28-31, 38, 40, 42, 34-36, 32, 45, 33, 49, 41, 39, 52, 54, 43, 44, 50, 48, 53, 46, 51, 37, 47. Bound in half-calf, *c.* 1860. Size 33 × 26.5 cm. Originally in the possession of Thomas Butts ; afterwards acquired by Lord Houghton, and sold at the Crewe sale, March 30, 1903 (lot 1, Quaritch, £300). Now in the possession of Mr. A. M. S. Methuen. (Sampson, 1905, copy M ; Nat. Gal. Cat., 1913, no. 87.)

V. *Songs of Experience* only. 27 plates on 27 leaves. No watermark. Printed in red-brown, the outlines touched with black ink. Brightly painted with water-colours. Foliated by Blake 1-27 in black. Arrangement : 1, 28-32, 38, 34-36, 42, 48, 37, 44, 39, 46, 43, 49, 50, 40, 47, 45, 51, 41, 33, 54, 52. Lacks 53. Loose leaves, originally sewn into grey-blue wrappers, one of which remains. Size 20.5 × 14 cm.

Flaxman's copy, sold at Christie's in the Denman sale, Feb. 26, 1883. A letter to Miss Denman from Ruskin accompanies the volume. Afterwards in the E. W. Hooper collection ; now in the possession of Mrs. R. S. Warner, Boston, Mass. The occurrence of this apparently separate copy of the *Songs of Experience* is probably to be explained by the fact that Flaxman already possessed an early copy of the *Songs of Innocence* (copy C). Blake has included the general title and pl. 54, but has omitted pl. 53. The irregular arrangement of the plates suggests that this copy was made up before 1808, but the evidence is inconclusive.

W. 8 plates. Coloured. Unbound.
A fragment, sold at Sotheby's, July 11, 1904 (Quaritch, £13).

X. A series of the coloured prints was lent to the Burlington Fine Arts Club Exhibition in 1876 by Miss E. J. Carey (items 277, 278).

---

* This index is written on a double leaf of quarto size, and is contained among a miscellaneous collection of prints by Blake, which are bound in at the end of a MS. copy of Cunningham's *Life of Blake* (see no. 249). This volume was formerly in the possession of Mr. William Muir who has published a lithographic facsimile of the MS. index at the end of his edition of *The Marriage of Heaven and Hell* (no. 217, e).

Y. A series of the uncoloured prints, contained in two frames, was lent to the Burlington Fine Arts Club Exhibition in 1876 (items 275, 276).

Z. A copy of the *Songs of Experience* was described by Mr. Richard Thomson in Smith's *Nollekens and his Times*, 1828, ii, 475-7 (no. 247) as follows: "Small "octavo; seventeen plates, including the title-page." The plates are then described in order and appear to consist of pl. 28-31, 38, 41, 33, 40, 53, 51, 34, 48, 54, 42, 46, 32, 52.

[*a-h*. POSTHUMOUS COPIES]

a. 54 plates on 54 leaves. Watermark *J Whatman* 1831 or 1832. Uncoloured. Ff. 1-40 and 42 are printed in grey ink on thick paper, 24.5 × 19 cm.; ff. 41, 43, 44 in darker ink on thinner paper, 28 × 20 cm.; ff. 45-54 in light brown on the thinner paper. The series lacks 15, but includes A Divine Image (pl. b). On pl. 28 can be seen traces of the plate-maker's stamp. Bound in morocco.
Acquired by the B.M. Reading Room, Jan. 7, 1864. (Sampson, 1905, copy X.)

b. 54 plates on 54 leaves. Watermark *J Whatman* 1831. Printed in red-brown. Uncoloured. No foliation. Consists of pl. 1-54. Bound in green seal-grain morocco, gilt, *c.* 1835, with the monogram H.B. in the centre of the cover. Size 18 × 14.5 cm. The plate-maker's stamp can be seen on several plates.
The monogram on the cover is probably that of Hannah Boddington, sister of the Contesse de Montebello, whose bookplate is inside the cover.
Offered for sale by Messrs. Maggs in 1910 (cat. 255, no. 513, 15 gns.). Now in the possession of Mr. W. E. Moss.

c. 54 plates on 54 leaves. Watermark *J Whatman* 1831. Printed in red-brown. Uncoloured. No foliation. The series lacks pl. 52, but includes A Divine Image (pl. b). Bound in red morocco, g.e. Size 18 × 15 cm.
Formerly in the library of Samuel Boddington and contains his bookplate. Afterwards the property of the late H. Stopford Brooke, but not sold with his library in 1918.

d. 42 plates on 42 leaves. Watermark *J Whatman* 1831. Printed in sepia. Uncoloured. No foliation. Consists of pl. 1-14, 16-29, 33-36, 38-43, 46, 49, 52, 53. Bound in russia together with Pickering's edition of the *Songs*, 1839 (no. 134). Size 18 × 11 cm.
On the title-page is the autograph of "Wm Odell Elwell 1840." This copy was sold at Sotheby's on March 16, 1909 (Tregaskis, £6 10*s.*), and was offered by Mr. Tregaskis in one of his catalogues shortly afterwards (36 gns.). Now in the possession of Mr. W. E. Moss.

e. 42 plates bound with Pickering's edition of the *Songs*, 1839. This volume is similar to copy *d.* Offered for sale by Messrs. Maggs in 1914 (cat. 325, 12 gns.).

f. 54 plates on 54 leaves. Watermark *J Whatman* 1831. Printed in red-brown. The first seven plates are touched with water-colours, possibly by Mrs. Blake; the rest are uncoloured. Foliated in pencil. Consists of pl. 1-54. Bound in black straight-grained morocco, with inlaid borders in red, g.e., by Leighton, 1869. Size 18.5 × 16.5 cm.

Inside the cover is the bookplate of Frederick Collins Wilson. A note on the fly-leaf states that a former owner had dated the book 1836. Sold at Sotheby's, Dec. 18, 1919 (Sabin, £39).

g. 41 plates on 41 leaves. Watermark *J Whatman* 1831. Printed in grey ink or sepia. The paper is not uniform. Uncoloured. Newly bound in two vols. in full maroon morocco, uncut, the leaves mounted on linen guards. Size given as 4°. This and the next copy formed together a pile of loose leaves which were formerly in the collection of H. Buxton Forman; sold with his library at the Anderson Galleries, New York, March 15, 1920.

h. 57 plates on 57 leaves. Watermark *J. Whatman* 1832. Printed in black or sepia. Three plates have been coloured in Blake's manner with water-colours and gold. General title and some other plates in duplicate. Newly bound in full maroon morocco, the leaves mounted on linen guards. Size given as 4°.

Formerly in the collection of H. Buxton Forman, together with copy *g*; sold with his library at the Anderson Galleries, New York, March 15, 1920.

Facsimile Reproductions: 16 plates in Gilchrist's *Life*, 1863 and 1880 (electro-types from the original plates); in *Works by William Blake*, 1876 (no. 212); W. Muir, 1885 (no. 217, a, d); Quaritch, 1893, plain or coloured (no. 222).

Typ. Reprints: Plates 18, 19, 42 first reprinted in Malkin's *Father's Memoirs of his Child*, 1806 (no. 80); pl. 4, 19, 42, 44 reprinted and translated into German in the *Vaterländisches Museum*, 1811 (no. 401); pl. 12 first reprinted in James Montgomery's *Chimney-sweeper's Friend, and Climbing-boy's Album,** 1824; pl. 16-18, 30, 44, 49 reprinted in the *London University Magazine*, 1830 (no. 408); pl. 4, 8, 12, 15, 19, 42 reprinted in Cunningham's *Life*, 2nd ed., 1830 (no. 250); pl. 4 reprinted in Dibdin's *Reminiscences*, 1836 (no. 254). First reprinted in full by Pickering, 1839 (no. 134). Later by Gilchrist, 1863; Pickering, 1866 (no. 138). Reprinted in full or in part by all subsequent editors.

* *The Chimney-sweeper's Friend, and Climbing-boy's Album . . . Arranged by James Montgomery. With illustrative designs by Cruickshank. London: Printed for Longman, Hurst, . . . 1824.* 8°, pp. xvi + 428 + [4] Woodcuts after designs by R. Cruickshank facing title, pp. 28 and 363. On pp. 343-4 is Blake's Chimney Sweeper, "communicated by Mr. Charles Lamb, from a very rare and curious little work." Second edition, Harvey and Darton, 1825. See also nos. 264 and 337 in the present work.

39 VISIONS / of / the Daughters of / Albion / The Eye sees more than the Heart knows. / Printed by Will.™ Blake: 1793.

Description: Frontispiece, title, *Argument*, 3 pl., *Visions*, 8 pl. = 11 plates, about 17 × 12 cm., relief etching, painted with water-colours. Plates 2, 3, 5, and 6 are numbered at the top right-hand corner.

Contents: [i] Frontispiece. Three nude figures at the mouth of a cave, one of them chained to a rock (Oothoon, Bromion, and Theotormon).

[ii] Title-page. *Visions*, etc. Decorated with various figures.

[iii] *The Argument*; 2 stanzas of 4 lines each. Below, a female figure is kissing the smaller figure of a man, who springs out of a flower (Oothoon plucking the flower of Leutha).

1. *Visions*. Begins: *Enslav'd, the Daughters of Albion weep*: Below, two recumbent figures. Five figures surround the letters of the heading.

2. Begins: *Now thou must marry Bromions harlot, and protect the child.* In the centre, a dark, recumbent figure (Theotormon in his sadness); to his right is a fallen tree against which leans a pickaxe.

3. Begins: *And none but Bromion can hear my lamentations.* Below, Theotormon's eagle rending the bosom of Oothoon.

4. Begins: *Wave shadows of discontent? and in what houses dwell the wretched.* Above, Oothoon, chained by one ankle, floats in a wave over the figure of Theotormon, who is seated at the water's edge.

5. Begins: *But when the morn arose, her lamentation renewd.* Near the bottom, a recumbent figure (Oothoon in despair).

6. Begins: *And a palace of eternity in the jaws of the hungry grave.* Below, Theotormon scourging Oothoon.

7. Begins: *In happy copulation; if in evening mild, wearied with work.* Above, four female figures seated (Daughters of Albion).

8. Begins: *Where the cold miser spreads his gold! or does the bright cloud drop.* Below, Oothoon, with outstretched arms, floats in a fiery cloud over three Daughters of Albion.

Note: The title-page of this work is dated 1793, but none of the copies known to me bears a watermark dated earlier than 1794. I have evidence of the existence of thirteen copies, though I have not been able to obtain detailed descriptions of all of them. The book is a folio, measuring about 36 × 26 cm. when uncut; its eleven plates, the constitution of which does not vary, are usually printed on both sides of the leaves in the earlier copies, but in five copies, one of which is dated 1794 and three others 1815, they are on one side only. The plates are printed in some shade of brown or green, and in every case except one (Q), a fragmentary copy, which is uncoloured, are painted with water-colours, some opaque pigments being added in two copies (A and I). The title-page is in most cases illuminated with a rainbow of bright colours, but the colouring in general is simple, and consists of solid washes. It is more elaborate in the later copies, gold being used.

In the *Prospectus* of 1793 the book was advertised as " Visions of the Daughters " of Albion, in Illuminated Printing. Folio with 8 designs, price 7s. 6d." In 1818 it was offered as " Visions 8 prints folio £3.3.0." In 1827 the price was £5 5s.

Copies:

A. 11 plates on 11 leaves. Watermark *J Whatman* 1794. Printed in golden-brown. Very beautifully coloured with opaque pigment and some water-colour. Size 38 × 28 cm., uncut. The leaves, which show Blake's stitch-holes, are now mounted on hinges in a volume bound in modern boards with leather back. Inserted are duplicate copies of pl. i-iii, printed in green on two leaves and painted with water-colours.

The Beaconsfield copy, probably bought from Blake by Isaac D'Israeli. Beaconsfield's library marks, dated 1856, show that the frontispiece was at that time missing; it was still missing when the library was sold at Sotheby's on March 20, 1882, the volume being bought for Mr. B. B. Macgeorge of Glasgow (Ellis and White, £34). The missing print came to light again, however, together with other Blake originals from an anonymous source, being sold at Hodgson's on Jan. 14, 1904 (Hopkins, £29), and was secured by Mr. Macgeorge. The leaf had been cut down to a somewhat smaller size, but has now been inlaid to its original size (cf. history of *Europe*, copy A). (Nat. Gal. Cat., 1913, no. 91; Manchester Cat., 1914, no. 152.)

B. 11 plates on 6 leaves. Watermark *J Whatman* without date. Printed in brown. Painted with water-colours. Size 36.5 × 25.5 cm. Bound in yellow morocco, together with *America*, copy E, and the *Song of Los*, copy D.

This volume belonged to Thomas Butts, and was sold with his collection at Sotheby's on March 26, 1852; it was bought by F. T. Palgrave (lot 54, £11), whose signature is on the recto of the frontispiece, dated 1852. It was acquired by the B.M. Reading Room in 1859. In 1852 the volume contained, in addition, *Europe*, copy D, which has since been separated from it.

C. 11 plates on 6 leaves. No watermark. Printed in golden-brown. Painted with water-colours. The frontispiece is at the end. Size of original leaf 30 × 21 cm.; now inlaid in leaves 36 × 25.5 cm. Bound in half-morocco, g.e., together with *Europe*, copy D.

Now in the B.M. Print Room, purchased from Messrs. Evans in 1847.

D. 11 plates on 6 leaves. Watermark on one leaf *J Whatman*. Printed in yellow.

Painted with solid water-colour washes; predominating tints blue and yellow. Size 38 × 27 cm., uncut. Unbound.

A copy sold at Sotheby's on July 1, 1895 (lot 503, Quaritch, £19). Now the property of Mr. W. A. White. (Grolier Cat., no. 14.)

E. 11 plates on 6 leaves. Watermark on one leaf *J Whatman*. Printed in green. Painted with solid water-colour washes; predominating tints purple, brown, and blue. Size 36 × 25 cm. Bound in old red half-morocco, together with the *Song of Los*, copy C, and *Europe*, copy C.

This volume was sold at Puttick and Simpson's on Nov. 19, 1900 (Quaritch, £225). It was acquired in that year by Mr. Marsden J. Perry, who sold it in 1908 to Mr. W. A. White (Grolier Cat., no. 15). It was afterwards given by Mr. White to his daughter, Mrs. William Emerson, Cambridge, Mass.

F. 11 plates on 6 leaves. No watermark. Printed in green. Painted with solid water-colour washes; predominating tints purple and blue. Size 34 × 25 cm. Bound in half-morocco, g.e.

This may be Sir William Tite's copy, sold at Sotheby's on May 19, 1874 (lot 293, Pearson, £30). It was afterwards in Thomas Gaisford's collection and contains his bookplate. It was sold with his library at Sotheby's on April 23, 1890 (lot 188, Ellis, £26 10s.), and is now the property of Mr. W. A. White. (Grolier Cat., no. 16.)

G. 11 plates on 6 leaves. No watermark. Printed in green. Delicately painted with water-colour washes. Size 38 × 26.5 cm., uncut. Bound in morocco by Rivière.

Probably to be identified with a copy sold at Sotheby's on June 1, 1905 (Leighton, £105), which had been in the collection of Mr. F. P. Osmaston. From 1906 to March 1920 it was in the possession of Dr. Greville MacDonald, by whom it was sold to Mr. Francis Edwards. (Manchester Cat., 1914, no. 151.)

H. 11 plates on 6 leaves. No watermark. Printed in green. Painted with water-colour washes, purple and green predominating. Arranged as above. Size 36 × 25 cm. Bound in half maroon morocco.

Sold at Sotheby's, July 28, 1919 (lot 222, Maggs, £195).

I. 11 plates on 6 leaves. No watermark. Printed in brown. Painted with water-colours; tints rich and dramatic. Arranged as above, except that pl. i is at the end. Size 29.5 × 15.5 cm. Bound in contemporary morocco with *Thel*, copy H, *q.v.*

In the possession of Miss Amy Lowell.

K. 11 plates on 6 leaves. No watermark. Printed in green. Vividly painted with water-colour washes. Size 37 × 26.5 cm. Olive morocco binding by Cockerell, 1904.

This copy, originally in the library of the Earl of Crewe, was sold with that collection at Sotheby's on March 30, 1903 (lot 4, Edwards, £122), and was acquired by Mr. A. M. S. Methuen, London. It is said to have been originally in the Butts collection, but see copy B. (Nat. Gal. Cat., 1913, no. 92.)

L. 11 plates on 11 leaves. Watermark *Ruse & Turners* 1815 on two leaves. Printed in brownish-red. Painted with water-colours, some opaque pigment, and gold. Foliated by Blake 1-11. Size 28.5 × 22.5 cm. Bound in red morocco by Rivière.

Frederick Locker's copy, though his bookplate has been removed. Sold with the Rowfant Library. Now in the possession of Mrs. H. H. Whitney.

M. 11 plates on 11 leaves. Watermark *Ruse & Turners* 1815. Printed in golden-brown. Painted with water-colours; colouring very fine and more elaborate than usual, gold being used on the frontispiece. Foliated by Blake 1-11 within a single line ruled round each plate. Size 28 × 22 cm. Bound in half-calf.

On the fly-leaf at the beginning is pasted a piece cut from the original grey wrapper bearing the signature H. C. Robinson (*i.e.*, Crabb Robinson) with a note added in a different hand: "bought by him from Blake for he thinks 1 guinea & presented by him to Edwin W. Field 2 June 1865."

At the beginning are the bookplates of Edwin Wilkins Field, Hampstead, and of A. G. E. Carthew; the frontispiece to Lavater's *Aphorisms* has been inserted at the end. This book was presented by the Misses Field to the Red Cross sale at Christie's, April 26, 1916 (£210). It is now the property of Miss A. G. E. Carthew, London.

N. 11 plates on 11 leaves. Watermark *Ruse & Turners* 1815. Printed in red-brown. Very finely and carefully painted with water-colours. Each plate has a single framing line. Numbered by Blake 1-11. Size 28 × 23 cm. Bound in maroon straight-grained morocco, g.e.

Formerly bound in calf together with *Thel*, copy M, and *The Marriage of Heaven and Hell*, copy G; this volume was sold at Sotheby's, Feb. 17, 1890 (lot 301, Robson). It was then divided up, and *Visions of the Daughters of Albion* was sold to the late Alexander Mackay for £60. After the decease of his widow it was resold at Christie's, April 26, 1921 (lot 5, Riches, £260). Now in the possession of Mr. T. H. Riches.

O. 11 plates on 11 leaves. Coloured. Size given as folio, uncut. Unbound. A copy sold at Sotheby's on Feb. 22, 1897 (Gerrard, £20 5s.).

P. 11 plates on 6 leaves. Coloured. Size given as folio. Bound in half-morocco, g.e. A copy sold at Hodgson's on April 14, 1904 (Quaritch, £39).

Q. A series of six fragments, consisting of the title-page, pl. i, and the designs from pl. iii, 4, 6, and 7. No watermark. Printed in dark brown. Uncoloured. Evidently cut from an uncoloured copy of the book. These fragments were contained in a scrap-book, which had belonged to the Chevalier family; it is there stated that the prints were done by Blake for the children of Thomas Chevalier, surgeon (1767-1824), who was a friend of Blake and is said to have attended him. The book was sold at Sotheby's, Dec. 1, 1910, and is now the property of Mr. W. E. Moss.

Facsimile Reproductions : In *Works by William Blake*, 1876 (no. 212) ; W. Muir, coloured, 1884 (no. 217, c) ; EY, iii.

Typ. Reprints : Extracts first given by Gilchrist, i, 102, and Swinburne, p. 105; later by LH, Pierce, 1915. In full by WBY, EJE, Sampson, 1913. Translated into German by Knoblauch, 1907 (no. 175), and von Taube, 1907 (no. 176).

40 AMERICA / a / PROPHECY / Lambeth / Printed by William Blake in the year 1793.

Description : Frontispiece, title, 2 pl., *Preludium*, 2 pl., *A Prophecy*, 14 pl. = 18 plates, about 24 × 17 cm., relief etching, sometimes painted with water-colours.

Contents :

i. Frontispiece. On the left is a winged giant seated with his head buried between his knees. On the right is a nude woman with two children. The figures are seated on the ruins of a massive wall, to which the giant is chained by the wrists. In the foreground is a cannon and a broken sword.

ii. Title-page. *America*, etc. In the centre two seated figures, reading ; smaller figures round them. Below, a woman striving to revive dead men with kisses.

1. *Preludium*. [This word is usually printed from a small separate plate, 2.5 × 8.5 cm.] Begins : *The Shadowy daughter of Urthona stood before red Orc*. Above, a naked boy is fettered by wrists and ankles to a rock beneath a great tree. A man and a woman stand beside him in attitudes of horror.* The roots of the tree extend down the left-hand margin of the plate. Below are a crouching figure and a coiling worm.

2. Begins : *Silent as despairing love, and strong as jealousy*. Below, a man is

---

* *Cf.* the engraving by Blake known as "The Chaining of Orc," 1813 (see Russell, *Engravings*, p. 93), and *The Four Zoas*, p. 30b.

emerging from the ground. On the left is a vine, its tendrils winding up the margin of the plate.

3. *A Prophecy*. Begins : *The Guardian Prince of Albion burns in his nightly tent*. Above are birds and a manacled figure floating upwards. In the centre is a figure blowing a trumpet from which flames issue. Below are three figures flying from tongues of flame.

4. Begins : *Appear to the Americans upon the cloudy night*. Above, a winged dragon pursues a draped and bearded man with a sceptre and book, who is plunging downwards into clouds. Below, two naked men, one of them clasping a draped figure, kneel in terror among fallen trees.

5. Begins : *Albions Angel stood beside the Stone of night, and saw*. Above, a man ascends a cloud, bearing another figure on his shoulders; on either side of him is a floating figure, one with a pair of scales, the other with a flaming sword. Below, two figures are falling headlong into flames, the central one in front of a spirally coiled serpent.

6. Begins : *The morning comes, the night decays, the watchmen leave their stations*. Above is a naked youth seated on a grave and gazing upwards ; beside him is a skull. Below, a thistle, newt, fly, toad, and worm, types of mortality (cf. *The Marriage of Heaven and Hell*, pl. 21, and illustrations to Blair's *Grave*, pl. 13).

7. Begins : *In thunders ends the voice. Then Albions Angel wrathful burnt*. Below is a ram and two children lying asleep. A tree rises up the left-hand margin and droops gracefully above ; birds are perched among the branches.

8. Begins : *The terror answerd: I am Orc, wreath'd round the accursed tree*. Above, a bearded man robed in white stretches out his arms upon the clouds. Below is a troubled sea (cf. *All Religions are One*, pl. 4).

9. Begins : *Sound! sound! my loud war-trumpets & alarm my Thirteen Angels!* Below, the corpse of a child is enveloped by huge overarching stalks of corn.

10. Begins : *Thus wept the Angel voice & as he wept the terrible blasts*. Below a naked man emerges with outstretched arms from masses of flames.

11. Begins : *Fiery the Angels rose, & as they rose deep thunder roll'd*. Above, a nude man rides on a flying swan. Below, three children astride a serpent (cf. *Thel*, pl. 6).

12. Begins : *So cried he, rending off his robe & throwing down his scepter*. Below an aged man on crutches is entering a stone doorway. To the right are the trunks of two trees, which extend up the left-hand margin and across the top. On the extreme right is seen a stormy landscape (cf. *The Gates of Paradise*, pl. 15, and illustrations to Blair's *Grave*, pl. 13).

13. Begins : *What time the thirteen Governors that England sent convene*. Above, a woman's body floating on the surface of the sea is being rent by a vulture. Below, at the bottom of the sea, fishes are devouring the body of a man.

14. Begins: *In the flames stood & view'd the armies drawn out in the sky.* In the centre a youth reclines with his elbows on two books, and listens to the words of a naked woman, who is seated with a serpent coiled about her at the foot of a great tree. Below is a fish-like animal with a tongue of flame.

15. Begins: *On Albions Angels: then the Pestilence began in streaks of red.* Below are five female figures among flames. A figure whose limbs end in roots extends up the left-hand margin, and above this is a woman seated beneath a tree.

16. Begins: *Over the hills, the vales, the cities, rage the red flames fierce.* Above is a draped female figure with long flowing hair kneeling in an attitude of supplication. About her are several small figures, and behind are fantastic tree forms. Below are flowers and a serpent inscribed *Finis*.

Cancelled plates:

a. *A Prophecy*. Begins: *The Guardian Prince of Albion burns in his nightly tent.* The design is similar to that on pl. 3, but differs from it in detail; on the left, opposite the flaming trumpet, is a figure which is omitted from the published design. There are variations in the text.

b. Begins: *Reveal the dragon thro' the human.* The design is similar to that on pl. 4, but differs in detail; the text takes up more room so that the figures are smaller.

c. Begins: *Then Albions Angel rose resolv'd.* The design of figures extending up the left-hand side is not found elsewhere.

Note: The title-page of *America* is dated 1793, but none of the fourteen copies known to me seems to have been printed before 1794. The book is a folio, about 36 × 26 cm., and consists of eighteen plates, which, except in the seven copies C-I, are printed on one side of the leaf only. Their constitution and arrangement do not vary. The plates are printed in a variety of tints—brown, green, blue, red, or black. One of the copies (B) printed in 1794 is painted with a combination of water-colours and opaque pigments, and three others, printed in 1799 (K), 1813 (M), and 1820 (N), are painted with water-colours only. Gold has been used in the second and third of these. There is a record of another coloured copy (I), but this has not been traced, and I can give no details of it. The remaining nine copies printed by Blake are uncoloured, though several of these have been touched up with grey or sepia washes; four of them (C-F) are printed on paper with watermark *E & P* and were evidently printed at the same time, probably about 1794, the date with which this watermark is elsewhere associated.* The plates were in existence after Blake's death, and one copy printed from them in 1832 is recorded below, but they have now

* See p. 17 of present work.

disappeared. The text, which is etched throughout in italic, does not vary in any of the copies issued by Blake, but at least three cancelled plates are known to me (a–c, above); one of these is similar in text and design to pl. 3, with variations in detail, but the text of the other two does not appear to have been published, and it is reprinted for the first time in an appendix to the present work. It is probable that these plates were executed earlier than the rest of the book as their style resembles that of *The French Revolution*, printed in 1791. A fragment of the original copper from which pl. a was printed is in existence and is described on p. 13 of the present work. It has been suggested * that one of the plates in *A Large Book of Designs* (see no. 44) was originally intended for *America*, but this is quite conjectural.

In the *Prospectus* of 1793 Blake advertised this work as "America a Prophecy in Illuminated Printing, Folio with 18 designs, price 10s. 6d." In 1818 he offered it as "America, 18 prints, folio £5.5.0," and in 1827 the price was £6 6s. The book is described by Mr. Richard Thomson in Smith's life of Blake,† and it is there stated to consist of "eighteen plates, or twenty pages including the frontispiece and title-page," but this is evidently a mistake.

Copies:

A. 18 plates on 18 leaves. Watermark *J Whatman* 1794. Printed in sepia. Uncoloured, except for grey wash on title-page. No foliation. Plate 1 lacks the word *Preludium* at the top. Size 37 × 25.5 cm. Bound in yellow morocco, inlaid, g.e., by Bedford.

Inscribed on the recto of the frontispiece is "From the author to C. H. Tatham Oct 7 1799." Later it was in the collection of Thomas Gaisford and contains his bookplate. It was sold with his library at Sotheby's on April 23, 1890 (lot 189, Quaritch, £61), and was acquired by Mr. B. B. Macgeorge of Glasgow. (Nat. Gal. Cat., 1913, no. 95; Manchester Cat., 1914, no. 162.)

B. 18 plates on 18 leaves. Watermark *J Whatman* 1794. Printed in brown. Painted with water-colours and opaque pigments; highly coloured with a good deal of prussian blue. Foliated by Blake. Size 32 × 24 cm. Sewn, but unbound.

This copy was originally bound up with the *Song of Los*, copy B, and other designs; it was sold at Hodgson's on Jan. 14, 1904 (lot 222, Quaritch, £207), and was acquired about 1909 for the Pierpont Morgan Library.

C. 18 plates on 10 leaves. Watermark *E & P* on one plate (*i.e.*, probably *c.* 1794). Printed in dull green and dull blue. Uncoloured. No pagination. Size 36.5 × 26 cm. Bound in half-morocco, g.e.

This copy was sold at Sotheby's on March 19, 1888 (Barnes, £23), and was acquired in 1891 by Mr. W. A. White. (Grolier Cat., no. 18.)

* See Russell, *Engravings*, pp. 69-70. † *Nollekens and his Times*, 1828, ii, 477.

D. 18 plates on 10 leaves. Watermark *E & P* on one plate (*i.e.*, probably about 1794). Printed in dull green. Uncoloured except for some grey wash on title-page. No pagination. Size 37.5 × 27 cm., uncut. Bound in morocco by the Club Bindery, 1908.

Purchased about 1895 by Mr. W. A. White. (Grolier Cat., no. 19.)

E. 18 plates on 10 leaves. Watermark *E & P* (*i.e.*, probably about 1794). Printed in grey-green. Uncoloured except for some sepia wash on title-page. Size 36.5 × 25.5 cm. Bound in yellow morocco together with *Visions of the Daughters of Albion*, copy B, and the *Song of Los*, copy D.

This volume belonged originally to Thomas Butts, and was sold with his collection at Sotheby's on March 26, 1852. It was bought by F. T. Palgrave (lot 54, £11), whose signature is on the recto of the frontispiece, dated 1852. It was acquired by the B.M. Reading Room in 1859. In 1852 the volume also contained *Europe*, copy D, which has since been separated from it.

F. 18 plates on 10 leaves. Watermark *E & P* (*i.e.*, probably about 1794). Printed in dull blue. Uncoloured. No pagination. Size 34.5 × 24.5 cm. Bound in half-morocco, g.e.

Now in the B.M. Print Room; purchased from Messrs. Evans in 1856.

G. 18 plates on 10 leaves. No watermark. Printed in dull blue and dull green. Uncoloured. No foliation. Size 36 × 25 cm. Bound in half maroon morocco, g.e. A copy sold at Sotheby's, July 28, 1919 (lot 221, Sabin, £100). This copy is similar to those of the series C-F, and probably belongs to the same period, *c.* 1794.

H 18 plates on 10 leaves. No watermark. Printed in dark green. Uncoloured. Size 37 × 25.5 cm. Bound in green morocco, g.e., by Bedford.

Locker-Lampson's copy, sold with the Rowfant Library to the late E. D. Church. Now in the library of Mr. H. E. Huntington. This copy probably belongs to the series A-F, printed about 1794.

I. 17 plates on 9 leaves. Coloured. Lacks frontispiece. In wrappers, uncut. Size 38 × 28.5 cm.

Sir Benjamin West's copy. Offered for sale by Mr. Tregaskis some years ago, having been bought by him at Christie's (£30). The frontispiece, with inscription from Blake to Sir Benjamin West, was sold separately at Hodgson's on Jan. 14, 1904 (lot 229, Maggs, £20 15*s.*). Not traced. This copy probably belongs to the series A-F, printed about 1794.

K. 18 plates on 18 leaves. Watermark on 5 leaves *Hayes & Wise* 1799. Printed in blue. Elaborately painted with water-colours. The last 16 leaves are foliated by Blake. The word *Preludium* on pl. 1 is painted by hand in blue instead of being printed. Size 37 × 27 cm., uncut. Bound in morocco by the Club Bindery, 1908.

T

This copy was formerly in the collection of the Earl of Crewe, and is referred to by Gilchrist, i, 109. It was sold at Sotheby's on May 30, 1903 (lot 3, Quaritch, £295), and was acquired by Mr. W. A. White. (Grolier Cat., no. 17.)

L. 18 plates on 18 leaves. Watermark *T Stains* 1813 on each leaf. Printed in black. Uncoloured, but touched with occasional sepia and grey water-colour washes. Foliated by Blake 1-18. Size 33.5 × 22.5 cm. Bound in grey calf together with *Europe*, copy G. The copper-plate maker's stamp can be seen on the title-page.

This volume was sold at Sotheby's on Feb. 20, 1913 (lot 59, Sabin, £66), having been for many years in the library of the late R. A. Potts. Its previous history is unknown, and the agent to whom Mr. Sabin sold the volume is unwilling to divulge its present whereabouts.

M. 18 plates on 18 leaves. Watermark *T Stains* 1813 on each leaf. Printed in black. Brightly painted with water-colours; gold has been used on pl. 19. Foliated by Blake 1-18. Size 26.5 × 22.5 cm. Recently bound in blue morocco, gilt, by Rivière. Three coloured drawings, enlarged from the designs on pl. ii and 17, are bound in at the end.

The history of this volume before 1913 is not known; it was acquired in that year by Mr. Herschel V. Jones, Minneapolis, and was sold with his library at the Anderson Galleries, New York, Dec. 2, 1918 (lot 183, Rosenbach, $3,600). It is now in the library of Mr. A. E. Newton.

N. 18 plates on 18 leaves. Watermark *J Whatman* 1818 and 1820. Printed in orange-red. Richly painted with water-colours and gold. Each plate has a single framing line in water-colour. Foliated by Blake 1-18. Size 30.5 × 23.5 cm. Bound in vellum together with *Europe*, copy I.

John Linnell's copy, sold with his collection at Christie's, March 15, 1918 (lot 172, Carfax, 750 gns.). Now in the possession of Mr. T. H. Riches. (Nat. Gal. Cat., 1913, no. 96; Manchester Cat., 1914, no. 145.)

O. 18 plates. Printed in blue. Uncoloured. Size given as f°. Bound in half-morocco, g.e.

A copy sold at the Anderson Galleries, New York, Oct. 27, 1911 (lot. 18, $625.00). Not traced.

P. Posthumous copy. 18 plates on 18 leaves. Watermark *J Whatman* 1832. Printed in red-brown. Uncoloured. Frontispiece follows title-page. Plate 1 lacks word *Preludium* at the top. Bound in contemporary morocco elaborately tooled, g.e., together with *Europe*, copy K. Size 28 × 22.5 cm. The copper-plate maker's stamp can be seen on several leaves.

Samuel Boddington's copy, with his bookplate inside the cover. Afterwards in the possession of Charles Fairfax Murray, who presented it in 1912 to the Fitzwilliam Museum, Cambridge.

TITLE-PAGE TO "EUROPE, A PROPHECY"
Variation in Water-colours, 1794

Facsimile Reproductions: In *Works by William Blake*, 1876 (no. 212); W. Muir, 1887 (no. 217, k); EY, iii, reduced.

Typ. Reprints: Extracts first printed and translated into German in the *Vaterländisches Museum*, 1811 (no. 401); extracts in Gilchrist, ii, 107, Swinburne, p. 235, and Pierce, 1915. In full by EJE, Sampson, 1913. Translated into German by Knoblauch, 1907 (no. 175).

41   EUROPE / a / PROPHECY / Lambeth / Printed by Will: Blake: 1794

Description: Frontispiece, title, 2 pl., Preface, 1 pl., *Preludium*, 2 pl., *A Prophecy*, 13 pl. = 18 plates, about 24 × 17 cm. (except pl. iii), relief etching, usually painted with water-colours.

Contents:

i. Frontispiece. The nude figure of the Almighty kneeling in the sun reaches his left hand with a huge pair of compasses down into the void; his hair and beard are streaming to his right, as though carried by a great wind. (Sometimes known as *The Ancient of Days* or as *The Act of Creation*.) See Russell, *Engravings*, p. 70.

ii. Title-page. *Europe, etc.* A large serpent coils about the page and raises its head among the words of the title. Part of one coil does not come on to the plate, as if it had been cut down after the design had been etched.

iii. Preface. Begins: *Five windows light the caverned Man; through one he breathes the air.* Found only in copies F and G. A smaller plate, 9.5 × 13.5 cm.

1. *Preludium*. Begins: *The nameless shadowy female rose from out the breast of Orc.* Above, a young traveller with a pack on his back walks towards the left; on the right a nude assassin with a dagger lies in wait for him in a cave. Below is a head with its arms wrapped round its ears and with bat's wings, and a nude man falling headlong with a weight fastened to his wrists.

2. Begins: *Unwilling I look up to heaven! unwilling count the stars.* At the right-hand margin a nude figure mounts the clouds; below, another nude figure is floating in the air with two others whom he has grasped by their throats.

3. *A Prophecy*. Begins: *The deep of winter came.* Below the heading an angel floats across the plate with her hands clasped at the back of her head; below her, at the right-hand margin, is a red globe with a figure seated in it. At the top various small figures.

4. Begins: *The shrill winds wake!* Below, a youth with flames radiating from his hair lies upon his face, and a nude girl, kneeling upon clouds, is spreading a mantle over him; above her are several small figures in ecstatic attitudes.

5. Begins: *Now comes the night of Enitharmons joy!* The greater part of the plate is taken up by a scaly figure, crowned and holding a large sword, who stands in front of two angels.

6. Full-page illustration. Two women, one crouching with her head buried between her knees, the other seated with clasped hands and upturned face, before a huge cauldron hung over a fire. A nude child is stretched on the ground at the feet of the second woman. (Sometimes known as *Famine.*)

7. Full-page illustration. A tall, dark-robed figure with a bell moves towards the left; in front of him a man supports a woman who is seated on the ground, and behind him is another woman in an attitude of passionate supplication. In some copies the words *Lord have mercy on us* appear on a door behind the figures. (Sometimes known as *Plague.*)

8. Begins: *Arise O Rintrah eldest born*: Below, a kneeling woman clasps the legs of an aged man, who is standing upright with his arms stretched out in front of him.

9. Begins: *Enitharmon slept.* Above, two nude figures, male and female, are blowing horns as they rush together through the air; the blast from the horns fills the air with black flakes, which light as mildew on some large ears of corn. The stalks of the corn curve about the plate.

10. Begins: *In thoughts perturb'd they rose.* A serpent coils up the left-hand margin of the plate.

11. Begins: *Albion's Angel rose upon the Stone of Night.* Above is seated a fat mitred Pope with bat's wings and with an open book on his knees; below him are two angels with lowered sceptres.

12. Begins: *And the clouds & fires pale rolld round in the night of Enitharmon.* Up the right-hand margin of the plate and across the centre are cobwebs with spiders and other insects; at the bottom is a reclining figure enmeshed in a net and gazing upwards.

13. Begins: *The red limb'd Angel siez'd in horror and torment.* Below, a nude figure with fettered ankles is seated in a dungeon; his hands are raised in horror and his face is turned to the right, looking after the dark, scaly figure of the jailor, who is ascending some steps with a large key in his hand.

14. Begins: *Ethinthus queen of waters.* The plate is decorated with birds, caterpillars, insects, snakes, etc.

15. Begins: *Shot from the heights of Enitharmon.* Below, a nude man carries an inanimate woman on his shoulder, and drags a child by the arm; they are flying from huge tongues of flame (cf. *Job*, pl. 3).

Note: *Europe* was executed and first printed in 1794. Only nine copies issued by Blake are known to me. The book is always on folio paper measuring about 36 × 26 cm. It consists usually of seventeen plates printed in the majority of copies on one side of the leaf only, but two copies, E and H, have an additional plate (numbered iii above); this plate was, no doubt, intentionally omitted from the other copies, and these cannot be regarded as incomplete. The position of the two full-page illustrations sometimes varies, but the arrangement of the plates is otherwise constant. Six of the copies (A-F) issued by Blake appear, from the watermarks, to have been printed about 1794; two of these are printed in brown and the other four in green; except for copy F, which is uncoloured, they are painted with opaque pigments, water-colours, or with a combination of the two. The next two copies (G and H) to which a definite date can be assigned are printed in black on paper with the unusual water-mark *T Stains* 1813; one is uncoloured, the other is painted with water-colours and gold. Next in order I have placed the second copy (I) containing the additional plate; it is printed in red, is elaborately and very beautifully painted with water-colours and gold, and has watermarks dated 1818-1820. One copy printed after Blake's death is known to me, but it does not contain the additional plate. I have not noticed any variations in the text, which is etched throughout in italic.

This book was not advertised in the *Prospectus* of 1793, but in 1818 it was offered by Blake as "Europe 17 prints folio £5.5.0.," and in 1827 the price was £6 6s. A copy was described in J. T. Smith's life of Blake in 1828 by Mr. Richard Thomson;* this, he writes, was "coloured to imitate the ancient fresco painting," and evidently was painted with opaque pigments. Very probably it is to be identified with copy B, but at the end were added a series of coloured prints without letterpress, which undoubtedly formed the series described here as *A Large Book of Designs* (see no. 44, *note*). The frontispiece, often known as *The Ancient of Days*, also occurs as a separate print; it was one of Blake's favourite designs, and Tatham relates that he was engaged in colouring a copy on his death-bed.† In the Linnell collection was a coloured example of the title-page, in which Blake had added a human figure to one side of the serpent;‡ this is now in the possession of Mrs. D. Y. Cameron, and is reproduced here by her permission. A sketch for the title-page, differing in detail from the plate, is contained in a miscellaneous collection of leaves from Blake's works, which is now in the Pierpont Morgan Library.

Copies:

A. 17 plates on 17 leaves. Watermark *J Whatman* 1794. Printed in olive-brown. Simply, but very beautifully coloured, with water-colours and opaque pigments, the frontispiece with the latter only. Foliated by Blake after the title-page 1-15. Plate 7 is placed between plates 10 and 11; otherwise arranged as above. Lacks pl. iii. Size 37.5 × 27 cm., uncut. The leaves, which show Blake's

---

* *Nollekens and his Times*, 1828, ii, 477-479.
† See Russell, *Letters*, p. 34.   ‡ Sold at Christie's, March 15, 1918 (lot 176, Robson, 22 gns.).

stitch-holes, are now mounted on hinges in a volume bound in modern boards with leather back.

The Beaconsfield copy, probably bought from Blake by Isaac D'Israeli. Beaconsfield's library marks, dated 1856, show that the first five plates were at that time missing. They were stil missing when the book was sold at Sotheby's on March 20, 1882 (Bain, £8 5s.); it was then acquired by Mr. B. B. Macgeorge of Glasgow. The missing plates came to light again, however, with other Blake originals, from an anonymous source, being sold at Hodgson's on Jan. 14, 1904 (lot 225, Hopkins, £80). They were secured by Mr. Macgeorge and restored to their original position. The leaves had been somewhat cut down, but they have now been inlaid to their original size (cf. history of *Visions of the Daughters of Albion*, copy A).

B. 17 plates on 17 leaves. Watermark *I Taylor* (3 leaves) or *J Whatman* 1794 (2 leaves). Printed in green or blue. Richly and sombrely painted with opaque pigments. Arranged as above, except that pl. 6 and 7 follow pl. 4 and 9. Lacks pl. iii. Foliated by Blake. Size 37 × 27 cm. Unbound, each leaf mounted on cardboard.

Formerly in the collection of the Earl of Crewe; it is said to have been bought from Butts by the first Lord Houghton. It was sold with the Crewe collection at Sotheby's on March 30, 1903 (lot 5, Quaritch, £203), and was acquired by Mr. W. A. White. (Grolier Cat., no. 21.)

C. 17 plates on 10 leaves. Watermark *I Taylor* (*i.e.*, probably about 1794). Printed in green or blue. Elaborately painted with water-colours. Arranged as above, but lacks pl. iii. Plates 1-15 paginated by Blake. Size 36 × 25 cm. Bound in half-morocco together with *The Song of Los*, copy C, and *Visions of the Daughters of Albion*, copy E. For history see the latter. (Grolier Cat., no. 22.)

D. 17 plates on 10 leaves. Watermark *I Taylor* (*i.e.*, about 1794). Printed in green. Coloured with opaque pigments and water-colour. Arranged as above, but lacks pl. iii. Plates 1-15 paginated by Blake in blue. Size 36 × 25.5 cm. Bound in half-morocco, g.e., together with *Visions of the Daughters of Albion*, copy C. On most of the plates are written in ink titles for the designs or quotations illustrating them from various authors; these are not in Blake's hand, but may possibly have been suggested by him, as the quotations are from authors with whose works he is believed to have been acquainted.

Probably the Butts copy, originally bound with three other works (*America*, copy E, *Visions of the Daughters of Albion*, copy B, and *The Song of Los*, copy D), and sold at Sotheby's on March 26, 1852 (lot 54, F. T. Palgrave, £11). Now in the B.M. Print Room, having been bought from F. T. Palgrave in 1859.

E. 17 plates on 10 leaves. Watermark *I Taylor* (*i.e.*, about 1794). Printed in shades of green, blue, and brown. Partly colour-printed with opaque pigments; finished with water-colours. Numbered by Blake 1-17. Arranged as above; lacks pl. iii. Size 37.5 × 26 cm. Bound in brown morocco by Bedford.

Thomas Gaisford's copy, and contains his bookplate. Sold at Sotheby's on April 23, 1890 (lot 190, Robson, £59). Next acquired by the late Alexander Mackay; after the decease of his widow, sold at Christie's, April 26, 1921 (lot 2, " Shoebridge," £600).

F. 18 plates on 18 leaves. Watermark *E & P* on two leaves (*i.e.*, about 1794). Printed in brown. Uncoloured, but freely retouched with sepia. Foliated in pencil. Arrangement: iii, ii, i, 1-6, 8-12, 7, 13-15. Size 36 × 25.5 cm. Originally bound in marbled boards, but now unbound. Contains the inscription "May 1835, H.E. Bohn N. 732." Afterwards Beckford's copy; sold with the Hamilton Palace library at Sotheby's on July 4, 1882 (pt. 1, lot 955, Ellis and White, £12 5s.). Next in the E. W. Hooper collection, and now in the possession of Mrs. John B. Potter, Boston, Mass. (Boston Mus. Cat., 1891, no. 6.)

G. 17 plates on 17 leaves. Watermark *T Stains* 1813 on each leaf. Printed in black. Uncoloured, but touched up with occasional sepia and grey water-colour washes. Arrangement: i, ii, 1, 2, 7, 6, 3-5, 8-15. Lacks pl. iii. Foliated by Blake 1-17 in black. Size 33.5 × 22.5 cm. Bound in grey calf together with *America*, copy L. This volume was sold at Sotheby's on Feb. 20, 1913 (lot 59, Sabin, £66), having been for many years in the library of the late R. A. Potts. Its previous history is unknown, and the agent to whom Mr. Sabin sold the volume is unwilling to divulge its present whereabouts. The stamp of the copper-plate maker can be seen on some leaves.

H. 17 plates on 17 leaves. Watermark *T Stains* 1813 on each leaf. Printed in black. Brightly painted with water-colours, gold being used on several plates. Arrangement: i, ii, 1, 2, 7, 6, 3-5, 8-15. Lacks pl. iii. Foliated by Blake 1-17. Size 27 × 22 cm. Recently bound in red morocco, gilt, by Rivière.

The history of this volume before 1913 is not known; in that year it was acquired by Mr. Herschel V. Jones, Minneapolis, and it was sold with his library at the Anderson Galleries, New York, Dec. 2, 1918 (lot 184, G. D. Smith, $4,600). It is now in the library of Mr. H. E. Huntington.

I. 18 plates on 18 leaves. Watermark *J Whatman* 1818, 1819, and 1820. Printed in orange-red. Very beautifully and elaborately painted with water-colours and gold. Arranged as above, except that pl. 6 and 7 are transposed. Foliated by Blake 1-18 in black. Size 30.5 × 23.5 cm. Bound in vellum together with *America*, copy N.

John Linnell's copy, sold with his collection at Christie's, March, 1918 (lot

172, Carfax, 750 gns.). Now in the possession of Mr. T. H. Riches. (Nat. Gal. Cat., 1913, no. 90; Manchester Cat., 1914, no. 145.)

K. Posthumous copy. 17 plates on 17 leaves. Watermark *J Whatman* 1832. Printed in red-brown. Uncoloured. Arranged as above. Size 28 × 22.5 cm. Bound in contemporary morocco, elaborately tooled, g.e., together with *America*, copy P.

Samuel Boddington's copy, with his bookplate inside the cover. Afterwards acquired by the late Charles Fairfax Murray, and presented by him in 1912 to the Fitzwilliam Museum, Cambridge. The copper-plate maker's stamp can be seen on many of the leaves.

Facsimile Reproductions: In *Works by William Blake*, 1876 (no. 212); W. Muir, coloured, 1887 (no. 217, 1); EY, iii, reduced and without pl. 6 and 7.

Typ. Reprints: An extract first printed and translated into German in the *Vaterländisches Museum*, 1811 (no. 401); extracts in Gilchrist, i, 126, and Swinburne, p. 242. Printed in full by EJE, Sampson, 1913. Extracts translated into German by Knoblauch, 1907 (no. 175), and von Taube, 1907 (no. 176).

42 **THE / FIRST BOOK / of / URIZEN /** Lambeth. Printed by Will Blake 1794.
Colophon: The End of the / first book of Urizen.

Description: Title, 1 pl., *Preludium*, 1 pl., *The First Book of Urizen*, chaps. i-ix, 16 pl., full-page illustrations, 10 pl. = 28 plates, about 16 × 11 cm., relief etching, painted with water-colours or opaque pigments. The text is etched in double columns.

Contents:

1. Title-page. *The First Book*, etc. An old man with a long beard is seated upon an open book with his knees drawn up to his shoulders; his eyes are closed, and in each hand he holds a pen with which he is writing in a book placed on either side of him. Behind him are the Tables of the Law; a leafless tree arches over him.

2. *Preludium to the First Book of Urizen*. Begins: *Of the primeval Priests assum'd power*. In the upper part of the plate floats a draped woman holding an infant by the hand. Below, the text is surrounded by flames.

3. *Chap: I*, 1-6, and *Chap: II*, 1-3. Begins: *Lo a shadow of horror is risen*. A nude youth (Orc) strides through a mass of flames.

4. *Urizen: C II.*, [3]-8, and *Chap: III*, 1-2. Begins: *Muster around the bleak desarts*. Below, a nude man is seated on the ground grasping his head between his

hands. Dark fumes stream up round him from the ground. The last line has been erased. Only found in copies A and B (cf. the design on pl. 8 of *There is No Natural Religion*, series b).

5. [*Chap: III*], [2]-8. Begins: *In living creations appear'd*. Above, an old man with a long beard (Urizen) holds open a large book, the pages of which are covered with Hebrew characters.

6. 1 *Urizen C: III*, [8]-11. Begins: *As the stars are apart from the earth*. Below, three figures with snakes coiled round them are falling head downwards through flames in which faces appear (cf. *Job*, pl. 16).

7. [*Chap: III*], 12-14. Begins: *Los howld in a dismal stupor*. Below, a huge figure kneeling among flames and hugging his face in his arms; his hair is on end, his eyes staring, and his mouth wide open.

8. *Chap: IV*, 1-6. Begins: *Los smitten with astonishment*. Below, a skeleton squatting with its head between its knees and its hands on its head.

9. Full-page illustration. A blind and aged man, with a long beard, crawling on hands and knees among masses of dark rock.

10. *Chap: IV*, 1-6. Begins: *Ages on ages roll'd over him*. Above, a nude man pushing his way through masses of rock.

11. 1 *Urizen* [*Chap: IV*], 7-10. Begins: *From the caverns of his jointed Spine*. Below, on the left, a chained and half-roasted figure is seated among flames and gazing upwards; on the right is seated a nude youth who is picking up a hammer.

12. Full-page illustration. A bearded old man with outstretched arms is floating up through dark water.

13. [*Chap: IV*], [10]-12, and *Chap: V*, 1-7. Begins: *Two Nostrils bent down to the deep*. In the centre, a vague female figure (Ahania) floating between masses of dark clouds (cf. *Ahania*, pl. 2).

14. Full-page illustration. A nude man balancing himself head downwards on his hands.

15. 1 *Urizen, C V*, [7]. Begins: *Thus the Eternal Prophet was divided*. Below, two youths and two bearded old men leaning out of the sky over the earth, from which one youth is pushing back the waters; an eagle is seen behind.

16. Full-page illustration. A nude youth, with his knees drawn up to his chin and his hands clasped behind his head, falling through fire.

17. Full-page illustration. A draped figure, with streaming hair and with the hands over the ears, bending over a crimson globe.

18. 1 *Urizen. C: V*, 8-10. Begins: *The globe of life blood trembled*. Below, a naked youth emerging from flames; in one hand he holds a hammer, the other rests on a rock.

19. [*Chap: V*], [10]-12, and *Chap: VI*, 1-10. Begins: *They call'd her Pity*

and fled. Above, a naked woman is rising from flames; beside her is a man kneeling with his head between his arms.   (Enitharmon and Los.)

20. 1 *Urizen C: VI,* [10]-11, *Chap: VII,* 1-10, and *Chap: VIII,* 1. Begins: *Stretch'd for a work of eternity.* Below, a naked child plunging headlong through flames.

21. Full-page illustration. Three naked figures; on the right a young bearded man, chained to the ground, rests his hands on a large hammer. Beside him is a woman holding a cloak behind her; a boy clasps her round the waist. In the background is a sunrise. (Los, Enitharmon, and Orc.)

22. Full-page illustration. A bearded old man, with tears on his cheeks, squats on the ground, to which he is fettered by ankles and wrists.

23. 1 *Urizen C: VIII,* [1]-5. Begins: *Of life on his forsaken mountains.* An old man in a long robe strides to the right, holding a radiating globe in his right hand and with his left stretched out in front of him; a lion meets him. Hills in the background.

24. Full-page illustration. Above is a head with flaming hair and outstretched arms, and underneath this floats a naked figure with a halo. Below, a naked man is struggling on to rocks out of dark water, from which emerges, on the left, a female head. (Thiriel, Fuzon, Grodna, and Utha.)

25. [*Chap: VIII*], [5]-9, and *Chap: IX,* 1-4. Begins: *The Ox in the slaughter house moans.* Above, three figures, half women, half reptiles, one with bat's wings, writhe together in a heap.

26. Full-page illustration. A boy standing in an attitude of prayer, and a large dog lying before a closed door.

27. Full-page illustration. An old man, in a long white robe and with hands upraised, seen from behind; he is floating away into clouds and fire.

28. 1 *Urizen C: IX,* [4]-9. Begins: *They lived a period of years.* Below, an old bearded man is seated with his arms resting on rocks at each side of him; he is enmeshed in a net of heavy rope.

Note: *The First Book of Urizen* was executed and first printed in 1794. Seven copies of the work are known to me, six of which I am able to describe in full. It usually forms a book of quarto size, measuring about 26 × 18 cm., but one copy (B) is a folio. The number of prints contained in it varies from twenty-four to twenty-eight. One of the plates, forming the full number of twenty-eight, is a plate of text * (pl. 4), which is found only in two of the earlier copies (A and B). The other plates, which have been omitted from copies containing less than twenty-

---

* This plate had not been reprinted or noticed until I discovered it in copy B. I then had it photographed, and sent a copy of the print to Mr. J. P. R. Wallis of Liverpool for use in his forthcoming edition of the Prophetic Books. The photograph was passed on by him to Dr. Sampson, who was thus enabled to print the text in his edition of the *Poetical Works,* 1913.

seven plates, are in most cases full-page illustrations. The changes in the positions of the full-page designs also account for most of the variations in the order of the plates recorded below. In one copy (F), printed in the year 1815, Blake has erased the word *First* from the plates of the title-page, *Preludium*, and colophon, as if by that date he had quite abandoned any intention he may ever have entertained of writing a *Second Book of Urizen* ; this copy is the latest to which a date can be assigned, and it may be the last that Blake executed. The word *First* has been left on the title-pages of all the remaining six copies, though it has been erased from the colophon of one of them (A). The text, which is etched throughout in italic, is divided into ten chapters, but the heading, "*Chap: IV*" occurs at the beginning both of the fourth and of the fifth chapters, so that there appear to be only nine. The last two lines of verse 6, plate 10, have been erased in some copies, and some of the designs have been altered during the painting in at least two copies (B and C). The plates, which are always on one side of the leaf only, are as a rule printed in brown, but in one copy (B) some of them are in green. In the earlier copies (A-C), which were probably executed about the year 1794, the plates are painted with opaque pigments, or with a combination of opaque pigments and water-colours. Later Blake used water-colours only, and the copy dated 1815 (F) is richly painted with water-colours and much gold. The book was evidently written after the *Prospectus* of 1793 had appeared, and it does not appear in this list. In 1818 it was offered as "Urizen "28 prints quarto £5.5.0," although there is no copy of that date extant containing the full number of twenty-eight plates. In 1827 the price was £6 6s.

The pages without text occasionally occur as separate designs. The Linnell collection, for example, included a print of pl. 21 very beautifully and carefully coloured (sold at Christie's, March 15, 1918, lot 177, Martin, £90). Further, a number of the plates, but with the text omitted, were used by Blake in his *Small* and *Large Books of Designs* (nos. 43 and 44).

Copies:

A. 28 plates on 28 leaves. No watermark. Printed in brown. Coloured with opaque pigments and some water-colour, though sparingly; parts of the designs are sometimes left uncoloured. Originally foliated by Blake in red, but most of these numbers have now been erased. The present arrangement is different: 1, 2, 22, 24, 3, 4, 12, 5-7, 17, 8, 10, 11, 14, 13, 18, 21, 19, 15, 16, 20, 9, 23, 26, 25, 28, 27. The leaves have evidently been put in this wrong order by the binder. The word *First* has been erased from the colophon after the plate was printed. Size 25.5 × 18 cm. Recently bound in straight-grained morocco by Cockerell.

In the possession of Baron Dimsdale of Meesdon Manor, Buntingford, Herts; it was acquired by the first Baron Dimsdale during Blake's lifetime.

B. 28 plates on 28 leaves. Watermark *I Taylor*, and *J Whatman* 1794. Printed in shades of brown and green. Very beautifully coloured, with water-colours chiefly, but occasionally with some opaque pigment in the backgrounds. Foliated by Blake 1-28. Arrangement: 1-4, 14, 5-7, 10, 12, 8, 11, 22, 13, 9, 15-19, 24, 20, 21, 23, 25-28. The last two lines have been erased from verse 10 on pl. 6, and on pl. 15 the left-hand figure has been omitted. Size 38 × 27 cm., uncut. The leaves, which show Blake's stitch-holes, are now mounted on hinges in a volume bound in boards with leather back.

The Beaconsfield copy, probably bought from Blake by Isaac D'Israeli. Contains Beaconsfield's library marks dated 1856. It was sold with the Beaconsfield collection at Sotheby's on March 20, 1882 (Ellis and White, £59), and was acquired by Mr. B. B. Macgeorge of Glasgow. (Nat. Gal. Cat., 1913, no. 99; Manchester Cat., 1914, no. 159.)

C. 26 plates on 26 leaves. Watermark *J Whatman* 1794. Printed in brown. Thickly coloured with opaque pigments. Arranged as above, but lacking pl. 4 and 16. Foliated by Blake 1-26. Two of the figures are painted out from pl. 24, and the two side figures from pl. 6. Size 26 × 18 cm. Bound in half-morocco.

Now in the B.M. Print Room; purchased from F. T. Palgrave in 1859.

D. 24 plates on 24 leaves. Watermark *J. Whatman* on one leaf. Printed in green. Coloured with opaque pigments. Arrangement: 1, 3, 5, 12, 2, 6, 14, 7, 10, 8, 11, 22, 13, 15, 18, 17, 19, 12, 20, 21, 23, 26-28. Lacks pl. 4, 9, 16, 24. Size 29.5 × 23.5 cm. Bound in brown morocco, gilt, by Clarke and Bedford. Contains the bookplate of Frederick Locker, to whom it came from Sir Charles Dilke. When the Rowfant Library was sold the book was acquired by the late E. D. Church. It is now in the possession of Mrs. H. H. Whitney, New York.

E. 26 plates on 26 leaves. No watermark. Printed in yellow-brown, except pl. 2. which is in green. Richly painted with opaque pigments and water-colours. Foliated in pencil. Arrangement: 1-3, 5, 12, 6, 7, 14, 10, 8, 9, 11, 13, 22, 15, 18, 17, 19, 16, 21, 23-28. Lacks pl. 4 and 20. Size 26.5 × 18.5 cm. Formerly bound in half-calf together with *Thel*, copy A, and *The Marriage of Heaven and Hell*, copy A; now unbound.

The volume belonged to George Cumberland and was afterwards in the Beckford library, being sold at Sotheby's, Nov. 29, 1883, in the Hamilton Palace sale (pt. 4, lot 764, Quaritch, £121); next in the collection of E. W. Hooper of Harvard. After his death the volume was divided up, and the *Urizen* is now in the possession of Mrs. Thorn, Boston, Mass.

F. 27 plates on 27 leaves. Watermark *Ruse & Turners* 1815. Printed in yellow-brown. Richly painted with water-colours and gold. Foliated by Blake 1-27.

Arrangement: 1-3, 9, 5, 12, 6, 14, 7, 8, 22, 10, 11, 16, 13, 15, 17-21, 23, 27, 24-26, 28. Lacks pl. 4. Size 26.5 × 23.5 cm. Bound in brown morocco, g.e., by the Club Bindery, 1908. The word *First* does not appear on the title-page, or *Preludium*, or in the colophon, having been erased from the plates. Formerly in the collection of the Earl of Crewe; sold at Sotheby's on March 30, 1903 (lot 6, Quaritch, £307), and acquired by Mr. W. A. White. (Grolier Cat., no. 27.)

G. 26 plates on 26 leaves. Coloured. Size given as royal 4°. Bound in brown morocco, g.e., by Bedford. A coloured drawing for the *Preludium* is inserted. Offered for sale in 1854 in a catalogue of John Pearson's stock (£55). Later in the library of Thomas Gaisford, and sold with his collection at Sotheby's on April 23, 1890 (lot 191, Nugent, £66). I have not been able to trace it farther.

Facsimile Reproductions: In *Works by William Blake*, 1876 (no. 212); W. Muir, coloured, 1888 (no. 217, m); EY, iii, reduced, without pl. 4.

Typ. Reprints: Extracts first given by Gilchrist, i, 127, and Swinburne, p. 246 ff. Also by Pierce, 1915. In full by EJE, Sampson, 1913. Translated into German by Knoblauch, 1907 (no. 175).

43 [A SMALL BOOK OF DESIGNS] Lambeth. Printed by Will Blake 1794

Description: 23 miscellaneous designs from the Illuminated Books without text, relief etchings of various sizes, painted with opaque pigments.

Contents: (As found in copy A)
1. From *Urizen*, pl. 1; lettered *Lambeth*, etc., as above.
2. From *The Marriage of Heaven and Hell*, pl. 11.
3. From *Urizen*, pl. 17.
4. From *The Marriage of Heaven and Hell*, pl. 16.
5. The same, pl. 14.
6. The same, pl. 20.
7. From *Urizen*, pl. 23.
8. The same, pl. 24, but differing from the usual design in that all the figures are painted out except the head emerging from the water. The sea is black and flecked with foam; behind is a stormy sunset.
9. The same, pl. 3.
10. From *Thel*, pl. ii.
11. From *Urizen*, pl. 26.

12. The same, pl. 2.
13. The same, pl. 8.
14. The same, pl. 19.
15. The same, pl. 10.
16. From *Thel*, pl. 4.
17. From *Visions of the Daughters of Albion*, pl. 7.
18. From *Urizen*, pl. 7.
19. The same, pl. 11.
20. From *Visions of the Daughters of Albion*, pl. iii.
21. From *Urizen*, pl. 5.
22. From *Thel*, pl. 5.
23. The same, pl. 2.

Note: There is no evidence to show that Blake ever made more than the two examples, which are recorded below, of this remarkable series of designs. One of these is probably the volume referred to by Blake in a letter to Dawson Turner, dated June 9, 1818, where he wrote: " I send you a list of the different works you have " done me the honour to enquire after . . . Those I printed for Mr. Humphry [*i.e.*, " Ozias Humphrey, miniaturist] are a selection from the different books of such as " could be printed without the writing, though to the loss of some of the best things; " for they, when printed perfect, accompany poetical personifications and acts, without " which poems they could never have been executed." (Russell, *Letters*, p. 207.)

Copy A was evidently executed about 1794, but the leaves of copy B, which did not consist of exactly the same series of prints as copy A, and contained titles below some of the designs in Blake's autograph, have been distributed, and I cannot give any indication of the date of its execution. The prints in both copies are elaborately coloured with opaque pigments, and some of them are exceedingly fine. Humphrey died in 1810, but the further history of whichever copy was done for him is not known. Later, in 1828, one copy, probably A, was described by Mr. Richard Thomson in J. T. Smith's life of Blake as follows: "Another publication by Mr. Blake " consisted only of a small quarto volume of twenty-three engravings of various shapes " and sizes, coloured as before, some of which are of extraordinary effect and beauty. " The best plates in this series are: the first of an aged man, with a white beard " sweeping the ground, and writing in a book with each hand, naked [no. 1 above]; " a human figure pressing out his brains through his ears [no. 3 above]; and the great " sea serpent [no. 6 above]; but perhaps the best is a figure sinking in a stormy sea " at sunset, the splendid light of which, and the foam upon the black waves, are " almost magical effects of colouring [no. 8 above]. Beneath the first design is " engraven *Lambeth printed by W. Blake* 1794." (*Nollekens and his Times*, 1828, ii, 480.) The volume is also described by Gilchrist, i, 419-420.

Copies:

A. 23 plates on 23 leaves. Watermark *J Whatman* 1794. All the designs are heavily painted with opaque pigments. Foliated in pencil. Plates arranged as above. Size 26 × 19 cm. Bound in half-morocco.
Now in the B.M. Print Room; acquired in 1856.

B. The leaves from this copy have been distributed, and only a few have come under my notice as below; these are all at the present time in frames, so that the watermarks cannot be seen. Each design is surrounded by three or four framing lines and is painted with opaque pigments. Some have inscriptions in Blake's hand, and the majority have been numbered by him.

1. No. 9 above. Unnumbered. In the possession of Mr. W. Graham Robertson.

2. From *Urizen*, pl. 9. Not represented in copy A. Numbered by Blake 13, and inscribed below in Blake's autograph, " Eternally I labour on." Formerly in the possession of the late H. Stopford Brooke. Sold at Sotheby's, April 9, 1919 (Tregaskis, £38).

3. No. 21 above. Numbered by Blake 19, and inscribed below in his autograph: " The Book of my Remembrance." Formerly in the possession of the late H. Stopford Brooke. Sold at Sotheby's, April 9, 1919 (Tregaskis, £20).

4. No. 15 above. Numbered by Blake 20, and inscribed below in his autograph:

> " Does the Soul labour thus
> " In Caverns of the Grave."

Formerly in the possession of the late H. Stopford Brooke. Sold at Sotheby's, April 9, 1919 (Edwards, £29).

5. No. 17 above. Numbered by Blake 22. In the possession of Dr. Greville MacDonald.

6. No. 2 above. Inscribed below in Blake's hand:

> " Death & Hell
> " Teem with Life."

Obtained by Carl Edelheim from Herbert Gilchrist about 1891. Now in the possession of his son-in-law, Mr. A. E. Newton.

44 [A LARGE BOOK OF DESIGNS. About 1794]

Description: 8 miscellaneous designs without text, line engravings and relief etchings of various sizes, coloured with opaque pigments.

Contents: (As found in copy A)

1. "Morning" or "Glad Day," 27 × 20 cm.; similar to an early line engraving described by Russell, *Engravings*, p. 54, but it is not the same as this, the two being different sizes.* The coloured print is reproduced in the present work.

2. "The Accusers of Theft, Adultery, Murder," from a line engraving, 21 × 12 cm. See Russell, *Engravings*, p. 66.

3. From *Urizen*, pl. 21.

4. From *Visions of the Daughters of Albion*, pl. 4.

5. The same, pl. i.

6. Joseph of Arimathea preaching to the inhabitants of Britain. 7.5 × 10.5 cm. See Russell, *Engravings*, p. 56.

7. From *Urizen*, pl. 14.

8. A semi-nude figure is seated with bowed head under a blasted tree; to the left a nude girl is kissing a small child which she holds high in the air. 12 × 17 cm. Part of a cancelled plate for one of the Illuminated Books, possibly for *America*. See Russell, *Engravings*, p. 69.

Note: This series of designs is similar in many respects to that which has been already described in the last entry, and was probably done about the same period (1794). It may have been first executed by Blake for Ozias Humphrey, but there are no definite records of its history. A copy of *Europe* coloured with opaque pigments was described in J. T. Smith's life of Blake in 1828 by Mr. Richard Thomson, who added: "At the end of this poem are seven separate engravings on folio pages, "without letterpress, which are coloured like the former part of the work, with a "degree of splendour and force, as almost to resemble sketches in oil colours. The "finest of these are a figure of an angel standing in the sun [no. 1 above], a group of "three furies surrounded by clouds and fire [no. 2 above], and a figure of a man sit- "ting beneath a tree in the deepest dejection [no. 8 above]; all of which are peculiarly "remarkable for their strength and splendour of colouring." (*Nollekens and his Times*, 1828, ii, 479-480.) The prints referred to are probably one of the two series A or B below, and were separated at a later date from the copy of *Europe* with which they were originally associated.

Copies:

A. 8 plates on 8 leaves. Watermark *J Whatman* 1794. Heavily painted with

* First pointed out by Mr. Laurence Binyon in the *Print Collector's Quarterly*, Dec. 1917 (see no. 646).

opaque pigments. Unnumbered. Arranged as above. Size 34.5 × 25 cm. Bound in half-morocco.

Now in the B.M. Print Room; acquired in 1856. Plate 1 has been recently restored, and shows an extraordinary brilliance of colouring.

B. 3 plates (nos. 2, 6, and 8), apparently from another example of this series, formed part of a collection of Blake's works sold at Hodgson's on Jan. 14, 1904 (no. 2, Quaritch, £15 10s.; no. 6, Quaritch, £26 10s.; no. 8, Osmaston, £42). They are coloured with opaque pigment and are on separate leaves, 32 × 24 cm. Nos. 2 and 6, numbered respectively 3 and 5, are now in the possession of Mr. W. A. White (Grolier Cat., nos. 39, 40). The text below no. 8 was not printed, but in this example was sufficiently clearly impressed on the paper to be deciphered by Mr. Russell from the back with the help of a mirror, and has been printed by him (*Engravings*, p. 69). It begins:

" As when a dream of Thiralatha flies the midnight hour."

An example of pl. 1 has been inserted in copy E of *The Song of Los*; this may have belonged to the same series.

45 THE / SONG of / LOS / Lambeth Printed by W Blake 1795
Colophon: The SONG of LOS is Ended. / Urizen Wept.

Description: Frontispiece, title, 2 pl., *Africa*, 2 pl., *Asia*, 2 pl., full-page illustrations, 2 pl. = 8 plates, about 24 × 17 cm. (title and illustrations), or 22 × 14 cm. (text), relief etching, coloured with opaque pigment.

Contents:

1. Frontispiece. A huge figure, heavily draped from the waist, and seen from behind, is kneeling at a stone altar before a fiery globe inscribed with hieroglyphics.

2. Title-page. *The Song*, etc. Below, an old man with flowing beard reclines on the ground and gazes upwards; his left hand rests on a skull. Hills in the background.

3. *Africa*. Begins: *I will sing you a song of Lôs*. A snake coils among the letters of the heading. Near the top are a child and some sheep lying asleep.

4. Begins: *These were the Churches*: Near the top, a flying figure with bat's wings. Below, a man and a woman, embracing one another, are running from left to right.

5. Full-page illustration. Two small figures, a man with crown and sceptre and a woman, are resting in two white lilies; behind is a dark sky with stars.

6. *Asia*. Begins: *The Kings of Asia heard*. Below the heading is a nude man

x

supporting an inanimate woman under a rocky archway.   Below, at the right-hand margin, a nude man is kneeling with his head buried in his arms.

7. Begins : *To cut off the bread from the city*.   At the right-hand margin, near the top, is a nude figure falling headlong.

8. Full-page illustration.   A nude man kneeling on clouds is about to plunge a huge iron mallet into a crimson sphere.

Note : Only five copies of *The Song of Los* are known to me, and these are very uniform in character.   They are all of folio size, measuring about 35 × 25 cm., and consist of eight plates, printed on one side of the leaves only.   The plates are printed in olive-green, and are thickly covered with opaque pigments.   The position of the full-page designs is not always the same, but the constitution of the plates does not vary.   The first five lines of the text are etched in minuscule roman ; the rest is in italic.   In none of the copies is any watermark visible, but their uniformity suggests that they were all executed about the same time, probably in 1795 or shortly afterwards.   This book does not appear in any of Blake's lists of works for sale.

Copies :

A. 8 plates on 8 leaves. No watermark. Printed in olive-green. Thickly coloured with opaque pigments.   Arranged as above.   Size 34.5 × 25 cm.   Bound in half-morocco, g.e.
Now in the B.M. Print Room ; purchased from Messrs. Evans in 1856.

B. 8 plates on 8 leaves. No watermark. Printed in olive-green. Coloured with opaque pigments. The leaves are loose, but some have been numbered by Blake.   Size 32 × 24 cm.
This copy was formerly bound up with *America*, copy B, and other designs ; it was sold at Hodgson's on Jan. 14, 1904 (lot 224, Quaritch, £144), and was acquired by Mr. W. A. White. (Grolier Cat., no. 30.)

C. 8 plates on 8 leaves. No watermark. Printed in olive-green. Coloured with opaque pigments and some water-colours.   Arrangement : 1, 8, 2-4, 6, 7, 5. Size 36 × 25 cm.   Bound in half-morocco together with *Europe*, copy C, and *Visions of the Daughters of Albion*, copy E.   For history see the latter (Grolier Cat., no. 31.)

D. 8 plates on 8 leaves. No watermark. Printed in olive-green. Thickly coloured with opaque pigments.   Arranged as above.   Size 36.5 × 25.5 cm. Bound in yellow morocco together with *America*, copy E, and *Visions of the Daughters of Albion*, copy B.
This volume was originally in the collection of Thomas Butts, and was sold at Sotheby's on March 26, 1852 (lot 54, F. T. Palgrave, £11). The autograph of its next owner, F. T. Palgrave, is on the recto of the first leaf, dated 1852.

It was acquired by the B.M. Reading Room in 1859. In 1852 the volume contained in addition *Europe*, copy D, which has since been separated from it.

E. 8 plates on 8 leaves. No watermark. Printed in green. Thickly coloured with opaque pigments. Arrangement: 1, 2, 3, 8, 4, 6, 5, 7; the leaves were unbound in 1903, so that this arrangement is arbitrary. A coloured copy of the design known as " Glad Day " has been added at the end; that it was not originally part of the book is shown by the fact that it consisted of only eight plates when it was sold in 1903. Size 36 × 26 cm. Bound in red levant morocco, gilt, by Rivière.

Formerly in the collection of the Earl of Crewe, and sold at Sotheby's, March 30, 1903 (lot 9, Sabin, £174). Afterwards in the Halsey collection, and now in the library of Mr. H. E. Huntington.

Facsimile Reproductions: In *Works by William Blake*, 1876 (no. 212); W. Muir, coloured, 1890 (no. 217, o); EY, iii, reduced and without pl. 1 and 8.

Typ. Reprints: Extracts first given by Gilchrist, i, 129, and Swinburne, p. 255. In full by EJE, Sampson, 1913.

46 THE / BOOK of / AHANIA / LAMBETH / Printed by W Blake 1795.

Description: Title, 1 pl., *Ahania*, ch. I-V, 4 pl. = 5 plates, about 13.5 × 7.5 cm., ordinary etching; the text finely etched in double columns; the designs coloured.

Contents:

1. Title-page. *The Book*, etc. Below, a spectral figure with flying hair and drapery is floating between clouds; the head is twisted round and the arms outstretched (cf. *Urizen*, pl. 13).

2. *Ahania, Chap: I*st, 1-9. Begins: *Fuzon on a chariot iron-wing'd*.

3. *Chap: II*^{d}, 1-10, and *Chap III*, 1-4. Begins: *But the forehead of Urizen gathering*.

4. [*Chap: III*], [4]-6, *Chap: IV*, 1-10, and *Chap: V*, 1-5. Begins: *Of iron from the dismal shade*.

5. [*Chap: V*] [5]-14. Begins: *But I wander on the rocks*. Tailpiece, a confused design of a giant lying crushed and bleeding among rocks.

Note: This and the entry following are the only books executed by Blake by the ordinary process of etching. The text is written in italic. The reproduction given in EY, iii, has a frontispiece representing a man seated, with his knees drawn up to his shoulders; his head is bowed, and his hands grasp the hair of a nude girl, who is kneeling between his legs. This design does not occur, however, in the copy of the book described below, which is believed to be the only one in existence, and it was evidently taken by Ellis from Blake's colour-print of this subject (13 × 10 cm.), formerly in the Crewe collection, or from the pencil drawing, which is to be found in the Print Room of the British Museum. The figures are interpreted in EJE as those of Urizen and Ahania, but I know of no other authority for connecting the design with *The Book of Ahania*. Proofs from the plates are exceedingly rare, but impressions from two of them are to be found in a miscellaneous collection of plates from Blake's works, which is now in the Pierpont Morgan Library.

Copy: 5 plates, printed in pale brown on one side of the leaf only. No watermark. Designs painted with water-colours, the title-page in blue, the tailpiece in red and brown. Unbound, sewed, g.e. Size 28.5 × 23 cm.

Sold at Sotheby's in 1855 (£1 13*s*.), and subsequently in the collection of the Earl of Crewe; sold at Sotheby's with the Crewe collection on March 30, 1903 (lot 7, Quaritch, £103), and acquired by Mr. W. A. White. (Grolier Cat., no. 29.)

Facsimile Reproductions: EY, iii; Griggs, 1892 (no. 221).

Typ. Reprints: Extracts first given by Gilchrist, i, 131, and Swinburne, p. 252. Also by Pierce, 1915. In full by WBY, EJE, Sampson, 1913. Translated into German by Knoblauch, 1907 (no. 175), and von Taube, 1907 (no. 176).

47　THE / BOOK of / LOS / Lambeth / Printed by W Blake 1795.
Colophon: The End of the / Book of LOS.

Description: Frontispiece, title, 2 pl., *Los*, ch. I-III, 3 pl. = 5 plates, about 13.5 × 10 cm., ordinary etching; the text finely etched in double columns; the designs coloured.

Contents:
1. Frontispiece. A woman with long, white hair sitting on a low stone seat, her knees drawn up to her chin. Dark rocks behind.
2. Title-page. *The Book*, etc. Near the bottom, a nude man, seen from behind, sitting huddled in a cave.
3. *Los. Chap. I*, 1-9. Begins: *Eno aged Mother*. In the central letter of the heading is an old man holding an open book; round him is a net, which spreads out below and involves the recumbent figures of a man and a woman.
4. [*Chap. I*], [9]-10, *Chap: II*, 1-9, and *Chap: III*, 1-4. Begins: *Darkness round Los: heat was not:*
5. [*Chap: III*], [4]-6, and *Chap: IV:*, 1-9. Begins: *An immense Fibrous Form,*

stretching out. Tailpiece, a small nude figure kneeling with outstretched arms above a globe.

Note: This book, of which the copy described below is the only one known to exist, is a companion work to the previous entry. The text is written in italic.

Copy: 5 plates on 5 leaves. No watermark. Printed in black. Designs coloured with opaque pigment. Size 29.5 × 24.5 cm. Bound in half-morocco.
Now in the B.M. Reading Room; acquired in 1866.

Facsimile Reproduction: EY, iii.

Typ. Reprints: *The Century Guild Hobby Horse*, 1890 (no. 497), EJE, Sampson, 1913. Extracts by Pierce, 1915. Translated into German by Knoblauch, 1907 (no. 175, in full), and von Taube, 1907 (no. 176, extracts).

48   MILTON a Poem / in 2 Books / The Author / & Printer W Blake / 1804 / To Justify the Ways of God to Men.

Description: Title, *Preface*, 2 pl., *Book the First*, 22 pl., *Book the Second*, 13 pl., full-page illustrations, 8 pl., additional plates, 5 pl. = 50 plates, about 16 × 11 cm., relief etching, painted with water-colours.

Contents:
1. Title-page. *Milton*, etc. The words are arranged round a central figure, which is that of a naked man seen from behind; he is passing into clouds with his right hand stretched out in front of him.
2. *Preface*. Begins: *The Stolen and Perverted Writings of Homer*. Below, four stanzas of four lines each, beginning: *And did those feet in ancient time*. At the bottom, a text from *Numbers*. xi. 29.
3. *Milton Book the First*. Begins: *Daughters of Beulah*! Above the heading is a large star shedding its rays over two figures, male and female, who recline below among corn and grapes.
4. Begins: *From Golgonooza the spiritual Four fold London*. Near the bottom, a man on horseback, passing through a colossal archway of three stones, is confronted by a huge boulder; stars and a young moon are in the sky (cf. *Jerusalem*, pl. 70).
5. Begins: *By Enitharmons Looms, & Spun beneath the Spindle of Tirzah.*
6. Begins: *Mean while wept Satan before Los.*
7. Begins: *And all Eden descended into Palamabrons tent.*

8. Full-page illustration. To the right is a naked man in flames standing on a pedestal; two other figures stand to the left.

9. Begins: *He set his face against Jerusalem.*

10. Begins: *For her light is terrible to me.*

11. Begins: *. . . Sick Couch bears the dark shades of Eternal Death.*

12. Begins: *According to the inspiration of the Poetic Genius.* Near the top, two figures under a tree.

13. Full-page illustration. A naked man with a nimbus is standing on a dark globe, behind which is seen the radiant edge of the sun; in his right hand he holds a pair of compasses, a cloak hangs from his left.

14. Begins: *As when a man dreams.* Near the bottom, a man bending backwards (cf. pl. 29) and a woman; flames and rocks between them.

15. Full-page illustration. In the upper part, a youth and four maidens with musical instruments. Below, an aged man with either hand resting on the stone tables of the law; a naked man is about to clasp him round the neck. Inscribed below: *To Annihilate the Self-hood of Deceit & False Forgiveness.*

16. Begins: *In the three females whom his wives, & these three whom his daughters.* Above, a group of six women, three of them seated. Below, a naked man stopped in his path by the branches of a mandragora.

17. Begins: *And he also darkend his brows.*

18. Begins: *Two yet but one: each in the other sweet reflected.*

19. Begins: *And down descended into Udan-Adan.*

20. Begins: *Tho driven away with the Seven Starry Ones.*

21. Full-page illustration. A naked man kneels in the centre and turns to look at another figure standing behind him in a fiery globe.

22. Begins: *Can you have greater Miracles than these?*

23. Begins: *Of Palamabrons Harrow.*

24. Begins: *But the Wine-press of Los is eastward of Golgonooza.* There is a row of lowly animals across the middle of the plate.

25. Begins: *Loud shout the Sons of Luvah.*

26. Begins: *These are the Sons of Los.* Lines of mountains extend across the plate near the top and at the bottom.

27. Begins: *Some Sons of Los surround the Passions with porches of iron & silver.*

28. Begins: *For in this Period the Poets Work is Done.* At the bottom: *End of the First Book.*

29. Full-page illustration. A naked man facing to the right and bending backwards (cf. pl. 14). Behind him are three steps; in front of him, close to his left leg, is a large falling star. Above him is the word *William* in capitals.

30. *Milton Book the Second.* Begins: *There is a place where Contrarieties are equally True.* Floating figures ascend and descend round the heading. At the top is

written backwards: *How wide the Gulf & Unpassable! between Simplicity & Insipidity;* and below *Milton*, also backwards: *Contraries are Positives. A Negation is not a Contrary.*

31. Begins: *Into this pleasant Shadow.*

32. Begins: *And the Divine Voice was heard in the Songs of Beulah.* Below is a fiery diagram of Milton's track through the Four Zoas.

33. Full-page illustration. A similar design to that on pl. 29, but reversed; the name at the top is *Robert*.

34. Begins: *And all the Songs of Beulah sounded.*

35. Begins: *Are here frozen to unexpansive deadly destroying terrors.*

36. Begins: *When on the highest lift of his light pinions.* Below is a sketch of a house and garden, inscribed: *Blakes Cottage at Felpham.* A man is standing in the garden, and above him is a figure descending from the sky.

37. Begins: *The Virgin answerd. Knowest thou of Milton.*

38. Full-page illustration. A man and a woman are lying exposed on a rock, at the foot of which is the sea; an eagle hovers over them.

39. Begins: *And the Forty-eight Starry Regions.*

40. Begins: *Till All Things become One.*

41. Full-page illustration. A naked man with a nimbus is stepping across a stream; a draped woman kneels at his feet and has placed one hand on his shoulder.

42. Begins: *Before Ololon Milton stood.* Below, a naked man in a cave pushing his way through monstrous serpents.

43. Begins: *To bathe in the waters of Life.* Above, a design of floating figures with joined hands (cf. *Job*, pl. 13).

44. Begins: *. . . Becomes a Womb? & is this the Death Couch of Albion.* Below, a naked woman floating over dark waters.

45. Text: *To go forth to the Great Harvest & Vintage of the Nations. Finis.* Below, in the centre is a sprouting stalk in the form of a naked woman with arms straining upwards; on either side is an ear of human corn.

Additional plates found only in copy C.

a. Numbered 3. Begins: *Beneath the Plow of Rintrah.* Below is a confused design of nude figures and stone archways.

b. Numbered 5. Begins: *By Enitharmons looms when Albion was slain upon his Mountains.*

c. Numbered 8*. Begins: *Then Los & Enitharmon knew.* Below, an old woman running with outstretched arms.

d. Numbered 17. Begins: *And Tharmas Demon of the Waters.*

e. Numbered 32*. Begins: *And Milton oft sat upon the Couch of Death.*

Note: *Milton* belongs to the period of Blake's residence at Felpham, and the five years succeeding this. The work is largely autobiographical, and some references to it in letters from Blake to Butts, written in April and July 1803,* show that the greater part of it was composed while he was actually at Felpham, but references in *Milton* to events which took place later show that additions were made to the poem after his return to London in the latter part of 1803. The title-page is dated 1804, but this is probably the date at which the etching of the plates was begun, since none of the three copies that are known to exist can have been printed before 1808, the date found in the watermarks of all of them; also a reference to the poem in connection with the first attack made upon him in the *Examiner*,† which occurs in the *Public Address*,‡ proves that the book had not yet been issued in August, 1808. The three copies of *Milton* described below are all quarto volumes, measuring about 24 × 17 cm. Two of them (A and B) contain forty-five plates printed in black on the same number of leaves, and are painted with water-colour washes, gold-leaf being added in the case of the second. The third copy (C) is of different constitution; Blake has omitted the *Preface* (pl. 2), but has inserted five additional plates, numbered a-e above, which do not occur anywhere else, so that the book contains in all forty-nine plates; it is printed and coloured in a manner similar to copy B. Nevertheless, it appears to have been Blake's intention that the complete work should consist of fifty plates, for in 1818 he offered it as: "Milton. 50 prints, quarto £10 10. 0." Except, however, for the reference from Lowndes given under the conjectural copy (D), there is no evidence that Blake ever issued a copy containing the full number of plates. The title-page has often been read as: *Milton a Poem in* 12 *Books*,§ but there can be no doubt that this is a mistake, part of one of the lines of decoration having been mistaken for the figure 1. A more extended account of this work will be found in the preface to the reprint, edited by Messrs. Russell and Maclagan in 1907 (no. 171).

Copies:

A. 45 plates on 45 leaves. Watermark *J Whatman* 1808. Delicately painted with water-colours. Arranged as above, but without pl. a-e. Foliated by Blake 1-45. Size 24 × 18 cm. Bound in half-morocco, g.e.
Now in the B.M. Print Room, having been bought from Francis Palgrave in 1859.

B. 45 plates on 45 leaves. Watermark *J Whatman* 1808. Painted with water-colours and gold; predominating tints pink, yellow, and blue. Arranged as above, but without pl. a-e. Foliated by Blake 1-45. Size 23.5 × 16.5 cm. Bound in calf, back repaired.
Probably the copy from the collection of Thomas Butts, sold at Sotheby's on

---

* See Russell, *Letters*, pp. 115, 121. † See no. 399.
‡ From the *Rossetti MS*. See Gilchrist, ii, 175.
§ See Sampson, 1905, p. 339; EJE, i, 437; Russell, *Letters*, p. 115.

March 26, 1852 (lot 53, Toovey, £9). Afterwards in the library of Robert Hoe, sold at the Anderson Galleries, New York, on April 23, 1911 (lot 393, Huntington, $9,000). Now in the collection of Mr. H. E. Huntington. (Grolier Cat., no. 34.)

C. 49 plates on 49 leaves. Watermark *J Whatman* 1808. Painted with watercolours and gold. Lacks pl. 2, but includes pl. a-e. Arrangement: 1, 3, 5, a, 4, b, 6-8, c, 9-16, d, 17-20, 22, 23, 25, 26, 24, 27-32, e, 33-42, 21, 43-45. The last two words, "and woven," on pl. 4, and the first line on pl. 5 have been erased by Blake. The title-page is not numbered; the remaining leaves are foliated by Blake 1-8, 8*, 9-32, 32*, 33-46. Size quarto. Bound in blue morocco, g.e., by J. Mackenzie.

The Beckford copy, sold at Sotheby's at the Hamilton Palace sale on July 4, 1882 (Quaritch, £230). Now in the New York Public Library (formerly the Lenox Library).

[D. Lowndes records a copy as follows: " 50 engraved pages coloured by the artist, 4to. 1804. Bohn's Cat. 10*l*. 10*s*." If the description is correct this copy cannot be identified with any of the above.]

Facsimile Reproductions: W. Muir, coloured, 1886 (no. 217, f); EY, iii, reduced.

Typ. Reprints: Extracts first given by Gilchrist, i, 241, and Swinburne, p. 249; later by WBY, LH, Sampson, 1913, Pierce, 1915. In full by EJE. Printed separately by Russell and Maclagan, 1907 (no. 171). Extracts translated into German by von Taube, 1907 (no. 176).

49 JERUSALEM / The / Emanation of / The Giant / Albion / 1804 / Printed by W. Blake S^th Molton S^t.
Colophon: The End of The Song / of Jerusalem.

Description: Frontispiece, title, 2 pl., text, 94 pl., full-page illustrations, 4 pl. = 100 plates, about 22 × 16 cm., relief etching, usually uncoloured.

Contents:
1. Frontispiece. A man clad in hat and cloak, with a fiery globe in his right hand, is going through a doorway. Inscriptions round and above the doorway have been erased.
2. Title-page. *Jerusalem*, etc. Various winged figures decorate the plate.
3. *To the Public*. Begins: *After my three years slumber*. Several lines and separate words have been erased from the plate.

4. *Jerusalem Chap:* 1. Begins: *Of the Sleep of Ulro!* Inscribed at the top Μονος ο Ισους. Below the heading, a cloaked woman grasps two men by the hair; naked figures mount upwards on the left. Line 23 and the last word of line 15 have been erased.

5. Begins: *The banks of the Thames are clouded.* Female figures extend up the right-hand margin.

6. Begins: *His Spectre driv'n by the Starry Wheels of Albions sons.* Below, a naked man leaning on a hammer and anvil is gazing up at a winged spectre which floats above him.

7. Begins: *Was living: panting like a frighted wolf.* Naked figures extend up the right-hand margin.

8. Begins: *Rose up against me thundering.* Below, a child is dragging the moon over the clouds by a string.

9. Begins: *Condens'd his Emanations.* Near the top, a shepherd piping to sheep and beasts of prey; in the centre, a child feeding a serpent; below, four women weeping beside the body of a man.

10. Begins: *Into the Furnaces & into the valleys of the Anvils of Death.*

11. Begins: *To labours mighty, with vast strength.* Above, a figure, half woman, half swan, kneeling on the surface of a lake; below, a flying figure with narrow, spiky wings.

12. Begins: *Why wilt thou give to her a Body.* Figures extend up the right-hand margin.

13. Begins: *And that toward Eden, four.* Moths and a kneeling figure along the right-hand margin.

14. Begins: *One hair nor particle of dust.* Below, a man lies asleep, and a small female figure with wings floats above him; a rainbow arches over them.

15. Begins: *And Hand & Hyle rooted into Jerusalem.* Below, a naked man running with outstretched arms; a smaller figure, enveloped by branching fibres, lies in his path.

16. Begins: *Hampstead Highgate Finchley Hendon.*

17. Begins: *His Spectre divides & Los in fury compells it to divide.*

18. Begins: *From every-one of the Four Regions.* Near the top, two winged figures, one with roses, the other with lilies in his hair; from their right hands proceed two smaller figures, which meet and kiss in the centre.

19. Begins: *His Children exil'd from his breast.* Below, a naked giant lying full-length on the ground, with women weeping at his head and feet; naked figures extend up the right-hand margin and along the top.

20. Begins: *But when they saw Albion fall'n.* Figures dragging flaming stars extend across the plate above and below the centre.

21. Begins: *O Vala! O Jerusalem! do you delight in my groans.* Below, a man scourging three naked women.

Both. mild Physician of Eternity. mysterious power.
Whose. springs are unsearchable & knowledge infinite.
Hereford. ancient Guardian of Wales, whose hands
Builded the mountain palaces of Eden. stupendous works!
Lincoln. Durham & Carlisle. Councellors of Los.
And Ely. Scribe of Los. whose pen no other hand
Dare touch: Oxford. immortal Bard! with eloquence
Divine. he wept over Albion: speaking the words of God
In mild perswasion: bringing leaves of the Tree of Life.

Thou art in Error Albion, the Land of Ulro:
One Error not removd. will destroy a human Soul
Repose in Beulahs night, till the Error is removd
Reason not on both sides. Repose upon our bosoms
Till the Plow of Jehovah. and the Harrow of Shaddai
Have passed over the Dead. to awake the Dead to Judgment.
But Albion turnd away refusing comfort.

Oxford trembled while he spoke. then fainted in the arms
Of Norwich. Peterboro. Rochester. Chester awful. Worcester.
Litchfield. Saint Davids. Landaff. Asaph. Bangor. Sodor.
Bowing their heads devoted: and the Furnaces of Los
Began to rage. thundering loud the storms began to roar
Upon the Furnaces. and loud the Furnaces rebellow beneath

And these the Four in whom the twenty-four appeard four-fold:
Verulam: London. York. Edinburgh. mourning one towards another
Alas!——The time will come. when a mans worst enemies
Shall be those of his own house and family: in a Religion
Of Generation. to destroy by Sin and Atonement. happy Jerusalem.
The Bride and Wife of the Lamb. O God thou art Not an Avenger!

JERUSALEM
Plate 46

22. Begins: *Albion thy fear has made me tremble.* Above, a naked woman and an angel; below, four angels floating above three huge cogwheels.

23. Begins: *Jerusalem! Jerusalem! deluding shadow of Albion!* Near the top, a winged female figure resting; below the centre, and at the bottom, a number of small figures crouching among rocks.

24. Begins: *What have I said? What have I done?* At the top, a crescent moon floating on dark waves.

25. Begins: *And there was heard a great lamenting in Beulah.* Below, a naked man, with the sun, moon, and stars on his limbs, is kneeling with his head thrust back and his arms behind him. Round him are three nude women.

26. Full-page illustration. On the left, a naked man in flames with outstretched arms; on the right, a robed figure in an attitude of astonishment. The names *Hand* and *Jerusalem* are inscribed below the figures. Two lines of text are inscribed at the sides and in the middle.

27. *To the Jews.* Begins: *Jerusalem the Emanation of the Giant Albion!* The greater part of the plate is occupied by twenty-two stanzas of four lines each beginning: *The fields from Islington to Marybone.*

28. *Jerusalem. Chap: 2.* Begins: *Every ornament of perfection.* Above, a man and a woman embracing on a lily.

29. Begins: *Then the Divine Vision like a silent Sun.* Nude figures along the right-hand margin.

30. Begins: *And the Two that escaped.* Above, two figures flying into the arms of a nude man.

31. Begins: *His western heaven with rocky clouds.* Below, two recumbent figures.

32. Begins: *Leaning against the pillars.* The greater part of the plate is occupied by a group of two women and three girls; the woman on the left is draped, the rest are nude. At the bottom on the left is a dome and a cross, on the right a gothic cathedral.

33. Begins: *Turning his back to the Divine Vision.* Near the centre, an old man ploughing; the plough is drawn by two human-headed lions.

34. Begins: *Elevate into the Region of Brotherhood.*

35. Begins: *Then the Divine hand found the Two Limits.* Above, a figure floating in flames and looking downwards; below, a woman rising out of the ribs of a sleeping man.

36. Begins: *Reuben return'd to his place.* At the top, the sun over an anvil between two figures, one shrinking away, the other about to strike the anvil with a sledge-hammer.

37. Begins: *And One stood forth from the Divine Family.* Above, Christ kneeling and supporting a naked man in his arms; on either side of them a palm and an oak

tree, and beneath their feet a winged globe. Below, a winged spectre hovering over a woman's body lying on a bier; the sun and moon at the sides.

38. Begins: *His face and bosom with petrific hardness.*

39. Begins: *By Satans Watch-fiends tho' they search.* Above, an old man with triple bow and arrow astride a winged horse. Below, a setting sun.

40. Begins: *Los shudder'd at beholding Albion.* Nude figures and decorations extend up the right-hand margin.

41. Begins: *Bath who is Legions.* Below, a seated figure with his head bowed between his knees; by his side is a scroll with an inscription in reversed writing.

42. Begins: *Thus Albion sat studious of others.* Up the right-hand margin a human vine.

43. Begins: *They saw their Wheels rising up poisonous.*

44. Begins: *With one accord in love sublime.* At the top, a winged ark and two angels.

45. Begins: *Bath, healing City!* Above, on the left a figure enveloped in fibres; a woman floats away holding a net, which is wrapped round the legs of the first figure. Two lines lower down is a big fish devouring smaller ones.

46. Begins: *Bath, mild Physician of Eternity.* Below, two figures seated in a chariot formed of serpents; the chariot is drawn by two human-headed oxen with demons seated on their backs.

47. Begins: *From Camberwell to Highgate where the mighty Thames shudders along.* In the middle, three naked figures in contorted attitudes. The first line of the text has been erased from the plate.

48. Begins: *These were his last words and the merciful Saviour in his arms.*

49. Begins: *The secret coverts of Albion & the hidden places of America.* In the right-hand margin is a female figure standing under a tree.

50. Begins: *The Atlantic Mountains where Giants dwelt.* Ends: *End of Chap: 2ᵈ.* Below, a man with three crowned heads is kneeling among rocks; a chain of figures proceeds from his body.

51. Full-page illustration. On the left, a seated figure, with robes, crown, and sceptre; in the centre, a naked man squatting with his head bowed between his legs; on the right, a naked man standing with bent head, and with chains hanging from his wrists. (Vala, Hyle, and Scofield; so inscribed in some impressions of the print.)

52. *To the Deists.* Begins: *He never can be a Friend to the Human Race.* At the bottom, seven stanzas of four lines each beginning: *I saw a Monk of Charlemaine.*

53. *Jerusalem Chap 3.* Begins: *But Los, who is the Vehicular Form.* Above is a figure, triple-crowned and seated on a throne with a canopy of celestial bodies, in the centre of a great sunflower.

54. Begins: *In Great Eternity every particular Form.* Near the centre, a boulder

From Camberwell to Highgate where the mighty Thames shudders along,
Where Loss Furnaces stand, where Jerusalem & Vala howl:
Luvah tore forth from Albions Loins, in fibrous veins, in rivers
Of blood over Europe a Vegetating Root in grinding pain.
Animating the Dragon Temples, soon to become that Holy Fiend
The Wicker Man of Scandinavia in which cruelly consumed
The Captives reard to heaven howl in flames among the stars
Loud the cries of War on the Rhine & Danube, with Albions Sons.
Away from Beulahs hills, & vales break forth the Souls of the Dead
With cymbal, trumpet, clarion: & the scythed chariots of Britain.

And the Veil of Vala, is composed of the Spectres of the Dead

Hark! the mingling cries of Luvah with the Sons of Albion
Hark! & Record the terrible wonder! that the Punisher
Mingles with his Victims Spectre, enslaved & tormented
To him whom he has murderd, bound in vengeance & enmity
Shudder not, but Write, & the hand of God will assist you!
Therefore I write Albions last words. Hope is banishd from me.

JERUSALEM
Plate 47

inscribed *Reason/Pity/Wrath/This World/Desire*; on either side of it small floating figures. Below, a fourfold head and five stars; moths flutter over them.

55. Begins: *When those who disregard all Mortal Things.*

56. Begins: *Then Los heaved his thund'ring Bellows on the valley of Middlesex.*

57. Begins: *And the voices of Bath & Canterbury & York & Edinburgh cry.* Above, two naked women among stars; fibres proceed from their hands. Immediately beneath the figures are small buildings inscribed *York* and *London*. Below, a similar figure, and over it a building inscribed *Jerusalem*.

58. Begins: *In beauty the Daughters of Albion divide.* Near the top, a winged head flying away. Near the bottom, a skeleton lying among flames.

59. Begins: *And formed into Four precious stones.* In the centre, three women round a spinning wheel.

60. Begins: *The clouds of Albions Druid Temples.*

61. Begins: *Behold: in the Visions of Elohim Jehovah, behold Joseph·& Mary.*

62. Begins: *Repose on me till the morning of the Grave.* The head and hands and the feet of a huge figure in anguish appear at the top and bottom. The head is surrounded by peacocks' feathers; there is a small figure between the feet.

63. Begins: *Jehovah stood among the Druids.* In the centre, a naked woman lying on the ground with a worm coiled about her body; a crescent moon is in the sky.

64. Begins: *Of the Mundane Shell which froze.* Above, two floating figures with a scroll beside a figure asleep. Below, an old man lying on the ground with an open book beside him.

65. Begins: *To decide Two Worlds with a great decision.* A chain extends up the right-hand margin.

66. Begins: *In awful pomp & gold, in all the precious unhewn stones of Eden.* Along the right-hand margin extend flames in which is a female figure, seated.

67. Begins: *By those who drink their blood.* Below, a man stretched out on his back, and chained down by his feet, hands, and middle.

68. *O Skofield why art thou cruel?*

69. Begins: *Then all the Males conjoined into One Male.* Below, two figures with a knife and a cup, and between them a mutilated victim; moon and stars above them; Druid stones in the background.

70. Begins: *And this the form of mighty Hand.* In the centre, a huge trilithon; three figures are passing under it along a road. A crescent moon is in the sky (cf. *Milton*, pl. 4).

71. Begins: *And above Albions land was seen the Heavenly Canaan.* Near the bottom, a winged spectre and a naked woman.

72. Begins: *And the Thirty-two Counties of the Four Provinces of Ireland.* Near the centre a boulder inscribed: *Continually Building. Continually Decaying because of Love & Jealousy*, with a weeping angel and flames on each side. At the bottom, a

serpent, below which is the line, in reversed writing: *Women the comforters of Men become the Tormentors & Punishers.*

73. Begins: *Such are Cathedrons golden Halls.* Near the centre, a man with a hammer is kneeling beside an anvil, on which is the sun.

74. Begins: *The Four Zoa's clouded rage.* Below, a naked man lying on the ground; fibres proceed from his head and body.

75. Begins: *And Rahab. Babylon the Great.* Near the top, a design of angels within circles. Below, a seven-headed serpent coiled about two women with crowns.

76. Full-page illustration. A man worshipping at the foot of a tree, on which is Christ crucified. At the foot of the plate the names *Albion* and *Jesus* can be seen in some copies.

77. *To the Christians.* Below the heading, a child holding one end of a long string, and a four-line stanza beginning: *I give you the end of a golden string.* To the left is inscribed: *Devils are False Religions.* "*Saul Saul Why persecutest thou me.*" Text begins: *We are told to abstain from fleshly desires.* At the bottom, three four-line stanzas beginning: *England! awake! awake! awake!*

78. *Jerusalem. C 4.* Begins: *The Spectres of Albions Twelve Sons.* Below the heading a man with a bird's head is seated on the right facing a setting sun.

79. Begins: *My tents are fall'n! my pillars are in ruins!*

80. Begins: *Encompass'd by the frozen Net.* Human figures and coiling worms extend up the right-hand margin.

81. Begins: *I have mock'd those who refused cruelty.* The greater part of the plate is occupied by a group; on the left is a naked woman pointing behind her to a five-line stanza in reversed writing, beginning: *In Heaven the only Art of Living*; on the right is a group of eleven other women.

82. Begins: *I have heard Jerusalems groans.* Up the right-hand margin, a worm.

83. Begins: *Corruptability appears upon thy limbs.* Clouds and two figures in the right-hand margin.

84. Begins: *Highgates heights & Hampsteads.* Below, an old man on crutches led by a child; in the background a cathedral.

85. Begins: *Became a Space & an Allegory.* Below, a man and a woman with a vine.

86. Begins: *I see thy Form O lovely mild Jerusalem.*

87. Begins: *Repelling weeping Enion blind & age-bent.* Above, a woman bent and groping after two smaller floating figures; over her is an aged man.

88. Begins: *Los answerd sighing like the bellows of his Furnaces.*

89. Begins: *Tho divided by the Cross & Nails & Thorns & Spear.* Two figures extend up the right-hand margin,

90. Begins: *The Feminine separates from the Masculine.*

JERUSALEM
Plate 76

91. Begins: *It is easier to forgive an Enemy.* Below, a man with head thrown back seated between two symbols. The first line of text has been erased.

92. Begins: *What do I see: The Briton Saxon Roman Norman.* In the centre, a woman seated in an attitude of despair; on the ground around her are four heads, and in the background Druid archways; on the right is the word *Jerusalem*.

93. Begins: *Enitharmon heard. She raisd her head.* Above, three men kneeling with pointing fingers; on their backs and thighs is inscribed: *Anytus Melitus & Lycon thought Socrates a Very Pernicious Man. So Caiphas thought Jesus.* Below, a woman lying in a fiery grave.

94. Begins: *Albion cold lays on his Rock.* Above, a threefold man supine. Below, a woman lying face downwards on the body of an old man; Druid stones in the background.

95. Begins: *Her voice pierc'd Albions clay cold ear.* Above, a young man arising among flames.

96. Begins: *As the Sun & Moon lead forward the Visions of Heaven & Earth.* On the right, an old man clasping a woman to his breast.

97. Begins: *Awake Awake Jerusalem!* Below, the vigorous figure of a young man with a globe of light in his left hand.

98. Begins: *Then each an Arrow flaming from his Quiver.* Above, a worm; below, various lowly animals.

99. Begins: *All Human Forms identified,* with colophon. Below, a naked woman is received into the arms of an old man among streaming fire.

100. Full-page illustration. Three naked figures, the central one with hammer and compasses; the figure on the left carries the sun on his shoulder; on the right is a woman with the moon at her side, and with a veil hanging from her right hand. In the background is a chain of Druid arches.

Note: *Jerusalem* is the last and greatest of the series of Blake's Illuminated Books. It is a large quarto volume, measuring about 33 × 27 cm., and consists of a hundred plates printed on one side of the leaf only. The title-page is dated 1804, but this is evidently the year in which Blake began the work. None of the six copies known to me can have been printed before 1818, and the book was probably not finished until this date. All the copies issued by Blake are printed on Whatman paper, with dates varying from 1818 to 1826. Five of them are printed in black and are uncoloured. The fifth (D) is printed in orange on paper dated 1820, and is very beautifully painted with water-colours and gold. It was probably this copy of which Blake wrote in 1827 to George Cumberland: " The last work I produced is a poem " entitled *Jerusalem, The Emanation of the Giant Albion,* but find that to print it will " cost my time the amount of twenty guineas. One I have finished, but it is not " likely I shall find a customer for it " (Russell, *Letters,* p. 222). Blake did not, in fact, find a customer for it, and it seems to have passed with his other effects to Frederick Tatham. It has usually been assumed, on the authority of this remark by Blake, that only one coloured copy of the work has ever existed, but I have been informed by Mr. Tregaskis that another coloured copy was sold by him to Ruskin about thirty-five years ago. I have communicated with the present owner of Ruskin's Library, Mr. Arthur Severn, and he states that he has a distinct recollection of there having been such a book in the collection, but that he believes Ruskin cut it up. A collection of miscellaneous water-colour drawings, which was recently deposited in the B.M. Print Room, contained some exquisitely coloured fragments, which had evidently been cut from leaves of a copy of *Jerusalem*, and these may possibly be some surviving evidence of Ruskin's extraordinary act of destruction.* Separate leaves coloured by Blake are also to be met with. Two of these, each with a plate printed on both sides, are in the B.M. Print Room and the Victoria and Albert Museum. Three other leaves, each printed and coloured on both sides, were formerly in the possession of H. Buxton Forman.† Another leaf, in the Linnell collection,‡ shows stitch-holes near the left-hand margin, and the plate printed on it is numbered 51, but there is no evidence to show that this was taken from a *complete* coloured example of the book; more probably Blake took this leaf from an uncoloured copy of the book, which he had been unable to sell, and coloured it, as a specimen, for John Linnell. Another coloured example of this plate (51) is in the possession of Mr. W. Graham Robertson.

The text of *Jerusalem* is etched throughout in italic, but the lettering is not uniform in size, as might be expected in a work the execution of which extended over some fourteen years. In all the copies, which I have myself examined, some words and passages on pl. 3, *To the Public*, have been erased; a few lines, however, quoted by Swinburne (*Critical Essay*, p. 284), have the gaps filled up, but I do not know whether the missing words were supplied by Swinburne, or whether he had access to a copy in which they had been filled in by Blake. The arrangement of the plates does not vary much, but, as is noted by Messrs. Russell and Maclagan in their edition of *Jerusalem* (p. 121), the order of the plates of Chapter II is not the same in all copies. I have adopted as a standard the order found in B and D. The plates were in existence after Blake's death, and two posthumous copies of the book, printed presumably by Tatham, are recorded below.

Jerusalem is not mentioned in the list of works offered by Blake in 1818, but a contemporary reference to it is to be found in the *London Magazine* for Sept.

---

* There is evidence that Ruskin was in the habit of cutting to pieces illuminated MSS., however valuable, that were in his possession. See *Catalogue of Fourteen Illuminated Manuscripts, the property of Henry Yates Thompson*. Sotheby's, June 22, 1921, p. 148.

† Sold with the Buxton Forman Library at the Anderson Galleries, New York, March 15, 1920.

‡ Sold with the Linnell collection at Christie's, March 15, 1918 (lot 158, Martin, 70 gns.).

1820 (see no. 402). Crabb Robinson has recorded that on July 24, 1811, Blake showed Southey "a perfectly mad poem called *Jerusalem*." *

Copies: [A-F, 1818-1826]

A. 100 plates on 100 leaves. Watermark *J. Whatman* 1818, 1819, or 1820. Printed in black. Several plates touched up with sepia and chinese white, and on pl. 16 there is some green tinting; otherwise uncoloured. Foliated by Blake 1-100. Arrangement: 1-28, 33-41, 43-46, 42, 29-32, 47-100. Bound in vellum. Size 32 × 25 cm.

John Linnell's copy, sold with his collection at Christie's, March 15, 1918 (lot 194, Edwards, £89). Now in the possession of Mr. Frank Rinder, London.

B. 100 plates on 100 leaves. Watermark *J Whatman* 1818, 1819, or 1820. Printed in black. Uncoloured except for occasional grey water-colour washes. Foliated by Blake 1-100. Arranged as above. Bound in half-morocco, g.e. Size 32.5 × 27 cm.

Now in the B.M. Print Room, having been purchased from Messrs. Evans in 1847.

C. 100 plates on 100 leaves. Watermark *J Whatman* 1820. Printed in black. Retouched with indian ink, and here and there lightly washed with brown; otherwise uncoloured. Unbound. Size 28.5 × 27 cm.

Formerly in the E. W. Hooper collection; now in the possession of the family of Mrs. R. S. Warner, Boston, Mass. (Boston Mus. Cat., 1891, no. 8.)

D. 100 plates on 100 leaves. Watermark *J Whatman* 1820. Printed in orange. Very beautifully and elaborately coloured with water-colours and gold. Foliated by Blake 1-100. Arranged as above. Bound in green morocco, with clasps, together with the MS., on twelve leaves, of Tatham's life of Blake. Size 33.5 × 27.5 cm. Bound with the MS. are a portrait of Mrs. Blake by George Richmond after Tatham, and drawings of Blake by Tatham at the ages of 28 and 69.

Frederick Tatham's copy, to whom it passed with Blake's other effects after his wife's death. It was sold at Christie's † on June 1, 1887 (lot 225, Quaritch, £166), and is now in the possession of General Archibald Stirling of Keir.

E. 100 plates on 100 leaves. Watermark *J Whatman* 1824 or 1826. Printed in black. Uncoloured. Foliated by Blake 1-100. Bound in red straight-grained morocco by Bedford. Size 36.5 × 26.5 cm.

From the Toovey collection. Now in the Pierpont Morgan Library.

---

* *Diary and Reminiscences*, i, 338.

† Usually stated to have been included in the Cosier Library, but reference to the sale catalogue shows that it was sold by another anonymous owner.

F. Copy in the possession of Mr. Felix Isman, New York. Printed in black and uncoloured. This copy is not available at the present time, so that no description can be given here.

[G, H posthumous]

G. 100 plates on 100 leaves. Watermark *J Whatman* 1831 or 1832. Printed in red brown. Uncoloured. No foliation. Bound in contemporary morocco, elaborately tooled, g.e. Size 28.5 × 23 cm.

Samuel Boddington's copy, with his bookplate. Sold at Sotheby's, Nov. 1895. Formerly in the possession of Charles Fairfax Murray; presented by him in 1912 to the Fitzwilliam Museum, Cambridge.

H. 100 plates on 100 leaves. Watermark *J Whatman* 1831 or 1832. Printed in red brown. Uncoloured. Some of the plates are numbered. Bound in morocco, g.e., by Leighton, with the Milnes crest on the front cover. Size 28.5 × 23.5 cm.

Formerly in the collection of Thomas Butts. Sold at Sotheby's on March 26, 1852 (R. Monckton Milnes, £10 15s.). In the Crewe collection until March, 1903, when it was sold at Sotheby's (lot 15, Quaritch, £83); it was then acquired by Mr. W. A. White. (Grolier Cat., no. 32.)

Facsimile Reproductions: Pearson, 1877 (no. 213); EY, iii, reduced.

Typ. Reprints: Extracts in Gilchrist, i, 226; Swinburne, p. 276; WBY, Sampson, 1905 and 1913; Pierce, 1915. In full in EJE. Printed separately by Russell and Maclagan, 1904 (no. 162). Extracts translated into German by von Taube, 1907 (no. 176).

50 ON HOMER'S POETRY [*and*] ON VIRGIL [about 1818-1822]

Description: A single plate, 11.5 × 10 cm.; relief etching; uncoloured.

Contents: 24 lines of prose, headed *On Homer's Poetry*, and beginning: *Every Poem must necessarily be a perfect Unity*, followed by 12 lines of prose, headed *On Virgil*, and beginning: *Sacred Truth has pronounced*. To the left of the second heading is a group of figures beside a tree; small decorations on other parts of the plate.

Note: This leaflet is one of the publications called by Gilchrist Blake's "Sibylline Leaves." Some of the opinions expressed in it are the same as are found engraved in *Laocoön* (no. 54), which is referred to in the sixth line of *On Homer's Poetry*, and probably belongs to about the years 1817-1818; in both of them occurs the same reference to Virgil's *Aeneid*, Bk. vi, l. 348. The plate is also similar in character to those of *The Ghost of Abel* (no. 51), which is dated 1822. *On Homer's Poetry* seems, therefore, to belong to the period 1818-1822, but it is not yet possible to assign to it a more accurate date. Six copies are known to me, four of which I have seen; they are all printed in black on paper which bears no watermark, and are uncoloured.

Copies:

A. No watermark. Printed in black. Uncoloured. Size 28.5 × 23.5 cm.
Probably from the collection of Thomas Butts. Afterwards in the collection of the Earl of Crewe, and sold at Sotheby's on March 30, 1903, together with *The Ghost of Abel*, copy A, and the engraving known as "The man sweeping the interpreter's parlour" (lot 8, Quaritch, £43); acquired by Mr. W. A. White. (Grolier Cat., no. 37b.)

B. No watermark. Printed in black. Uncoloured. Size 34 × 24.5 cm.
John Linnell's copy, sold with his collection at Christie's, March 15, 1918, together with *The Ghost of Abel*, copy B, and *Laocoön* (lot 199, Quaritch, 36 gns.). Now in my own possession.

C. Similar to copy B. Also in the Linnell collection, but not included in the sale.

D. No watermark. Printed in black. Uncoloured. Size 31 × 21.5 cm.
In the collection of Mr. B. B. Macgeorge of Glasgow.

E. Similar to copy D. Size 33 × 23 cm. Also in the possession of Mr. Macgeorge.

F. A copy was included in a volume of miscellaneous prints by Blake from the collection of Mr. Henry White of Queen's Gate, which was sold at Sotheby's in April, 1902 (Roberts, £87); it was resold at Sotheby's on Dec. 9, 1905 (£80), and again on Dec. 15, 1906. It is now in the Pierpont Morgan Library.

Facsimile Reproductions: W. Muir, 1886 (no. 217, h); EY, iii.

Typ. Reprints: Gilchrist, ii, 179-180; EJE; Sampson, 1913. Extracts in LH, JS.

51 The GHOST OF ABEL / A Revelation In the Visions of Jehovah / Seen by William Blake.
Colophon: 1822, W Blakes Original Stereotype was 1788

Description: 2 plates about 16.5 × 12.5 cm.; relief etching; uncoloured.

Contents:

1. Heading, *The Ghost of Abel, etc.*; begins: *To Lord Byron in the Wilderness.* The plate is decorated with small figures.

2. Begins: *Alive & not Dead: were it not better to believe Vision.* Along the left-hand margin are small figures. Below, Eve, naked except for a skin about her

middle, is stretched out upon Abel's body; above her floats a figure inscribed: *The Voice of Abel's Blood.* At the bottom is the colophon.

Note: This short dramatic piece was included by Gilchrist among the so-called "Sibylline Leaves." It begins with four lines addressed *To Lord Byron in the Wilderness.* Blake's stage directions state that the *Scene* is *A rocky Country. Eve fainted over the dead body of Abel which lays near a Grave. Adam kneels by her. Jehovah stands above.* The speakers are Jehovah, Adam, Eve, The Voice of Abel's Blood, and Satan. At the end: *On each side a Chorus of Angels entering sing the following*, these directions being followed by five lines of blank verse. Finally: *The Curtain falls.* The date, 1788, in the colophon, evidently refers, as was first pointed out by Dr. Sampson (1905, p. 341), to Blake's earliest use of his relief-etching process in the illuminated books, and not, as had been commonly supposed, to a previous issue of *The Ghost of Abel.* Only three copies of the work are known to me. These are all printed in black and uncoloured; one is on paper with a watermark dated 1821.

Copies:

A. 2 plates on 2 leaves. Watermark *J Whatman* 1821. Printed in black. Uncoloured. Size 28.5 × 23 cm. Unbound; sewn.
Copy from the collection of Thomas Butts, sold at Sotheby's on March 26, 1852 (R. Monckton Milnes, £2). Afterwards in the collection of the Earl of Crewe, and was again sold at Sotheby's on March 30, 1903, together with *On Homer's Poetry*, copy A, and the engraving known as "The man sweeping the interpreter's parlour" (lot 8, Quaritch, £43); it was acquired by Mr. W. A. White. (Grolier Cat., no. 37a.)

B. 2 plates on 2 leaves. No watermark. Printed in black. Uncoloured. Size 34.5 × 24.5 cm. Unbound.
Formerly in John Linnell's collection, sold at Christie's, March 15, 1918, together with *On Homer's Poetry*, copy B, and *Laocoön* (lot 199, Quaritch, 36 gns.). Now in my own possession. (Nat. Gal. Cat., 1913, no. 103; Manchester Cat., 1914, no. 93.)

C. Similar to copy B. Also in the Linnell collection. Sold at Christie's, March 15, 1918 (lot 200, Edwards, £29 8s.).

Facsimile Reproduction: EY, iii.

Typ. Reprints: Gilchrist, ii, 181-184; Swinburne, pp. 295-297; EJE; Sampson, 1913.

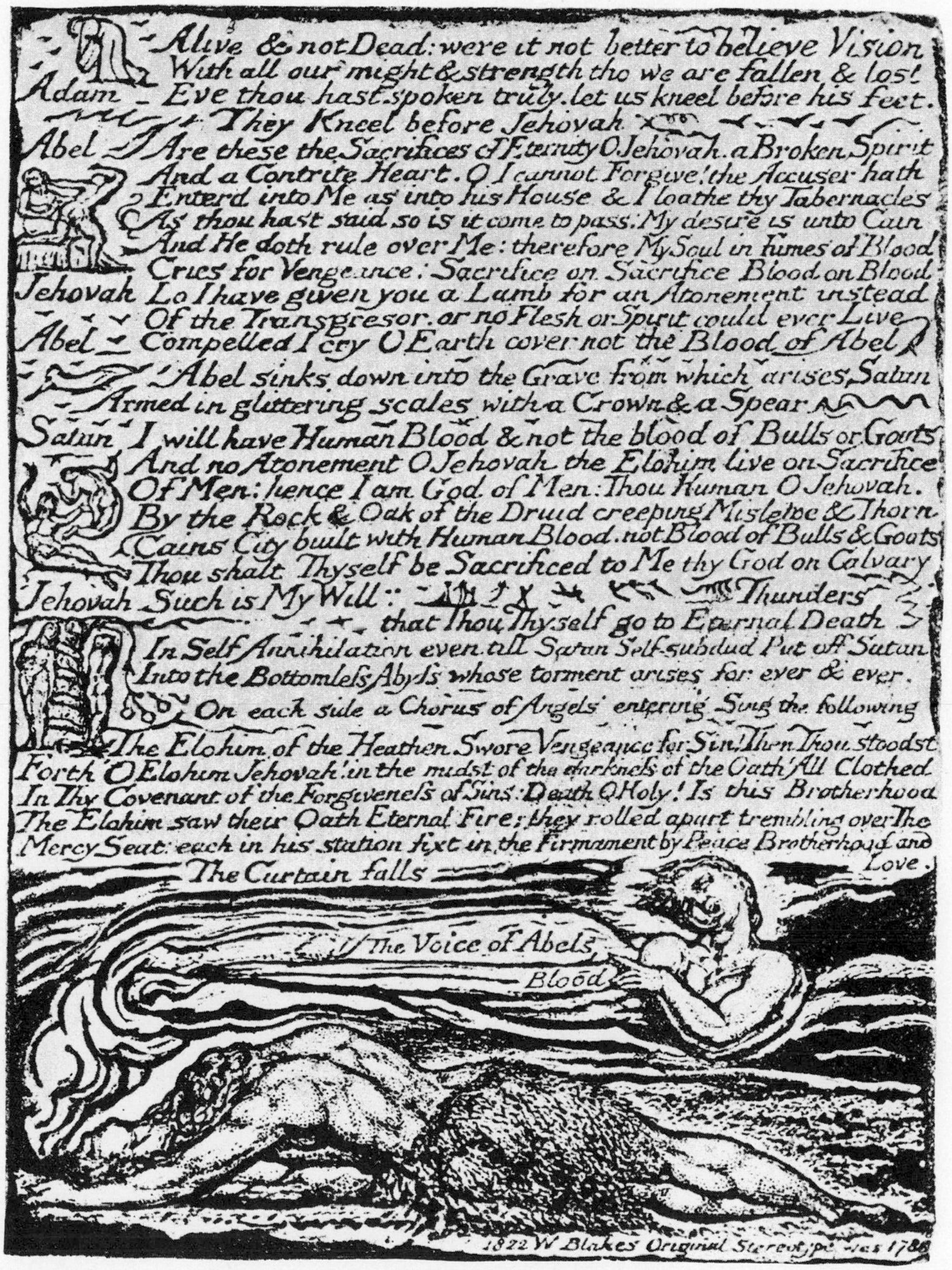

Alive & not Dead: were it not better to believe Vision
With all our might & strength tho we are fallen & lost.

Adam — Eve thou hast spoken truly. let us kneel before his feet.

They Kneel before Jehovah

Abel — Are these the Sacrifices of Eternity O Jehovah. a Broken Spirit
And a Contrite Heart. O I cannot Forgive! the Accuser hath
Enterd into Me as into his House & I loathe thy Tabernacles
As thou hast said so is it come to pass. My desire is unto Cain
And He doth rule over Me: therefore My Soul in fumes of Blood
Cries for Vengeance: Sacrifice on Sacrifice Blood on Blood

Jehovah — Lo I have given you a Lamb for an Atonement instead
Of the Transgresor. or no Flesh or Spirit could ever Live

Abel — Compelled I cry O Earth cover not the Blood of Abel

*Abel sinks down into the Grave from which arises Satan
Armed in glittering scales with a Crown & a Spear*

Satan — I will have Human Blood & not the blood of Bulls or Goats
And no Atonement O Jehovah the Elohim live on Sacrifice
Of Men: hence I am God of Men: Thou Human O Jehovah.
By the Rock & Oak of the Druid creeping Mistletoe & Thorn
Cains City built with Human Blood. not Blood of Bulls & Goats
Thou shalt. Thyself be Sacrificed to Me thy God on Calvary

Jehovah — Such is My Will: *Thunders*
that Thou. Thyself go to Eternal Death
In Self Annihilation even till Satan Self-subdud Put off Satan
Into the Bottomless Abyss whose torment arises for ever & ever.

On each side a Chorus of Angels entering Sing the following

The Elohim of the Heathen Swore Vengeance for Sin Then Thou stoodst
Forth O Elohim Jehovah! in the midst of the darkness of the Oath All Clothed
In Thy Covenant of the Forgiveness of Sins: Death O Holy! Is this Brotherhood
The Elohim saw their Oath Eternal Fire; they rolled apart trembling over The
Mercy Seat: each in his station fixt in the Firmament by Peace Brotherhood and
Love.

The Curtain falls

The Voice of Abels
Blood

1822 W Blakes Original Stereotype was 1788

THE GHOST OF ABEL

Plate 2

F. *LINE ENGRAVINGS*

52 FOR CHILDREN: THE GATES OF PARADISE

Title-page: For Children / [a flying figure] / The / Gates / of / Paradise / [rule] / 1793 / Published by W Blake Nº 13 / Hercules Buildings Lambeth / and / J. Johnson Sᵗ. Pauls Church Yard.

Description: Frontispiece, title, 2 pl. (unnumbered), *The Gates of Paradise*, 16 pl. (numbered 1-16) = 18 plates, 6.5 to 9.5 × 4 to 7.5 cm., line engraving, uncoloured, printed in black on one side only of separate leaves.

Plates : Of various sizes according to the measurements given below. In addition to the legend printed below, each plate, except no. 13, is inscribed : *Publishd 17 May 1793 by W Blake Lambeth*, or with some variation of this, often without the word *Lambeth*.

[i]. *Frontispiece. What is Man!* A caterpillar on a leaf ; lying on a second leaf below is a chrysalis with a child's face. 9.5 × 6 cm.

[ii]. Title-page. *For Children* etc. 7 × 4 cm.

1. *I found him beneath a Tree.* A woman under a weeping willow is pulling a child out of the ground by its hair ; she holds a second child in her apron. 8 × 6.5 cm.

2. *Water.* A nude man sitting beneath a leafless tree in a deluge of rain. 8 × 7.5 cm.

3. *Earth.* A nude man struggling out of a crevice in a rock. 8 × 7.5 cm.

4. *Air.* A man seated among clouds, clasping his forehead with both hands and staring steadfastly before him ; a background of dark sky and stars. 8.5 × 7.5 cm.

5. *Fire.* A nude figure among flames, armed with shield and spear. 9 × 7 cm.

6. *At length for hatching ripe | he breaks the shell.* A cherub breaking out of an egg shell. 6 × 5 cm.

7. *Alas!* A boy in a garden, hat in hand, is running after a small figure in the air ; another small figure lies face downwards on the ground at his feet. 8 × 5 cm.

8. *My Son! my Son!* A nude boy brandishing a spear ; an old man holding a sword sits by in an attitude of sorrow. 9.5 × 6 cm.

9. *I want! I want!* A man essays to climb by a ladder to the moon ; two lovers look on. 7 × 5 cm.

10. *Help! Help!* The arm of a drowning man is raised from the water in the midst of sea and sky. 7 × 5 cm.

11. *Aged ignorance.* An old man with spectacles, seated under a tree, clips the wings of a nude struggling boy with a large pair of scissors. 7 × 6.5 cm.

12. *Does thy God O Priest take such vengeance | as this?* An old man and four other figures in a dungeon in attitudes of dejection. 7 × 6 cm.

13. *Fear & Hope are—Vision.* A man, a woman, and two children are watching by the body of an old man, whose spirit, with finger pointing upward, floats at the foot of the couch. No imprint. 8 × 7 cm.

14. *The Traveller hasteth in the | Evening.* A man carrying a staff strides along a lane. 7 × 4.5 cm.

15. *Death's Door.* An old man with a crutch entering the massive stone doorway of a tomb. 7.5 × 5 cm. (cf. illustrations to Blair's *Grave*, pl. 13).

16. *I have said to the Worm, Thou | art my mother & my sister.* A woman draped in white and seated on the ground ; huge worms crawl at her feet. 6.5 × 5 cm.

Note : Only four copies of *For Children: The Gates of Paradise* are known to me. These are on small leaves, measuring about 14 × 10 cm., and all consisted originally of eighteen plates, though three plates from a later work have been added to copy D. The plates in copy A are in an early state before the addition of the imprints. The book was advertised by Blake in his prospectus of 1793 as : " The Gates of Paradise, a small book of engravings. Price 3s.", but very few copies can have been sold. At a later period, about 1805-1810, Blake used pl. i and 1-16 again, though with alterations and additions, in another work with the title *For the Sexes : The Gates of Paradise* (see next entry). Sketches for all the designs in *The Gates of Paradise* are found in the *Rossetti MS.*, and two water-colours resembling pl. 12 and 16 are recorded by Russell (*Engravings*, pp. 63-64).

Copies :
A. 18 plates on 18 leaves. Watermark *Mafrins* (? ; very indistinct). The lettering on the title-page after the word *Paradise* has been erased ; the other plates have their numbers and titles, but no imprints. Size 14 × 9.5 cm. Bound in old red morocco, g.e.
One of the Beckford copies, sold at Sotheby's in the Hamilton Palace sale on July 4, 1882 (Bain, £16). It was then acquired by Mr. B. B. Macgeorge of Glasgow. A fly-leaf is inscribed, probably in Beckford's handwriting, " Handest [?] July 1838." Another fly-leaf is watermarked 1805. (Nat. Gal. Cat., 1913, no. 94 ; Manchester Cat., 1914, no. 156.)
B. 18 plates on 18 leaves. No watermark visible. Size of original leaf 13.5 × 10.5 cm. ; now mounted on leaves 21 × 17 cm. Bound in half-morocco, g.e.

Now in the B.M. Print Room, having been bought from Messrs. Colnaghi and Co. in 1862.

C. 18 plates on 18 leaves. No watermark. Size 13 × 10.5 cm. Bound in half-calf, lettered on back : *Blake's Work.* In purple morocco case.

Formerly in the Beckford Library. On the fly-leaf is an inscription in Beckford's handwriting : "A present from H. G. Bohn, 19th May, 1835." Inside the cover is the bookplate of Thomas Brooke, F.S.A. Sold at Sotheby's with the library of Lady Brooke, Nov. 24, 1913 (Spencer, £91). Acquired by Mr. Herschel V. Jones, Minneapolis, and resold at the Anderson Galleries, New York, Dec. 2, 1918 (lot 185, Rosenbach, $610). Now in the collection of Mr. A. E. Newton.

D. 21 plates on 21 leaves. No watermark. Plates ii, 17, and 18 from *For the Sexes: The Gates of Paradise* have been inserted after the title-page. Size 13 × 10 cm. Bound in green morocco, g.e., by F. Bedford.

Formerly in the possession of Frederick Tatham, by whom the three additional leaves were probably inserted. It was sold by him to Frederick Locker, who inserted his Kate Greenaway bookplate and a pencil note recording its history. Sold with the Rowfant Library, and acquired in April, 1905, by Mr. W. A. White.

53 FOR THE SEXES: THE GATES OF PARADISE

Title-page : For the Sexes / The / Gates / of / Paradise / [Prologue 10 lines, beginning:] Mutual Forgiveness of each Vice . . . [about 1805-1810]

Description : Frontispiece, title, 2 pl. (unnumbered), *The Gates of Paradise*, 16 pl. (numbered 1-16), *The Keys of the Gates*, 2 pl., epilogue *To The Accuser*, 1 pl. = 21 plates, 6.5 to 9.5 × 4 to 7.5 cm., line engraving, uncoloured, printed in black on one side only of separate leaves.

Plates : Plates i and 1-16 are the same as in *For Children: The Gates of Paradise*, though with alterations and with additions to the legends; the imprints are unaltered.

[i]. *Frontispiece. What is Man ! | The Sun's Light when he unfolds it | Depends on the Organ that beholds it.* Design as before.

[ii]. Title-page. *For the Sexes* etc., with prologue.

1. As in *For Children: The Gates of Paradise.*

2. *Water | Thou Waterest him with Tears.* Design as before.

3. *Earth | He struggles into Life.* Design as before.

4. *Air | On Cloudy Doubts & Reasoning Cares.* Design as before.

5. *Fire | That end in endless Strife.* The figure has been blinded in this issue.

6. As in *For Children: The Gates of Paradise.*

7. *What are these? Alas! the Female Martyr | Is She also the Divine Image.* Design as before.

8, 9, 10. As in *For Children: The Gates of Paradise.*

11. *Aged Ignorance | Perceptive Organs closed, their Objects close.* Design as before.

12-16. As in *For Children: The Gates of Paradise.*

[17]. *The Keys | of the Gates.* 21 lines, beginning: *The Catterpiller on the Leaf . . .*

[18]. 29 lines, beginning: *He meets his Saviour in the Grave . . .*

[19]. *To The Accuser who is | The God of This World.* Epilogue, 8 lines, beginning: *Truly, My Satan, thou art but a Dunce.* . . . Below, a figure of Satan, with sun, moon, and stars emblazoned on his wings, hovers over the prostrate body of a traveller with a staff beside him.

Note: Most of the plates of *For the Sexes: The Gates of Paradise* were first used in the earlier work entitled *For Children: The Gates of Paradise*, which was issued in 1793 (see last entry). Later, about 1805-1810, alterations and additions were made in these plates, a new title-page was engraved, and three plates of text (17-19) were added to form the total number of twenty-one. I have definite evidence of the existence of only five complete copies of the book thus constituted. The earlier work, *For Children*, was a duodecimo, but *For the Sexes* is usually larger, measuring up to 34 × 24 cm. The plates of this work exist in three states, two of which were first differentiated by Dr. Sampson (1905, p. 368); the third of these contains alterations in the text on pl. ii and 17 as follows:

	First State	*Third State*
Pl. ii, l. 5.	Jehovah's fingers wrote the Law	Jehovah's Finger wrote the Law
Pl. ii, ll. 7-8.	And in the midst of Sinais heat	And the Dead Corpse from Sinais heat
	Hid it beneath His Mercy Seat	Buried beneath his Mercy Seat
Pl. 17, l. 15.	A dark Hermaphrodite I stood	A dark Hermaphrodite We stood

The first state appears to be found only in copy A. The second state, found only in copy B, has the first of these alterations, but not the others. According to Russell (*Engravings*, p. 60) the plates in copy E have been still further worked upon and perhaps constitute a fourth state.

Gilchrist was the first to print the text of this work, but, like most of Blake's later editors, did not realize that it must have been written long after the first appearance of *For Children: The Gates of Paradise* in 1793. Dr. Sampson pointed out, however, in 1905, that the work has much in common with *Milton* and *Jerusalem*, and evidently belongs to the same period.* The best text † is given by Dr. Sampson, who states that he followed copy D.

* For evidence see Sampson, 1905, pp. 372-377.

† Dr. Sampson's text of 1905 contains two bad readings in pl. 17, l. 13, and pl. 19, l. 5. These have been corrected in his edition of 1913.

Copies:

A. First state. 21 plates on 21 leaves. No dated watermark. Size 16 × 11 cm. John Linnell's copy; it passed to John Linnell junr., and was in his possession when Dr. Sampson was writing in 1905, but later it was not to be found in the Linnell collection. I have not been able to trace it any farther.

B. Second state. 21 plates on 21 leaves. Watermark *J. Whatman* 1818. Plates 17 and 18 are not numbered and are placed after the title-page. Size about 17 × 11 cm. Bound in plain brown morocco by Zaehnsdorf.
This is probably the copy referred to by Dr. Sampson (1905, p. 368) and stated by him to be in the possession of Mr. James T. Linnell. It was bought by Mr. Edwards from a member of the Linnell family in 1906, and was then acquired by Miss A. G. E. Carthew, London.

C. Third state. 21 plates on 21 leaves. Watermark *J Whatman* 182 . . .
The frontispiece is placed after the title-page. Plates 17-19 have been numbered by Blake in ink at the right-hand lower corner. Size 22.5 × 14 cm. Bound in old green morocco, gilt.
Formerly in the library of Samuel Boddington, and contains his bookplate. Later in the collection of R. A. Potts, by whom it was sold in 1908 to its present owner, Mr. T. J. Wise.

D. Third state. 21 plates on 21 leaves. Watermark dated 1825. Plates 17-19 numbered by Blake. Size 23 × 14 cm. Bound in half-calf.
Formerly in the library of Thomas Boddington, and contains his bookplate; sold with this collection at Sotheby's, Nov. 4, 1895 (Quaritch, £21). Now in the possession of Mr. W. A. White.

E. Third state. 21 plates on 21 leaves. No watermark. Size 26 × 19 cm. Bound in brown morocco, g.e., by F. Bedford. Evidently a late copy as the plates have been more worked upon than in copy D.
Frederick Locker's copy; sold with the Rowfant Library and acquired in April, 1905, by Mr. W. A. White.

F. Third state. 19 plates on 19 leaves. Watermark *J Whatman* 1826. Lacks pl. [17] and [18]. Size 34.5 × 24 cm. Stitched into green paper wrappers.
On the front wrapper is the inscription: "Frederick Tatham [from *del.*] to Mr Bird on his attendance at the Funeral, Oct 23rd, 1831, being the day on which the widow of the author was Buried in Bunhill Fields church yard."
Formerly in the library of the late T. G. Arthur, Ayr; sold at Sotheby's, July 21, 1914 (lot 260, G. D. Smith, £72). Now in the library of Mr. H. E. Huntington.

G. 10 of the plates in proof condition on folio leaves, including pl. ii, 1, 2, 5, and 7, are contained in a miscellaneous collection of pages from Blake's works which is now in the Pierpont Morgan Library.

[H. 21 plates. Size given as 8°, uncut. Said to contain an alteration in Blake's hand.

A copy sold at Sotheby's, June 27, 1906 (£22 1s.). It was resold at Puttick and Simpson's on Aug. 1, 1906, and was then seen by Mr. T. J. Wise, who states that it was a tattered copy in grey paper wrappers. It is possibly to be identified with copy A above.]

Facsimile Reproductions: W. Muir, 1888 (no. 217, 1; incomplete); W. A. White, 1913 (no. 237).

Typ. Reprints: Gilchrist, i, 100-102; Swinburne, pp. 26-27; WMR, JS, EY, iii, WBY, LH, EJE, Sampson, 1905 and 1913; translated into German by von Taube, 1907 (no. 176).

54 [LAOCOON] יה & his two Sons Satan & Adam as they were copied from the Cherubim of Solomons Temple by three Rhodians & applied to Natural Fact or History of Ilium

[*On the pedestal of the group*] Drawn & Engraved by William Blake. [*about* 1818]

Description: A single plate, 27.5 × 23 cm., line engraving. In the centre is the Laocoön group, below which is inscribed the title given above. Over the head of the central figure is the word: "Ophiouchos," * in Greek characters, and above this again: "The Angel of the Divine Presence." The two serpents are named "Good" and "Evil." The whole of the space surrounding the group is filled with a series of sentences, chiefly concerning Art and the Imagination, which are engraved in all directions wherever Blake could find room.

Note: The central group was no doubt engraved from the drawing, now in the possession of Mr. W. Graham Robertson, which Blake made from a cast in the antique school at the Royal Academy.† This drawing was done in 1815, and in the same year Blake made a small engraving from it to illustrate an article in Ree's *Cyclopædia* (see no. 132). In the present engraving, which was probably executed about 1818, the same year as *On Homer's Poetry* (no. 50), the Laocoön group is invested by Blake with a symbolical meaning, and the sentences surrounding it epitomize his philosophy. The engraving was not known to Gilchrist or W. M. Rossetti, but it is described by Mr. Russell (*Engravings*, p. 94). Only a single impression of the print is at present known to exist.

* *i.e.,* "Serpent-holder," a constellation which is mentioned again by Blake in *Milton*, pl. 37, l. 50.
† See Gilchrist, i, 297.

LAOCOÖN

Line engraving, about 1818

Copy: A single leaf without watermark. Printed in black. Uncoloured. Size 38 × 27.5 cm.

Formerly in the Linnell collection; sold at Christie's, March 15, 1918, together with *On Homer's Poetry*, copy B, and *The Ghost of Abel*, copy B (lot 199, Quaritch, 36 gns.). Now in my own possession.

Facsimile Reproductions: EY, iii (much reduced), and in the present work (slightly reduced).

Typ. Reprints: EJE, i, 433; Russell, *Engravings*, pp. 95-96; Sampson, 1913.

55

> # ILLUSTRATIONS
> ## OF THE
> # 𝔅𝔬𝔬𝔨 𝔬𝔣 𝔍𝔬𝔟,
> ### IN TWENTY-ONE PLATES, INVENTED AND ENGRAVED BY
> # WILLIAM BLAKE,
> *Author of Designs to " Blair's Grave," "Young's Night Thoughts," &c.*
>
> ## 𝔏𝔬𝔫𝔡𝔬𝔫:
> PUBLISHED BY THE AUTHOR, 3, FOUNTAIN COURT, STRAND, AND
> MR. J. LINNELL, 6, CIRENCESTER PLACE, FITZROY SQUARE.
>
> ### MARCH, 1826.
>
> *Prints £*   *Proofs £*

Engraved Title: ספר איוב / Illustrations of / The / Book / of / Job / Invented & Engraved / by William Blake / 1825

Description: Engraved title and 21 pl. (numbered 1-21) = 22 plates, about 19 × 15 cm., line and stipple engraving, usually uncoloured, printed in black on one side only of separate leaves.

Plates:

[i]. Title-page, *Illustrations*, etc., with a design of angels.
1. Job and his family praising God.
2. Satan before the Lord.
3. The destruction of Job's sons and daughters.
4. "And there came a Messenger unto Job."
5. "Then went Satan forth from the presence of the Lord."
6. Satan smiting Job with boils.
7. Job and his friends. "And when they lifted up their eyes afar off and knew him not they lifted up their voice and wept."
8. "Let the day perish wherein I was born."
9. The vision of Eliphaz.
10. "The just upright man is laughed to scorn."
11. Job's terrific dreams.
12. Elihu's intervention.
13. "Then the Lord answered Job out of the whirlwind."
14. "When the morning stars sang together, and all the Sons of God shouted for joy."
15. Behemoth and Leviathan.
16. Satan's fall from Heaven.
17. Job with his wife and friends in the presence of God.
18. Job's sacrifice for his friends.
19. "Everyone also gave him a piece of money."
20. Job and his three daughters.
21. Job and his family praising God with music.

In the centre of each plate is a rectangular design, about 13 × 10 cm., surrounded by a symbolical border containing quotations from the Book of Job. The plate-mark measures about 22 × 17 cm. Each plate is signed *W Blake invenit & sculpᵗ*, or with some abbreviation of this. At the bottom each plate is lettered: *London Published as the Act directs March 8: 1825 by William Blake Nᵒ 3 Fountain Court Strand*, with the exception of pl. 1, which has been erroneously dated 1828.

Note: This series of engravings represents Blake's most widely known achievement. The original series * of water-colour designs was the last work bought by his patron, Thomas Butts. A second set and the engravings after them were commissioned by John Linnell, and the agreement made between Blake and Linnell has been preserved; it runs as follows:

March 25, 1823—Mem. of agreement between W. B. and J. L. W. B. to

* Afterwards in the Crewe collection and sold at Sotheby's, March, 1903 (Sabin, £5,600).

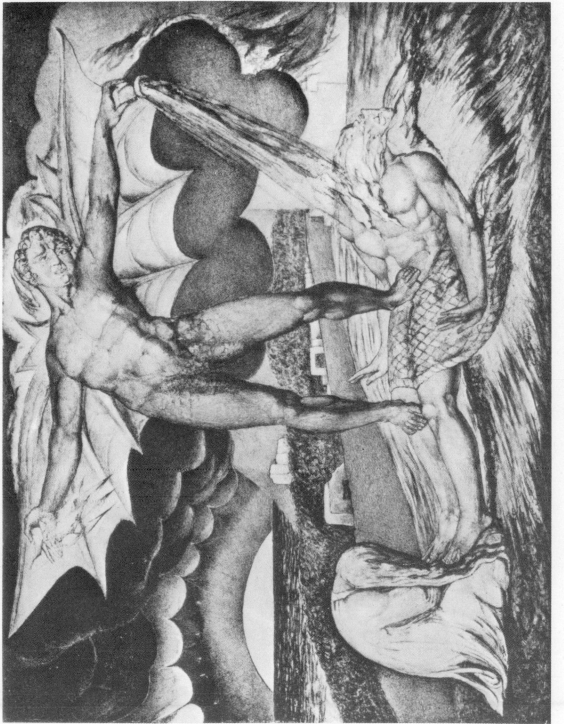

SATAN SMITING JOB WITH BOILS

Tempera, about 1820

"*WHEN THE MORNING STARS SANG TOGETHER*"
Pencil Sketch for the Engraving, about 1825

engrave the set of plates from his designs to Job, in number 20, for J. L.   J. L. to pay W. B. £5 per plate, part before, and the remainder when the plates are finished. Also, J. L. to pay Mr. B. £100 out of the profits of the work as the receipts will admit of it.   J. L. to find copper-plates.

W. B., J. L.

Blake was therefore paid £100 for the plates, and, although no profits resulted, Linnell paid Blake an additional £50 between March, 1823, and Oct. 1825.   Blake's receipt for the £150 is dated July 14, 1826, and states that the money was paid "for the copyright and plates (22 in number) of the Job, published March, 1825, by William Blake, author." *   The series of water-colour designs, the reduced pencil sketches † which Blake made for the engravings, and the copper-plates were, until 1918, in the possession of the Linnell family, who issued a few series of prints up to recent times.   The actual date of issue was March, 1826, as stated on the outer label, and not March 8, 1825, as on the plates.   It has been stated on the authority of John Linnell, jun., that "the proofs were published at 10 guineas the set, and the "prints at 5 guineas the set, bound in cardboard covers of terra-cotta colour, with white "labels pasted in the middle, upon which the price is written in pencil." ‡   On the other hand, such copies in original boards as I have seen have been marked: "Prints £3.3.0 Proofs £6.6.0."

At the sale of the Linnell collection at Christie's on March 15, 1918, the water-colour designs were sold for £3,990 (Sabin), and the pencil sketches for £504 (Carfax; now in the possession of Mr. T. H. Riches).   Eighteen proof sets on India paper and fifty in print state were sold to various buyers.   The original copper-plates have been deposited by the Linnell trustees in the British Museum.

The existing prints show several states of the engravings, the main divisions of which may be classified as follows:

i. Proofs of the central design alone before the addition of borders and inscriptions. Examples in B.M. Print Room and in the Linnell collection.

ii. Proofs of the complete designs unfinished and without any imprint.   These proofs show many interesting variations.   The paper on which they are printed has a watermark of an open device surmounted by a T.   A complete set is in the possession of Mr. T. H. Riches.

iii. Proofs with imprint: *Published as the Act directs March 8: 1825 by J. Linnell N 6 Cirencester Place Fitzroy Square*, or some variation of this.   Examples in the Linnell collection.

iv. Proofs on India paper with imprint as given above.   The plates are printed

* See Story's *Life of Linnell*, i, 169-170.
† One of these is here reproduced by permission of Mr. T. H. Riches.
‡ Ellis, p. 409.

on leaves measuring about 43 × 32 cm., and bearing the watermark *J Whatman Turkey Mill* 1825. The plates are marked *Proof* at the lower right-hand corner.*

v. Proofs similar to state iv, but printed on smaller paper.

vi. Ordinary issue on leaves measuring about 40 × 28 cm., with watermark *J Whatman* 1825; bound in boards with the label reproduced above pasted on the front cover. Some copies have paper watermarked *J Whatman Turkey Mill* 1825 †; in others the paper has no watermark at all. In all these the word *Proof* has been erased.

For further accounts of these designs see Gilchrist, i, 327-336, and Russell. *Engravings*, pp. 103-115. An elaborate study of the designs and an explanation of their symbolism will be found in *Blake's Vision of the Book of Job* by J. H. Wicksteed, 1910 (no. 361).

Facsimiles: Gilchrist, ii, 1863 and 1880; Methuen, 1903 (no. 227); Lane, 1907 (no. 233); Gowans and Gray, 1912 (no. 236) [all reduced]. Osgood, 1875 (no. 211); Dent, 1902 (no. 225); Methuen, 1906 (no. 230) [all the size of the originals]. Evans, 1914 (no. 238) [enlarged].

56

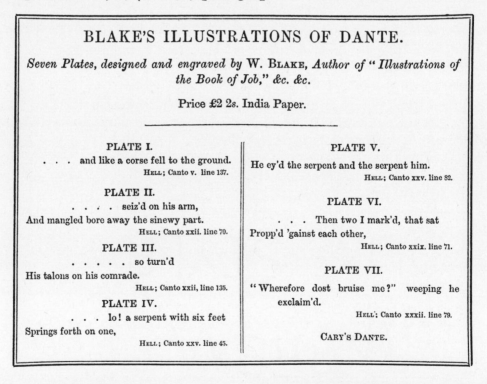

BLAKE'S ILLUSTRATIONS OF DANTE.

Seven Plates, designed and engraved by W. Blake, *Author of " Illustrations of the Book of Job," &c. &c.*

Price £2 2s. India Paper.

PLATE I.

. . . and like a corse fell to the ground.
Hell; Canto v. line 137.

PLATE II.

. . . . seiz'd on his arm,
And mangled bore away the sinewy part.
Hell; Canto xxii. line 70.

PLATE III.

. . . . . so turn'd
His talons on his comrade.
Hell; Canto xxii, line 135.

PLATE IV.

. . . lo! a serpent with six feet
Springs forth on one,
Hell; Canto xxv. line 45.

PLATE V.

He ey'd the serpent and the serpent him.
Hell; Canto xxv. line 82.

PLATE VI.

. . . Then two I mark'd, that sat
Propp'd 'gainst each other,
Hell; Canto xxix. line 71.

PLATE VII.

"Wherefore dost bruise me?" weeping he
exclaim'd.
Hell; Canto xxxii. line 79.

Cary's Dante.

* A set of India paper proofs is in existence, which has been tinted, possibly by Blake himself, with water-colours; it was formerly in Sir F. Burton's collection. Offered by Mr. Tregaskis, cat. 493, 1901.

† *e.g.*, George Richmond's copy, now in the possession of Mr. Frank Rinder.

THE CIRCLE OF THE FALSIFIERS, Dante's "Inferno," Canto XXIX, line 71

Line Engraving, 1826

Description: 7 unnumbered plates, line engraving; the engraved surface measures about 24 × 33 cm., and the impress of each plate about 28 × 36 cm.; printed in black on separate leaves about 34 × 54 cm. Issued as loose leaves together with the above label, or bound up as an oblong folio volume with the label pasted on to the outer cover.

Plates:

1. The Circle of the Lustful. Paolo and Francesca. Dante has swooned with pity. In the right-hand lower corner Blake has lightly engraved in reversed writing: *The Whirlwind of Lovers from Dante's Inferno Canto V*. He first began to engrave these words higher up, but not having had room has erased them.

2. The Circle of the Corrupt Officials. The Devils tormenting Ciampolo.

3. The same. The Devils mauling each other. The group in the background on the right-hand side has only been sketched in.

4. The Circle of the Thieves. Agnolo Brunnelleschi attacked by a six-footed serpent.

5. The same. Buoso Donati attacked by a serpent.

6. The Circle of the Falsifiers. Dante and Virgil are holding their noses because of the stench.

7. The Circle of the Traitors. Dante's foot striking Bocca degli Abati, who is frozen into the ice.

The plates bear no signature nor, except in the case of the first, any other lettering.

Note: Blake was engaged upon the engraving of the Dante plates at the time of his death, and these seven, some of them unfinished, were the only ones that he had been able to execute. The original water-colour designs number 98, most of them unfinished and many of them only just begun. The series was commissioned by Linnell, and Gilchrist states (i, 375) that Blake began the designs in 1824. According to more recent information received by E. J. Ellis from John Linnell, jun. (*The Real Blake*, p. 410), Linnell began his payments towards the end of the year 1825, and the last payment was made on Aug. 2, 1827. The same authority states that Blake received altogether £103 5s. 6d. for the designs and plates, and that Mrs. Blake received a further sum of about £26 after her husband's death. All the designs and plates were in the possession of the Linnell family until March, 1918, and they had issued only a very limited number of sets of the prints up to that date. On March 15, 1918, when the Linnell collection was put up to auction at Christie's, the original designs were sold for £7,665 (lot 148, "Martin"), and have now been distributed among several public galleries, including the British Museum, the National Gallery of British Art, the Ashmolean Museum, Oxford, and the Melbourne Art Galleries; the majority of the designs have been sent to Australia for the last-named gallery. At the same time eleven sets of the prints were sold to various buyers. The original copper-plates have been deposited by the Linnell trustees in the British Museum. The engravings, which are characterized by an extraordinary precision and delicacy of line, are executed in a freer style than those for the *Book of Job*. By the courtesy of Mr. J. I. Davis I have recently seen a series of the prints which has been finely painted with water-colours. It seems unlikely that the colouring was done by Blake himself, who was fully occupied up to the time of his death with the original water-colours and the engravings from them, but it may have been executed by Mrs. Blake. More probably, however, it was done by Birket Foster,* whose bookplate is pasted upon the verso of the first print.

It is related (*Literary Gazette*, 1827, no. 405) that at the age of sixty-six Blake began the study of Italian in order that he might read Dante in the original, a task which he accomplished. He makes several references to his designs in his letters to Linnell, as follows:

c. March, 1826. I am going on with Dante and please myself. (Russell, *Letters*, p. 213.)

2 July, 1826. I intend to bring with me . . . only my book of drawings from Dante, and one plate shut up in the book. (*ib.*, p. 215.)

Feb. 1827. I go on as I think improving my engravings of Dante more and more; and shall soon get proofs of these four which I have; and beg the favour of you to send me the two plates of Dante which you have, that I may finish them sufficiently to make show of colour and strength. (*ib.*, p. 219.)

c. March 1827. I am still far from recovered . . . Dante goes on the better, which is all I care about. Mr. Butts is to have a proof copy for three guineas; this is his own decision quite in character. (*ib.*, p. 221.)

25 April 1827. I am too much attached to Dante to think much of anything else. I have proved the six plates, and reduced the fighting devils ready for the copper. (*ib.*, p. 225.)

Crabb Robinson also refers twice to the Dante in his *Diary*:

Dec. 17, 1825. I found [him] at work on Dante. The book (Cary) and his sketches before him. He shewed me his designs . . . (Symons, p. 261).

Feb. 2, 1827. Götzenberger, the young painter from Germany, called on me, and I accompanied him to Blake. We look over Blake's Dante. Götzenberger seemed highly gratified by the designs . . . (*ib.*, p. 271).

In his *Reminiscences*, Feb. 26, 1852, he also remarks of the engravings that " they are in the hands of Linnell the painter, and, it has been suggested, are reserved " by him for publication when Blake has become an object of interest to a greater " number than he could be at this age " (Symons, p. 294); but he adds later on, March 22, 1852, " Linnell has not found the market I took for granted he would

* Myles Birket Foster, water-colourist, 1825-1899.

seek for Blake's works" (*ib.*, p. 306). Linnell is, further, entirely cleared of Crabb Robinson's imputations by a letter written by him to Lord Egremont. Linnell sends his lordship a copy of "a work by the late Mr Blake," probably the *Illustrations of the Book of Job*, and at the same time offers him the Dante drawings. "Many," he writes, "are in an unfinished state, but the greater number are, and are more power-" fully, coloured and finished than he usually did. They were done for Mr Linnell in "return for moneys advanced to Mr Blake when he had no other resources. The sum, "however, was inconsiderable, compared to the value of the drawings; and Mr Linnell's "object being only to relieve the necessities of his friend as far as he was able, he is "now willing to part with the drawings for the benefit of his widow, and if he can "obtain a price something more adequate, he will engage to hand over the difference "to Mrs Blake." (Story's *Life of Linnell*, i, 245.)

A list of the original designs is given in Rossetti's annotated catalogue, Gilchrist, ii, 227. A series of articles by W. B. Yeats on "William Blake and his Illustrations to the Divine Comedy," with reproductions, appeared in *The Savoy*, 1896 (no. 518), and was reprinted in *Ideas of Good and Evil*, London, 1903 (no. 331). No facsimile reproductions of the engravings have ever been issued, but the entire series of water-colour designs is now in process of reproduction for the National Art Collections Fund, and will be issued to subscribers.

G. *WORKS LOST OR CONJECTURAL*

57 THE BIBLE OF HELL, in Nocturnal Visions collected. Vol. I, Lambeth [? about 1793]

Note: This title is written on the back of a drawing in title-page form, and is mentioned in EY, i, 46. The work is also referred to by Blake in *The Marriage of Heaven and Hell*, pl. 24, where he wrote: "I have also The Bible of Hell which the "world shall have whether they will or no." Nothing further is known of any work of this name, but Dr. Sampson (1913, p. xxx) points out that the date of the title given above cannot be earlier than 1793, the year of Blake's removal to Lambeth.

58 THE HISTORY OF ENGLAND [? about 1793]

Note: No copy of this work is known to exist, but at the end of the list of works offered for sale in Blake's prospectus of Oct. 10, 1793 (no. 37), are the two items following:

"9. The History of England, a small book of Engravings. Price 3*s*.
"10. The Gates of Paradise, a small book of Engravings. Price 3*s*."

It may therefore be supposed that *The History of England*, if it was ever actually issued, resembled *The Gates of Paradise* (no. 52). It is probable, as was suggested by Dr. Sampson, that the rough draft of a list of twenty-six subjects for a history of England, written on page 116 of the *Rossetti MS.*, gives some idea of the contents of the missing work. This list is printed in Sampson, 1905, pp. 366-367, and in Russell, *Engravings*, p. 66.

59 FOR CHILDREN : THE GATES OF HELL [? about 1793]

Note: W. M. Rossetti, in his annotated catalogue (Gilchrist, ii, 269, no. 135), refers to a slight sketch inscribed as above. The drawing and inscription, which is written out by Blake in pencil as for a title-page, formerly belonged to Frederick Tatham, and are now in the possession of Mr. W. Graham Robertson. If a work with this title ever existed it has been lost; or it may only have been projected. In any case it was evidently intended as a companion work to *For Children: The Gates of Paradise*, which was first issued in 1793 (see no. 52).

60 OUTHOON [? 1793]

Note: No copy of this work is known, but Gilchrist (i, 410) states that it occurs in a list of works by Blake offered for sale by his widow to Mr. James Ferguson, an artist of Tynemouth, with whom Gilchrist was in correspondence. The work was described in this list as follows: " Outhoon. 12 Plates, 6 inches, more or less. Price £2. 2s. 0."

Gilchrist (ii, 284) adds the following note: " I have never seen a copy of this, " nor been able to find anyone who has. Even Mr. Linnell had never heard of it. " But the above must be taken, I think, as indisputable evidence that such a book " does or did exist. An ingenious friend suggested that ' Outhoun ' might be another " title for *Visions of the Daughters of Albion*, in which one Oothoon plays a prominent " part. But the number of plates in the two not corresponding decisively negatives " such a supposition."

There is no evidence which can help in assigning a date to this work, except the similarity of its title to the name in the *Visions of the Daughters of Albion*, 1793. It is possible that a copy of this work will eventually be found.

61 **THE BOOK OF ENOCH** [after 1796]

Note: In the Linnell collection was a set of five large sheets, 52.5 × 37 cm., bearing pencil sketches of naked figures. At the top of each sheet is written *The Book of Enoch*, and one sheet has in addition at the side *N° 26 next at p.* 43. Two of the sheets have a watermark dated 1796. The designs are mentioned in W. M. Rossetti's annotated catalogue (Gilchrist, ii, 270), and they were sold with the Linnell collection at Christie's, March 15, 1918 (lot 161, Parsons, 25 gns.). There is no other reference to a work of this name, but the indications on these designs suggest that *The Book of Enoch* may have been a projected work, and that these five designs represent only a small portion of the whole series. An alternative explanation may be that Blake began in the last years of his life a series of illustrations to the apocalyptic book of the same name, of which a translation from the Ethiopic appeared in 1821.

62 [A WORK ON ART. About 1809]

Note: In a letter to George Cumberland, dated Dec. 18, 1808, Blake wrote: " I " have the satisfaction to inform you that I have myself begun to print an account of " my various inventions in Art, for which I have procured a publisher, and am deter- " mined to pursue the plan of publishing, that I may get printed without disarranging "my time, which in future must alone be designing and painting. When I have got "my work printed I will send it you first of anybody." (Letter 62.)

In his advertisement, dated May 15, 1809, of his exhibition, he again refers to this work: "The Art [of Fresco Painting] has been lost: I have recovered it. How "this was done, will be told, together with the whole Process, in a Work on Art, now "in the Press." (See no. 28.)

Another reference, possibly to the same work, is to be found in the *Descriptive Catalogue*, 1809: "Let the works of modern Artists since Rubens' time witness the "villainy of some one at that time, who first brought Oil Painting into general opinion "and practice: since which we have never had a Picture painted that could show itself "by the side of an earlier production. Whether Rubens or Vandyke, or both, were "guilty of this villainy, is to be inquired in another work on Painting. . . ."

The first two references are sufficiently definite to make it probable that this work was at any rate written, but, if it was ever printed, no copy has yet been discovered, nor does the manuscript appear to have survived.

63 ADVERTIZEMENT TO BLAKE'S CANTERBURY PILGRIMS from Chaucer, containing anecdotes of Artists [about 1810]

Note: The above title is taken from an undated entry on p. 56 of the *Rossetti MS.* as follows: "This day is Publish'd Advertizement to Blake's Canterbury Pilgrims "from Chaucer, containing anecdotes of Artists."

The date given above is assigned to it by Dr. Sampson owing to its position in the MS., and to the fact that the engraving of *The Canterbury Pilgrims* was published in 1810. If the publication actually took place it seems that no copy has survived. The text is found written in scattered fragments on pp. 1-67 of the *Rossetti MS.*, and on p. 65 is another title: *Chaucer's Canterbury Pilgrims. Being a complete Index of Human Characters as they exist age after age.* It is usually known by the title of *Public Address*, given to it by D. G. Rossetti. EY state (i, 232), apparently on MS. authority, that the price of the publication was 6*d.*, but this is probably an error. This *Advertizement* is distinct from the short *Prospectus* (no. 31) which was published May 15, 1809.

Typ. Reprints: Gilchrist, ii, 164, with title *Public Address*, though inaccurately, and with the fragments arbitrarily arranged by the editor; Ellis, *The Real Blake*, pp. 302-312.

64 VISION *or* VERSION OF GENESIS. [about 1825]

Note: This work is referred to by Crabb Robinson, under the date Feb. 18, 1826, in his *Diary and Reminiscences* (see Symons, pp. 267 and 302) as follows: " He " showed me his Vision [*altered to* Version *in the Reminiscences*] (for so it may be " called) of Genesis—' as understood by a Christian Visionary,' in which in a style " resembling the Bible the spirit is given. He read a passage at random. It was " striking."

Ellis also notes (*The Real Blake*, p. 432) that the prose fragment on p. 86 of the *Rossetti MS.* (II, 155), beginning: " The Combats of Good & Evil is eating of the " Tree of Knowledge . . ." may have belonged to this work. The fragment is crossed out in pencil, as if it had been copied elsewhere. It is, on the other hand, possible that no work of this name ever existed, Crabb Robinson having substituted this, to him, more intelligible title for that of an earlier illuminated book, such as *The Book of Urizen.*

65 THE BOOK OF MOONLIGHT [date unknown]

Note: This work is known only by the reference on p. 46 of the *Rossetti MS.* (II, 156) as follows: " Delicate Hands & Heads will never appear While Titian &c " as in the Book of Moonlight, p. 5." This statement is sufficiently definite, and it is probable that the work existed, at any rate in MS. It may have been one of the works supposed to have been destroyed by Tatham.

66 BARRY: A POEM [date unknown]

Note: This work is known only from a reference on p. 60 of the *Rossetti MS.* (I, 136). At the end of the piece beginning: " I askèd my Dear Friend Orator Prig," and ending: " But look yonder—that house is the house of Rembrandt! &c.," Blake has written the words: " to come in Barry: a Poem." Dr. Sampson suggests that another piece on p. 61 of the *Rossetti MS.* (I, 137), beginning: " O dear Mother " Outline! of wisdom most sage . . ." may be a continuation of the first fragment.

II. BOOK ILLUSTRATIONS

BIBLIOGRAPHICAL PREFACE

THE beginning of Blake's career as a book illustrator dates from 1771, the year in which he was apprenticed to James Basire, the engraver, who worked in Great Queen Street, Lincoln's Inn Fields. During the seven years of his apprenticeship he must have worked upon many plates which do not bear his name and cannot now be identified. Some of these have been conjecturally attributed to him, but his only contribution of which we have direct evidence is in Gough's *Sepulchral Monuments*, published in 1786; I have made no attempt to seek out the others, as the uncertain value of the results does not seem to me to justify the labour that the completion of the task would entail. Even during his apprenticeship and immediately afterwards Blake had begun to express his originality in the separate engravings dealt with by Mr. Russell, and from 1788 onwards in the illustrations to his own writings described in the earlier pages of the present work. It was, however, in keeping with his character that he did not always find it a congenial occupation to illustrate the books or compositions of other people whose work was on a lower plane than his own, and consequently his original designs were sometimes unsuccessful.

His earliest original book illustration is the frontispiece to Commins' *Elegy set to Music*, 1786, and he published no more until 1791, when he made a number of designs for Mary Wollstonecraft's *Original Stories from Real Life*. During the succeeding years he made his ambitious series of water-colour drawings for Young's *Night Thoughts*, the engravings from some of these being published in 1797, but in doing so he somewhat over-taxed his powers of invention, and the book was abandoned after the issue of the first part, containing forty-three plates. To the same period belong his designs for Gray's *Poems*, but none of these was engraved, and so they do not come within the scope of this section, though they have been included in Section I among the manuscripts. In 1796 he also made three illustrations for a translation of Bürger's *Leonora*. From 1800 to 1805 his book illustrations were done chiefly to please his patron, William Hayley, and some of them were evidently made under constraint. The best of this period are his head- and tail-pieces for the ballad of *Little Tom the Sailor*. After freeing himself from Hayley's influence he designed in 1806 a frontispiece for Dr. Malkin's *Father's Memoirs of his Child*, and at the same time was making at Cromek's instigation the well-known series of designs for Blair's *Grave*, published in 1808. In 1812 he engraved the frontispiece for a small reprint of Chaucer's *Canterbury Pilgrims*, which appears to have been intended to promote the sale of his larger engraving of this subject. About 1816 he made drawings and engravings for a catalogue of Wedgwood's hardware, but it is only the demands of consistent bibliography that compel the inclusion of these plates among Blake's own designs. At last, in 1821, in illustrating a modern imitation of an ancient author, Blake found his best means of expression as a book illustrator, and the woodcuts for Dr. Thornton's *Virgil* atone for any partial failures of previous years. In 1825 he executed another very beautiful engraving for *Remember Me*, an obscure "annual" edited by Dr. Thornton. Finally, after Blake's death, John Linnell made some engravings from his drawings of "The Ghost of a Flea," which appeared in Varley's *Zodiacal Physiognomy*, 1828.

This completes the account of those of Blake's original book illustrations that found a publisher, and it is evident that some of them do not greatly add to his reputation as an artist. Even the illustrations for Blair's *Grave*, splendid as they are, have lost much of their value by having been transferred to the copper-plates by the hand of another. Nevertheless, Blake's potentialities as a book illustrator were immense, and it is due to lack of opportunities rather than to lack of genius that he was not more successful. Had he been commissioned to engrave his designs for *Paradise Lost* and Milton's other poems, or some of his many illustrations of the Bible, for publication in editions of those works, then he must have come to be regarded as one of the greatest of book illustrators, even though his earlier style of engraving had not allowed his plates to reach quite the same level of achievement as he attained at the end of his life in the *Illustrations to the Book of Job*, described in the previous section.

It is probable that, in addition to these greater works, he made other book illustrations which were not engraved; an exceedingly good example of these is to be found in the sepia wash drawing here reproduced by permission of Mr. W. Bateson, F.R.S. The subject has not been identified with

UNPUBLISHED BOOK ILLUSTRATION
Sepia Drawing, date unknown

certainty, but it seems probable that it was intended to illustrate an incident in *The Vicar of Wakefield*.

Although Blake did not find much outlet for his originality in book illustrations he nevertheless found a ready market for his technical skill as a journeyman engraver, and it is with the work done in this capacity for the publishers that the present section is largely concerned. Blake had served his apprenticeship with conscientious application, and he was afterwards as good as the best engravers of the period, and a great deal better than most. An opportunity of comparing Blake's work with that of thirty-two of his contemporaries is afforded by the volume of plates in illustration of Shakespeare issued by Boydell in 1803, which is here described for the first time. Blake's plate after a painting by Opie is almost, if not quite, the best in the book. Joseph Johnson, bookseller in St. Paul's Churchyard, was his most frequent employer, but he worked also for more than a dozen other publishers, and he produced for them altogether considerably more than 200 engraved plates. The great majority of these were executed during the period 1779-1806, after which he applied himself almost entirely to his own compositions. The plates described here are not always signed, but they can nearly all be regarded as his work with some degree of confidence. Many other engravings in books, such as those in illustration of Mrs. Trimmer's histories for children, have been attributed to him, but without any show of evidence or even of probability. A motive for fathering upon Blake the inferior productions of his rivals is to be found in the increased value which any book, however dull or unimportant, acquires from the association with it of his name. One book, however, containing plates which have been persistently attributed to Blake by generations of booksellers, is neither dull nor unimportant, and must be mentioned here. This is Lamb's *Tales from Shakespeare*, 2 vols., 8°, 1807. The illustrations, though they have some qualities suggesting Blake's work, were certainly not designed by him and are, indeed, known to have been done by William Mulready. By whom they were engraved it is difficult to say, but an examination of the technique employed does not support the view that they were executed by Blake. Mr. Russell, who gives at the end of his work a brief list of books containing plates wrongly attributed to Blake, concurs in this belief.

It has been my aim in this section to provide a complete bibliographical record of all the books containing engravings which are, in my opinion, to be regarded as Blake's work. Most of the prints have been already described by Mr. Russell in his book on *The Engravings of William Blake*, 1912, to which constant reference is made in the present work, but it was not part of his plan to deal with the more bibliographical details of the books containing them. Several of the engravings and a number of the books were not known to Mr. Russell in 1912, so that the present work gives a more complete record than is to be found elsewhere. Mr. Russell's book will remain the chief authority for the separate engravings which do not fall within the scope of this bibliography, though several more, as was inevitable, have been discovered since his book was published. It is probable that, as time passes, other books containing authentic plates by Blake will also be discovered, though these are unlikely to be of much importance.

In some of the books here described Blake's share is of so trivial a nature that they may be thought to receive more space and attention than they merit. Yet it is remarkable how often Blake has added something of his own personality and feeling to these engravings, though working, as he sometimes must have done, with contempt for the subject and with indignation in his mind. In any case, everything which can be authenticated as his work has a biographical interest, and therefore may not be neglected. A possible source of confusion lies in the fact that there may have existed at the same time another engraver of Blake's name, who worked in Exchange Alley, Cornhill. One book with a plate so signed is included here with a warning annotation, since proof of the identity of this other obscurer Blake is still to be obtained.

A. *DESIGNED AND ENGRAVED BY BLAKE*

67 SEPULCHRAL MONUMENTS IN GREAT BRITAIN . . . from the Norman Conquest to the Seventeenth Century . . . Part I. Containing the First Four Centuries . . . [By Richard Gough, F.S.A.] London, . . . MDCCLXXXVI.

Collation: F°. Part I, pp. [iv] + 14 + [ii] + cciv + [ii] + 78, 3 leaves inserted between pp. 15-16, 32-33, and 36-37. Part II, pp. [ii] + 79-265.

Illustrations: Eighty-three plates and many smaller engravings in the text. Some of the plates were drawn and engraved by Blake during his apprenticeship to Basire.

   i. Pl. xxii, p. 57. *Portrait of Henry III. from his Monument.*

   ii. Pl. xxiii*, p. 63. *Portrait of Queen Eleanor from her Monument.*

   iii. Pl. xlix, p. 125. *Portrait of Queen Philippa from her Monument.*

   iv. Pl. lv, p. 139. *Portrait of Edward III. from his Monument.*

   v. Pl. lxiii, p. 165. *Portrait of Richard II. from his Monument.*

   vi. Pl. lxiv, p. 167. *Portrait of Anne Queen of Richard II. from her Monument.*

At the top of each plate are the numbers of the plate and page. Lettered below: *Portrait* etc. / *Basire del. & sc.*, or some variation of this. Plate-mark about 40 × 28.5 cm.

Note: Basire was engaged in executing plates for this publication during the years of Blake's apprenticeship, from 1771 to 1778. It is related by Dr. Malkin* that, owing to disagreements with his fellow apprentices, Blake was sent out to draw the tombs and effigies in Westminster Abbey and other churches in London, and the results of these labours are partly represented by the six plates mentioned above. It is further recorded by J. T. Smith that the drawing of the " Portrait of Queen Philippa " was particularly mentioned by Stothard as Blake's, and with praise.† The engraving of this and of the other Portraits is characteristic and may with certainty be attributed to Blake; they are on a large scale, only the head and shoulders of the subject being represented. Each Portrait is preceded by an engraving of the whole monument, and it is probable that the drawings for these, too, were made by Blake; Malkin also mentions that Blake made drawings of the tomb of Aymer de Valence, and probably

---

* *A Father's Memoirs of his Child*, 1806, pp. xx-xxi.   † *Nollekens and his Times*, 1828, ii, 471.

many others were engraved from Blake's work. With the exception, however, of the Portraits, none of the plates show the characteristics of Blake's style of engraving, and they have therefore not been included in the above list. In vol. II of this work, published in 1796, are some further Portraits, evidently done in imitation of Blake's earlier plates, but executed much less effectively by another hand.

The National Gallery Exhibition, 1913, included two water-colour drawings, lent by the Society of Antiquaries, of tombs in Westminster Abbey,* which it was suggested were Blake's work; but in Mr. Russell's opinion they were not actually done by Blake, though they may have been executed from his sketches. Mr. Russell also records (*Engravings*, pp. 191-3) other books containing prints signed by Basire, which may be Blake's work; these attributions are, however, conjectural, and the books are not included here.

68   *Heading on second leaf*: AN ELEGY, SET TO MUSIC by Thos Commins, Organist of Penzance, Cornwall.   London.   Printed & Sold by J. Fentum, No 78, corner Salisbury St Strand [1786]

Collation: 33 × 24 cm., uncut.   Engraved frontispiece, verso blank + 5 engraved plates of music; 4 leaves.

Frontispiece: An oval engraving surrounded by a fillet of rushes.   The design represents the return of a sailor to his wife and child; he is leaping from the bow of a small boat into the arms of his wife, who is waiting with the child on the shore. Lettered:

W. Blake delt & Sculpt

| *The shatter'd bark from adverse winds* | *And when the storms of life are past* |
| *Rest in this peaceful haven finds* | *Hope drops her anchor here at last.* |

Publish'd July 1. 1786 by J. Fentum No 78 Corner of Salisbury Street Strand.

The engraving measures 17.5 × 14 cm., the plate-mark 28 × 20 cm.

Note: This early and characteristic design appears to have been unknown to Gilchrist. The complete publication is very rare. The original sketch for the design was in 1913 in the hands of Messrs. Robson.

Copies: B.M. Print Room (the design has been tinted). A copy formerly in my own possession is now in the library of Mr. W. E. Moss. An example of the design without the *Elegy* was formerly in the possession of Mr. A. G. B. Russell.

* Nat. Gal. Cat., 1913, item 113.

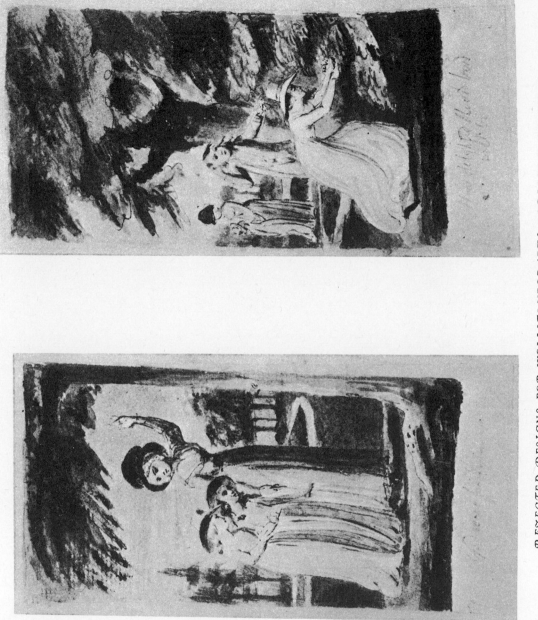

REJECTED DESIGNS FOR WOLLSTONECRAFT'S "ORIGINAL STORIES"

Sepia Drawings, about 1791

69 ORIGINAL STORIES FROM REAL LIFE; with Conversations, Calculated to Regulate the Affections, and Form the Mind to Truth and Goodness. By Mary Wollstonecraft. London: Printed for J. Johnson, No. 72, St. Paul's Church-Yard. 1791.

Collation: A⁶, B-H¹², I⁶; 96 leaves. Pp. viii Title, Preface, Introduction + [iv] Contents + 177 + [3] A Catalogue of Books.

Illustrations: Six plates designed and engraved by Blake.

i. Frontispiece. *Look what a fine morning it is.—Insects, Birds, & Animals, are all enjoying existence.* Mrs. Mason, with Mary and Caroline on either side of her.

ii. Facing p. 24. *The Dog strove to attract his attention.—He said, Thou wilt not leave me!* A man in a prison cell is gazing at the dead bodies of his two children, while a dog is licking his hand.

iii. Facing p. 74. *Indeed we are very happy!—*Mrs. Mason with Mary and Caroline in the cottage of a Sailor, who is telling the story of his life.

iv. Facing p. 94. *Be calm, my child, remember that you must do all the good you can the present day.* Mrs. Mason, with her two girls, looking at a ruined mansion.

v. Facing p. 114. *Trying to trace the sound, I discovered a little hut, rudely built.* Mrs. Mason, under a starry sky is approaching a hut in which is a man playing on a harp.

vi. Facing p. 173. *Œconomy & Self-denial are necessary, in every station, to enable us to be generous.* Mrs. Mason and her two children visiting a poor family in a garret.

Each plate is lettered: [*Quotation*] | *Published by J. Johnson, Septr 1, 1791.* The frontispiece is also signed: *Blake d. & sc.* Plate-mark about 16 × 9 cm.

Note: Ten sepia drawings were made by Blake to illustrate the *Original Stories*, but four of them were not engraved; the drawings were formerly in Gilchrist's possession, and one of the unpublished designs was reproduced as a wood engraving in the *Life*, i, 90. They were afterwards in the collection of H. Buxton Forman, and were sold with his library at the Anderson Galleries, New York, March 15, 1920. They are now in the collection of Mr. A. E. Newton, by whose permission two of the unpublished designs are reproduced here.

A New Edition of the *Original Stories* was issued by Johnson in 1796 (A⁶, B-G¹², H⁶; pp. viii + [iv] + 155 + [1]) with the same plates retouched. The book has been recently reprinted (Oxford, 1906; see no. 231) with reproductions of five of Blake's plates. The stories were first published in 1788, but without Blake's illustrations.

70 **THE COMPLAINT, AND THE CONSOLATION;** or, Night Thoughts by Edward Young, LL.D.

—*fatis contraria fata rependens.* Virg.

London: Printed by R. Noble, for R. Edwards, No. 142, Bond-Street, MDCCXCVII.

Collation: 43 × 33 cm., uncut; 56 separate leaves, no signatures. Pp. viii Title, Advertisement + [2] Frontispiece to Night the First + 95 + [2] Explanation of the engravings.

Illustrations: Forty-three engravings designed and executed by Blake. The designs are on the pages of the book, surrounding the text, which is enclosed in a ruled panel, 23.5 × 17 cm. The following brief descriptions of the designs are based on those given on the sheet of explanation of the engravings:

    i. Frontispiece to Night the First: Death gathering up a family to immortality.

    ii. Page 1: Sleep with his wand shedding his influence on a flock of sheep.

    iii. Page 4: A sleeper and the various antics of his dreaming soul.

    iv. Page 7: Death, with his bell, summoning a man from sleep to the grave.

    v. Page 8: Death plucking down the Sun.

    vi. Page 10: An evil genius, with two phials, scattering germs of disease over a shepherd and his flock.

    vii. Page 12: A man dying of a snake-bite beside his unheeding wife and child.

    viii. Page 13: Death with a dart about to strike a mother and her child.

    ix. Page 15: The poet, bound down by thorns and chains, lamenting to the midnight hours.

    x. Page 16: The poet with a lyre is striving upwards, but is held down by a chain.

    xi. Frontispiece to Night the Second, page 17: Time defending Friendship from the arrow of Death.

    xii. Page 19: An angel with a trumpet awakening a skeleton.

    xiii. Page 23: A man measuring an infant with the span of his hand.

    xiv. Page 24: Time creeping along with hidden wings.

    xv. Page 25: Time speeding away.

    xvi. Page 26: Time mowing down humanity with his scythe.

    xvii. Page 27: Conscience, as a recording angel, and a drunkard.

    xviii. Page 31: A good man conversing with his past hours.

    xix. Page 33: Belshazzar and the writing on the wall.

    xx. Page 35: A parent instructing his family.

DESIGN FOR YOUNG'S "NIGHT THOUGHTS"
Water-colour, about 1794

xxi. Page 37: The good Samaritan.

xxii. Page 40: Angels attending the deathbed of a righteous man.

xxiii. Page 41: His spirit conveyed by angels to heaven.

xxiv. Frontispiece to Night the Third, page 43: A female figure on a crescent, and a serpent with its tail in its mouth, emblem of eternity.

xxv. Page 46: Death throwing his pall over a nude female figure.

xxvi. Page 49: The poet presenting his daughter to the Sun in his chariot.

xxvii. Page 54: Darkness brooding over the river of death.

xxviii. Page 55: A mourner, beside a grave, reproved by an angel.

xxix. Page 57: Death striking at a group of drinkers.

xxx. Page 63: Death as the Prince of Peace.

xxxi. Frontispiece to Night the Fourth, page 65: The resurrection of Christ.

xxxii. Page 70: Death as a huntsman.

xxxiii. Page 72: The figures of Sense and Reason directing the poet through a doorway.

xxxiv. Page 73: Christ, with the emblems of torture, in the furnace of affliction.

xxxv. Page 75: The Sun hiding his face in his hands.

xxxvi. Page 80: The poet questioning the thunder.

xxxvii. Page 86: A figure in the clouds with one hand fixed in the sky, the other touching the earth.

xxxviii. Page 87: Christ instructing all ages and sexes.

xxxix. Page 88: Jacob wrestling with the angel.

xl. Page 90: Christ healing a sick man with a touch.

xli. Page 92: Faith writing down the dictates of Reason.

xlii. Page 93: Angels leaving an infidel in grief and wonder.

xliii. Page 95: The goddess Truth bursting forth in thunder and in flame.

All the plates except nos. i, ii, iii, vi, viii, xi, and xxxiv are signed: *inv & s | W.B.*; all except nos. vii, xii, xxi, xxiv, xxviii, xxix, xxx, xxxiv, xxxv, xxxvii, xxxviii, xl, xli, and xliii are lettered below: [*London*] *Pub^d* [*Pub*] [*date*] *by R. Edwards, N° 142, New Bond Street*. The majority of these are dated *June* 27, 1796; but no. x is dated *June* 21, 1796; nos. xxv, xxxi, xxxiii, xxxvi, xxxix, and xlii are dated *Jan.* 1, 1797; no. xxii is dated *Jan.* 4, 1797; and nos. xxiii and xxvii are dated *March* 22, 1797. Plate-mark about 41 × 32.5 cm.

Note: A very rare prospectus, a copy of which was in Mr. Dobell's possession in 1914, was issued by the publisher and runs as follows:

Edwards's
Magnificent Edition
of
Young's Night Thoughts.

Early in JUNE will be published, by subscription, part the first of a splendid edition of this favourite work, elegantly·printed, and illustrated with forty very spirited engravings from original drawings by BLAKE.

These engravings are in a perfectly new style of decoration, surrounding the text which they are designed to elucidate.

The work is printed in atlas-sized quarto, and the subscription for the whole, making four parts, with one hundred and fifty engravings, is five guineas;—one to be paid at the time of subscribing, and one on the delivery of each part;—The price will be considerably advanced to non-subscribers.

Specimens may be seen at Edwards's, No. 142 New Bond-Street; at Mr Edwards' Pall-Mall; and at the Historic Gallery, Pall-Mall: where subscriptions are received.

The venture did not meet with success, and these forty-three designs of very varying merit are the only part of the original series of 537 coloured designs that was ever engraved. One copy of the *Night Thoughts* was richly coloured by Blake for Thomas Butts,* and others coloured by him are said to exist, but several that I have seen are feebly tinted, and were probably done by Mrs. Blake.† The book is well printed on Whatman paper with watermark dated 1794, but the register of text and design is sometimes imperfect. The plates are often almost the same size as the page, so that the designs are only to be found intact in uncut copies of the book. In the *Advertisement*, possibly written by Fuseli (Gilchrist, i, 135), Blake's merit as a designer and engraver is spoken of in the highest terms: "... while a taste for the arts of "design shall continue to exist, the original conception, and the bold and masterly "execution of this artist cannot be unnoticed or unadmired." The "Explanation of the Engravings" is not by Blake, but may also have been written by Fuseli.

Blake's series of water-colour designs are contained in two large volumes, which are now in the possession of Mr. W. A. White. The designs are on leaves, 43 × 32 cm., watermarked *J Whatman* 1794, in the centre of which are inlaid the pages of an earlier quarto edition of the *Night Thoughts*. Some of the designs were described by the late Frederick Shields (Gilchrist, ii, 289-307), but the majority are undescribed. Two of them are here reproduced by permission of Mr. White.

Facsimile Reproduction: Liverpool, 1911, reduced, Nights I and II (no. 234).

---

* Sold with the Crewe Collection, Sotheby's, March 30, 1903 (lot 13, Edwards, £170).

† One such copy was sold with the library of R. A. Potts at Sotheby's, Feb. 20, 1913 (lot 64, £50); another is to be seen in Sir John Soane's Museum, Lincoln's Inn Fields.

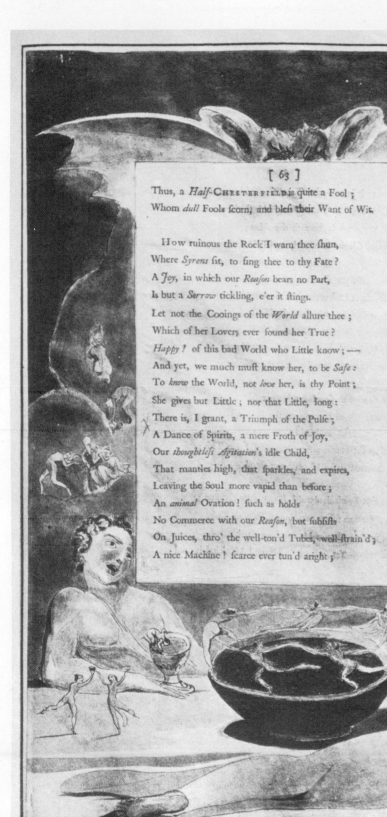

[63]

Thus, a *Half*-CHESTERFIELD is quite a Fool ;
Whom *dull* Fools scorn, and bless their Want of Wit.

How ruinous the Rock I warn thee shun,
Where *Syrens* sit, to sing thee to thy Fate ?
A *Joy*, in which our *Reason* bears no Part,   1170.
Is but a *Sorrow* tickling, e'er it stings.
Let not the Cooings of the *World* allure thee ;
Which of her Lovers ever found her True ?
Happy ! of this bad World who Little know ;——
And yet, we much must know her, to be *Safe* :
To *know* the World, not *love* her, is thy Point ;
She gives but Little ; nor that Little, long :
There is, I grant, a Triumph of the Pulse ;
A Dance of Spirits, a mere Froth of Joy,
Our *thoughtless Agitation*'s idle Child,   1180.
That mantles high, that sparkles, and expires,
Leaving the Soul more vapid than before ;
An *animal* Ovation ! such as holds
No Commerce with our *Reason*, but subsists
On Juices, thro' the well-ton'd Tubes, well-strain'd ;
A nice Machine ! scarce ever tun'd aright ;

                                                  And

DESIGN FOR YOUNG'S "NIGHT THOUGHTS"
Water-colour, about 1794

71 *Broadside, headed*: LITTLE TOM THE SAILOR. *Lettered below*: Printed for & Sold by the Widow Spicer of Folkstone / for the Benefit of her Orphans / October 5, 1800.

Description: A leaf, about 56 × 19 cm., with a Ballad by Hayley and two designs by Blake. The Ballad, designs, and lettering were executed by Blake on four plates as follows:

    i. Head-piece, engraved on pewter, representing Little Tom "aloft in the shrouds"; above him, in the midst of clouds and lightning, watches the spirit of his father. Plate-mark 11 × 16 cm.

    ii. Ballad, *Little Tom the Sailor*, twelve stanzas of four lines each, executed in Blake's usual method of relief etching. Plate-mark 22.5 × 11 cm.

    iii. Tail-piece, engraved on pewter, representing the Widow Spicer leaving to Tom's care her cottage and her two other children. There is a background of trees and downs. Signed at right-hand lower corner: *W Blake Inv*. Plate-mark 11 × 16 cm.

    iv. A small plate at the bottom, lettered: *Printed for*, etc.; relief etching. Plate-mark 3.5 × 12 cm.

    The broadside is printed in black and is usually uncoloured; some copies were painted with water-colours by Blake or by his wife.

Note: The Ballad was written by Hayley on Sept. 22, 1800; it was engraved shortly afterwards and is referred to by Blake in a letter to Hayley, Nov. 26, 1800: "*Little Tom* has been of late unattended to, and my wife's illness not being quite gone "off, she has not printed any more since you went to London. But we can muster a "few in colours and some in black, which I hope will be no less favoured, though "they are rough like rough sailors. We mean to begin printing again to-morrow." (Russell, *Letters*, p. 85.)

    The broadside is referred to in the *Memoirs of Hayley*, ii, 22-23 (no. 245), where it is stated that: "The ballad was successfully devoted to relieve the necessities of a "meritorious poor woman on the Kentish coast, whose misfortunes Mrs. Rose had "imparted to Hayley, and whose heroic sea-boy was the hero of the ballad."

    The designs are two of the few existing examples of the process called by Blake "wood-cutting on pewter"; for his description see p. 12 of the present work. The pencil sketch for the head-piece is now in the Victoria and Albert Museum.

Facsimile Reproduction: W. Muir, about 1887 (no. 217, i).

Reproductions of the cuts: William Blake Society, 1917 (no. 239)

72 DESIGNS TO A SERIES OF BALLADS, Written By William Hayley, Esq. And founded on Anecdotes Relating to Animals, Drawn, Engraved, and Published, by William Blake. With the Ballads annexed, by the Author's Permission. Chicheſter: Printed by J. Seagrave, and ſold by him and P. Humphry; and by R. H. Evans, Pall-Mall, London, for W. Blake, Felpham. 1802.

Collation: 29.5 × 23.5 cm., uncut. A²⁺¹, B⁴, C¹, D-F⁴, G²⁺¹, H⁴, I²; 29 leaves. Title, pp. iv Preface + 52 Ballads I to IV.

Illustrations: Six plates designed and engraved by Blake and eight vignettes in the text, of which the majority were designed, and all engraved, by Blake.

i. Facing title. Adam naming the beasts. Adam is seated at the foot of a tree, surrounded by animals. The design is bordered by a rectangular frame, the lower part of which contains 6 lines from *Cowper's Task Book VI*. Lettered: *Blake d & s / Publiſhd June* 1 1802 *by W Blake Felpham*. The design measures 12 × 11.5 cm., the plate-mark 17.5 × 16 cm.

ii. Vignette at bottom of p. iv. A landscape showing Chichester Cathedral surrounded by trees. Lettered: *W B d & s / [etc. as in no.* i]. Plate-mark 6 × 14.5 cm.

iii. Facing p. 1. Frontispiece to Ballad no. 1, "The Elephant." An elephant is lifting a native gardener high in the air with his trunk; on the right is a vegetable stall, in the background Indian temples. Lettered: *Blake d & sc / [etc. as in no.* i]. The design measures 14 × 10 cm., the plate-mark 16 × 11 cm.

iv. Oval vignette at top of p. 1. A tiger on the ground is snarling at a man, who is climbing in at the window of a building. Lettered: *Blake d & s [etc. as in no.* i]. Plate-mark 8 × 11 cm.

v. Oval stippled vignette at bottom of p. 9. A study of an elephant after a drawing by Thomas Hayley. In the left-hand lower corner is a small blank oval, inscribed: *Size of the gem*. Lettered: *Blake sc / From an Antique Gem [etc. as in no.* i]. Plate-mark 8 × 11 cm.

vi. Facing p. 11. Frontispiece to Ballad no. 11, "The Eagle." The mother with outstretched arms kneels on a rock above an eagle's eerie, where the bird is resting with a child. Lettered: *Blake d & s / Publiſhd July* 1 1802 *by W Blake / Felpham*. The design measures 14 × 10 cm., the plate-mark 16 × 11.5 cm.

vii. Vignette at top of p. 11. An eagle is swooping down upon a child lying asleep outside a cottage. Lettered: *Blake d & s / [etc. as in no.* vi]. Plate-mark 8 × 11 cm.

viii. Vignette on p. 26. A child is triumphing over the dead body of an eagle among rocks and mountains. Lettered: *Blake in. / [etc. as in no.* vi]. Plate-mark 8 × 11 cm.

THE DOG

Line Engraving, 1802

Hayley's Ballads, 1802

ix. Facing p. 28. Frontispiece to Ballad no. III, "The Lion." A negress has just pinned a lion to the trunk of a tree by an arrow through its throat; her husband is among the branches of the tree, and at her side is their son applauding. Lettered: *Publish'd Aug^st 5. 1802 by W Blake Felpham Blake in & s.* The design measures 15.5 × 12.5 cm., the plate-mark 17 × 14 cm.

x. Oval vignette at top of p. 28. The negress and her boy are setting out armed with bow and arrows; native huts in the background. Lettered: *Blake inv & sc | Publish'd Aug^st 5: 1802 by W Blake Felpham.* Plate-mark 8 × 10.5 cm.

xi. Oval stippled vignette at bottom of p. 39. A study of a lion after a drawing by Thomas Hayley. Lettered: *T. H. del: Blake sc | From an Antique | [etc. as in no. x].* Plate-mark 7 × 9.5 cm.

xii. Facing p. 41. Frontispiece to Ballad no. IV, "The Dog." A dog is leaping off the bank of a river into the jaws of a crocodile, while his master stops himself in horror. Round the design is a border containing figures in the lower part of the sides and a water scene below. Lettered: *Publish'd Septr 9. 1802 by W Blake Felpham | Blake inv. & sc.* The engraving measures 15 × 11.5 cm., the plate-mark 16.5 × 14 cm.

xiii. Oval vignette at top of p. 41. A woman and a soldier caressing a dog. The design is surrounded by a rose vine. Lettered: *Publish'd [etc. as in no. xii] | Blake inv s.* Plate-mark 8 × 11 cm.

xiv. Facing p. 52. Lucy caressing the statue of Fido in her room; there is a tracery of leaves around the bottom of the design. Lettered: *Publish'd [etc. as in no. xii] | Blake inv: Sc.* The engraving measures 13 × 9 cm., the plate-mark 15 × 10.5 cm.

Note: These four ballads were published separately as quarto pamphlets in blue paper covers during 1802, the second year of Blake's residence at Felpham. On the front cover of no. 1 is printed: *A Series of Ballads. Number 1. The Elephant. Ballad the First. Price 2s. 6d.* On the covers of the succeeding numbers the price is omitted, but an imprint is added as on the title-page. The Preface, written by Hayley in a vein of triumphant patronage, gives "an ingenuous history" of the origin of the publication. Hayley tells how Blake came from London through friendship on purpose to engrave the plates for the *Life of Cowper*, but remarks that: "there is hardly any kind of ingeni-"ous employment in which the mind requires more to be cheared and diverted, than the "slow, and sometimes very irksome, progress of engraving; especially, when that art is "exercised by a person of varied talents and of a creative imagination." In order, there-fore, "to amuse the Artist in his patient labour" he composed a few ballads, which "succeeded perfectly as an amusement to [his] Friend; and led him to execute a few "rapid sketches, that several judges of his talent are desirous of converting to his honour "and emolument. . . . It is proposed to publish every month, a Number, containing "three Engravings, with one Ballad, at the price of Half-a-crown; and to complete the "whole series in fifteen Numbers, so that the purchaser will ultimately obtain a quarto

" Volume containing forty-five Engravings, not to mention the Ballads." Hayley then refers to his " native city," to " its Printer (who has a laudable ambition to distinguish himself in his profession)," and to his dead friend, Cowper ; finally he inscribes the ballads to the " Inhabitants of Chichester." Hayley also refers to these designs in his letters to Dr. Johnson (*Memoirs of Hayley*, 1823, no. 245) as follows :

Aug. 6, 1801. " Our good Blake is actually *in labour with a young lion*. The " new-born cub will probably kiss your hands in a week or two. The Lion is his 3d " ballad, and we hope his plate will surpass its predecessors."

May 16, 1802. " Blake . . . is at this moment by my side, representing on copper " an Adam, of his own, surrounded by animals, as a frontispiece to the projected " ballads."

June 28, 1802. " Our alert Blake is preparing, *con spirito*, to launch his eagle, " with a lively hope of seeing him superior to the elephant. . . ."

From these references it appears that some of the plates were executed during 1801. Blake himself does not make many references to this issue of the ballads in his letters, though he sent the first four numbers to Butts on Nov. 22, 1802 (Russell, *Letters*, p. 112), and again on April 25, 1803, for his doctor, Mr. Birch (Russell, *Letters*, p. 113). These four were, however, the only numbers of the projected fifteen that were issued. On Jan. 30, 1803, he sent ten copies of ballad no. 4 to his brother with a letter, which is first printed in an appendix to the present work. At this time he was hopeful that the *Ballads* would be profitable, " for we have sold all that we have had " time to print," but they did not find favour with the public or were not sufficiently advertised, and Blake writes in a letter to Hayley, Oct. 26, 1803: " I called on " Mr. Evans, who gives small hopes of our *Ballads*; he says he has sold but fifteen " numbers at the most, and that going on would be a certain loss of almost all the expenses." (Russell, *Letters*, p. 132.)

This edition of the ballads, and especially the fourth part, is now extremely rare, but in 1805 an octavo edition was issued, containing three of the same designs reduced in size (see no. 74).

Copies : H. E. Huntington ; B. B. MacGeorge ; W. A. White. I have seen several other copies consisting of parts ɪ to ɪɪɪ only.

73 THE LIFE . . . OF WILLIAM COWPER, . . . By William Hayley . . . Chichester . . . 1803

Note : One of the plates in vol. ɪɪ was designed as well as engraved by Blake. See no. 124.

74 BALLADS, BY WILLIAM HAYLEY, ESQ. Founded on Anecdotes relating to Animals, with Prints, Designed and Engraved By William Blake. Chichester: Printed by J. Seagrave; for Richard Phillips, Bridge-Street, Blackfriars, London. 1805.

Collation: 17 × 11 cm., uncut. [a]⁴, A-N⁸, O⁴; 112 leaves. First leaf blank, pp. [vi] Half-title, Title, Preface + 212 + [1] Index, last leaf blank.

Illustrations: Five plates designed and engraved by Blake.
i. Facing p. 1. *The Dog* [Ballad the First]. The same subject as in pl. 12 of no. 72, though without the ornamental border and with variations in detail.
ii. Facing p. 21. *The Eagle* [Ballad the Third]. The same subject as in pl. 6 of no. 72.
iii. Facing p. 100. *The Lion* [Ballad the Ninth]. The same subject as in pl. 9 of no. 72.
iv. Facing p. 123. *The Hermit's Dog* [Ballad the Eleventh]. The body of a knight lies stretched upon the ground at the foot of two trees, with a drawn sword by his side; a dead vulture is spread over his body, and on the top of this crouches a dog, which is defending its dead master from the attacks of another vulture. A man in monkish clothes is approaching on the left.
v. Facing p. 204. *The Horse* [Ballad the Sixteenth]. A woman stands fearlessly between her frightened children and a white horse, which has stopped before her in awe.
Each plate is lettered: *Blake inv & sc | [title] | Pubᵈ June* 18, 1805, *by R. Phillips Nº 6 Bridge Street Black Friers*. Each engraving measures about 11 × 7 cm., and the plate-mark 15 × 9.5 cm.

Note: These *Ballads* were originally intended to have been issued separately in fifteen quarto parts with numerous illustrations by Blake, and for the benefit of the artist. Four parts were issued (no. 72) in 1802, but the series did not meet with success and was then discontinued. Later it was arranged to issue them in the present form, again for Blake's benefit. The history of the volume is contained in the following extracts from Blake's letters to Hayley:
Jan. 22, 1805. "I must now express my thanks for your generous manner of pro-
"posing the *Ballads* to him [Mr. Phillips] on my account, and inform you of his advice
"concerning them; and he thinks they should be published all together in a volume the
"size of the small edition of the *Triumphs of Temper* [see no. 125], with six or seven
"plates. That one thousand copies should be the first edition, and, if we choose, we
"might add to the number of plates in a second edition. And he will go equal shares
"with me in the expense and the profits, and that Seagrave is to be the printer. That

"we must consider all that has been printed as lost, and begin anew, unless we can
"apply some of the plates to the new edition. I consider myself as only put in trust
"with this work, and that the copyright is for ever yours." (Russell, *Letters*, p. 179.)

April 25, 1805. "This morning I have been with Mr. Phillips, and have entirely
"settled with him the plan of engraving for the new edition of the *Ballads*. The prints,
"five in number, I have engaged to finish by 28th May. They are to be as highly
"finished as I can do them, the size the same as the seven plates, the price twenty
"guineas each, half to be prepared by P. The subjects I cannot do better than those
"already chosen, viz.: the Lion, the Eagle, the Horse, the Dog. Of the dog species, the
"two ballads are so pre-eminent, and my designs for them please me so well, that I have
"chosen that design in our last number, of the dog and the crocodile, and that of the
"dog defending his dead master from the vultures. Of these five I am making little high
"finished pictures, the size the engravings are to be, and I am hard at it to accomplish
"in time what I intend. Mr. P says he will send Mr. Seagrave the paper directly. . . .
"P.S.—Your desire that I should write a little advertisement at the beginning of the
"*Ballads* has set my brains to work, and at length produced the following. Simplicity,
"as you desire, has been my first object. I send it for your correction or condemnation,
"begging you to supply its deficiency or to new create it according to your wish: 'The
"'public ought to be informed that the *Ballads* were the effusions of friendship to
"'countenance what their author is kindly pleased to call talents for designing and to
"'relieve my more laborious engagement of engraving those portraits which accom-
"'pany the *Life of Cowper*. Out of a number of designs, I have selected five, and hope
"'that the public will approve of my rather giving a few highly laboured plates than a
"'greater number and less finished. If I have succeeded in these, more may be added
"'at pleasure. Will. Blake.'" (Russell, *Letters*, p. 180.)

June 4, 1805. "I have fortunately, I ought to say providently, discovered that I
"have engraved one of the plates for that ballad of 'The Horse' which is omitted in
"the new edition; time enough to save the extreme loss and disappointment which I
"should have suffered had the work been completed without that ballad's insertion. I
"write to entreat that you would contrive so as that my plate may come into the work,
"as its omission would be to me a loss that I could not now sustain, as it would cut
"off ten guineas from my next demand on Phillips, which sum I am in absolute want
"of; as well as that I should lose all the labour I have been at on that plate, which I
"consider as one of my best; I know it has cost me immense labour. The way in
"which I discovered this mistake is odd enough. Mr. Phillips objects altogether to
"the insertion of my Advertisement, calling it an appeal to charity, and says it will
"hurt the sale of the work." (Russell, *Letters*, p. 184.)

Blake refers again to the *Ballads* in a letter dated Nov. 27, 1805, which is printed for the first time in an appendix to the present work.

Three of the designs—The Dog, The Eagle, and The Lion—are repetitions from the earlier issue; the other two are new. The plates in this book occur in two states, in the second of which they have been carefully worked over.* Gilchrist (i, 219-225), who considers that the plates have more than Blake's ordinary hardness of manner, states that this issue also was a failure. A notice of this edition of the *Ballads* appeared in vol. xx (part II for 1805) of Phillips's *Monthly Magazine*, pp. 614-615; it is favourable to Hayley, but makes no mention of Blake's designs. Another notice appeared in the *Annual Review* for 1805 (see no. 395); it is unsigned, but is known to be by Robert Southey, who ridicules the ballads and adds: " The poet has had the " singular good fortune to meet with a painter capable of doing full justice to his con- " ceptions; and, in fact, when we look at the delectable frontispiece to this volume " which represents Edward starting back, Fido *volant*, and the crocodile *rampant*, with " a mouth open like a boot-jack to receive him, we know not whether most to admire " the genius of Mr William Blake or of Mr William Hayley." Southey concludes his review: " We could not help quoting O'Keefe's song—Hayley-gaily gamborayly " higgledy piggledy galloping draggle-tail'd dreary dun."

Several of the plates were subsequently used in a small volume of miscellaneous engravings, but I have not seen a copy of this book.

75 THE PROLOGUE AND CHARACTERS OF CHAUCER'S PIL-GRIMS, selected from his Canterbury Tales; intended to illustrate A Particular Design of Mr William Blake, which is engraved by himself. And may be seen at Mr Colnaghi's, Cockspur Street; at Mr Blake's, No. 28, Broad Street, Golden Square; and at the Publisher's, Mr Harris Bookseller, St. Paul's Church Yard. Price two shillings and sixpence. M.DCCC.XII.

Collation: A², B-I⁴; 34 leaves. Pp. iv Title, Preface + 61 + [1] Errata, last leaf blank.

Illustrations: Frontispiece and vignette designed and engraved by Blake.

i. Frontispiece. A portion of the left-hand end of the larger engraving of the *Canterbury Pilgrims*, but with variations in detail. The names of the characters represented are engraved below. Lettered:

> Reeve Chaucer Oxford Cook Miller Wife of Merchant
> Scholar   Bath   W Blake
> Publish'd Decr 26 1811 by Newberry St Pauls Ch: Yard   inv & sc

Plate-mark 13 × 8 cm.

* This fact was pointed out to me by Mr. A. G. B. Russell.

E E

THE

PROLOGUE AND CHARACTERS

OF

𝕮𝖍𝖆𝖚𝖈𝖊𝖗'𝖘 𝕻𝖎𝖑𝖌𝖗𝖎𝖒𝖘,

SELECTED FROM HIS

CANTERBURY TALES;

INTENDED TO ILLUSTRATE

A PARTICULAR DESIGN

OF

Mr. WILLIAM BLAKE,

WHICH IS ENGRAVED BY HIMSELF.

And may be seen at Mr. COLNAGHI's, Cockspur Street; at
Mr. BLAKE's, No. 28, Broad Street, Golden Square; and at the
Publisher's, Mr. HARRIS, Bookseller, St. Paul's Church Yard.

◆

PRICE TWO SHILLINGS AND SIXPENCE.

◆

M.DCCC.XII.

ii. Rectangular vignette at bottom of p. 58, probably representing Canterbury Cathedral. No lettering. Plate-mark 5 × 7.5 cm.

Note: This publication is now very rare. It contains the Introduction to Chaucer's *Canterbury Tales*, and the volume was intended to be an advertisement of Blake's large engraving. On the left-hand pages is Chaucer's text from Speight's edition of 1687; on the opposite pages a modernized version from Ogle's edition of 1741. The Preface, most of which is quoted by Gilchrist, i, 292, contains an appreciation of Blake and of his large engraving of the *Pilgrims*; Gilchrist suggests that it was from the hand of Dr. Malkin (see no. 80). Blake's address given on the title-page is that of his brother James, and it was in this house that he had held the exhibition in 1809 (see no. 30).

Copies: BM, H. E. Huntington (Hoe and Edelheim copies), W. E. Moss.

76 WEDGWOOD'S CATALOGUE of Earthenware and Porcelain. [About 1816-1820]

Illustrations: Eighteen plates representing various pieces of crockery—tea and dinner services, egg-cups, jugs, basins, etc., drawn and engraved by Blake. Heading: *Wedgwood* [number of plate]; lettered below: *Blake d & sc*. Plate-mark 22.5 × 17 cm.

Note: A complete set of the plates, which are mentioned by Gilchrist, i, 34, was in the Linnell collection (sold at Christie's, March 15, 1918, lot 190), and is now in the B.M. Print Room together with four proofs, one of which is watermarked 1816 *Whatman*. Another set of four proofs, formerly belonging to Frederick Tatham, is in the possession of Mr. Graham Robertson. A note by Tatham attached to these states that the pottery depicted was designed by Flaxman, and that it was Flaxman who introduced Blake to Wedgwood. I have not seen a copy of the catalogue for which the plates were, presumably, executed.

77 THE PASTORALS OF VIRGIL, with a Course of English Reading, Adapted for Schools: in which all The Proper Facilities are given, enabling youtm [*sic*] to acquire The Latin Language in the Shortest Period of Time. Illustrated by 230 Engravings. By Robert John Thornton, M.D. . . . Third Edition. Vol. I.[II.] London: Stereotyped and Printed by J. M'Gowan, . . . Published by F. C. & J. Rivingtons; . . . and may be had of all Book-

sellers in the United Kingdom; or of Mr. Harrison, . . . Agent for Dr. Thornton. 1821. *N.B. The Price of Thornton's Pastorals of Virgil, is* 1 5*s. bound.* A full Allowance to the Trade and Schoolmasters.

Collation: 17.5 × 10.5 cm. Vol. I. [✱]¹⁺⁸, a-b⁶, B-S⁶, T¹⁺⁴; 129 leaves. Pp. vi Title and verso, Dedication, Two woodcuts, Address to school-masters & parents + ix-xii Quotation, Opinions in favour of the present plan of teaching, The only objection to our Virgil answered + 12 Contents + v-xxiv Preface + 214 A discourse on pastoral poetry by Alexander Pope (pp. 1-4), Eclogues i-iv.

Vol. II [✱]¹, T6, U-Z⁶, AA-ZZ⁶, 3A-3D⁶, 3E²; 190 leaves. Title, pp. 215-592 Eclogues v-x, Concluding Remark.

Illustrations: Vol. i. Woodcut frontispiece, four plates drawn and engraved by Blake, three lithographed maps, and seventy-four pages of woodcuts, of which seven were drawn and five executed by Blake. Vol. ii. Woodcut frontispiece, two plates drawn and engraved by Blake, and forty-three pages of woodcuts.

A. Six engravings drawn and executed by Blake:
   i. Vol. i. Facing p. 3. Bust of *Theocritus*.
   ii. Vol. i. Facing p. 4. Bust of *Publius Virgilius Maro*.
   iii. Vol. i. Following no. 2. Bust of *Octavius Augustus Cæsar*.
   iv. Vol. i. Facing no. 3. In the centre a bust of *Agrippa*; in each corner an engraving from a coin representing *Pollio, Gallus, Varus,* and *Mecænas*.
   v. Vol. ii. Facing p. 229. Bust of *Caius Julius Cæsar*.
   vi. Vol. ii. Facing p. 360. Bust of *Epicurus*.
Each plate is lettered: *Blake, del. et Sculp.* / [Subject, with an account of his life] / *London, Published by Dr Thornton*, 1821. Each engraving without the lettering measures about 10 to 13 × 8 cm.

B. Twenty woodcuts on six pages, illustrating Phillips' *Imitation of Eclogue I*, which were all designed, but of which only seventeen were executed, by Blake:
   i. Facing p. 13. Frontispiece. Thenot and Colinet; the former with his crook is leaning against a tree, and behind him is a flock of sheep. The woodcut measures 6 × 8.5 cm. Below it is the following note: "The Illustrations of this English Pastoral are by the famous BLAKE, the illustrator of *Young's* Night Thoughts, and *Blair's* Grave; who designed and engraved them himself. This is mentioned, as they display less of art than genius, and are much admired by some eminent painters."

   ii-v. Facing p. 14.
   ii. Colinet addressing Thenot; at Colinet's feet is a dog, behind Thenot a flock of sheep.

DESIGNS FOR THORNTON'S "VIRGIL"
Proofs from woodcuts, 1821

DESIGNS FOR THORNTON'S "VIRGIL"
Proofs from woodcuts, 1821

iii. Thenot seated beneath a tree addressing Colinet, who is reclining on a bank; in the background are sheep and a cottage.

iv. Colinet and Thenot, each leaning against a tree. Between them are two sheep, and in the background another shepherd and his dog, running.

v. Thenot and Colinet regarding a riven tree. Colinet speaks. Behind are sheep and lambs.

vi-ix. Facing p. 15.

vi. A stunted tree, and a field of corn beaten down; in the sky is a partially eclipsed moon.

vii. Thenot chasing a wolf away from his fold; at his feet is a dead sheep.

viii. A hut on the bank of a winding stream; sheep are feeding on the other side of the stream.

ix. Colinet walking along a road; by the roadside is a milestone and, at a bend, a sign-post. A building is dimly seen in the distance among the hills.

x-xiii. Facing p. 16.

x. A man dragging a stone roller on a path in front of a large house.

xi. Colinet lying on the ground on the bank of a stream with his back against a tree. Behind him are three sheep, and in the sky is a young moon.

xii. Two youths mocking Colinet, who tries to hide among the trees.

xiii. Maidens dancing on a lawn; two musicians are seated on chairs at the side.

xiv-xvi. Facing p. 17. Designed by Blake, but executed by another.

xiv. *First Comparison*. Birds flying over a cornfield.

xv. *Second Comparison*. Ships sailing on the sea.

xvi. *Third Comparison*. A winding river with buildings on its banks.

xvii-xx. Facing p. 18.

xvii. Thenot inviting Colinet to fold his flock with his own.

xviii. Thenot and Colinet seated at a table in a hut, eating their evening meal.

xix. A peasant is unyolking two oxen from a plough; two other peasants with musical instruments are preparing to return home. Behind is the setting sun.

xx. A peasant with two oxen leaving a plough in the light of the setting sun.

Nos. ii-xx measure 32 to 35 × 70 to 75 mm. None is signed, but below each, except nos. xiv-xvi, is *Thenot* or *Colinet*, indicating the speaker of the lines illustrated.

C. A full-page woodcut, facing p. 21 of vol. 1, after a drawing by Blake of a painting by Poussin. It represents a landscape; in the background is a mountain, on the top of which Polyphemus is seated with his pipes and crook. Heading: *Illustration of Eclogue I. | Introductory.* Lettered below: *Blake, del. Byfield, sculps. | The Giant Polypheme, from a Famous Picture by N. Poussin.* The woodcut measures 8 × 11 cm.

Most of the other woodcuts are unsigned, but the engravers include Bewick, Byfield, Hughes, Thompson, and Thurston.

Note: The extraordinary merit of these woodcuts is now generally recognized, although they are the only designs that Blake executed on wood. Another subject was drawn by him on a wood block ready for cutting, but was never actually carried out.* The volume containing the woodcuts was used as a school book, and has become scarce. There were two previous editions in 1812 (with illustrations published separately in 1814) and in 1819, but Blake's designs are found only in the present edition. In the Linnell collection was a small oblong sketch book containing twenty Indian ink drawings for the woodcuts, without the frontispiece, but with one additional design.† It is related (Gilchrist, i, 318) that Dr. Thornton and his publishers were horrified at Blake's rough and amateurish work, and that the blocks would all have been re-cut by professionals, but for the intercession of Linnell and some other artists. Three of the blocks (nos. xiv-xvi) were in fact executed by a professional hand and lost all character and beauty in the process; the note, given above, was also inserted below the frontispiece as an apology for the rest. One of the latter (no. iii) was actually re-cut, and prints from the two blocks are to be seen side by side in the *Athenæum* for Jan. 21, 1843 (see no. 413). All the blocks, except the first, after they left Blake's hands were found to be too large for the page for which they were intended, and were cut down regardless of the designs; proofs taken from the blocks before this was done show that they originally measured 35 to 40 × 84 mm., and have therefore lost about 5 × 10 mm. Proofs from the blocks in this state are extremely rare; those which are in existence show that the designs were cut four at a time on single blocks of wood, which were afterwards divided up. Proofs of two sheets with designs nos. ii-v and vi-ix are in the B.M. Print Room, and are here reproduced; similar sheets are in the possession of Mr. Herbert Linnell. A sheet with the first set, ii-v, formerly in the Linnell collection, is now in the possession of Mr. Frank Rinder; some of the designs seem to have been further worked upon after this proof was taken. A sheet with the second set, vi-ix, is inserted in the MS. in the Fitzwilliam Museum, Cambridge, known as *An Island in the Moon* (no. 2). Several other sets of so-called proofs of the blocks after they were cut down are also to be met with, but some of these were probably taken in recent times from the blocks which are still in the possession of the Linnell trustees. Reproductions of prints from the blocks before they were cut down, side by side with the designs as they appeared in the book, are given in the *Burlington Magazine*, 1920 (see no. 664).

Facsimiles: Mosher, 1899 (no. 223); Binyon, 1902 (no. 224); Evans, 1912 (no. 235; enlarged).

---

* See National Gallery Cat., item 77.
† National Gallery Cat., item 79. Sold at Christie's, March 15, 1918 (lot 205, Parsons, £113).

THE HIDING OF MOSES
Water-colour, 1825

78 REMEMBER ME! A New Years Gift or Christmas Present. 1825
London. I. Poole. 8. Newgate Street. Fenner 50 Paternoster Row.

Collation: 13.2 × 8.5 cm. a², b¹², B-P¹², *⁴, *⁴, Q-S⁶; engraved title, pp. xxiv
Contents, Introduction + 372 text, Kalendar and Album for 1825.

Illustrations: Frontispiece and ten other plates, one designed and engraved by
Blake, facing pp. 1, 32, 42, 73, 88, 89, 93, 148, 149, and 275.

Blake's plate, facing p. 32, represents the hiding of Moses among the bullrushes. The infant Moses is lying in a basket which has been placed in the water
close to the bank among a clump of bullrushes. On the right of the picture, on the
bank, are the infant's mother and father; the mother, on her knees beside the basket,
is overcome with grief and, falling backwards, is supported by her husband. The
Nile winds away into the distance, and projecting into it, behind the central figures,
is a massive stone building, which rises from the water in a series of ledges; on the
lowest ledge is a Sphinx, on an upper ledge is the figure of the father's sister watching against witnesses of the scene. Beyond, on the left bank, are pyramids, and in the
distance on the right bank are other buildings. On the extreme right of the picture
close to Moses' father is a palm tree. Lettered: *Blake del et sculpt, / Hiding of Moses.*
The engraving measures 7 × 10 cm.; the plate-mark about 8 × 12.5 cm.

Note: This plate is briefly described by W. M. Rossetti in his list of engravings, Gilchrist, ii, 280, but the volume containing it has only been recorded by
Mr. Russell (*Engravings*, p. 102). The book, which seems to be rare, is well printed
and produced; it was issued in boards, enclosed in a cardboard case, with a coloured
design of *Children Gleaning* on the side. The text consists of a miscellaneous collection of anecdotes, essays, and verses, and Blake's design is in illustration of an
unsigned account, extending over four pages, of *The Hiding of Moses*, and in the
course of it (p. 34) the designer is referred to in the following terms: " None but an
" artist possessing the imagination and abilities of Mr. Blake could possibly accom-
" plish a task so replete with difficulty. . . ." The original water-colour design, which
is much larger than the engraving (28.5 × 39.7 cm.), was in the possession of the
Linnell family, and is reproduced here by permission of the trustees.*

Blake's association with this "annual" is explained by the fact that it was produced under the auspices of Dr. Thornton (see nos. 22 and 77) and with the help
of Linnell. Dr. Thornton wrote the Introduction, which breaks off " To be concluded in next year's *Remember Me*," and the majority of the other contributions are
either from his pen or from that of Miss Thornton.

* Sold at Christie's, March 15, 1918 (lot 156, Robson, 115 gns.).

B. *DESIGNED BY BLAKE, ENGRAVED BY OTHERS*

79 LEONORA. A Tale, translated and altered from the German of Gottfried Augustus Burger. By J. T. Stanley, Esq. F.R.S. &c. [two quotations] A New Edition. London: Printed by S. Gosnell, for William Miller, Old Bond Street. 1796.

Collation: 29.5 × 23 cm. a-c², B-E²; 14 leaves. Pp. xi half-title, title, Advertisement, Preface + 16 text.

Illustrations: A frontispiece and two vignettes engraved by Perry in line and stipple after designs by Blake.

i. Frontispiece. Leonora and her bridegroom dashing through the air on the back of a horse; imps and devils are hovering above and dancing below. Lettered: *Blake inv. Perry sc:/[Eight lines] Alter'd from Young.* The engraving measures 20 × 16.5 cm.

ii. Vignette on p. 1. A procession of Prussian soldiers escorted by their friends; Leonora and her mother searching in vain for the missing William. Lettered: *Blake in. Perry sc.* The plate-mark measures 14 × 18 cm.

iii. Vignette on p. 16. William is rushing into the arms of Leonora, who is just waking from her dream; beside her is her mother. Lettered: *Blake in. Perry sc.* The plate-mark measures 10 × 15 cm.

Note: The translation is very unfaithful, having been "altered and added to" for the sake of "the cause of religion and morality." Blake's original designs for the first two engravings are not known; his water-colour design* for the third was formerly in the possession of Mrs. Dew-Smith, and a sketch for it, with additions, belongs to Mr. W. Graham Robertson. The engravings are described by Gilchrist, i, 234-235.

An ordinary copy of the book, uncut, has the measurements given above; some copies, on large paper, measure 36 × 25.5 cm., uncut. The book was issued in boards bound up with the German original, which was published with it for the purpose of comparison. *Title*: Leonora. Ein Gedicht. Von Gottfried August Bürger. [quota-

---

* Sold at Sotheby's, Nov. 18, 1920 (lot 16).

tion] London : Gedrucht bey S. Gosnell. 1796. *Collation*: A-D²; 8 leaves. One leaf blank, title, pp. 12 text. *Illustrations*: Frontispiece engraved by J. Harding after Chodowiecki, and two vignettes on pp. 1 and 12 designed and engraved by the former.

80 A FATHER'S MEMOIRS OF HIS CHILD.   By Benj. Heath Malkin, Esq. M.A. F.A.S.

> Great loss to all that ever him did see ;
> Great loss to all, but greatest loss to me.
>
> ASTROPHEL.

London: Printed for Longman, Hurst, Rees, and Orme, Paternoster Row; by T. Bensley, Bolt Court, Fleet Street. 1806.

Collation: 25 × 15.5 cm., uncut. [*]², a-c⁸, B-L⁸, M⁶; 112 leaves. Half-title, Title, pp. xlviii Introductory Letter + 172.

Illustrations: Frontispiece, engraved by Cromek after Paye and Blake, and three other plates.

i. Frontispiece. An oval stippled portrait of the child, T. W. Malkin, at the age of two years, from a miniature by Paye, surrounded by a design by Blake, which represents an angel conducting the child heavenward; the child takes leave of his mother, who is kneeling on the edge of a cliff (earth's edge), and beside her are a book, a compass, two pens, and a pencil. Lettered: *Wᵐ Blake invᵗ R. H. Cromek ſc. | London Publiſhed by Longman Cᵒ February 1ˢᵗ 1806.* The oval portrait measures 7.5 × 6 cm., the plate-mark 22 × 14.5 cm.

ii. Facing p. 33. Six engravings of "little landscapes" after drawings by T. W. Malkin.

iii. Facing p. 54. Facsimiles of two of the child's letters.

iv. Facing p. 95. A large folding plate inscribed: *A Correĉted | and Revised Map of the | Country of Allestone | from the best Authorities | by Thomas Williams Malkin | done 1 Oĉtober 1801, with all the Names | of the Towns and Islands round it.* Plate-mark 30 × 36.5 cm.

Biographical references and poems: The preface, which is in the form of an Introductory Letter addressed to Thomas Johnes, of Hafod, Esq., M.P., contains (pp. xviii-xli) an account of Blake, consisting of a short biographical sketch of his early years and a criticism of his poetry. The following poems by Blake are reprinted in full for the first time:

1. Laughing Song (*Songs of Innocence*).

2. The Divine Image (the same).
3. Holy Thursday (*Songs of Experience*).
4. The Tiger (the same).
5. " I love the jocund dance " (*Poetical Sketches*).

Their texts are very accurate, but no. 4 contains a variant reading of the last line of the third stanza: " What dread hand forged thy dread feet? " instead of " What dread hand? & what dread feet? "

On pp. 33-34 is quoted Blake's somewhat extravagant criticism of the child's drawings and maps.

Note: This book is an account of an infant prodigy, who died at the age of seven, by his father, Benjamin Heath Malkin, headmaster of Bury Grammar School and a friend of Blake. Many specimens of the child's compositions, letters, and stories are included, some of which are very entertaining. The account of Blake in the preface is the earliest available, and his later biographers have derived substantial help from it. The facts recorded in it were obtained from Blake himself, and this gives an additional importance to the variant reading of " The Tiger." Gilchrist states (i, 256-257) that the frontispiece was originally engraved by Blake, but was subsequently erased and re-engraved by Cromek. The other plates are unsigned, but presumably were also executed by Cromek.

Blake's poetry did not find much favour with the contemporary reviewers. A notice of the book appeared in *The Monthly Review* for Oct. 1806 (see no. 397), concluding as follows: " In the long dedication to Mr. Johnes of Hafod, a bio-" graphical notice is inserted of Mr. William Blake the artist, with some selections " from his poems, which are highly extolled: but if ' Watts seldom rose above the " ' level of a mere versifier ' [Introductory Letter, p. xxxi], in what class must we " place Mr. Blake, who is certainly very inferior to Dr. Watts? " Another short notice appeared in Philips's *Monthly Magazine* for Jan. 25, 1807 (see no. 398); it concludes: " Mr. Malkin's *Memoirs of his Son* contain proofs of early genius, " astonishing even to those who are without the partiality of parents; . . . The " poetry of Mr. Blake, inserted in the dedication, does not rise above mediocrity; as " an artist he appears to more advantage."

Reprint: That part of the Introductory Letter which is concerned with Blake has been reprinted in full by Symons.

REJECTED DESIGN FOR TITLE-PAGE OF BLAIR'S "GRAVE"
Pencil Sketch, about 1806

81 BLAIR'S GRAVE

Engraved title-page: The Grave, A Poem. Illustrated by twelve Etchings Executed by Louis Schiavonetti, From the Original Inventions of William Blake. 1808.

Printed title-page: The Grave, a Poem. By Robert Blair. Illustrated by Twelve Etchings Executed from Original Designs. London: Printed by T. Bensley, Bolt Court, for the Proprietor, R. H. Cromek, Nº 64, Newman Street; and sold by Cadell and Davies, J. Johnson, T. Payne, J. White, Longman, Hurst, Rees, and Orme, W. Millar, J. Murray, and Constable and Co. Edinburgh. 1808.

Collation: 36 × 29.5 cm., uncut. a², b⁴, c¹, B-F⁴; 27 leaves. Pp. xiv title with quotation on verso, Dedication "To the Queen" by William Blake, List of Subscribers, Advertisement by R. H. Cromek, Remarks upon the designs by Henry Fuseli + 36 text, "Of the Designs" + [4] Prospectus of the engraving of Stothard's *Canterbury Pilgrims*.

Illustrations: Frontispiece, engraved title, and eleven plates.

i. Frontispiece. Portrait of Blake after the painting by Phillips, now in the National Portrait Gallery. Blake is seated, and is holding a pencil in his right hand. Lettered: *Painted by T. Phillips R.A. Engraved by L. Schiavonetti V.A. | William Blake | London, Published by R. H. Cromek, 64, Newman Sᵗ May 1ˢᵗ 1808*. Plate-mark 35.5 × 26 cm.

ii. Engraved title, facing frontispiece: [The Skeleton Reanimated]. The left half of the engraving is inscribed as above; lettered below: *Drawn by W. Blake. Etched by L. Schiavonetti. | London, Published May 1, 1808, by R. H. Cromek, . . . | Subscribers' Copy*. Plate-mark 35.5 × 27.5 cm.

iii. Facing p. 1. *Christ descending into the Grave. | [quotation]*. Plate-mark 27.5 × 20 cm.

iv. Facing p. 4. *The meeting of a Family in Heaven*. Plate-mark 27.5 × 15.5 cm.

v. Facing p. 11. *The Counseller [sic], King, Warrior, Mother & Child, in the Tomb*. Plate-mark 21 × 26.5 cm.

vi. Facing p. 12. *Death of the Strong Wicked Man. | [quotation]*. Plate-mark 24 × 28 cm.

vii. Facing p. 16. *The Soul hovering over the Body reluctantly parting with Life. | [quotation]*. Plate-mark 22 × 26.5 cm.

viii. Facing p. 21. *The descent of Man into the Vale of Death. | [quotation]*. Plate-mark 27.5 × 16.5 cm.

ix. Facing p. 28. *The Day of Judgment.* Plate-mark 31.5 × 25 cm.

x. Facing p. 29. *The Soul exploring the receſses of the Grave.* Plate-mark 28 × 15.5 cm.

xi. Facing p. 30. *The Death of The Good Old Man.* / [*quotation*]. Plate-mark 23.5 × 27 cm.

xii. Facing p. 32. *The Reunion of the Soul & the Body.* Plate-mark 29.5 × 23 cm.

xiii. Following no. xii. *Death's Door.* / [*quotation*]. Plate-mark 29.5 × 17 cm.

At the top of each plate, except no. iv, is *P.1*, *P.11*, etc.; pl. iii-xiii are lettered below: *Drawn by W. Blake Etched by L. Schiavonetti.* / [*Title etc.*] / *London, Published May 1ˢᵗ 1808, by Cadell & Davies, Strand.*

Note: This book is not rare and contains one of Blake's most widely known series of designs. The designs were produced during 1805, and in that year Cromek issued a Prospectus (Gilchrist, i, 247), in which it was stated that Blake was himself to be the engraver. An account of the transaction is found in a letter written by Blake to Hayley, Nov. 27, 1805, which is printed for the first time in an appendix to the present work. This is confirmed by a statement in a letter from Flaxman to Hayley, dated Oct. 18, 1805*. Eventually, however, Cromek assigned the task to Schiavonetti, who produced a conscientiously executed series of engravings, but if his somewhat woolly rendering of "The Skeleton Reanimated" be compared with Blake's exuberant version of a similar design in Young's *Night Thoughts* (no. 70) it may be realized how much of Blake's original vigour has been lost. Blake also made a water-colour design, now in the B.M. Print Room, for the Dedication, but this was rejected by Cromek, who in returning the design wrote the insolent letter which was first printed in *The Gentleman's Magazine* for Feb. 1852 (see no. 417). Another water-colour design, dated 1806, and evidently intended for the title-page of Blair's *Grave*, is in the possession of Mr. B. B. Macgeorge. A third, also probably intended for the title-page, is in the B.M. Print Room; the pencil sketch for this belongs to Mr. W. Bateson, F.R.S. Flaxman also mentions with approbation two designs which were not engraved, entitled: "The Gambols of the Ghosts according with their "affections previous to the final Judgment," and "A widow embracing the turf which "covers her husband's grave." According to Russell (*Engravings*, p. 129) the first of these has not survived; the second belongs to Miss Louisa Salaman. Several studies for the designs are known; most of the finished drawings have disappeared, but that for pl. **v**, which differs considerably from the engraving, belongs to Mrs. D. Y. Cameron, by whose permission it is reproduced here.

The book was handsomely printed on Whatman paper, and was issued to the 589 subscribers at 2½ guineas, some proof copies also being issued at 4 guineas. It

* See Russell, *Letters*, p. 185. The letter is now in the Pierpont Morgan Library.

THE COUNSELLOR, KING, WARRIOR, MOTHER AND CHILD IN THE GRAVE
Sepia Drawing, about 1806

was bound in boards with a label pasted on the front cover. Ordinary copies, uncut, have the measurements given above. The proof copies were issued with the following label on the front cover: *Blake's Illustrations of Blair's Grave, Engraved by Schiavonetti. 13 Plates.—Price Four Guineas.* These copies have the portrait printed on India paper and mounted, and the engraved title-page is marked at the bottom: *Proof copy R.H.C. Price £5.5.0*; they are also on larger paper than the ordinary issue, measuring 41.5 × 32.5 cm., uncut. Blake received 20 guineas from Cromek for the designs (see Cromek's letter, Russell, *Letters*, p. 196). In my own possession are proofs of most of the plates in which the lettering is absent or incomplete. One of pl. xii has the imprint: *London, Published by R H Cromek, June 1ˢᵗ 1806.* Another of pl. xiii, recorded by Russell (*Engravings*, p. 130), has a similar imprint with date: *February 1ˢᵗ 1806.*

Blake's poem of dedication "To the Queen" consists of two stanzas of ten lines each; it was first reprinted by Garth Wilkinson in 1839 (see no. 134). Fuseli's remarks on the designs were translated into German shortly after the publication of *The Grave*, being incorporated in Crabb Robinson's article on Blake in the *Vaterländisches Museum*, 1811 (no. 401). The explanation of the designs, which follows the text, was presumably written by Cromek; they are there arranged in a different order, in which, it is stated, they "form of themselves a most interesting Poem." The publication of these designs was made the excuse for a violent attack on Blake in *The Examiner* for Aug. 7, 1808 (see no. 399).

The plates were used for the second time in Ackermann's reissue of *The Grave* in 1813 (next entry), and for the third time in 1826 by the same publisher to illustrate a Spanish poem by Jose Joaquin de Mora (no. 84). They are said (Gilchrist, i, 271) then to have passed to America and to have been used in an edition of Martin Tupper's *Proverbial Philosophy*; I have not met with this publication, but see no. 419.

Facsimile Reproductions: EY, iii; Methuen, 1903 (no. 226); Routledge, 1905 (no 228), all reduced. Scattered reproductions of one or more of the designs have frequently appeared.

82 BLAIR'S GRAVE

Printed title-page: The Grave [etc., as in no. 81], To which is added a Life of the Author. London: Printed by T. Bensley, Bolt Court, for the Proprietor, R. Ackermann, 101, Strand; and sold by Cadell and Davies, . . . 1813.

Collation: 35 × 28 cm. a², b⁴, c², d-h⁴, B-F⁴, G¹; 49 leaves. Title with quotation on verso, pp. liv Dedication, List of Subscribers, Advertisement, Remarks upon the designs, Biographical Sketches of Robert Blair, Louis Schiavonetti, and Robert Hartley Cromek + 42 text, "Of the Designs."

Illustrations: Frontispiece, engraved title, and eleven plates as in no. 81, except that the lettering at the bottom has been altered so as to read: *London, Published [Pub⁴] Mar. [March] 1ˢᵗ [1], 1813, by R. Ackermann, 101, Strand.* The date on the engraved title has not been altered.

Note: The impressions of the plates are weak compared with those in the original edition; this issue nevertheless included a few "proof copies" on large paper. It will be noticed that a life not only of the author has been added, but also of Schiavonetti and Cromek, who had both died in the interval. In the account of the latter no mention is made of Blake's picture of the *Canterbury Pilgrims*, the original conception of this picture being attributed entirely to Cromek.

83 **THE SERAPH**
Engraved title-page with design: Vol. 1. [2.] The Seraph, A Collection of Sacred Music, . . . adapted to Words from Milton, . . . &c. To which are added Many Original Pieces, . . . by John Whitaker . . . London, Printed by Whitaker and Compʸ . . . [1818]

Collation: 25 × 17 cm. Vol. I. Engraved title, pp. 4 Advertisement + 240 Engraved music and words + [4] Index. Vol. II. Engraved title-page, pp. [2] To vocal, and instrumental, performers + 240 Engraved music and words + [4] Index.

Designs: Vol. 1. The engraved title is surrounded by a design of angels somewhat in the style of Blake, but lettered: *Mills delin. Jones sc.* . . .
Vol. II. The design on the engraved title is entitled *Conscience & the recording Angel,* and is copied from Blake's illustrations to Young's *Night Thoughts* (no. 70), p. 27; lettered: *Drawn by the late W. Blake Esqʳ R.A. Engᵈ by P. Jones 36, Theobald's Rd.* Each engraving measures about 20 × 14 cm.

Note: Russell (*Engravings*, p. 131) assigns these volumes to *c.* 1830, because of the reference to "the *late* W. Blake Esq." in the imprint. It is, however, probable that Blake was in 1818 so little known to the general public that the epithet was applied in ignorance by the engraver; the date 1818 at the end of the Advertisement may, therefore, be the actual year of publication.

84 MEDITACIONES POETICAS. Por Jose Joaquin de Mora. Londres: Lo Publica R. Ackermann, No. 101, Strand; y en su Establecimiento en Megico: Asimismo en Colombia, en Buenos Ayres, Chile, Peru, y Guatemala. 1826.

Collation: 4° a², B-E⁴. Pp. iii title, Advertencia + 31 text.

Illustrations: The same plates as in the two editions of Blair's *Grave* (nos. 81 and 82) but with altered titles and lettering:

i. Frontispiece. Lettered: *T. Phillips R.A. Pinxᵗ L. Schiavonetti, V.A. Sculpᵗ | Guillermo Blake.*

ii. Engraved title: *Meditaciones | Poeticas, | por | Jose Joaquin de Mora.*

iii. Facing p. 1. *La Eternidad y el Espacio.*

iv. Facing p. 4. *El Sepulcro.*

v. Facing p. 7. *La Muerte del Impio.*

vi. Facing p. 10. *La Muerte del Justo.*

vii. Facing p. 13. *La Separacion.*

viii. Facing p. 17. *La Puerta de la Muerte.*

ix. Facing p. 19. *El Valle de la Muerte.*

x. Facing p. 21. *La Caverna.*

xi. Facing p. 24. *La Resurreccion.*

xii. Facing p. 26. *El Juicio.*

xiii. Facing p. 30. *La Reunion.*

Nos. 2-13 are lettered: *Drawn by W. Blake. Etched by L. Schiavonetti | [title] | Pub. por R. Ackermann, Londres, y en Megico.*

Note: The impressions of the plates are very weak.

85 A TREATISE ON ZODIACAL PHYSIOGNOMY . . . By John Varley . . . London . . . 1828 [see no. 248]

Note: Contains engravings by Linnell after Blake's "Ghost of a Flea" and "Coin of Nebuchadnezzar."

C. *ENGRAVED BY BLAKE AFTER DESIGNS BY OTHERS*

86 A SYSTEM OF GEOGRAPHY. 1779

Frontispiece: "The Four quarters of the World. Frontispiece to a system of Geography, 1779. Stothard del^t Blake sc." A group of figures representing various nationalities. 18 × 12.5 cm.

Note: The volume in which this plate occurs is unknown to me. The Balmanno collection of Stothard's works in the B.M. Print Room contains a proof of the engraving inscribed as above in pencil. The same collection contains also a proof of an unknown subject after Stothard, engraved by Blake and dated 1779, which may belong to the same book (for description see Russell, *Engravings*, p. 136).

87 FENCING FAMILIARIZED: or A New Treatise on the Art of Small Sword. . . . A New Edition, Revised, Corrected, and Augmented by an original Set of Prints. By Mr. Olivier, Educated at the Royal Academy of Paris, and Professor of Fencing, N° 8, Serle-street, Lincoln's Inn Fields. . . . London: Printed for John Bell, at the British Library, Strand. M DCC LXXX.

Collation: 8°. pp. [iv] Half-title, Titles in English and French, Dedication to the Earl of Harrington + xlvii Dedication (continued), Contents, List of plates, Advertisement "To my Scholars," Preface, Introduction + [1] + 205 text. The whole book is printed in English and French on opposite pages.

Illustrations: Engraved frontispiece, engraved vignettes on pp. [iv] and i, and thirteen folding plates at the end, one of which was engraved by Blake.
Plate 4. Lettered below: *J. Roberts del^t ad vivum | W. Blake Sculp | 4e Position de l'allongement du Coup de quarte*. 15 × 21 cm. Plate-mark 19.5 × 23 cm.

Note: This plate, which was first noticed by Mr. W. E. Moss, has not been previously recorded. According to Thimm's *Bibliography of Fencing*, 1896, the first edition of *L'Art des Armes Simplifié*, or *Fencing Familiarized*, was published by John Bell in 1771-2, with a frontispiece and eight plates engraved by Ovenden. The majority of the plates in the present edition were engraved after J. Roberts by D. Jenkins; two were done by Grignion, and one each by Goldar and Blake.

88 *Engraved title*: THE PROTESTANTS FAMILY BIBLE. Containing the Old and New Testament, with the Apocrypha, illustrated by explanatory notes. With A Compleat Concordance, and general index. By a Society of Protestant Divines. [vignette] London: Printed for Harrison and Co. No. 18, Paternoster-Row. [1780]

 Collation: 4°. Engraved title, pp. iii-vi Preface, Contents + B-9C² text (no pagination).

 Illustrations: Engraved frontispiece and thirty-six plates, five of which. were engraved by Blake after Raphael and Rubens.
  i. Facing E2*b*. *Genesis xviii.* 2. | *Abraham & the Three Angels* | *Raphael de Urbin del. Blake Sculp.* | *Publish'd etc.*
  ii. Facing F1*b*. *Gen. xix.* 26. | *Lot's Escape* | *Rubens del. Blake sculp.* | *Publish'd, etc.*
  iii. Facing L1*b*. *Gen. xxvii.* 28. | *Joseph sold to the Ishmeelites* | *Rubens del. Blake sculp.* | *Publish'd etc.*
  iv. Facing Y2*b*. *Exodus xxxii.* 19. | *The Israelites Idolatry* | *Raphael de Urbin del. Blake sculp.* | *Publish'd etc.*
  v. Facing Eee2*a*. *Joshua. iv.* 16. | *Joshua passing over Jordan* | *Raphael de Urbin del. Blake sculp.* | *Publish'd etc.*
 Each design measures 14.5 × 10.5 cm., and is surrounded by an ornamental border. The text reference is above, the title below. At the bottom is the imprint: *Publish'd as the Act directs by Harrison & Co. No.* 18 *Paternoster Row.* The frontispiece is in addition dated: *Sep.* 2, 1780. The plate-mark measures 20 × 15 cm.

 Note: These engravings are recorded only by Russell (*Engravings*, p. 154), but are there dated 1790. The only copy of this book that I have seen is now in the B.M. Reading Room.

89 THE SPEAKER: or, Miscellaneous Pieces, selected from the Best English Writers . . . By William Enfield, LL.D. . . . London: Printed for Joseph Johnson, St. Paul's Church-Yard M DCC LXXIV [1780]

 Collation: 12°. Pp. xxxiv Title, Dedication, Essay on Elocution, Contents + 421.

Illustrations: Frontispiece and three plates after Stothard, one engraved by Blake. Facing p. 302. Heading: *Clarence's Dream | Book VII. Chap.* 22. Lettered below: *Stothard del. Blake sc.* | [six lines from *Shakespeare*] | *Publish'd . . . by J. Johnson . . .* 1 *Aug.* 1780. Clarence is kneeling on the ground; an angel and three demons are flying towards him from behind. 12.5 × 7.5 cm. Plate-mark 18 × 11 cm.

Note: Although the title-page is dated 1774 all the plates are dated 1780. There is no mention of plates on the title-page, and evidently the book was first issued without the plates, which were inserted in the unsold copies in 1780. A new edition issued in 1785 is without the plates, but they appear again in editions issued in 1795, 1799, 1805, and 1820. Blake's plate is much worn in the later editions, and appears to have been worked over by him at least three times; proofs of three states are in the possession of Mr. W. E. Moss, and in one of these the head of the angel is turned so that half the face is visible. Mr. Moss also has Stothard's original sketch for the design. The other plates were engraved by Heath and Sharp.

90 **AN INTRODUCTION TO MENSURATION AND PRACTICAL GEOMETRY**: By John Bonnycastle. 1782. 12°

Illustration: The frontispiece (or vignette on the title?) represents a group of six cherubs among ruins practising geometry. Lettered: *Stothard del. Blake sc.* 6.5 × 8.5 cm.

Note: The writer has not seen a copy of this volume. A proof of the engraving is in the Balmanno collection of Stothard's works in the B.M. Print Room. The plate was re-engraved by various hands for later editions of the book.

91 **THE LADY'S POCKET BOOK.** Edited by Dodsley for J. Johnson. 1782.

Illustrations: Contains two plates engraved by Blake after Stothard.
i. Lettered: *A Lady in the full Dress, & another in the most fashionable Undress now worn.* | *T. S. del. W.B. sc.* 9.5 × 6.5 cm.
ii. Lettered: *The Morning Amusements of her Royal Highness the Princess Royal & her 4 Sisters.* | *Published by J. Johnson . . . Nov*ʳ 1, 1782 | *Stothard del Blake Sc.* 9.5 × 12 cm.

Note: This volume is mentioned by Gilchrist, i, 51, but I have been unable to find a copy. The Balmanno collection of Stothard's works in the B.M. Print Room contains examples of Blake's plates printed side by side on one piece of paper.

92 *Engraved title*: THE NOVELIST'S MAGAZINE. Vol. VIII. [IX, X,] Containing Don Quixote [etc.] [vignette] London: Printed for Harrison and C⁰ . . . 1782.[1783.]

> *Collation*: 22 × 14 cm. Vol. VIII. Engraved title, pp. xxiv + 25-589 Don Quixote. Vol. IX. Engraved title, pp. 58 Sterne's Sentimental Journey + 140 Swift's Gulliver's Travels + 157 Miss Fielding's David Simple + 125 Smollett's Sir Lancelot Greaves + 88 de Grafigny's Peruvian Princess + 101 Fielding's Jonathan Wild the Great. Vol. X. Engraved title, pp. viii + 9-611 Richardson's Sir Charles Grandison, vols. 1-4.

> *Illustrations*: Fifteen or sixteen plates in each volume, of which eight in all were engraved by Blake, after Stothard.
> 　　i. Vol. VIII. Don Quixote, pl. ix, facing p. 257. Don Quixote and the barber's bason (*May* 4, 1782).
> 　　ii. Ditto, pl. xv, facing p. 587. The last testament of Don Quixote (*June* 15, 1782).
> 　　iii. Vol. IX. Sentimental Journey, pl. ii, facing p. 52. Peasants dancing before Yorick (*July* 6, 1782).
> 　　iv. Vol. IX. David Simple, pl. i, facing p. 66. David paying the rent of the distressed couple (*Aug.* 10, 1782).
> 　　v. Vol. IX. Sir Lancelot Greaves, pl. iii, facing p. 45. Sir Lancelot addressing a crowd at a General Election (*Sep.* 21, 1782).
> 　　vi. Vol. X. Sir Charles Grandison, pl. xxiii, facing p. 329. Miss Byron visiting Miss Emily Jervoise (*Apr.* 5, 1783).
> 　　vii. Ditto, pl. vi, facing p. 351. The duel in the parlour (*Dec.* 7, 1782).
> 　　viii. Ditto, pl. xii, facing p. 443. Grandison's interview with Lady Clementina and her mother (*Jan.* 18, 1783).
> Each engraving is surrounded by an ornamental border, and is lettered below: *Stothard del. Blake sculp.*/[*No. of plate*] *Publifhed . . . by Harrifon & C⁰* [*date*]. Plate-mark 17.5 × 11 cm. The other engravings were executed by Angus, Birrel, Grignion, Heath, and Walker.

93 THE POETICAL WORKS OF GEOFF. CHAUCER. In Fourteen Volumes. . . . Vol. XIII. Edinburg: At the Apollo Prefs, by the Martins. Anno 1782.

> *Collation*: 13 × 8 cm. Pp. 202 Title, Sub-title, Text, Contents.

Frontispiece: (recto) Sampson and Dalila; a circular design (diameter 6.5 cm.) within a rectangular frame (10.5 × 6.5 cm.). Engraved by Blake after Stothard. Lettered above design: *Bell's Edition | The Poets of Great Britain | Complete From | Chaucer to Churchill.* Below design: *Chaucer Vol XIII. | [quotation].* Below frame: *Stodhard del Blake ſculpᵗ | London Printed for John Bell . . . May 24ᵗʰ 1783.*

Note: The engraving is very similar in style to those executed by various hands for the other 108 volumes of Bell's edition of the British Poets. None of the published engravings in the rest of the series is by Blake, though there is a print by him which was apparently intended for the Milton (see Russell, *Engravings* p. 142).

94 THE POETICAL WORKS OF JOHN SCOTT ESQ. [Oval engraved portrait by Hall after Townsend] London Printed for J. Buckland, MDCCLXXXII.

Collation: 8°. Engraved title, pp. vi Advertisement, Contents + [ii] List of the Engravings, Errata + 341 + [1] Books by the same author.

Illustrations: Frontispiece, six plates, and four vignettes. Two of the plates and two of the vignettes were engraved by Blake after Stothard.
   i. Vignette on p. 21. Two shepherds listening to Damon's complaint. A rectangular design at the end of Eclogue iv. Plate-mark 7 × 10 cm.
   ii. Facing p. 23. Contentment and the four Seasons. An oval allegorical design illustrating Elegy iv. Plate-mark 8 × 12 cm.
   iii. Facing p. 247. Olmedo, chaplain to Cortes, holding back the Spanish warriors. An oval design illustrating "The Mexican Prophecy." Plate-mark 9 × 11 cm.
   iv. Vignette on p. 335. A female figure laying a scroll on a monument, which is inscribed "Sacred to Simplicity." A rectangular allegorical design, forming a tail-piece to "Conclusion." Plate-mark 9 × 8.5 cm.
   Each engraving is lettered: *Stothard del.* [d] *Blake sc.* . . . The frontispiece was executed by Bartolozzi; the other engravings (facing pp. 3, 49, 59, 125, 259, 313, and on pp. 59, 89) by Heath, Taylor, Watts, Page, Godfrey, and Wollett.

Note: Mr. W. E. Moss has a series of proofs of these plates before letters printed on India paper. A second edition, with the same plates, was published in 1786.

95 MEMOIRS OF ALBERT DE HALLER, M.D. . . . Compiled, . . . By Thomas Henry, . . . Warrington, Printed by W. Eyres, for J. Johnson, . . . London. MDCCLXXXIII.

Collation: 8°. Pp. xvii Title, Dedication + 161 + [3] Errata and Advertisement, Books printed for J. Johnson.

Frontispiece: A circular engraving (diameter 6 cm.), lettered: *Dunker. d Blake. sc. / Albert de Haller.* Plate-mark 13 × 8.5 cm.

Note: An example of this engraving was shown at the Burlington Club's exhibition in 1876, and in the *Catalogue* (no. 667) is included in exhibit no. 271. It is also recorded in Russell, *Engravings*, p. 143.

96 ORLANDO FURIOSO: Translated from the Italian of Ludovico Ariosto; With Notes: By John Hoole. In Five Volumes. Vol. I. [etc.] London: Printed for the Author: Sold by . . . J. Dodsley; . . . J. Stockdale; and J. Phillips. M.D.CC.L.XXXIII.

Collation: 8°. Vol. I. Half-title, Title, pp. [iv] Dedication, Advertisement + cxxxi Preface, etc. + 335. Vol. II. Half-title, Title, pp. 407. Vol. III. Half-title, Title, pp. 427. Vol. IV. Half-title, Title, pp. 438. Vol. V. Half-title, Title, pp. 322 + vi Postscript + [lv] Index, Errata.

Illustrations: Three plates in vol. 1, and one in each subsequent volume, of which one was engraved by Blake after Stothard.
Vol. III, facing p. 164. Orlando in a fury tearing up trees; his horse is tethered close by. Lettered: *Stothard del. Blake sc.* 15 × 11 cm.
The other engravings were executed by Hall, Bartolozzi, Collyer, Anker Smith, Heath, and Caldwall.

Note: This edition was re-issued in 1785. An abridged edition in two volumes was published by Dodsley in 1791; Blake's plate is lettered at the top *Vol. I facing Page* 461. A new edition in five volumes was published by Otridge & Son in 1799. Blake's plate is in the same position as before, but is lettered in addition: *Published by Vernor & Hood Dec* 1, 1798.

97 A SELECT COLLECTION OF ENGLISH SONGS. [By Joseph Ritson] In Three Volumes. Volume the First [etc.] [vignette and quotation] London: Printed for J. Johnson. . . . MDCCLXXXIII.

Collation: 8°. Vol. I. Half-title, Title, pp. xiv Preface + lxxii A Historical Essay on National Song + [ii] Sub-title to Part I + 264. Vol. II. Half-title, Title, Sub-title to Part III, pp. 342 + [32] Index, etc. Vol. III. Half-title, Title, pp. [ii] Advertisement + [301] Airs to the Songs in Vols. I and II.

Illustrations: Allegorical frontispiece and ten vignettes in vol. I; six vignettes in vol. II. Of the vignettes nine were engraved by Blake.

 i. Vol. I, p. 1. A lover kneeling before his lady. Headpiece to "Love Songs, Class I."

 ii. Vol. I, p. 85. A lady seated on a rock and looking out to sea, in which is floating a man's body. Tailpiece to "Love Songs, Class I."

 iii. Vol. I, p. 86. Cupid playing on the lute before Venus and three attendants. Headpiece to "Love Songs, Class II."

 iv. Vol. I, p. 108. A lover parting from his angry mistress. Heading to "Love Songs, Class III."

 v. Vol. I, p. 156. A group of country people dancing round a maypole. Tailpiece to "Love Songs, Class III."

 vi. Vol. I, p. 157. A lady is seated writing at a desk, while a cupid holds up a lamp behind her. The moon is shining in at the door of the terrace, but the artist has omitted to indicate the moonlight. Headpiece to "Love Songs, Class IV."

 vii. Vol. I, p. 170. Two cupids are flying away from a young lady, who is seated on a rock in an attitude of dejection. Tailpiece to the same.

 viii. Vol. I, p. 171. Two lovers in an arbour. Trees and a church spire in the background. Headpiece to "Love Songs, Class V."

 ix. Vol. II, p. 1. A group of men seated round a table, drinking. Headpiece to "Drinking Songs."

Each vignette, except nos. iii, iv, is lettered: *Stothard del. Blake sc.* Each plate-mark measures about 7.5 × 10 cm.

The other vignettes are on pp. 107, 254 of vol. I, and on pp. 77, 81, 183, 187, 337 of vol. II. They are all unsigned except that on p. 77 of vol. II, which is by Heath.

Note: Gilchrist, i, 51-52, describes these engravings, and specially mentions one "at the head of the *Love Songs*, a Lady singing, Cupids fluttering before her, a "singularly refined composition." The book does not, however, contain an engraving answering to this description, and it is probably a mistake, as the other references are very inaccurate. As was noted by Russell (*Engravings*, p. 144), nos. iii and iv are unsigned as they appear in the book, but proofs of them in the Balmanno collection of Stothard's works in the B.M. Print Room bear Blake's name. It is possible that some of the other unsigned engravings are also by him. Later editions of Ritson's *English Songs* are without the engravings, some small woodcuts being substituted.

98 THE WIT'S MAGAZINE; or, Library of Momus. Being a Compleat Repository of Mirth, Humour, and Entertainment . . . Vol. I [II] [device] London: Printed for Harrison and Co, . . . MDCCLXXXIV

Collation: 8°. Vol. I. Pp. vi Title, Preface, Apologue + 7-486 XII numbers (Jan.-Dec., 1784), Contents, List of Correspondents. Vol. II. Pp. 194 Title, v numbers (Jan.-May, 1785), Contents, List of Correspondents.

Illustrations: A folding plate at the beginning of each number, of which the first five were engraved by Blake.
i. *The Temple of Mirth*, after Stothard.
ii. *Tythe in Kind; or the Sow's Revenge*, after Collings.
iii. *The Discomfited Duellists*, after Collings.
iv. *The Blind Beggars Hats*, after Collings.
v. *May-Day in London*, after Collings.
Each engraving measures about 17 × 23 cm., and is lettered: *Stothard* [or *Collings*] *del. Blake ſculp.* / [Title] / *Published* . . ., *by Harriſon & Cᵒ Febʸ* [etc] 1. 1784. Plates 6 and 7 were engraved by Smith and Thomas, after Collings; the rest are unsigned.

Note: These engravings are mentioned by Gilchrist, i, 53-54. A proof of the frontispiece before letters is in the possession of Mr. W. E. Moss.

99 A NEW SYSTEM OF GEOGRAPHY: . . . By the late D. Fenning and J. Collyer. A New Edition, . . . by Frederick Hervey, Esq; . . . Vol. I. London: Printed for J. Johnson, Nᵒ 72, and G. and T. Wilkie Nᵒ 71, in St. Paul's Church-Yard. M.DCC.LXXXV.

Collation: F°. Pp. iv Title, Preface + 5-620-?

Illustrations: 20 plates, of which two were engraved by Blake, and six engraved maps.

i. Heading: *Engraved for Hervey's New System of Geography | Frontispiece | Vol. I.* Lettered below: *Asia and Africa | Characterised by a representation of their | Various Inhabitants | Published June 6th 1784, by G. Wilkie* . . . A group of people in an archway; with an ornamental border. Plate-mark 27.5 × 18 cm.

ii. Heading: *Engraved etc. | Vol. I. page 583.* Lettered below: *Blake Sc | Publish'd April 16th 1785 by G. & T. Wilkie, . . . | No 16.* Five heads of savages in ovals, with an inscription below each. Plate-mark 23 × 20 cm.

The other engravings are by Hall, Page, Rooker, and Tookey.

Note: First recorded by Russell (*Engravings*, p. 135). The copy of the book seen by the writer in the B.M. Reading Room is imperfect.

100 **THE WHOLE GENUINE AND COMPLETE WORKS OF FLAVIUS JOSEPHUS, . . .** To Which is Added Various Useful Indexes, . . . Also a Continuation of the History . . . By George Henry Maynard, LL.D. . . . Embellished with upwards of sixty beautiful Engravings, taken from original Drawings of Messrs. Metz, Stothard, and Corbould, . . . and other eminent Artists; and engraved by Grignion, Collier, Heath, Tookey, Taylor, &c. London: Printed for C. Cooke, . . . [*about* 1786]

Collation: F°. Pp. vi Title, Royal Licence, Josephus's Preface + 7-723 + [1] Directions to the Binder.

Illustrations: Frontispiece and 59 plates, of which three were engraved by Blake.

i. Facing p. 13. Lettered: *Metz delin. Blake sculp. | The Parting of Lot and Abraham, | after seperating* [sic] *their Flocks &c.*

ii. Facing p. 65. Lettered: *Stothard delin. Blake sculp. | The Battle of Ain, & the Destruction of | the City, by the Army of Joshua.*

iii. Facing p. 76. Lettered: *Metz delin. Blake sculp. | The Fugitive Shechemites | Burnt and Suffocated in the Holds of their Retreat, | by order of King Abimelech.*

Each engraving has an ornamental border inscribed at the top: *Engraved for | Maynard's | Josephus.* Plate-mark 29 × 17 cm.

Note: The plates facing pp. 125 and 398 are dated Jan. 14, 1786, and Dec. 31, 1785 respectively. It will be noticed that in the engraving of *The Battle of Ain* the combatants are holding their weapons in their left hands, that is to say the design has been reversed. A proof of another version of the plate, which is in the collection of **Mr. W. E. Moss**, has the design the right way round, but this engraving seems to have been rejected by Blake. Some copies of the book contain a slightly different title-page, and a Translator's Preface instead of the Royal Licence, but are otherwise similar to the above.

101 APHORISMS ON MAN: Translated from the Original Manuscript of The Rev. John Caspar Lavater, Citizen of Zuric.

—*è cælo descendit* γνωθι σεαυτον

Juv. Sat. ix.

London: Printed for J. Johnson, St. Paul's Church-Yard. MDCCLXXXVIII.

Collation: 8°. Pp. vi Title, Dedication "To Henry Fuseli, A.M.", Advertisement + [ii] Errata + 224.

Frontispiece: A seated figure allegorical of Meditation, above whose head floats a cupid with a tablet inscribed ΓΝΩΘΙ ΣΕΑΥΤΟΝ. Engraved by Blake after Fuseli. Lettered: *Blake. sc* Plate-mark 15 × 9 cm.

Note: At the bottom of p. 224 are the words "End of Vol. I," since the editor intended to add another volume of *Aphorisms on Art* (see p. vi). For a description of Blake's own copy of the *Aphorisms on Man*, see no. 13. A second edition, 8°, *London, for J. Johnson* (pp. viii + 224) was issued in 1789; it contains sundry alterations in the text, but the frontispiece is the same as before. A third edition was issued in 1794; it is similar to the second edition, except that the plate has been worked over and that aphorism no. 529 of the previous editions has been omitted. Another edition, also called the third, was published in Dublin (*Printed by W. Sleater, and P. Byrne*, 12°, pp. vi + 222) in 1790.

102 ESSAYS ON PHYSIOGNOMY, . . . By John Caspar Lavater, . . . Illustrated by more than Eight Hundred Engravings . . . Executed by, or under the Inspection of, Thomas Holloway. Translated from the French by Henry Hunter, D.D. . . . Volume I. [etc.] [vignette] London: Printed for John Murray, . . . MDCCLXXXIX.

Collation: Imp. 4°. Vol. I. Half-title, Title, pp. [x] List of Subscribers + iv Contents + [xviii] Dedication, Author's Preface, Translator's Preface + 281. Vol. II, part 1, pp. xii + 238; part 2, pp. [vi] + 239-444. Vol. III, part 1, pp. xii + 252; part 2, pp. [vi] + 253-437.

H H

Illustrations: Numerous plates and vignettes, of which three in vol. I were executed by Blake.

i. Plate 25, facing p. 159. A head and shoulders of Democritus. Lettered: *Rubens delin. Blake sculp. / Democritus. / 25.* The engraving measures 17 × 14 cm., the plate-mark 27.5 × 22.5 cm.

ii. Vignette on p. 206. A female hand and arm holding a lighted candle round which moths are fluttering; emblematical of science dissipating ignorance. Lettered: *Blake sc.* Plate-mark 14 × 7 cm.

iii. Vignette on p. 225. A head of Spalding in profile. Lettered: *Blake sculp.* Plate-mark 13.5 × 10.5 cm.

Note: These engravings are of no special interest. No. iii is recorded only in Russell, *Engravings*, p. 152.

103 **THE BOTANIC GARDEN**; A Poem, in Two Parts. Part I. Containing the Economy of Vegetation. Part II. The Loves of the Plants. With Philosophical Notes. [By Erasmus Darwin, M.D., F.R.S.] London, Printed for J. Johnson . . . MDCCXCI . . .

Collation: 4°. Part I, pp. xii Title, Sub-title to part I, Advertisement, Apology, Verses to the Author of "The Loves of the Plants" by the Rev. W. B. Stephens, Argument + 214 + 126 Additional notes + [2] Errata, etc. Part II, pp. vii Half-title to part II, Sub-title to part II (dated 1789), Proem + [i] Errata + viii Advertisement, Preface + 184.

Illustrations: Part I. Engraved frontispiece and eight plates, of which five were engraved by Blake. Part II. Engraved frontispiece, seven plates, and one vignette in the text.

i. The engraving signed by Blake is the second plate in part I, facing p. 127, and is entitled *Fertilization of Egypt*. In the centre of the picture a dog-headed man, Anubis, stands astride a stream, with his hands held in a supplicating attitude towards a large star, Sirius. To his left, on the ground, is a *sistrum*; to his right are pyramids. In the background, above a waterfall, is a winged and bearded representation of God, with outstretched arms holding thunderbolts.* Lettered: *H. Fuseli, R.A. inv. W Blake sc. / [Title] / London Publish'd Dec* 1*st* 1791. *by J. Johnson* . . . The engraving measures 20 × 15 cm.

---

* A kind of caricature of this design is to be found in *Sketches from St. George's Fields*, by Giorgione die Castel Chiuso [Peter Bayley], 1821, 8°, p. 95. A pump is here substituted for the figure of Anubis.

ii-v. Four large engravings of the Portland Vase, unsigned. They are entitled respectively: *The Portland Vase* (facing p. 53), *The first Compartment* (facing p. 54), *The second Compartment* (facing p. 55), and *The Handles & Bottom of the Vase* (facing p. 58). Each is lettered below: *London, Published Decr 1st, 1791, by J. Johnson . . .* , and the plate-mark of each measures about 28 × 20 cm.

The other plates were engraved by Anker Smith, Holloway, Nodder, Conder, and Alken.

Note: Part II of this work appears to have been published separately in 1789, and this edition of *The Loves of the Plants* appears in some copies of the complete work; in other copies it is replaced by the second and third editions, dated respectively 1790 and 1791, and to these editions two more plates are added. On the other hand the second edition of part I seems only to occur with the third edition of part II, and the third edition of part I with the fourth edition of part II. An 8° edition in two volumes, published in 1799, was called the fourth edition of *The Botanic Garden*. An unillustrated edition in two volumes, 8°, was published in Dublin in 1793. The work has been translated into French and German.

Fuseli's original sketch for *The Fertilization of Egypt* is in the B.M. Print Room, together with the sepia-wash drawing made after it by Blake. Fuseli's sketch shows only the figure of Anubis and the star, the other details having been added by Blake. It is referred to by W. M. Rossetti (Gilchrist, ii, 282) as "a good engrav- "ing, softer in style and effect than usual." A reduced engraving of the same design appeared in the 8° edition of 1799, and is probably also by Blake. Another engraving by Blake after Fuseli was added to the third 4° edition of the work (see no. 108). The engravings of the Portland Vase in the notes to part I are unsigned, but are in my opinion certainly by Blake; the style of engraving is typical of his work, and this attribution is supported by the fact that the reduced engravings of the same subject in the octavo edition of 1799 were engraved by him (see no. 118).

104 ELEMENTS OF MORALITY, for the Use of Children; with an Introductory Address to Parents. Translated from the German of the Rev. C. G. Salzmann. Illustrated with Fifty Copper Plates. In Three Volumes. Vol. I. [etc.] London: Printed by J. Crowder, for J. Johnson in St. Paul's Church-Yard. M,DCC,XCI.

Collation: 12°. Vol. I. Half-title, Title, pp. xxxii Advertisement by Mary Wollstonecraft, Introductory Address, Directions for placing the plates + 168.

Vol. II. Half-title, title, pp. 190+[1] Directions for placing the plates. Vol. III. Half-title, Title, pp. 200+[4] Directions for placing the plates, Catalogue of books.

Illustrations: Fifty-one plates, of which about sixteen were engraved by Blake after Chodowiecki.

Vol. i.	i.	Pl. 2, facing p.	15.	*Health is dearer to me than a whole Sack full of Gold.*
	ii.	„ 5, „ „	28.	*Stop! Stop!*
	iii.	„ 6, „ „	41.	*There he is! There comes our dear Father.*
	iv.	„ 8, „ „	60.	*Pompey is dead!*
	v.	„ 9, „ „	81.	*Patience can soften every pain.*
	vi.	„ 12, „ „	124.	*Is there any Hope?*
	vii.	„ 13, „ „	130.	*Your Compassion has saved my life.*
	viii.	„ 15, „ „	144.	*If we love others, they will love us in return.*
Vol. ii.	ix.	„ 26, „ „	85.	*Through Perseverance we may do many things, which we thought impossible.*
	x.	„ 32, „ „	177.	*We loathe a Slanderer as we do a Viper.*
Vol. iii.	xi.	„ 36, „ „	37.	*He who can torment a little helpless animal, has certainly a bad heart.*
	xii.	„ 37, „ „	50.	*A wicked man is more to be pitied than a cripple.*
	xiii.	„ 39, „ „	76.	*See how much good a Single man can do!*
	xiv.	„ 41, „ „	93.	*How happy it is that there are rich men in the world.*
	xv.	„ 47, „ „	164.	*Oh God! Thou art just!*
	xvi.	„ 49, „ „	180.	*See Children how powerful God is!*

At the top of each plate is the number of plate and volume. Each plate is lettered below: [*Title*] / *Published by J. Johnson,* [*date*]. The frontispiece and pl. 1-16, 27, 28, are dated Octr 1 1790; pl. 17-26, 29-32, Jany 1 1791; pl. 33-50, *March* 15, 1791. Plate 10 is in addition signed *W.P:C fec^t* 1790. Each engraving measures about 12 × 7 cm., and the plate-mark 15 × 9 cm.

Note: All the plates in this book except one are unsigned, but Gilchrist stated in the first edition of the *Life*, i, 91-92, that the illustrations were designed and engraved by Blake. This was corrected in the second edition, i, 91, a writer in *Notes and Queries* for June 19, 1880, having pointed out that all the illustrations except two (pl. 27 and 28) were copied from Daniel Chodowiecki's designs in Salzmann's *Moralisches Elementarbuch*, Leipzig, 1785; this book contains 70 plates, of which 49 were copied in the English edition. Since 1880 it has been usual to attribute all the plates to Blake, but if they be examined critically it becomes evident that only the minority are his work. The 16 plates in the above list are the only ones which I am able to assign to Blake with any degree of certainty; some of the others may be by Blake, but I think it is unlikely, although my list will be found to be in several instances in disagreement with that given by Russell (*Engravings*, pp. 156-158). The other plates were executed by at least two other engravers, one of whom, as noted above, has signed his initials *W.P: C fec*ᵗ * on pl. 10. The compiler of the Grolier Club Catalogue (no. 674) states (p. 102) that the two plates not copied from Chodowiecki were designed by Blake; the treatment of the trees and vines in the second of these (pl. 28) certainly suggests Blake's work, but as the plates were obviously not engraved by him, it seems unlikely that he was their designer.

The *Elements of Morality* were first published by Johnson in two volumes in 1790 "illustrated with copperplates." A duplicate two-volume edition, with a new title-page and without the plates, was issued in 1793. A second edition containing Blake's plates, which have been worked over, was published in 1792; it is called the third edition. The third edition with the plates, called the fourth, was published in 1799. A two-volume edition, 12°, containing the plates was published about 1820, It has the imprint: *London: Printed for John Sharpe, Juvenile Library, London Museum, Piccadilly*, and is undated.

105 OBSERVATIONS ON MAN, . . . In Two Parts. . . . By David Hartley, M.A. Reprinted from the Author's Edition in 1749. To which are now added, Notes and Additions to the Second Part; . . . Also . . . a Head of the Author. London: Printed for J. Johnson, . . . MDCCXCI.

Collation: 4°. Title, pp.[ii] Booksellers Advertisement + viii A Sketch of the Life and Character of Dr. Hartley + xx Preface, Contents, Table of Propositions + iv Introduction + 756 + [7] Index.

Frontispiece: A bust of Hartley in an oval, 15 × 11 cm. Lettered: *Blake sc. | David Hartley, M.A. | From a Painting by Shackelton. | Published by J. Johnson*, . . . *March 1*ˢᵗ. 1791.

Note: Other editions of the work do not contain this portrait. Blake refers to Hartley in contemptuous terms in his annotations to Watson's *Apology for the Bible*, 1798 (see appendix to the present work).

* The *P* of this signature has a very long lower serif, and Mr. W. E. Moss has made the ingenious suggestion that it should read *W.B: C fec*ᵗ, i.e., *W. Blake: Chodowiecki fec*ᵗ, but I find it impossible to accept this plate as Blake's work.

106 FABLES BY JOHN GAY With a Life of the Author and Embellished with Seventy Plates [device] Vol. I. London Printed for John Stockdale, Piccadilly. 1793

Collation: Roy. 8°, 25.5 × 15.5 cm., uncut, and imp. 8°. Vol. I. Engraved title, pp. xi Dedication, Contents + 225 Introduction, Fables + [1]. Vol. II. Engraved title, pp. vii Advertisement, Contents + 187 Fables, Life of Gay, List of Subscribers + [2] Advt. of Stockdale's edition of Barlow's *Aesop's Fables* + [1].

Illustrations: Frontispiece and 67 plates, of which 12 were engraved by Blake:
Vol. I. i. Facing p. 1. Introduction. The Shepherd and the Philosopher.
    ii.   „   „ 29. Fable vi. The Miser and Plutus.
    iii. „   „ 59. Fable xiii. The Tame Stag.
    iv.   „   „ 73. Fable xvi. The Pin and the Needle.
    v.   „   „ 99. Fable xxii. The Goat without a Beard.
    vi.   „   „ 109. Fable xxiv. The Butterfly and the Snail.
    vii. „   „ 125. Fable xxviii. The Persian, the Sun, and the Cloud.
    viii. „   „ 133. Fable xxx. The Setting-dog and the Partridge.
    ix.   „   „ 181. Fable xli. The Owl and the Farmer.
Vol. II. x. „   „ 1.   Fable i. The Dog and the Fox.
    xi.   „   „ 105. Fable xii. Pan and Fortune.
    xii. „   „ 145. Fable xvi. The Ravens, the Sexton, and the Earthworm.
Each engraving is lettered: *Blake sc.*, and each measures 7.5 × 9.5 cm. The other engravings are by Audinet, Cook, Grainger, Lovegrove, Mazell, Skelton, and Wilson.

Note: The plates are often stated to have been designed as well as engraved by Blake, but the illustrations to earlier editions of the *Fables* seem to have been adopted as a basis for all the designs, though in some the resemblance is slight. The first plate is the most characteristic example of Blake's work. The List of Subscribers includes the name of " Mr. Blake."

The edition of *Aesop's Fables* published by Stockdale in the same year is said to contain plates designed or engraved by Blake. This is, however, not the case, and the mistake may be due to the fact that Blake's name occurs in the list of engravers given in the advertisement of this work at the end of Gay's *Fables*, vol. ii. The plates for *Aesop's Fables* were after designs by Barlow.

A new edition of Gay's *Fables* was published by Stockdale in 1810; the paper on which it is printed has the date 1809 or 1810 in the watermark, though the date on the title-page is still 1793. The List of Subscribers and Advt. are omitted from vol. ii. The plates are somewhat worn.

107 ANECDOTES OF MARY; or, the Good Governess. By the Author of The History of the Davenport Family . . . London: Printed for E. Newbery, Corner of St. Paul's Church-Yard. M,DCC,XCV.

Collation: 12°. Half-title, Title, pp. 159 text + [1] blank + [4] books printed for E. Newbery.

Frontispiece: *The Pleasures of Benevolence*. 13.5 × 7.5 cm. Unsigned, but probably engraved by Blake.

Note: This book is included on the authority of Russell (*Engravings*, p. 161), who was the first to record it.

108 THE BOTANIC GARDEN. A Poem, in Two Parts . . . The Third Edition. London: Printed for J. Johnson, . . . MDCCXCV . . .

Collation: 4°. Part I. Pp. xx + 218 + 124 + [2]. Part II. Half-title, Sub-title, pp. viii + 200 + [2].

Illustrations: The same plates as in no. 103, with another plate engraved by Blake after Fuseli, entitled *Tornado*, added to part I, facing p. 168. This represents the nude figure of a hideous demon, with a serpent coiled round his left leg and his body, and looking over the top of his head. He is poised on a coil of the serpent, and his wings, with water streaming from their points, are stretched out on either side, while the serpent's tail is lashing up the sea below. His left hand is lost in black clouds, and lightning is blazing from his right. Lettered: *H. Fuseli RA: inv: W Blake: sc: | Tornado | London, Published Augt 1st 1795, by J. Johnson,* . . . The engraving measures 21 × 17 cm.

Note: This edition of *The Botanic Garden*, which is considerably scarcer than the other two (see no. 103), consists of the third edition of part I, dated 1795, and the fourth edition of part II, dated 1794. The additional plate was probably known to W. M. Rossetti only by the proof now in the B.M. Print Room, and he refers to it (Gilchrist, ii, 283) as: " Subject apparently from the Scandinavian Mythology (Thor " battering the Serpent [?]). Fuseli. Forcibly executed plate."

109 THE ELEMENTS OF MEDICINE OF JOHN BROWN, M.D. Translated from the Latin, with comments and illustrations, by the Author. New Edition revised and corrected. With a biographical preface by Thomas Beddoes, M.D. and a head of the Author. . . . In Two Volumes . . . London: Printed for J. Johnson, . . . MDCCXCV.

Collation: 8°. Vol. I. Pp. clxviii Half-title, Title, Dedication, Prefaces + 312 Text; folding leaf before p. 1. Vol. II. Pp. [iv] Half-title, Title + 366 Text + [8] Index + 1 leaf blank.

Frontispiece to vol. I: Half-length portrait of Dr. John Brown in an oval 13 × 11 cm. Inscribed below: *Donaldson Pinx^t Blake Sculp^t | John Brown, M.D. | London, Published May 1, 1795, by J. Johnson, St. Paul's Church Yard.*

Note: The frontispiece is described by Russell (*Engravings*, p. 162), but the book has not been recorded before. A copy containing the initials of S. T. Coleridge was sold with the Buxton Forman library at the Anderson Galleries, New York, on March 15, 1920. There is no copy of the work in the British Museum.

110 THE POEMS OF CAIUS VALERIUS CATULLUS, in English Verse: with the Latin text revised, and classical notes. Prefixed are Engravings of Catullus, and his friend Cornelius Nepos; In Two Volumes . . . London: Printed for J. Johnson, St. Paul's Church-Yard. MDCCXCV.

Collation: 8°. Vol. I. Pp. xxxvi Half-title, Title, Preface, Life of Catullus, Metres of Catullus, Ancient writers who make mention of Catullus + 223 + [3] Errata. Vol. II. Half-title, Title, pp. 236 + [2] Errata.

Illustrations: A frontispiece to each volume stippled by Blake.
    i. Heading: *Frontispiece to Vol. I.* Lettered below: *Xaverius Della Rosa, Veronae, delin. Blake sculpsit. | C: Val: Catullus | Apud effigiem antiquam curiae senatûs veronensi superpositam | London Published March 19, 1795, by J. Johnson . . .* 16 × 9.5 cm.
    ii. Heading: *Frontispiece to Vol. II.* Lettered below: *Xaverius Della Rosa, Veronae, delin. Blake sculpsit. | Cornel: Nepos | (etc. as in no. i).* 16.5 × 10.5 cm.

Note: The frontispieces, representing full-length statues of Catullus and Nepos, are described by Russell (*Engravings*, pp. 161-2), but the volumes containing them are very rare and have not been recorded before.

THE SKINNING OF THE ABOMA SNAKE, SHOT BY CAPTAIN STEDMAN

Line Engraving, 1791

111 NARRATIVE, OF A FIVE YEARS' EXPEDITION, against the Revolted Negroes of Surinam, . . . from the year 1772, to 1777: elucidating the History of that Country, and describing its Productions, . . . with an account of the Indians of Guiana, & Negroes of Guinea. By Captn J. G. Stedman. illustrated with 80 elegant Engravings, from drawings made by the Author. Vol. I.[II.] . . . London. Printed for J. Johnson, . . . & J. Edwards, . . . 1796.

Collation: 4°. Vol. 1. Engraved title, pp. vi Dedication, Preface + [viii] List of Subscribers + 407 + [8] Index, Directions for facing the plates, Errata. Vol. II. Engraved title, pp. iv Contents + 404 + [8] Index, Directions for facing the plates, Errata.

Illustrations: Frontispiece to vol. 1, and forty plates in each volume, of which eight in each volume were engraved by Blake.

Vol. 1.	i. Pl.	VII, facing p.	80.	*A Coromantyn Free Negro, or Ranger, armed.*
	ii. „	XI, „	„ 110.	*A Negro hung alive by the Ribs to a Gallows.*
	iii. „	XIII, „	„ 132.	*A private Marine of Col. Fourgeoud's Corps.*
	iv. „	XVIII, „	„ 166.	*The Mecoo & Kishee Kishee Monkeys.*
	v. „	XIX, „	„ 174.	*The skinning of the Aboma Snake, shot by Cap. Stedman.*
	vi. „	XXII, „	„ 200.	*Group of Negros, as imported to be sold for Slaves.*
	vii. „	XXV, „	„ 227.	*The Sculls of Lieu^t Leppar, & Six of his Men.*
	viii. „	XXXV, „	„ 326.	*Flagellation of a Female Samboe Slave.*
Vol. 11.	ix. „	XLII, „	„ 10.	*The Quato & Saccawinkee Monkeys.*
	x. „	XLIX, „	„ 56.	*A Surinam Planter in his Morning Dreſs.*
	xi. „	LII, „	„ 74.	*Limes, Capsicum, Mammy Apple etc.*
	xii. „	LV, „	„ 104.	*March thro' a swamp or Marsh in Terra-firma.*
	xiii. „	LXVIII, „	„ 280.	*Family of Negro Slaves from Loango.*
	xiv. „	LXXI, „	„ 296.	*The Execution of Breaking on the Rack.*
	xv. „	LXXVI, „	„ 348.	*The celebrated Graman Quacy.*
	xvi. „	LXXX, „	„ 394.	*Europe supported by Africa & America.*

The majority of the plates are lettered: *Blake sculp^t* / [*Title*] / *London, Published Decr 2^d 1793, by J. Johnson* . . . / [*no. of plate*]. Plates vii, xii, and xiv are without the signature; pl. 2, 13, and 16 are dated *Decr 1st* 1792, and pl. 12, *Decr 1st* 1794. The plate-marks measure about 27 × 20 cm., the engravings about 18 × 13 cm.

The other 65 plates were executed by Bartolozzi, Benedetti, Barlow, Conder, Holloway, and Smith.

Note: Three of the plates, as mentioned above, do not bear Blake's signature, but there can be no doubt that they are his work.* Some copies of the book were issued with the plates coloured by hand. The name of " Blake (Mr. Wm.) London " appears in the List of Subscribers.

A second edition, in which the plates are differently placed, was published in 1806; some copies have the plates coloured as before. The unsold copies of the second edition were issued with a new title-page in 1813.

112　**THOUGHTS ON OUTLINE**, Sculpture, and the System That Guided the Ancient Artists in Composing their Figures and Groupes: Accompanied with Free Remarks on the Practice of The Moderns, and Liberal Hints Cordially Intended For their Advantage. To which are Annexed Twenty-four Designs of Classical Subjects Invented on the Principles Recommended in the Essay by George Cumberland. . . . London. Printed by W. Wilson, . . . and Sold By Messrs. Robinson . . . and T. Egerton, . . . MDCCXCVI.

Collation: 4°. Pp. [iv] Quotation, Title + iii To the Reader + 52 + [2] Books by the Same Author.

Illustrations: 24 engravings at the end, of which 8 were executed by Blake.
　i. No. 12. *Psyche Disobeys.*
　ii. 　„　13. *Psyche Repents.*
　iii. 　„　14. *Venus Councels Cupid.*
　iv. 　„　15. *The Conjugal Union of Cupid.*
　v. 　„　16. *Cupid and Psyche.*
　vi. 　„　18. *Iron Age.*
　vii. 　„　19. *Aristophanes, Clouds, Scene* 1.
　viii. 　„　23. *Anacreon, Ode LII.*
Nos. i-vi are lettered : [*Title*] / *From an original Invention by G: Cumberland: Eng^d by W. Blake: Publish'd as the Act directs November* [*Nov^r*] 5: 1794. Nos. vii-viii are

* Although pl. xii is omitted by Russell (*Engravings*, p. 163).

lettered: *From an original Invention by G: C: Eng^d by W: B: Publishd January.* [*Jan^y*] 1: 1795. Plate-mark about 15 × 21 cm.

Note: For a short account of Blake's relations with Cumberland see Russell, *Letters*, p. 53, note 1. Blake thought very highly of the *Outlines* and refers to them several times in letters written to Cumberland between 1795 and 1799 (Russell, *Letters*, pp. 56, 66). In an appendix to this work, in the course of some remarks on the illustrations, Cumberland writes (pp. 47-48): ". . . but one thing may be "asserted of this work, which can be said of few others that have passed the hands of "an engraver, which is, that *Mr. Blake* has condescended to take upon him the "laborious office of making them, I may say, fac-similes of my originals: a compli- "ment, from a man of his extraordinary genius and abilities, the highest, I believe, I "shall ever receive:—and I am indebted to his generous partiality for the instruction "which encouraged me to execute a great part of the plates myself; enabling me "thereby to reduce considerably the price of the book." Four of the plates appeared again in a later work by Cumberland, published in 1829 (see no. 133).

---

113 **ELEMENTS OF ALGEBRA, BY LEONARD EULER.** Translated from the French, . . . In Two Volumes. . . . London: Printed for J. Johnson, . . . 1797.

Collation: 8°. Vol. I. Pp. xliii Title, Preface, Life of Euler, Advertisement, Contents + [i] Errata + 461. Vol. II. Pp. viii Title, Contents + 552.

Frontispiece: Vol. 1. A head of Euler, 11 × 7 cm., engraved in line and stipple. Lettered: *Blake Sculp.* | *Leonard Euler.* | *From a Medalion, as large as life,* | *by Ruchotte, in the poſſeſſion of* | *John Wilmot Esqr.*

Note: This engraving is referred to by Blake in a letter to Hayley dated May 4, 1804: "Mr. Flaxman agrees with me that somewhat more than outline is necessary "to the execution of Romney's designs, . . . I should propose to etch them in a "rapid but firm manner, somewhat, perhaps, as I did the 'Head of Euler'" (Russell, *Letters*, p. 154).

---

114 **THE MONTHLY MAGAZINE,** and British Register, for 1797. From July to December, inclusive. Vol. IV. London: Printed for R. Phillips, No. 71, and Sold by J. Johnson, No 72 St Pauls Church-yard. 1798.

Collation: 8°. Pp. [viii] Title, Index + 566.

Illustrations: Seven plates, one of which was engraved by Blake. Heading: *For the Monthly Magazine*, *Sept.* 1797. Lettered below: *Blake: s | The late Mr Wright | of Derby.* A bust of the subject looking to the right; 8.5 × 6 cm. Plate-mark 17.5 × 11 cm.

Note: First recorded by Russell (*Engravings*, p. 166).

115 **A NEW AND IMPROVED HISTORY OF ENGLAND, . . .** By Charles Allen, A.M. Author of the Roman History, &c. The Second Edition, Embellished with Four Copper Plates, and a Chronological Chart . . . London: Printed for J. Johnson, . . . 1798.

Collation: 12°. Pp. iv Title, Preface + [iv] Contents, Advts. of books + 551 + [1] Remarks. A folding table faces the title.

Illustrations: Four plates engraved by Blake after Fuseli.
   i. Facing p. 15. *Alfred and the Neat-herd's Wife.*
   ii.   ,,   ,,   78. *King John absolved by Pandulph.*
   iii.   ,,   ,, 128. *Wat Tyler and the Tax-gatherer.*
   iv.   ,,   ,, 224. *Queen Elizabeth and Essex.*
Each plate is lettered: *Blake: s.* [*sc.*] | [*Title*] | *London, Published Dec^r* 1, 1797, *by J. Johnson,* . . . Each engraving measures 14.5 × 8 cm.

Note: Although these illustrations do not bear Fuseli's signature there can be no doubt that they were engraved after his designs. Four similar plates are found in the *Roman History* by the same author (see next entry).

116 **A NEW AND IMPROVED ROMAN HISTORY, . . .** By Charles Allen, A.M. Author of the History of England, &c. The Second Edition. Embellished with Four Copper Plates. London: Printed for J. Johnson, . . . 1798.

Collation: 12°. Pp. viii Title, Advertisement, Preface, Contents + 496.

Illustrations: Four plates engraved by Blake after Fuseli.
   i. Facing p. 2. *Mars and Rhea Silvia.*
   ii.   ,,   ,,   33. *The Death of Lucretia.*
   iii.   ,,   ,, 174. *C. Marius at Minturnum.*
   iv.   ,,   ,, 292. *The Death of Cleopatra.*

Each plate is lettered: *Blake: sc.* / [Title] / *London, Published Dec* 1, 1797, *by J. Johnson*, . . . Each engraving measures 15 × 8 cm.

Note: These plates, like those in the *History of England* by the same author (see preceding entry), were doubtless designed by Fuseli, although they do not bear his name.

117 THE POETRY OF VARIOUS GLEES, Songs, &c. as Performed at the Harmonists. London: Printed at the Philanthropic Reform, London-Road, St. George's Fields, 1798.

    Collation: 21 cm., in fours. Pp. [iv] Title, Dedication + viii Index + 115 + [1].

    Frontispiece: Representing three cherubs, seated among clouds, and singing together. Over their heads is the word *Harmonists*, and above this is a lyre surmounted by an irradiated head. Lettered: *Blake sc. Change Alley*. Plate-mark 17.5 × 11 cm.

    Note: It is possible that this engraving is not the work of William Blake, since the lettering gives an address at which it is not known that he ever lived; it may be that of an occasional employer, and if so it would appear that Blake's connexion with this employer lasted over a long period. In the list of subscribers in vol. II of *Bell's Shakspere*, an elaborately illustrated work in twenty volumes, published 1786-1788, is the name of: "Blake, Mr., Engraver, No. 6 Exchange-alley, Cornhill—4 copies." Further, in the B.M. Print Room are two other engravings with the same lettering, dated 1800 and 1809, but these do not come within the scope of the present work (see Russell, *Engravings*, pp. 169, 179). The style of engraving of all three is conventional and inconclusive, and it is quite possible that they are all the work of another engraver of the same name, but the proof is still lacking.

    There is another issue of the *Harmonists'* volume with the same title-page, in which certain misprints in the text have been corrected; the frontispiece has been re-engraved, but is not signed.

118 THE BOTANIC GARDEN, A Poem. In Two Parts . . . The Fourth Edition. London: Printed for J. Johnson, . . . 1799.

    Collation: 8°. Part I, pp. xx + 492. Part II, pp. xii + 282.

    Illustrations: Part I. Frontispiece, ten plates, five of which were probably engraved by Blake, and one vignette. Part II. Frontispiece and ten plates.

i. Part I, facing p. 145. A reduced and reversed engraving of the *Fertilization of Egypt*. Unsigned, but probably engraved by Blake. 13 × 8 cm. Plate-mark 20.5 × 13 cm.

ii-v. Part I, facing pp. 352, 355, 357, 362. Reduced engravings of *The Portland Vase*, *The first Compartment*, *The second Compartment*, and *The Handle & Bottom of the Vase*. The third of these is signed on the base, *Blake*, and they were probably all engraved by him.

These five engravings are lettered below: *London, Published Decr 1st 1791, by J. Johnson . . .*

Note: It will be noticed that these plates were executed at the same time as those in the quarto edition of *The Botanic Garden* (see no. 103), though not published until 1799; this makes it all the more probable that they were engraved by Blake. The frontispieces, on the other hand, are dated June 1st, 1799, and are certainly not by him. The *Fertilization of Egypt* was re-engraved by another hand for a second octavo edition, published in 1824.

119 **A LETTER TO THE COMMITTEE** for Raising the Naval Pillar, or Monument, . . . By John Flaxman, Sculptor. London: Printed for **T. Cadell**, jun. and **W. Davies**, . . . 1799.

Collation: 4°. Pp. 14 Title, A Letter &c. + [2] Explanation of the Plates.

Illustrations: Frontispiece and two plates at the end engraved by Blake after Flaxman.

i. Frontispiece. A Statue of Britannia Triumphant. Lettered: *Blake sculp. | A Colofsal Statue 230 feet high; proposed to be erected on Greenwich Hill*. The engraving measures 19 × 15 cm.

ii. Plate II. Lettered: *A View of Greenwich Hospital with the Statue of Britannia on the hill*. The engraving measures 10 × 19 cm.

iii. Plate III. Illustrations of six ancient monuments, each with its name below. The engraving measures 19 × 15 cm.

Note: Plates II and III are unsigned, but they appear to have been engraved by Blake. All three plates are very trivial examples of his work. They are mentioned by Gilchrist, i, 41.

120 AN ESSAY ON SCULPTURE: in a Series of Epistles to John Flaxman, Esq. R.A. With Notes. . . . By William Hayley, Eſq. London: Printed by A. Strahan, . . . for T. Cadell jun. and W. Davies, . . . 1800.

Collation: 4°. Pp. xi Half-title, Title, Introductory Letter + [1] errata slip + 358.

Illustrations: Three plates engraved by Blake.

i. Frontispiece. A circular engraving of a head of Pericles. Lettered: *Pericles. | from a Bust in the Poſseſsion of Charles Townley Esq. | Publiſhd June 14. 1800 by Cadell & Davis Strand.* Plate-mark 22.5 × 16 cm.

ii. Facing p. 126. An engraving after a drawing by Thomas Hayley. Lettered: *T. H. invenit   W. Blake sc. | The Death of Demosthenes. | [quotation] | Publiſhd* &c. Plate-mark 16.5 × 21 cm.

iii. Facing p. 163. An engraving after a drawing by Howard of a medallion of Thomas Hayley by Flaxman. Lettered: *Blake. sc | Thomas Hayley, | the Disciple of | John Flaxman. | from a Medallion. | Publiſhd* &c. Plate-mark 22.5 × 16 cm.

Note: These engravings are all trivial examples, the best of them being that of the medallion of Thomas Hayley, illegitimate son of William Hayley. In letters to Hayley, dated April 1 and May 6, 1800 (Letters 6 and 7), shortly after Thomas Hayley's death, Blake refers to this engraving; in the second letter he also mentions the frontispiece.

The plates are also referred to by Flaxman in his letters * to Hayley:

Jan. 29, 1800—" I have delivered the drawing of Demosthenes to Mr. Blake with " the right orthography of the Dedication to Neptune."

March 26, 1800—" It is equally surprising & unaccountable that you have had " no further news of the engravings, for Mr. Howard finished a beautiful drawing from " the Medallion of my Friend Thomas I think four weeks ago, since which time it has " been in the hands of Mr. Blake & the copper plate from it is most likely done by " this time, as well as that of the head of Pericles but perhaps you are not acquainted " with Mr. Blake's direction? it is No. 13 Hercules Buildings near the Asylum, Surry " side of Westminster Bridge."

In my possession is Hayley's own copy of the *Essay,* in which he has made a few corrections. Inserted is Thomas Hayley's pencil sketch for *The Death of Demosthenes*; in this the dedication of the statue, at the base of which Demosthenes is lying, is written ΠΟΣΕΙΔΑΩΝΙ; the reference in Flaxman's letter given above is thus explained.

* Fairfax Murray collection, Fitzwilliam Museum, Cambridge. For other interesting extracts from the same source see *The Real Blake* by E. J. Ellis, London, 1907, pp. 187-8, 260, and 267.

121   GYMNASTICS FOR YOUTH: or a Practical Guide to Healthful and Amusing Exercises for the Use of Schools. . . . Freely Translated from the German of C. G. Salzmann, . . . Illustrated with Copper Plates. London: Printed for J. Johnson, . . . 1800.

Collation: 8°. Pp. xvi Title, Dedication, Preface, Contents + 433 + [1].

Illustrations: Ten engravings probably executed by Blake.
i. Frontispiece. Folding plate, 19 × 23 cm., representing various gymnastic appliances.
ii-x. Facing pp. 196, 218, 226, 237, 247, 264, 286, 314, and 339. Nine plates, 11.5 × 7 cm., representing boys engaged in various forms of sport—leaping, running, shooting, wrestling, etc. Each engraving is lettered: [Title] / *Publiſh'd by J. Johnson,* . . . *Feb*ʸ 1 1800.

Note: These engravings are usually attributed to Blake. They are unsigned, but their style shows strong evidence of Blake's work. In the B.M. Print Room is a set of proofs of the same subjects, but some are reversed, and all are badly engraved by a different hand; these are perhaps the originals from which those in the book were engraved, considerable changes being made in the process. A writer in *Notes & Queries*, April 17, 1897, p. 302, discusses the authenticity of this attribution, and concludes that neither the drawing nor the engraving is by Blake; Russell (*Engravings*, p. 195) is also of this opinion. The present writer does not agree with this as regards the engraving. Another edition was issued in Philadelphia in 1803.

122   LECTURES ON PAINTING, Delivered at the Royal Academy March 1801, By Henry Fuseli, P.P. With Additional Observations and Notes. [*vignette*] London: Printed for J. Johnson, . . . 1801. . . .

Collation: 4°. Pp. [vi] Title, Dedication, Sub-title to First Lecture, Argument + 151 + [1].

Illustrations: Two vignettes after Fuseli, one of which was engraved by Blake:
i. On title-page. An oval vignette, lettered: *F. Legat ſculp*ᵗ.
ii. On p. 151. A rectangular vignette representing Michelangelo standing before the Coliseum. Lettered: *Blake: sc / Ancora imparo. / M: Angelo Bonarroti.* Plate-mark 14 × 8 cm.

Note: Blake's engraving is reduced and considerably altered from Fuseli's original wash drawing, which was seen recently by the writer. Gilchrist (i, 161)

Variation

ROMEO AND JULIET, ACT IV, SCENE V
Line Engraving, 1799

describes the engraving, and suggests that the inspiration of the vignette on the title-page was owed by Fuseli to Blake. That the former was the actual designer there can be no doubt, since a proof in the B.M. is lettered with his name also.

Some copies of the book were bound up later with a second part issued in 1820; this volume has as frontispiece a portrait of Fuseli engraved by Sievier after Houghton. In a new edition of the work, published in 1830, Blake's vignette is re-engraved by Engelheart.

123 BOYDELL'S GRAPHIC ILLUSTRATIONS OF THE DRAMATIC WORKS, OF SHAKSPEARE; consisting of a series of prints Forming an elegant and useful Companion to the Various Editions of his Works, Engraved from Pictures, purposely printed By the very first Artists, and lately exhibited at The Shakspeare Gallery. London Published by Messrs Boydell & Co. Cheapside [1803]

Collation: 44 × 34 cm. Pp. [iv] List of Plates, Advertisement + [vi] Index, with Frontispiece, Engraved title, and ninety-nine plates.

Plates: One was engraved by Blake.
[Pl. 95] Capulet finds Juliet dead. Lettered below: *Painted by J. Opie. Variation Engrav'd by W. Blake. | Shakspeare. | Romeo and Juliet, | Act IV. Scene V. | Pub^d March 25, 1799, by John & Josiah Boydell, at the Shakspeare Gallery Pall Mall, & N° 90, Cheapside.* The engraving measures 17 × 24 cm. The other plates were executed by thirty-two different engravers, and bear dates varying from 1791 to 1803.

Note: Hitherto unrecorded. Plate 94, preceding Blake's engraving, was executed by Simon from another painting by Opie of the same subject. The two larger volumes of Boydell's *Collection of Prints*, 1803, do not contain any plates by Blake. The only copy of the present volume that I have seen is in the collection of Mr. W. E. Moss.

124 THE LIFE AND POSTHUMOUS WRITINGS, OF WILLIAM COWPER, ESQR. . . . . By William Hayley Esqr. . . . . Vol. I [*etc.*] Chichester: Printed by J. Seagrave; For J. Johnson, . . . 1803 [1804].

Collation: 4°. Vol. I. Pp. xxii Title, Introductory Letter + 413 + [8] Contents. Vol. II. Title, pp. 422 + [6] Contents + 1 leaf blank (pp. 415-416 are on a leaf inserted between G G G 3 and 4). Vol. III. Title, pp. xxxi Desultory Remarks + 416 + [4] Contents + [2] blank.

Illustrations: Five plates engraved, and one illustration in the text designed and engraved, by Blake.

i. Vol. i. Frontispiece. A bust of Cowper. Lettered: *From a Portrait in Crayons Drawn from the Life by Romney in* 1792 *Engravd by W Blake* 1802 | *William, Cowper.* | . . . *Publish'd Novemb* 5, 1802, *by J. Johnson* . . . Plate-mark 26 × 19.5 cm.

ii. Vol. i. Facing p. 4. A bust of Cowper's mother within an oval surrounded by a rectangular frame. Lettered: *D. Heins pinx   W Blake sculp* | *M* *Cowper* | *Mother of the Poet* | *Publish'd* etc. The engraving measures 15.5 × 13 cm.

iii. Vol. ii. Frontispiece. A bust of Cowper in a night-cap, stippled after Lawrence and inscribed *William Cowper—Author of "The Task."* Lettered: *T Lawrence RA: ad vivum del:* 1793   *W. Blake sculp* 1802 | *Publish'd Nov* 5, 1802 etc. The stipple measures 23 × 16.5 cm.

iv. Vol. ii. On p. 415, below a " Motto on a Clock." A design drawn and executed by Blake.   The upper part represents the " weather-house," in the left hand compartment of which is a cloaked man with a storm in the background, and in the right a girl, with sheep, a cottage, and the sun behind.   The stand of the " weather-house " is inscribed with lines from Cowper's *Task. B*1, *line* 200[-204].   Below the stand is a garland with a scroll inscribed *The Peasants Nest,* and below this is a circular design inscribed *Puss Tiney & Bess* | *Cowper's tame Hares.*   Lettered, below the stand: *Blake d & sc*; and at the bottom of the plate *Publish'd* etc. Plate-mark 23 × 17 cm.

v. Vol. iii. Frontispiece. Lettered: *Francis Stone del: W Blake sculp* | *A View of S* *Edmund's Chapel,* | *in the Church of East Dereham,* | *Containing the Grave of William Cowper Esq* | *Publish'd by J. Johnson* . . . 25 *March* 1804.   The engraving measures 20 × 14.5 cm.

vi. Vol. iii. Facing the frontispiece. Lettered: *A Sketch of the Monument* | *Erected in the Church of East Dereham in Norfolk* | *In Memory of William Cowper Esq* | *Etch'd by W Blake from the original Model* | *by John Flaxman Esq* . . . | *Publish'd* etc. The design and lettering measure 18 × 15 cm.

Note: In a letter to Thomas Butts, Sept. 11, 1801, Blake remarks that: " my " principal labour at this time is engraving plates for Cowper's *Life,* a work of " magnitude, which Mr. Hayley is now labouring at with all his matchless industry " (Russell, *Letters,* p. 93).   Later he writes to Hayley, Feb. 23, 1804: " The plates of " Cowper's monument are both in great forwardness, and you shall have proofs in " another week. I assure you that I will not spare pains, and am myself very much " satisfied that I shall do my duty and produce two very elegant plates " (Russell, *Letters,* p. 145).   For another letter to Hayley, hitherto unpublished, chiefly concerning these plates, and dated March 16, 1804, see appendix to present work. There is a MS. note by John Linnell as follows: "The copper-plates which Blake " engraved to illustrate Hayley's life of Cowper were, as he told me, printed entirely " by himself and his wife in his own press—a very good one which cost him forty " pounds." In my own possession is a proof of the stippled portrait in vol. II (no. iii above); it differs from the published print only in details. A supplementary volume was issued in 1806; it has a frontispiece representing *Judith, or Cowper's Oak*, engraved by Caroline Watson.

I have noticed at least three states of Blake's " Weather-house " design. One of these belongs to the second edition of the book, which was issued in the same year as the first. The typographical part of the leaf, which, as noted above, is an insertion, has been reset. A reproduction of this engraving is to be found in *The Poems of William Cowper. Ed. J. C. Bailey Methuen and Co. London* [1905]; this volume also contains reproductions of a recently discovered miniature portrait of Cowper by Blake after the painting by Romney, and of Blake's designs "Winter" and "Evening," done for the sides of a fireplace at Yaxham Rectory.

125 **THE TRIUMPHS OF TEMPER. A Poem: In Six Cantos. By William Hayley, Esq . . . The Twelfth Edition, Corrected. With New Original Designs, By Maria Flaxman. Chichester: Printed by J. Seagrave; For T. Cadell and W. Davies, . . . 1803.**

Collation: 8°. Pp. xii Half-title, Title, Preface + 165 + [1].

Illustrations: Six plates, facing pp. 2, 48, 61, 97, 105, 154, engraved by Blake after Maria Flaxman, sister of the sculptor. Each plate is lettered: *Canto I, verse* 29 [etc.] | *Maria Flaxman inv. & del. W. Blake sculp* [*sc.*] | *Publish'd May* 1. 1803. *by Cadell & Davies. Strand.* Plate-mark 15.5 × 9.5 cm. See Russell, *Engravings*, p. 174.

Note: In a letter to his brother dated Jan. 30, 1803, Blake mentions that he is receiving 10 guineas each for these plates (see appendix to present work). Some copies were issued on large paper, measuring 24 × 14.5 cm., uncut. The copy of the book, which had belonged to Hayley's son, was given to Blake by Hayley after his son's death; in it the author wrote the two stanzas beginning—

" Accept, my gentle visionary Blake . . ."

These verses are recorded by J. T. Smith in his biography of Blake,* the book being in Mrs. Blake's possession in 1828 when he was writing. Blake's engravings were also included in the thirteenth edition of *The Triumphs of Temper*, published in 1807; the plates are there somewhat worn.

126 ACADEMIC CORRESPONDENCE, 1803 . . . Published by desire of the Academy, by Prince Hoare, . . . London: Printed for Robson, Old Bond Street; Payne, Mews-gate; Hatchard, Piccadilly, and Barker, Great Russel-street. 1804

> *Collation*: 4°. Pp. viii Half-title, Title, Introduction + 9-28.
>
> *Frontispiece*: Two views of a statue of Ceres engraved by Blake after Flaxman. Lettered below: *J Flaxman R.A. del: W Blake. sc: | Fragment of an Antique Statue of Ceres, found in the Ruins of Eleusis and now placed in the Public Library at Cambridge.* The plate-mark measures 19.5 × 21 cm.
>
> *Note*: Not recorded elsewhere. The statue is referred to on p. 25 of the *Academic Correspondence* in a letter on a different subject from Flaxman to Hoare; Flaxman, instead of a description, sends a sketch, no doubt the original from which Blake's engraving was executed.

127 THE ILIAD OF HOMER Engraved from the Compositions of John Flaxman R.A. Sculptor, London. . . . Printed for Longman, Hurst, Rees & Orme, . . . March 1, 1805.

> *Collation*: Oblong f°., 13 × 27 cm. Engraved title + 39 designs = 40 plates.
>
> *Plates*: Three were engraved by Blake.
> i. Heading: *Plate 1. Homer Invoking the Muse 1.1.*
> ii. Heading: *Plate 2. Minerva Repressing the Fury of Achilles.*
> iii. Heading: *Plate 5. Thetis Entreating Jupiter to Honor Achilles.*
> Each plate is lettered below: *Blake sculp. | [quotation].* Plate-mark about 25 × 36 cm. The majority of the other plates were engraved by Piroli, and a few by Parker.
>
> *Note*: Published together with a new issue of the *Odyssey*, the plates for the latter being engraved by Parker and Neagle. Blake refers to these engravings in a letter to Hayley as follows: May 4, 1804 " . . . the price I receive for engraving "Flaxman's outlines of *Homer* is five guineas each" (Russell, *Letters*, p. 154). Gilchrist

* *Nollekens and his Times*, 1828, ii, 465-6.

(i, 111) states that the plates for the original edition of Flaxman's *Odyssey*, 1793, were engraved by Blake, those by Piroli having been lost on the way to England. The plates, however, bear Piroli's name, and, as there does not seem to be any evidence beyond Gilchrist's statement for attributing them to Blake, they have not been included here.

128 THE PLAYS OF WILLIAM SHAKSPEARE, Accurately printed from the Text . . . left by the late George Steevens, Esq. With a Series of Engravings, From Original Designs of Henry Fuseli, Esq. R.A. . . . and . . . Notes, . . . &c. By Alexander Chalmers, A.M. In Ten Volumes . . . London: Printed for F. C. and J. Rivington; J. Johnson; . . . 1805

Collation: 8°. Vol. VII. Title, pp. 402. Vol. X. Title, pp. 463.

Illustrations: Three engravings after Fuseli, one of which is by Blake, in each volume.
   i. Vol. VII. Facing p. 235. Queen Katherine's Dream. Heading: *Act iv. King Henry VIII. Sc. II.* Lettered below: *Fuseli inv. Blake sculp.* / [quotation] / *Publish'd May* 12, 1804, *by F. & C. Rivington*, . . . The engraving measures 15.5 × 9.5 cm.
   ii. Vol. X. Facing p. 107. Romeo and the Apothecary. Heading: *Act I Romeo and Juliet Sc I.* Lettered below: *H. Fuseli R.A. inv. W. Blake sc.* / [quotation] / *Publish'd by C & F Rivington . . . Jan* 14. 1804. The engraving measures 17 × 9 cm.
   The other engravings in these volumes are by Neagle, J. Smith, and Rhodes.

Note: These engravings were undertaken by Blake towards the end of the year 1803, and several references to them are found in his letters to Hayley, including the following, dated Dec. 18, 1804: "I cannot omit observing that the price " Mr. Johnson gives for the plates of Fuseli's 'Shakespeare' . . . is twenty-five guineas " each. On comparing them with mine of the 'Shipwreck' [see no. 130], you will " perceive that I have done my duty and put forth my whole strength" (Russell, *Letters*, p. 173). The other references show that the work was issued in parts, which were sent by Blake to Hayley in four batches on Feb. 23, March 16, Sept. 20, and Dec. 18, 1804. Blake subsequently made three water-colour drawings of *Queen Katherine's Vision*, which are dated 1807.
   Another edition in nine volumes containing the same plates was issued in the same year; Blake's plates are in vol. VI, facing p. 263, and vol. IX, facing p. 1.

129 AN INQUIRY into the Requisite Cultivation and Present State of the Arts of Design in England. By Prince Hoare. London: Printed for Richard Phillips, . . . 1806. . . .

Collation: 8°. Pp. xxiii Title, Dedication, Preface, Contents + [i] Erratum + 270 + [2] Books published by R. Phillips.

Frontispiece: Heading: *The Graphic Muse*. A rectangular engraving, representing a female figure seated upon clouds, and holding in one hand a scroll inscribed *Theory*. Lettered below: *Sr Josh^a Reynolds pinx^t   Blake. sc.* / [quotation] / *Sketched from the Picture by Sir Joshua Reynolds on the ceiling of the Library of* / *the Royal Academy.* / *Pub^d Feb^r 21, 1806, by R. Phillips*, . . . The engraving measures 9 × 8.5 cm., the plate-mark 17.5 × 11.5 cm.

Note: Prince Hoare was a painter, and the author of many essays on subjects connected with the fine arts; he was made Foreign Secretary of the Royal Academy in 1799. Blake was acquainted with him, and in a letter to Hayley dated Feb. 23, 1804, expressed admiration for his work. The engraving was first described by Miss K. A. McDowall in *The Burlington Magazine*, 1907 (see no. 576).

130 THE LIFE OF GEORGE ROMNEY, ESQ. . . . By William Hayley, Esq. Chichester: Printed by W. Mason For T. Payne, Pall Mall, London. 1809.

Collation: 4°. Pp. [ii] Title + 2 Dedication + [4] Preface + 416 + [6] Contents.

Illustrations: Frontispiece and eleven plates, of which one was engraved by Blake after Romney:
Facing p. 84. Engraving after an oil sketch of a horseman rescuing the victims of a shipwreck from the sea; it is in illustration of a story told in the travels of Thunberg. Lettered: *Sketch of a Shipwreck after Romney.* / *Engraved by Blake.* / *Published April 14th 1809 by Thomas Payne*, . . . The engraving measures 13 × 18 cm.
Most of the other plates were engraved by Caroline Watson, and the remainder by Haines, Raimbach, Meadows, and Cooper.

Note: Blake also engraved a portrait of Romney for this work, but the plate was not used. These two engravings are the subjects of several references in Blake's letters to Hayley:
June 22, 1804. "I have got the three sublime designs of Romney now in

" my lodgings and find them all too grand as well as too undefined for mere outlines
" . . . It is certain that the pictures deserve to be engraved by the hands of angels, and
" must not by any means be done in a careless or too hasty manner . . . My ' Head
" ' of Romney ' is in very great forwardness. Parker commends it highly." (Russell,
Letters, p. 162.)

    " Sept. 20, 1804. " I hope you will excuse my delay in sending the books
" which I have had some time, but kept them back till I could send a proof of ' The
" ' Shipwreck,' which I hope will please. It yet wants all its last and finishing touches,
" but I hope you will be enabled by it to judge of the pathos of the picture . . . The
" favour of ten pounds more will carry me through this plate and the ' Head of
" ' Romney,' for which I am already paid. You shall soon see a proof of him in a very
" advanced state." (*Ibid.*, p. 166.)

    Oct. 23, 1804. " In a short time I shall make my assertion good that I am
" become suddenly as I was at first, by producing the ' Head of Romney ' and ' The
" ' Shipwreck,' quite another thing from what you or I ever expected them to be. In
" short I am now satisfied and proud of my work, which I have not been for the above
" long period." (*Ibid.*, p. 172.)

    Dec. 18, 1804. " I am again in want of ten pounds; hope that the size and
" neatness of my plate of ' The Shipwreck,' will plead for me the excuse for troubling
" you before it can be properly called finished, though Flaxman has already pronounced
" it so." (*Ibid.*, p. 173.)

    Dec. 28, 1804. " As to the price of the plates . . . I consulted Mr. Parker
" on the subject before I decided on ' The Shipwreck,' and it was his opinion, and he
" says it still is so, that a print of that size cannot be done under thirty guineas, if
" finished, and, if a sketch, fifteen guineas . . . I am very far from showing the portrait
" of Romney as a finished proof. Be assured that with our good Flaxman's help, and
" with your remarks on it in addition, I hope to make it a ' supernaculum.' ' The
" ' Shipwreck,' also, will be infinitely better the next proof. (*Ibid.*, p. 189.)

    Dec. 11, 1805. " A very few touches will finish ' The Shipwreck '; those few
" I have added upon a proof before I parted with the picture. It is a print that I feel
" proud of, on a new inspection." (*Ibid.*, p. 189.)

    Romney was familiar with Blake's early compositions, and he is said by
Flaxman, in a letter written to Hayley about 1783, to have regarded his historical
drawings as ranking with those of Michael Angelo (*ibid.*, p. 52). For a note on
Blake's influence on Romney see the catalogue of the National Gallery exhibition
of Blake's works, 1913 (no. 676), p. 69.

131 COMPOSITIONS FROM THE WORKS DAYS AND THEOGONY OF HESIOD. Designed by John Flaxman, R.A. P.S. Engraved by William Blake. . . . [lettered below] Published by Longman, Hurst, Rees, Orme & Brown, London, Jan. 1, 1817.

Collation: Oblong f°, 42 × 27 cm. Engraved half-title and title + 36 designs = 38 plates.

Plates: Engraved chiefly in dotted lines. They represent groupings of classical deities, etc., in Flaxman's usual style. Heading on some plates: [*No. of plate*] [*Title*] [*Reference*]. Lettered below: [*Quotation*] / *Published* . . . *November* 1 1816 [or *Jan* 1 1817]. The engravings vary in size.

Note: The method of execution renders these engravings softer in effect than those in Flaxman's previous volumes (see no. 127). A small reproduction of this book was published in 1881 (see no. 213). In the possession of Mr. W. E. Moss is a series of the plates, of which all but ten are proofs before letters. These were formerly in the possession of Thomas Reader, a member of the firm of Longman, who has dated each print in pencil as he received it from Blake. The dates range from Oct. 1814 to Dec. 1816.

132 THE CYCLOPAEDIA; or, Universal Dictionary of Arts, Sciences and Literature. By Abraham Rees, D.D.F.R.S. . . . Plates Vol. I [etc.] . . . London: Printed for Longman, Hurst, Rees, Orme, & Brown, . . . 1820

Collation: 4 vols. 4°. Half-title and title in each vol. followed by a varying number of plates (186-234).

Plates: One or more plates in each vol. were engraved by Blake.
  i. Vol. I. Armour, pl. IV and V (on one plate). Ten figures, representing various types of armour. Lettered: *Blake sc.* / *Published* . . . *Dec* 10, 1818, . . .
  ii. Vol. II. Basso Relievo, pl. IV. Eight pieces of ancient sculpture are represented on the plate. Lettered: *Blake sc.* / *Published* . . . *Novem* 11th 1818.
  iii. Vol. III. Miscellany, Gem Engraving, pl. XVIII. Figs. 16, 17, and 18 only were engraved by Blake; they illustrate a finished cameo and two stages in its manufacture. Lettered: *Drawn by Farey. Published* . . . 1819. *Engraved by W. Blake & W. Lowry*.
  iv. Vol. IV. Sculpture, pl. I. Engraved in stipple, representing six pieces of Greek sculpture. Lettered: *Blake sc. London Published* . . . *Feb* 1, 1816 . . .

v. Ditto, pl. II. Representing three pieces of Greek sculpture. Lettered: *Blake. sculp. Published . . . Jan* 1, 1816 . . .

vi.* Ditto, pl. III. Representing Venus de Medici, Apollo Belvedere, and Laocoon. Lettered: *Blake del et sc. Published . . . Oct* 1, 1815 . . .

vii. Ditto, pl. IV. Representing five pieces of sculpture and an Etruscan patera. Lettered: *Blake sculp. Published . . . March* 1, 1816, . . .

Plate-mark in each case about 28 × 22 cm. The majority of the other plates were engraved by Wilson Lowry.

Note: The article on " Basso Relievo " was written by Flaxman; a reference to this and to the engraving for it (no. ii above) is found in a letter from Flaxman to Hayley, dated Jan. 2, 1804 (see Russell, *Letters*, p. 136). The subjects of the third plate for the article on " Sculpture " (no. vi above) were drawn as well as engraved by Blake, and in order to draw the Laocoön group he is said to have visited the Royal Academy's antique school (Gilchrist, i, 297). Blake afterwards engraved this group again, probably from the same drawing, in the centre of his single plate, usually known as *The Laocoon* (no. 54).

A note from Blake accepting an offer to engrave some " of Mr Parr's drawings for the antiquities of Athens " has been preserved in the Linnell collection (letter no. 64), and is printed in an appendix to the present work.

133 **OUTLINES FROM THE ANTIENTS . . . With an Introductory Essay by George Cumberland Esq London Septimus Prowett MDCCCXXIX.**

Collation: 4°. Pp. [iv] Title, Dedication + xxiv Introduction + 44 + [2] Appendix.

Illustrations: 81 engraved plates. Of these nos. 1-43 are lettered *F.C. Lewis Sc*; nos. 44-77 are unsigned. The last four plates were engraved by Blake in 1794-5 and appeared as pl. 14, 15, 19, and 23 in Cumberland's *Thoughts on Outline*, 1796 (see no. 112). The plates are unaltered except that they have been numbered at the top 78-81.

Note: The impressions from Blake's plates are weak, although they were retouched by him, as appears from a letter from Cumberland to his son George, dated June 17, 1824:

" And as to the possibility of its being done [*i.e.*, satisfactory outline engraving] " I need only refer to all those engraved by Blake from my drawings, particularly

---

* The original drawing for this plate is in the possession of Mr. W. E. Moss. It is vouched for as Blake's work by Frederick Tatham. It has a watermark dated 1813.

"plates 14 and 19, of which I sent up the plates to be carefully, I hope, repaired by
"Blake if they are worn by printing. He understands me, and how to keep a free and
"equal outline, which is always best. I send you, with this, one from Blake's etching
"with my own design . . . I don't want the outlines mended, I don't expect that,
"except from such a man as Blake; they may be, and certainly are, defective even as
"contours, but if they are copied with feeling they will do very well to explain my
"ideas of the system of composition, and we must be content to get them done as
"well as we can in this age of very bad engravers . . ." (B.M. MSS. Cumberland
Correspondence).

III. EDITIONS OF BLAKE'S WORKS

BIBLIOGRAPHICAL PREFACE

BLAKE was known to few as a poet during his lifetime, and after his death in 1827 his poetic fame was almost completely obscured. It was not until 1839 that his name was brought again before the public, when a Swedenborgian homoeopathist, J. J. Garth Wilkinson, was sufficiently impressed by their merit to print an edition of the *Songs of Innocence and of Experience*; to him and to William Pickering, the publisher, is due the credit of producing the first typographical reprint of any of Blake's works. Wilkinson's attractive volume was probably issued in a small and semi-private edition, and it is now become scarce. There were two issues of it, one of which has not been recorded before. After 1839 Blake's poetry was again neglected for more than twenty years, and no edition was published until the selection edited by D. G. Rossetti appeared in 1863 in the second volume of Gilchrist's *Life*. Wilkinson's reprint had been substantially correct, but Rossetti took considerable liberties with Blake's text, and the evil tradition of his numerous " emendations " has persisted until quite recent years.

Interest in Blake having been stimulated by Gilchrist's biography, the time was evidently ripe for further editions of his poems, and several volumes edited by R. H. Shepherd were published successively by Basil Montagu Pickering. The series began with the *Songs of Innocence and of Experience* in 1866, and this was followed by the first separate reprint of the *Poetical Sketches* in 1868; these were combined in one volume in 1874. In the same year appeared a rival edition prepared by W. M. Rossetti for Bell's Aldine Poets. Some jealousy was exhibited by the publishers concerning the copyright of a few poems, but as regards accuracy Shepherd's text is greatly to be preferred. Rossetti's volume, however, was more complete, and proved to be the more popular, and, since this or D. G. Rossetti's selection served for many years as the basis upon which other editors founded their texts, it is natural that many corrupt readings survived for a long time. They have left their mark upon the volumes of selections edited by Joseph Skipsey in 1885, by W. B. Yeats in 1893, and by Laurence Housman in the same year.

Up to this time Blake's editors had been content with selecting poems chiefly from the *Songs of Innocence and of Experience*, the *Poetical Sketches*, the *Rossetti MS.*, and the *Pickering MS.* W. M. Rossetti had printed the early work, *Tiriel*, but the other mystical poems had only been drawn upon to a very small extent, so that a definite advance in public appreciation was heralded by the appearance in 1893 of the three large volumes edited by E. J. Ellis and W. B. Yeats, which contained lithographed reproductions of all the Illuminated Books together with the first printed version of *The Four Zoas*. The texts given by the editors suffer by reason of the many inaccuracies they contain, but to have produced these volumes at all was a remarkable achievement. No new collected edition of any importance appeared during the next twelve years, but in 1905 a further great advance was made by the publication at Oxford of Dr. Sampson's edition of the Poetical Works. In this volume real bibliographical and textual scholarship was applied to Blake's poems for the first time; his texts were at last freed from inaccuracies and arbitrary emendations and so were placed upon a secure foundation for future generations of readers. Dr. Sampson did not then choose to include the symbolical books among the Poetical Works, but he afterwards remedied the omission by printing all the shorter books, with selections from *The Four Zoas*, *Milton*, and *Jerusalem*, in the new Oxford edition published in 1913; this volume also contained the first reprint of *The French Revolution*, which had been lately re-discovered. An almost complete edition in two volumes, edited by E. J. Ellis, had appeared in 1907, but although this supplies the best text of *The Four Zoas* at present available, it again leaves much to be desired in point of accuracy. Dr. Sampson's is, therefore, to be regarded as the standard edition of Blake's poems at the present time, and little remains to be done by future editors beyond the work of selection.

Meanwhile, since 1884, separate reprints of some of Blake's works had appeared at frequent intervals. By far the greater number of these are booklets containing the *Songs of Innocence* and the *Songs of Experience*, either together or separately. Most of them were catch-penny editions, and some contain " illustrations " which are an impertinence both to Blake's memory and to the intelligence of the reader. Among the other separate reprints are *Poetical Sketches*, 1899, *Jerusalem*, 1904, *The Marriage of Heaven and Hell*, 1906 and 1911, *Milton*, 1907, and *Auguries of Innocence*, 1914.

Several smaller volumes of selections have appeared from time to time, among which the most notable is that from the Symbolical Poems, edited by F. E. Pierce for the Yale University Press, 1915. Blake's poems have been placed within the reach of everyone in the volumes published at three-pence each by the Clarendon Press, 1908, and by Stead's Publishing House, 1920.

Blake's works have not been extensively translated into foreign languages. A few were put into German by Dr. Julius for Crabb Robinson in 1811 (see no. 401), but no further selections in this language appeared until 1907, when two were published in Berlin and Jena respectively. The first work to appear in French was *Le Mariage du Ciel et de l'Enfer*, Paris, 1900. Translations of many poems are contained in Berger's *William Blake, Mysticisme et Poesie*, 1907 (no. 344), but no separate volume of selections in French has yet been issued. "The Tiger" from *Songs of Experience* has been translated into Italian, and was published in 1906, but there do not seem to be any other poems by Blake in this language. A few were translated into Swedish by Osterling, and were included in a volume published at Stockholm in 1912. Finally, it is said that the whole of Blake's poems have been translated by a young journalist of Petrograd named Morshak, but no printed text in Russian has yet reached me.

At the end of the present section are added a few entries dealing with musical settings for Blake's poems. Nearly all of these are taken from the *Songs of Innocence and of Experience*, but in addition the lines from *Milton*, " And did those feet in ancient time," have been twice set to music. The setting by Sir Hubert Parry has been sung several times in public places in England.

The section concludes with entries recording all the facsimile reproductions of Blake's works that have appeared up to the present time. The most notable of these are *The Marriage of Heaven and Hell*, coloured by hand for Camden Hotten in 1868, *Jerusalem*, published by Pearson in 1877, the series of nearly all the Illuminated Books done by Mr. William Muir between the years 1884 and 1894, and the *Songs of Innocence and of Experience*, published by Quaritch in 1893. The *Illustrations to the Book of Job* have been several times reproduced, and also the woodcuts for Thornton's *Virgil*. Lithographic reproductions of the illustrations of Milton's *Comus*, of *The Book of Ahania*, and of the original edition of *Poetical Sketches* were done by William Griggs in the years 1890-1892. Among the more recent volumes must be mentioned the admirable facsimile of *The Gates of Paradise* done for Mr. W. A. White in 1913.

A. *TYPOGRAPHICAL REPRINTS*

134 SONGS OF INNOCENCE AND OF EXPERIENCE, Shewing the Two Contrary States of the Human Soul. By William Blake. London: W. Pickering, Chancery Lane, and W. Newbery, 6, Chenies Street, Bedford Square. 1839.

Collation: 19 × 11.5 cm. [A]⁸ [*]⁴, B-E⁸, F⁴, G²; 50 leaves. Pp. xxi Title Preface + [ii] Half-title to *Songs of Innocence* + 76.

Contents: Songs of Innocence.
            Songs of Experience.
            Dedication of the Poem of the Grave.

Note: The editor of this volume, whose name does not appear, was James John Garth Wilkinson (1812-1899), homœopathist and translator of Swedenborg. The circumstances which led to its publication were as follows: " In 1838 Mr. Charles " Augustus Tulk, then Member of Parliament for Poole, lent Mr. Wilkinson a copy " of William Blake's *Songs of Innocence and of Experience*, a copy of Blake's own " making. . . . The delicacy and spiritual simplicity of the *Songs* made a deep im- " pression on Garth Wilkinson who was himself to do somewhat similar work in his " *Improvisations from the Spirit.** His brother William, holding no lower opinion " came forward with the necessary funds; subscribers were sought for high and low; " a preface was written and the edition, a thin cloth-bound octavo, was published " jointly by Pickering and Newbery on July 9, 1839." †
Wilkinson was supposed by Gilchrist (i, 121) and by Dr. Sampson (1905, p. 78) to have adopted an arrangement of his own, but it is evident that he printed the poems as they were given in Tulk's copy of the original (see copy I, p. 121 of the present work), which, as is mentioned above, was lent to him in 1838; the text contains a number of emendations, but not so many as were introduced by later editors.

* *Improvisations from the Spirit*. London: W. White, 36 Bloomsbury Street. Manchester : Dunhill and Palmer, 1857. 12.5 cm., pp. viii + 408. The book is scarce. My own copy bears the autographs of D. G. Rossetti and W. M. Rossetti.
    † *Memoir of J. J. Garth Wilkinson*. By Clement John Wilkinson. London, 1911. P. 25.

M M

The preface, which was his first published work, gives an account of Blake, the facts of which were derived from Cunningham's memoir. He quotes a few lines from the *Poetical Sketches* and *The Book of Thel*, and gives an extract from the *Descriptive Catalogue*. The volume was printed by Walton and Mitchell, 24 Wardour Street, on Whatman paper with watermark dated 1838 or 1839. It is of much bibliographical interest, but the edition was probably a small one, and the book is now somewhat rare. The last two sheets, F and G, of part of the edition seem to have been cancelled and reprinted in order that "The Little Vagabond" might be omitted (see next entry). A copy of the first issue, in my own possession, has the inscription: "J. Ogle, from "the Editor, J. J. G. Wilkinson, July, 1840. *Sui monumentum et pignus amoris.* "Virgil." However much Wilkinson appreciated Blake's genius, it was only with the milder manifestations of Blake's mind that he found himself in sympathy. In Nov. 1838 he was introduced to Tatham, who showed him some of Blake's productions and soon afterwards he wrote: Nov. 6, 1838. "On the whole, I must say, "the series of drawings, giving me an idea that Blake was inferior to no one who "ever lived in terrific tremendous power, also gave me the impression that his whole "inner man must have been in a monstrous and deformed condition—for it teemed "with monstrous and horrid productions . . ." July 17, 1839. "I received the Designs "etc. of Blake's from Mr Clarke; comprising I fancy all those I saw. I almost wish I "had not seen them. The designs are disorder rendered palpable and powerful and "give me strongly the impression of their being the work of a madman. Insanity "seems stamped on every one of them . . . The Book of Thel is partly an exception "to the general badness or unintelligibility of his verse and designs. I *can* see some "glimmer of meaning in it, and some warmth of religion and of goodness; but "beginning to be obscured and lost under the infatuating phantasies which at length "possessed the author" (*loc. cit.*). Later, on April 17, 1848, Wilkinson was introduced to Crabb Robinson who "entertained him beyond measure about the great "artist," and invited him to call upon him to see original poems and pictures by Blake (*loc. cit.*, p. 52). Crabb Robinson records a breakfast party on May 13, 1848, at which Wilkinson was present, and says of him: "His love of Blake is delightful" (*Diary and Reminiscences*, iii, 318). Many years later, in 1868, Wilkinson seems to have modified his opinion of 1839, for Swinburne records that the *Critical Essay* had "shown him [Wilkinson] a quite new outlet of revelation." *

* In a letter from Swinburne to Seymour Kirkup.

135 SONGS OF INNOCENCE AND OF EXPERIENCE, Shewing the Two Contrary States of the Human Soul. By William Blake. London: W. Pickering, Chancery Lane, and W. Newbery, 6, Chenies Street, Bedford Square. 1839.

Collation: 19 × 11.5 cm. [A]⁸ [∗]⁴ B-E⁸, F⁴, G²; 50 leaves. Pp. xxi Title, Preface + [ii] Half-title to *Songs of Innocence* + 74 + 1 leaf blank.

Contents: The same as in no. 134 with the omission of "The Little Vagabond" from the end of the *Songs of Experience*, p. 71.

Note: This and the preceding issue containing "The Little Vagabond" occur, in my experience, with equal frequency, although the completer issue seems to have been unknown to Dr. Sampson.

136 [SONGS OF INNOCENCE AND OF EXPERIENCE. *About* 1840].

Description: 4°, 17.5 × 13.5 cm. Bound in dark purple morocco in the style of 1840; it is lettered "Blake's Songs," and contains the book-plate of H. F. R. Yorke. There is no title-page or printer's imprint. The *Songs* are printed on one side only of thick drawing paper, and are interleaved.

Note: This unique copy of a private reprint of the *Songs of Innocence and of Experience* is described by Dr. Sampson in *Notes and Queries* for Dec. 1, 1906 (Series 10, Vol. VI). He concludes from internal evidence, partly typographical, that the text was printed either for Garth Wilkinson or for Pickering, and that it was set up at the same press as their edition of 1839 (no. 134), which appears to have been used as a basis; but the present text is more accurate, for Blake's readings have mostly been restored, and "The Little Vagabond," omitted by Wilkinson from his second issue, has been included. Dr. Sampson suggests that it may have been intended to add facsimiles of Blake's designs. The volume is now in the library of the University of Liverpool.

137 LIFE OF WILLIAM BLAKE, "Pictor Ignotus." With Selections from his Poems and Other Writings by . . . Alexander Gilchrist, . . . London and Cambridge: Macmillan and Co. 1863 . . .

Selection: In vol. II; for list see no. 270, *Contents*.

138 SONGS OF INNOCENCE AND EXPERIENCE with other Poems By W Blake [Pickering's device] London Basil Montagu Pickering 196 Piccadilly 1866.

Collation: 17 × 11 cm.   A⁶, B-N⁴, O⁶; 60 leaves.   Pp. xii Half-title, Title, Contents, Preface + 108.

Contents: Songs of Innocence.
Songs of Experience, including " A Divine Image."
Miscellaneous Poems: Pickering MS., 1-10.
Dedication of the Poem of the Grave.

Note: This edition was printed at the Chiswick Press, and was issued in brown cloth with a paper label along the back. The short critical Preface is not signed, but it is by the editor, Richard Herne Shepherd. It is there stated that the poems are, with the exception of some alterations in spelling and punctuation, now printed for the first time in their integrity, and this claim is justified by the accuracy of the text. " A Divine Image " is here printed for the first time, and was probably taken from the posthumous copy of the *Songs* in the B.M. Of the poems from the *Pickering MS.*, which was at this time in Pickering's possession, nos. 7 and 9 are printed for the first time. As is mentioned in the Preface, the fifth stanza of "Mary" and lines 113-114 of " Auguries of Innocence " have been suppressed, but copies of the book exist, in which the omissions have not been made (*Notes and Queries*, Series 7, Vol. VIII, p. 147); it seems probable that the sheets, N and O, on which the omissions occur, were cancelled and reset after a few copies containing the offending lines had been circulaed (*loc. cit.*, p. 216).

139 SONGS OF INNOCENCE AND OF EXPERIENCE Showing the Two Contrary States of the Human Soul By William Blake Edited and Prefaced by Richard Herne Shepherd [Pickering's device] London Basil Montagu Pickering 196 Piccadilly 1868

Collation: 17 × 11 cm. [a]-[b⁴], B-P⁴; 64 leaves.* Pp. [ii] Advertisements + xiv Half-title, Title, Preface, Contents + 112 *Songs*, Index of first lines.

Contents: Same as in no. 138, and, in addition, among the Miscellaneous Poems:
Song by a Shepherd.
Song by an Old Shepherd.

* The signatures on a-b are erratic; a has none, b1 has signature c, and b4 has signature A2. The pagination shows that these are due to the printer's, not the binder's, error.

Note: The two additional poems are here printed for the first time. These, together with a third poem, " Song by a Young Shepherd," another version of which appeared as " Laughing Song" among the *Songs of Innocence*, were copied with the editor's usual accuracy from a MS. written, in Blake's hand as was then believed, on the fly-leaves of a copy of the original edition of the *Poetical Sketches*, which was lent to Pickering about 1868 (see no. 26, *note*). All subsequent editors have followed the text in the present edition, as, until recently, the volume containing the original MS. became lost to sight. The Preface in this edition, dated " Brompton, July, 1866," has been re-written and extended. Printing and binding as before.

140 **POETICAL SKETCHES** By William Blake Now first reprinted from the original Edition of 1783 Edited and Prefaced by Richard Herne Shepherd [Pickering's device] London Basil Montagu Pickering 196 Piccadilly 1868

> *Collation*: 17 × 11 cm. a-b⁴, B-N⁴; 56 leaves. Pp.[ii] Advertisements + xiv Half-title, Title, Contents, Preface + 96.

> *Note*: The text of this edition is very accurate. The original title-page and advertisement are printed, but Blake's general heading, " Miscellaneous Poems," is omitted; there is a half-title not in the original before " King Edward the Third." The volume was printed at the Chiswick Press, and issued in brown cloth with a paper label along the back.

141 **THE POEMS OF WILLIAM BLAKE** Comprising Songs of Innocence and of Experience together with Poetical Sketches and some copyright Poems not in any other Edition [Pickering's device] London Basil Montagu Pickering 196 Piccadilly 1874 17 × 10.5 cm., pp. iii-xx + 165 + [1].

> *Contents*: Same as in nos. 139 and 140, with the addition, among the Miscellaneous Poems, of the following from the Illuminated Books:
>> To the Jews, To the Deists, To the Christians (from *Jerusalem*).
>> " And did those feet in ancient time . . . " (from *Milton*).

> *Note*: The Introduction in this edition is signed " R. H. Shepherd, Brompton, July, 1874." The lines which had been suppressed in Shepherd's previous editions (nos. 138 and 139) are here restored. The name in the first line of the " Song by an Old Shepherd " has been altered from " Sylvio " to "Sylvia"; the former is the MS.

reading. The copyright of three poems, *Pickering MS.*, 9, "Song by a Shepherd," and "Song by an Old Shepherd," first printed in nos. 138-9, belonged to Pickering, and they could therefore not appear in Rossetti's Aldine Edition, published in the same year. A leaflet concerning the rival claims of the two books was printed by Pickering in Sept. 1874 (see no. 280). This edition was reissued in 1887; see no. 147. In my own copy is an inscription showing that it was sent by the publisher to the editor of the Academy; it is also inscribed "To W. M. Rossetti 1874," in Rossetti's hand.

142 THE POETICAL WORKS OF WILLIAM BLAKE, Lyrical and Miscellaneous. Edited, with a Prefatory Memoir, by William Michael Rossetti.

> He wanders, like a day-appearing dream,
> Through the dim wildernesses of the mind.
> SHELLEY.

London: George Bell and Sons, York Street, Covent Garden. 1874. [The Aldine Edition.] 17 × 10.5 cm., pp. [iv] + cxxxiii + [iii] + 231 + [1].

Frontispiece: Portrait of Blake engraved on steel by Jeens, after Phillips, with facsimile of Blake's signature.

Contents:
Poetical Sketches: Advertisement, 1-23, 26.
The Book of Thel.
Rossetti MS., 49 (A Motto).
Songs of Innocence.
Songs of Experience, including "A Divine Image" and "A Cradle Song" (Rossetti MS., 24).
Rossetti MS., 9 (The Tiger, second version).
Rossetti MS., 53 (Lafayette).
The Gates of Paradise: Introduction, The Keys, Epilogue.
Five Poems from letters nos. 10, 14, 22, 26.
From Jerusalem: To the Public, To the Jews, To the Deists, To the Christians.
From Milton: "And did those feet in ancient time."
Dedication of the Designs to Blair's Grave.
The Everlasting Gospel (Rossetti MS., 152).

Rossetti MS., 19, 21-23, 25, 27, 28-32, 36, 44, 54, 58, 60, 64, 94, 135, 145, 149, 150.

Pickering MS., 1-8, 10.

Couplets and Fragments: Rossetti MS., 37, 41, 42, 48, 50, 52.ii, 66, 70, 78, 80, 82, 90, 97(ll. 1-2), 103, 106-108, 116, 125, 129, 132, 134, 141, 143, 146. From the Marriage of Heaven and Hell: Proverbs of Hell, last 2 ll.

Epigrams and Satirical Pieces on Art and Artists: Rossetti MS., 65, 74, 79, 95, 98, 101, 110, 112, 118, 125(ll. 3-4), 127, 131, 136-138, 142.

Annotations to Reynolds' Discourses, epigrams, 2, 5, 6.

Tiriel.

Note: The text of this popular selection has been very generally adopted as a standard since 1874, but its quality varies. That of the *Poetical Sketches* is derived from Shepherd's edition of 1868 (no. 140), and is very accurate, though Rossetti chose to print " Samson " as blank verse. On the other hand, in the case of the *Songs of Innocence and of Experience*, the editor followed the very inaccurate versions given by D. G. Rossetti in Gilchrist, and in the poems from the *Rossetti* and *Pickering MSS.* he generally follows the same text. In his preface Rossetti states (p. cxxx) that he includes the whole body of Blake's poetry with the exception of the bulk of the Prophetic Books, one poem (no. 9) from the *Pickering MS.*, and the two songs " By a Shepherd " and " By an Old Shepherd," the last three of these being Pickering's copyright. Reference to the list of contents above shows, however, that only a selection of the poems from the *Rossetti MS.* is printed, poems being omitted as too slight or too fragmentary at the editor's discretion. The Prefatory Memoir gives a biographical and critical account of Blake. The volume has been reissued with a fresh date on the title-page at frequent intervals up to the present time. Some textual alterations were made in the earlier reissues. It has also been reprinted in another series with additions (see no. 195). It is referred to elsewhere in the present work as WMR. The original issue of 1874 was printed at the Chiswick Press, and bound in green cloth with gilt lettering on the back. In my own possession is a copy of the issue of 1875 with the inscription: " Dante Gabriel Rossetti with William's " love. March 1880." The elder Rossetti has added many marginal annotations.

143 LIFE OF WILLIAM BLAKE with Selections from his Poems and other Writings by Alexander Gilchrist . . . London Macmillan and Co. 1880 . . .

Selection: In vol. II; as in no. 137 with a few additions. For list see nos. 270 and 285, *Contents*.

144   THE JEWEL POETS WILLIAM BLAKE. Edinburgh: Macniven
      & Wallace 1884 9 cm., pp. 96.

>   *Note*: A selection of poems, with a preface by Henry T. Nicoll.

145   THE POEMS, WITH SPECIMENS OF THE PROSE WRITINGS
      OF WILLIAM BLAKE. With a Prefatory Notice, Biographical and
      Critical. By Joseph Skipsey. London: Walter Scott, . . . 1885. [The
      Canterbury Poets.]   14 × 10.5 cm., pp. viii + 9-282 + [6].

>   *Contents*:
>   Poetical Sketches: Advertisement, 1-23, 26 (printed as blank verse).
>   Songs of Innocence.
>   Songs of Experience, including " A Divine Image."
>   Later Poems:
>   Rossetti MS., 9, 19, 23, 25, 29, 30, 32, 36, 52.i, 54, 64, 135, 145.
>   Pickering MS., 1-8, 10.
>   The Gates of Paradise: Introduction, The Keys of the Gates.
>   Dedication of the Designs to Blair's Grave.
>   Prose Extracts: From the Descriptive Catalogue.
>   From the Public Address (Rossetti MS., 153).
>   Proverbs, from the Marriage of Heaven and Hell.

>   *Note*: The text is fairly accurate, but the editor has in many cases followed that
      of WMR. Reissued in 1904; see no. 161.

146   SONGS BY WILLIAM BLAKE H. Daniel: Oxford. 1885. 10.5 ×
      7.5 cm., pp. 27 + [13].

>   *Note*: At the beginning—" Rachel and Ruth to their child friends these with
      " Christmas Greetings." A list of the children is printed at the end.

147   THE POEMS OF WILLIAM BLAKE . . . A New Edition   London
      Pickering and Chatto 66 Haymarket 1887 17 cm., pp. iii-xx + 165 + [1].

>   *Contents*: As in no. 141.

>   *Note*: A reissue, with a fresh title-page, of the sheets of R. H. Shepherd's
      edition of 1874 (no. 141).

148 THE LAMB Printed by Rachel Daniel Oxford 1889 10.5 × 9 cm., pp. [8].

el Press.

149   Printed by H. Daniel:
                                                 38 + [2]; 4 ll. blank at

150   ic, Symbolic, and Critical
                                                 Interpretation by Edwin
                                                 . In Three Vols. . . .
                                                 × 16 cm. Vol. I. pp. xvi
                                                 l. III. pp. ix + [i] + 97 +

                                                 MS.
                                                 spaces.
                                                 d.
v   ture of the poems.

v   ke's illustrations to Blair's

v   s:
                                                 40.

                                                 22, 26 (both printed as

                                                 S., synopsis, and extracts,

                                                 ith quotations: 26, 34,

---

ECKANKAR
A Way Of Life

"*Truth is never denied any man if in his heart he asks for it. He will be led to the temple within which is far greater than any temple man can build.*"

Sri Darwin Gross
Your Right to Know

35, 38, 46, 51, 52.iv, 55-57, 67, 71-73, 75-78, 83-93, 95-103, 105, 108, 109, 111-115, 117-126, 128-131, 133, 135 (stanza 5), 142, 144, 147, 150, 155.

The Symbolic System.

Vol. II. Interpretation and Paraphrased Commentary of some Minor Poems, the Prophetic Books, etc., including the following quotations:

Rossetti MS., 53, 54, 152.

Pickering MS., 3.

Preface from Europe.

To the Deists, from Jerusalem, together with Rossetti MS., 59.

Blake the Artist, including the following:

Annotations to Reynolds's Discourses.

A Descriptive Catalogue.

Rossetti MS., 153, 154.

Some References.

Vol. III. Poetical Sketches, 1-23.

Songs of Innocence.

Songs of Experience, including "A Divine Image" and "A Cradle Song" (Rossetti MS., 24).

The Gates of Paradise: Introduction, The Keys, Epilogue.

Poems from letters nos. 10, 14, 22.

Rossetti MS., 19, 21-23, 25, 27, 28-30, 32, 36, 52-i, 58, 60, 64, 94, 135, 145, 149.

Pickering MS., 1, 2, 4-6, 8-10.

"Song by a Shepherd" and "Song by an Old Shepherd."

Couplets and Fragments: Rossetti MS., 37, 41, 42, 50, 52-ii, 65, 66, 70, 74, 80, 107, 110, 116, 125 (ll. 5-6), 127, 129, 134, 136-138, 143, 146.

Notes to the above.

All Religions are One.

Lithographic reproductions of: There is No Natural Religion, a, without title, and b, pl. 3-4; The Laocöon; On Homer's Poetry; The Ghost of Abel; The Marriage of Heaven and Hell; The Book of Los; The Book of Urizen; Ahania.

Tiriel.

Lithographic reproductions of: Thel; Visions of the Daughters of Albion; The Song of Los; America; Europe; Jerusalem; Milton; Vala (18 pp.); The Ghost of a Flea; Rossetti MS. (3 pp.).

Vala [The Four Zoas].

Note: The chief value of these volumes lies in the interpretation of the symbolism, the paraphrased commentaries, and the lithographic reproductions which they contain. The memoir advances a new theory of Blake's ancestry, according to which he is supposed to be of Irish origin. The value of the printed texts is reduced by the large number of inaccuracies which occur in them; some of these are intentional alterations, but the majority are mistakes made in copying. This applies especially to the poems from the *Rossetti MS.*, a transcript of which was made apparently without sufficient care. *Vala* [*The Four Zoas*] was printed here for the first time, but the text is so inaccurate, that the revised text printed in EJE is to be preferred; the poem was first set up in a different form from that in which it finally appeared, and the sheets of two copies printed in the earlier form are in existence, one belonging to Mr. Yeats, the other to Mr. E. R. D. Maclagan.

This edition is generally referred to as EY in the present work.

151 THE POEMS OF WILLIAM BLAKE   Edited by W. B. Yeats . . .
London: Lawrence & Bullen, . . . New York: Charles Scribner's Sons
. . . 1893. [The Muses' Library] 15 × 9.5 cm., pp. liii + [i] + 251 + [1].

Frontispiece: Photogravure portrait of Blake after a drawing.

Contents:
    Poetical Sketches, 1-6, 8-16, 19, 20.
    Songs of Innocence.
    Songs of Experience, including " A Divine Image " and " A Cradle Song "
        (Rossetti MS., 24).
    Ideas of Good and Evil:
      The Island in the Moon, 5, 8, 9.
      Rossetti MS., 19-23, 25, 27, 28, 30-32, 34, 36, 44, 54, 58, 60, 64,
        145, 149, 150, 152.
      Pickering MS., 1-7, 8 (part printed separately as " Proverbs "), 10.
      Poems from letters nos. 10, 14, 22 (with title " Los the terrible ").
      Dedication of the Designs to Blair's Grave.
      The Gates of Paradise: Introduction, The Keys, Epilogue.
      Couplets and Fragments: Rossetti MS., 37, 41, 42, 50, 52.ii, iv, 70,
        76, 78, 80, 88, 90, 101, 107, 116, 125 (last 2 ll.), 129, 143, 146.
      The Prophetic Books: Tiriel; The Book of Thel; The Marriage of Heaven
        and Hell; Visions of the Daughters of Albion; Ahania; extracts from
        Vala, Jerusalem, and Milton.
    Prose Fragments: Descriptive Catalogue, extracts.
    Rossetti MS., 153 and 154, extracts; 155.

There is no Natural Religion, a and b mixed.
All Religions are One.
The Notes also contain:
Poetical Sketches, Advertisement, 23.
Rossetti MS., 9, 14 (6 stanzas), 30, 49, 54 (3 stanzas).

Note: The text of this edition is more accurate than that in the volumes produced by the editor in collaboration with E. J. Ellis, with the exception of the poems from the *Rossetti* and *Pickering MSS.* In the case of the *Rossetti MS.* Mr. Yeats has followed Ellis's transcript, and in the case of the *Pickering MS.* he could only follow the texts given by the Rossettis, the original MS. not being available. The lack of arrangement of the poems given under the general heading "Ideas of Good and Evil," is confusing; in other respects the selection is a very useful one. The introduction contains a biographical account of Blake. Two hundred numbered copies were printed on large paper, 17 × 11 cm., with a different title-page, bearing the imprint of the London publisher only. This edition was reprinted in the same series in 1905; see no. 165. It is referred to elsewhere in the present work as WBY.

152 SELECTIONS FROM THE WRITINGS OF WILLIAM BLAKE
With an Introductory Essay By Laurence Housman . . . London Kegan
Paul, Trench, Trübner, & Co. Ltd. MDCCCXCIII 16 × 10 cm., pp. xxxi +
[i] + 259 + [1].

Frontispiece: Photogravure after *Illustrations to Job*, pl. 2.

Contents:
Poetical Sketches, 1-5, 8-16, 18, 20.
Songs of Innocence.
Songs of Experience, including "A Divine Image."
The Book of Thel.
The Gates of Paradise: Introduction, The Keys.
Dedication of the Designs to Blair's Grave.
Later Poems:
    An Island in the Moon, 5.
    Rossetti MS., 19, 21, 23, 25, 30, 32, 36, 54, 58, 64, 135, 152 (extract).
    Pickering MS., 1-8, 10.
    Fragments: Rossetti MS., 37, 41, 42, 52.i, 90, 120, 129, 145.
The Marriage of Heaven and Hell.
[There is No] Natural Religion, a and b mixed.
Extracts from Visions of the Daughters of Albion and Milton.

Prose Extracts:
    An Island in the Moon, chaps. 1, 2, 5.
    Descriptive Catalogue, extracts.
    On Homer's Poetry.
    Rossetti MS., 154.

Note: The text of this edition is fairly accurate, though Mr. Housman seems to have followed WMR to some extent. The extracts from *An Island in the Moon* were taken directly from the original MS. This edition is referred to elsewhere in the present work as LH.

153 *Colophon*: Here ends the BOOK OF THEL, SONGS OF INNOCENCE & SONGS OF EXPERIENCE. By William Blake. With decorations designed and cut on the wood by Charles Ricketts, under whose supervision the book has been printed at the Ballantyne Press. This edition consists of two hundred and ten copies. Sold by Messrs. Hacon & Ricketts at the Sign of the Dial, LII Warwick Street, Regent Street, London. mdcccxcvii 19.5 × 13 cm., in fours; pp. lxxxi + [iii].

Note: This text contains most of the same inaccuracies as WMR.

154 *Colophon*: Here ends this edition of POETICAL SKETCHES by William Blake, with decorations . . . Press [as in no. 153] M.D.CCC.XCIX Sold by Messrs. Hacon and Ricketts . . . London. 19.5 × 13 cm., in fours; pp. xciii + [iii].

155 THE SONGS OF INNOCENCE By William Blake . . . With Designs by Celia Levetus Wells Gardner Darton & Co London [1899] [The Midget Series] 7.5 × 6 cm., pp. 118 + [6].

Illustrations: 20 full-page plates and numerous small designs among the text.

156 WILLIAM BLAKE LE MARIAGE DU CIEL ET DE L'ENFER Traduction Française avec Introduction par Charles Grolleau Paris Lucien Chamuel Editeur 5, Rue de Savoie, 5 . . . 1900. 8°. Pp. 53 + [3].

Illustrations: Portraits of Blake (frontispiece) and six reproductions in the text from the Prophetic Books.

157 SELECTIONS FROM THE WORKS OF WILLIAM BLAKE
With an Introduction and Notes By Mark Perugini . . . London Methuen
& Co. . . . MDCCCI [The Little Library] 15 × 9.5 cm., pp. xlii + 147 + [1].

> *Frontispiece*: Photogravure after Deville's life-mask of Blake.

> *Note*: The text of this selection is accurate except in the poems from the
> *Rossetti MS.* and *Pickering MS.*, where the editor has followed versions given in
> Gilchrist, WMR, and WBY.

158 SONGS OF INNOCENCE AND SONGS OF EXPERIENCE by
William Blake   London: R. Brimley Johnson. Guildford: A. C. Curtis.
MDCCCCI.   12.5 × 10 cm., pp. [viii] + 72.

> *Frontispiece*: "The Tyger."

159 THE SONGS OF EXPERIENCE.   By William Blake.   With Designs
by Celia Levetus.   Published by David Nutt . . . London. [1902] 22.5 ×
14.5 cm., pp. 84.

> *Illustrations*: 9 full-page plates, and small designs in the text.

160 SONGS OF INNOCENCE by William Blake   With Illustrations by
Geraldine Morris   John Lane: . . . London and New York MDCCCCII.
[The Flowers of Parnassus, no. xii]   14 × 11 cm.   pp. 61 + [3]

> *Illustrations*: 6 full-page plates, headpiece, and tailpiece.

161 THE POEMS, WITH SPECIMENS OF THE PROSE WRITINGS,
of William Blake.   With a Prefatory Notice by Joseph Skipsey.   The
Walter Scott Publishing Co., Ltd., London . . . [1904] [The Canterbury
Poets]   13.5 × 10 cm., pp. viii + 9-282 + [2].

> *Contents*: As in no. 145.

> *Note*: A reissue of no. 145.   Part of the edition contains a photogravure
> frontispiece.

162 THE PROPHETIC BOOKS of William Blake Jerusalem Edited by
E. R. D. Maclagan and A. G. B. Russell London: A. H. Bullen . . .
1904 25.5 × 19 cm., pp. [ii] + xxii + 127 + [1].

> *Note*: This volume is the first of a projected series of reprints of Blake's works,
> though at present *Milton* (no. 171) is the only other one that has been issued. This
> is the first complete typographical reprint of *Jerusalem*, and the editors have taken
> pains to make it as accurate as possible, retaining even Blake's peculiarities of spell-
> ing. The introduction contains a valuable summary of Blake's symbolic system.

163 SONGS OF INNOCENCE Lyrics from the Works of William Blake.
Thomas B. Mosher Portland Maine U.S.A. 1904 [The Old World Series,
no. 35] 18 × 10 cm., pp. viii + 112.

> *Note*: 925 copies printed on Van Gelder hand-made paper, and 100 copies on
> Japanese vellum. Contains *Songs of Innocence and of Experience* and most of the
> *Poetical Sketches*; the texts printed are those of EY.

164 THE BROADWAY BOOKLETS SONGS OF INNOCENCE by
William Blake . . . London George Routledge & Sons, Limited New
York: E. P. Dutton & Co. [1905] 14 × 11 cm., pp. 47 + [1].

165 POEMS OF WILLIAM BLAKE Edited by W. B. Yeats London:
George Routledge & Sons, Limited New York: E. P. Dutton & Co.
[1905] [The Muses' Library] 15 × 9.5 cm., pp. xlix + [i] + 277 + 7.

> *Contents*: As in no. 151.

> *Note*: A reprint of no. 151. Reissued in 1910; see no. 179.

166 THE POETICAL WORKS of William Blake A New and Verbatim
Text from the Manuscript Engraved and Letterpress Originals with
Variorum Readings and Bibliographical Notes and Prefaces by John

Sampson Librarian in the University of Liverpool Oxford At the Clarendon Press 1905 22 × 14 cm., pp. xxxvi + 384.

Illustrations: Two folding plates, collotype reproductions of pp. 109 (reversed) and 52 of the *Rossetti MS*.

Contents:

Poetical Sketches, 1-19; (in appendix I) 20-26; (in appendix II) "Song by a Shepherd" and "Song by an Old Shepherd."

An Island in the Moon, 4-9; (in appendix) 10-17, 19-21.

Songs of Innocence and of Experience; (in appendix) "A Divine Image."

Rossetti MS., 14, 19-61, 64-127, 129-152.

Pickering MS., 1-10.

Poems from letters nos. 9, 10, 14 (two poems), 22, 26, and the fragment "A fairy leapt upon my knee."

Dedication of Blake's Illustrations of Blair's Grave.

Annotations to Reynolds's Discourses, epigrams 1-9.

Poems from the Prophetic Books:

Thel's Motto, from The Book of Thel.

Two ll. of the Proverbs of Hell, from The Marriage of Heaven and Hell.

The Argument, from Visions of the Daughters of Albion.

Extracts from The Four Zoas.

"And did those feet in ancient time," from Milton.

To the Public, "Such visions have appear'd to me," To the Jews, "Each Man is in his Spectre's power," To the Deists, To the Christians, Especially to the Female, from Jerusalem.

The Gates of Paradise: Prologue, The Keys, Epilogue, Verses from the legends to the plates.

Note: In this volume the public was for the first time enabled to read accurate texts of Blake's poetical works. It contains all of Blake's writings, with the exception of the Prophetic Books, that can possibly be regarded as poetry, and the texts were prepared with great labour from the originals, whenever these were still in existence. In the footnotes all MS. variations are recorded, and every mistake or emendation made by previous editors is exposed. Each section is preceded by a useful Bibliographical Preface, to which, in the present work, the reader has frequently been referred. It is to be hoped that this or the subsequent Oxford edition (no. 192) will be used as a standard text by the editors of the future. This edition is referred to elsewhere in the present work as "Sampson, 1905."

167 THE LYRICAL POEMS of William Blake Text by John Sampson
with an Introduction by Walter Raleigh Oxford At the Clarendon Press
1905 17 × 11 cm., pp. li + [i] + 196.

> *Frontispiece*: Half-tone reproduction of *Milton*, pl. 29.

> *Contents*: Same as in no. 166, though with some omissions and without the
notes and prefaces.

168 THE LYRICAL POEMS of William Blake . . . Oxford . . . 1906
17 × 11 cm., pp. li + [i] + 203 + [1].

> *Frontispiece, contents*: Same as in no. 167.

> *Note*: A reissue of no. 167, to which an index of first lines has been added.

169 THE MARRIAGE OF HEAVEN AND HELL By William Blake
London E. Grant Richards 1906 [The Venetian Series II] 13 × 9.5 cm.,
pp. 39 + [1].

> *Note*: The text, except in details of spelling, is very accurate.

170 THE POETICAL WORKS of William Blake Edited and Annotated by
Edwin J. Ellis In Two Volumes . . . London Chatto & Windus 1906
20 × 14 cm. Vol. I pp. xxiv + 551 + [1] + leaf of errata. Vol. II pp. [vi]
+ 492.

> *Frontispieces*: Vol. I. Portrait of Blake after a drawing by E. J. Ellis. Vol. II.
" Reunion of Soul & Body," from Blair's *Grave*, pl. 12.

> *Contents*:
Vol. I. The Passions (pp. xxv-xxxii).
>> Poetical Sketches, 1-26.
>> Songs of Innocence and of Experience, the notes to which include Rossetti MS.,
>>> 14, 20, 24, 28, 30, 34, 35, 49, 52.v; Pickering MS., 4; "A Divine Image";
>>> " Song by a Shepherd"; and " Song by an Old Shepherd."

o o

Ideas of Good and Evil:
    Rossetti MS., 19, 21, 22, 23, 25, 27, 29, 32, 36, 40, 44, 54, 60, 64, 133, 135, 145, 150.
    Pickering MS., 1-3, 5-7, 9, 10.
    Fragment, " A fairy leapt upon my knee."
Further Ideas of Good and Evil:
    The Gates of Paradise.
    Introduction, The Keys, Epilogue.
    Pickering MS., 8.
    Rossetti MS., 58, 94, 149.
    Poems from letters nos. 10, 14, 22.
Miniatures: Rossetti MS., 26, 37, 41, 42, 52-ii, 90.
Gallantries and Mockeries: Rossetti MS., 38, 50, 51, 52.iv, 55, 57, 102, 116, 130, 134, 135 (last stanza), 146.
An Island in the Moon, 4-10, 12-21.
Resentments:
    Rossetti MS., 31, 46, 48, 56, 65-83, 86-89, 91-93, 95, 97-101, 103-114, 117-127, 129, 131, 132, 136-140, 142-144, 147.
    Poem from letter no. 26.
    Annotations to Reynolds's Discourses, epigrams 1-5.
The Everlasting Gospel: Rossetti MS., 152.
La Fayette (Rossetti MS., 53).
Blake's Earliest Explanation: There is No Natural Religion, a & b, All Religions are One.
On Homer's Poetry.
On Virgil.
The Prophetic Books:
    The Ghost of Abel, The Book of Thel, The Marriage of Heaven and Hell, A Song of Liberty, Tiriel, Visions of the Daughters of Albion, America, The Book of Urizen, Europe, The Book of Ahania, The Book of Los, The Song of Los, The Laocoon, Milton (the notes to which include brief explanations of the designs).

Vol. II. Vala.
    Jerusalem.

Note: The arrangement of the poems in this edition is somewhat confusing to anyone not familiar with the editor's system of interpretation, and the text contains most of the same inaccuracies as EY. Otherwise the edition is an extremely useful one; it is the only one which gives the text of the Prophetic Books in full, and the only one besides EY which gives *Vala* (*The Four Zoas*).   The early poem known as *The Passions* is here reprinted from the *Monthly Review* for the first time (see no. 1). This edition is referred to elsewhere in the present work as EJE.

171 THE PROPHETIC BOOKS of William Blake Milton Edited by E. R. D. Maclagan and A. G. B. Russell London: A. H. Bullen . . . 1907 25.5 × 18.5 cm., pp. xix + 57 + [1].

   Note: This is the first separate reprint of *Milton*, and is the second of a projected series of reprints of Blake's works (see no. 162).   The greater part of the text has been printed from the British Museum copy and is very accurate.   There is an introductory account of the book by the editors; on p. 57 is a symbolic diagram from *Milton*, pl. 32.

172 SONGS OF INNOCENCE William Blake Illustrated by Olive Allen . . . London T. C. & E. C. Jack and Edinburgh [1906] [The English Masterpieces] 15 × 11.5 cm., pp. 31 + [1].

   Illustrations: Frontispiece and three plates in colours.

173 SONGS OF INNOCENCE AND OF EXPERIENCE by William Blake Showing the two contrary states of the human Soul [device] Ralph Fletcher Seymour Company The Alderbrink Press Chicago MDCCCCVI 19.5 cm., pp. 62 + [2].

   Note: The title-page has an elaborate decorative border. The type was designed by George F. McKiernan and Co. The edition consisted of 300 copies on hand-made paper, and twelve on Japanese vellum. The description was kindly supplied by Mrs. Joseph N. Damon.

174 TIGRE DI GUGLIELMO BLAKE (1756-1827) *Dated*: Il 28 Febbraio 1906 2 ll.

   Note: A double leaf with a translation of "The Tiger" into Italian, preceded by a short note signed E. T[eza].

175 WILLIAM BLAKE AUSGEWAHLTE DICHTUNGEN Ubertragen von Adolf Knoblauch Oesterheld & Co. Verlag Berlin 1907 25 × 20 cm. Vol. I. pp. 95 + [1]. Vol. II. pp. 84.

Contents:
Vol. I. Dichtungen:
      Songs of Experience, 30, 31, 47.
      Dedication of the designs to Blair's Grave.
      Poems from letter no. 14 (To my Friend Butts I write).
      Rossetti MS., 47, 152.
      Pickering MS., 7(stanza 8), 10(stanzas 12-13).
      Freiheits-Gesang (from The Marriage of Heaven and Hell).
      Extracts from the Prophetic Books.
   Weissagungen der Unschuld: Pickering MS., 8.
   Sprüchwörter der Hölle (from The Marriage of Heaven and Hell).
   Thel.
   Visionen der Tochter Albions.
   America.
Vol. II. Los (The Book of).
   Urizen.
   Ahania.
   Europa (without Preface or Preludium).
   Los und Enitharmon (from The Four Zoas).

Note: Of this edition 670 numbered copies were printed in Leipzig, the first twenty on Japanese vellum, the rest on hand-made paper. It was originally intended that the selection should be printed in one volume, but owing to technical difficulties this idea had to be abandoned.

176 WILLIAM BLAKE DIE ETHIK DER FRUCHTBARKEIT zusammengestellt aus seinen Werken und Aufzeichnungen übersetzt und eingeleitet von Otto Freiherrn von Taube Verlegt bei Eugen Diederichs Jena 1907 22 × 15 cm., pp. [iv] + li + [i] + 147 + [5].

Contents:
   Das Buch von Thel.
   Aus der Vermahlung von Himmel und Hölle (almost in full).
   Das Gesicht der Töchter Albions.
   Aus Europa, die Herrschaft des Weibes (21 ll.).

Aus dem Buch von Los, Anfangsverse vom Kapitel I (26 ll.).
Ahania.
Aus Vala, aus Milton, aus Jerusalem (extracts).
Die Pforten des Paradises.
Gedichte:
>   Songs of Experience, 31 (stanzas 4-5), 43, 44, 47, 48.
>   Rossetti MS., 20-22, 29, 31, 32, 54, 152.
>   Pickering MS., 8 (32 ll.).

Aus Prosaschriften, Notizen und Briefen:
>   Es giebt Keine Religion aus der Natur: There is No Natural Religion, a, b; All Religions are One.
>   Allgemein Ethisches: Rossetti MS., 37, 154 (extracts), 155.
>   Erotik, including Rossetti MS., 42, 43, 52.iv.
>   Religion, Gesetz, und Kirche, including Rossetti MS., 33, 52.v, 144, Das Vater-Unser from annotations to Dr. Thornton's pamphlet.
>   Phantasie, Inspiration, Genie und deren Gegentheil; über den inneren Beruf; vom Vorrange der Kunst und von ihrer Forderung; über Kunst: prose fragments, including Rossetti MS., 85, 90, and Gates of Paradise, legend to frontispiece.

Note: Twenty numbered copies were printed on Japanese vellum.

177 WILLIAM BLAKE Poems Selected by A. T. Quiller-Couch Oxford at the Clarendon Press [1908][Select English Classics]   16.5 × 12.5 cm., pp. 32.

178 THE MARRIAGE OF HEAVEN AND HELL By William Blake Chelsea: MCMX   20.5 × 14 cm., pp. [ii] + 21 + 4 bl. ll. at each end.

Note: This edition consisted of twenty-four copies privately printed at the Ashendene Press, Chelsea, by J. P. Raverat in Jan. 1910.   The text contains many inaccuracies.

179 MR WILLIAM BUTLER YEATS introduces the Poetical Works of William Blake, . . . as the second volume in the series of "Books that marked Epochs," published in the year 1910 by George Routledge & Sons, Limited.   15 × 9.5 cm., pp. xlix + [i] + 277 + [1].

Contents: As in no. 151.

Note: A reissue of no. 165, with a new title-page and half-title; the type has not been re-set.

180 THE MARRIAGE OF HEAVEN AND HELL and A Song of Liberty By William Blake With an Introduction by Francis Griffin Stokes Published for the Florence Press by Chatto and Windus . . . London 1911 19 × 13 cm., pp. 79 + [1].

Note: The text is very accurate, though the punctuation has been amended.

181 POEMS BY WILLIAM BLAKE Selected with an Introduction by Alice Meynell Blackie and Son Ld. London [September 1911] [Red Letter Library] 15 × 10 cm., pp. xvi + 225 + [1].

182 SONGS OF INNOCENCE by William Blake With a Preface by Thomas Seccombe and Twelve Coloured Illustrations by Honor C. Appleton Herbert & Daniel . . . London, W. [1911] 20.5 × 15.5 cm., pp. xvii + [iii] + 49 + [3].

183 SONGS OF INNOCENCE By William Blake London Arthur L. Humphreys 1911 14.5 × 12 cm., pp. viii + 64.

184 SONGS OF INNOCENCE by William Blake Siegle, Hill & Co. . . . London, W. [1911] [Langham Booklets] 8.5 × 5.5 cm., pp. 55 + [5].

185 SONGS OF EXPERIENCE by William Blake Siegle, Hill & Co. . . . London, W. [1911] [Langham Booklets] 8.5 × 5.5 cm., pp. 74.

186 ANDERS JOHANN OSTERLING: Fränder och främlingar: ett häfte lyriska öfversättningar. Stockholm: A. Bonnier. [1912] 12° pp. 64.

Contents: The translations include Blake's "Till våren" (In Spring), "En Sorgens sang," "Kristalbrummet" (Crystal Cabinet), "Kärlekens lund" (Land of Dreams).

Note: The title of this in English is "Friends and Strangers: a few literary poems translated."

187 SONGS OF INNOCENCE And Other Poems by William Blake . . . London Samuel Bagster & Sons Limited . . . [1912] 12 × 9 cm., pp. viii + 125 + [3].

188 SONGS OF INNOCENCE by William Blake Decorated by Charles Robinson & Mary H. Robinson London J. M. Dent & Sons, . . . New York E. P. Dutton & Co [1912] 19.5 × 14 cm., pp. viii + 56 + [2].

> *Illustrations*: Six in colours.

189 SONGS OF INNOCENCE by William Blake London The St Catherine Press . . . [1912] [The Arden Books] 13.5 × 11 cm., pp. 37 + [3].

190 SONGS OF EXPERIENCE by William Blake London The St Catherine Press . . . [1912] [The Arden Books] 13.5 × 11 cm., pp. 45 + [3].

191 The Gravure Series [No. 2] SONGS OF INNOCENCE by W. Blake London: Simpkin, Marshall, Hamilton, Kent & Co. Ltd. [1913] 18 × 11.5 cm., pp. 47 + [1].

> *Illustrations*: Cover design and frontispiece in colours.

192 **OXFORD EDITION THE POETICAL WORKS** of William Blake Including the unpublished French Revolution together with the Minor Prophetic Books and Selections from The Four Zoas, Milton & Jerusalem Edited with an Introduction and Textual Notes by John Sampson Hon. D.Litt. Oxon. Oxford University Press . . . Humphrey Milford MDCCCCXIII 18.5 × 12 cm., pp. lvi + 453 + [3].

> *Illustrations*: Portrait of Blake after Phillips and fifteen reproductions of title-pages in half-tone.

> *Contents*:
> Poetical Sketches, 1-26; (in appendix) " Song by a Shepherd " and " Song by an Old Shepherd."

Songs from " An Island in the Moon," 4-14, 16, 19, 20.

Songs of Innocence and of Experience; (in appendix) A Divine Image.

Poems from the Rossetti MS.:

    I. Earlier Poems, 14, 19-25, 27-32, 36, 39, 40, 49, 53; (in appendix) " A fairy leapt upon my knee."

    II. Later Poems, 54, 56, 58-60, 64, 66, 94, 133, 135, 147, 149, 150; (addendum) To the Queen.

    III. 152 (The Everlasting Gospel).

Pickering MS., 1-10.

Poems from letters nos. 9, 10, 14 (two poems), 22, 26.

Gnomic Verses, Epigrams, and short Satirical Pieces:

    Annotations to Reynolds's Discourses, 1-9.

    Rossetti MS., 26, 33-35, 37, 38, 41, 42, 44, 46-48, 50-52, 55, 57, 61, 65, 67-83, 85-93, 95-114, 116-127, 129-132, 134, 136-140, 142-146, 148, 151.

[The Prophetic Books]:

    Tiriel, The Book of Thel, The Marriage of Heaven and Hell, The French Revolution, A Song of Liberty, Visions of the Daughters of Albion, America, Europe, The First Book of Urizen, The Song of Los, The Book of Los, The Book of Ahania.

    Selections from The Four Zoas, Milton, Jerusalem.

    Verses from the Gates of Paradise.

    The Ghost of Abel.

    Appendix: There is No Natural Religion, All Religions are One, The Laocoon, On Homer's Poetry, On Virgil.

From the Descriptive Catalogue: Sir Geffrey Chaucer.

Note: Dr. Sampson prints here for the first time *The French Revolution* and pl. 4 of *The First Book of Urizen*. This edition was issued in several forms; in the more expensive ones the frontispiece is in photogravure. This edition is referred to elsewhere in the present work as " Sampson, 1913."

193 **THE WILLIAM BLAKE CALENDAR** A quotation from the works of William Blake for every day in the year selected by Thomas Wright London Frank Palmer Red Lion Court [1913] 17 cm., pp. 99 + [5].

Frontispiece: Portrait of Blake after Phillips.

194 AUGURIES OF INNOCENCE By William Blake
Colophon: These are the Proverbs by William Blake called Auguries of Innocence, here written out by Lilian Frost and printed from plates at the Pear Tree Press by James Guthrie & S. J. Housley. Spring MCMXIV. Flansham. 16 cm., in fours, ff. 16.

Note: Etched plates printed in two colours on one side of the leaf only.

195 THE POETICAL WORKS of William Blake. Edited, with a Prefatory Memoir, by William Michael Rossetti. London. G. Bell and Sons, Ltd. 1914 [Bohn's Popular Library] 16 × 10.5 cm., pp. [iv] + viii + 233 + [1].

Contents: As in WMR, with the addition of Pickering MS., 9, "Song by a Shepherd," and "Song by an Old Shepherd" at the end.

196 SELECTIONS FROM THE SYMBOLICAL POEMS of William Blake Frederick E. Pierce, Ph.D. Assistant Professor of English in Sheffield Scientific School, Yale University New Haven: Yale University Press London: Humphrey Milford Oxford University Press MDCCCCXV 25.5 × 19 cm., pp. xvi + 79 + [1].

Contents: Extracts, with explanatory headings, from: *The Marriage of Heaven and Hell, Daughters of Albion, America, The Book of Urizen, The Book of Los, The Book of Ahania, Vala [The Four Zoas], Milton,* and *Jerusalem.*

197 SONGS AND POEMS by William Blake The Poet of Childhood. With an Introduction by Michael Kingsdown. London: Stead's Publishing House, . . . [1920] [Stead's Poets, no. 75] 18 cm., pp. 48.

Note: Forty poems, issued in wrappers at threepence.

P P

B. *MUSICAL SETTINGS*

198 FOUR "SONGS OF INNOCENCE" by William Blake set to Music by Arthur Somervell Price Two Shillings nett Stanley Lucas Weber & Co 84 New Bond Street London [1889] 4° pp. [ii] + 9 + [1].

> *Contents*: Settings for "The Shepherd," "The Blossom," "The Lamb," "Nurse's Song."

199 A SONG OF INNOCENCE by William Blake Set to Music by H. Walford Davies (Op 3, No. 5) Price Two Shillings Net London & New York Novello, Ewer & Co Copyright 1897 . . . 4° pp. [ii] + 5 + [1].

> *Contents*: A setting for "The Lamb."

200 FOUR SONGS OF INNOCENCE for female voices The poems written by William Blake the music composed by H. Walford Davies Price one shilling London: Novello and Company Limited . . . Copyright, 1900 . . . 8° pp. [ii] + 21.

> *Contents*: Settings for "The Lamb," "A Cradle Song," "Infant Joy," and "The Shepherd."

200A THE SONGS OF INNOCENCE of William Blake (1788) Set to Music by Sir Vincent Caillard. Price Three Shillings . . . London: Novello and Company Limited . . . [1904] 4° pp. [ii] + 72.

201 I LOVE THE JOCUND DANCE Song Words by William Blake Set to Music by H Walford Davies (Op. 18, No. 4) Price Two Shillings Net. London: Sidney Riorden, . . . Copyright, 1905, . . . 4° pp. [ii] + 4.

202 ENGLAND'S PLEASANT LAND. Three Part Songs . . . Set to Music
by H Walford Davies Op. 22 . . . London: Sidney Riorden . . . Copyright, 1907 . . . 8° pp. [iv] + 22.

    Contents: Pp. 10-22, a setting for "And did those feet in ancient time" (*Milton*, pl. 2).

203 Stainer & Bell's Modern Songs. No. 2. TIGER, TIGER Words by
Blake Composed by Alan Gray . . . London . . . [1909] F°. pp. 7 + [1].

204 THREE SONGS OF INNOCENCE 1. The Shepherd 2. The Lamb
3. Spring Words by William Blake Music by Harold E. Darke. Price
2/- net. London Stainer & Bell, Ltd. . . . [1911] 4° pp. 14.

205 JERUSALEM ("And did those feet in ancient time") Stanzas From
William Blake's "Prophetic Books" Set to Music by Sir Hubert H. Parry
Price Twopence London: J. Curwen & Sons Ltd., 24 Berners Street, W. . . .
Copyright 1916 . . . 27 × 19 cm., pp. [4].

    Note: Sung in Trafalgar Square on May 6, 1919, by the League of Arts
Choir of 500 voices. The poem is taken from *Milton*, pl. 2, not from *Jerusalem*,
as stated on the title-page.

206 SEVEN POEMS from Blake's "Songs of Innocence." Decorated in
Colours by G. Spencer Watson. Set to Music by Geoffrey Gwyther.
Price 9ᵈ net each. The set complete in Decorated Portfolio, 6/- net.
(Postage 6ᵈ.) . . . The Poetry Bookshop, . . . London, W.C. [1917]
Seven double sheets, 29 × 23 cm.

    Contents: i. Piping down the Valleys Wild.
           ii. The Shepherd.   iii. Nurse's Song.
           iv. Spring.   v. Opportunity [*Rossetti MS.*, 52.i].
           vi. Infant Joy.   vii. Night.

207   THE TIGER.   Words by Wm. Blake, Music by E. T. Potter   Copyright E. T. Potter.   For sale by C. E. Hammett, 124 Thames St., Newport R.I. [N.D.]

208   FIVE "SONGS OF INNOCENCE" by William Blake set to Music by Arthur Somervell   Price two shillings and sixpence nett   E. Hatzfeld . . . London W. [N.D.]   4° pp. 19+[1].

   Contents: Settings for "Piping down the valleys wild," "The Shepherd," "The Blossom," "The Lamb," and "Nurse's Song."

209   SACRED LULLABIES and Other Songs Set to Music by H. Walford Davies . . . London: Sidney Riorden, . . . [N.D.]   8° pp. [ii]+39+[3].

   Contents: Pp. 25-29.   Setting for "Infant Joy."

C. *FACSIMILE REPRODUCTIONS*

210 THE MARRIAGE OF HEAVEN AND HELL [1868] 24.5 × 19 cm.,
27 leaves + 4 blank leaves at each end.

Description: Lithographed facsimiles, coloured by hand, of the 27 plates of the
original (no. 36). The plates are printed in dark brown on one side of the leaf only;
they lack the outer line round the margin.

Note: This facsimile was made by Camden Hotten in 1868, and three of the
plates, nos. 1, 8, and 20, were used by the same publisher in the several issues of
Swinburne's *Critical Essay* (no. 273), also published in that year. The plates
are printed on thick paper which was "expressly made to resemble that used by
Blake." The flesh tints have in some copies turned very dark, and the paper is often
much foxed. The original, from which this facsimile was made, was lent by D. G.
Rossetti to Swinburne, by whom it was passed on to Camden Hotten, but I have not
been able to identify the copy; possibly it was copy B.

211 WILLIAM BLAKE'S ILLUSTRATIONS OF THE BOOK OF JOB.
With Descriptive Letterpress, and a Sketch of the Artist's Life and Works.
By Charles Eliot Norton . . . Boston: James R. Osgood and Company,
. . . 1875. 34.5 × 27.5 cm., pp. [2] + 79 + [1].

Illustrations: Photographic reproductions, the size of the originals.

212 WORKS BY WILLIAM BLAKE Songs of Innocence 1789 Songs of
Experience 1794 Book of Thel 1789 Visions of the Daughters of Albion
1793 America: A Prophecy 1793 Europe: A Prophecy 1794 The First
Book of Urizen 1794 The Song of Los 1794 Reproduced in Facsimile

from the Original Editions One hundred Copies printed for Private Circulation 1876 38 × 27.5 cm., 147 ll.

Note: These lithographed plates, which were done for F. S. Ellis, are poorly executed, and the text is inaccurate.

213 JERUSALEM The Emanation of The Giant Albion 1804 Printed by W. Blake S^th Molton S^t [1877] 34.5 × 27 cm., 100 leaves.

Description: Photo-lithographed plates, the size of the originals, printed in black and uncoloured.

Note: 100 numbered copies of this facsimile in printed wrappers were issued by Pearson in 1877. William Muir (see no. 217) did not issue a facsimile of *Jerusalem* from his "Blake Press" at Edmonton, since this one had already appeared.

214 WILLIAM BLAKE ETCHINGS FROM HIS WORKS by William Bell Scott. With Descriptive Text. London: Chatto and Windus, . . . 1878. 42 × 28 cm., pp. 8.

Illustrations:

1. Part of a rejected design for Blair's *Grave*; water-colour.
2. "And the Waters prevailed upon the Earth an hundred and fifty days"; indian ink drawing.
3. A comic sketch on the back of the former (lithographed).
4. The Nativity; tempera.
5. St Mathew and the Angel; tempera.
6. The Queen of Evil; water-colour.
7. The Creation of Eve; water-colour.
8. Adam and Eve in Paradise; water-colour.
9. Eve eating the Forbidden Fruit; water-colour.
10. The Dream of Eve; water-colour (lithographed).

215 COMPOSITIONS from the "Works and Days" and "Theogony" of Hesiod. Designed by John Flaxman, R.A., Sculptor. Engraved by William Blake. London: George Bell and Sons, . . . 1881. 13 × 21 cm., 39 leaves.

Note: A small lithographed reproduction of no. 131.

216 SONGS OF INNOCENCE William Blake Reproduced by photography from a perfect black and white copy of the original issue of 1789, Containing all the Poems afterwards called Songs of Innocence, and three more which were afterwards issued among the Songs of Experience. Boston Little, Brown & Co. 1883. 18 cm.

Note: Reproduced from copy T of the original, which was then in the collection of E. W. Hooper, Treasurer of Harvard College. It is an uncoloured copy printed before 1818, but the evidence is insufficient to date it more accurately than this.

217 THE EDITION OF THE WORKS OF WILLIAM BLAKE PRE-PARED BY THE BLAKE PRESS AT EDMONTON [1884-1894]

Note: Under this title Mr. William Muir, with the help of several others whose names appear below, produced between 1880 and 1890 a series of hand-coloured facsimiles of Blake's illuminated books, which were issued from 1884 onwards. The complete set consists of three folio volumes, nine quarto volumes, and two single sheets; these are described below, lettered *a-o*. Fifty copies of most of the volumes were made, and were numbered and signed by Mr. Muir on the outside wrapper. A prospectus of the whole series was issued about 1884 by John Pearson, who had published the facsimile of *Jerusalem* (no. 213) in 1877, but only the first four volumes were issued by him. Bernard Quaritch acted as Mr. Muir's agent for the other volumes, and prospectuses, each 4 pp. quarto, were issued by him in May, 1885, and May, 1887. The edition of the *Songs of Innocence* and *Songs of Experience* was soon exhausted, but some of the other volumes did not find so ready a market, and copies are still to be obtained from Quaritch, having been recently coloured by Mr. Muir. In two of the volumes (*g* and *m*) the plates were etched on zinc in imitation of Blake's method, and in one (*n*) were engraved on copper; in the rest the plates were lithographed. Volumes *a-g*, *l*, *m*, and *o* have the plates coloured by hand, water-colour being used except in the case of *The Song of Los* (*o*), which was coloured with an opaque medium, containing glue and varnish, to resemble that used by Blake; volume *k* is sometimes coloured. The remainder are uncoloured. Volumes *e* and *g* contain a preface addressed to H.S.H. Prince Victor of Hohenlohe-Langenburg, Count Gleichen.

a. Songs of Innocence . . . *Colophon*: . . . produced by Wm. Muir Emily J. Druitt J. W. Watts Joseph B. Muir Hannah T. Muir . . . published by Jno. Pearson . . . 1884. 4° 33 ll.

Note: Done from Flaxman's copy (C) of the separate issue.

b. The Book of Thel . . . [Pearson, 1884] 4° & f° 8 ll.

Note: Done from the B.M. copy (D) of the original.

c. Visions of the Daughters of Albion [Pearson, 1884] 4° 13 ll.

Note: Done from the Butts copy (B) of the original. Seven copies were printed on "antique note-paper."

d. Songs of Experience . . . [Pearson, 1885] 4° 30 ll.

Note: Done from the Hamilton Palace copy (N) of the complete issue. An appendix was issued with volume *e.*

e. The Marriage of Heaven and Hell . . . [Quaritch, 1885] 4° 32 ll.

Note: Done from the Hamilton Palace copy (A) of the original. The first leaf is a preface addressed by Mr. Muir to Prince Hohenlohe-Langenburg. At the end is an appendix to volume *d*, consisting of three leaves with facsimiles of Blake's MS. index to the *Songs of Innocence and of Experience*, and of " A Divine Image," from a proof on a scrap of paper. On the recto of the back wrapper is a " Programme " addressed to the same patron as the preface.

f. Milton, a Poem in 2 Books, By Wm. Blake, 1804, facsimilied at Edmonton, anno 1886, by Wm. Muir, J. D. Watts, H. T. Muir, and E. Druitt. For whom Bernard Quaritch of 15, Piccadilly, W., is agent. [1886] 4° 51 ll.

Note: Done from the B.M. copy (A) of the original. The title-page and preface (5 pp.) are in ordinary typography. On two leaves at the end is a lithographed facsimile of a letter from Blake to Hayley, dated March 16, 1804 (letter no. 35). On the recto of the back wrapper is the same Programme as appeared in volume *e.*

g. There is No Natural Religion. By Wm. Blake. Facsimilied at Edmonton Anno 1886 by Wm. Muir, E. Druitt, H. T. Muir, and J. D. Watts.

> A Machine is not a man nor a work of art. It is destructive of humanity and of art.
> Commerce cannot endure individual merit. Its insatiable maw must be fed by what all can do equally well.
> A man puts a model before him and copies. Is this Art? Who could not do this?
> He who copies does not execute. He only imitates what is already executed.   W. BLAKE.

4° 23 ll.

Note: Contains both series *a* and *b*, done from the B.M. copy (A) of the original, supplemented with facsimiles of some additional plates which were then in Mr. Muir's possession. Instead of pl. 5 of series *b*, no copy of which is known to exist, is inserted a plate invented by Mr. Muir. The arrangement of the two series is virtually that adopted in the present work. The first leaf is a

Preface addressed to Prince Hohenlohe-Langenburg. The last leaf is a facsimile of the plate *On Homer* (*h,* below). The plates were etched on zinc in imitation of Blake's method.

h. On Homer's Poetry *and* On Virgil. [1886]

Note: A single leaf, 28 × 21 cm., uncoloured. Issued separately, but was also inserted in the *Century Guild Hobby Horse*, 1887 (see no. 492), and at the end of volume *g* above.

i. Little Tom the Sailor. [1886]

Note: A single sheet, 56 × 23 cm., uncoloured. Issued separately, but was also inserted in the *Century Guild Hobby Horse*, 1886 (see no. 490).

k. America, A Prophecy, by William Blake, 1793 Facsimilied at Edmonton, Anno 1887. By W. Muir, H. T. Muir, E. Druitt, & M. Hughes. This is the first part of the second volume of my edition of 50 copies of the Works of William Blake . . . Mr Quaritch, of 15, Piccadilly, W. is my only Agent. W. Muir. January, 1887. f° 20 ll.

Note: Printed in dull blue, in most cases uncoloured. About six copies have been coloured in recent years after copy B of the original.

l. Europe, A Prophecy, By William Blake, 1794. Facsimilied at Edmonton, Anno 1887, By W. Muir, S. E. Muir, H. T. Muir, & M. Hughes . . . Mr Quaritch is my only agent. Wm. Muir. September, 1887. f° 18 ll.

Note: Plates 1 and 3 were done from originals in Mr. Muir's possession; pl. 2, 4, 5, and 7 from the B.M. copy (D) of the original, and the remainder from the Beaconsfield copy (A), which was at that time imperfect. Plate 1, known as "The Ancient of Days," was also issued by Mr. Muir as a separate plate, but done from a different example (copy D).

m. The First Book of Urizen, By William Blake, 1794. Facsimilied at Edmonton in 1888 by Wm. Muir, H. T. Muir, J. D. Watts, and A. F. Westcott . . . 4° 28 ll.

Note: Done from the Beaconsfield copy (B), and therefore contains pl. 4, which is not found in most copies of the original. Only about twenty-five copies were done; the plates, which were etchings on zinc, have since been lost.

Q Q

n. The Gates of Paradise, By Wm. Blake, Lambeth, 1793. Facsimilied at Edmonton, Anno 1888, By Mary Hughes and Wm. Muir. Bernard Quaritch, Agent, 15, Piccadilly, W. 4° 21 ll.

> *Note*: On the first two leaves are the Prologue and the Keys of the Gate in ordinary type; nineteen plates, engraved on copper, follow. The title-page is from *For Children: The Gates of Paradise*; the other plates are from *For the Sexes*.

o. The Song of Los, By William Blake, 1795. Facsimilied at Edmonton, Anno 1890, by W. C. Ward, E. Druitt, H. T. Muir, S. E. Muir, and Wm. Muir. f° 8 ll.

> *Note*: Done from the B.M. copy (A) of the original. Coloured with an opaque medium in imitation of Blake's method. Only about twenty-five copies of this volume were made. Some additional copies have been executed recently.

218 **THERE IS NO NATURAL RELIGION** By W. Blake. Privately Printed. London Pickering & Co. 1886. 20 × 14.5 cm., 12 ll., unbound.

> *Description*: The plates are printed in light brown on one side of separate leaves; some are coloured by hand.

> *Note*: Fifty copies of this facsimile were issued in the same year as Muir's more complete edition (no. 217, *g*). It consists of no. 32, a, pl. 1-10; and b, pl. 3-4.

219 **ILLUSTRATIONS OF MILTON'S COMUS** Eight Drawings by William Blake Reproduced by William Griggs Bernard Quaritch . . . 1890 [Facsimiles of Choice Examples Selected from Illuminated Manuscripts Unpublished Drawings and Illustrated Books of Early Date, Part II] 29 cm., 8 ll.

> *Illustrations*:
> 1. Comus and his Revel Rout surprise the Lady.
> 2. Comus disguised as a rustic, addresses the Lady in the wood.
> 3. The Brothers gathering grapes. Comus looking on.
> 4. The Brothers passing the night in the wood; the Guardian-spirit as a Shepherd.
> 5. Comus, with the Lady spell-bound in the chair.
> 6. The Brothers rush in to save their Sister; Comus flies.

7. Sabrina disenchanting the Lady.
8. The Lady restored to her Parents.

Note: These coloured lithographs are facsimiles of the set of water-colours which was in 1890 in Quaritch's possession, but it is not indicated which one of the two existing sets (Gilchrist, ii, 245-6) this is.

220 POETICAL SKETCHES. By W. B. London: Printed in the Year MDCCLXXXIII.
Colophon: 50 copies reproduced in facsimile by W. Griggs, May, 1890. No. 1 [etc.] 22.5 × 14.5 cm., pp. [6] + 70 + [4].

Note: An accurate lithographic facsimile.

221 THE BOOK OF AHANIA Lambeth Printed by W Blake 1795 [1892] 28 × 19 cm., 4 ll., unbound.

Note: A lithographic facsimile by William Griggs, with headpiece and tailpiece in colours; issued by Quaritch in 1892.

222 FACSIMILE OF THE ORIGINAL OUTLINES before Colouring of The Songs of Innocence and of Experience Executed by William Blake With an Introduction By Edwin J. Ellis . . . London Bernard Quaritch, . . . 1893 31 × 24.5 cm., pp. xxi + 54 pl.

Note: These plates are photographic reproductions of Blake's relief-etchings; in cases where uncoloured copies of the originals were not available for reproduction, the outlines of the facsimiles are necessarily somewhat blurred. In addition to the uncoloured issue there were fifty copies coloured by hand; these were executed by Mr. Laing, of Lavender Hill, S.W., after copy O of the original, and were retouched by Mr. Ellis. Recently (1919) two copies have been coloured for Messrs. Quaritch by Mr. Wm. Muir.

223   WILLIAM BLAKE XVII DESIGNS TO THORTON'S VIRGIL Reproduced from the original wood-cuts MDCCCXXI [woodcut] Portland, Maine Thomas B. Mosher MDCCCXCIX 26 × 16.5 cm., pp. xx + 59 + [1].

> *Note*: 450 copies printed on Van Gelder hand-made paper, and twenty-five copies on Japanese vellum. Headbands and tailpieces from designs by Selwyn Image in the *Century Guild Hobby Horse*. Issued in cardboard slip-case with paper labels. On p. xvi is a reproduction of Blake's third design recut by another, which first appeared in the *Athenæum*, 1843 (see no. 413).

224   LITTLE ENGRAVINGS Classical & Contemporary Number II William Blake Being all his Woodcuts Photographically Reproduced in Facsimile with an Introduction By Laurence Binyon At the Sign of the Unicorn . . . London MDCCCCII 28.5 × 22.5 cm., pp. [vii] + [40].

225   ILLUSTRATIONS OF THE BOOK OF JOB . . . By William Blake, . . . 1000 copies issued in facsimile by J. M. Dent & Co., London, and G. P. Putnam's Sons, New York. 1902 . . . 37.5 + 27.5 cm. 22 ll.

> *Description*: Photographic reproductions, the size of the originals.

226   THE GRAVE A Poem By Robert Blair Illustrated by Twelve Etchings Executed by L. Schiavonetti from the Original Inventions of William Blake A New Edition Methuen & Co. London 1903 [The Illustrated Pocket Library of Plain and Coloured Books] 17 × 10.5 cm., pp. xx + 44 + 12 pl.

> *Note*: Also a large paper edition, 20 × 13 cm., limited to 100 copies for England. The plates were also issued separately in a portfolio.

227   ILLUSTRATIONS OF THE BOOK OF JOB Invented and Engraved by William Blake A New Edition Methuen & Co. London 1903 [The Illustrated Pocket Library of Plain and Coloured Books] 17 × 10.5 cm., pp. [iv] + 21 pl.

> *Note*: Also a large paper edition, 20 × 13 cm., limited to 100 copies for England. The plates were also issued separately in a portfolio.

228 THE GRAVE A Poem by Robert Blair With Eleven Photogravures and One Half-tone Reproduction after Designs by William Blake A Photogravure Portrait after T. Phillips R.A., . . . London George Routledge & Sons, Limited New York: E. P. Dutton & Co. [1905] [The Photogravure and Colour Series] 8° pp. 94 + 12 pl.

229 PARADISE LOST By John Milton Illustrations by William Blake . . . Printed at the Lyceum Press, Liverpool, and Published by the Liverpool Booksellers' Co., Limited 1906 26 × 19 cm., pp. ix + 397 + 1 l. blank at each end.

Illustrations: Twelve colour-printed reproductions, 14 × 12 cm., of the Liverpool set of illustrations to Paradise Lost (see Gilchrist, ii, 218).

Note: Two of the original water-colours belonged to Mr. J. A. Bryce, the rest to Mr. Sydney Style; they measure about 25 × 20 cm., and are dated 1807. The text of this edition is that prepared by Dr. David Masson for Messrs. Macmillan and Co.

230 WILLIAM BLAKE VOLUME I. ILLUSTRATIONS OF THE BOOK OF JOB With a General Introduction by Laurence Binyon Methuen & Co. . . . London [1906] 32 × 25.5 cm., pp. [iv] + 62 + 22 pl.

Illustrations: Photogravure reproductions, the size of the originals.

Note: This volume was intended to be the first of a series of reproductions, but it is the only one issued up to the present time.

231 MARY WOLLSTONECRAFT'S ORIGINAL STORIES With Five Illustrations by William Blake With an Introduction by E. V. Lucas London Henry Frowde 1906 17 × 11 cm., pp. xxiv + 88.

Note: A reprint of no. 69. The second illustration of the original editions is omitted.

232 MRS. Q— AND " WINDSOR CASTLE " With a Note on the Plates by Joseph Grego and Memoirs of the Life of the Celebrated Mrs. Q— by Edward Eglantine, Esq. London Kegan Paul, Trench, Trübner & Co. Limited . . . 1906 f° pp. 27.

> *Illustrations*:
> 1. Frontispiece. Coloured stipple of " Windsor Castle," drawn by I. B., engraved by G. Maile.
> 2. Facing p. 15. Coloured stipple, lettered: *Mrs Q Drawn by Huet Villiers. Engraved by W. Blake. London, Published 1ˢᵗ June 1820, by I. Barrow* . . .
>
> *Note*: Blake's plate was published separately, and is therefore not described in the present work, but see Russell, *Engravings*, p. 187. The *Memoirs of Mrs. Q—, by Edward Eglantine, Esq.*, were first published by Benbow in 1822 as an 8° pamphlet, " embellished with a striking likeness," which is an unsigned engraving of the same drawing as in Blake's larger plate. The edition containing the present reproductions was limited to 500 copies.

233 THE HERESY OF JOB By Francis Coutts With the Inventions of William Blake London: John Lane, . . . New York: . . . mcmvii 22 × 17 cm., pp. v + [iv] + 137 + [2] + 22 pl.

> *Illustrations*: Half-tone reproductions, reduced.

234 WILLIAM BLAKE, MYSTIC a study by Adeline M. Butterworth together with Young's Night Thoughts: Nights I & II with illustrations by William Blake . . . 1911 (see no. 368)

235 WILLIAM BLAKE'S ILLUSTRATIONS TO THORNTON'S PASTORALS OF VIRGIL in Ambrose Phillips' Imitation of Virgil's First Eclogue 1821 Enlarged Fac-similes in Platinotype from the scarce original edition by Frederick H. Evans Privately printed in 1912. Issue limited to 25 copies . . . 29 × 26 cm., ff. 37.

> *Note*: The photographs are nearly twice the size of the originals. Each is mounted on a separate page with the lines illustrated printed on the page opposite.

236 ILLUSTRATIONS OF THE BOOK OF JOB Invented and Engraved by William Blake Reproduced in facsimile from impressions in the British Museum London and Glasgow: Gowans & Gray, Ltd., 1912 15.5 × 12 cm., pp. 48.

237 FOR THE SEXES. THE GATES OF PARADISE [Facsimile, privately printed for W. A. White, New York, 1913] 23 × 14 cm., 21 ll.

Note: 100 copies of this facsimile were made from copy D of the original, which is in the collection of Mr. W. A. White. The leaves are unbound, and are contained in a slip-case with morocco back, lettered: "William Blake The Gates of Paradise (1793)."

238 WILLIAM BLAKE'S ILLUSTRATIONS TO THE BOOK OF JOB Enlarged Facsimiles in Platinotype from the original edition by Frederic H. Evans. Privately printed in 1914.

Note: Issue limited to twenty-five copies.

239 LITTLE TOM THE SAILOR . . .
Colophon: Munificenti Jacksoni . . . William Blake's "Little Tom the Sailor," now first cast in type and printed in book form . . . has been printed at the costs and charges made [sic] Richard C. Jackson, founder and president of the William Blake Society of Art and Letters . . . by way of celebrating his one-hundredth and sixty birthday; in Blake's beloved Lambeth, by George Vincent Steer, senior, of which one hundred copies (with ten proofs) have been taken, printed upon "Queen of Scots" fine hand made paper, . . . [1917] 27 × 20 cm., pp. [16].

Note: With a portrait, and reproductions of the cuts from the original broadside printed in monochrome.

240 THE BOOK OF THEL. Wm Blake [Facsimile, hand coloured by William Muir. London, Bernard Quaritch. 1920] 28 × 22.5 cm., 8 ll.

Note: Inside the wrapper is the following note: "This Book is copied from a " very richly coloured Original, which was lent to me by Mr Bernard Quaritch of " 15 Piccadilly in 1887. I now issue this edition of fifty copies through Messrs " Quaritch of Grafton Street, London, August, 1920. Wm Muir." The previous facsimile made by Mr. Muir in 1884 was done from another copy (D) of the original; the colouring in the present volume is quite different.

240A BRITISH MUSEUM Set 44 Prints and Drawings by William Blake 15 Pictorial Postcards Price 1s. [1920]

Note: Collotype reproductions of works by Blake in the British Museum with a leaf of description.

IV. BIOGRAPHY AND CRITICISM

BIBLIOGRAPHICAL PREFACE

THE task which confronts a future biographer of Blake is not an easy one, and it is probable that he will arrive at the conclusion that the fullest revelation of Blake's personality and life is to be found in his own works and correspondence. Never at any time did he have many intimate friends, and even with these few he was inclined to quarrel, so that some of his friendships lasted only for a few years. In consequence, although many of his contemporaries recognized in him an eccentric man of genius, little intimate biographical record has survived. His life, too, was uneventful in the ordinary sense of the word, as it consisted of long stretches of hard work, only broken by the successive removals of his home. The chief incidents of his life were adventures of the spirit, in which none of his friends could share, and with which few were even able to sympathize. The result of this isolation has been that the existing contemporary records are anecdotal rather than truly biographical, and therefore unsatisfying. Anecdote is exceedingly prone to be falsely coloured by sentiment or by exaggeration, and it is partly due to this that Blake has tended to become a legendary figure, sometimes even tinged with absurdity.

Of his contemporary biographers Dr. Benjamin Heath Malkin, head master of Bury Grammar School, has provided the best record of his early years,* and a vivid impression of him at the end of his life has been left by Henry Crabb Robinson.† Some of the gaps have been filled in by the biographies written by John Thomas Smith (no. 247), Allan Cunningham (no. 249), and Frederic Tatham (no. 339), but in each case lack of sympathy has produced a certain distortion of perspective. Illuminating side-lights are cast by the references scattered through the memoirs of Blake's friends, William Hayley (no. 245), John Linnell (no. 306), Samuel Palmer (no. 307), and Edward Calvert (no. 310). These, not being deliberately biographical,

* *A Father's Memoirs of his Child*, 1806 (no. 80).
† *Diary and Reminiscences*, 1869 (no. 275).

bear the stamp of sincerity, and so may be contrasted with a biography such as that by Allan Cunningham, whose veracity has been questioned by so credible a witness as John Linnell. Further facts are provided by the documents concerning his well-known trial for treason in 1804, which have all been printed within recent years, and some additional anecdotes are to be found in Varley's *Zodiacal Physiognomy*, 1828, Cunningham's *Cabinet Gallery of Pictures*, 1833, Dibdin's *Reminiscences*, 1836, Lady Charlotte Bury's *Diary*, 1839, Miss Jane Porter's *Scottish Chiefs*, 1840, J. T. Smith's *Book for a Rainy Day*, 1845, and Bray's *Life of Stothard*, 1851. Several of these have not been used hitherto by any of Blake's biographers, and they are therefore reprinted in an appendix to the present work.

If this had been the whole of the material at the command of Alexander Gilchrist when he undertook the writing of an exhaustive biography of Blake about 1856, his task would have been difficult indeed; but at that date there were still people living who could supply him with personal reminiscences of Blake, so that his book contains more biographical matter than can be found anywhere else, though he was exceedingly remiss in recording the sources of his information. His *Life* will therefore always remain the classic to which all students of Blake must turn. Whatever views may be held as to Gilchrist's literary style, his sentiments, or his accuracy in details, it must always be admitted that his book is a work of piety and enthusiasm, and much may be forgiven to a writer actuated by these motives in the face of an apathetic world. Other biographies have been more recently compiled, notably by E. J. Ellis and by W. B. Yeats, but Gilchrist's *Life* has not been superseded.

There is one part of Blake's life, the obscurity of which even Gilchrist's researches did not penetrate. His exhibition in 1809 having quite failed to attract the attention of the public, Blake seems to have retired into a more complete isolation than before, which lasted until he first met John Linnell in 1818. Of the incidents of the intervening nine years almost no record now remains. Not a single letter written in the years 1810 to 1817 is known to exist. Even his artistic output seems to have been small, and his account with Thomas Butts ends in December 1810.* His smaller engraving of the Canterbury Pilgrims was published in 1812 (no. 75). One engraving of a subject from *America* dated 1813 is known,† and

* See p. 75 of the present work.   † See Russell, *Engravings*, p. 93.

copies of several of the Illuminated Books were issued about 1815.* No book illustrations are known to have been done for the publishers between 1809 and 1817, except the plates for Flaxman's *Hesiod* (no. 131), the proofs of which bear dates ranging from October 1814 to December 1817. Further evidence of the obscurity in which Blake was living in 1817 is to be found in William Carey's appreciation (no. 244) of the designs for Blair's *Grave*; this is here noticed for the first time and is reprinted in an appendix. It is difficult to understand upon what resources he depended for his living during these years, and a theory which would supply an explanation has been founded upon a passage printed in the *Revue Britannique* in 1833 (see no. 411). An account is given in this article of an undated visit to Bethlem Hospital, and of an interview purporting to have been held there with Blake, the Seer, as he is said to have been named. The story has been fully investigated by Mr. W. T. Horton, but no confirmation of the truth of the assertion that Blake was ever an inmate of Bedlam can be discovered. If it be true, it is strange that none of his friends has left any hint that such was the fact. The story is probably a fabrication, but it cannot be lightly passed over, and the original article is therefore reprinted with the other contemporary records.

This section aims at giving a bibliographical account of every source of information concerning Blake's life, but it will have been inferred from the foregoing remarks that these sources are not numerous. Nevertheless, the section is a large one, its bulk being partly due to repetitions of certain well-known stories, and partly to the very large amount of criticism and speculation to which Blake's genius and peculiarities have given rise. Biography and criticism cannot be dissociated, and the present section attempts therefore to cover the whole ground. Criticism of Blake begins adversely with the violent attacks made upon him in Leigh Hunt's *Examiner* in 1808 and 1809, and, although active hostility subsided, it never during his lifetime gave place to any audible chorus of approval. Critical appreciation was, indeed, almost dumb for thirty years after Blake's death until, stimulated by Gilchrist's biography in 1863, it suddenly burst forth in Swinburne's *Critical Essay* in 1868. Never again since that date has Blake had so wholehearted and undiscriminating an advocate; but criticism has poured out in a steady stream, the volume of which has

* See p. 17 of the present work.

shown a periodic increase coincident with the stimulation of public interest by the appearance of certain books and by the successive exhibitions or sales at auction of his works. The entries, which number nearly 430, cannot be here analysed in detail, but attention may be drawn to the few works on Blake which have been written in countries other than England or America. The German public was first made acquainted with Blake by an article from the pen of Crabb Robinson, which appeared in the *Vaterländisches Museum* in 1811 (no. 401). A further account of him was given in *Zeitgenossen* in 1830 (no. 409), and he was included in 1835 in Nagler's *Neues Algemeines Künstler-Lexicon* (no. 252), fourteen years before his name was to be found in any similar work published in England. Nothing more appeared in German until the essay written by Rudolf Kassner in 1900 (no. 328), which was followed in 1906 by a study by Helena Richter (no. 343), and in 1907 by von Taube's introduction to his volume of translations from Blake's works (no. 176). The first critic to notice Blake in France was Milsand, who published an essay in 1863 (no. 422); another short work by Prof. Benoit appeared in 1906 (no. 341). One of the most valuable works on Blake in this or any other language is the volume by Prof. Berger of Bordeaux, which appeared in 1907 (no. 344), and was afterwards translated into English. In Italy, so far as is known to me, only one small pamphlet has appeared (no. 356). In Denmark considerable interest is being taken in Blake at the present time; for this Prof. Grönbech of Copenhagen is chiefly responsible (no. 386). Blake's affinity with the art of the East is evident when it has been pointed out, and expression has been given to this in a large book in Japanese by M. Yanagi, published at Tokyo in 1915 (no. 381).

The pages following record the books dealing only with Blake or containing essays or articles about him, and in addition all that could be found with any reference to him that might be considered to be of interest. It cannot be supposed that the list is even approximately complete, but great pains have been taken to avoid the omission of anything that is of real importance. For bibliographical convenience books and periodicals are given in separate lists. Both subdivisions are arranged in chronological order, but for purposes of reference among so large a number of entries the index will probably be found the simplest method of approach.

A. BOOKS

241 DISCOURSES ON VARIOUS SUBJECTS, By Jacob Duché, M.A. Rector of Christ-Church and St. Peters, in Philadelphia; and formerly of Clare-Hall, Cambridge. Vol. I [II] London: . . . J. Phillips . . . M.DCC.LXXIX. 2 vols. 8°.

> *Reference*: In the list of subscribers, at the beginning of vol. i, occurs the name of "Mr William Blake."

> *Note*: In 1779 Blake was aged twenty-two, and no doubt already interested in religious matters, so that he may well have been a subscriber to this work. Duché was intimately connected with the Female Orphan Asylum, St. George's Fields, Lambeth, which is within a very short distance of 13 Hercules Buildings, Blake's home from 1793 to 1800; I do not, however, know of any other reference connecting Duché with Blake, so that this apparent association may be only a coincidence. Second and third editions of Duché's *Discourses* were published in 1780 and 1790. This reference was first recorded by the late Charles Higham in an article in *The New-Church Magazine*, vol. xv, London, 1896, p. 460 (reprinted in *The New-Church Review*, Boston, April, 1915).

242 A FATHER'S MEMOIRS OF HIS CHILD. By Benj. Heath Malkin, Esq. . . . London . . . 1806. [See no. 80.]

> *Note*: Contains an account of Blake's early years.

243 CRITICAL DESCRIPTION of the Procession of Chaucer's Pilgrims to Canterbury, painted by Thomas Stothard, Esq. R.A. Respectfully addressed, by permission, to John Leigh Philips, Esq. . . . By William Carey. London, . . . T. Cadell and W. Davies, for R. H. Cromek, 64, Newman Street. 1808. Price two shillings. 8°. Pp. 77 + [3].

> *Reference*: Pp. 10-11, footnote: " It is but justice to note that we are indebted "to Mr Cromek for the first intention of employing Mr Stothard to paint the "picture of the Procession of Chaucer's Pilgrims. The same spirit conceived the

" idea of employing that extraordinary Artist, Blake, to compose his grand designs
" for Blair's Grave."

Note: The author of this pamphlet, William Paulet Carey, 1759-1839, was an
engraver, art critic, and dealer in prints and pictures. His admiration for Blake's
genius was very great, though he seems only to have known his designs for Blair's
Grave, and to have based his opinion on these. He was evidently unaware of Blake's
grievance against Cromek with regard to the " Canterbury Pilgrims," and he makes
no further reference to Blake in this connexion, but later, in 1817, he wrote another
much longer appreciation of Blake in a work on Benjamin West's " Death on the
Pale Horse " (see next entry). My attention was first drawn to the *Critical Description*
by Mr. W. E. Moss, who pointed out that Blake's description of his own "Canterbury
Pilgrims " in the *Descriptive Catalogue*, 1809, may have been regarded by him as a
counter-blast to Carey's pamphlet.

Mr. Moss states that the *Critical Description* was first published in an edition of
200 copies at Liverpool (G. Harris, 1808), but I have not seen a copy of this issue.
A second edition was published in 1818 (London, 35 Mary-la-bonne Street, 8⁰).

244   CRITICAL DESCRIPTION and analytical review of " Death on the Pale Horse,"
painted by Benjamin West, P.R.A. with desultory references to the works of some
ancient masters, and living British Artists. Respectfully addressed to the most noble
The Marquis of Stafford. By William Carey. . . . London: Published at 35, Mary-
la-bonne Street, Piccadilly. Price 3s. 6d. sewed. Large Copy, 4s. Dec. 31, 1817.
8⁰. Pp. xii + 172 + 4.

References:
1. P. 9. Reference to Blake's designs for Blair's *Grave*.
2. Pp. 128-136, in the " Desultory references to the works of . . . living
British Artists " is a long appreciation of the designs for Blair's *Grave*, and some
remarks on Blake's circumstances; these afford striking evidence of the obscurity
in which he was living at this date. Reprinted in an appendix to the present work.

Note: An earlier reference to Blake by William Carey is to be found in his
Critical Description of Stothard's Canterbury Pilgrims, 1808 (see preceding entry), the
second edition of which is advertised at the end of this later work. These references
have not been noticed before.

245   MEMOIRS OF THE LIFE AND WRITINGS OF WILLIAM HAYLEY,
Esq. the friend and biographer of Cowper, written by himself. With extracts from
his Private Correspondence and Unpublished Poetry. And Memoirs of his Son

Thomas Alphonso Hayley, the young sculptor. Edited by John Johnson, LL.D. Rector of Yaxham with Welborne in Norfolk. In Two Volumes. Vol. I. London: Printed for Henry Colburn and Co. Conduit Street, and Simpkin and Marshall, Stationers-Hall-Court. 1823. 4° 28.5 cm. Vol. I. pp. xii + 484. Vol. II. pp. vi + 515 + [1].

Illustrations: 1. Frontispiece to vol. I. Portrait of William Hayley. Line engraving by Cooper after Engleheart. 12 × 10 cm.

2. Frontispiece to Vol. II. Mezzotint by Caroline Watson after Romney, representing Flaxman, William Hayley, and Thomas Alphonso Hayley. 22 × 18 cm.

References: All in vol. II:

1. Pp. 22-23. Blake's designs for *Little Tom the Sailor* (see no. 71).

2. P. 32. Blake's designs for Hayley's *Ballads*, 1802 (see no 72). Mentions Blake's miniatures, and his portrait of Dr. Johnson.

3. Pp. 37-38. The form of publication of the *Ballads*.

4. P. 42. Extract from Hayley's diary, March 26-27, 1803, where he mentions reading Klopstock to Blake (see no. 10).

5. Pp. 46-47. A description of Blake's quarrel with the soldier, and of his subsequent trial and acquittal (see no. 319).

6. Pp. 123-142. Eleven references to Blake in letters written by Hayley, the majority to the Rev. Dr. Johnson, under the dates: Aug. 6, Sept. 3, Oct. 1, Nov. 8, Nov. 18, Nov. 22, 1801; Feb. 3, Feb. 25, March 11, May 16, June 28, 1802. Several of these refer to Blake's designs for the *Ballads* (see nos. 72 and 74).

Note: William Hayley played so large a part in Blake's life that these references, which have all been reprinted in Gilchrist, i, 166-177, are of considerable importance. They give an interesting picture, from Hayley's point of view, of Blake's life at Felpham during the years 1800-1803. Blake's feelings of gratitude towards Hayley are warmly expressed in the numerous letters which he wrote to him in the years 1803-1805 after he had left Felpham; on the other hand, Hayley's character and condescending patronage produced in Blake, as long as he remained with him, an increasing irritation, which found a private outlet in the scurrilous verses and epigrams written in the *Rossetti MS*. The large number of references to Hayley that occur in the present work in connection with his *Ballads*, his *Life of Cowper*, and other writings, will be found by reference to the index.

246 THE LIBRARY COMPANION; or, Young Man's Guide, . . . By the Rev. T. F. Dibdin, F.R.S., A.S. . . . London: Printed for . . . J. Major . . . MDCCCXXIV 8° large paper. Vol. I. pp. [iv] + lii + 400. Vol. II. pp. [ii] + 512.

Reference: Vol. II, p. 334, to Blake's designs for Young's *Night Thoughts*, and in a footnote, to Isaac D'Israeli's collection of Blake's works.   (Small paper edition, p. 734; second edition, 1824, p. 742.)

Note: This reference to Blake was greatly amplified in Dibdin's *Reminiscences of a Literary Life*, 1836 (no. 254).

247   NOLLEKENS AND HIS TIMES: comprehending a Life of that Celebrated Sculptor; and Memoirs of several Contemporary Artists, from the Time of Roubiliac, Hogarth and Reynolds, to that of Fuseli, Flaxman, and Blake.   By John Thomas Smith, . . . In Two Volumes . . . London: Henry Colburn, . . . 1828. 8° 22 cm. Vol. I. pp. x+424.   Vol. II. pp. vi+488.

Frontispiece to vol. 1: Portrait of Nollekens, engraved by Bond after Jackson.

Memoir: The last memoir in vol. II, pp. 454-488, gives an account of Blake. It includes the following quotations:

   1. Song " How sweet I roamed " (*Poetical Sketches*).
   2. Four concluding lines of the " Address to the Deists " (*Jerusalem*).
   3. Four lines of the " Address to the Christians " (*Jerusalem*).
   4. A letter from Blake to Flaxman, Sept. 21, 1800 (letter no. 12).
   5. A letter from Blake to Ozias Humphrey, Jan. 18, 1808 (letter no. 61).
Smith also prints Mr. Richard Thomson's description of the *Songs of Experience*, *America*, *Europe*, and *A Small Book of Designs*.

Note: Smith had known Blake as a young man, and this memoir gives more facts at first hand than any other account.   It was largely used by Cunningham (no. 249) and by Gilchrist in the compilation of their biographies.   It has been reprinted in full by Symons.   A second edition of *Nollekens and his Times* was issued in 1829 (memoir of Blake, ii, 461-494), and a new edition, edited by Edmund Gosse, in 1894.   Re-edited by Wilfred Whitten, 1920 (John Lane, 2 vols., 8°).

248   A TREATISE ON ZODIACAL PHYSIOGNOMY; . . . By John Varley. London: . . . 1828 . . . [type facsimile opposite]

Collation: 25.5 × 16 cm., uncut.   A², B-H⁴, I²; 32 leaves.   Pp. iv Title, Preface +60.

Contents: Zodiacal Physiognomy (p. 1).
         A Brief Sketch of Astrology (p. 4).
         Tables of Signs and Degrees which rise each hour (p. 10).
         Explanation of the Signs (p. 41).
         On Physiognomy (p. 56).

A TREATISE

ON

ZODIACAL PHYSIOGNOMY;

ILLUSTRATED BY

ENGRAVINGS OF HEADS AND FEATURES;

AND ACCOMPANIED BY

TABLES OF THE TIME OF RISING OF THE TWELVE SIGNS OF THE ZODIAC;

AND

CONTAINING ALSO NEW AND ASTROLOGICAL EXPLANATIONS OF SOME REMARKABLE PORTIONS OF

ANCIENT MYTHOLOGICAL HISTORY.

By JOHN VARLEY.

LONDON:

PUBLISHED BY THE AUTHOR, 10½, GREAT TICHFIELD STREET;

AND SOLD BY

LONGMAN AND CO., PATERNOSTER ROW.

1828.

[ENTERED AT STATIONERS' HALL.]

Illustrations: Six plates in illustration of the text, engraved by Linnell in line and stipple. On the last three plates are engravings of *Cancer*, and two versions of the *Ghost of a Flea* after Blake's "visionary heads":

1. Two heads named *Scorpio* and *Aries*. Inscribed above: *Pl.* 2, and below: *J. L. fec^t*

2. Various astrological diagrams and signs. Lettered below: *J. Varley inv.* / *Published . . . by J. Varley, London, Decr 1 1828.*

3. Two rows of heads, each with a name inscribed below: *Self-will, Goodness, Masked Eyeball, Gemini (Cochabiel), A Cur, Pride, Conceit, The Genius Cochabiel.*

4. Ditto: *Taurus, Capella, Bellatrix, Cochabiel, Cancer* [after Blake], *Scorpio, Capella as transmitted from Taurus, Gemini.*

5. Three heads: *Gemini, Cancer, Ghost of a Flea from Blake's vision* [with the mouth open].

6. Two heads: *Ghost of a Flea from Blake's vision* [with the mouth shut and tongue protruded], *Taurus (fair class)*; and *Reverse of the coin of Nebuchadnezzar after Blake.*

Plates 3-6 are lettered below: *J. Linnel sc. J. Varley inv.* No. 1 faces p. 1; the rest are together at the end.

Reference: On pp. 54-55 Varley explains the significance of Blake's vision of the Ghost of a Flea, and describes the circumstances in which the drawings were made.

Note: This pamphlet is extremely rare; it was issued in grey wrappers, on which was printed, in addition to the title given above, the information that it was "To be completed in four parts" and was "Price five shillings," but this is the only part that was published. A portion of the passage referring to Blake was quoted by Southey in *The Doctor* (no. 260), and by Gilchrist, i, 303-304, and it has been reprinted in full by Symons. Gilchrist (i, 304) states that one of the heads of Cancer is after a "visionary head" by Blake; this evidently refers to the head on pl. 4, which bears close resemblance to Blake's drawing of "Cancer" formerly in the Linnell collection.* It is also worth noting that this head of Cancer and the head of Gemini on pl. 5 have a definite resemblance to Blake's sketches of himself and of his wife in the *Rossetti MS.*† In *The Portfolio* for July, 1871, the late W. B. Scott has described "A Varley-and-Blake Sketch-book," which was then in his possession. Among other sketches and "visionary heads" in this book there is a full-length drawing of the Ghost of a Flea, which is very similar to the tempera painting of this subject in the possession of Mr. W. Graham Robertson. The head of the Ghost of a Flea, engraved on pl. 5 above, is the one which is usually reproduced; the second

---

* Sold at Christie's, March 15, 1918 (lot 164, Carthew, 52 gns.).

† See the plate in Gilchrist, i, facing p. 374.

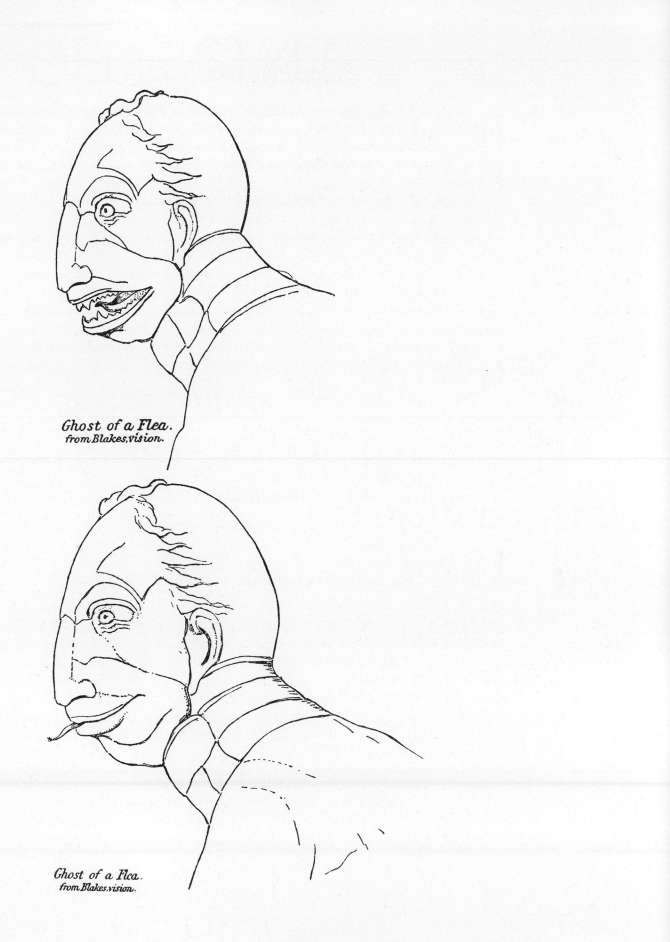

Ghost of a Flea.
from Blakes vision.

Ghost of a Flea.
from Blakes vision.

head is given on the plate of reproductions in *The Portfolio*, together with the full-length drawing and other sketches. Both heads are reproduced on p. 317. In the Linnell collection was a drawing of the head with the mouth closed and with the mouth alone, open, below,* and probably it was from this drawing that Linnell; executed the engravings for the *Zodiacal Physiognomy*. There is no mention in the text of any coin of Nebuchadnezzar, but probably the explanation of the engraving on pl. 6 would have been supplied by the second part of the *Zodiacal Physiognomy*, had it been published. In the possession of Mr. W. E. Moss is a proof, formerly in the Linnell collection, of an engraving hitherto unrecorded, which was evidently intended for the *Zodiacal Physiognomy*. It represents, on the left, a coin (diameter 11 cm.) bearing the bearded head of an old man in profile with a crown, and, on the right, another grotesque head in profile. The coin represents the obverse of the " coin of Nebuchadnezzar," and the original drawings for both sides of the coin were in the Linnell collection † on a single piece of paper marked " coin of Nebuchadnezzar seen " by Mr Blake in a vision." The second head may also have been drawn by Blake.

Copies: B.M. (with duplicate of pl. 5, but lacking pl. 6); G. L. Keynes (2 copies); W. E. Moss.

249 THE LIVES OF THE MOST EMINENT BRITISH PAINTERS, SCULP-TORS, AND ARCHITECTS. By Allan Cunningham. Vol. II. London: John Murray, ... MDCCCXXX. [The Family Library, No. X.] 8°. 15.5 cm., pp. [iv] + 320.

Illustrations: Engraved frontispiece and six other portraits, including one of Blake, facing p. 142, after the painting by Phillips. Lettered: *T. Phillips Esqʳ R.A. W. C. Edwards | Will Blake* [signature in facsimile] | *London*, ... 1830. The engraving measures 8.5 × 7 cm.

Memoir: Cunningham's biography of Blake occupies pp. 142-179. It contains the following quotations:
1. To the Muses (*Poetical Sketches*).
2. The Tiger (*Songs of Experience*).
3. 29 lines from " King Edward the Third " (*Poetical Sketches*).
4. " Introduction " to *Songs of Innocence*.
5. A letter from Blake to Flaxman, dated " Felpham, Sept. 21, 1800 " (letter no. 12).

Note: This volume is the second of a series of six issued between 1829 and

* Now in the possession of Miss A. G. E. Carthew, London.
† Sold at Christie's, March 15, 1918 (lot 163, Parsons, 42 gns.).

BLAKE AND VARLEY ARGUING
Pencil Drawing by John Linnell, 1821

1833. The memoir, although it contains a number of facts and anecdotes not recorded elsewhere, was largely made up from the account in J. T. Smith's *Nollekens and his Times* (no. 247). It is written in a lively style, and the author, who was at that time well known as a poet, novelist, biographer, and art critic, had, in his younger days, known Blake. In Story's *Life of John Linnell* (no. 306), i, 246, is printed a letter from Cunningham to Linnell, dated July 20, 1829, in which he states that "much valuable information" has been received from Varley, and asks for more from Linnell; he writes further: "I know Blake's character for I knew the man. I "shall make *judicious* use of my materials, and be merciful where sympathy is "needed."

Cunningham does not seem, however, to have taken full advantage of Linnell's help, for in a letter to Bernard Barton, dated April 3, 1830, Linnell writes: "Mr. Blake never was reduced to live in a garret, as asserted in the Memoir; and I "am sorry Mr. Cunningham did not avail himself of the information I offered him, "as he might have made his very interesting Memoir still more instructive, and far "more creditable to Mr. Blake by the alteration of some things and the addition of "others with which I could have furnished him" (Russell, *Letters*, p. 227).

A contemporary reviewer in the *London University Magazine* for 1830 (no. 408), who seems himself to have known Blake, also charges Cunningham with having introduced incidents which are falsely coloured, and complains of his somewhat contemptuous view of Blake's character. Another more general review appeared in the *Edinburgh Review* in 1834 (no. 412), where it is remarked: "that Blake, the "able, but, alas! insane author of some very striking and original designs, could "scarcely be considered a painter."

Gilchrist gives several extracts from Cunningham's memoir, and it is reprinted in full by Symons.

In the possession of Mr. B. B. Macgeorge of Glasgow is a MS. copy of the memoir bound up in a quarto volume; it is illustrated with portraits and with engravings and drawings by Blake, which include a pencil portrait of Thomas Hayley. Bound in at the end are a large number of rare prints by Blake, with a prefatory note signed "G.A.S. 1855"; these include proofs, coloured prints, cancelled plates, and some posthumous impressions from the Illuminated Books. In addition to these there is Blake's MS. index of the *Songs of Innocence and of Experience*. The volume formerly belonged to Mr. William Muir, and was acquired by Mr. Macgeorge from Quaritch (*General Catalogue*, p. 935).

Cunningham's memoirs of other artists contain occasional references to Blake, among them the following, which seem not to have been noticed:

Vol. ii, p. 309. "When Blake, a man infinitely more wild in conception than "Fuseli himself, showed him one of his strange productions, he said, 'Now some "'one has told you this is very fine.' 'Yes,' said Blake, 'the Virgin Mary appeared

" ' to me, and told me it was very fine: what can you say to that ?' ' Say ?' exclaimed
" Fuseli, ' why nothing—only her ladyship has not an immaculate taste.' "

Vol. v, p. 2. ". . . students of threescore years and more are not unknown to
" academies. I have seen William Blake, within a few years of his death, studying at
" Somerset House with all the ardour of youth ; and other names not less dis-
" tinguished might be cited."

Cunningham's *Lives* were reissued in 1830-1837 with additions (see next entry)
and were reprinted in *Harper's Family Library* (New York, 1844, 3 vols., 12°), and
later in *Bohn's Standard Library* (London, George Bell, 1879, 8°), edited by Mrs.
Charles Heaton ; this editor adds numerous footnotes, among which is the anecdote
of Blake and the Archangel Gabriel, given under Cunningham's *Cabinet Gallery of
Pictures* (no. 251).

250　THE LIVES OF THE MOST EMINENT BRITISH PAINTERS, . . .
Second Edition. Vol. II. London : John Murray . . . MDCCCXXX. 8°. 15.5 c.m.,
pp. [iv] + 349 + [1].

Illustrations : As in first edition.

Memoir : The memoir, occupying pp. 143-188, has been somewhat extended in
this edition. On pp. 169-170 Cunningham includes a quotation concerning Blake
from a letter from Charles Lamb to Bernard Barton (dated May 15, 1824; see
no. 337). At the end he appends a more detailed criticism of Blake's poetry
(pp. 183-188), and states in the last paragraph that Blake " has left volumes, amounting
" it is said to nearly an hundred, prepared for the press." This edition contains the
following additional quotations :

   1. The Chimney Sweeper (*Songs of Innocence*).
   2. Holy Thursday (the same).
   3. Laughing Song (the same).
   4. The Lamb (the same).
   5. " I love the jocund dance " (*Poetical Sketches*).
   6. Gwin, King of Norway, several stanzas beginning " The husbandman now
" leaves the plough " (the same).

Note : This edition was issued in six volumes between 1830 and 1837. The
additions have not been previously noticed.

251 THE CABINET GALLERY OF PICTURES, . . . with Biographical and Critical Descriptions by Allan Cunningham. Vol. I. [II.] . . . London: John Major, . . . MDCCCXXXIII. 8°. Vol. I. pp. [viii]+204. Vol. II. pp. [x]+192.

Illustrations: Each volume contains 36 engravings after various masters.

Reference: In vol. I, pp. 11-13, in connexion with the angels in a picture of "Christ in the Sepulchre" by Guercino, Cunningham gives an anecdote of Blake and the painter Phillips, in which, in the course of a conversation, Blake tells how the Archangel Gabriel appeared to him. It is reprinted in full in an appendix to the present work.

Note: This story has been reprinted in Mrs. Heaton's edition of Cunningham's *Lives of the Painters*, but it does not seem to have been noticed elsewhere. Mrs. Heaton found it among the Cunningham MSS., the writer having heard it, apparently from Linnell (see Mrs. Heaton's index), too late for insertion in his memoir of Blake. It is probable that Cunningham has somewhat improved upon the story in the telling.

252 NEUES ALGEMEINES KUNSTLER - LEXICON . . . Bearbeitet von Dr. G. K. Nagler . . . München, 1835. Verlag von E. A. Fleischmann. 22 cm.

Article: Vol. 1 (A-Boe), pp. 519-522. "Blake, William."

Note: References are given to *Vaterländisches Museum*, 1811 (no. 401), and *Zeitgenossen*, 1830 (no. 409), from which the article was probably compiled.

253 THE STUDENT. A Series of Papers, . . . [By Bulwer Lytton] London . . . 1835 2 vols. 8°. 19 cm. Vol. I. pp. xi+ [iii]+335+[1]. Vol. II. pp. viii+ 361+[1].

Reference: Vol. II, pp. 152-3. "Of all enthusiasts, the painter Blake seems to " have been the most remarkable. With what a hearty faith he believed in his faculty " of seeing spirits and conversing with the dead! And what a delightful vein of mad- " ness it was—with what exquisite verses it inspired him! . . . And what engravings! " I saw, a few days ago, a copy of the Night Thoughts, which he had illustrated in a " manner at once so grotesque, so sublime—now by so literal an interpretation, now " by so vague and disconnected a train of invention, that the whole makes one of the " most astonishing and curious productions which ever balanced between the conception " of genius and the raving of insanity."

T T

254 REMINISCENCES OF A LITERARY LIFE; by the Reverend Thos. Frognall Dibdin, D.D. . . London : John Major, . . . MDCCCXXXVI.   8°.   22.5 cm.   Pt. I. pp. xxxii + [iv] + 556.   Pt. II.   pp. 557-982 + 44.

Illustrations : Pt. I. Frontispiece and four engraved plates. Pt. II. Five engraved plates.

Reference : In pt. II, pp. 784-789, there is a passage concerning Blake, giving Dibdin's impressions of him and his recollections of a visit paid to him by Blake about 1816.   In footnotes he gives the " Introduction " from the *Songs of Innocence*, the first line of which he misquotes, and a letter from Isaac D'Israeli about Blake. The passage is printed in full in an appendix to the present work.

Note : This passage, though apparently of great interest, is not mentioned by any of Blake's biographers. This is explained by the following extract from a memoir of *Anne Gilchrist*, London, 1887, p. 132 (no. 294), consisting of a passage from a letter from Anne Gilchrist to Rossetti, and a note by the editor of the memoir : " Only think of Mr. Disraeli's collection turning out such a mare's nest, and Dibdin's " whole account a mere fabrication. [The antiquarian said that Disraeli (Beacons- " field) possessed original drawings by Blake; so W. M. Rossetti wrote to Disraeli, " and he replied in the most courteous spirit, showing that he possessed only some of " the published books.] " The letter to Dibdin is not from Beaconsfield, but from Isaac D'Israeli, who states that he possesses 160 of Blake's designs. It is almost incredible that Dibdin should have deliberately forged such a letter from D'Israeli, who was himself a subscriber for two copies of the *Reminiscences*. Moreover, a previous reference to Blake's illustrations to Young's *Night Thoughts* and to D'Israeli's collection of Blake's works is to be found in Dibdin's *Library Companion*, 1824 (no. 246), though no mention of the visit is made there. I am inclined to believe in the authenticity of the greater part of Dibdin's account ; it has been mentioned else-where in the present work (p. 18) that D'Israeli possessed six of the illuminated books, and these, together with the *Night Thoughts* and the *Job*, would account for the large number of designs mentioned in the letter. A writer in the *Times Literary Supplement* for July 15, 1920, has inferred from Dibdin's account that the D'Israeli collection still remains to be discovered, but the explanation given above makes it unlikely that any such collection exists. All D'Israeli's copies of the illuminated books are now in the possession of Mr. B. B. Macgeorge of Glasgow.

255 DIARY ILLUSTRATIVE OF THE TIMES OF GEORGE THE FOURTH, Interspersed with Original Letters [By Lady Charlotte Bury] . . . Edited by John Galt, Esq. . . . In Four Volumes. . . . London: Henry Colburn, . . . MDCCCXXXIX . . . 8°. Vol. I. pp. [ii] + 391 + [1]. Vol. II. pp. [ii] + 415 + [1]. Vol. III. pp. ix + [i] + 402. Vol. IV. pp. [ii] + 392.

Illustrations: Vol. III. Frontispiece. Facsimile of a letter. Vol. IV. Frontispiece. Portrait of H.R.H. the Princess of Wales.

Reference: Vol. III, pp. 345-348. Under the date Jan. 20 [1820], Lady Charlotte Bury gives an account of a dinner party at Lady C. L—'s, in the course of which she conversed with Blake. She conveys in an entertaining manner her impressions of " the eccentric little artist."

Note: Vols. I and II were published in 1838, vols. III and IV in 1839. The passage containing the reference to Blake has been reprinted by W. M. Rossetti in the *Athenæum*, 1891 (no. 499), and by Symons. Rossetti identifies Lady C. L— with Lady Caroline Lamb.

256 A TREATISE ON WOOD ENGRAVING, Historical and Practical. [By W. A. Chatto.] With upwards of three hundred illustrations, engraved on wood, by John Jackson. London: Charles Knight and Co. Ludgate Street. 1839. 8°. 26 cm., pp. xvi + 749 + [3].

Reference: Pp. 715-717 give an account of Blake's methods of engraving and etching. The facts are derived chiefly from Cunningham.

Note: In the second edition (London, H. G. Bohn, 1861) a wood engraving by W. J. Linton after Blake's " Death's Door " is inserted facing p. 591*. The references to Blake are on pp. 632-633.

257 THE SCOTTISH CHIEFS. By Miss Jane Porter. Revised, Corrected, and Illustrated with A New Retrospective Introduction, Notes, &c., by the Author . . . London: George Virtue [1841]. 8°. 22.5 cm. Vol. I. pp. [ii] + 488. Vol. II. pp. [ii] + 481 + [1].

Illustrations: Vol. I. Frontispiece, engraved title, and ten other steel engravings. Vol. II. Engraved title, and nine other engravings.

Reference: Vol. II, pp. 466-470, in a postscript, written in May, 1841, to a " Note respecting the personal Conformation of Sir William Wallace and King " Robert Bruce " is an account of Blake's vision of Wallace. The facts were related to Miss Porter by an unnamed friend, who was in the habit of visiting Blake's studio.

Note: Attention was first drawn to this anecdote by Mr. William Muir, who made it the subject of a paper read to the Blake Society on Sept. 11, 1917. It has not been anywhere reprinted, and is given in an appendix to the present work. Miss Porter's note implies that Blake was familiar with her book, which was first published in 1810.

258 A NEW VIEW OF INSANITY. The Duality of the Mind . . . By A. L. Wigan, M.D. . . . London: . . . 1844. 21.5 cm., pp. xii+459+[3].

Reference: On p. 169 is a passage about "a celebrated artist of the present day" and his visionary drawings, which evidently refers to Blake.

Note: In addition to the above, on pp. 123-6 is an account of a visionary artist based on personal knowledge, which has been supposed to refer to Blake (see, for instance, Elam's *A Physician's Problems*, 1869, no. 276), but it evidently refers to someone else, possibly the individual described in the *Revue Britannique*, 1833 (see no. 411).

259 A BOOK FOR A RAINY DAY: or, Recollections of the Events of the Last Sixty-six Years. By John Thomas Smith, . . . London Richard Bentley, . . . 1845. 8°. 20 cm., pp. iv+306.

Reference: On pp. 81-82, under the date 1784, Smith tells how he first met Blake at Mrs. Mathew's house. In a footnote on p. 82 he predicts the avidity with which Blake's works will be sought after in the future, and describes Stothard's and Flaxman's opinions of Blake.

Note: Two later editions were issued in 1845 and 1861. In 1905 Methuen published a new edition, annotated by Mr. W. Whitten, and with 47 illustrations. The passages relating to Blake are reprinted in full by Symons, pp. 387-8.

260 THE DOCTOR, &c. . . . [By Robert Southey] . . . London: . . . 1837-1847. 7 vols. 8°. Vol. VI. pp. xxxviii+386. Vol. VII. pp. xli+630.

References:
1. Vol. VI, p. 108. The latter part of the heading to Chap. CLXXXI is as follows: "William Blake the Painter, and the Welsh Triads.—Curious extract from

" that very curious and rare book, the Descriptive Catalogue of his own pictures,—
" and a painful one from his Poetical Sketches."

After a paragraph (quoted by Gilchrist, i, 276) beginning: " That painter of
" great but insane genius, William Blake," is quoted the greater part of " The Ancient
Britons " from the *Descriptive Catalogue*. The concluding paragraph on p. 126 is as
follows: " My regard for thee, dear Reader, would not permit me to leave untran-
" scribed this very curious and original piece of composition. Probably thou hast never
" seen, and art never likely to see either the ' Descriptive Catalogue ' or the ' Poetical
" ' Sketches ' of this insane and erratic genius, I will therefore end the chapter with the
" *Mad Song* from the latter."

The " Mad Song " is printed on p. 127; it contains Blake's emendation in
stanza 1, line 7, " rustling birds of dawn " for " rustling beds of dawn." (See no. 26,
note.)

2. Vol. VII, p. 157. The heading to Chap. CCXIV ends: " Question concerning
" inferior apparitions—Blake the painter, and the Ghost of a Flea." The passage
(pp. 161-163) begins:

" O Dove, ' my guide, philosopher and friend! ' that thou hadst lived to see
" what I have seen, the portrait of the Ghost of a Flea, engraved by Varley, from the
" original by Blake! The engraver was present when the likeness was taken, and
" relates the circumstances thus in his Treatise on Zodiacal Physiognomy."

Then follows a quotation from Varley's *Treatise* (no. 248) beginning: " This
" spirit visited his imagination . . .", and ending, ". . . and should not be lost."
The passage concludes with a few lines in praise of the wisdom and benevolence of
the Almighty Creator in not creating such monsters as the Flea would be, if, as the
Ghost suggested, it were the size of a horse.

Note: Southey was probably one of the few visitors to Blake's exhibition in
1809. He also knew Blake personally, and, though he admired his genius, he seems
to have failed entirely to understand it, as is shown by the following passage from
Crabb Robinson's *Diary and Reminiscences*, vol. I, p. 338:

July 24, 1811—" Late at C. Lamb's. Found a large party there. Southey had
" been with Blake and admired both his designs and his poetic talents. At the same
" time he held him to be a decided madman. Blake, he said, spoke of his visions with
" the diffidence which is usual with such people, and did not seem to expect that he
" should be believed. He showed Southey a perfectly mad poem called ' Jerusalem.'
" Oxford Street is in Jerusalem."

261 SACRED AND LEGENDARY ART. By Mrs. Jameson. London: Longman, Brown, Green, and Longmans. 1848. 2 vols. 4°.

> *Reference* in vol. 1, pp. 50-51, to Blake's angels, with wood engravings after Blake on pp. 1 and 51.

> *Note*: Second and third editions published in 1850 and 1857.

262 DICTIONARY OF PAINTERS AND ENGRAVERS By Michael Bryan. Ed. George Stanley London: H. G. Bohn 1849 4°.

> *Article*: P. 81. "Blake, William" (short notice).

> *Note*: Amplified in later editions. See nos. 293A and 332A.

263 LIFE OF THOMAS STOTHARD, R.A. With Personal Reminiscences By Mrs. Bray, . . . London: John Murray, . . . 1851. 4°. 21.5 cm., pp. xxiv + 246.

> *Illustrations*: Frontispiece, and numerous reproductions of Stothard's designs in the text.

> *Reference*: A passage on pp. 20-21 relates how Blake with Stothard and Ogleby, while on an expedition up the Medway, were arrested as spies. It is reprinted in full in an appendix to the present work.

> *Note*: The description of this incident has not been noticed by any of Blake's biographers.* Stothard's drawing of the scene, which is now in the possession of Miss L. Sharpe, was also etched on copper, and concerning this Mrs. Bray has the following footnote (p. 21): " In the British Museum, amongst the folios containing " Stothard's works in the Print Room, an etching from this drawing may be seen, " called a Boating Excursion. The etching is there stated to be by Blake; but Alfred " Stothard says it was by his father. . . ." This etching, here reproduced from a print in the collection of Mr. W. E. Moss, is referred to in Rossetti's list (Gilchrist, ii, 282) as: " Stothard and Friends Prisoners during a Boating Excursion. Stothard " and Blake "; it possesses, however, no characteristics by which it can be identified as Blake's work, and in view of Mrs. Bray's statement, the attribution to him is probably wrong.

> * I owe this reference, through Mr. J. H. Wicksteed, to the notes of the late B. Kirkman Gray, who had himself contemplated writing a biography of Blake.

BLAKE, STOTHARD, AND OGLEBY MADE PRISONERS DURING A BOATING EXCURSION ON THE MEDWAY

Etching by Stothard, about 1780

264 MEMOIRS OF THE LIFE AND WRITINGS OF JAMES MONT-
GOMERY, . . . by John Holland and James Everett. Vol. I [-VII] London:
. . . 1854. 19.5 cm.

Reference: Vol. 1, p. 38: "When the *Grave* was long afterwards published,
"with Blake's splendid illustrations, he became the possessor of a copy; but, as
"several of the plates were hardly of such a nature as to render the book proper to
"lie on a parlour table for general inspection, he sold his copy for the subscription
"price; a circumstance which he often regretted, as the death of the artist soon after-
"wards rendered the work both scarce and proportionately more valuable. Those
"persons who have once seen these illustrations will readily recollect the print repre-
"senting the angel of the 'last trump' descending to awake the dead. . . . The
"solemn absurdity of this conception, and the ingenious manner in which it is
"executed, afforded Montgomery a very amusing topic of conversation on one
"occasion when we were present."

Note: James Montgomery, 1771-1854, poet, hymn-writer, and journalist, compiled in 1824 his *Chimney Sweeper's Friend, and Climbing-boy's Album*, to which Lamb
contributed Blake's "Chimney Sweeper" from the *Songs of Innocence*. In the same
work Montgomery paraphrased and extended, without acknowledgments, "A
Dream" from the same source. See pp. 128 and 354 of the present work.

265 A HANDBOOK FOR YOUNG PAINTERS. By C. R. Leslie, R.A. . . .
London: John Murray, . . . 1855. 19 cm., pp. xiv + 313 + [1].

Reference on p. 58 to Blake's objectiveness.

Note: Reprinted in the second edition, 1870, p. 57.

266 THE ELEMENTS OF DRAWING . . . By John Ruskin M.A. . . . London:
Smith, Elder, and Co. . . . 1857. 19 cm., pp. xxii + [ii] + 350 + [2].

Reference on p. 342 in: "Appendix. Things to be studied."

267 A CRITICAL DICTIONARY OF ENGLISH LITERATURE . . . By
S. Antin Allibone . . . Philadelphia . . . London . . . 1859. 26 cm.

Article: Vol. 1, p. 203. "Blake, Wm." A list of his works with a few critical
quotations from other authors, including Lamb.

268 NIGHTINGALE VALLEY. A Collection, including a great number of the Choicest Lyrics and Short Poems in the English Language. Edited by Giraldus [William Allingham] . . . London: Bell and Daldy, . . . 1860. 8°. 17 cm., pp. xvi + 288.

>   *Essay and Selection*: Note J, pp. 273-276, gives a short account of Blake's life. The poems include: *Songs of Innocence and of Experience* 4, 19, 34 (MS. version), 42.

>   *Note*: This book was reissued in [1871] with the title: *Choice Lyrics and Short Poems; or, Nightingale Valley. Edited by William Allingham.*

269 BRITISH ARTISTS FROM HOGARTH TO TURNER; being a Series of Biographical Sketches by Walter Thornbury, . . . In Two Volumes. . . . London: . . . 1861 . . . 8°. Vol. I. pp. viii + 343 + [1]. Vol. II. pp. iv + 318 + [6].

>   *Essay*: Vol. II, ch. ii, pp. 26-44. "The Prophet in Carnaby Market—Blake the Visionary."

270 LIFE OF WILLIAM BLAKE, "Pictor Ignotus." With Selections from his Poems and Other Writings by the late Alexander Gilchrist, of the Middle Temple, Barrister-at-Law; Author of "The Life of William Etty, R.A." Illustrated from Blake's own Works, in Facsimile by W. J. Linton, and in Photolithography; with a few of Blake's original plates. In Two Volumes. Vol. I. [II.] London and Cambridge: Macmillan and Co. 1863 . . .

>   *Collation*: 8°. 23 × 15 cm. Vol. I. pp. xiv Half-title, Title, Preface, Contents of Vol. I, Errata, List of illustrations + [ii] Sub-title + 389 + [1]. Vol. II. pp. viii Half-title, Title, Contents of Vol. II + 268.

>   *Illustrations*:
> Vol. I. Frontispiece: Engraving by Jeens after a portrait of Blake painted on ivory by J. Linnell.
>   Four full-page woodcuts by Linton: 1, 2. Facing p. 4. *Job*, pl. 8, 14.
>   3.   „   „ 54 Plague.
>   4.   „   „ 286 *Job*, pl. 5.
>   Six plates in monochrome: 1. Facing p. 112. *America*, pl. 5.
>   2, 3.   „   pp. 126, 129. *Europe*, pl. 7, 10.
>   4-6.   „   „ 182, 194. *Jerusalem*, pl. 78, 39, 76.
>   Folding plate, facing p. 230: Engraving by Simms after Blake's plate of the *Canterbury Pilgrims* (sometimes bound in as frontispiece to vol. II).

Fifty-six small woodcuts by Linton in the text:

Pp. [i], 112. From *America*. Pp. 1, 291. From *Job*.

Pp. 27, 50, 51, 75, 186-7-8, 193-4, 209, 216. From *Jerusalem*.

Pp. 60, 89, 137, 172, 182. From the *Rossetti MS*.

P. 91. An unpublished illustration to Wollstonecraft's *Original Stories*.

Pp. 98, 105, 241. From *Visions of the Daughters of Albion*.

Pp. 99, 100-1-2-3. Eight plates from the *Gates of Paradise*.

P. 154. Blake's cottage at Felpham. P. 198. From *Milton*.

Pp. 224, 362. From Blair's *Grave*. Pp. 249, 252-3-4. Five "Visionary Heads."

P. 255. The Ghost of a Flea. P. 256. The Three Accusers.

P. 318. Portrait of Mrs. Blake after a drawing by Tatham.

P. 334. From Illustrations to Dante, pl. 7.

P. 356. Mr. Cumberland's card-plate.

Pp. 11, 42, 118, 126, 160, 233, 248, 269, 304, 367. Unidentified.

Impressions, on p. 271, from Blake's wood blocks for Thornton's *Pastorals of Virgil*, nos. 5, 9, and 6.

Vol. II. Between pp. 266 and 267: Photo-lithographic reproductions (reduced) of the *Illustrations of the Book of Job* (22 plates).

Impressions from electrotypes of sixteen of Blake's original copper-plates for the *Songs of Innocence and of Experience*, comprising pl. 3, 5, 7, 15, 21, 17, 25, 29, 40, 35, 36, 46, 51, 54, 49, 50.

Seven small woodcuts by Linton in the text:

Pp. 1, 268. From *Visions of the Daughters of Albion*.

P. 2. From *Jerusalem*. P. 71. From *Thel*. Pp. 24, 97, 116. Unidentified.

Contents:

Vol. I. The Life of William Blake, including the following quotations:

U U

Ch. xxi. Extracts from *Jerusalem, Milton.*

„ xxii. Letter from Cromek to Blake, May, 1807. *Rossetti MS.*, 81, 82, 121.

„ xxiii. Blake's remarks on T. H. Malkin's drawings, from Malkin's *Father's Memoirs of his Child*, 1806. Letter 61.

„ xxiv. Dedication from Blair's *Grave*; extracts from Fuseli's remarks on the designs.

„ xxv. Prospectus of *The Canterbury Pilgrims*, May 15, 1809.

„ xxviii. Extract from Varley's *Zodiacal Physiognomy*, 1828.

„ xxix. Extracts from Blake's Annotations to Reynolds's *Discourses*, including epigrams 1, 2, 4-6. Blake's Annotations to Bacon's *Essays. Rossetti MS.*, 114, 117, 142, 65.

„ xxxi. Extract from the *London Magazine*, Sept. 1820.

„ xxxiii. Letter no. 67.

„ xxxiv. *Rossetti MS.*, 150, 90.

„ xxxvi. Letter no. 69. Extracts from Crabb Robinson's *Reminiscences.* Extracts from Blake's Annotations to Wordsworth's *Poems.* Letters nos. 71, 73-76, 78, 80, 82, 87.

„ xxxvii. Letter no. 88.

Vol. ii. Selections:

1. Poetical Sketches, 1, 2, 5, 8-13, 16, 19, 20.

2. Songs of Innocence and Songs of Experience; to the latter is added Rossetti MS., 24.

3. The Book of Thel.

4. Poems hitherto unpublished: Pickering MS., 1-6, 8, 10. Rossetti MS., 19, 21, 23, 25, 27-29, 30 (final version, with two deleted lines added), 32, 36, 52.i, 54, 58, 59 (stanza 2 omitted, the last two stanzas from Pickering MS., 7), 60, 64, 135, 145, 152 (extracts, with title " The Woman Taken in Adultery ").

Couplets and Fragments: Rossetti MS., 37, 42, 48, 50, 52.ii, 80, 97, 101, 107, 116, 125 (lines 5-6), 129, 143, 146.

Epigrams and Satirical Pieces on Art and Artists: Rossetti MS., 74, 79, 98, 110, 118, 125 (lines 3-4), 127, 136, 137.

5. Prose Writings: Descriptive Catalogue; Rossetti MS., 153, 159.iii; On Homer's Poetry; On Virgil; Rossetti MS., 154.

Appendix:

1. Letters nos. 13, 14, 17, 18, 20, 22, 24-26 (Butts collection).

2. Annotated Catalogue of Blake's Paintings and Drawings.

3. Account between Blake and Mr. Butts (see no. 25).

4. Annotated List of Blake's Engravings.
5. List of Blake's Writings.
6. Prospectus of 1793 (see no. 37).
Index.

Note: Until the appearance of Gilchrist's biography the general public had had no means of knowing more about Blake and his works than is contained in Cunningham's or Smith's short essays, but these volumes once and for all rescued Blake's name from obscurity. Alexander Gilchrist began to work at the life of Blake about 1856, but he died in 1861 and so did not live to see the book completed. The greater part, however, had been written, and, with the help of the Rossettis, Gilchrist's widow was able to see the book through the press in 1863. D. G. Rossetti wrote the Supplementary Chapter, which was based on Gilchrist's memoranda, and edited the Selections in vol. II; W. M. Rossetti compiled the Annotated Catalogue of Blake's works. Correspondence and information bearing on the production of the book is to be found in *Anne Gilchrist, her Life and Writings*, 1887 (no. 294), and in the *Rossetti Papers*, 1903 (no. 332); further references to Gilchrist and to Blake will be found in the *Letters of Dante Gabriel Rossetti to William Allingham*, 1897 (no. 326), and a series of letters from D. G. Rossetti to Anne Gilchrist concerning the biography were in the possession of Messrs. Maggs a few years ago, who printed extracts in their catalogue.

The biography contains much material which cannot be found elsewhere, so that its value must always remain very great, but it can never be relied upon for accuracy of detail. It has also been adversely criticized by so competent an authority as John Linnell, senr., who wrote, " several matters related therein are, in my opinion, great exaggerations " (Story's *Life of Linnell*, i, 160); he gave the Adam and Eve story (Gilchrist, i, 115) as an example of an evident absurdity. The value of the Selections in vol. II is also very much reduced by the liberties taken by D. G. Rossetti in his editing of Blake's texts; he corrected what he considered were imperfections in the metre, and supplied emendations, often quite unnecessary, so that his text is very untrustworthy. Later editors have frequently followed this text, and so corrupt versions have been perpetuated. Rossetti did not, however, adopt all the changes which he had made in his first transcript of the *Rossetti MS.*, and stated later that, if the work were still before him, he would not then have made so many alterations as were actually printed.* The Annotated Catalogue also contains many inaccuracies, but is useful as a preliminary list.

---

* *Letters of D. G. Rossetti to William Allingham*, 1897, p. 265. See no. 326.

271 A CENTURY OF ENGLISH PAINTERS of the English School; . . . By Richard Redgrave, R.A. . . . and Samuel Redgrave. . . . Vol. I. [II.] London: Smith Elder and Co., 65 Cornhill. 1866. 22 cm. Vol. I. pp. xvi + 543 + [1]. Vol. II. pp. xvi + 643 + [1].

Critical account : Pp. 440-448 " William Blake " (in chap. xv—Book Illustrators and Designers).

272 ENGLISH ECCENTRICS AND ECCENTRICITIES. By John Timbs, . . . In Two Volumes . . . London: Richard Bentley, . . . 1866. 8°. Vol. I. pp. viii + 319 + [1]. Vol. II. pp. vii + [i] + 320.

Essay : Vol. ii, pp. 60-72. " Eccentric Artists. William Blake Painter and Poet."

Note : An illustrated edition, published by Chatto and Windus, 1875, has the account of Blake at pp. 339-350.

273 WILLIAM BLAKE. A CRITICAL ESSAY. By Algernon Charles Swinburne. [*vignette, with legend* : Zamiel. From the Book of Job] With illustrations from Blake's designs in facsimile, coloured and plain. London: John Camden Hotten, Piccadilly. 1868. [All rights reserved.]

Collation : 8°. 22 cm., pp. iv Title, Dedication to D. G. Rossetti + [iv] Contents, List of Illustrations, List of Authorities + 304.

Illustrations : 9 plates made in facsimile of Blake's designs, and printed on paper specially made to resemble that used by him. Nos. 1-4, 6, and 7 are coloured by hand:

    1. Frontispiece. *Jerusalem*, pl. 70 (reduced).
    2. Extra title, facing no. 1. *William Blake, A Critical Essay*, with a border of designs taken from *Jerusalem*, and with minor details from *The Marriage of Heaven and Hell*, and *Thel*.
    3. Facing p. 200. *Thel*, pl. [ii].
    4-6. Facing pp. 204, 208, and 224. *The Marriage of Heaven and Hell*, pl. 1, 8, and 20.*
    7. Facing p. 258. *Milton*, pl. 8.
    8-9. Facing pp. 276 and 282. *Jerusalem*, pl. 81 and 33 (reduced).

   * These plates were used again in Hotten's edition of *The Marriage of Heaven and Hell*, 1868. See no. 210.

Contents: The essay is divided into: 1. Life and Designs. 2. Lyrical Poems. 3. The Prophetic Books. The first two parts contain numerous quotations from Blake's poems, mostly fragmentary, but some in full, including the following:

Rossetti MS., 14, 20, 22, 40, 49, 87, 88, 95, 149, 150, 152.

The Gates of Paradise: Epilogue.

Fragment: " A fairy leapt upon my knee " (p. 143).

The third part contains numerous quotations from the Prophetic Books. On pp. 62-63. Blake's letter " To the Editor of the *Monthly Magazine*" (see letter no. 59, p. 67) is reprinted for the first time.

Note: Many of Swinburne's quotations from the *Rossetti MS.* are from poems which were not included in D. G. Rossetti's selection in Gilchrist, and these are therefore printed here for the first time. Swinburne's text is now the only authority for the fragment " A fairy leapt upon my knee " (see no. 4).

This work was begun by Swinburne in 1864, and was finished in 1866, but owing to the large number of additions and alterations made by him, it was not published until Aug. 1868. The delay in publication was also due in part to the fact that the work was originally printed for Moxon, the sheets being transferred, when almost complete, to Camden Hotten.* Swinburne made several successive alterations in the title-page, and two proofs, one believed to be unique, are in the possession of Mr. T. J. Wise. The first of these has no vignette, and is without the words " coloured and plain." The second has the vignette, but the legend below it runs: *Ithuriel. From the Book of Job*; probably not more than six copies of this were printed. In the title-page as actually issued *Ithuriel* was altered to *Zamiel*, and later the legend *Going to and fro in the Earth* was substituted for it. Copies of the book containing the last alteration, which is the form most frequently met with, may therefore be regarded as the second issue of the first edition. It is stated by Mr. Wise that 1,500 copies of the book were printed, and that 500 of these were bound up later with a reprint title-page marked *Second Edition* (see next entry). Further details concerning the book will be found in *A Bibliography of A. C. Swinburne. By T. J. Wise, London*, 1919, pp. 180-190, which is the authority for some of the facts given above. It was while engaged upon the *Critical Essay* in 1864 that Swinburne first met Seymour Kirkup, whose reminiscences of Blake " modified Swinburne's views on some points."† A few of the letters which passed between Swinburne and Kirkup, containing some interesting references to Blake, have been recently printed by Mr. Edmund Gosse. ‡

A new edition of the *Critical Essay*, with a preface added, was published in 1906 (no. 342).

* See Gosse's *Life of Swinburne*, 1917, p. 154. † *Ibid.*, p. 180.

‡ In *The London Mercury*, Dec. 1920; see no. 665. For letters from Kirkup to Monckton Milnes and Rossetti see nos. 300 and 332.

274 WILLIAM BLAKE. A CRITICAL ESSAY. By Algernon Charles Swinburne. [*vignette, with legend*: Going to and fro in the Earth] With illustrations from Blake's designs in facsimile, coloured and plain. Second Edition. London: John Camden Hotten, Piccadilly. 1868. [All rights reserved.]

Collation, illustrations, contents: As in no. 273.

Note: A reissue of the original edition with a cancel title-page. It is therefore really the third issue of the first edition. See note to preceding entry.

275 DIARY, REMINISCENCES, AND CORRESPONDENCE OF HENRY CRABB ROBINSON, . . . Selected and Edited by Thomas Sadler, Ph.D. In Three Volumes. . . . London: Macmillan and Co. 1869. . . . 8°. 22 cm. Vol. I. pp. xxiii + [i] + ii[errata slip] + 509 + [1]. Vol. II. pp. iv + 529 + [1]. Vol. III. pp. v + [i] + 598.

Frontispiece: In vol. 1. Portrait of Crabb Robinson.

References:

Vol. I. P. 299. Crabb Robinson's account of his paper on Blake (see no. 401).

P. 338. An account of Southey's visit to Blake (see no. 260).

P. 385. Wordsworth's opinion of Blake's poetry (see no. 21).

P. 472. A conversation with Flaxman about Blake.

Vol. II. Pp. 301-310. Several meetings with, and calls on, Blake. Crabb Robinson's impressions of him. Blake's opinions on religion, on the evil of education, on good and evil, on art, on fame, on Swedenborg, on Wordsworth, on Jacob Boehme, on suffering, on Dante, on Atheism, on the Mannichean doctrine, on the Fall of Man. Aphorisms by Blake. A description of Blake's manners, and of his house in Fountain Court.

P. 314. A call on Blake.

Pp. 316-318. A call on Blake. His opinions on Wordsworth's paganism, on reason and inspiration, on Voltaire's mission. Blake's account of his own writings. His horror of money.

Pp. 322-325 (in a letter to Miss Wordsworth). A description of Blake. His religious opinions. His estimate of Wordsworth. Milton, Dante, and Wordsworth atheists. Blake's poverty and refinement.

P. 330. A call on Blake. "As wild as ever with no great novelty."

Pp. 370-371. A call on Blake. How he received the news of Flaxman's death. More religious opinions.

Pp. 379-383. The last visit to Blake, accompanied by Gotzenberger. Various reminiscences of Blake. His engraving of the *Canterbury Pilgrims*, and

Lamb's opinion of the description in the *Descriptive Catalogue*. Blake's remarks on himself. Hazlitt's opinion of Blake. Blake's notes on Wordsworth. A call on Mrs. Blake and a description of her.

Vol. III. P. 318. J. J. Garth Wilkinson's love of Blake.

Note: These extracts constitute one of the most valuable sources of information about Blake that we possess, since they give by the hand of an unprejudiced observer so many of Blake's opinions and actual words. Crabb Robinson had visited Blake's exhibition in 1809, but it was not until 1825 that he met him at the house of Mr. Aders. The bulk of the reminiscences were printed by Gilchrist (i, 381-393), who had access to Crabb Robinson's MS. before any of it had been published. Most of the extracts relating to Blake have been transcribed, though not very accurately, from the MS., and reprinted by Symons. Later editions of the *Diary* were as follows: Second edition, 3 vols., 1869; third edition, 2 vols., 1872; fourth edition, 2 vols., 1874. Also published by Houghton, Mifflin & Co., Boston, Mass., 1898.

276 A PHYSICIAN'S PROBLEMS. By Charles Elam, M.D., M.R.C.P. London: Macmillan and Co., 1869. 19 cm., pp. viii + 424.

References on pp. 299, 366, to Blake's visions, and to his supposed residence in Bethlem Hospital, derived from Brierre de Boismont (see no. 411), and from Wigan's *Duality of the Mind*, 1844 (no. 258).

277 WALTER SAVAGE LANDOR. A Biography. By John Forster. London: Chapman and Hall. . . . 1869. 8°. Vol. I. pp. vi + [ii] + 532. Vol. II. pp. vi + 596.

Reference: Vol. II, pp. 322-3. (1836) " At an old bookseller's in Bristol he " picked up some of the writings of Blake, and was strangely fascinated by them. He " was anxious to have collected as many more as he could and enlisted me in the " service; but he as much wanted patience for it as I wanted time, and between us it " came to nothing. He protested that Blake had been Wordsworth's prototype, and " wished they could have divided his madness between them; for that some accession " of it in the one case, and something of a diminution of it in the other would very " greatly have improved both."

Note: Elsewhere, in a MS. notebook,* Landor recorded his opinion of Blake as follows: " Blake: Never did a braver or a better man carry the sword of justice."

* From the Browning and Fairfax Murray Libraries; sold at Sotheby's, July 7, 1919 (Maggs, £5 10*s*.).

278 CHILDREN IN ITALIAN AND ENGLISH DESIGN. By Sidney Colvin, M.A. . . . With illustrations after Luca della Robbia, Marc Antonio, Correggio, Blake, Stothard, and Flaxman. Seeley, Jackson, and Halliday, Fleet Street, London. MDCCCLXXII. 4°. 24.5 cm., pp. [iv] + 60.

> *Essay*: Pp. 21-29. "Blake."

> *Illustrations*: 12 photographic reproductions of drawings, etc., two of them after designs by Blake in *The Book of Urizen* and *America*, and numerous reproductions of sketches in the text.

> *Note*: The essay on Blake was first printed in *The Portfolio*, 1871 (no. 449).

279 HOMES, WORKS, AND SHRINES OF ENGLISH ARTISTS By Frederick William Fairholt F.S.A. London Virtue & Co. 1873 4°. 22.5 cm., pp. x + 182 + [2].

> *Essay*: Pp. 94-100. "William Blake." With wood-engravings of "Blake's House, Fountain Court," "Spirit of a Flea," and "Scene from Dante."

> *Note*: First printed as an article in *The Art Journal*, 1858 (no. 418).

280 WILLIAM BLAKE AND HIS EDITORS [B. M. Pickering] 196, Piccadilly, Sept. 18, 1874. 17 × 10.5 cm., pp. 4.

> *Note*: This leaflet was printed by B. M. Pickering in answer to a notice of his edition of the *Poems*, 1874 (no. 141), which was written by W. M. Rossetti for *The Academy*, Sept. 5, 1874. Pickering probably intended it for insertion in the later copies of his edition. He explains why he withheld from W. M. Rossetti permission to reprint the poems from the *Pickering MS*. in their correct form, and protests against the liberties taken by the Rossettis with Blake's poems in the text which they edited for Gilchrist, vol. ii.

281 STUDIES IN LITERATURE 1789-1877. By Edward Dowden, LL.D. . . . London: C. Kegan Paul & Co. . . . 1878 20 cm., pp. xii + 523 + [1].

> *Reference*: Pp. 15-17. William Blake and the Revolution.

282 CATALOGUE OF A COLLECTION of Engravings, Etchings, and Woodcuts. [By Richard Fisher. Privately printed] 1879 Imp. 8°. Pp. x + 352 + [2].

> *Article*: P. 341. "William Blake" (a short account of).

283 ESSAYS ON ART By J. Comyns Carr London Smith, Elder, & Co. ... 1879 . . . 19.5 cm., pp. [viii] + 253 + [3].

>*Essay*: Pp. 35-76. "William Blake, Poet and Painter."

>*Note*: First published in *Belgravia*, May, 1876 (see no. 459).

284 THE ENGLISH POETS Selections with critical introductions by Various Writers and a general introduction by Matthew Arnold Ed. T. H. Ward, M.A. Vol. III Addison to Blake London Macmillan & Co. 1880 8°. Pp. [iv] + xii + 608.

>*Essay*: Pp. 596-608. "William Blake." Selection, with introduction by J. Comyns Carr.

285 LIFE OF WILLIAM BLAKE with Selections from his Poems and other Writings by Alexander Gilchrist . . . A New and Enlarged Edition Illustrated from Blake's own Works with Additional Letters and a Memoir of the Author In Two Volumes Vol. I. [II.] London Macmillan and Co. 1880 The Right of Translation is Reserved

Collation: 8°. 23 × 15 cm. Vol. I. pp. xxi Half-title, Title, Preface to Second Edition, Preface to First Edition, Contents of Vol. I, List of Illustrations + [iii] + 431 + [1]. Vol. II. pp. ix Half-title, Title, Contents of Vol. II + [v] + 383 + [1].

Illustrations: The majority are from the same blocks as were used in the first edition, 1863 (no. 270), though some of these are omitted and several new ones added. Most of the larger blocks are printed on india paper and mounted.

Vol. I. Frontispiece: As in 1st edition.
Ten full-page woodcuts:
>1. Facing p. 54. Plague (by Linton).
>2-4. „ pp. 98, 100, 102. Eight plates from *The Gates of Paradise* (by Linton).
>5. Facing p. 128. Elijah in the Chariot of Fire.
>6. „ p. 134. Young burying Narcissa (by Hellawell).
>7, 8. „ pp. 269, 270. Pl. 13, 5 from Blair's *Grave*.
>9. „ p. 272. Design for Hamlet (by Cooper).
>10. „ p. 300. Four "Visionary Heads."

Nine plates in monochrome:
>1, 2. Facing pp. 108, 110. *America*, pl. 11, 5.
>3, 4. „ „ 124, 126. *Europe*, pl. 7, 10.
>5-9. „ „ 227, 230, 236, 238, 240. *Jerusalem*, pl. 78, 51, 32, 39, 76.

x x

Four reproductions of drawings:

1. Facing p. 150. Blake's cottage at Felpham, after a drawing by H. H. Gilchrist.
2. Facing p. 348. Blake's work-room, after a drawing by H. H. Gilchrist.
3. On p. 361. Catherine Blake, from a drawing by F. J. Shields after Blake.
4. Facing p. 374. Catherine and William Blake from a drawing by F. J. Shields after pencil outlines in the *Rossetti MS.*

Thirty-two small woodcuts in the text, mostly by Linton:

P. [i]. From *America.* P. 1, 336. From *Job.*

Pp. 27, 50, 51, 115, 232, 233, 234, 239, 240, 264. From *Jerusalem.*

P. 28. Glad Day. P. 68. *Songs of Innocence,* pl. 2 (by Jungling).

P. 90. An unpublished illustration to Wollstonecraft's *Original Stories.*

Pp. 88, 141, 225. From the *Rossetti MS.*

Pp. 97, 103, 155. From *Visions of the Daughters of Albion.*

P. 245. From *Milton.* P. 298. Visionary Heads. P. 303. The Ghost of a Flea. P. 304. The Accusers. P. 322. Plan of Blake's room in Fountain Court, from a drawing by F. J. Shields. P. 377. From Illustrations to Dante, pl. 7. P. 399. Mr. Cumberland's card-plate. P. 406. From Blair's *Grave.* P. 412. Mrs. Blake, after a drawing by Tatham. P. 431. Unidentified.

Impressions, facing p. 320, from Blake's wood blocks as in 1st edition.

Vol. II. Frontispiece: Portrait of Blake after the engraving by Schiavonetti.

Folding plate, facing p. 144: The *Canterbury Pilgrims* as in vol. 1 of 1st edition.

Between pp. 204-205: Reproductions of the *Illustrations of the Book of Job* and 16 plates from the *Songs of Innocence and of Experience,* as in 1st edition (the latter sometimes bound in between pp. 76-77).

Five small woodcuts by Linton in the text:

Pp. [i], 376. From *Visions of the Daughters of Albion.* P. [ii]. From *Jerusalem.* P. 77. From *Thel.* P. 25. Unidentified.

Contents:

Vol. I. The Life of William Blake. Various minor corrections have been made in this edition, and letters nos. 7, 13-15, 17, 18, 20-22, 24-26, 29, 31-34, 38-42, 47, 48, 50, 53, 54, 56, 59, 61 have been incorporated in the text, chap. XVI-XXIII. Of these, letters nos. 13, 14, 17, 18, 20, 22, 24-26 were printed in an appendix to vol. II of 1st edition ; the rest are new.

Vol. II. Selections, revised by the editor:

1-3. As in 1st edition.
4. General title altered to " Ideas of Good and Evil ": As in 1st edition with the

addition of *Rossetti MS.*, 34, 35 (printed together, with title "Love and Deceit").

5. As in 1st edition, with the addition of *The Ghost of Abel*.

Note on Blake's Engraved Designs by D. G. Rossetti (not in 1st edition).

[Appendix]: 1-5 the same as 2-6 in 1st edition ; the Butts letters are omitted, having been incorporated in vol. 1; various additions are made to the Annotated Catalogue. The following are also added:

6. Descriptive notes of the Designs to Young's *Night Thoughts* by F. J. Shields.

7. Essay on Blake by James Smetham (reprinted from the *London Quarterly Review*, Jan. 1869. See no. 445).

8. In Memoriam F. O. Finch by Samuel Palmer (printed as a footnote in 1st edition, i, 298-300; reprinted in *Memorials of Francis Oliver Finch*, London, 1865).

9. Memoir of Alexander Gilchrist by Anne Gilchrist.
Index.

Note : The additions and corrections made in this edition have been noted above. The book is printed on handmade paper, and the illustrations have been improved. In the present work this has been adopted as the standard edition, and all references to Gilchrist must be looked for among its pages.

---

286 BALLADS AND SONNETS By Dante Gabriel Rossetti. London: Ellis and White. 1881. 8°. Pp. xii + 335 + [1].

> *Sonnet* : P. 314. "Five English Poets II. William Blake (To Frederic Shields, "on his sketch of Blake's work-room and death-room, 3 Fountain Court, Strand.)" "This is the place. Even here the dauntless soul . . ."

Note : Rossetti's first version of the Sonnet, together with an account of how it came to be written, will be found in an article, "Some Notes on Dante Gabriel Rossetti," by Frederic Shields in *The Century Guild Hobby Horse*, vol. 1, 1886, pp. 144-5.

287 THE LIBRARY by Andrew Lang with a chapter on Modern English Illustrated Books by Austin Dobson London Macmillan & Co. 1881 . . . 18 cm., pp. xvi + 184 + [8].

References : Pp. 125-133, in "Illustrated Books" (illustrated).

288 ESSAYS FROM "THE CRITIC" by John Burroughs Edmund C. Stedman Walt Whitman R. H. Stoddard F. B. Sanborn E. W. Gosse and Others Boston . . . 1882 8°. Pp. 185+[1].

> *Essay*: Pp. 21-28. "William Blake, Poet and Painter," by E. C. Stedman.

> *Note*: Reprinted in Stedman's *Genius and Other Essays*, New York, 1911.

289 THE LITERARY HISTORY OF ENGLAND in the end of the Eighteenth and the beginning of the Nineteenth Century By Mrs Oliphant In Three Volumes Vol. II London Macmillan & Co 1882 8°. Pp. [vi]+392.

> *Critical account* of Blake, pp. 285-294.

290 LANDMARKS OF ENGLISH LITERATURE. By Henry J. Nicoll . . . London: John Hogg, . . . 1883. 8°. 18 cm., pp. xiv+460.

> *Reference*: P. 281, a short notice of Blake.

291 SHELLEY, A POEM: with other Writings relating to Shelley, by the late James Thomson('B.V.'): to which is added an Essay on The Poems of William Blake, by the same Author. Printed for Private Circulation, . . . at the Chiswick Press. 1884. 8°. 22.5 cm., pp. xii+128.

> *Essay*: Pp. 101-128. "The Poems of William Blake." The article concludes with a poem of four stanzas on Blake.

> *Note*: First published in the *National Reformer*, 1866 (no. 438). Later reprinted in *Biographical and Critical Studies By James Thomson*, London, Dobell, 1896, pp. 240-269. The poem on Blake is reprinted in Thomson's *Poetical Works*, 2 vols., London, 1895, i, 305. Of *Shelley, a Poem*, 190 copies were printed, of which 30 are on handmade paper.

292 MINUTES OF THE FIRST SEVEN SESSIONS of the General Conference of the New Church, signified by the New Jerusalem in the Revelation . . . Reprinted from the original editions. London: James Spiers, . . . 1885. 8°. Pp. xl+296.

> *Reference*: P. xx. The names W. Blake and C. Blake are among those subscribed to a declaration stating belief in the divine origin of the writings of Swedenborg, and approving the establishment of the New Church, dated April 13, 1789.

Note: Attention was first drawn to this by Mr. Charles Higham in *Notes and Queries*, 1915 (see no. 639), who pointed out that the names are probably those of William Blake and his wife. The original minute book has unfortunately been lost, so that the signatures cannot now be verified.

293 DICTIONARY OF NATIONAL BIOGRAPHY 1886

Article: Vol. v, pp. 180-184. "Blake, William." By A[nne] G[ilchrist].

Note: Reprinted, with two or three lines added, in the new edition, 1908, vol. ii, pp. 642-646.

Reference: Vol. xvii, p. 376. Ensom, William (1796-1832), engraver, was awarded in 1815 the silver medal of the Royal Society of Arts for a pen-and-ink portrait of William Blake.

Note: This reference was brought to my notice by Mr. W. E. Moss; enquiries addressed by him to the Secretary of the Royal Society of Arts in Dec. 1919 only elicited the information that no further details are given in the Society's records, and that the drawing cannot now be traced.

293A DICTIONARY OF PAINTERS AND ENGRAVERS By Michael Bryan Ed. R. E. Graves London George Bell and Sons 1886 4°.

Article: Vol. i, pp. 132-134. "Blake, William." By M. M. H[eaton].

Note: Re-written in a later edition. See no. 332A.

294 ANNE GILCHRIST Her Life and Writings Edited by Herbert Harlakenden Gilchrist With a Prefatory Notice by William Michael Rossetti. London: T. Fisher Unwin 1887 8°. 22.5 cm., pp. xxi + [i] + 368.

Illustrations: 12 plates and one illustration in the text, including the following:
On p. 131. William Blake, sketched from memory by Frederick Tatham for Alexander Gilchrist one evening at 6, Great Cheyne-row, in 1860.
Facing p. 154. William Hayley. From a sketch by Romney.
„   284. Angel of Hope. Designed in water-colours by Blake.

References: Anne Gilchrist was the wife of the author of the *Life of Blake*, and this memoir contains frequent references to Blake and to the *Life*; see especially:
Pp. 129-131. Tatham's and Linnell's relations with Mrs. and Miss Blake.
Pp. 258-262. George Richmond's memories of Blake and of his home.

295 APPRECIATIONS with an Essay on Style   By Walter Pater . . . London   Macmillan and Co. . . . 1889 8°. 20 cm., pp. [viii] + 264 + [2].

   Reference: Pp. 98-99. Blake and Coleridge.

296 PRINCIPLE IN ART etc. By Coventry Patmore London George Bell and Sons, . . . 1889 8°. Pp. viii + 219 + [1].

   Essay: Pp. 97-102. " Blake."

297 THROUGH THE IVORY GATE: Studies in Psychology and History. By William W. Ireland, M.D. Edin.; . . . Edinburgh: Bell & Bradfute, . . . London: Simpkin, Marshall & Co., . . . MDCCCLXXXIX. 22.5 cm., pp. viii + 311 + [1].

   Essay: Pp. 130-134. " William Blake."

298 THE TREASURY OF SACRED SONG . . . By Francis T. Palgrave . . . Oxford At the Clarendon Press MDCCCLXXXIX 8°. Pp. x + 374.

   Selection and note: Pp. 186-188. Four poems by Blake.
   Pp. 353-354. A note on Blake.

299 SIX PORTRAITS Della Robbia, Corregio, Blake, Corot, George Fuller, Winslow Homer by Mr. Schuyler van Rensselaer . . . Boston and New York . . . 1899 8°. Pp. [viii] + 277 + [1].

   Essay: Pp. 113-138. " Blake."

300 THE LIFE OF RICHARD MONCKTON MILNES, first Lord Houghton. By T. Wemyss Reid. In two volumes. Cassell & Company, Limited; London . . . 1890. 8°. Vol. I. pp. xvi + 527 + [1]. Vol. II. pp. vii + [1] + 544.

   Reference: Pp. 222-223. Letter from Seymour Kirkup to Lord Houghton, dated Florence, March 25, 1870, describing his friendship with Blake and Blake's picture of " The Ancient Britons."   " It made so great an impression on me that I

WILLIAM BLAKE
Pencil Drawing by John Linnell, 1820

" made a drawing of it fifty years afterwards, which I gave to Swinburne. You can
" see it."

Note: For another letter from Kirkup to W. M. Rossetti on the same subject
see no. 332. Enquiries, kindly made on my behalf by Mr. Edmund Gosse (May,
1919), have failed to recover any trace of Kirkup's drawing among Swinburne's papers.

301 THE PAINTER POETS. Selected and edited, with an introduction and notes,
by Kineton Parkes. London. Walter Scott . . . [1890] [The Canterbury Poets]
16°. 14.5 cm., pp. xxx + [ii] + 255 + [11].

Critical note on Blake, p. 244, with selection from poems, pp. 13-21.

302 THE MAN OF GENIUS. By Cesare Lombroso, . . . with illustrations. London:
Walter Scott, . . . 1891. 18 cm., pp. xvi + 370.

References: Pp. 6, 56.

303 THE POETS AND THE POETRY OF THE CENTURY George Crabbe
to Samuel Taylor Coleridge Edited by Alfred H. Miles Hutchinson & Co . . .
London [1891] 8°. Pp. [ii] + xvi + [ii] + 556.

Essay and selection: Pp. 85-94, a short account of Blake's life; pp. 95-122,
Poetical Sketches, Songs of Innocence and of Experience, and seven later poems.

Note: Second edition, 1898; new issue [1899]; third edition, 1905.

304 AUTOBIOGRAPHICAL NOTES of the Life of William Bell Scott . . . Edited
by W. Minto . . . Vol. I[II] London James R. Osgood, McIlvaine & Co. . . .
MDCCCXCII. 22.5 cm. Vol. I. pp. x + [ii] + 356. Vol. II. pp. viii + [ii] + 346 + [2].

References: Vol. 1, pp. 21-24, with a sonnet on Blake by W. B. Scott.

Note: See nos. 214 and 319 for Scott's *Etchings from Blake's Works*, 1878, and
his steel engraving after Phillips's portrait of Blake.

305 CHAMBERS'S CYCLOPÆDIA of English Literature . . . originally edited by Robert Chambers, LL.D. Fourth Edition. Revised by Robert Carruthers, LL.D. In two volumes . . . W. & R. Chambers, Limited London and Edinburgh 1892 Roy 8°

Article: Vol. ii, pp. 57-58. "William Blake." With quotations from *Poetical Sketches* and *Songs of Innocence and of Experience*.

306 THE LIFE OF JOHN LINNELL by Alfred T. Story . . . In Two Volumes . . . London Richard Bentley and Son . . . 1892 . . . 8°. 22.5 cm. Vol. I. pp. xi + [i] + 308. Vol. II. pp. xi + [i] + 284.

Illustrations: Vol. i. Frontispiece and 16 illustrations in the text. Vol. ii. Frontispiece and 5 illustrations in the text. Those in vol. i include the following sketches by Linnell:

    1. P. 162. William Blake and John Varley arguing.
    2. P. 230. Half-length portrait of Blake.
    3. P. 243. Head of Blake.

References:

Vol. i. Pp. 147-151. Blake's visits to Hampstead. His designs for Thornton's *Virgil*.

    Pp. 158-173. Beginning of Linnell's friendship with Blake. Linnell's opinions of Gilchrist's statements about Blake. Blake and Varley. Illustrations of the *Book of Job*. *Vala*. First letter from Blake. Memoranda about Blake.

    Pp. 175-179, 192. Correspondence with Bernard Barton about Blake.

    P. 194. Barton's sonnet on Blake and Linnell (see no. 337).

    Pp. 224-247. Blake and Mrs. Aders. Blake's method of engraving. Blake and the theatre. Blake's last days. Illustrations of *Dante*. Letters from Blake. His visits to Hampstead. His death. Frederick Tatham. Mrs. Blake. Sale of Blake's works. Cunningham's *Life*. Linnell's opinion of Blake's beliefs, recorded in 1855.

Vol. ii. Pp. 48-52. Blake's influence on Linnell.
    Pp. 125-127. The origin of Blake's dragons.

Note: John Linnell was Blake's intimate friend and benefactor from 1818 until the latter's death in 1827, and these references have very great biographical value. His collection of Blake's works remained in the possession of the family until March, 1918 (see no. 683); it included the originals of the above sketches of Blake, which

WILLIAM BLAKE AT HAMPSTEAD
Pencil Drawing by John Linnell, 1821

now belong to Mr. T. H. Riches. References to Linnell will be found in the present work *passim*.

307 THE LIFE AND LETTERS OF SAMUEL PALMER ... Written and Edited by A. H. Palmer ... London Published by Seeley & Co., ... 1892 4°. Pp. xv +[i]+422.

> *Illustrations*: Frontispiece and 18 plates.

> *References*: The early part of the memoir contains many references to Blake ; see especially:
> > Pp. 8-10. Palmer's first impressions of Blake (in 1824).
> > Pp. 15-16. His early opinions of Blake.
> > Pp. 21-28. Blake's influence on his followers, and the question of his sanity.
> > P. 171. Blake's character.
> See also pp. 240-246 for two letters written by Palmer to Mrs. Gilchrist in 1862. The first is concerning *The Marriage of Heaven and Hell*; the second contains some reminiscences of Blake.

> *Note*: Samuel Palmer, 1805-1881, landscape painter, was one of a small band of artists, including Edward Calvert (see no. 310), Oliver Finch, George Richmond, and Henry Walter, who were intimately associated with Blake during the last years of his life. His reminiscences of Blake, written in 1855, were printed by Gilchrist, i, 344-347. After Blake's death several of his books seem to have passed into Palmer's possession, including the annotated copies of Lavater's *Aphorisms* (no. 13), Watson's *Apology for the Bible* (no. 16), and Berkeley's *Siris* (no. 19).

308 JOSEPH MILSAND Litterature Anglaise et Philosophie Dijon Lamarche, Editeur Place Saint-Etienne 1893 24.5 cm., pp. 502+[2].

> *Essay*: Pp. 305-346. " W. Blake."

> *Note*: First printed in *Le Revue Moderne*, 1863 (see no. 422).

309 THE LITERARY WORKS OF JAMES SMETHAM Edited by William Davies London ... 1893 ... 8°. Pp. viii+288+[2].

> *Essay*: Pp. 98-194. " William Blake."

> *Note*: First published as a review of Gilchrist, 1st edition, in the *London Quarterly Review*, 1869 (no. 445); part was reprinted in Gilchrist, 2nd edition, some account of Smetham being given by D. G. Rossetti, i, 428-429.

310 A MEMOIR OF EDWARD CALVERT Artist by his Third Son . . . London Sampson Low, Marston and Company . . . 1893 37 × 27 cm., pp. xix + [i] + 236.

Illustrations : Frontispiece, 30 plates, and 43 illustrations in the text. The latter include (p. 30) a reproduction of one of Blake's woodcuts for Thornton's *Virgil*.

References : Pp. 17-58, including several anecdotes and reminiscences of Blake. See also p. 155 for Blake's three Principles of painting.

Note : Edward Calvert, 1799-1883, was, like Samuel Palmer, an admirer of Blake during the last years of his life, and was greatly influenced by him in his art. He is referred to by Gilchrist, i, 343, who did not, however, utilize such reminiscences of Blake as he might have supplied. The anecdotes recorded in this memoir have not been reprinted.

311 UNDER THE EVENING LAMP By Richard Henry Stoddard London Gay and Bird 1893 8°. Pp. viii + 284.

Essay : Pp. 164-181. " William Blake."

312 WILLIAM BLAKE His Life Character and Genius By Alfred T. Story . . . London Swan Sonnenschein & Co. New York : Macmillan & Co. 1893 8°. 16.5 cm., pp. [viii] + 160.

Illustrations : Photogravure frontispiece after Linnell's miniature of Blake. Large paper copies with four additional illustrations in photogravure.

Note : The large paper edition on handmade paper consisted of 280 copies.

313 ENGLISH POETRY from Blake to Browning By William MacNeile Dixon Methuen & Co. . . . London 1894 8°. Pp. viii + 204.

References to Blake, pp. 26-44.

314 A HISTORY OF ENGLISH LITERATURE for Secondary Schools By J. Logie Robertson, M.A. . . . William Blackwood and Sons Edinburgh and London MDCCCXCIV 18.5 cm., pp. vi + [ii] + 372.

Biographical account : Pp. 190-191.

315 JAMES HOLMES AND JOHN VARLEY By Alfred T. Story . . . London
Richard Bentley and Son . . . 1894 8°. Pp. x + 303 + [1].

References: Pp. 259-268. Chap. VI. "Blake and Linnell."

Note: Very little is added to what had already been recorded in the author's
Life of Linnell, 1892 (no. 306).

315A LETTERS OF EDWARD FITZGERALD In Two Volumes . . . London . . .
1894 8°. Vol. I. pp. xiv + 348 + [4]. Vol. II. pp. [iv] + 368.

Reference: Vol. 1, pp. 25-26, in a letter to W. B. Donne, dated Oct. 25, 1833,
Fitzgerald writes: ". . . I have lately bought a little pamphlet which is very difficult
"to be got, called The Songs of Innocence, written and adorned with drawings by
"W. Blake (if you know his name) who was quite mad, but of a madness that was
"really the elements of great genius ill-sorted: in fact, a genius with a screw loose,
"as we used to say. I shall shew you this book when I see you: to me there is
"particular interest in this man's writing and drawing, from the strangeness of the
"constitution of his mind. He was a man that used to see visions and make draw-
"ings and paintings of Alexander the Great, Cæsar, etc., who, he declared, stood
"before him while he drew . . ."

Note: From 1821 to 1826 Fitzgerald was at King Edward VIth's School, Bury
St. Edmunds, under Dr. Malkin, author of *A Father's Memoirs of his Child*, 1806
(no. 80), and may first have heard of Blake during this period. Later, no doubt,
others, such as Southey and Crabb Robinson, who had themselves known Blake,
introduced him to Fitzgerald's notice, but there are no further references to him in
the *Letters*. I have not been able to identify Fitzgerald's copy of the *Songs of
Innocence*; his autographed copy of *A Father's Memoirs of his Child* was sold with the
library of William Cowan at Sotheby's, Dec. 4, 1912 (lot 852, Dobell, £4).

316 LETTERS OF SAMUEL TAYLOR COLERIDGE Edited by Ernest Hartley
Coleridge In Two Volumes . . . London . . . 1895 8°. Vol. I. pp. xix +
[iii] + 444. Vol. II. pp. vii + [iii] + 445-813 + [1].

Illustrations: Vol. I. Frontispiece and 8 plates. Vol. II. Frontispiece and
6 plates.

Reference: On pp. 685-688 is a letter dated "Highgate, Thursday evening, 1818,"
and addressed to Charles Augustus Tulk, an eminent Swedenborgian, in which

Coleridge remarks that he returns "Blake's poesies, metrical and graphic, with "thanks." He appends a criticism of the *Songs of Innocence and of Experience* and a list of the poems, with symbols indicating the degree to which he enjoyed each of them.

Note: At this date (1818) Coleridge evidently did not know Blake personally, but that he met him later appears from a footnote to an anonymous article on Blake in the *London University Magazine* for March, 1830 (see no. 408), as follows: "Blake and Coleridge when in company, seemed like congenial beings of another "sphere, breathing for a while on our earth ; which may easily be perceived from the "similarity of thought pervading their works." Crabb Robinson also refers to this meeting in a letter to Dorothy Wordsworth, dated Feb. 20, 1826, as follows: "Coleridge has visited Blake, and, I am told, talks finely about him" (Symons, p. 276). The copy (I) of the *Songs* lent by Tulk to Coleridge is still extant (see p. 121 of the present work).

317 PIERS PLOWMAN A Contribution to the History of English Mysticism By J. J. Jusserand Translated from the French by M.E.R. London T. Fisher Unwin MDCCCXCIV 8°. (65 copies on Japanese vellum).

References to Blake, pp. 218-219, with reproductions of three of the *Illustrations of the Book of Job* facing pp. 212, 216, 218.

317A DANTE GABRIEL ROSSETTI his family-letters with a memoir by William Michael Rossetti . . . Vol. I [II] London Ellis and Elvey 1895 8°. Vol. I. pp. xxx +[iv]+440. Vol. II. pp. [x]+436.

References : *Passim*, but see especially :
Vol. I, pp. 109-110. The MS. Book.
　　　　p. 251. Rossetti's opinion of the poem " My Spectre " (*Rossetti MS.*, 54).
Vol. II, pp. 314-315. His edition of the poems in Gilchrist.
　　　　p. 359. Blake's " Visionary Heads."

318 THE LIFE OF THE SPIRIT in the Modern English Poets By Vida D. Scudder Boston and New York Houghton Mifflin and Company The Riverside Press, Cambridge 1895 19.5 cm., pp. vi+ 349 +[3].
References : Pp. 25, 31, 57, 63, 196, 269.

319 LITERARY ANECDOTES OF THE NINETEENTH CENTURY: Contributions towards a Literary History of the Period Edited by W. Robertson Nicoll, M.A., LL.D., and Thomas J. Wise London: Hodder & Stoughton Paternoster Row MDCCCXCV 8°. 21 cm., pp. xii + 634 + [2].

Illustrations: Engraved frontispiece and twenty facsimiles of letters, etc. The frontispiece is a portrait of Blake engraved on steel by W. B. Scott after the finished oil sketch made by T. Phillips for the large portrait now in the National Portrait Gallery. The plate-mark measures 19 × 13.5 cm.

Records: Pp. 2-17. "The Trial of William Blake for Sedition." A short introductory note, with transcripts of three unpublished documents:
  i. The information of John Scofield.
  ii. Blake's Memorandum in refutation of the information and complaint of John Scholfield, a private soldier, etc.
  iii. The speech of Counsellor Rose. In defence of Blake the Artist, at the Chichester Sessions, January 11th, 1804, taken in shorthand by the Rev. Mr. Youatt.

Note: The three documents here printed for the first time were not known to Gilchrist, who derived his information concerning the trial from the brief notice in the *Sussex Advertiser* (no. 394), from the reference in *Hayley's Memoirs* (no. 245), and from Blake's letter to Butts, dated Aug. 16, 1803 (letter no. 26). These documents provide a very much fuller account; among other new facts they show that the soldier Scofield, or Scholfield, had a companion of the name of Cock, a fact which explains various references in the *Rossetti MS.* and in *Jerusalem*.

The original MSS. from which these records were printed were formerly among William Hayley's papers, and were sold at Sotheby's, May 20, 1878 (lot 34, Quaritch, 12s.); in 1895 they belonged to the late H. Buxton Forman, who also owned the oil painting from which the frontispiece was engraved; this engraving is said to be one of Scott's best plates. Further documents concerning the trial, namely, the official Indictment and Acquittal, were printed in 1910 in an article by Mr. Herbert Jenkins in *The Nineteenth Century* (see no. 608). A reference to the episode in a letter * from Flaxman to Hayley, dated Jan. 2, 1804, is printed by Mr. Russell (*Letters*, p. 134).

320 THAT DOME IN AIR Thoughts on Poetry and the Poets By John Vance Cheney . . . Chicago A. C. McClurg and Company 1895 18 cm., pp. 236 + [4].

Essay: Pp. 169-187. "William Blake."

* Now in the Pierpont Morgan Library.

321 WILLIAM BLAKE PAINTER AND POET By Richard Garnett, LL.D. . . . London Seeley and Co. . . . New York Macmillan and Co. [October] 1895 [The Portfolio Monographs, no. 22] 8°. 26.5 cm., pp. 80.

Illustrations: Photogravure frontispiece, six plates in colour, and twenty-two reproductions in the text of Blake's designs and engravings.

322 ESSAYS By Arthur Christopher Benson London William Heinemann. 1896 8°. Pp. xvi + 312.

Essay: Pp. 147-179. "William Blake."

323 SOCIAL ENGLAND. By Various Writers. Edited by H. D. Traill, D.C.L. Vol. V. Cassell and Company, Limited. London. 1896. 8°. Pp. viii + 636.

References: Pp. 445-446, 567-568. Critical remarks about Blake as poet and artist.

324 A DICTIONARY OF ENGLISH AUTHORS Biographical and Bibliographical By R. Farquharson Sharp London George Redway 1897 8°. Pp. vi + 2 + 310.

Article: Pp. 27-28. "Blake (William)."

325 ENGLISH LITERATURE from A.D. 670 to A.D. 1832 By Stopford Brooke, M.A. . . . London Macmillan and Co., Limited . . . 1897 8°. Pp. 192.

Reference: Pp. 148-149. "William Blake."

326 LETTERS OF DANTE GABRIEL ROSSETTI to William Allingham 1854-1870 By George Birkbeck Hill, D.C.L., LL.D. . . . London T. Fisher Unwin . . . 1897 22 cm., pp. xxviii + 307 + [1].

References:
    pp. 158-9, 165. The illustrations in Hayley's *Ballads*, 1805.
    p. 237. Rossetti's first dealings with Alexander Gilchrist, Nov. 1860.
    p. 241. Gilchrist's death. The purchase of the *Rossetti MS.*
    p. 259. Gilchrist's *Life of Blake.*
    pp. 262-5. Garth Wilkinson's poems. The emendations in Rossetti's edition of Blake's poems, Gilchrist, ii.

Note: For further references connected with Rossetti see nos. 317A and 332.

327 GREAT ENGLISH POETS. By Julian Hill. Philadelphia. [1898].

    Essays : Contains two essays on Blake.

    Note : Reference from Mr. S. Foster Damon. Not verified.

328 RUDOLF KASSNER Die Mystik die Künstler und das Leben Uber Englische Dichter und Maler im 19. Jahrhundert. accorde Verlegt in Leipzig 1900 bei Eugen Diederichs. 8°. Pp. [iv]+289+[1].

    Essay : Pp. 14-56. "William Blake" (Visionen, Mystik, Mythus, Kunst).

329 THE HAMPSTEAD ANNUAL 1902 [etc.] Edited by Greville E. Matheson and Sydney C. Mayle. London . . . 27 cm. 1902, pp. 180. 1903, pp. 143+[3]. 1904-5, pp. 139+[1].

    Articles :
    1. 1902, pp. 9-21. "John Linnell and William Blake at Hampstead." By Richard Garnett, C.B., LL.D.
    2. 1903, pp. 54-69. "Letters of William Blake to George Cumberland." Edited by Richard Garnett, C.B., LL.D.
    3. 1903, pp. 110-134. "Wyldes and its Story." By Mrs. Arthur Wilson.
    4. 1904-5, pp. 110-123. "Gleanings from the Cumberland Papers. Blake and Poole." By Richard Garnett, C.B., LL.D.

    Note : Blake's letters to Cumberland were here printed for the first time. In the fourth article Dr. Garnett has collected most of the few references to Blake that are to be found in the Cumberland correspondence (B.M. MSS.). They consist of a letter concerning Cumberland's *Outlines* (see nos. 112 and 133), and some correspondence between Cumberland, his son George, and John Linnell, about the small cardplate engraved by Blake for Cumberland, and about a copy of the *Job*, which Cumberland had been trying to dispose of in Bristol on Blake's behalf. A letter from Linnell dated Nov. 12, 1827, states that Mrs. Blake was then living in his house. A supplementary collection of references was printed by Mr. Symons in the *Saturday Review* 1906 (no. 568).

330 THE LIBRARY OF LITERARY CRITICISM of English and American Authors. Vol. V. 1825-1854 Ed. C. W. Moulton. The Moulton Publishing Company Buffalo New York 1902 8°. 25 cm., pp. 768+[2].

    Critical extracts : Pp. 56-64. "William Blake." Many extracts from books mentioned in the present work. A MS. note by David Scott, 1844, in a copy of Blair's *Grave*, is quoted.

331 IDEAS OF GOOD AND EVIL. By W. B. Yeats A. H. Bullen, . . . London, W.C. MCMIII 8°. Pp. vii + [i] + 341 + [1].

> *Essays*: Pp. 168-175. "William Blake and the Imagination."
> Pp. 176-225. "William Blake and his Illustrations to The Divine Comedy."

Note: The second of these was first published in *The Savoy*, 1896, illustrated with half-tone reproductions of Blake's designs (see no. 518). A second edition was issued in 1903.

332 ROSSETTI PAPERS 1862 to 1870 A Compilation by William Michael Rossetti . . . London Sands & Co . . . 1903 8°. 22.5 cm., pp. xxiii + [i] + 559 + [1].

References: Frequent references to Blake and his works and to Gilchrist's *Life of Blake*. See especially the following letters, all addressed to W. M. Rossetti:

No. 15. From Tatham, describing Blake's method of colour-printing.
16. From John Linnell jr., describing the Dante designs.
18. From Tatham, describing Blake's death.
19. From John Linnell jr., describing the designs for Thornton's *Virgil*.
20. From Anne Gilchrist, discussing Blake's method of colour-printing.
21. From John Linnell sen., concerning the origin of Blake's dragons.
23. From William Haines, containing a description of some of Blake's works in the Petworth collection.
33. From Anne Gilchrist, concerning some Blake MSS. which she seems to have burnt.
112. From Seymour Kirkup, containing some recollections of Blake and of his picture of "The Ancient Britons."
115. The same.

Note: For another letter from Kirkup concerning "The Ancient Britons," addressed to Lord Houghton, see no. 300.

332A BRYAN'S DICTIONARY OF PAINTERS AND ENGRAVERS. Edited by G. C. Williamson. London George Bell & Sons 1903 4°.

Article: Vol. 1, pp. 140-142. "Blake, William." By E. J. O[ldmeadow].

333 A HISTORY OF CRITICISM and Literary Taste in Europe . . . By George Saintsbury In Three Volumes . . . William Blackwood and Sons Edinburgh and London MCMIV 8°.

> *Critical account* of Blake, vol. III, pp. 266-269.

334 THE MASTERS OF ENGLISH LITERATURE By Stephen Gwynn London Macmillan and Co., Limited New York: The Macmillan Company 1904 . . . 17.5 cm., pp. xiii + [iii] + 424.

> *References*: Pp. 257, 271-3.

335 WILLIAM BLAKE A Study of his Life and Art Work by Irene Langridge London George Bell and Sons 1904 8°. 23 cm., pp. xii + 198.

> *Illustrations*: 50 half-tone reproductions, after designs selected almost entirely from the works by Blake contained in the National Art Collections.

336 OLD MASTERS AND NEW Essays in Art Criticism By Kenyon Cox New York Fox, Duffield and Co. 1905 18 cm., pp. [viii] + 311 + [1].

> *Essay*: Pp. 127-132. " William Blake."

337 THE WORKS OF CHARLES AND MARY LAMB Edited by E. V. Lucas Volume VII. Letters 1821-1834 Methuen & Co . . . [1905] 22 cm., pp. [ii] + xxii + [ii] + 549-1029 + [1].

> *Illustrations*: 30 plates in photogravure and half-tone, the latter including " The Death of the Strong Wicked Man " from Blair's *Grave*, 1808.

> *Reference*: On pp. 642-643, in a letter to Bernard Barton, dated May 15, 1824, Lamb refers to Blake in a passage, of which the main part is as follows: " Blake is a
> " real name, I assure you, and a most extraordinary man, if he be still living. He is the
> " Robert [*sic*] Blake, whose wild designs accompany a splendid folio edition of the
> " ' Night Thoughts ' . . . He paints in water colours marvellous strange pictures,
> " visions of his brain, which he asserts that he has seen. They have great merit. He
> " has *seen* the old Welsh bards on Snowdon . . . and has painted them from memory
> " (I have seen his paintings) . . . His Pictures—one in particular, the Canterbury
> " Pilgrims (far above Stothard's)—have great merit, but hard, dry, yet with grace. He
> " has written a Catalogue of them with a most spirited criticism on Chaucer, but mystical

"and full of Vision . . . There is one [song] to a tiger, which I have heard recited
". . . which is glorious, but, alas! I have not the book; for the man is flown, whither
"I know not—to Hades or a Mad House. But I must look on him as one of the most
"extraordinary persons of the age. . . ."

Note: There is no evidence that Lamb ever met Blake, but he had, as he implies above, been to his exhibition, probably after he had been given a copy of the *Descriptive Catalogue* by Crabb Robinson, who records that Lamb considered Blake's description of his Canterbury Pilgrims "the finest criticism he had ever read of Chaucer's "poem" (Symons, p. 284). Lamb obtained "The Chimney Sweeper" from the *Songs of Innocence* for James Montgomery's *Chimney-Sweeper's Friend and Climbing-boy's Album*, 1824,* and regarded it as "the flower of the set." In the same volume were some verses by Montgomery entitled "The Climbing-boy's Soliloquies"; the second of these, headed "The Dream," is a version of Blake's poem extended, or, as Lamb calls it in the same letter which has been already quoted, "awkwardly paraphras'd from "B." Crabb Robinson records that on Jan. 8, 1828, he bought two prints of Chaucer's pilgrimage at 2½ guineas each from Mrs. Blake, meaning one for Lamb, who actually received the print on May 22 of the same year. The passage here reprinted was first quoted in Cunningham's *Lives of the Painters*, 2nd edition, 1830 (see no. 250), and later by E. V. Lucas in his *Lives of Charles and Mary Lamb*, 1906, ii, pp. 255-256.

Bernard Barton's interest in Blake was re-aroused after the latter's death, and he addressed a sonnet † to John Linnell concerning his friendship with Blake. A long and interesting letter ‡ from Linnell to Barton, dated April 3, 1830, describing his relations with Blake is printed by Mr. Russell (*Letters*, p. 226).

338　ENGLISH COLOUR BOOKS By Martin Hardie Methuen and Co. . . . London [1906] (The Connoisseur's Library)　8°.　Pp. xxiv + 340.

Essay: Chap. VIII, pp. 72-86. "William Blake" (illustrated with reproductions of two pages from the Prophetic Books, one in colour).

339　THE LETTERS OF WILLIAM BLAKE Together with a Life by Frederick Tatham　Edited from the Original Manuscripts with an Introduction and Notes by Archibald G. B. Russell　With twelve illustrations　Methuen & Co . . . London [1906]　8°.　21 cm., pp. xlvii + [i] + 237 + [1].

* See pp. 128 and 327 of the present work.
† Printed in Story's *Life of John Linnell*, i, 194, with letters from Barton containing references to Blake.
‡ Now in the Pierpont Morgan Library.

Note: The Life by Frederick Tatham is printed here for the first time, though extracts were given by Swinburne, and later by others. The main facts of Tatham's life are now fairly well established, but owing to his having destroyed a quantity of Blake's MSS. after his death, his character has attracted more suspicion than he has, perhaps, deserved; in his introduction (pp. xlv-xlvii) Mr. Russell attempts, as far as is possible, to vindicate him. Tatham was in communication with W. M. Rossetti and Mrs. Gilchrist (see *Rossetti Papers*, no. 332, and *Anne Gilchrist*, no. 294) at the time of the publication of the first edition of Gilchrist's *Life*, and about 1860 he visited Dr. Richard Garnett, who records his recollections of the occasion on pp. 71-72 of his monograph (no. 321). Owing to his intimacy with Blake and his wife, Tatham should have had many opportunities of gathering information and impressions, but in spite of this his Life does not contain a great deal of importance that is not recorded elsewhere; nor does it possess much literary form. It is, nevertheless, a valuable document as a source of evidence, and it is an important addition to the number of the contemporary records of Blake that are available.

The MS. of the Life, after Tatham had parted with it, was for some time lost sight of, but it appeared again at the Blamire sale in 1863, bound up with the only illuminated copy of *Jerusalem* that Blake ever finished; the volume also contains a portrait of Mrs. Blake by Richmond, and two portraits of Blake, one at the age of twenty-eight years, drawn by Tatham after Mrs. Blake, the other by Tatham at the age of sixty-nine. This volume was resold at Sotheby's in 1887, and is now the property of General Archibald Stirling of Keir.

The letters were collected by Mr. Russell from all the sources then available, and include a few which had not been previously printed, notably two to Dr. Trusler, nos. 5 and 6, and one to Flaxman, no. 10, containing the lines " To my dearest " friend, John Flaxman." Several extracts relating to Blake from the letters of his friends, Flaxman, Hayley, Butts, Linnell, and Cumberland, are also printed.

This book is referred to elsewhere in the present work as: Russell, *Letters*.

340 SHELBURNE ESSAYS By Paul Elmer More Fourth Series G. P. Putnam's Sons New York and London 1906 18.5 cm., pp. [viii] + 283 + [5].

Essay: Pp. 212-238. " William Blake."

Note: First printed in the *New York Evening Post* as a review of Sampson, 1905.

341   1757-1827 UN MAITRE DE L'ART Blake le Visionnaire par François Benoit Professeur d'Histoire de l'Art à l'Université de Lille . . . Lille Au Siège de l'Université Paris H. Laurens . . . [1906] 4°. 32 cm., pp. 76.

Illustrations: Frontispiece in colours, 24 plates in half-tone, and numerous illustrations in the text.

Note: The 24 half-tone plates are printed on the pages of the book, but they are not included in the pagination.

342   WILLIAM BLAKE A CRITICAL ESSAY By Algernon Charles Swinburne A New Edition London Chatto & Windus 1906 8°. 19 cm., pp. x + [ii] + 340.

Frontispiece: Photogravure portrait of Blake after Schiavonetti's engraving of the painting by Phillips.

Note: A reprint of the original edition of 1868 (no. 273) with a new preface by the author.

343   WILLIAM BLAKE von Helene Richter. Mit 13 Tafeln in Lichtdruck und einem Dreifarbendruck.

> Die Welt zu sehen im Körnchen Sand
> Und den Himmel aus wilder Blumen Grunde;
> Die Unendlichkeit in der flachen Hand
> Zu erfassen, die Ewigkeit in der Stunde.
>   W. BLAKE, *Auguries of Innocence.*

Strassburg J. H. Ed. Heitz (Heitz & Mündel) 1906 8°. 23.5 cm., pp. viii + 404 + [4].

Note: Contains numerous translations of poems, etc., into German, the original text being given in footnotes. In my own possession is a copy given by the authoress to W. M. Rossetti, with inscription.

343A   DIE VISIONARE KUNST PHILOSOPHIE DES WILLIAM BLAKE. Englisch v Archibald B. G. Russell Deutsch von Stefan Zweig Leipzig 1906 Verlag von Julius Zeitler 8°. Pp. 30 + [2].

343B   THE ART OF WILLIAM BLAKE His Sketch-book His Water-colours His Painted Books By Elisabeth Luther Cary With Numerous Illustrations New York Moffat, Yard & Company 1907 26.5 cm., pp. xi + [i] + 56.

Illustrations: Photogravure frontispiece and 50 plates in half-tone, including reproductions of seven pages from the *Rossetti MS.*, which have not been reproduced elsewhere.

344 P. BERGER Docteur ès Lettres Professeur Agrégé d'Anglais au Lycée de Bordeaux. WILLIAM BLAKE MYSTICISME ET POESIE Paris Société Française d'Imprimerie et de Librairie Ancienne Librairie Lecène, Oudin et Cie 15, Rue de Cluny, 15 1907 8°. 25.5 cm., pp. [viii] + 480 + [4].

Note: Written as the author's "thèse de doctorat," and it is stated that not more than fifty copies found their way into the market. In my own possession is a presentation copy from the author to A. C. Swinburne, with inscription dated 18 Mai, 1907. The work contains numerous translations into French from Blake's poems and Prophetic Books, the English text being given in footnotes. A translation into English by D. H. Conner was published in 1914 (no. 379).

345 THE LIFE OF WILLIAM BLAKE by Alexander Gilchrist Edited with an Introduction by W. Graham Robertson and Numerous Reproductions from Blake's Pictures many hitherto unpublished London John Lane The Bodley Head New York John Lane Company MDCCCCVII 8°. 22 × 14 cm., pp. xxii + [ii] + 533 + [3].

Illustrations: 54 half-tone reproductions, including Linnell's portrait of Blake, designs by William and Robert Blake, etc.

Contents:
Introduction, by W. Graham Robertson.
The Life of William Blake, by Alexander Gilchrist.
The Colour Prints [by W. Graham Robertson].
W. M. Rossetti's Annotated Lists of Blake's Paintings, Drawings, and Engravings.
Account between Blake and Mr. Butts.
List of Blake's Writings.
Prospectus of 1793.
Supplementary List of Blake's Works.
Blake's Descriptive Catalogue.
Index.

Note: This is a faithful reprint of the second edition of Gilchrist's *Life of Blake*, 1880, though without the Selections contained in vol. II of that issue. Many of the illustrations were chosen from Mr. Graham Robertson's collection of Blake's works, and had not been previously reproduced. In his account of the Colour Prints the Editor gives a conjectural reconstruction of the processes by which Blake produced them.

346 THE REAL BLAKE A Portrait Biography by Edwin J. Ellis With 13 Illustrations London Chatto & Windus [New York Maclure, Phillips and Company] MCMVII 8°. 22 cm., pp. xviii + [ii] + 443 + [1].

> *Contents*: In the course of the biography the following are printed:
> 1. *An Island in the Moon* (no. 2).
> 2. Blake's annotations to Swedenborg's *Divine Wisdom* (no. 14).
> 3. Blake's annotations to Lavater's *Alphorisms* (no. 13).
> 4. *A Descriptive Catalogue* (no. 30).
> 5. Public Address (*Rossetti MS.*, 153).
> 6. The Last Judgement (*Rossetti MS.*, 154).
> 7. Blake's annotations to Dr. Thornton's pamphlet (no. 22).
> 8. Blake's annotations to Reynolds's *Discourses* (no. 18).

> *Illustrations*: Reproductions of four photographs of Deville's life-mask of Blake, of two MS. pages of *An Island in the Moon*, and of seven engravings by Blake.

347 STUDIES IN POETRY by Stopford A. Brooke London Duckworth and Company . . . 1907 8°. Pp. [vi] + 253 + [1].

> *Essay*: Pp. 1-54. "William Blake."

348 WILLIAM BLAKE by Arthur Symons London Archibald Constable and Company Ltd. [New York E. P. Dutton and Company] 1907 8°. 22 cm., pp. xviii + [ii] + 433 + [3].

> *Contents*: In part II Mr. Symons reprints the following in full:
> 1. Extracts from the Diary, Letters, and Reminiscences of Henry Crabb Robinson, transcribed from the original MSS. in Dr. Williams's Library, 1810-1822 (see no. 275).
> 2. From Malkin's *A Father's Memoirs of his Child*, 1806 (no. 80).
> 3. From Lady Charlotte Bury's Diary, 1820 (no. 255).
> 4. Blake's Horoscope, 1825 (no. 403).
> 5. Obituary Notices in *The Literary Gazette* and *The Gentleman's Magazine*, 1827 (nos. 405 and 404).
> 6. Extract from Varley's *Zodiacal Physiognomy*, 1828 (no. 248).
> 7. Biographical Sketch of Blake by J. T. Smith, 1828 (no. 247).
> 8. Life of Blake, by Allan Cunningham, 1830 (no. 249).

Note: Mr. Symons includes in his essay the results of some new researches into Blake's family, which he first published in *The Athenæum*, April 28, 1906 (see no. 557). Most of the contemporary records are here reprinted in full for the first time. On p. 338 is given Blake's Horoscope from *Urania*, but in a simplified form as copied by Dr. Garnett.

349 THE FAME OF WILLIAM BLAKE by Lewis Nathaniel Chase Reprint from The South Atlantic Quarterly, January, 1908 8°. Pp. 9+[1].

350 THE SANITY OF WILLIAM BLAKE By Greville MacDonald, M.D. . . . With six illustrations of Blake's drawings . . . London A. C. Fifield, . . . 1908 8°. 17 cm., pp. 59+[5].

    Note: Contains "the substance of a lecture given before the Ruskin Union, "November, 1907, now illustrated and amplified." First printed in *Saint George*, 1908 (no. 596).

351 WILLIAM BLAKE Seer, Poet, & Artist By W. P. Swainson London C. W. Daniel . . . [1908] [Christian Mystics, no. 8] 18°. 15 cm., pp. 30+[6].

352 ALLGEMEINES LEXICON der Bildenden Künstler. Ed. Prof. Ulrich Thieme & Dr. Felix Becker. Leipzig. 1909.

    Article: Vol. IV, pp. 84-88. "William Blake." By A. G. B. Russell.

353 EGOISTS A Book of Supermen By James Huneker London T. Werner Laurie [New York C. Scribner's Sons] 1909 19 cm., pp. [viii]+372.

    Essay: Pp. 277-290. "Mystics: Mad, Naked Blake."

354 MANUAL OF ENGLISH LITERATURE by Prof George Lillie Craik (with some new additions) [by Eleanor Urquhart] London: Published by J. M. Dent & Co and in New York by E. P. Dutton & Co [1909] (Everyman's Library) 17.5 cm., pp. xii+356.

    Article: Pp. 312-313. "William Blake."

355 MEMORIALS OF OLD SUSSEX Edited by Percy D. Mundy . . . London George Allen & Sons . . . 1909 8°. Pp. xiii + [i] + 304.

>*Essay*: Pp. 174-188. "Hayley and Blake at Felpham." By E. Sage.

>*Illustrations*: A drawing of Blake's cottage at Felpham, and portraits of Blake and Hayley.

356 PIERO MISCIATELLI Un Poeta Pittore: Villiam Blake Estratto dal No. 23 della "Vita d'Arte" Rivista Mensile Illustrata d'Arte . . . Siena Stabilimento Tipografico Ditta L. Lazzeri 1909 4°. Pp. 16.

>*Illustrations*: 12 half-tone reproductions of designs from Young's *Night Thoughts*.

357 THE ROMANTIC MOVEMENT in English Poetry by Arthur Symons London Archibald Constable & Co. Ltd. 1909 8°. Pp. [iv] + xi + [i] + 344 + [2].

>*Essay*: Pp. 37-51. "William Blake."

358 THE TREATMENT OF NATURE in English Poetry between Pope and Wordsworth By Myra Reynolds Chicago The University of Chicago Press 1909 21.5 cm., pp. xxii + 388 + [2].

>*References*: Pp. 152, 177-180, 222, 342, 344, 362.

359 WILLIAM BLAKE by Basil de Sélincourt . . . London: Duckworth and Co. New York: Charles Scribner's Sons 1909 [The Library of Art] 8°. 19.5 cm., pp. xi + [i] + 298.

>*Illustrations*: 40 half-tone reproductions of Blake's designs, many of which have not been reproduced elsewhere.

360 ART AND LIFE By T. Sturge Moore With Eight Illustrations Methuen & Co. . . . London [1910] 8°. Pp. xi + [i] + 314 + [2].

>*Illustrations*: 8 half-tone reproductions, 7 of which are after Blake's designs.

>*Essays*: Pp. 193-216. "Blake and his Aesthetic."
>   Pp. 217-241. "Visionary Art."

>*Note*: The rest of the book is concerning Flaubert.

361 BLAKE'S VISION OF THE BOOK OF JOB With Reproductions of the Illustrations   A Study by Joseph H Wicksteed M.A. London: J. M. Dent & Sons Limited New York: E. P. Dutton & Co.   MCMX   8°.   21.5 cm., pp. 168.

362 THE ENCYCLOPÆDIA BRITANNICA.   Ed. 11.   1910.

>   *Article*: Vol. IV, pp. 36-38. "Blake, William." By J. C[omyns] C[arr].

>   *Note* : First appeared in the ninth edition, Edinburgh, 1875.

362A ENGLISH LITERATURE AND RELIGION   1800-1900 by Edward Mortimer Chapman London Constable & Co. Limited Boston and New York Houghton Mifflin Company 1910   21 cm., pp. xii + [ii] + 578 + [2].

>   *References* to Blake, pp. 58-60.

363 A HISTORY OF ENGLISH PROSODY . . . By George Saintsbury . . . Vol. III From Blake to Mr. Swinburne . . . Macmillan and Co . . . London 1910 8°. Pp. xii + [ii] + 562 + [2].

>   *Critical study* of Blake as a prosodist, pp. 8-29. Professor Saintsbury gives numerous quotations, among them 13 lines from *The French Revolution* (no. 27), which is here quoted and criticized for the first time.

364 WILLIAM BLAKE   By G. K. Chesterton . . . London: Duckworth & Co. New York E. P. Dutton & Co. [1910] [The Popular Library of Art] 8°. 15 cm., pp. vi + 210 + [2].

>   *Illustrations*: Frontispiece in colours, and 31 half-tone reproductions of designs selected chiefly from Blake's Illuminated Books.

365 JAMES JOHN GARTH WILKINSON; a Memoir of his Life, with a Selection from his Letters; by Clement John Wilkinson. . . . London Kegan Paul, Trench, Trübner & Co., Ltd. . . . 1911 8°. 22 cm., pp. [vi] + 304.

>   *Reference*: Pp. 25-31. Wilkinson's edition of the *Songs of Innocence and of Experience*, 1839 (no. 134), and his opinions of Blake.

3 A

366 MYSTICISM A Study in the Nature and Developement of Man's Spiritual Consciousness By Evelyn Underhill . . . Methuen & Co. Ltd. . . . London [1911; 2nd edition, 1912]. 8°.

References: References to Blake *passim*; a list is given in the index.

367 WILLIAM BLAKE in his Relation to Dante Gabriel Rossetti. A Dissertation presented to the Philosophical Faculty of the University of Zurich for the Acquisition of the Degree of Doctor of Philosophy by J. C. E. Bassalik-de-Vries. Basel Buchdruckerei Brin & Cie. 1911. 22.5 cm., pp. 58 + [6].

368 WILLIAM BLAKE, MYSTIC A Study by Adeline M. Butterworth together with Young's Night Thoughts: Nights I & II with illustrations by William Blake and frontispiece Death's Door, from Blair's " The Grave " Liverpool The Liverpool Booksellers Co., Ltd. London Simpkin, Marshall, Hamilton, Kent & Co., Ltd. 1911 26.5 cm. 47 leaves.

Note: The edition was limited to 250 copies.

369 THE ENGRAVINGS OF WILLIAM BLAKE by Archibald G. B. Russell London Grant Richards Ltd. MDCCCXII 25 cm., pp. 229 + [3].

Illustrations: Thirty-two reproductions of Blake's works in half-tone.

Note: This volume contains a detailed catalogue of Blake's engravings, with an introductory essay by the compiler. It is referred to in other parts of the present work as : Russell, *Engravings*. It contains much information which is not to be found elsewhere. 500 copies were printed for sale in England.

370 ESSAYS AND STUDIES by Members of the English Association Vol. III Collected by W. P. Ker Oxford At the Clarendon Press 1912 8°. Pp. 152.

Essay: Pp. 136-152. " Blake's Religious Lyrics." By Canon H. C. Beeching.

371 PRIMITIÆ Essays in English Literature by Students of the University of Liverpool Liverpool The University Press London Constable & Company Ltd 1912 8°. Pp. [viii] + 287 + [1].

Essay: Pp. 1-42. "Blake's symbolism and some of its recent interpreters." By John P. R. Wallis.

372 A SURVEY OF ENGLISH LITERATURE 1780-1830 By Oliver Elton ... Professor of English Literature in the University of Liverpool . . . In Two Volumes Vol. I   London Edward Arnold 1912 ... 8°. Pp. xv + [i] + 456.

Essay: Chap. v, pp. 137-171. "William Blake."

373 CHAMBERS'S ENCYCLOPÆDIA A Dictionary of Universal Knowledge New Edition Vol. II . . . London: . . . William & Robert Chambers, Limited Edinburgh: . . . J. B. Lippincott Company, Philadelphia ... [1913] Imp. 8°.

Article: Pp. 209-210. "Blake, William." [By J. M. Gray.]

374 COWPER AND BLAKE A Paper Read at the 13th Annual Meeting of the Cowper Society, Held at the Mansion House, London, 23rd April, 1913 by Dr. Hubert J. Norman . . . Olney: Thomas Wright [July 1913] 8°. 18.5 cm., pp. viii + 9-62 + [2].

Illustrations : Six half-tone reproductions of portraits of persons mentioned in the paper, including Joseph Johnson, the bookseller.

375 THE FIRST MEETING OF THE BLAKE SOCIETY Papers read before the Blake Society at the First Annual Meeting, 12th August, 1912. Olney: Thomas Wright. [January, 1913] In fours, 21 cm., pp. 62.

Contents:
"William Blake, the Practical Idealist." By Dr. Greville Macdonald.
"The Teaching of William Blake." By Herbert Jenkins.
"Blake and Hampstead." By Walter K. Jealous.
"The Art of William Blake." By Prof. G. H. Leonard, M.A.
"Blake's Burden." By F. C. Owlett.

376 MYSTICISM IN ENGLISH LITERATURE By Caroline F. E. Spurgeon . . . Cambridge: at the University Press 1913 [Cambridge Manuals of Science and Literature] 16 cm., pp. [viii]+168.

> *References*: Pp. 129-147. A critical account of Blake as a mystic, with other references *passim*.

377 THE PRACTICE & SCIENCE OF DRAWING By Harold Speed . . . London Seeley, Service & Co. Limited . . . 1913 8°. Pp. xvi+17-296.

> *References* to Blake's drawing, pp. 51, 145-147, 155, 169, with small reproductions of eight plates from *Illustrations of the Book of Job*.

378 MODERN ENGLISH LITERATURE from Chaucer to the Present Day By G. H. Mair . . . London Williams & Norgate . . . 1914 22 cm., pp. [x]+310 +[2].

> *References*: Pp. 200-203. Blake's relations to his contemporaries.

379 WILLIAM BLAKE POET AND MYSTIC By P. Berger Docteur-ès-Lettres Professor of English Language and Literature in the Lycée and Lecturer in the University of Bordeaux Authorized Translation from the French by Daniel H. Conner. London Chapman & Hall, Ltd. 1914 8°. 22 cm., pp. xii+420.

> *Note*: For the original edition in French see no. 344. At the end of this edition is a useful bibliographical list. Among the additions to the text is a description of *The French Revolution* with a quotation from it. Three of the appendices to the original edition, "Editeurs et critiques," "Remarques sur la versification de Blake," and "Notes sur Swedenborg," are here omitted.

380 FLAXMAN BLAKE COLERIDGE and other Men of Genius Influenced by Swedenborg Together with Flaxman's Allegory of the "Knight of the Blazing Cross" By H. N. Morris Published by the New-Church Press, Limited . . . London 1915 8°. 21 cm., pp. viii+166+[2].

> *Essay*: Pp. 77-104. "William Blake Artist and Poet." With two portraits and five other reproductions.

381

柳宗悦著

ヰリアム・ブレーク

彼の生涯と製作
及びその思想

洛陽堂發行

[1915] 8°. 22 cm., pp. xxiii + [i] + 754 + [24].

Illustrations: Frontispiece after Deville's life-mask, fifty-nine reproductions of Blake's works in half-tone, and one of a fragment of Michael Angelo's "Last Judgment." Each illustration is preceded by a leaf with the title in English.

Note: By M. Yanagi, Abiko, Chibaken, Japan. Printed in Japanese except for proper names, titles of books, and quotations from Blake's works. At the end is a bibliographical list, a catalogue of Mr. Hollyer's reproductions, and an index.

382 ANTHOLOGY OF MODERN VERSE for 1916. Edited by William Stanley Braithwaite. New York. 1916. 22 cm., pp. xx + 266.

Poem: Pp. 43-44. "Mad Blake." By Wm. Rose Benét.

Note: First printed in *The Burglar of the Zodiac*, Yale University Press. Also printed in *Reedy's Mirror*, St. Louis, Mv., Oct. 1, 1915, and in *The Second Book of Modern Verse*, Houghton Mifflin and Co., 1919.

383 INTERPRETATIONS OF LITERATURE By Lafcadio Hearn Selected and edited with an introduction by John Erskine, Ph.D. . . . With Frontispiece. Volume I [II] London William Heinemann 1916 23 cm. Vol. I. pp. xiv+[ii]+ 406+[2]. Vol. II. pp. [viii]+379+[1].

Essay: Vol. 1, ch. vi, pp. 51-71. "Blake—The First English Mystic."

384 VISION & VESTURE A Study of William Blake in Modern Thought By Charles Gardner . . . London, . . . J. M. Dent & Sons Limited MCMXVI 8°. 19 cm., pp. xii+226.

385 LIFE AND WORKS OF OZIAS HUMPHREY, R.A. By George C. Williamson, Litt.D. London: John Lane . . . MCMXVIII 4°. pp. xx+[2]+329+[1].

References to Blake's friendship with Humphrey, pp. 216-217. Numerous illustrations, but none connected with Blake.

386 DET NITTENDE AARHUNDREDES KUNST. Emil Hannover. Gyldendalske Boghandel, Nordisk Forlag. [Copenhagen] 1918. (No. 26 of Det Nittende Aarhundrede.)

Reference: Pp. 62-64.

Note: Published simultaneously in Stockholm. Reference from Mr. S. Foster Damon; not verified. Mr. Hannover remarks that Blake was "ganske blottet for Talent." In another volume of *Det Nittende Aarhundrede*, which is to appear soon, Professor Grönbech of Copenhagen will devote several pages to Blake in an article on "Religiöse Stromninger i det Nittende Aarhundrede." Later the same author will publish a series of lectures on Blake.

387 THE MYSTICAL POETS of the English Church By Percy H. Osmond . . . London Society for Promoting Christian Knowledge New York: The Macmillan Co. 1919 21.5 cm., pp. x+[ii]+436.

Essay: Pp. 278-289. "William Blake" (as mystic).

388 PICTURES OF THE FLOATING WORLD [By Amy Lowell] New York, the Macmillan Co. 1919 18 cm., pp. xx + 257 + [1].

> *Poems*: 1. P. 181. "William Blake."
> 2. Pp. 182-3. "An Incident" (Blake's marriage).

> *Note*: No. 1 was first printed in *The Yale Review*, 1917 (see no. 649); no. 2 had not appeared before. Reference supplied by Mr. Thos. Ollive Mabbott.

389 WILLIAM BLAKE THE MAN by Charles Gardner author of "Vision and Vesture," "The Redemption of Religion," etc.

> "The men that were with me saw not the vision."—DANIEL.

London: J. M. Dent & Sons Limited New York: E. P. Dutton & Co. MCMXIX 8°. 21 cm., pp. 202 + [2].

> *Illustrations*: Twelve reproductions in half-tone of Blake's paintings and engravings, several hitherto unpublished.

390 BLAKE AND MILTON. Denis Saurat. Bordeaux, Imprimerie de l'Université. 1920. 25 cm., pp. 74.

391 A MISCELLANY OF AMERICAN POETRY, 1920. New York, Harcourt, Brace & Howe. 1920. 8°.

> *Poem*: P. 46. "Blake." By John Gould Fletcher.

> *Note*: Reference supplied by Mr. S. Foster Damon.

392 THE SACRED WOOD Essays on Poetry and Criticism by T. S. Eliot Methuen & Co. Ltd. . . . London [1920] 17 cm., pp. viii + [ii] + 155 + [1].

> *Essay*: Pp. 137-143. "Blake."

393 VISION AND DESIGN by Roger Fry London Chatto & Windus 1920 28.5 cm., pp. viii + 204.

> *Essay*: Pp. 140-144. "Three Pictures in Tempera by William Blake."

> *Note*: Illustrated with a reproduction of Blake's "Bathsheba." First printed in *The Burlington Magazine*, 1904 (no. 546).

B. PERIODICALS

394 SUSSEX ADVERTISER, The. Chichester. January 16, 1804.

    Reference: This number of the local journal contains a brief account of Blake's trial at Chichester for sedition on Jan. 11, 1804.

    Note: The account is reprinted by Gilchrist, i, 196-197. For further sources of information concerning the trial see no. 319.

395 ANNUAL REVIEW, The, for 1805. Vol. IV. London. 1806.

    Reference to Blake's designs in an unsigned review of Hayley's *Ballads*, 1805, by Robert Southey. See no. 74.

396 MONTHLY MAGAZINE, The. Vol. XXI. London: Richard Philips. 1806.

    Letter: In the number for July 1, 1806, pp. 520-521 is a letter addressed " To " the Editor of the Monthly Magazine" and signed " Wm. Blake." It consists of a defence, with Blake's own criticism, of Fuseli's picture of Count Ugolino, which had been attacked in *Bell's Weekly Messenger* of May 25.

    Note. This letter was discovered and first reprinted by Swinburne in his *Critical Essay*, 1868. The MS. of the letter is not known to have survived. Blake wrote a second letter to Sir Richard Philips on Oct. 14, 1807, calling attention to the harsh treatment of an astrologer by a Mr. Blair, a surgeon, but this was not published. See letters nos. 59 and 60.

397 MONTHLY REVIEW, The. Vol. LI. London. 1806.

    Reference on p. 217 to Blake's poetry, in a review of Malkin's *Father's Memoirs of his Child*, 1806 (see no. 80).

398 MONTHLY MAGAZINE, The. Vol. XXII. London: Richard Philips. 1807.

Reference on p. 633 to Blake's poetry, in a review of Malkin's *Father's Memoirs of his Child*, 1806 (no. 80).

399 EXAMINER, The, a Sunday Paper, . . . for the Year 1808. . . . London: Printed and Published by John Hunt, . . . 1808. 4°. Pp. [iv] + 832 + [4].

Review: On pp. 509-510, in no. 32, for Sunday, Aug. 7, 1808, is an article headed—"Fine Arts. Blake's Edition of Blair's Grave"; it occupies nearly a page and is signed " R.H." The article praises Blair's poetry and Schiavonetti's engraving, but speaks disparagingly of Fuseli's prefatory note and ridicules Blake's designs.

Note: This article is the first of two attacks on Blake which appeared in *The Examiner* (see next entry), a paper at that time edited by Leigh Hunt. The initials with which it is signed are those of Robert Hunt, a brother of the editor, as was established by Mr. Arthur Symons in *The Athenæum*, 1907 (no. 571), and Ellis suggests (*The Real Blake*, p. 270) that it may have been the same critic who found fault with Fuseli's work and was dealt with by Blake in the *Monthly Magazine* (see no. 396) two years previously. The terms of this review certainly sound more like the ravings of spite than the opinions of a genuine critic. Extracts from the article are given by Swinburne (*Critical Essay*, p. 59).

400 EXAMINER, The . . . for the Year 1809. . . . London: . . . 1809. 4°. Pp. [iv] + 850 + [4].

Review: On pp. 605-606, in no. 90, for Sunday, Sept. 17, 1809, is an article headed—"Fine Arts. Mr. Blake's Exhibition." The article, which occupies rather more than a page, is unsigned; it constitutes a most violent attack on Blake referring to him as "an unfortunate lunatic, whose personal inoffensiveness secures him from "confinement." The *Descriptive Catalogue*, some extracts from which are given, is described as "a farrago of nonsense, unintelligibleness, and egregious vanity, the "wild effusions of a distempered brain."

Note: This is the second attack on Blake by *The Examiner* and is even more violent than the first (see last entry); both may be attributed to the same writer, for again more spite than criticism is apparent in the terms of the article. Extracts are given by Swinburne (*Critical Essay*, p. 60). These attacks were very much resented by Blake, who refers to them in his *Advertisement* [*Public Address, Rossetti MS.*, 153] in a passage printed by Gilchrist, i, 230, and by Sampson, 1905, p. 214, which begins: "The manner in which my character has been blasted these thirty years "both as an Artist and as a Man may be seen particularly in a Sunday paper called

"the Examiner, published in Beaufort's Buildings, and the manner in which I have
"rooted out the nest of villains will be seen in a poem concerning my three years'
"Herculean labours at Felpham, which I shall soon publish." The poem referred to
may be *Jerusalem*, or it may be the fragment in the *Rossetti MS.*, 68, containing the
following lines, in which "Death" is Blake's nickname for himself:

> The Examiner whose very name is Hunt,
> Call'd Death a Madman, trembling for the affront;
> Like trembling Hare sits on his weakly paper
> On which he used to dance & sport & caper.

Dr. Sampson also points out (1905, p. 205) that the couplet "To H——," *Rossetti
MS.*, 73:

> You think Fuseli is not a great painter. I'm glad.
> This is one of the best compliments he ever had.

is probably addressed to Hunt, since in this volume of *The Examiner* (no. 75,
June 4, 1809, pp. 366-7) occur disparaging remarks by "R.H." about Fuseli also.
In the volume of *The Examiner* for 1810, p. 414, is a long obituary account of
Schiavonetti by R. H. Cromek. Blake is mentioned as the author of designs engraved
by Schiavonetti, but the passage is not of any interest.

401   VATERLANDISCHES MUSEUM. Erster Band. [Zweiter Band Erstes Heft.]
Hamburg, bey Friedrich Perthes. 1810. [1811.] 8°. Vol. I. pp. [vi] + 769 + [1].
Vol. II. pp. [iv] + 131 + [1].

Article: Vol. II, pp. 107-131, headed—"William Blake, Künstler, Dichter und
religiöser Schwärmer." In the course of the article the following poems are printed,
together with German translations (pp. 121-130):

1. To the Muses: An die Musen.
2. Piping down the valleys wild; Pfeifend ging ich durch das Thal (omitting
stanzas 2 and 3).
3. Holy Thursday; Gründonnerstag.
4. The Tyger; Der Tyger.
5. The Garden of Love; Der Garten der Liebe.
6. Six lines from *America*, pl. 10, beginning—"On these vast shady hills . . .";
"Auf jenem weiten Hayngebürge . . ."
7. Four lines from *Europe, Preludium*, beginning—"I wrap my turban of thick
clouds . . ."; "Ich winde die dunkeln Wolken zu einem Bund . . ."

In the earlier part of the article is a translation of Fuseli's remarks on Blake in

Blair's *Grave*, and of several extracts from the *Descriptive Catalogue*. On p. 120 is an anecdote of Blake and the Angel Gabriel which is not found elsewhere.*

Note: This publication consisted of six numbers issued in 1810, Feb. to Dec., and one final number in Jan. 1811. The article on Blake, stated in the contents list to be "Aus dem Englischen," is unsigned, but it is known to have been written by Crabb Robinson and translated by Dr. Julius, these facts being recorded by the former in his *Diary and Reminiscences*; he writes as follows, under the date 1810:

"I was amusing myself this spring by writing an account of the insane poet, "painter and engraver, *Blake*. Perthes of Hamburg had written to me asking me to "send him an article for a new German magazine, entitled Vaterländische Annalen, "which he was about to set up, and Dr. *Malkin* having in his Memoirs of his son "given an account of this extraordinary genius with specimens of his poems, I "resolved out of these to compile a paper. And this I did, and the paper was trans-"lated by Dr. Julius, who, many years afterwards, introduced himself to me as my "translator. It appears in the single number of the second volume of the Vaterländische "Annalen. For it was at this time that Buonaparte united Hamburg to the French "Empire, on which Perthes manfully gave up the magazine, saying [Schluss-"Anmerkung], as he had no longer a Vaterland, there could be no Vaterländische "Annalen. But before I drew up the paper I went to see a gallery of Blake's paint-"ings . . . I afterwards became acquainted with Blake [1825]. . . ." (*Diary and Reminiscences*, ii, 299.)

Some of the translations of the songs, nos. 2-5, are reprinted in Sampson, 1905, and again in an article by K. A. Esdaile in *The Library*, 1914 (no. 631), which includes an annotated translation of the greater part of Crabb Robinson's paper.

402 LONDON MAGAZINE, The. July to December, 1820. . . . Vol. II. London: . . . 1820. 8°. Pp. viii + 712.

Reference: On p. 300 in the number for Sept. 1820, in the course of an article headed "Mr. Janus Weathercock's Private Correspondence," is a frivolous reference to *Jerusalem*.

Note: The writer of this article was Thomas Griffiths Wainewright, an artist, who was at one time a friend of Blake, Lamb, Coleridge, and de Quincey, but who

---

* "Er [Blake] erzählte jemand, aus dessen Munde wir es haben, dass als er einst ein Gemählde, "welches er für eine Dame von Stande verfertigt, nach Hause getragen, und sich dabey in einem Wirths-"hause habe ausruhen wollen, habe ihm der Engel Gabriel auf die Schulter geklopft und gesprochen: "Blake, warum weilst Du hier? Geh zu, Du sollst nicht müde werden! Er sey darauf auch weiter "gegangen, ohne zu ermüden,"

afterwards committed murder and forgery and died in Australia. Some account of his life is given by Gilchrist, i, 322-326, who also prints the extract in question. For Wainewright's copy of the *Songs of Innocence and of Experience* see p. 124 of the present work.

403

Urania;

OR, THE

ASTROLOGER'S CHRONICLE,

AND MYSTICAL MAGAZINE.

—

EDITED BY

MERLINUS ANGLICUS, Jun.

THE ASTROLOGER OF THE NINETEENTH CENTURY,

ASSISTED BY

THE METROPOLITAN SOCIETY OF OCCULT PHILOSOPHERS.

——

No. I.

CONTENTS.

——

LONDON:

PRINTED BY A. SWEETING, ALDERSGATE STREET;

PUBLISHED BY

COWIE AND STRANGE, 24, FETTER LANE;

AND SOLD BY SHERWOOD, JONES, AND CO. PATERNOSTER

ROW, AND ALL BOOKSELLERS.

1825.

Collation: 15 × 9 cm. [A]^1, B^1, C^{1+8} (sign. on C$_2$ and C$_4$), D^{1+8} (sign. on D$_{2-5}$, D$_5$ signed D$_3$), E^{1+8} (sign. on E$_2$ and E$_4$), F^{1+6} (sign. on F$_2$ and F$_3$) = 36 leaves. Pp. [ii] Title, The Caduceus + 1-2, 5-72 (pp. 3 and 4 are omitted in the pagination).

Article: The last article, pp. 71-72, is headed "Nativity of Mr. Blake, The "Mystical Artist." It begins with "Planet's Latitude," and goes on with a short description of Blake and of his peculiarities; it ends with an interpretation of his Horoscope, which is reproduced here from p. 70 of *Urania*.

NATIVITY OF MR. BLAKE,

𝔗𝔥𝔢 𝔐𝔶𝔰𝔱𝔦𝔠𝔞𝔩 𝔄𝔯𝔱𝔦𝔰𝔱.

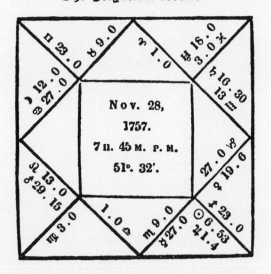

Note: This is the first and only number of a very rare astrological magazine, edited by R. C. Smith under the pseudonym given on the title-page. The date of Blake's birth, which is the correct one, was probably derived from Varley. The *Nativity* has been reprinted by Symons, together with a simplified version of the Horoscope from a drawing by Dr. Garnett. The copy here described is in the British Museum.

404   GENTLEMAN'S MAGAZINE, The. Vol. XCVII. London. 1827.

Pp. 377-8. Obituary notice in the number for Oct. 1827, headed: " MR WILLIAM " BLAKE Aug. 13. Aged 68, Mr. William Blake, an excellent, but eccentric artist." Except for the opening sentences, which have been reprinted by Symons, it seems to have been taken from the notice which had appeared in the *Literary Gazette* (no. 405).

405   LITERARY GAZETTE, The. London. 1827.

Pp. 540-1. Obituary notice in the number for Saturday, Aug. 18, 1827, giving a short account of his life and works. Reprinted by Symons.

406   MONTHLY MAGAZINE, The, or British Register. Vol. IV. New Series. London. 1827.

P. 435. Obituary notice in the number for Oct. 1827. It states that Blake was "born about the year 1761," but all the other facts seem to have been taken from the account in the *Literary Gazette* (no. 405).

407 ANNUAL REGISTER, The. London. 1828.

Pp. 253-4. Obituary notice in the appendix to the *Chronicle*. It is merely an abridgement of the notice which had appeared in the *Gentleman's Magazine* (no. 404).

408 LONDON UNIVERSITY MAGAZINE, The. . . . London: . . . 1829 . . . 8°. Vol. I. pp. [ii] + viii + 384 (Oct.-Dec. 1829). Vol. II. pp. 492 (Jan.-April, 1830).*

Illustrations: 5 engraved plates in vol. I.

Article: Vol. II, in the number for March, 1830, pp. 318-323, contains an unsigned article headed: "The Inventions of William Blake, Painter and Poet." The writer begins with a criticism of Cunningham's biography of Blake (see no. 249), in the course of which he complains "first, of the insertion of stories which are falsely "coloured; then of the stealing, borrowing, or copying a considerable portion of the "life from Nollekens Own Times; and, last of all, of a smile of contempt when "speaking of Blake's private sentiments and feelings. . . ." He then indulges in an enthusiastic appreciation of Blake's genius both as painter and poet. A footnote at the end of the article concerning Blake and Coleridge is given at p. 348 of the present work. In the course of the article the following quotations are made:

1. Introduction to Songs of Experience.
2. The Poison Tree.
3. A Cradle Song.
4. The Divine Image.
5. The Garden of Love.
6. Thirty-seven lines from *Thel*.

Note: This article was first recorded by Bertram Dobell in *Notes and Queries* for Feb. 3, 1906 (no. 564). There is no indication whatever of the identity of the author, but evidently it was written by one who had first-hand knowledge of Blake and of his life, and who had seen him and Coleridge in company. A writer in *Notes and Queries* for Feb. 17, 1906, suggests that it may have been by Crabb Robinson, who was intimately connected with University College; but the opinions expressed are not

---

* Collated from an incomplete copy in the British Museum.

those of Crabb Robinson, who regarded Blake as a madman, and his works as unintelligible, and the clumsy style is that of a less literary writer. It is more likely that the article must be attributed to one of Blake's younger friends, Palmer, Richmond, or Calvert.

409 ZEITGENOSSEN. Ein biographisches Magazin für die Geschichte unserer Zeit Dritte Reihe. Herausgegeben . . . von F. C. A. Hasse . . . Zweiter Band. Leipzig: F. A. Brockhaus. 1830. 8°.

No. 6, pp. 170-178. "Züge aus dem Leben des Künstler's Blake." (Compiled from Cunningham's *Life*, 1830.)

410 NEW JERUSALEM MAGAZINE, The. Vol. V. Boston. [Mass.] 1832.

Pp. 192-199. "Memoirs of William Blake." (A biographical account compiled from Cunningham's *Life*, 1830.)

411 REVUE BRITANNIQUE . . . Troisième Serie. Tome Quatrième. Paris . . . [July] 1833. 8°. Pp. 382.

Reference: On pp. 179-187, under the heading "Statistique," is an article on "Hôpital des fous à Londres." On pp. 183-186 is an account of a visit to Bethlem Hospital and of an interview with Blake, who is said to have been an inmate there.

Note: This account was first discovered by Mr. W. T. Horton, from a reference to it which occurs in *Des Hallucinations* by A. Brierre de Boismont (3rd ed., 1862, p. 89). Mr. Horton published a translation of the passage in the *Occult Review* in 1912 (see no. 619), and discussed its authenticity. The records of the asylum from 1815 to 1835 have been searched on behalf of Mr. Horton, but no mention of Blake can be discovered. The author of the article is anonymous and does not mention the date of his supposed visit to Bethlem; it is most probable that the account is not founded on fact. The original article is reprinted in an appendix to the present work.

412 EDINBURGH REVIEW, The. Vol. 59. London. April, 1834.

P. 53. Reference to Blake in a general review of Cunningham's *Lives of the Painters* (no. 249).

413 ATHENÆUM, The. Vol. XLIII. London. January, 1843.

Pp. 65-68. "The Vicar of Wakefield. With 32 illustrations by W. Mulready, R.A." (Review, with references to Blake's engraving and impressions from a wood block made by Blake for Thornton's *Virgil*, 1821, and from the same design recut by another. See p. 214 of the present work.)

414 GRAHAM'S MAGAZINE. Vol. XXIX. Philadelphia. Sept. 1846.

P. 151. "Blake's Visitants." Poem by William H. C. Hosmer. (Reprinted in Hosmer's *Poetical Works*, Redfield, New York, 1854. 8°. Vol. II, pp. 317-318.)

415 HOWITT'S JOURNAL. Vol. II. London. 1847.

Pp. 321-2. "Death's Door. By William Blake." With woodcut reproduction of Blake's design.

416 HOGG'S WEEKLY INSTRUCTOR. Vol. II. New Series. Edinburgh. 1849.

Pp. 17-20. "Some Chat about William Blake." By William Allingham.

417 GENTLEMAN'S MAGAZINE, The. Vol. XXXVII. New Series. London. 1852.

Pp. 149-150. In an anonymous article on Bray's *Life and Works of Thomas Stothard*, is a reference to Blake's engraving of the *Canterbury Pilgrims*, followed by an attempt to throw discredit on his character. A letter to him from R. H. Cromek, dated 64 Newman Street, May, 1807, is printed in full. This letter is now well known in connexion with the controversy concerning Cromek's dealings with Blake over his picture of the *Canterbury Pilgrims*, but it was here printed for the first time. It is reprinted in Gilchrist, i, 252-254, and Russell, *Letters*, p. 193; extracts are given in Ellis's *Real Blake*, 1907 (no. 346).

418 ART JOURNAL, The. Vol. IV. London. 1858.

P. 236. "Tombs of English Artists, no. 7.—William Blake." By F. W. Fairholt. (Illustrations include one of Blake's house in Fountain Court.)

419   LITTELL'S LIVING AGE. [Vol. LIX.] Third Series. Vol. III. Boston and New York. 1858.

> Facing p. 723. *Death's Door*, engraved by A. L. Dick after Blake.
> „   p. 787. Portrait of Blake, engraved by A. L. Dick after Schiavonetti.
> „   p. 851. *The Soul Exploring the Recesses of the Grave*, engraved by A. L. Dick after Blake.
> P. 848. A short account of Blake from a quarto edition of Blair's *Grave*, illustrated by Blake and published by Stanford and Delisser, New York.

420   ATHENÆUM, The.   London.   1863.

> No. 1880, Nov. 7, pp. 599-601.   Review of Gilchrist's *Life of Blake*.
> No. 1881, Nov. 14, pp. 642-644.   Ditto, second notice.
> No. 1886, Dec. 19, p. 838.   "Stothard and Blake." By Robert T. Stothard. Gives a personal anecdote of Blake and a rambling statement about his relations with Stothard and Cromek by the former's son. This is of some importance in connexion with the controversy concerning the *Canterbury Pilgrims*, and has not been noticed elsewhere.   It is reprinted in an appendix to the present work.

421   LITERATURE, THE SCIENCES, AND THE ARTS.   London.   1863.

> Pp. 673-680. "Life of William Blake." By W. B. Scott (review).

422   REVUE MODERNE, Le.   Paris.   1863.

> "W. Blake." By Joseph Milsand [reference from Berger's *William Blake*, 1915. Not verified].
> Reprinted in *Littérature Anglaise et Philosophie*, 1893 (see no. 308).

423   SPECTATOR, The.   No. 1847.   London, 21 Nov., 1863.

> Pp. 2771-3. "William Blake" (review of Gilchrist, 1863).
> Reprinted in *Littell's Living Age*, vol. XXIII, Third Series [LXXIX], Boston, 1863, pp. 579-583.

424   ART JOURNAL, The.   N.S.   Vol. III.   London.   1864.

> Pp. 25-6. "William Blake" (review).

425   ATLANTIC MONTHLY, The.   Vol. XIII.   Boston, Mass.   1864.

> Pp. 443-447. "Pictor Ignotus" (review). By Gail Hamilton (Mary Abigail Dodge).

426 COLBURN'S NEW MONTHLY MAGAZINE. Vol. 130. London. 1864.

    Review of Gilchrist's *Life of Blake* [reference from Berger's *William Blake*, 1915. Not verified].

427 ECLECTIC REVIEW, The. N.S. Vol. VI. London. 1864.

    Pp. 373-391. "William Blake" (review).

428 FINE ARTS QUARTERLY REVIEW, The. Vol. III. London. Oct., 1864.

    Pp. 56-79. "The Life and Works of William Blake." By W. F. Rea (review, illus.).

429 MACMILLAN'S MAGAZINE. Vol. XI. London. Nov., 1864.

    Pp. 26-33. "William Blake" (review).

430 NEW MONTHLY MAGAZINE, The. Vol. 130. London. 1864.

    Pp. 309-319. "Pictor Ignotus: A Biography" (review).

431 NEW QUARTERLY MAGAZINE, The. London. 1864.

    Pp. 466-501. "William Blake: Artist, Poet, and Mystic." By the editor.

432 NORTH AMERICAN REVIEW, The. Vol. XCIX. Boston. 1864.

    Pp. 465-482. Gilchrist's *Life of William Blake* (review).

433 NOTES AND QUERIES. 3 Series, V. London. 9 April, 1864.

    P. 312. Notice of Gilchrist's *Life of Blake.*

434 WESTMINSTER REVIEW, The. N.S. Vol. XXV. London. Jan., 1864.

    Pp. 101-118. "Gilchrist's Life of William Blake" (review).

435 BLACKWOOD'S MAGAZINE. Vol. LXXVII. Edinburgh. March, 1865.

    Pp. 291-307. "William Blake" (review).

436   FINE ARTS QUARTERLY REVIEW, The. Vol. III. London. 1865.

Pp. 56-79. "The Life and Works of William Blake." By W. F. Rae. A review of Gilchrist, 1st edition, with strictures on the author's style and method. Illustrated with two reproductions from *America* and *Jerusalem*.

437   QUARTERLY REVIEW, The. Vol. CXVII. London. January, 1865.

Pp. 1-27. "Gilchrist's Life of William Blake" (review, illus.). [? By Francis Palgrave.]

438   NATIONAL REFORMER, The. Vol. VII. New Series. London. 1866.

14 Jan., pp. 22-23; 21 Jan., pp. 42-43; 28 Jan., pp. 52-54; 4 Feb., pp. 70-71. "The Poems of William Blake." By B. V. [James Thomson]. Reprinted in 1884 with *Shelley, a Poem* (see no. 291).

439   TEMPLE BAR. Vol. XVII. London. April, 1866.

Pp. 95-105. "William Blake, Seer and Painter" [By A. T. Storey].

440   LIGHT BLUE, The. Vol. II. Cambridge. 1867.

Pp. 146-151. "William Blake.   i. Blake the Author"
216-226.   „   „   ii. Blake the Artist" } By P. M.
286-294.   „   „   iii. ditto, concluded.
Includes three poems from *An Island in the Moon* (no. 2) printed for the first time.

441   SHARPE'S LONDON MAGAZINE. Vol. XXXI. N.S. London. [1867.]

Pp. 19-28. "Pictor Ignotus" (including a review of Gilchrist, 1863).

442   BROADWAY REVIEW. London. 1868.

Pp. 723-730. "Mr. Swinburne's Essay on Blake" (review).

443   FORTNIGHTLY REVIEW, The. Vol. III. New Series [IX]. London. 1868.

Pp. 216-220. "Swinburne's William Blake: A Critical Essay." By Moncure D. Conway (review).

444   RADICAL, The. Vol. III. Boston. 1868.

Pp. 378-382. "William Blake." By W. A. Cram.

445 LONDON QUARTERLY REVIEW, The. Vol. XXI. London. Jan., 1869.

Pp. 265-311. " Gilchrist's Life of William Blake." By James Smetham. (Reprinted in Gilchrist, 1880, and in Smetham's *Works*, 1893, no. 309.)

446 NORTH AMERICAN REVIEW, The. Vol. CVIII. Boston, Mass. 1869.

Pp. 641-646. Critical notices of Pickering's *Songs of Innocence and Experience* and *Poetical Sketches*, and of Hotten's *Marriage of Heaven and Hell*, 1868. [By C. E. Norton.]

447 HOURS AT HOME. Vol. XI. New York. May, 1870.

Pp. 55-65. " William Blake. Poet and Painter." [By E. P. Evans.]

448 ILLUSTRATED REVIEW, The. Vol. I, no. 13. London. April, 1871.

Pp. 435-437. " William Blake: a Critical Essay. By Charles Algernon " Swinburne" (review).

449 PORTFOLIO, The. Vol. II. London. 1871.

Pp. 103-105. " A Varley-and-Blake Sketch-Book." By W. B. Scott (illus.).
Pp. 138-143. " Children in Italian and English Design. Pt. II. Blake." By Sidney Colvin (illus.).

450 CHAMBERS'S JOURNAL. Fourth Series. London. 1872.

P. 326. In an unsigned essay on " Hallucinations " is an exaggerated description of Blake's method of making portraits from visions, and a statement that he was insane for thirty years. This was quoted in the *Cornhill*, 1875 (no. 456), and refuted by Samuel Palmer in the *Athenæum*, 1875 (no. 454).

451 OLD AND NEW MAGAZINE, The. Vol. VII. Boston, Mass. 1873.

Pp. 67-82. " William Blake, Painter and Poet." By Thomas M. Clark.

452 NEW QUARTERLY MAGAZINE, The. Vol. II. London. April, 1874.

Pp. 466-501. " William Blake: Artist, Poet, and Mystic." By the Editor [Oswald Crawfurd].

453 ACADEMY, The. Vol. 7. London. 1875.

Jan. 16, p. 66. "Blake's Etchings." By F. York Powell. [A note on Blake's Nebuchadnezzar in *The Marriage of Heaven and Hell*; the figure is stated to have been derived from pl. 146 in *The Bible Commentary*, Richard Blome, 1703, which was probably drawn by G. Freeman and engraved by a Dutch or Flemish artist.]

June 19, p. 636. "Blake's Songs of Innocence." By R. H. Shepherd. [A note on the Samuel Rogers copy.]

454 ATHENÆUM, The. No. 2498. London. 11 Sept., 1875.

Pp. 348-9. "Fictions Concerning William Blake." By Samuel Palmer. Denying a statement in the *Cornhill* (see no. 456) that Blake was insane for thirty years, with letters from John P. Wright and John Linnell, sen.

455 ATLANTIC MONTHLY, The. Vol. XXXV. Boston & New York. 1875.

Pp. 482-488. "William Blake" By T. S. Perry.

456 CORNHILL, The. Vol. 31-32. London 1875.

Vol. 31, pp. 721-736. "William Blake." By J. C[omyns] C[arr]. Describes several of the original designs for Young's *Night Thoughts*, with one woodcut illustration.

Vol. 32, pp. 167-8. In an essay "On Some Strange Mental Feats" is a quotation from another essay in *Chambers's Journal*, 1872 (no. 450) here ascribed to a Dr. Richardson, which contains erroneous statements about Blake's sanity; it was refuted by Samuel Palmer in the *Athenæum*, 1875 (no. 454).

457 NOTES AND QUERIES. 5 Series, IV. London. 1875.

Aug. 14, p. 129. A query re Blake's sanity. By O. C. (See also Oct. 16, p. 316.)

Dec. 4, pp. 449-450. "William Blake: Book of Thel." By W. Smith (a note on the Bodleian copy).

458 ACADEMY, The. Vol. 9. London. 1876.

March 11, p. 248. "Blake at the Burlington Club." By W. M. Rossetti.

April 15, pp. 364-5. "The Blake Catalogue [of the Burlington Exhibition]." By W. M. Rossetti.

April 22, p. 385. "The Blake Catalogue." By W. B. Scott.

459 BELGRAVIA. Vol. XXIX. London. May, 1876.

Pp. 366-379. "William Blake." By J. Comyns Carr. (Reprinted in *Essays on Art*, 1879, no. 283.)

460 CONTEMPORARY REVIEW, The. Vols. XXVIII-XXIX. London. 1876-1877.

Vol. xxviii, pp. 756-784.) "Imperfect Genius : William Blake." By H. G.
Vol. xxix, pp. 207-228. ∫ Hewlett.

461 ECHO. London. 1876.

"The Blake Exhibition" [reference from Berger's *William Blake*, 1915. Not verified].

462 ECLECTIC MAGAZINE, The. Vol. XXIII, New Series. New York. 1876.

P. 567. Reference to Blake in "Modern British Poetry," by W. M. Rossetti (from *Macmillan's Magazine*).

463 MACMILLAN'S MAGAZINE. Vol. XXXIV. London. May, 1876.

Pp. 55-68. "The Blake Drawings at the Burlington Fine Arts Club." By H. H. Statham.

464 PENN MONTHLY. Vol. VII. Philadelphia. 1876.

"Blake's Poems" [reference from Berger's *William Blake*, 1915. Not verified].

465 PORTFOLIO, The. Vol. VII. London. 1876.

Pp. 69-71. "Exhibition of Works of William Blake at the Burlington Fine Arts Club." By J. Beavington Atkinson.

466 SATURDAY REVIEW, The. Vol. XLI. London. April 15, 1876.

Pp. 492-3. "An Exploded Idol" (notice of Burlington Club Exhibition).

467 ATHENÆUM, The. No. 2597. London. Aug. 4, 1877.

P. 155. An adverse notice of Pearson's reproduction of *Jerusalem*. [Notices of Muir's reproductions appeared in the *Athenæum* as they were issued, see no. 489.]

468   SPECTATOR, The. Vol. 50. London. 1877.

Dec. 29, pp. 1660-1. "Etchings from Blake." (Review of W. B. Scott's *William Blake*.)

469   AMERICAN ARCHITECT, The. Vol. VIII. Boston, Mass. 1880.

"The Works of William Blake." By M. G. van Rensselaer [reference from Berger's *William Blake*, 1915. Not verified].

470   JOURNAL OF PSYCHOLOGICAL MEDICINE AND MENTAL PATHOLOGY. New Series. Vol. VI, part 1. London. 1880.

Pp. 40-46. "William Blake," in an article headed "Mad Artists." (This has been attributed to Dr. W. F. A. Browne, but it is unsigned.)

471   MIDLAND MAGAZINE, The. Birmingham. Sept.—Dec., 1880.

1. "William Blake, as Poet." ⎫ By Edward J. Shaw.
2. "William Blake, as Painter."⎭

472   NOTES AND QUERIES. 6 Series, II. London. July 24, 1880.

P. 77. "Gilchrist's Life of Blake." By Ralph Thomas.

473   SCRIBNER'S MONTHLY. Vol. XX. New York. 1880.

Pp. 225-240. "William Blake. Painter and Poet." By Horace E. Scudder (illus.).

474   ACADEMY, The. Vol. 19. London. 1881.

March 12, p. 196. A note on the purchase by Messrs. Colnaghi of the original plate of the *Canterbury Pilgrims*.
March 19, pp. 212-214. Review of Gilchrist's *Life of Blake* by John M. Gray.

475   ATHENÆUM, The. No. 2811. London. 10 Sept., 1881.

P. 345. "William Blake" (review of Gilchrist, 1880).

476   ATLANTIC MONTHLY, The. Vol. XLVII. Boston. 1881.

   Pp. 717-719. "The New Edition of Gilchrist's Blake."

477   BULLETIN OF THE BOSTON PUBLIC LIBRARY. Vol. IV, no. 10. Boston, Mass. April, 1881.

   P. 335. Bibliographical list of Blake's Works.

478   CRITIC, The. Vol. I. New York. 1881.

   P. 3. "William Blake. Poet and Painter." By E. C. Stedman. (Reprinted in *Essays from The Critic*, 1882, no. 288.) With portrait of Blake after Phillips, and reproduction of "Reunion of Soul and Body" from Blair's *Grave*.

479   LONDON QUARTERLY REVIEW, The. Vol. LVI. London. 1881.

   Pp. 249-255. "Gilchrist's Life of William Blake" (review).

480   MAGAZINE OF ART, The. Vol. IV. London. 1881.

   Pp. 478-481. "Artist and Wife." By John Oldcastle.

481   MODERN REVIEW, The. Vol. II. London. 1881.

   Pp. 565-577. "William Blake." By Charles Hargrove (review of Gilchrist, 1880).

482   NOTES AND QUERIES. 6 Series, III. London. 1881.

   Jan. 15, p. 59. Notice of Gilchrist's *Life of Blake*.
   March 5, p. 200. Note on Messrs. Colnaghi's purchase of the original plate of Blake's *Canterbury Pilgrims*.

483   SCRIBNER'S MONTHLY REVIEW. Vol. XXI. New York. April, 1881.

   Pp. 249-255. "Gilchrist's Life of William Blake" (review). By H. E. Scudder.

484 TEMPLE BAR. Vol. CVI. London. May, 1881.

Pp. 52-63. "William Blake." By Frederick Wedmore. (Reprinted in *Littell's Living Age*, vol. CXLIX, pp. 557-563, Boston, Mass., 1881, and in *The Eclectic Magazine*, New York, 1881.)

485 WESLEYAN METHODIST MAGAZINE, The. Vol. CIV. London. June, 1881.

Pp. 423-429. "William Blake, Poet and Painter." By the Rev. Jabez Marrat (review).

486 SPECTATOR, The. Vol. 55. London. 1882.

Oct. 21, pp. 1351-2. "Mr. Gilchrist's Blake" (review).

487 ATHENÆUM, The. No. 2948. London. April 26, 1884.

P. 536. "Places and Men." By William Allingham (verses in appreciation of Blake and Collins).

488 BUILDER, The. London. Oct. 18, 1884.

Notice of William Muir's facsimiles of Blake's works.

489 ATHENÆUM, The. London. 1886.

No. 3061, June 26, p. 849. Notice of Muir's reproductions of Blake's *Milton*, etc.
No. 3070, Aug. 28, p. 280. Notice of Muir's reproductions of *The Marriage of Heaven and Hell* and *Songs of Experience*.

490 CENTURY GUILD HOBBY HORSE, The. Vol. I. London. 1886.

1. Facing p. 121. "Little Tom the Sailor" [facsimile by William Muir].
2. Pp. 159-160. A note on the same by H. H. Gilchrist, together with letter no. 15.

491 TIMES, The. London. July 29, 1886.

Notice of William Muir's facsimiles of Blake's works.

492　CENTURY GUILD HOBBY HORSE, The. Vol. II. London. 1887.

　　1. P. 29. "The Life Mask of William Blake." By Herbert P. Horne (with photogravure reproduction).
　　2. Facing p. 112. *On Homer* [facsimile by William Muir].
　　3. Pp. 115-6. "Blake's Sibylline Leaf On Homer and Virgil." By Herbert P. Horne.
　　4. Pp. 135-157. *The Marriage of Heaven and Hell*, with an introductory note by the Editor [Herbert P. Horne].

493　NEW CHURCH MAGAZINE, The. Vol. VI. London. 1887.

　　Pp. 204-211. "Blake the Visionary." }
　　Pp. 253-259. "Blake, Artist and Poet." } By James Spilling.

494　SATURDAY REVIEW, The. Vol. 63. London. April 9, 1887.

　　Pp. 522-3. "William Blake" (a notice of Muir's facsimiles).

495　CENTURY GUILD HOBBY HORSE, The. Vol. III. London. 1888.

　　Facing p. 108. Facsimiles of three illustrations to the *Pastorals of Virgil*, by William Blake.

496　NOTES AND QUERIES. 7 Series, VIII. London. 1889.

　　Aug. 24, pp. 147-8. A query re Pickering's *Songs of Innocence and Experience*, 1866. (See also Sept. 14, p. 216.)

497　CENTURY GUILD HOBBY HORSE, The. Vol. V. London. 1890.

　　Pp. 82-9. *The Book of Los*, with an introduction by F. York Powell.

498　UNIVERSAL REVIEW, The. Vol. VI. London. Feb., 1890.

　　Pp. 209-222. "Blake as an Impressionist." By Laurence Housman (illus.).

499　ATHENÆUM, The. No. 3309. London. March 28, 1891.

　　Pp. 407-8. "William Blake." By W. M. Rossetti, giving in full the reference to Blake which occurs in Lady Charlotte Bury's *Diary* (see no. 255) ; it was here reprinted for the first time.

500 NOTES AND QUERIES. 7 Series, XI. London. 1891.

May 16, p. 386. A query re Blake's Holy Thursday. By C. C. Bell. (See also 7 S., xi, 1891, June 13, p. 475, and June 27, p. 514; 7 S., xii, 1891, July 18, p. 58; 8 S., ii, 1892, Sept. 10, p. 214; 8 S., ix, 1896, May 16, p. 394.)

501 SUN, The. Vol. IV. Paisley and London. 1891.

"William Blake, Poet, Painter, and Seer." By A. L. Salmon [reference from Berger's *William Blake*, 1915. Not verified].

502 BELGRAVIA. Vol. LXXVII. London. April, 1892.

Pp. 357-377. "William Blake." By Emilia Aylmer Gowing.

503 ACADEMY, The. Vol. 44. London. 1893.

Aug. 26, pp. 163-165. Review of EY by Lionel Johnson.

504 ART JOURNAL, The. Vol. XLV. London. 1893.

Pp. 43-4. "The Royal Academy Exhibition of Old Masters. William Blake "and his Disciples." By A. T. Story.

505 BOOKMAN, The. Vol. IV. London. August, 1893.

Pp. 146-7. "The Writings of William Blake." By W. B. Yeats (review of LH).

506 NATION, The. Vol. LVII. New York. 1893.

Pp. 376-7. "William Blake" (review of Story's *Life of Blake*). [By K. Cox.]

507 POET LORE. Vol. V. Boston, Mass. 1893.

Pp. 93-96. "A Prophecy of America [Blake's]. From the Correspondence of "—— —— and * * *."

Pp. 363-371. *America: A Prophecy* [By W. Blake]. The text printed from Muir's facsimile.

Pp. 481-488. "A Phase of William Blake's Romanticism." By Lucy Allen Paton.

508   REVIEW OF REVIEWS, The. Vol. VII. London. 1893.

    P. 197. Review of EY.

509   SATURDAY REVIEW, The. Vol. LXXV. London. 1893.

    P. 126. Review of EY.

510   BOOKMAN, The. Vol. VI. London. April, 1894.

    Pp. 22-3. " A New Blake " (notice of WBY).

511   CALIFORNIAN ILLUSTRATED MAGAZINE, The. Vol. IV. San Francisco. 1894.

    Article on William Blake. By J. V. Chesney [reference from Berger's *William Blake*, 1915. Not verified].

512   GENTLEMAN'S MAGAZINE, The. Vol. CCLXXVI. London. 1894.

    Pp. 429-431. "Table Talk: William Blake—Blake's Prophetic Books—"Blake's Lyrics."

513   NOTES AND QUERIES. 8 Series, V. London. Jan. 27, 1894.

    Pp. 79-80. Notice of WBY.

514   TEMPLE BAR. Vol. 106. London. December, 1895.

    Pp. 525-537. "William Blake." By Alfred T. Story. (Reprinted in *Littell's Living Age*, vol. 208, Boston, Mass., 1896, and in *The Eclectic Magazine*, vol. 126, New York, 1896.)

515   ART JOURNAL, The. New Series. London. 1896.

    P. 30. Notice of formation of Blake Society.
    Pp. 237-8. "William Wynne Ryland and Blake." By Ernest Radford.

516   BOOKMAN, The. Vol. X. London. April, 1896.

    P. 21. "William Blake." By W. B. Yeats (review of Garnett's *William Blake*, 1896).

517 DAILY CHRONICLE, The. London. 1896.

"Blake & Messrs W. H. Smith and Son." A letter from Dr. Richard Garnett on their refusal to supply *The Savoy*.

518 SAVOY, The. London. 1896.

"William Blake and his Illustrations to Dante." By W. B. Yeats.
  i. No. 3, pp. 41-57. His Opinions upon Art (with four illustrations after Blake).
  ii. No. 4, pp. 25-41. His Opinions on Dante (with four illustrations after Blake).
  iii. No. 5, pp. 31-36. The Illustrations of Dante (with two illustrations after Blake).
(Reprinted in Yeats's *Ideas of Good and Evil*, 1903 (no. 331), and in *Collected Works*, 1908, vol. VI.)

519 ACADEMY, The. Vol. 51. London. 1897.

June 19, pp. 634-5. "Academy Portraits. XXXII. William Blake." By W. B. Yeats. With portrait after Phillips.

520 NOTES AND QUERIES. 8 Series, XI. London. 1897.

April 17, pp. 302-3. Engravings attributed to William Blake. By Ralph Thomas. (See also 9 S., I, June 4, 1898; 10 S., v, Feb. 3, 1906, p. 86; 10 S., xi, April 10, 1909, p. 287.)

521 SEWANEE REVIEW, The. Vol. V. Sewanee, Tenn. 1897.

Pp. 328-348. "William Blake: Poet and Artist."
Pp. 438-456. "William Blake: Mystic." By William Norman Guthrie.
(Both reprinted in *The Vital Study of Literature*. Chicago, 1912.)

522 UNIVERSITY MAGAZINE AND FREE REVIEW, The. Vol. VIII. London. 1897.

Pp. 204-213. "William Blake and Modern Problems." By Edward Willmore.

523 CHRISTIAN GLOBE, The. London. April 20, 1899.

"William Blake. The Proposed Memorial."

524 HARVARD MONTHLY, The. Vol. 28. Cambridge, Mass. June, 1899.

Pp. 145-151. "The lyrics of William Blake." By Walter C. Arensberg.

525 LITERATURE. London. August 26, 1899.

Pp. 207-8. " William Blake." By M. R. Hoste.

526 DAILY TELEGRAPH, The. London. 1899.

" A Memorial to William Blake."

527 POET LORE. Vol. XI (Vol. III, New Series). Boston, Mass. 1899.

Pp. 25-28. " A Sheaf of Poetry and Prose by William Blake."

528 SUNDAY TIMES, The. London. September 24, 1899.

" The William Blake Memorial." By Mark Perugini.

529 CENTURY ILLUSTRATED MONTHLY MAGAZINE, The.   Vol. LX (Vol. XXXVIII, New Series). New York and London. 1900.

Pp. 284-291. " The Poetry of William Blake." By Henry Justin Smith (prize essay).

530 OUTLOOK, The. London. 23 June, 1900.

Pp. 845-6. " The Carfax Exhibition of Blake's Works." By T. Sturge Moore.

531 ACADEMY, The. Vol. 61. London. 1901.

July 6, pp. 15-16. " The Poetry of William Blake."

532 BRIXTONIAN, The. London. Jan. 11, 25, *et seq.* 1901.

" The Portraiture of William Blake." By Richard C. Jackson, F.S.A.

533 CURRENT LITERATURE. Vol. 32. New York. 1902.

" The Poetry of William Blake " [reference not verified].

534 GRAPHISCHEN KUNSTE, Die. Vol. XXV. Vienna. 1902.

Pp. 96-101. " William Blake und Edward Calvert."   By Laurence Binyon (illus.).

535 NOTES AND QUERIES. 9 Series, X. London. Nov. 8, 1902.

    Pp. 365-6. "Glowworms and Fireflies" (reference in Blake's "A Dream"). By C. Lawrence Ford.

536 ART JOURNAL, The. London. 1903.

    P. 114. "William Blake." A Sonnet by D. G. Rossetti to Frederic Shields on his sketch of Blake's work-room, 3 Fountain Court, Strand (with a reproduction of the sketch). From Rossetti's *Ballads and Sonnets*, 1881 (see no. 286).

    Pp. 114-118. "Some British Illustrators of the Bible. Blake's Illustrations of the Book of Job." By R. E. D. Sketchley (illus.).

537 ATHENÆUM, The. No. 3928. London. Feb. 7, 1903.

    P. 185. Notice of the sale of the Crewe Collection of Blake's works.

538 CRITIC, The. Vol. XLII. New York. 1903.

    Pp. 463-4. "Lord Crewe's Blake Collection." By Thomas Nutt (contains a reference to a MS. poem by Blake which is not recorded anywhere else. See no. 10).

539 MONTHLY REVIEW, The. Vol. XII. August, 1903.

    Pp. 123-129. "Blake's 'The Passions.'" By W. M. Rossetti. (First printed text of the MS. known as *The Passions*. See no. 1.)

540 MORNING LIGHT. Vol. XXVI. London. 1903.

    P. 109. A letter on Blake and Swedenborg from the Rev. J. G. Dufty.

    P. 119. A note by George Trobridge, containing the following passage: "Many "years ago I visited an exhibition of Blake's work at the Burlington Fine Arts Club. "On one of the sketches I noticed a 'list of books to be read,' and first on the list "was Swedenborg's *Worship and Love of God*." This sketch cannot now be identified, and Blake's "list of books" is not anywhere recorded. For other works by Swedenborg read by Blake see nos. 14 and 15.

541 NOTES AND QUERIES. 9 Series, XI. London. April 11, 1903.

    P 285. "The Crewe Collection." By B. C. A.

542 PLUME, La. Paris. 1903.

    Article by M. Stokoe [reference not verified].

543 ALLGEMEINES ZEITUNG, Supplement to the. 23 March 1904.

    "The Prophetic Books of William Blake." By H. von Keyserling.

544 ART JOURNAL, The. Vol. LVI. London. 1904.

    Pp. 349-350. "The Art of William Blake" (illus.).

545 ATHENÆUM, The. London. 1904.

    No. 3976, Jan. 9, p. 58. Notice of the Carfax Exhibition of Blake's works.
    No. 4004, July 23, pp. 102-3. Review of Maclagan and Russell's edition of Blake's *Jerusalem* [by Arthur Symons].
    No. 4020, Nov. 12, p. 664. Notice of Langridge's *William Blake*.

546 BURLINGTON MAGAZINE, The. Vol. IV. London. 1904.

    Pp. 204-211. "Three Pictures in Tempera by William Blake." By Roger Fry (with three reproductions. Reprinted in *Vision and Design*, 1920; no. 393).
    P. 298. "Discovery of the Missing Leaves of the Beaconsfield Blakes."

547 BURLINGTON MAGAZINE, The. Vol. VI. London. 1904-1905.

    P. 163. Notice of Langridge's *William Blake*.

548 DAILY CHRONICLE, The. London. 1904.

    "Blake the Prophet" (review).

549 INDEPENDENT REVIEW, The. Vol. II. London. April, 1904.

    Pp. 407-415. "The Art of Blake." By Laurence Binyon. (Reprinted in *Littell's Living Age*, vol. ccxli, Boston, Mass., 1904, and in *The Eclectic Magazine*, vol. cxliii, New York, 1904.)

550 NOTES AND QUERIES. 10 Series, II. London. Oct. 1, 1904.

    P. 278. Notice of Maclagan and Russell's *Jerusalem*.

551 SPEAKER, The. London. 8 October 1904.

    "Blake's Jerusalem." By A. Clutton-Brock.

552 CATHOLIC WORLD, The. Vol. 81. New York. 1905.

    "Was Blake a Poet?" By Percy C. Standing [reference from Berger's *William Blake*, 1915. Not verified].

553 COMMONWEALTH, The. Vol. X, no. 10. London. September, 1905.

    Pp. 270-274. "The Social Teaching of William Blake." By Helen M. Blagg.

554 CRITIC AND LITERARY WORLD, The. Vol. XLVI. New York. 1905.

    Pp. 214-216. "William Blake as an Illustrator." By Elisabeth Lúther Cary (illus.).

555 MONTHLY REVIEW, The. Vol. XXI. London. Nov., 1905.

    Pp. 123-129. "William Blake at Felpham." By Herbert Ives [Herbert Jenkins].

556 ACADEMY, The. Vols. 70-71. London. 1906.

    Vol. 70, June 23, pp. 600-1. "The Paintings of William Blake."
    Vol. 71, Sept. 29, pp. 307-309. "Swinblake: A Prophetic Book, with home "Zarathrusts." By Robert Ross.
    Vol. 71, Nov. 24, pp. 524-526. "A Literary Causerie. The Poetry of William "Blake." By A. Clutton-Brock.

557 ATHENÆUM, The. London. 1906.

    No. 4083, Jan. 27, pp. 100-102. Review of Sampson, 1905, and *Lyrical Poems*. [By Arthur Symons.]
    No. 4096, April 28, pp. 515-6. "The Family of William Blake." By Arthur Symons. These researches into Blake's antecedents were afterwards incorporated in the author's *William Blake*, 1907 (see no. 348).
    No. 4111, Aug. 11, pp. 149-150. Critical review of Swinburne's *William Blake*.
    No. 4125, Nov. 17, pp. 611-2. Review of Russell's *Letters of Blake*, and EJE. [By Arthur Symons.]
    No. 4216, Nov. 24, p. 659. A note on Frederick Tatham. By S. S.
    No. 4131, Dec. 29, p. 828. Notice of Robertson's edition of Gilchrist's *Life*.

558 BOOKMAN, The. Vol. XXX, no. 180. London. Sept., 1906.

Pp. 201-211. "William Blake." By Alfred Noyes (with two portraits of Blake, sixteen reproductions from his works, and two photographs of his dwelling places).

559 BURLINGTON MAGAZINE, The. Vol. IX. London. 1906.

Pp. 150-167. "The Place of William Blake in English Art." By Robert Ross (with six reproductions).

560 DAILY CHRONICLE, The. London. 1906.

Review of Sampson, 1905. By A. G. B. Russell.

561 EDINBURGH REVIEW, The. Vol. CCIII. London. Jan., 1906.

Pp. 161-179. "The Visionary Art of William Blake." By A. G. B. Russell.

562 INDEPENDENT REVIEW, The. Vol. IX. London. May, 1906.

Pp. 215-226. "The Poetry of Blake." By G. L. Strachey.

563 LIVERPOOL COURIER, The. Liverpool. Nov. 27, 1906.

"Liverpool and Blake." (Reprinted as a leaflet, pp. 4.)

564 NOTES AND QUERIES. 10 Series, V. London. 1906.

Jan. 13, p. 38. Notice of Sampson's *Lyrical Poems of Blake*.
　　　　p. 89. "William Blake and S. T. Coleridge." By B. Dobell (see also Feb. 17, p. 135).
Feb. 10, pp. 108-9. A query re Tatham's *Life of Blake*. By Charlotte Mowbray.

565 NOTES AND QUERIES. 10 Series, VI. London. 1906.

Sept. 22, p. 226. "Blake's Tiger." By W. B.
Sept. 29, p. 254. "Blake in Great Queen Street." By R. L. Moreton.
Nov. 17, pp. 398-9. Notice of Ellis's *Blake's Works*.
Dec. 1, pp. 421-2. "Blake's Songs: An Early Private Reprint." By John Sampson. (See also Dec. 15, p. 473; Dec. 29, p. 511; 10 S., VII, Jan. 19, 1907, p. 56.)

566 MANCHESTER GUARDIAN, The. 1 November 1906.

"William Blake" (unsigned).

567 OCCULT REVIEW, The. Vol. X. London. July, 1906.

Pp. 26-35. "William Blake." By E. J. Ellis (continued in nos. following).

568 SATURDAY REVIEW, The. Vol. 102. London. 1906.

Pp. 231-2 (Aug. 25). "Some Notes on Blake" (from the Cumberland Papers). By Arthur Symons. Gives other references to Blake supplementary to the letters printed by Dr. Garnett in the *Hampstead Annual*, 1902 (see no. 329).
Pp. 708-9 (Dec. 8). "William Blake" (reviews).

569 SPECTATOR, The. Vols. 96-97. London. 1906.

Vol. 96, Feb. 17, pp. 259-260. "The Text of Blake" (review of Sampson, 1905).
Vol. 97, Nov. 24, pp. 826-7. "William Blake" (reviews).

570 TRIBUNE, The. London. 6 November, 1906.

"Tatham's Life of Blake." By A. Clutton-Brock.

571 ATHENÆUM, The. London. 1907.

No. 4136, Feb. 2, pp. 139-140. Review of Binyon's edition of Blake's *Job*.
No. 4151, May 18, pp. 598-9. Review of Ellis's *Real Blake*.
No. 4161, July 27, pp. 89-90. Review of Berger's *William Blake*.
No. 4177, Nov. 16, p. 618. "Blake's 'Nest of Villain's' Unearthed." By Arthur Symons. This establishes the identity of R.H., Blake's critic in the *Examiner*, 1808 (see no. 399), with Robert Hunt, brother of Leigh Hunt.

572 BEILAGE DER NEWEN FREIEN PRESSE. Vienna. 27 January 1907.

"William Blakes Auferstehung." Von Stefan Zweig.

573 BIBBY'S ANNUAL. Liverpool. Summer 1907.

P. 12. "On Dreams." By A. G. B. Russell (with a reproduction in colours of Blake's "Vision of Jacob's Ladder").

574 BOOKLOVER'S MAGAZINE, The. Vol. VI. London. 1907.

Pp. 238-243. "Blake as a Book Illustrator." By Lewis Melville (illus.).

575 BURLINGTON MAGAZINE, The. Vol. X. London. 1907.

Pp. 290-293. " The Creation of Eve by William Blake " (illus.).

576 BURLINGTON MAGAZINE, The. Vol. XI. London. 1907.

Pp. 113-115. " Theory, or The Graphic Muse, engraved by Blake after " Reynolds." By Katharine A. McDowall (illus.).

577 CONNOISSEUR, The. Vol. XIX. London. 1907.

No. 74, Oct., pp. 92-96. " Mr. Butts, the Friend and Patron of Blake." By Ada E. Briggs (sister-in-law of Capt. Butts). With reproductions of engravings by Thomas Butts, jun., under Blake's teaching, etc.

578 CURRENT LITERATURE. Vol. 42-43. New York. 1907.

Vol. 42. " The Simple and Fantastic Genius of William Blake."
Vol. 43. " William Blake : Pontiff of a New Spiritual Dispensation " [references from Berger's *William Blake*, 1915. Not verified].

579 DAILY TELEGRAPH, The. London. 1907.

P. 423. Review of Symons' *William Blake*.

580 DEUTSCHEN ALMANACK VON DR. JULIUS ZEITLER FUR 1907. Leipzig.

" Ein Brief von William Blake, übersetzt von Stefan Zweig " [reference from Mr. S. Foster Damon. Not verified].

581 HUMANE REVIEW, The. Vol. VII. London. 1907.

Pp. 73-83. " Blake as Humanitarian." By Carl Heath.

582 LITERARISCHES ZENTRALBLATT FUR DEUTSCHLAND. 4 May, 1907.

Reviews by Helene Richter.

583 NATION, The. London. 26 October, 1907.

" Blake and the Imagination." By A. G. B. Russell (review).

584 NATION, The. Vol. LXXXV. New York. 1907.

   Pp. 286-7. Review of Symons's *William Blake*.
   P. 401. Review of Ellis's *Real Blake*.

585 OUTLOOK, The. Vol. 87. New York. 1907.

   Review of Symons's *William Blake* [reference not verified].

586 PUTNAM'S MONTHLY. Vol. III. New York. 1907-1908.

   Pp. 410-417. "Blake's Work as a Painter." By Laurence Binyon (illus.).

587 QUARTERLY REVIEW, The. Vol. 207. London. 1907.

   Pp. 455-457. Blake as poet and mystic, in "Mysticism in English Poetry." By Caroline F. E. Spurgeon.

588 SCRIP, The. Vols. 2-3. New York. 1907.

   "Notes on William Blake." By Elizabeth Luther Cary.
   1. Vol. 2, no. 9, pp. 273-283. The Manuscript Book.
   2. Vol. 2, no. 12, pp. 396-399. Blake's Water-colours in the Print Room of the Boston Museum of Fine Arts.
   3. Vol. 3, no. 1, pp. 1-15. Some Characteristics of his Design.
   4. Vol. 3, no. 3, pp. 69-79. His Literary Sympathies.

589 SPEAKER, The. London. 16 February, 1907.

   Pp. 585-6. "William Blake: His Critics and Interpreters." By R. A. Scott James.

590 WESTMINSTER GAZETTE, The. London. 12 November, 1907.

   Notice of Symons's *William Blake* by A. G. B. Russell.

591 ANNALS OF PSYCHICAL SCIENCE. London. 22 January, 1908.

   "William Blake." By Francois Benoit.

592 ATHENÆUM, The. No. 4219. London. Sept. 5, 1908.

   P. 267. Review of Maclagan and Russell's edition of Blake's *Milton* [by Arthur Symons].

593 BIBLIOPHILE, The. Vol. II, no. 8. London. October, 1908.

Pp. 86-89. "An Eighteenth Century Occult Magazine and a Query as to "William Blake." By Mark Perugini. (A note on an article in the *Conjuror's Magazine*, London, 1792, on p. 80 of which is "a list of the numbers and correspondent names "attributed to the planets"; these include 45 Zazel, 1225 Bne Seraphim, 260 Tiriel. The writer draws attention to the second and third of these, and suggests that they may have some relation to the first line of *Thel* and to the title of *Tiriel*. The name Zazel, which he does not notice, occurs frequently in the latter work.)

594 QUARTERLY REVIEW, The. Vol. 208. London. 1908.

Pp. 24-53. "William Blake." By T. Sturge Moore.

595 REVUE DE L'ART ANCIEN ET MODERNE, La. Paris. 10 March, 1908.

Pp. 219-236. "Un Peintre-Poète Visionaire. William Blake." Par Paul Alfarsa (a suivre).

596 SAINT GEORGE. Vol. XI. London. 1908.

Pp. 1-31. "The Sanity of William Blake." By Greville Macdonald, M.D. (Reprinted as a separate work. See no. 350.)

597 BIBLIOPHILE, The. Vol. III, no. 14. London. April, 1909.

Pp. 91-98. "The Most Perfect Wife on Record, Catherine Blake." By Herbert Ives [Jenkins] (illus.).

598 BURLINGTON MAGAZINE, The. Vol. XVI. London. 1909-1910.

Pp. 84-87. "A Recent Criticism of Blake." By Robert Ross (review of de Sélincourt's *William Blake*).

599 DIAL, The. Vol. XLV. Chicago. 1909.

Pp. 34-36. "William Blake — Poet, Artist, and Man." By Frederick W. Gookin.

600 MORNING LIGHT. Vol. XXXII. London. 1909.

P. 444. "The Real Blake." Review by C. G. C[avit].

601 QUARTERLY REVIEW, The. Vol. 211. London. 1909.

Pp. 415-417. Blake's illustrations to Dante, in "Illustrators of Dante." By Paget Toynbee. With reproductions of two of Blake's engravings.

602 VITA D'ARTE. No. 23. Siena. November, 1909.

"Un Poeta Pittore : William Blake" (with illustrations reproduced from Young's *Night Thoughts*). By Piero Misciatelli. (Also reprinted separately. See no. 356.)

603 BEAU, The, on the Science of Pleasure. Vol. I, no. 2. Nov., 1910.

Pp. 78-85. *The Marriage of Heaven and Hell.* By W. Blake (lacks the Song of Liberty).

604 CAMBRIDGE REVIEW, The. Cambridge. Dec. 1, 1910.

Pp. 169-170. Reviews of Wicksteed's *Blake's Job* and Chesterton's *William Blake*. By G. L. K[eynes].

605 CURRENT LITERATURE. Vol. 49. New York. 1910.

"Vital Import of Esthetics as Illustrated by Flaubert and Blake" [reference from Berger's *William Blake*, 1915. Not verified].

606 FORTNIGHTLY REVIEW, The. Vol. LXXXVII, N.S. London. Jan.-June, 1910.

Pp. 569-574. "William Blake as a Teacher." By Herbert Jenkins.

607 NATION, The. London. Dec. 17, 1910.

Pp. 506-7. "Blake Read and Misread" (review).

608 NINETEENTH CENTURY, The. Vol. LXVII. London. May, 1910.

Pp. 849-861. "The Trial of William Blake for High Treason." By Herbert Ives [Herbert Jenkins]. (Prints the Indictment and Acquittal. See no. 319.)

609   NOTES AND QUERIES. 11 Series, II. London. Sept. 24, 1910.

> Pp. 241-2. "William Blake's Laughing Song: A New Version." By G. L. Keynes.

610   CAMBRIDGE REVIEW, The. Cambridge. Oct. 19, 1911.

> P. 40. Review of *The Marriage of Heaven and Hell*. Ed. Stokes. [By Cosmo Gordon.]

610A NATION, The. Vol. 93. New York. 1911.

> P. 240. "An Allusion to Blake." By Thurman Los Hood (suggesting that a poem by Robert Browning may be a burlesque of Blake's *Milton*).

611   NINETEENTH CENTURY, The. Vol. LXX. London. July, 1911.

> Pp. 163-169. "The Grave of William Blake." By Herbert Jenkins.

612   QUEST, The. Vol. III. London. Oct., 1911.

> Pp. 81-99. "The So-called 'Madness' of William Blake." By J. H. Wicksteed, M.A.

613   TIMES, The. London. July 6, 1911.

> "Blake's Grave." A letter, suggesting the exhumation of Blake's remains and their transference to Westminster Abbey, from Sir William Blake Richmond.

614   TIMES LITERARY SUPPLEMENT, The. London. July 6, 1911.

> Pp. 249-250. "Blake as an Artist" (review).

615   VINEYARD, The. Nos. 8-9. London. May-June, 1911.

> "William Blake: his Critics and his Masters." By Greville Macdonald, M.D.
> Pp. 558-571. i. "His Critics" (an examination of Swinburne's interpretations).
> Pp. 626-642. ii. "His Masters" (Blake's relation to contemporary mystics and philosophers).

616 GAZETTE DES BEAUX-ARTS, La. Paris. Fevrier 1912.

Pp. 113-130. "William Blake." By Jeanne Doin.

617 HAMPSTEAD AND HIGHGATE EXPRESS, The. London. Aug. 17, 1912.

"Blake Society at Hampstead," and "Hampstead in the time of Blake." By Walker K. Jealous. (Reprinted in *The First Meeting of the Blake Society*, Olney, 1912, see no. 375).

618 QUEST, The. Vol. III. April 1912.

Pp. 422-442. "The Method of William Blake." By J. H. Wicksteed, M.A.

619 OCCULT REVIEW, The. Vol. XVI. London. Nov., 1912.

Pp. 266-269. "Was Blake ever in Bedlam? A Strange Discovery." By William T. Horton. (See no. 411.)

620 TIMES, The. London. 1912.

Aug. 13. "The Blake Society." An account of the first meeting.
Sept. 6. "A Blake Museum for London." A letter from Thomas Wright.
Dec. 12. "The Engravings of William Blake."

621 VINEYARD, The. Third Year, no. 2. Nov., 1912.

Pp. 98-110. "William Blake, the Practical Idealist." By Greville Macdonald, M.D. (The introductory paper read before the inaugural meeting of the Blake Society, Aug. 12, 1912.)

622 ATHENÆUM, The. London. 1913.

No. 4448, Jan. 25, p. 105. Reviews of Russell's *Engravings of William Blake*, and F. H. Evans's edition of Blake's *Illustrations to Thornton's Virgil*.
No. 4487, Oct. 25, p. 462. "Blake at the Tate Gallery."
No. 4494, Dec. 13, p. 705. Account of a meeting of the William Blake Society of Art and Letters.

623 BURLINGTON MAGAZINE, The. Vol. XXIV. London. 1913-1914.

Pp. 184-5. "Blake's ' Riposo ': a Note" (with reproduction).

624 DAILY TELEGRAPH, The. London. 1913.

"Blake at the Tate Gallery." By Claude Phillips.

625 HARVARD MUSICAL REVIEW, The. Vol. 2. Cambridge, Mass. Dec., 1913.

Pp. 3-8, 28-9. "The Unwritten Music of a Great Man." By S. Foster Damon (illustrated with four reproductions of Blake's designs).

626 NATION, The. Vol. XCVII. New York. 1913.

Pp. 573-4. "William Blake at the Tate Gallery." By N. N.

627 NOTES AND QUERIES. 11 Series, VII. London. May 31, 1913.

P. 425. "Blake and his Friend Butts." A query by M. L. R. Breslar. (See also 11 S., VII, June 21, 1913, p. 492, and 11 S., VIII, July 12, 1913, p. 35.)

628 TIMES, The. London. Oct. 16, 1913.

P. 12. "William Blake. Exhibition at the Tate Gallery."

629 BOGNOR OBSERVER, The, and West Sussex Recorder. Bognor. 27 May, 1914.

"Felpham and the poet-painter Blake." (The thirty-fourth meeting of the William Blake Society of Arts and Letters.)

630 BURLINGTON MAGAZINE, The. Vol. XXVI. London. 1914-1915.

Pp. 138-140. "William Blake's Nelson." By M. A. (with reproduction of Blake's "Spiritual Form of Nelson guiding Leviathan").

631 LIBRARY, The. Third Series. Vol. V. London. 1914.

Pp. 229-256. "An Early Appreciation of William Blake." By K. A. Esdaile. (Includes an annotated translation of Crabb Robinson's article in the *Vaterländisches Museum*, 1811; see no. 401.)

632 SHIRAKABA REVIEW, The. Vol. V, no. 4. Tokyo. April, 1914.

> Pp. 1-137. "William Blake." By M. Yanagi (with eighteen illustrations).
> Pp. 462-471. "Notes on William Blake." By B. Leach.
> The first article is printed in Japanese with quotations in English; it concludes with a series of parallel passages from Blake and Walt Whitman. The second article is printed in English.

633 SPECTATOR, The. London. 4 April, 1914.

> P. 567. "The Poetry of Blake" (review of Sampson, 1913).

634 TIMES LITERARY SUPPLEMENT, The. London. Feb. 5, 1914.

> P. 61. "Blake's French Revolution" (review of Sampson, 1913).

635 ATHENÆUM, The. No. 4557. London. Feb. 27, 1915.

> P. 186. Review of Conner's translation of Berger's *William Blake* (original edition reviewed in the *Athenæum*, July, 1907; see no. 571).

636 JOURNAL OF MENTAL SCIENCE, The. Vol. LXI, no. 253. London. April, 1915.

> Pp. 198-244. "William Blake." By Hubert J. Norman, M.B., Ch.B., D.P.H. Edin. (With a portrait of Blake after Phillips, and a list of references. Blake's supposed residence in Bethlem is discussed on p. 226.)

637 LAND AND WATER. London. October 2, 1915.

> P. 15. "Blake's Songs of Battle." By Anna Bunston.

638 NORTH AMERICAN REVIEW, The. Vol. 202. New York. 1915.

> Pp. 576-591. "William Blake and Catherine." By Margaret Sherwood.

639 NOTES AND QUERIES. 11 Series, XI. London. 1915.

> Feb. 27, p. 179. Review of Morris's *Flaxman, Blake, Coleridge*, etc. (no. 380), by Charles Higham. (Reprinted in *Morning Light*, vol. 38, 1915, p. 92.)
> April 10, pp. 276-7. "Blake and the Swedenborgians." By Charles Higham. (Reprinted in *Morning Light*, vol. 38, 1915, p. 168.)

640 PRINT-COLLECTOR'S QUARTERLY, The. Vol. 5, no. 1. Boston. Feb., 1915.

Pp. 38-58. "William Blake, and his Water-color Drawings in the Museum of Fine Arts, Boston." By Elisabeth Luther Carey (with eleven reproductions).

641 STANDARD, The. London. March 9, 1915.

"William Blake. The Poet of Mystery and Simplicity" (review of Berger's *William Blake*, translated by Conner).

642 POETRY REVIEW, The. Vol. VII. London. Jan. to Dec., 1916.

1. Pp. 125-132. "An Analysis of Blake's Attitude to War." By A. K. C.
2. Pp. 317-8. "The Mystical Note in Poetry." By Theodore Maynard (references to Blake).

643 TIMES LITERARY SUPPLEMENT, The. London. April 6, 1916.

"Blake and Religion" (review of Gardner's *Vision and Vesture*).

644 LONDON QUARTERLY REVIEW, The. Vol. XIII. London. 1917.

Pp. 215-226. "Imagination and William Blake." By S. E. Keeble.

645 NEW CHURCH WEEKLY, The. Vol. XL. London. 1917.

P. 413. "Swedenborg and Blake." By Charles Higham.

646 PRINT-COLLECTOR'S QUARTERLY, The. Vol. VII, no. 4. Boston. Dec., 1917.

Pp. 305-332. "The Engravings of William Blake and Edward Calvert." By Laurence Binyon (with fifteen reproductions).

647 SHIRAKABA REVIEW, The. Vol. VIII, no. 4. Tokyo. April, 1917.

P. 226. Short explanatory notes by M. Yanagi of ten illustrations from Blake (one in colours).

648 TIMES LITERARY SUPPLEMENT, The. London. Nov. 22, 1917.

"Blake and Hayley" (review of reprint of *Little Tom the Sailor*).

649 YALE REVIEW, The. N.S. Vol. VI. New Haven. 1917.

P. 397. " William Blake." Poem by Miss Amy Lowell. (Reprinted in *Pictures of the Floating World*, 1919; see no. 388.)

650 ARTS & DECORATION. New York. January, 1918.

Pp. 100-105, 130. "An Unknown Collection of Portraits by William Blake; " the Genius of the Pre-Raphaelite Movement." By J. E. Robinson. (Describing a collection of portraits and MSS., supposed to be by Blake, in the possession of Dr. J. W. Bartlett of New York; with twelve reproductions which show conclusively that Blake cannot be their author.)

651 CATHOLIC EDUCATIONAL REVIEW, The. Vol. XV. Washington. 1918.

Pp. 306-308. "Francis Thomson and Blake." By Florence Moynihan.

652 COUNTRY LIFE. Vol. XLIII. London. 1918.

1. P. 172, Feb. 16. "An Imaginary Portrait by William Blake." A letter from F. W. Bourdillon, drawing attention to the likeness between the German Emperor and one of the devils in pl. 2 of Blake's *Illustrations of Dante* (no. 56); with reproductions of the engraving.

2. P. 199, Feb. 23. "Blake's Prophetic Portrait." A letter from F. Carruthers Gould, with a sketch of two of the other figures in Blake's engraving adapted to represent the German Crown Prince and Admiral von Tirpitz.

3. Pp. 249-252, March 9. "William Blake: For few or all?" By Frank Rinder (with eight reproductions in half-tone).

653 GRAPHIC, The. London. April 27, 1918.

P. 524. "William Blake A Portrait Painter" (a note on the article in *Arts & Decoration*, no. 650, with seven reproductions).

654 NEW CHURCH WEEKLY, The. Vol. XLI. London. 1918.

P. 73. "Swedenborg annotated by Blake." By Charles Higham.

655 SOCIALIST REVIEW, The. Vol. XV. London. 1918.

Pp. 359-364. "William Blake as Lyric Poet and Humanist." By Samuel J. Looker.

656 TIMES LITERARY SUPPLEMENT, The. London. Nov. 28, 1918.

"William Blake's House at Lambeth." A letter concerning its demolition from Alfred G. Hopkins.

657 HIBBERT JOURNAL, The. Vol. XVII, no. 4. London. July, 1919.

Pp. 660-671. "The Ethics of William Blake." By the Rev. Richard Roberts.

658 PUBLISHERS' WEEKLY, The. London. Dec. 20, 1919.

P. 1611. "An exhibition of the works of William Blake" (at the Grolier Club, New York).

659 QUEST, The. Vol. XI. London. 1919.

Pp. 69-82. "Blake and Swedenborg." By H. N. Morris. (An address given before the Blake Society, Sept. 11, 1917.)

660 SHIRAKABA REVIEW, The. Vol. X, no. 11. Tokyo. Nov., 1919.

P. 180. Short explanatory notes by M. Yanagi of six illustrations from Blake.

661 SPHERE, The. Vol. 77, no. 1013. London. June 21, 1919.

P. vi. "Blake, by Himself." Reproduction of a newly discovered drawing believed to be Blake, as a young man, by himself. The drawing is probably by Barry.

662 TIMES LITERARY SUPPLEMENT, The. London. October, 1919.

Oct. 9, 16, 23, and 30. "A Textual Point in Blake." Letters from H. J. C. Grierson, John Sampson, Geoffrey Keynes, G.B., and T. J. Wise concerning a reading in Blake's Mad Song. See also no. 666.
Oct. 23. "A Religious Blake" (review of Gardner's *William Blake the Man*).

663 TIMES, The. London. November, 1919.

Nov. 4. "Blake's Designs for Gray. Discovery in Hamilton Palace." A letter, with a description of Blake's volume, from Prof. H. J. C. Grierson. Contains the first printed text of Blake's lines "To Mrs. Anna Flaxman" and couplet, "Around the "Springs of Gray . . ."
Nov. 5. "Blake's Designs for Gray. Light on their history." (From a correspondent).

664　BURLINGTON MAGAZINE, The. Vol. XXXVII. London. 1920.

　　No. 208, July, pp. 27-39. "The Graham Robertson Collection." By Archibald G. B. Russell, Rouge Croix (with a catalogue of the paintings and drawings by Blake contained in the collection, and six reproductions in half-tone).

　　No. 213, Dec., pp. 284-5. "Blake's Woodcuts." By Laurence Binyon (with reproductions of prints from the blocks before and after they were cut down).

665　LONDON MERCURY, The. London. 1920.

　　Vol. I, no. 3, pp. 283-290. "On Blake as a Prophet." By A. Clutton-Brock.

　　Vol. III, no. 14, pp. 156-165. "Swinburne and Kirkup." By Edmund Gosse, C.B. (containing references to Blake).

666　TIMES LITERARY SUPPLEMENT, The. London. 1920.

　　Feb. 12. "A Textual Point in Blake." Letter from Geoffrey Keynes concerning lines in the *Poetical Sketches*. See also no. 662.

　　July 15, p. 460. A note on Dibdin's reference to D'Israeli's collection of Blake's works (see no. 254).

V. MISCELLANEOUS

BIBLIOGRAPHICAL PREFACE

IN this final section are collected the few volumes which did not seem to fit easily into any position earlier in the book. The Exhibition Catalogues recorded here do not represent every exhibition of Blake's works that has been held, for some of which a catalogue has not been printed. They do, however, include most of the exhibitions which were devoted entirely to Blake's art, together with a few containing smaller collections of his works. More of these exhibitions have been held in London than elsewhere, beginning in 1876 with the exhibition at the Burlington Fine Arts Club, where Blake was for the first time since 1809 presented to the public view, and culminating in the magnificent collection shown at the Tate Gallery in 1913. Exhibitions have also been held at Birmingham, Manchester, and Edinburgh. Two exhibitions were held at Boston in 1880 and 1891, and two very fine collections, which were greatly enriched by Mr. W. A. White's copies of the Illuminated Books, were shown at the premises of the Grolier Club in New York in 1905 and 1919. An exhibition of Blake's designs was held at Tokyo in 1919, but this consisted entirely of reproductions.

Only three sale catalogues are included here, since Blake's works have usually been offered for sale singly or in small collections, which have been incidentally mentioned in the earlier pages of this book. The dispersal of the collections formed by Thomas Butts, John Linnell, and Richard Monckton-Milnes were, however, events of enough importance to warrant their being recorded among the entries following.

In a previous section, pp. 49-55, have already been described those of Blake's books which gain an additional value by having his annotations on their pages. The present section is concluded by a series of eleven entries describing books which show evidence of having been at one time in his possession, but contain usually nothing more than his signature. These books have the interest of their associations, and at the same time give some indications of what were Blake's interests in literature; they may also be of help in the elucidation of references in his writings. Blake no doubt possessed at different times of his life many other books in addition to those here described, but some of these may have been destroyed, and others may never have contained the signature or annotations by which alone they may be identified. It remains for a future bibliographer to render this list more complete.

A. EXHIBITION CATALOGUES

667 Burlington Fine Arts Club Exhibition of the Works of William Blake . . . 1876 27.5 cm., pp. 71 + [1].

> *Note*: The introductory remarks (pp. 3-11) are by W. B. Scott. 333 items were exhibited.

668 Boston Museum of Fine Arts Print Department. Catalogue of an Exhibition of Drawings, Water Colors, and Engravings by William Blake . . . Boston . . . 1880. 8° pp. 24.

> *Note*: See Gilchrist, ii, 276, and *Bibliography of Books on Engraving*, by H. C. Levis, London, 1912. The writer has not seen a copy of this catalogue.

669 Museum of Fine Arts Print Department Exhibition of Books, Water Colors, Engravings, etc. by William Blake. February 7 to March 15, 1891 Boston: Printed for the Museum . . . 1891 8° pp. iv + [ii] + 53 + [1].

> *Note*: 147 items were exhibited. A short bibliography is given at the end.

670 Catalogue of the Second Loan Exhibition of Pictures, Sculpture, etc., in the Art Gallery and Museum, . . . Walsall, . . . 1893 . . . 16° pp. 32

> *Note*: On pp. 21-32 is a catalogue of an exhibition of 77 items connected with Blake lent by Mr. E. J. Shaw, who also wrote the introductory note on Blake (pp. 22-24).

671 Exhibition of Works by the Old Masters and by Deceased Members of the British School; including a collection of Water Colour Drawings, &c., by William Blake, Frederick Calvert, Samuel Palmer, . . . Winter Exhibition . . . MDCCCXCIII. London . . . the Royal Academy 8° pp. 59 + [1].

> *Note*: Pp. 41-45. Water-colour drawings, nos. 1-29, by W. Blake, consisting of part of the series of illustrations to Dante's *Inferno*, lent by the Linnell family.

672 Exhibition of Works by the Old Masters and by Deceased Members of the British School; including special collections of the works of Thomas Stothard, R.A., of William Blake, and of John Pettie, R.A. Winter Exhibition . . . MDCCCXCIV. London . . . the Royal Academy 8° pp. 68.

Note: Pp. 62-64. Water-colour drawings, nos. 47-67, by W. Blake, consisting of the replica set of illustrations for the *Book of Job*, lent by the Linnell family.

673 Exhibition of Works by William Blake January 1904 . . . Carfax & Co., Ltd. 17 Ryder Street. S. James's Price one shilling. 8° pp. [ii] + 8 + [ii].

Note: The introductory note, "The Art of William Blake," is by A. G. B. Russell. 41 items were exhibited.

674 Catalogue of Books, Engravings Water-colors & Sketches by William Blake Exhibited at the Grolier Club from January 26 to February 25 MCMV 17.5 cm., pp. xvii + [iii] + 147 + [1].

Note: 148 items were exhibited, including the whole of Mr. W. A. White's collection of the Illuminated Books.

675 Carfax Exhibition of Works by William Blake . . . 14 June to 31 July 1906 Carfax & Co., Ltd. 24 Bury St., St. James's, London, S.W. Price one shilling 24.5 cm., pp. 40.

Note: 80 items were exhibited. In an appendix (pp. 25-40) are given extensive quotations from Blake's *Descriptive Catalogue*.

676 The National Gallery, British Art. Catalogue of Loan Exhibition of Works by William Blake. October to December, 1913. London: Printed under the authority of His Majesty's Stationery Office, . . . 1913. Price sixpence. 20.5 cm., pp. 75 + [1].

Note: 144 items were exhibited, including many from the Linnell collection which had not been exhibited before. The catalogue was compiled by Mr. A. G. B. Russell, who also contributed an account of Blake as painter and engraver. A second edition was issued in 1913.

677 The Manchester Whitworth Institute. Catalogue of a Loan Collection of Works by William Blake. February to March, 1914. London: . . . 1914. Price sixpence. 20 cm., pp. 92.

Note: 208 items were exhibited. The collection was for the most part the same as was exhibited at the Tate Gallery in 1913 (see no. 676), but with a number of additions; the greater part of the previous catalogue was reprinted.

678 National Gallery of Scotland Catalogue of Loan Exhibition of Works by William Blake and David Scott May 22nd to July 4th, 1914 Edinburgh: . . . [1914] Price 3d. 20 cm., pp. 32.

Note: 140 of the exhibits were by Blake, from the same collection as had already been exhibited in London and Manchester, the remainder by David Scott. Mr. Russell's account of Blake is reprinted, but the annotations are abridged.

679 An Annotated Catalogue of an Exhibition of the Reproductions from the Works of William Blake at the Russian Gallery Tokyo Nov. 7-11, 1919, and The Imperial University Y.M.C.A. Hall, Kyoto, Nov. 18-22, 1919. The Shirakaba Society, Tokyo, Japan. 19 cm., pp. [iv] + xxii.

Note: With three reproductions, one in colours. The above translation of the title-page was supplied by Mr. M. Yanagi, the author of the annotations. Seventy-four reproductions were exhibited.

680 William Blake An Exhibition The Grolier Club New York MCMXIX 18 cm., pp. viii + 12.

Note: In printed wrappers, on the front of which is a reproduction of pl. 5 from *For the Sexes, the Gates of Paradise*. The catalogue contains 58 items; several copies of most of the illuminated books were exhibited. At the end is a note on the arrangement of the plates of *There is No Natural Religion*.

B. *SALE CATALOGUES*

681 Catalogue of a Choice Selection of the Original Productions of William Blake the property of the Rt. Hon. the Earl of Crewe, . . . Which will be sold by auction, by Messrs. Sotheby, Wilkinson & Hodge, . . . at their House, No. 13, Wellington Street, Strand, W.C. On Monday, the 30th day of March 1903 . . . 25.5 cm., pp. [ii] + 4.

Note: The 18 lots included copies of most of the Illuminated Books, the Butts set of the original designs for the *Book of Job* (£5,600), and the set of twelve designs for *L'allegro* and *Il Penseroso* (£1,960). The collection here dispersed had been formed by Richard Monckton-Milnes, first Lord Houghton.

682 Catalogue of Drawings by William Blake, the property of Captain Butts, Grandson of Thomas Butts, Muster Master General, the Friend and Patron of Blake. Which will be sold by auction by Messrs. Sotheby, Wilkinson & Hodge, . . . at their House, No. 13, Wellington Street, Strand, W.C. On Wednesday; the 24th day of June, 1903, . . . 25.5 cm., pp. 8.

Note: The 42 lots consist of 23 from the Butts collection, 18 from the collection of Alexander Gilchrist, and one from another property. The majority of the books, paintings, and drawings which formed the Butts collection had already been dispersed at auction fifty years earlier; for these see the catalogues issued by Sotheby, March 26-27, 1852, and by Foster, Pall Mall, June 29, 1853.

683 Catalogue of the John Linnell Collection of highly important works by William Blake Obtained direct from the Artist . . . The Remaining Pictures & Drawings by John Linnell, Senr. and Pictures by Old Masters which . . . Will be Sold by Auction by Messrs. Christie, Manson & Woods .. at . . . 8 King Street, St. James's Square London on Friday, March 15, 1918 . . . 25 cm., pp. 30 + [2].

Note: Works by Blake were catalogued in 68 lots (148-215), which included the designs for the *Divina Comedia* (7,300 gns.), designs for the *Book of Job* (3,800 gns.), designs for *Paradise Regained* (2,100 gns.), *The French Revolution* 1791 (125 gns.), and *Vala* (400 gns.).

684   Reflections on the Painting and Sculpture of The Greeks: with Instructions for the Connoisseur, and An Essay on Grace in Works of Art. Translated from The German Original of the Abbé Winkelmann, . . . By Henry Fusseli, A.M. [vignette] London: Printed for the Translator, and Sold by A. Millar, in the Strand. 1765. 8°

    Description: Bound in contemporary calf. On the fly-leaf is the inscription:

    Note: Blake worked with Basire, the engraver, in Great Queen Street, Lincoln's Inn Fields, from 1771 to 1778, and this book was no doubt in his possession at that time. He probably did not become acquainted with Fuseli until about 1780.

    This volume is now in my own library. I obtained it from Mr. P. J. Dobell in 1914. I do not know of any other example of Blake's signature belonging to the period before 1778, but this signature closely resembles those of later dates.

685   The Tragedies of Æschylus, translated by R. Potter. Second edition. London. W. Strahan and T. Cadell. 1779. 2 vols. 8°

    Description: In original boards, uncut. On the half-title of each volume is the autograph signature of "William Blake." Inside the cover is the inscription "Samuel Palmer, 1833."

Note: Inserted in vol. 1 is a note by F. G. Stephens as follows: "Given me, "July 15, 1890, by Herbert Palmer, son of Samuel Palmer, containing the autographs "of William Blake and Samuel Palmer, to whom they belonged." The volumes were sold at Sotheby's, June 17, 1918 (£11). They were offered by Mr. Tregaskis in Oct. 1919 (cat. 819, £20).

686   Poems, supposed to have been written at Bristol, by Thomas Rowley, and others, in the Fifteenth Century. [By Thomas Chatterton] The Third Edition; . . . London: Printed for T. Payne and Son, at the Mews-Gate. MDCCLXXVIII. 8°

Description: In original boards, uncut. At the top of the title-page is the autograph of "William Blake" in ink. Inside the cover is the autograph of "Samuel Palmer" in pencil.

Note: Sold at Sotheby's. Now in the possession of Mr. Sydney Cockerell, Director of the Fitzwilliam Museum, Cambridge. Chatterton is referred to in chapters V and VII of *An Island in the Moon* (no. 2).

687   An Account of a Series of Pictures in the Great Room of the Society of Arts, Manufactures, and Commerce, at the Adelphi. By James Barry, R.A. . . . London: Printed for the Author, . . . MDCCLXXXIII 8°

Description: In original wrappers, uncut. Presumably Blake's copy, since it contains a drawing by him of Barry.

Note: This volume belonged to the late H. Buxton Forman, C.B., who has inserted a note (3 pp.) on Barry and Blake. It was sold with the Buxton Forman Library at the Anderson Galleries, New York, March 15, 1920 (lot 36). Gilchrist (i, 48) writes: "This was the year, too, in which Barry published his *Account* "of the *Pictures in the Adelphi*. On one copy I have seen a characteristic pencil "recollection, from Blake's hand, of the strange Irishman's ill-favoured face: that "of an idealized bulldog, with villainously low forehead, turn-up nose, and squalid "*tout-ensemble*." He does not record who was then the owner of the book.

Blake's annotations to Reynolds's *Discourses* (see no. 18) contain references to Barry, who, he considered, was "equal to Raphael or Michael Angelo or any of the Italians" (Gilchrist, i, 306). The *Rossetti MS.* contains passages from a work by Blake, called *Barry: a Poem*, but this has not survived (see no. 66).

A three-quarter length pencil drawing of Blake by Barry is in the collection of Mr. E. J. Shaw of Walsall; this has never been reproduced.

688 A Catalogue of the Royal and Noble Authors of England, with Lists of their Works. [By Horace Walpole] In Two Volumes . . . A New Edition, . . . Edinburgh: . . . 1792 2 vols. 8°

Description: Bound in contemporary calf. The autograph of William Blake is on the fly-leaf of each volume, that in vol. 1 being dated 1795.

These volumes are in the library of the late H. E. Widener of Philadelphia (see *A Catalogue of the Library of Harry Elkins Widener, Philadelphia*, 1910); this library was bequeathed to Harvard University in 1912.

689 The Complaint; or, Night Thoughts . . . By Edward Young, LL.D. . . . London: . . . MDCCXCVI. 8°

Description: On the fly-leaf is the autograph of William Blake.

Note: This volume was offered in a bookseller's catalogue some years ago, together with the edition of the *Night Thoughts* illustrated by Blake, for 10 guineas. I do not know its present whereabouts.

690 Sonnets, and Other Poems, by the Reverend W. L. Bowles, A.M. of Trinity-College, Oxford. Sixth Edition. To which is added Hope, an allegorical sketch on recovering slowly from sickness . . . Printed for C. Dilly, Poultry, and T. Cadell, jun. . . . London . . . M DCC XCVIII. 8°

Description: Bound in contemporary tree calf. The autograph of " William Blake " is on the half-title. At the top of the title is the inscription: " Jeremiah " & M. E. Awdry, Dec^{br} 29, 1799."

Note: Bought by Mr. Everard Meynell in 1914, and now in my own possession.

691 Ballads, by William Hayley, Esq. . . . with Prints, . . . By William Blake. Chichester: . . . 1805. [see no. 74]

Description: Bound in contemporary marbled calf, with marbled end-papers. On the fly-leaf is written in Blake's autograph in ink: " Mr. Weller. With kind " Remembrances from William Blake."

Note: In the possession of Mr. W. T. Spencer in 1914. The " Mr. Weller " of the inscription is no doubt the same friend as is referred to by Blake in a letter written to Flaxman from Felpham, Oct. 19, 1801 (Russell, *Letters*, p. 96). His name also appears in the *Memoirs of Hayley*, ii, 150, and from this reference it may be inferred that he was a carver in wood; a Miss Augusta Weller of Chichester is recorded in Graves's *Dictionary of Painters and Engravers* as exhibiting at the Royal Academy and elsewhere in 1836-39.

692 Tragedies by William Sotheby, Esq. The Death of Darnley. Ivan. Zamorin and Zama. The Confession. Orestes. London: Printed for John Murray, Albemarle-Street; . . . 1814. 8°

Description: Bound in contemporary calf, gilt. On the blank leaf facing the title is the inscription: "Wm Blake Esqr. From the Author."

Note: In my own library; obtained from Messrs. Maggs in 1921. William Sotheby, 1757-1833, was a dilettante poet and dramatist of exactly Blake's own age. Probably he did not cultivate Blake's acquaintance for long, and nothing further is known of their relations.

693 Reliques of Ancient English Poetry: . . . [Edited by Bishop Percy] Volume the First [etc.] London: Printed for J. Dodsley . . . MDCCLXV. 3 vols. 8°

Description: On the fly-leaf is the inscription: "Mary Ann Linnell, the gift of "Mr. W. Blake."

Note: Offered in a bookseller's catalogue some years ago, and now in the possession of Prof. G. H. Palmer, Newton, Mass. It is not stated if the inscription is in Blake's autograph or not. The books must have been given by him to Mrs. Linnell after 1818, the year in which he first became acquainted with John Linnell.

694 The Whole Works of Homer, prince of Poets, in his Iliads and Odysses, translated according to the Greeke, by Geo. Chapman. London. [1616] F°.

Note: "He [John Linnell] was also a great lover of Homer, and took especial "delight in Chapman's robust translation, of which he subsequently bought William "Blake's fine folio copy" (Story's *Life of Linnell*, i, 78). I do not know the present whereabouts of this copy, or whether it contains evidence of having been in Blake's possession.

APPENDIX I

BLAKE'S ANNOTATIONS TO WATSON'S *APOLOGY*
FOR THE BIBLE

Blake's Annotations to: *An Apology for the Bible in a Series of Letters addressed to Thomas Paine by R. Watson, D.D., F.R.S. London,* 1797 (see no. 16)

The passages underlined by Blake are here printed in italics; his annotations are printed below the extracts from Bishop Watson's text, with numbers indicating the passages to which they refer. Necessary punctuation has been supplied.

On the back of the title-page Blake has written:

Notes on the B. of L's. Apology for the Bible
by William Blake.

To defend the Bible in this year 1798 would cost a man his life.

The Beast & Whore rule without control.

It is an easy matter for a Bishop to triumph over Paine's attack, but it is not so easy for one who loves the Bible.

The Perversions of Christ's words & acts are attack'd by Paine & also the perversions of the Bible: Who dare defend either the Acts of Christ or the Bible Unperverted?

But to him who sees this mortal pilgrimage in the light that I see it, Duty to his country is the first consideration & safety the last.

Read patiently: take not up this Book in an idle hour: the consideration of these things is the whole duty of man & the affairs of life & death trifles, sports of time. But these considerations [are the] business of Eternity.

I have been commanded from Hell not to print this, as it is what our Enemies wish.

Page [iii].

[Bishop Watson's Preface]

This edition of the Apology for the Bible is published, in compliance with the earnest solicitations of many serious persons of all ranks. They have remarked to me, that the deistical writings of Mr Paine are circulated, with great and pernicious industry, amongst the unlearned part of the community, especially in large manufacturing towns; and they have been pleased to think, that this Defence of Revealed Religion might, if generally distributed, be efficacious in stopping that torrent of infidelity which endangers alike the future happiness of individuals, and the present safety of *all Christian states* [1] . . .

Calgarth Park,

May 10, 1796.

[1] Paine has not attacked Christianity. Watson has defended Antichrist.

Page [iv].

[List of books by Bishop Watson] [1]

7. The Wisdom and Goodness of God, in having made both *Rich and Poor* [2]: a Sermon, preached before the Stewards of Westminster Dispensary, at the Anniversary Meeting in Charlotte-street Chapel . . .

[1] Read the xxiii Chap. of Matthew & then condemn Paine's hatred of Priests if you dare. [2] God made Man happy & Rich, but the Subtil made the innocent Poor. This must be a most wicked & blasphemous book.

Page 1.

LETTER I. [1]

SIR,

I have lately met with a book of your's, entitled—"The Age of Reason," part the second, being an investigation of true and of fabulous theology;—and I think it not inconsistent with my station, and the duty I owe to society, to trouble you and the world with some observations on so extraordinary a performance. Extraordinary I esteem it; not from any novelty in the objections which *you have produced against revealed religion, (for I find little or no novelty in them,)* [2] but from the zeal with which you labour to disseminate your opinions, and from the confidence with which you esteem them true. You perceive, by this, that I give you credit for your sincerity, *how much soever I may question your wisdom,* [3] in writing in such a manner on such a subject: and I have no reluctance in acknowledging, that you possess a considerable share of energy of language, and acuteness of investigation; though I must be allowed to lament, that these *talents have not been applied in a manner more useful to human kind, and more creditable to yourself.* [4]

I begin with your preface. You therein state—that you had long had an intention of publishing your thoughts upon religion, but that you had originally reserved it to a later period in life. I hope there is no want of charity in saying, that it would have been fortunate for the Christian world, *had your life been terminated before you had fulfilled your intention.* [5] In accomplishing your purpose you will have unsettled the faith of thousands; rooted from the minds of the unhappy virtuous all their comfortable assurance of a future recompence; have annihilated in the minds of the flagitious all their fears of future punishment; you will have given the reins to the domination of every passion, and have thereby contributed to the introduction of the public insecurity, and of the private unhappiness usually and almost necessarily accompanying a state of corrupted morals. [6]

[1] If this first Letter is written without Railing & Illiberality I have never read one that is. To me it is all Daggers & Poison; the sting of the serpent is in every Sentence as well as the glittering Dissimulation. Achilles' wrath is blunt abuse: Thersites' sly imprication; such is the Bishop's. If such is the characteristic of a modern polite gentleman we may hope to see Christ's discourses Expung'd. I have not the Charity for the Bishop that he pretends to have for Paine. I believe him to be a State trickster. [2] Dishonest Misrepresentation. [3] Priestly Impudence. [4] Contemptible Falsehood & Detraction. [5] Presumptuous Murderer. Dost thou, O Priest, wish thy brother's death when God has preserved him? [6] Mr Paine

has not extinguish'd, & cannot Extinguish, Moral rectitude; he has Extinguish'd Superstition, which took the Place of Moral Rectitude. What has Moral Rectitude to do with Opinions concerning historical fact?

Page 2.

No one can think worse of confession to a priest and subsequent absolution, as practised in the church of Rome, than I do: but I cannot, with you, attribute the *guillotine-massacres to that cause. Men's minds were not prepared,* [1] as you suppose, for the commission of all manner of crimes, by any doctrines of the church of Rome, corrupted as I esteem it, *but by their not thoroughly believing even that religion. What may not society expect from those, who shall imbibe the principles of your book?* [2]

A fever, which you and those about you expected would prove mortal, made you remember, with renewed satisfaction, that you had written the former part of your Age of Reason—and you know therefore, you say, by experience, the conscientious trial of your own principles. I admit this declaration to be a proof of the sincerity of your persuasion, but I cannot admit it to be any proof of the truth of your principles. What is conscience? It is, as has been thought, an internal monitor implanted in us by the *Supreme Being*, and dictating to us, on all occasions, what is *right or wrong? Or is it merely* our own judgment of the moral rectitude or turpitude of our own actions? I *take the word* (with Mr. Locke) in the latter, *as in the only intelligible* sense. [3] Now who sees not that our judgments of virtue and vice, right and wrong, are not always formed from an enlightened and dispassionate use of our reason, in the investigation of truth? They are more generally formed from the nature of the religion we profess; from the quality of the civil government under which we live; from the general manners of the age, or the particular manners of the persons with whom we associate; from the education we have had in our youth; from the books we have read at a more advanced period; and from other accidental causes. Who sees not that, on this account, conscience may be conformable or repugnant to the law of nature?—may be certain, or doubtful?—and that it can be no criterion of moral rectitude, even when it is certain, because the certainty of an opinion is no proof of it's being a right opinion? A man may be certainly persuaded of an error in reasoning, or of an untruth in matters of fact. It is a maxim of every law, human and divine, that a man ought never to act in opposition to his conscience:

[1] To what does the Bishop attribute the English Crusade against France? Is it not the State Religion? Blush for shame.   [2] Folly & Impudence. Does the thorough belief of Popery hinder crimes, or can the man who writes the latter sentiment be in the good humour the bishop Pretends to be? If we are to expect crimes from Paine & his followers, are we to believe that Bishops do not Rail?   [3] I should Expect that the man who wrote this sneaking sentence *would be as good an inquisitor as any other Priest.* Conscience in those that have it is unequivocal. It is the voice of God. Our judgment of right & wrong is Reason. I believe that the Bishop laught at the Bible in his slieve & so did Locke.

Page 3.

but it will not from thence follow, that he will, in obeying the dictates of his conscience, *on all occasions act right.* [1] An inquisitor, who burns jews and heretics; a Robespierre, who massacres innocent and harmless women; a robber, who thinks that all things ought to be in common, and that a state of property is an unjust infringement of natural liberty:—these, and a thousand perpetrators of different crimes, may all follow *the dictates of conscience*; [2] and may, at the real or supposed approach of death, remember " with renewed satisfaction " the worst of their transactions, and experience, without dismay, " a conscientious trial of their principles." But this their con- scientious composure can be no proof to others of the rectitude of their principles, and ought to be no pledge to themselves of their innocence, in adhering to them.

I have thought fit to make this remark, with a view of suggesting to you a consideration of great importance—whether you have examined calmly, and according to the best of your ability, the arguments by which the truth of revealed religion may, in the judgment of learned and impartial men, be established? [3] . . .

If you have made the best examination you can, and yet reject revealed religion as an imposture, I pray that God may pardon what I esteem your error. And whether you have made this examination or not, does not become me or any man to determine. That gospel, which you despise, has taught me this moderation; it has said to me—" Who art thou that judgest another man's servant? To his own master he standeth or falleth."—I think that you are in an error; but whether that error be to you a vincible or an invincible error, I presume not to deter- mine [4] . . .

[1] Always, or the Bible is false. If Conscience is not a Criterion of Moral Rectitude, What is it? He who thinks that Honesty is changeable knows nothing about it. [2] Contemptible Falshood & Wickedness. Virtue & honesty, or the dictates of Conscience, are of no doubtful Signification to anyone. Opinion is one Thing. Principle another. No Man can change his Principles. Every Man changes his opinions. He who supposes that his Principles are to be changed is a Dissembler, who Disguises his Principles & calls that change. [3] Paine is either a Devil or an inspired man. Men who give themselves to their Energetic Genius in the manner that Paine does are no Examiners. If they are not determinately wrong they must be Right or the Bible is false; as to Examiners in these points they will (always be found to be neither cold nor hot & will *del*) be spewed out. The Man who pretends to be a modest enquirer into the truth of a self evident thing is a Knave. The truth & cer- tainty of Virtue & Honesty, *i.e.* Inspiration, needs no one to prove it; it is Evident as the Sun & Moon. (*six words deleted*) He who stands doubting of what he intends, whether it is Virtuous or Vicious, knows not what Virtue means. No man can do a Vicious action & think it to be Virtuous. No man can take darkness for light. He may pretend to do so & may pretend to be a modest Enquirer, but he is a Knave. [4] Surpentine Dissimulation.

Pages 4-5.

You hold it impossible that the Bible can be the Word of God, because it is therein said, that the Israelites destroyed the Canaanites by the express command of God: and to believe the Bible to be true, we must, you affirm, unbelieve all our belief of the moral justice of God; for wherein, you ask, could crying or smiling infants offend?—I am astonished that so acute a reasoner should attempt to disparage the Bible, by bringing forward this exploded and frequently refuted objection of Morgan, Tindal, and Bolingbroke. [1] You profess yourself to be a deist, and to believe that there is a God, who created the universe, and established the laws of nature, by which it is sustained in existence. You profess that from the contemplation of the works of God, you derive a knowledge of his attributes; and you reject the Bible, because it ascribes to God things inconsistent (as you suppose) with the attributes which you have discovered to belong to him; in particular, you think it repugnant to his moral justice, that he should doom to destruction the crying or smiling infants of the Canaanites.—Why do you not maintain it to be repugnant to his moral justice, that he should suffer crying or smiling infants to be swallowed up by an earthquake, drowned by an inundation, consumed by a fire, starved by famine, or destroyed by a pestilence? The Word of God is in perfect harmony with his work; crying or smiling infants are subjected to death in both. We believe that the earth, at the express command of God, opened her mouth, and swallowed up Korah, Dathan, and Abiram, with their wives, their sons, and their little ones. This you esteem so repugnant to God's moral justice, that you spurn, as spurious, the Book in which the circumstance is related. When Catania, Lima, and Lisbon, were severally destroyed by earthquakes, men with their wives, their sons, and their little ones, were swallowed up alive:—why do you not spurn, as spurious, the book of nature, in which this fact is certainly written, and from the perusal of which you infer the moral justice of God? You will, probably, reply, that the evils which the Canaanites suffered from the express command of God, were different from those which are brought on mankind by the operation of the laws of nature.— Different! in what?—Not in the magnitude of the evil—not in the subjects of sufferance—not in the author of it—for my philosophy,

[1] To me, who believe the Bible & profess myself a Christian, a defence of the Wickedness of the Israelites in murdering so many thousands under pretence of a command from God is altogether Abominable & Blasphimous. Why did Christ come? Was it not to abolish the Jewish Imposture? Was not Christ marter'd because he taught that God loved all Men & was their father & forbad all contention for Worldly prosperity in opposition to the Jewish Scriptures, which are only an Example of the wickedness & deceit of the Jews & were written as an Example of the possibility of Human Beastliness in all its branches? Christ died as an Unbeliever & if the Bishops had their will so would Paine: see page 5: but he who speaks a word against the Son of man shall be forgiven. Let the Bishop prove that he has not spoken against the Holy Ghost, who in Paine strives with Christendom as in Christ he strove with the Jews.

Page 6.

at least, instructs me to believe, that God not only primarily formed, but that he hath through all ages executed, the laws of nature; and that he will through all eternity administer them, for the general happiness of his creatures, whether we can, on every occasion, discern that end or not. [1]

I am far from being guilty of the impiety of questioning the existence of the moral justice of God, as proved either by natural or revealed religion; what I contend for is shortly this—that you have no right, in fairness of reasoning, to urge any apparent deviation from moral justice, as an argument against revealed religion, because you do not urge an equally apparent deviation from it, as an argument against natural religion: you reject the former, and admit the latter, without considering that, as to your objection, they must stand or fall together. [2]

As to the Canaanites, it is needless to enter into any proof of the depraved state of their morals; they were a wicked people in the time of Abraham, and they, even then, were devoted to destruction by God; but their iniquity was not then full. In the time of Moses, they were idolaters; sacrificers of their own crying or smiling infants; devourers of human flesh; addicted to unnatural lust; immersed in the filthiness of all manner of vice. Now, I think, it will be impossible to prove, that it was a *proceeding contrary to God's moral justice, to exterminate so wicked a people.* [3] He made the Israelites the executors of his vengeance; and, in doing this, he gave such an evident and terrible proof of his abomination of vice, as could not fail to strike the surrounding nations with astonishment and terror, and to impress on the minds of the Israelites what they were to expect, if they followed the example of the nations whom he commanded them to cut off. " Ye shall not commit any of these abominations—that the land spue not you out also, as it spued out the nations that were before you." How strong and descriptive this language! the vices of the inhabitants were so abominable, that the very land was sick of them, and forced to vomit them forth, as the stomach disgorges a deadly poison. [4]

[1] The Bible says that God formed Nature perfect, but that Man perverted the order of Nature, since which time the Elements are fill'd with the Prince of Evil, who has the power of the air.   [2] Natural Religion is the voice of God & not the result of reasoning on the Power of Satan.   [3] Horrible! The Bishop is an Inquisitor. God never makes one man murder another nor one nation.   [4] There is a vast difference between an accident brought on by a man's own carelessness & a destruction from the designs of another. The Earthquakes at Lisbon etc. were the Natural result of Sin, but the distruction of the Canaanites by Joshua was the Unnatural design of wicked men.   To Extirpate a nation by means of another is as wicked as to destroy an individual by means of another individual, which God considers (in the Bible) as Murder & commands that it shall not be done. Therefore the Bishop has not answer'd Paine.

Pages 6-7.

I have often wondered what could be the reason that men, not destitute of talents, should be desirous of undermining the authority of revealed religion, and studious in exposing, with a malignant and illiberal exultation, every little difficulty attending the scriptures, to popular animadversion and contempt. I am not willing to attribute this strange propensity to what Plato attributed the atheism of his time—to profligacy of manners—to affectation of singularity—to gross ignorance, assuming the semblance of deep research and superior sagacity;—I had rather refer it to an impropriety of judgment, respecting the manners, and mental acquirements, of human kind in the first ages of the world. Most unbelievers argue as if they thought that man, in remote and rude antiquity, in the very birth and infancy of our species, had the same distinct conceptions of one, eternal, invincible, incorporeal, infinitely wise, powerful, and good God, which they themselves have now. This I look upon as a great mistake, and a pregnant source of infidelity. Human kind, by long experience; by the institutions of civil society; by the cultivation of arts and sciences; by, as I believe, divine instruction actually given to some, and traditionally communicated to all; *is in a far more distinguished situation, as to the powers* of the mind, than it was in the childhood of the world. [1] . . .

[1] That mankind are in a less distinguished Situation with regard to mind than they were in the time of Homer, Socrates, Phidias, Glycon, Aristotle, etc., let all their words witness. Painc (the Devil *del.*) says that Christianity put a stop to improvement & the Bishop has not shewn the contrary.

Pages 7-8.

It appears incredible to many, that God Almighty should have had colloquial intercourse with our first parents; that he should have contracted a kind of friendship for the patriarchs, and entered into covenants with them; [1] that he should have suspended the laws of nature in Egypt; should have been so apparently partial, as to become the God and governor of one particular nation; [2] and should have so far demeaned himself, as to give to that people a burdensome ritual of worship, statutes and ordinances, many of which seem to be beneath the dignity of his attention, unimportant and impolitic. . . .

[1] That God does & always did converse with honest Men Paine never denies. He only denies that God conversed with Murderers & Revengers such as the Jews were & of course he holds that the Jews conversed with their own [self will *del*] State Religion which they call'd God & so were liars as Christ says. [2] That the Jews assumed a right to the Everlasting benefits of God will be a lasting witness against them & the same will it be against (of *del*) Christians.

Pages 8-9.

... I own to you, that when I consider how nearly man, *in a savage state, approaches to the brute creation*, as to intellectual excellence; [3] and when I contemplate his miserable attainments, as to the knowledge of God, in a civilized state, when he has had no divine instruction on the subject, or when that instruction has been forgotten, (for all men have known something of God from tradition,) I cannot but admire the wisdom and goodness of the Supreme Being, in having let himself down to our apprehensions; in having given to mankind, in the earliest ages, sensible and extraordinary proofs of his existence and attributes; in having made the jewish and Christian dispensations mediums to convey to all men, through all ages, that knowledge concerning himself, which he had vouchsafed to give immediately to the first. [4]

[3] Read the Edda of Iceland, the Songs of Fingal, the accounts of North American Savages (as they are call'd). Likewise read Homer's Iliad. He was certainly a Savage in the Bishop's sense. He knew nothing of God in the Bishop's sense of the word & yet he was no fool. [4] The Bible or Peculiar Word of God, Exclusive of Conscience or the Word of God Universal, is the Abomination, which, like the Jewish ceremonies, is for ever removed & henceforth every man may converse with God & be a King & Priest in his own house.

Page 9.

I own it is strange, very strange, that he should have made an immediate manifestation of himself in the first ages of the world; but what is there that is not strange? It is strange that you and I are here—that there is water, and earth, and air, and fire—that there is a sun, and moon, and stars—that there is generation, corruption, reproduction. [1] I can account ultimately for none of these things, without recurring to him who made every thing. I also am his workmanship, and look up to him with hope of preservation through all eternity; I adore him for his word as well as for his work; his work I cannot comprehend, but his word hath assured me of all that I am concerned to know—that he hath prepared everlasting happiness for those who love and obey him. This you will call preachment:—I will have done with it; but the subject is so vast, and the *plan of providence*, in my opinion, so obviously *wise and good*, [2] that I can never think of it without having my mind filled with piety, admiration, and gratitude.

In addition to the moral evidence (as you are pleased to think it) against the Bible, you threaten, in the progress of your work, to produce such other evidence as even a priest cannot deny. A philosopher in search of truth forfeits with me all claim to candour and impartiality, when he introduces railing for reasoning, vulgar and illiberal sarcasm in the room of argument. I will not imitate the example you set me; but examine what you shall produce, with as much

[1] It is strange that God should speak to man formerly & not now, because it is not true; but the Strangeness of Sun, Moon, & Stars is Strange on a contrary account. [2] The Bible tells me that the plan of Providence was Subverted at the Fall of Adam & that it was not restored till Christ.

coolness and respect, *as if you had given the priests no provocation; as if you were a man of the most unblemished character*, subject to no prejudices, actuated by no bad designs, not liable to have abuse retorted upon you with success. [3]

[3] Is not this Illiberal? Has not the Bishop given himself the lie in the moment the first words were out of his mouth? Can any man who writes so pretend that he is in a good humour? Is not this the Bishop's cloven foot? Has he not spoil'd the hasty pudding?

Page 11.

LETTER II. [1]

This distinction between the genuineness and authenticity of a book, will assist us in detecting the fallacy of an argument, which you state with great confidence in the part of your work now under consideration, and which you frequently allude to, in other parts, as conclusive evidence against the truth of the Bible. Your argument stands thus—If it be found that the books ascribed to Moses, Joshua, and Samuel, were not written by Moses, Joshua, and Samuel, every part of the authority and authenticity of these books is gone at once.—I presume to think otherwise. The genuineness of these books (in the judgment of those who say that they were written by these authors) will certainly be gone; but their authenticity will remain; they may still contain a true account of real transactions, though the names of the writers of them should be found to be different from what they are generally esteemed to be. [2]

[1] The trifles which the Bishop has combated in the following Letters are such as do nothing against Paine's Arguments, none of which the Bishop has dared to Consider. One, for instance, which is that the books of the Bible were never believ'd willingly by any nation & that none but designing Villains ever pretended to believe— That the Bible is all a State Trick, thro' which tho' the People at all times could see, they never had the power to throw off. Another Argument is that all the Commentators on the Bible are Dishonest Designing Knaves, who in hopes of a good living adopt the State religion; this he has shewn with great force, which calls upon His Opponent loudly for an answer. I could name an hundred such.

[2] He who writes things for true which none would write but the actor; such are most of the acts of Moses, [who] must either be the actor or a fable writer or a liar. If Moses did not write the history of his acts, it takes away the authority altogether; it ceases to be history & becomes a Poem of probable impossibilities, fabricated for pleasure, as moderns say, but I say by Inspiration.

Pages 12-13.

Had, indeed, Moses said that he wrote the five first books of the Bible; and had Joshua and Samuel said that they wrote the books which are respectively attributed to them; and had it been found, that Moses, Joshua, and Samuel, did not write these books; then, I grant, the authority of the whole would have been gone at once; these men would have been found liars, as to the genuineness of the books; and this proof of their want of veracity, in one point, would have invalidated their testimony in every other; these books would have been justly stigmatized, as neither genuine nor authentic. [1] . . .

As to your assertion, that the miracles recorded in Tacitus, and in other profane historians, are quite as well authenticated as those of the Bible—it, being a mere assertion destitute of proof, may be properly answered by a contrary assertion. I take the liberty then to say, that the evidence for the miracles recorded in the Bible is, both in kind and degree, so greatly superior to that for the prodigies mentioned by Livy, or the miracles related by Tacitus, as to justify us in giving credit to the one as the work of God, and in with-holding it from the other as the effect of superstition and imposture. This method of derogating from the credibility of Christianity, by opposing to the miracles of our Saviour, the tricks of ancient impostors, seems to have originated with Hierocles in the fourth century; and it has been adopted by unbelievers from that time to this; with this difference, indeed, that the heathens of the third and fourth century admitted that Jesus wrought miracles; but lest that admission should have compelled them to abandon their gods and become Christians, they said, that their Apollonius, their Apuleius, their Aristeas, did as great; whilst modern deists deny the fact of Jesus having ever wrought a miracle. [2] . . .

[1] If Paine means that a history, tho' true in itself, is false when it is attributed to a wrong author, he's a fool. But he says that Moses, being proved not the author of that history which is written in his name & in which he says I did so & so, Undermines the veracity intirely. The writer says he is Moses; if this is proved false, the history is false (Deut. xxxi v 24). But perhaps Moses is not the author & then the Bishop loses his Author.

[2] Jesus could not do miracles where unbelief hindered, hence we must conclude that the man who holds miracles to be ceased puts it out of his own power to ever witness one. The manner of a miracle being performed is in modern times considered as an arbitrary command of the agent upon the patient, but this is an impossibility, not a miracle, neither did Jesus ever do such a miracle. Is it a greater miracle to feed five thousand men with five loaves than to overthrow all the armies of Europe with a small pamphlet? Look over the events of your own life & if you do not find that you have both done such miracles & lived by such you do not see as I do. True, I cannot do a miracle thro' experiment & domineer over & prove to others my superior power, as neither could Christ. But I can & do work such as both astonish & comfort me & mine. How can Paine, the worker of miracles, ever doubt Christ's in the above sense of the word miracle? But how can Watson ever believe the above sense of a miracle, who considers it as an arbitrary act of the agent upon an unbelieving patient, whereas the Gospel says that Christ could not do a miracle because of Unbelief?

If Christ could not do miracles because of Unbelief, the reason alledged by Priests for miracles is false; for those who believe want not to be confounded by miracles. Christ & his Prophets & Apostles were not Ambitious miracle mongers.

Page 14.

. . . The Bible is not the only book which has undergone the fate of being reprobated as spurious, after it had been received as genuine and authentic for many ages. It has been maintained that the history of Herodotus was written in the time of Constantine; and that the Classics are forgeries of the thirteenth or fourteenth century. These extravagant reveries amused the world at the time of their publication, and have long since sunk into oblivion. You esteem all prophets to be such lying rascals, that I dare not venture to predict the fate of your book. [1]

[1] Prophets, in the modern sense of the word, have never existed. Jonah was no prophet in the modern sense, for his prophecy of Nineveh failed. Every honest man is a Prophet; he utters his opinion both of private & public matters. Thus: If you go on so, the result is so. He never says, such a thing shall happen let you do what you will. A Prophet is a Seer, not an Arbitrary Dictator. It is man's fault if God is not able to do him good, for he gives to the just & to the unjust, but the unjust reject his gift.

Pages 15-16.

What possible doubt can there be that Moses wrote the books in question? I could accumulate many other passages from the scriptures to this purpose; but if what I have advanced will not convince you that there is affirmative evidence, and of the strongest kind, for Moses's being the author of these books, nothing that I can advance will convince you.

What if I should grant all you undertake to prove (the stupidity and ignorance of the writer excepted)?—What if I should admit, that Samuel, or Ezra, or some other learned jew, composed these books, *from public* records, many years after the death of Moses? Will it follow, that there was no truth in them? According to my logic, it will only follow, that they are not genuine books; every fact recorded *in them may be true*, whenever, or by whomsoever they were written. [1] It cannot be said that the jews had no public records; the Bible furnishes abundance of proof to the contrary. I by no means admit, that these books, as to the main part of them, were not written by Moses; but I do contend, that a book may contain a true history, though we know not the author of it, or though we may be mistaken in ascribing it to a wrong author.

[1] Nothing can be more contemptible than to suppose Public RECORDS to be True. Read, then, & Judge, if you are not a Fool.

Of what consequence is it whether Moses wrote the Pentateuch or no? If Paine trifles in some of his objections it is folly to confute him so seriously in them & leave his more material ones unanswered. Public Records! As If Public Records were True! Impossible; for the facts are such as none but the actor could tell. If it is True, Moses & none but he could write it, unless we allow it to be Poetry & that poetry inspired.

If historical facts can be written by inspiration, Milton's Paradise Lost is as true as Genesis or Exodus; but the Evidence is nothing, for how can he who writes what he has neither seen nor heard of be an Evidence of The Truth of his history.

3 K

Page 17.

. . . I do not call you a vain and arrogant coxcomb for vindicating your character, when in the latter part of this very work you boast, and I hope truly, "that the man does not exist that can say I have persecuted him, or any man, or any set of men, in the American revolution, or in the French revolution; or that I have in any case returned evil for evil." I know not what kings and priests may say to this; you may not have returned to them evil for evil, because they never, I believe, did you any harm; but you have done them all the harm you could, and that without provocation. [1]

[1] Paine says that Kings & Priests have done him harm from his birth.

Page 22.

LETTER III.

Having done with what you call the grammatical evidence that Moses was not the author of the books attributed to him, you come to your historical and chronological evidence; and you begin with Genesis. [1]

[1] I cannot concieve the Divinity of the books in the Bible to consist either in who they were written by, or at what time, or in the historical evidence which may be all false in the eyes of one man & true in the eyes of another, but in the Sentiments & Examples, which, whether true or Parabolic, are Equally useful as Examples given to us of the perverseness of some & its consequent evil & the honesty of others & its consequent good. This sense of the Bible is equally true to all & equally plain to all. None can doubt the impression which he receives from a book of Examples. If he is good he will abhor wickedness in David or Abraham; if he is wicked he will make their wickedness an excuse for his & so he would do by any other book.

Page 25.

. . . The destruction of the Canaanites exhibits to all nations, in all ages, a signal proof of God's displeasure against sin; it has been to others, and it is to ourselves, a benevolent warning. Moses would have been the wretch you represent him, had he acted by his own authority alone; but you may as reasonably attribute cruelty and murder to the judge of the land in condemning criminals to death, as butchery and massacre to Moses in executing the command of God. [1]

[1] All Penal Laws court Transgression & therefore are cruelty & Murder. The laws of the Jews were (both ceremonial & real) the basest, most oppressive of human codes, & being like all other codes given under pretence of divine command were what Christ pronounced them, The Abomination that maketh desolate, *i.e.* State Religion, which is the source of all Cruelty.

Page 29.

LETTER IV.

. . . And who told you that the jews had no records, or that they did not preserve them with singular care? . . . If any one, having access to the journals of the lords and commons, to the books of the treasury, war-office, privy council, and other public documents, should at this day write an history of the reigns of George the first and second, and should publish it without his name, would any man, three or four hundreds or thousands of years hence, [1] question the authority of that book, when he knew that the whole British nation had received it as an authentic book, from the time of it's first publication to the age in which he lived? . . .

If I am right in this reasoning, [2] (and I protest to you that I do not see any error in it,) all the arguments you adduce in proof that the book of Joshua was not written by Joshua, nor that of Samuel by Samuel, are nothing to the purpose for which you have brought them forward: these books may be books of authority, though all you advance against the genuineness of them should be granted.

[1] Hundreds or Thousands of Years! O, very fine Records! As if he knew that there were Records! The Ancients Knew Better.   [2] As if Reasoning was of any Consequence to a Question! Downright Plain Truth is Something, but Reasoning is Nothing.

Page 31.

Whoever wrote the gospel of St. Matthew, it was written not many centuries, probably (I had almost said certainly) not a quarter of one century after the death of Jesus; [1]

Page 33.

It seems to me that you do not perfectly comprehend what is meant by the expression—the Word of God—or the divine authority of the scriptures: I will explain it to you in the words of Dr Law, late bishop of Carlisle, and in those of St. Austin. [2]

Page 35.

. . . The two books of Samuel come next under your review. You proceed to shew that these books were not written by Samuel, that they are anonymous, and thence you conclude without authority. [3]

[1] There are no Proofs that Mathew, the Earliest of all the writings of the New Testament, was written within the first century (see p. 94 & 95).   [2] They seem to Forget that there is a God of this World, A God worship'd in this World as God & set above all that is call'd God.   [3] Who gave them the Name of Books of Samuel? It is not of Consequence.

Page 36.

. . . Very little certainty, I think, can at this time be obtained on this subject: but that you may have some knowledge of what has been conjectured by men of judgment, I will quote to you a passage from Dr. Hartley's Observations on Man. [4]

[4] Hartley a Man of Judgment! Then Judgment was a Fool. What Nonsense!

Page 48.

LETTER V.

. . . As to the sins and debaucheries of Solomon, we have nothing to do with them but to avoid them; and to give full credit to his experience, when he preaches to us his admirable sermon on the vanity of every thing but piety and virtue. [1]

Page 49.

. . . I have read also Isaiah's burden of Babylon, and I have compared it with the past and present state of Babylon, and the comparison has made such an impression on my mind, that it will never be effaced from my memory. I shall never cease to believe that the Eternal alone, by whom things future are more distinctly known than past or present things are by man, that the eternal God alone could have dictated to the prophet Isaiah the subject of the burden of Babylon. [2]

[1] Piety & Virtue! Is Seneca Classical, O Fine Bishop?   [2] The Bishops never saw the Everlasting Gospel any more than Tom Paine.

Page 95.

LETTER IX.

Did you ever read the apology for the Christians, which Justin Martyr presented to the emperor Antoninus Pius, to the senate, and people of Rome? I should sooner expect a falsity in a petition, which any body of persecuted men, imploring justice, should present to the king and parliament of Great Britain, than in this apology.—Yet in this apology, which was presented not fifty years after the death of St. John, [1] not only parts of all the four gospels are quoted, but it is expressly said, that on the day called Sunday, a portion of them was read in the public assemblies of the Christians. I forbear pursuing this matter farther; else it might easily be shewn, that *probably the gospels*, and certainly some of St. Paul's epistles, were known to Clement, Ignatius, and Polycarp, contemporaries with the apostles. These men could not quote or refer to books which did not exist: and therefore, though you could make it out that the book called the New Testament did not formally exist under that title, till 350 years after Christ; *yet I hold it to be a certain fact, that all the books*, of which it is composed, were written, and most of them received by all Christians, within a few years after his death. [2]

[1] A:D: 150.   [2] This is No Certain Fact. Presumption is no Proof.

Page 108.

LETTER X.

. . . The moral precepts of the gospel [1] are so well fitted to promote the happiness of mankind in this world, and to prepare human nature for the future enjoyment of that blessedness, of which, in our present state, we can form no conception, that I had no expectation they would have met with your disapprobation.

Page 109.

. . . Two precepts you particularize as inconsistent with the dignity and the nature of man —that of not resenting injuries, and that of loving enemies. [2] —Who but yourself ever interpreted literally the proverbial phrase—"If a man smite thee on thy right cheek, turn to him the other also?"—Did Jesus himself turn the *other cheek when the officer of the high priest smote him*? [3] It is evident, that a patient acquiescence under *slight* [4] personal injuries is here enjoined; and that a proneness to revenge, which instigates men to savage acts of brutality, for every trifling offence, is forbidden.

Page 117.

. . . The importance of revelation is by nothing rendered more apparent, than by the discordant sentiments of learned and good men (for I speak not of the *ignorant and immoral*) [5] on this point.

[1] The Gospel is Forgiveness of Sins & has No Moral Precepts; those belong to Plato & Seneca & Nero. [2] Well done, Paine! [3] Yes, I have no doubt he Did. [4] O Fool! Slight Hippocrite & Villain! [5] O, how Virtuous! Christ came not to call the Virtuous.

Pages 118-119.

We are all, of every rank and condition, equally concerned in knowing—what will become of us after death;—and, if we are to live again, we are interested in knowing—whether it be possible for us to do any thing [1] whilst we live here, which may render that future life an happy one.—Now, "that thing called Christianity," as you scoffingly speak—that last best gift of Almighty God, as I esteem it, the gospel of Jesus Christ, has given us the most clear and satisfactory information on both these points. It tells us, what deism never could have told us, that we shall certainly be raised from the dead—that, whatever be the nature of the soul, we shall certainly live for ever—and that, whilst we live here, it is possible for us to do much towards the rendering that everlasting life an happy one.—These are tremendous truths to bad men; [2] they cannot be received and reflected on with indifference by the best; and they suggest to all such a cogent motive to virtuous action, as deism could not furnish even to Brutus himself.

[1] Do or Act to Do Good or to do Evil. Who dares to Judge but God alone? [2] Who does the Bishop call Bad Men? Are they the Publicans & Sinners that Christ loved to associate with? Does God Love the Righteous according to the Gospel, or does he not cast them off?

Some men have been warped to infidelity by viciousness of life; and some may have hypocritically professed Christianity from prospects of temporal advantage: but, being a stranger to your character, I neither impute the former to you, nor can admit the latter as operating on myself. The generality of unbelievers are such, from want of information on the subject of religion; having been engaged from their youth in struggling for worldly distinction, or perplexed with the incessant intricacies of business, or bewildered in the pursuits of pleasure, they have neither ability, inclination, nor leisure, to enter into critical disquisitions concerning the truth of Christianity. [3] . . .

[3] For who is really righteous? It is all Pretension.

On the last page (p. 120) Blake has written:

It appears to me Now that Tom Paine is a better Christian than the Bishop.
I have read this Book with attention & find that the Bishop has only hurt Paine's heel while Paine has broken his head. The Bishop has not answer'd one of Paine's grand objections.

APPENDIX II

BLAKE'S ANNOTATIONS TO BERKELEY'S *SIRIS*

Blake's Annotations to: *Siris: A Chain of Philosophical Reflexions and Inquiries Concerning the Virtues of Tar Water, And divers other Subjects.* [*By Bishop Berkeley*] *Dublin.* 1744. (See no. 19*.)

P. 203. *Berkeley*: God knoweth all things, as pure mind or intellect, but nothing by sense, nor in nor through a sensory. Therefore to suppose a sensory of any kind, whether space or any other, in God would be very wrong, and lead us into false conceptions of his nature.
Blake: Imagination or the Human Eternal Body in Every Man.

P. 204. *Berkeley*: But in respect of a perfect spirit, there is nothing hard or impenetrable: there is no resistance to the deity. Nor hath he any body: Nor is the supreme being united to the world, as the soul of an animal is to its body, which necessarily implieth defect, both as an instrument and as a constant weight and impediment.
Blake: Imagination is the Divine Body in Every Man.

P. 205. *Berkeley*: Natural phænomena are only natural appearances . . . They and the phantomes that result from those appearances, *the children of imagination* [underlined by Blake] grafted upon sense, such for example as pure space, are thought by many the very first in existence and stability, and to embrace and comprehend all beings.
Blake: [in margin] The All in Man. The Divine Image or Imagination.
[at bottom] The Four Senses are the Four Faces of Man & the Four Rivers of the Water of Life.

P. 212. *Berkeley*: Plato and Aristotle considered God as abstracted or distinct from the natural world. But the Aegyptians considered God and nature as making one whole, or all things together as making one universe.
Blake: [in margin] They also considered God as abstracted or distinct from the Imaginative World, but Jesus, as also Abraham & David, considered God as a Man in the Spiritual or Imaginative Vision.
[at bottom] Jesus considered Imagination to be that Real Man & says I will not leave you Orphans as I will manifest myself to you; he says also the Spiritual Body or Angel as little Children always behold the Face of the Heavenly Father.

* Under no. 19 the date is printed in error as 1749.

P. 213. *Berkeley*: The perceptions of sence are gross: but even in the senses there is a difference. Though harmony and proportion are not objects of sense, yet the eye and the ear are organs, which offer to the mind such materials, by means whereof she may apprehend both the one and the other.

Blake: Harmony and Proportion are Qualities & Not Things. The Harmony & Proportion of a Horse are not the same with those of a Bull. Every Thing has its own Harmony & Proportion, Two Inferior Qualities in it. For its Reality is Its Imaginative Form.

P. 214. *Berkeley*: By experiments of sense we become acquainted with the lower faculties of the soul; and from them, whether by a gradual evolution or ascent, we arrive at the highest. These become subjects for fancy to work upon. Reason considers and judges of the imaginations. And these acts of reason become new objects to the understanding.

Blake: Knowledge is not by deduction, but Immediate by Perception or Sense at once. Christ adresses himself to the Man not to his Reason. Plato did not bring Life & Immortality to Light. Jesus only did this.

P. 215. *Berkeley*: There is according to Plato properly no knowledge, but only opinion concerning things sensible and perishing, not because they are naturally abstruse and involved in darkness: but because their nature and existence is uncertain, ever fleeting and changing.

Blake: [in margin] Jesus supposes every Thing to be Evident to the Child & to the Poor & Unlearned. Such is the Gospel.

[at bottom] The Whole Bible is filld with Imagination & Visions from End to End & not with Moral Virtues; that is the baseness of Plato & the Greeks & all Warriors. The Moral Virtues are continual Accusers of Sin & promote Eternal Wars & Dominency over others.

P. 217. *Berkeley*: Aristotle maketh a threefold distinction of objects according to the three speculative sciences. Physics he supposeth to be conversant about such things as have a principle of motion in themselves, mathematics about things permanent but not abstracted, and theology about things abstracted and immoveable, which distinction may be seen in the ninth book of his metaphysics.

Blake: God is not a Mathematical Diagram.

P. 218. *Berkeley*: It is a maxim of the Platonic philosophy, that the soul of man was originally furnished with native inbred notions, and stands in need of sensible occasions, not absolutely for producing them, but only for awakening, rousing or exciting, into act what was already pre-existent, dormant, and latent in the soul.

Blake: The Natural Body is an Obstruction to the Soul or Spiritual Body.

P. 219. *Berkeley*: . . . Whence, according to Themistius, . . . it may be inferred that all beings are in the soul. For, saith he, the forms are the beings. By the form every thing is what it is. And, he adds, it is the soul that imparteth forms to matter, . . .

Blake: This is my Opinion, but Form must be apprehended by Sense or the Eye of Imagination. Man is All Imagination. God is Man & exists in us & we in him.

P. 241. *Blake*: What Jesus came to Remove was the Heathen or Platonic Philosophy, which blinds the Eye of Imagination, The Real Man.

APPENDIX III

LETTERS HITHERTO UNCOLLECTED

[None of these letters is to be found in the collection edited by A. G. B. Russell in 1906. Number 8 has been printed by E. J. Ellis in *The Real Blake*, 1907, p. 206; the rest have not been printed before.]

LETTERS HITHERTO UNCOLLECTED

LETTER 6

To William Hayley Esqr., Eartham, Near Chichester, Sussex.

HERCULES BUILDINGS, LAMBETH.
1, April, 1800.

DEAR SIR,

With all possible Expedition I send you a proof of my attempt to Express your & our Much Beloveds Countenance.* Mr. Flaxman has seen it & approved of my now sending it to you for your remarks. Your Sorrows and your dear sons, May Jesus and his Angels assuage & if it is consistent with his divine providence restore him to us & to his labours of Art & Science in this world. So prays a fellow sufferer & Your humble Servant,

WILLM. BLAKE.

LETTER 8

To Mr. Cumberland, Bishopsgate, Windsor Great Park.

13, HERCULES BUILDINGS, LAMBETH.
2 July, 1800.

DEAR CUMBERLAND,

I have to congratulate you on your plan for a National Gallery being put into execution. All your wishes shall in due time be fulfilled; the immense flood of Grecian light & glory which is coming on Europe will more than realize our warmest wishes. Your honour will be unbounded when your plan shall be carried into execution as it must be if England continues a Nation. I hear that it is now in the hands of Ministers, That the King shews it great Countenance & encouragement, that it will soon be before Parliament, & that it *must* be extended & enlarged to take in Originals both of Painting & Sculpture by considering every valuable original that is brought into England or can be purchased abroad as its objects of acquisition. Such is the Plan as I am told & such must be the plan if England wishes to

---

* An engraving after a medallion portrait of Thomas Alfonso Hayley by Flaxman, done for Hayley's *Essay on Sculpture*, 1800 (see no. 120).

447

continue at all worth notice, as you have yourself observed, only now we must possess Originals as well as France or be Nothing.

Excuse, I entreat you, my not returning Thanks at the proper moment for your kind present. No perswasion could make my stupid head believe that it was proper for me to trouble you with a letter of meer compliment & expression of thanks. I begin to emerge from a deep pit of Melancholy. Melancholy without any real reason for it, a Disease which God keep you from & all good men. Our artists of all ranks praise your outlines * & wish for more. Flaxman is very warm in your commendation & more & more of a Grecian. Mr. Hayley has lately mentioned your work on outline in Notes to [Epistles on Sculpture *del*.] an Essay on Sculpture in Six Epistles to John Flaxman. I have been too little among friends which I fear they will not excuse & I know not how to apologize for. Poor Fuseli sore from the lash of envious tongues praises you & dispraises with the same breath; he is not naturally good natured, but he is artificially very ill natured yet even from him I learn the estimation you are held in among artists & connoisseurs.

I am still employed in making Designs & little Pictures with now & then an engraving & find that in future to live will not be so difficult as it has been. It is very extraordinary that London in so few years from a city of meer Necessaries or at l[e]ast a commerce of the lowest order of luxuries should have become a City of elegance in some degree & that its once stupid inhabitants should enter into an emulation of Grecian manner. There are now I believe as many Booksellers as there are Butchers & as many Printshops as of any other trade. We remember when a Print shop was a rare bird in London & I myself remember when I thought my pursuits of Art a kind of criminal dissipation & neglect of the main chance, which I hid my face for not being able to abandon as a Passion which is forbidden by Law & Religion, but now it appears to be Law & Gospel too, at least I hear so from the few friends I have dared to visit in my stupid Melancholy. Excuse this communication of sentiments which I felt necessary to my repose at this time. I feel very strongly that I neglect my Duty to my Friends but it is not want of Gratitude or Friendship but perhaps an excess of both.

Let me hear of your welfare.

Remember My & My Wife's Respectful Compliments to Mrs. Cumberland & family & believe me to be for ever yours

WILLIAM BLAKE.

* Cumberland's *Thoughts on Outline*, 1796 (see no. 112).

LETTER 23

[To James Blake]

FELPHAM
Jan.ʸ 30, 1803.

DEAR BROTHER,

Your Letter mentioning Mr Butts' account of my Ague surprized me because I have no Ague but have had a Cold this Winter. You know that it is my way to make the best of everything. I never make myself nor my friends uneasy if I can help it. My Wife has had Agues & Rheumatisms almost ever since she has been here but our time is almost out that we took the Cottage for. I did not mention our Sickness to you & should not to Mr Butts but for a determination which we have lately made namely To leave This Place because I am now certain of what I have long doubted Viz that H. is Jealous as Stothard was & will be no further My friend than he is compelld by circumstances. The truth is As a Poet he is frightened at me & as a Painter his views & mine are opposite; he thinks to turn me into a Portrait Painter as he did Poor Romney, but this he nor all the devils in hell will never do. I must own that seeing H. like S. envious (& that he is I am now certain) made me very uneasy, but it is over & I now defy the worst & fear not while I am true to myself which I will be. This is the uneasinefs I spoke of to Mr Butts but I did not tell him so plain & wish you to keep it a secret & to burn this letter because it speaks so plain.

I told Mr Butts that I did not wish to explore too much the cause of our determination to leave Felpham because of pecuniary connexions between H. & me— Be not then uneasy on any account & tell my Sister not to be uneasy for I am fully Employ'd & Well Paid. I have made it so much H's interest to employ me that he can no longer treat me with indifference & now it is in my power to stay or return or remove to any other place that I choose, because I am getting beforehand in money matters. The Profits arising from Publications are immense & I now have it in my power to commence publication with many very formidable works, which I have finish'd & ready. A Book price half a guinea may be got out at the Expense of Ten pounds & its almost certain profits are 500 G. I am only sorry that I did not know the methods of publishing years ago & this is one of the numerous benefits I have obtain'd by coming here for I should never have known the nature of Publication unless I had known H. & his connexions & his method of managing. It now would be folly not to venture publishing. I am now engraving Six little plates for a little work * of Mr H's for which I am to have 10 Guineas each & the certain profits

---

* Hayley's *Triumphs of Temper*, 1803 (no. 125) for which Blake engraved six plates after designs by Maria Flaxman.

of that work are a fortune such as would make me independent supposing that I would substantiate such a one of my own & I mean to try many. But I again say as I said before We are very Happy sitting at tea by a wood fire in our Cottage the wind singing about our roof & the Sea roaring at a distance but if sickness comes all is unpleasant.

But my letter to Mr Butts appears to me not to be so explicit as that to you for I told you that I should come to London in the Spring to commence Publisher & he has offered me every afsistance in his power without knowing my intention. But since I wrote yours we had made the resolution of which we inform'd him viz to leave Felpham entirely. I also told you what I was about & that I was not ignorant of what was doing in London in works of art. But I did not mention Illness because I hoped to get better (for I was really very ill when I wrote to him the last time) & was not then persuaded as I am now that the air tho warm is unhealthy.

However this I know will set you at Ease. I am now so full of work that I have had no time to go on with the Ballads, & my prospects of more & more work continually are certain. My Heads of Cowper for Mr H's life of Cowper have pleas'd his Relations exceedingly & in Particular Lady Hesketh & Lord Cowper— to please Lady H. was a doubtful chance who almost adord her Cousin the poet & thought him all perfection & she writes that she is quite satisfied with the portraits & charmd by the great Head in particular tho she never could bear the original Picture.

But I ought to mention to you that our present idea is, To take a house in some village further from the Sea, Perhaps Lavant, & in or near the road to London for the sake of convenience. I also ought to inform you that I read your letter to Mr H. & that he is very afraid of losing me & also very afraid that my Friends in London should have a bad opinion of the reception he has given to me. But My Wife has undertaken to Print the whole number of the Plates for Cowper's work which she does to admiration & being under my own eye the prints are as fine as the French prints & please everyone. In short I have Got everything so under my thumb that it is more profitable that things should be as they are than any other way, tho not so agreeable because we wish naturally for friendship in preference to interest. The Publishers are already indebted to My Wife Twenty Guineas for work deliverd; this is a small specimen of how we go on. Then fear nothing & let my Sister fear nothing because it appears to me that I am now too old & have had too much experience to be any longer imposed upon, only illnefs makes all uncomfortable & this we must prevent by every means in our power.

I send with this 5 Copies of N4 of the Ballads * for Mrs Flaxman & Five more two of which you will be so good as to give to Mrs Chetwynd if she should call or

* Hayley's *Ballads*, 1802 ; see no. 72.

send for them. These Ballads are likely to be Profitable for we have Sold all that we have had time to print. Evans the Bookseller in Pall Mall says they go off very well & why should we repent of having done them; it is doing Nothing that is to be repented of & not doing such things as these.

Pray remember us both to Mr Hall when you see him.

I write in great haste & with a head full of botheration about various projected works & particularly a work now Proposed to the Public at the End of Cowper's Life, which will very likely be of great consequence. It is Cowper's Milton the same that Fuseli's Milton Gallery was painted for, & if we succeed in our intentions the prints to this work will be very profitable to me and not only profitable but honourable at anyrate.* The Project pleases Lord Cowper's family, & I am now labouring in my thoughts Designs for this & other works equally creditable. These are works to be boasted of & therefore I cannot feel deprefsd tho I know that as far as Designing & Poetry are concernd I am envied in many Quarters, but I will cram the dogs for I know that the Public are my friends & love my works & will embrace them whenever they see them. My only Difficulty is to produce fast enough.

I go on Merrily with my Greek & Latin: am very sorry that I did not begin to learn languages early in life as I find it very Easy, am now learning my Hebrew אבב, I read Greek as fluently as an Oxford scholar & the Testament is my chief master: astonishing indeed is the English Translation, it is almost word for word & if the Hebrew Bible is as well translated, which I do not doubt it is, we need not doubt of its having been translated as well as written by the Holy Ghost.

My wife joins me in Love to you both

I am

Sincerely yours

W Blake

LETTER 35

To William Hayley Esq.

16 March, 1804.

Dear Sir,

According to your Desire I send proofs of the Monumental Plates † tho as you will perceive they have not the last touches especially the Plate of the Monument which I have drawn from Mr. Flaxman's Model with all the fidelity I could & will

---

* These prints were never executed.

† This and the succeeding paragraphs refer to the plates for Hayley's *Life of Cowper*, 1803 (see no. 124).

finish with equal care, the writing being exactly copied from the tracing paper which was traced on the marble. The inscriptions to the Plates I must beg of you to send to me that I may engrave them immediately.

The drawing of the Monument which Mr. Johnson sent has the following Inscription—"Monument Erected to the Memory of William Cowper Esqre. in St. Edmunds Chapel East Dereham by the Lady Hesketh 1803"—But it strikes me that St. Edmunds Chapel East Dereham may be understood to mean a Chapel in East Dereham *Town* & not to express sufficiently that the Monument is in *East Dereham Church*. Owing to my determination of sending you Proofs I have not been able to consult Mr. Flaxman about the Designs of Mr. Romney which are at Saunders. I called once of [on] Mr. F. but he was not at home so could not spare more time but will now immediately proceed in that business. The Pleasure I received from your kind Letter ought to make me assiduous & it does so. That Mr. John Romney is so honest as to expose to you his whole absurd prejudice gives hopes that he may prove worthy of his father & that he should tell such inconsistent surmizes proves that they will soon be eradicated & forgotten. You who was his father's best friend will I hope become the most respected object of his love & admiration.

I called on Mr. Hoare * with your Elegant & Heart lifting Compliment; he was not at home. I left it with a short note, have not seen him since.

Mr. Rose † I am happy to hear is getting quite well.

Hope to hear the same good account of our most admirable & always anxiously remembered Miss Poole.

Mr. Braithwaite called on me & brought two Prints which he desires may be sent to you (with his Compliments) (which you will find enclosed) one is a copy from that Miniature you kindly suffered me to make from the Picture of Romney which I am now engraving: & which was lent by Mr. Long ‡ for the purpose of being engraved for the European Magne. The other is Mrs. Siddons from the Picture by Romney in Mr. Braithwaite's possession, but as much unlike the original as possible.

My Wife joins me in best affections to you & I remain

Sincerely Yours,

WILL BLAKE.

I enclose also No. 23 of the Shakspeare.

* Prince Hoare (see no. 129).
† Samuel Rose, Blake's counsel at his trial.   ‡ William Long, surgeon; see p. 79.

LETTER 57

To Mr. Hayley

27 Nov., 1805.

DEAR SIR,

Mr Cromek the Engraver came to me desiring to have some of my Designs; he named his Price & wishd me to Produce him Illustrations of The Grave A Poem by Robert Blair.* In consequence of this I produced about twenty Designs which pleasd so well that he with the same liborality with which he set me about the Drawing, has now set me to Engrave them. He means to Publish them by Subscription with the Poem as you will see in the Prospectus which he sends you in the Pacquet with the Letter. You will I know feel as you always do on such occasions, not only warm wishes to promote the Spirited Exertions of my friend Cromek. You will be pleased to see that the Royal Academy have Sanctioned the Style of work. I now have reason more than ever to lament your Distance from London as that alone has prevented our Consulting you in our Progress, which is but of about two Months Date. I cannot give you any Account of our Ballads † for I have heard nothing of Phillips this Age. I hear them approved by the best, that is the most serious people, & if any others are displeased it is also an argument of their being Successful as well as Right, of which I have no Doubt for what is Good must succeed first or last: but what is bad owes success to something beside or without itself if it has any.

My Wife joins me in anxious wishes for your health & Happiness desiring to be particularly remembered by You & our Good Lady Paulina‡ over a dish of Coffee. I long to hear of your Good Health & that our dear friend of Lavant § & of all our frinds (to whom we are grateful & desire to be rememberd) In Sussex

I am Dear Sir,

Yours ever affectionately,

WILL. BLAKE.

* See no. 81. † Hayley's *Ballads*, 1805 (see no. 94).
‡ Mrs. Paulina Lushington. § Miss Harriet Poole of Lavant.

LETTER 63

To Ozias Humphrey, Esqre.

[*C.* 1809.]

DEAR SIR,

You will see in this little work * the cause of difference between you & me. You demand of me to Mix two things that Reynolds has confessed cannot be mixed. You will perceive that I not only detest False Art, but have the Courage to say so Publickly & to dare all the Power on Earth to oppose—Florentine & Venetian Art cannot exist together. Till the Venetian & Flemish are destroyed the Florentine & Roman cannot Exist; this will be shortly accomplished, till then I remain your Grateful altho Seemingly otherwise I say your Grateful & Sincere,

WILLIAM BLAKE.

I inclose a ticket of admission if you should honour my Exhibition with a Visit.

LETTER 64

To Mr. Blake, Engraver.

[*C.* 1818.]

Mr. Reveley's Compts. to Mr. Blake if he wishes to engrave any of Mr. Parr's drawings for the antiquities of Athens † & can do them by the end of January Mr. R. will be glad to [send] some to him.

GREAT TITCHFIELD ST.
Oct. 18.

[*To Mr. Reveley.*]

Mr. Blake's Compts. to Mr. Reveley; tho full of work he is glad to embrace the offer of engraving such beautiful things & will do what he can by the end of January.

* Evidently the *Descriptive Catalogue* (see no. 30).
† Probably refers to the engraving executed by Blake in 1818 for vol. ii of Rees' *Cyclopædia*, 1820 (see no. 132).

LETTER 68

To J. Linnell Esqr., Cirencester Place, Fitzroy Square.

12 o'clock Wednesday [1825].

A return of the old shivering fit* came on as soon as I awakened and I am now in bed, Better and as I think almost well. I will be at Laker's [?] tomorrow morning. These attacks are too serious at the time to permit me to be out of bed, but they go off by rest which seems to be all that I want. I send the Pilgrims under your care with the Two First plates of Job.

I am, yours sincerely,
WILLM. BLAKE.

LETTER 70

To Mrs. Linnell

London Sunday morning [? 1825].

DEAR MADAM,
Mr. Linnell will have arrived at his Journeys end before the time I now write. He set off last night before eight o'clock from the Angel Inn near St. Clements Church Strand on one of the strongest & handsomest Built horses I ever saw. I should have written Last Night, but as the Dr. would not come before now I do as Mr. Linnell desired I would by the first stage. My Wife desires her kindest remembrances to you

I am
Yours sincerely,
WILLM. BLAKE.

Excuse the writing. I have delayed too long.

* Probably gall-stone colic, from which Blake frequently suffered during the last years of his life. He eventually died from biliary obstruction.

LETTER 77

To Mr. Linnell, 6, Cirencester Place, Fitzroy Square.

29 July, 1826.

DEAR SIR,

Just as I had become well that is subdued the disease tho not its Effects, Weakness etc., comes Another to hinder my Progress, called the Piles, which, when to the degree I have had them, are a most sore plague and on a Weak body truly afflictive. These Piles have now also as I hope run their period and I begin to again feel returning Strength. On this account I cannot yet tell when I can start for Hampstead like a young Lark without feathers. Two or Three days may be sufficient or not. All now will depend on my bones and sinews and Muscle. I have none, but a few days may do, and have done, miracles in the case of a Convalescent who prepares himself ardently for his return to Life and its Business among his Friends

With whom he makes his first effort

Dear Sir,
Yours ever
WILLIAM BLAKE.

LETTER 79

To Mr. Linnell, 6, Cirencester Place, Fitzroy Square.

Saturday Night, Jany. 27, 1827.

DEAR SIR,

I ought to have acknowledged the Rect. of Five Pounds from you on 16 Jany. 1827; that part of your Letter in which you desired I would send an acknowledgement I did not see till the next morning, owing to its being writ on the outside double of your letter. Nevertheless I ought to have sent it, but must beg you to excuse such Follies which tho I am enough ashamed of and hope to mend can only do so at present by owning the Fault

I am dear Sir,
Yours sincerely,
WILLIAM BLAKE.

LETTER 81

To J. Linnell Esq.

[? Feb. 1827.]

Dear Sir,

I called this Morning for a Walk and brought my Plates* with me to prevent the trouble of your being thro [word illegible] to see what I was about. I have got on very forward with four Plates and am getting better or I could not have come at all.

Yours
WILLM. BLAKE.

* Engravings of the illustrations to Dante (see no. 56).

APPENDIX IV

CANCELLED PLATES FOR *AMERICA*, 1793

[These three plates are printed in sepia on two leaves, and bound up together with other plates from the Illuminated Books and a manuscript copy of Cunningham's life of Blake (see no. 249). The prints are uncoloured, and the paper has no watermark. The text of the plates, which has never been reprinted before, is given here by permission of Mr. B. B. Macgeorge of Glasgow. For a brief description of the designs see p. 135 of the present work.]

AMERICA

Plate a

A PROPHECY

The Guardian Prince of Albion burns in his nightly tent,
Sullen fires acrofs the Atlantic glow to America's shore:
Piercing the souls of warlike men, who rise in silent night,
Washington, Hancock, Paine & Warren, Gates, Franklin, & Green;
Meet on the coast glowing with blood stood Albions fiery Prince.   5
Washington spoke: Friends of America look over the Atlantic sea:
A bended bow in heaven is lifted, & a heavy iron chain
Descends link by link from Albions cliffs acrofs the sea to bind
Brothers & sons of America till our faces pale and yellow;
Heads deprest, voices weak, eyes downcast, hands work-bruis'd,   10
Feet bleeding on the sultry sands, and the furrows of the whip
Descend to generations that in future times forget.—
The strong voice ceas'd: for a terrible blast swept over the heaving sea.
The eastern cloud rent: on his cliffs stood Albions fiery Prince
A dragon form clashing his scales at midnight he arose,   15
And flam'd fierce meteors round the band of Albion beneath.
His voice, his locks, his awful shoulders, and his glowing eyes,   17

> *Published version (America,* pl. 3):
>
> 4 [Washington, Hancock, . . . Franklin & Green] Washington, Franklin, . . .
> Hancock & Green
>
> 7 [A bended bow in heaven is lifted] A bended bow is lifted in heaven
>
> 14 [stood Albions fiery Prince] from Albions wrathful Prince
>
> 16 [And flam'd fierce meteors round the band of Albion] And flam'd red
> meteors round the land of Albion

Plate b

Reveal the dragon thro' the human; coursing swift as fire
To the close hall of counsel, where his Angel form renews.
In a sweet vale shelter'd with cedars, that eternal stretch
Their unmov'd branches, stood the hall; built when the moon shot forth,
In that dread night when Urizen call'd the stars round his feet;   5
Then burnt the center from its orb, and found a place beneath;
And Earth conglob'd, in narrow room, roll'd round its sulphur Sun.
To this deep valley situated by the flowing Thames;
Where George the third holds council & his Lords & Commons meet:
Shut out from mortal sight the Angel came; the vale was dark   10
With clouds of smoke from the Atlantic, that in volumes roll'd
Between the mountains, dismal visions mope around the house
On chairs of iron, canopied with mystic ornaments
Of life by magic power condens'd; infernal forms art-bound
The council sat; all rose before the aged apparition;   15
His snowy beard that streams like lambent flames down his wide breast
Wetting with tears, & his white garments cast a wintry light.
Then as arm'd clouds arise terrific round the northern drum;
The world is silent at the flapping of the folding banners;
So still terrors rent the house: as when the solemn globe   20
Launch'd to the unknown shore, while Sotha held the northern helm,
Till to that void it came & fell; so the dark house was rent,
The valley mov'd beneath; its shining pillars split in twain,
And its roofs crack acrofs down falling on th' Angelic seats.   24

Plate c

Then Albions Angel rose resolv'd to the cove of armoury:
His shield that bound twelve demons & their cities in its orb,
He took down from its trembling pillar; from its cavern deep,
His helm was brought by Londons Guardian, & his thirsty spear
By the wise spirit of Londons river; silent stood the King breathing with flames: 5
And on his shining limbs they clasp'd the armour of terrible gold.
Infinite Londons awful spires cast a dreadful gleam
Even to rational things beneath and from the palace walls
Around Saint James's glow the fires, even to the city gate.
On the vast stone whose name is Truth he stood, his cloudy shield   10
Smote with his scepter, the scale bound orb loud howld; the eternal pillar

Trembling sunk, an earthquake roll'd along the mofsy pile.
In glittering armour, swift as winds; intelligent as flames;
Four winged heralds mount the furious blasts & blow their trumps
Gold, silver, brafs & iron ardors clamoring rend the shores.   15
Like white clouds rising from the deeps, his fifty-two armies
From the four cliffs of Albion rise, glowing around their Prince;
Angels of cities and of parishes and villages and families,
In armour as the nerves of wisdom, each his station fires.
In opposition dire, a warlike cloud the myriads stood   20
In the red air before the Demon; seen even by mortal men:
Who call it Fancy, & shut the gates of sense, & in their chambers,
Sleep like the dead. But like a constellation ris'n and blazing
Over the rugged ocean; so the Angels of Albion hung
Over the frowning shadow, like a King in arms of gold.   25
Who wept over a den, in which his only son outstretch'd
By rebels hands was slain; his white beard wav'd in the wild wind,
On mountains & cliffs of snow the awful apparition hover'd;
And like the voices of religious dead, heard in the mountains:
When holy zeal scents the sweet valleys of ripe virgin blifs;   30
Such was the hollow voice that o'er the red Demon lamented.   31

The pencil corrections and additions on pl. c in Blake's handwriting are as follows:

1 [Then Albions Angel] *del.*   5 [Londons river; silent stood] *an addition
after* river, *but illegible*   [with flames] fear forth *del.*, damp mists   6 [shining
limbs] aged limbs   7 [dreadful gleam] dreadful cold   8 [Even to rational] Even
on rational   9 [Around Saint James's glow the fires] Around Saint James's chill
& heavy, *a previous correction is deleted and illegible*   11 [th' eternal pillar] eternal *del.*,
but correction illegible   13 [intelligent as flames] intelligent as clouds   15 [iron
ardors clamoring] iron clangors clamoring   17 [glowing around] mustering
around   19 [his station fires] his station holds   21-23 [seen even by mortal
men . . . sleep like the dead] *del.*   22 [& shut . . . & in their chambers] or
shut . . . or in their chambers   24 [Over the] *del.*   25 [like a King] like an
aged King   31 [o'er the red Demon lamented] o'er America lamented.
     A vertical pencil line has been drawn through the text from l. 10 *to the bottom.*

On the verso of the leaf on which this plate is printed is pl. 13 of *America.*

APPENDIX V
CONTEMPORARY RECORDS

[The extracts reprinted here have not been used by any of Blake's biographers, and were too long to be given in section IV of the present bibliography to which they belong.]

Extracts from: *Critical description and analytical review of "Death on the Pale Horse," painted by Benjamin West, P.R.A. with desultory references to the works of some ancient masters, and living British Artists . . . By William Carey . . . London . . . 1817. (See no. 244.)*

i. P. 9. "If Blake had designed a series of subjects from heathen story, his genius could not have made so deep and lasting an impression upon the public, as it has done, by his solemn and affecting series of designs, for *Blair's* poem of The Grave, engraved by that lamented artist, *Schiavonetti*."

ii. Pp. 128-136. "Fuseli in his just and forcible introduction to Blake's noble series of designs for Cromek's edition of Blair's poem of the Grave, remarks that, through frequent repetition—'The Serpent, with its tail in its mouth, from a type of eternity, has become a *child's bauble;* even the nobler idea of Hercules pausing between Virtue and Vice, or the *varied imagery of Death leading his patients to the grave,* owe their effect upon us more to *technical excellence* than allegoric utility.' The context and the prints may warrant a conclusion that it was, from this conviction, Blake, in those imperishable designs, did not attempt to give any defined form of Death the Destroyer, to whom almost any other artist would have assigned a most conspicuous place. The skeleton rising out of the shroud, laid beside the grave, over which an angel sounds the last trumpet, is an emblem of the resurrection of the Dead, not a personification of Death, the insatiate Devourer.

"Having mentioned these drawings, by Blake, I feel their strong hold upon me and must obey the impulse. It would be impossible to enumerate, in a restricted space, the succession of beauties, in these affecting groups; yet I cannot, without self-reproach, and an abandonment of a public duty, pass them in silence. . . . The heart follows the rapt Enthusiast with pleasing sadness, and shares in the more rapid delight of his journey, while his placid but melancholy fancy bids the bloom of Beauty triumph over the shadows of Death; breathes a nameless loveliness on things unearthly; and sheds a mild and holy illumination on the night of the grave.

"I have applied the term 'placid' to the finely tempered genius, as it appears in those affecting compositions, and in the deep serenity expressed in his portrait by the masculine graver of the elder Schiavonetti, from the painting by Phillips. I never had the good fortune to see him; and so entire is the uncertainty, in which he is involved, that after many inquiries, I meet with some in doubt whether he is still in existence. But I have accidentally learned from a Lady, since I commenced these remarks, that

467

he is, certainly, now a resident in London. I have, however, heard enough to warrant my belief that his professional encouragement has been very limited, compared with his powers.

"One fact is clear, that the purchaser of his drawings for the ' Grave,' was not a person of *rank* and *independent fortune*. The world is indebted to the superior taste and liberal spirit of that ingenious engraver, Cromek, as a printseller and publisher for the engravings of these designs. Beyond the circle of artists, I anxiously look round for the Designer's *Patrons*. In an Engraver, now no more, he found a purchaser, and in the Royal Academy, a recommendation to his country. *Posterity will inquire the rest.* . . .

" I would fail in my sense of duty, were I not here to notice a fact, which does honour to the Royal Academy. If my information be not erroneous, and I think it is not, Blake is one of those highly gifted men, who owe the vantage ground of their fame, solely to their own powers. I have heard that he was, originally, an engraver of book-plates. Yet, far from endeavouring to keep him in the background, or question his merits, in 1808, when he executed the drawings for the ' Grave,' eleven Members of the Royal Academy bore testimony, in a public advertisement, to their extraordinary excellence. The name of the Venerable President, West, appeared at the head of the list, followed by Sir William Beechey, Richard Cosway, John Flaxman, Thomas Lawrence, Joseph Nollekens, William Owen, Thomas Stothard, Martin Archer Shee, Henry Thomson and Henry Tresham, Esquires. . . . Phillips, whose best portraits unite a *correct definition of details*, and an admirable truth of resemblance, with grace, spirit, and a noble breadth and harmony of effect, bore testimony to the merits of Blake's drawings, by painting his head for Cromek, the intended publisher of the plates. The vigorous character of nature, in this masterly picture, is a fine lesson for the florid and flimsy *Mannerists* of the day. The countenance expresses the deep calm of a spirit, lifted above the little concerns of this world, and, already, in imagination, winging its way beyond the skies. In this honourable effort of the Royal Academicians to draw the attention of the public to the highest department of invention, portrait painters, sculptors, and historical designers liberally co-operated."

Extract from: *The Cabinet Gallery of Pictures . . . by Allan Cunningham London:* 1833. (See no. 251.)

Vol. 1, pp. 11-13, in connexion with the angels in a picture of " Christ in the Sepulchre" by Guercino, Cunningham gives an anecdote of Blake as follows:

"Blake, who always saw in fancy every form he drew, believed that angels descended to painters of old, and sat for their portraits. When he himself sat to Phillips for that fine portrait so beautifully engraved by Schiavonetti, the painter, in order to obtain the most unaffected attitude, and the most poetic expression, engaged his sitter in a conversation concerning the sublime in art. 'We hear much,' said Phillips, 'of the grandeur of Michael Angelo; from the engravings, I should say he has been over-rated; he could not paint an angel so well as Raphael.' 'He has not been over-rated, Sir,' said Blake, 'and he could paint an angel better than Raphael.' 'Well, but' said the other, 'you never saw any of the paintings of Michael Angelo; and perhaps speak from the opinions of others; your friends may have deceived you.' 'I never saw any of the paintings of Michael Angelo,' replied Blake, 'but I speak from the opinion of a friend who could not be mistaken.' 'A valuable friend truly,' said Phillips, 'and who may he be I pray?' 'The arch-angel Gabriel, Sir,' answered Blake. 'A good authority surely, but you know evil spirits love to assume the looks of good ones; and this may have been done to mislead you.' 'Well now, Sir,' said Blake, 'this is really singular; such were my own suspicions; but they were soon removed—I will tell you how. I was one day reading Young's Night Thoughts, and when I came to that passage which asks "who can paint an angel," I closed the book and cried, "Aye! who can paint an angel?" A voice in the room answered, "Michael Angelo could." "And how do *you* know," I said, looking round me, but I saw nothing save a greater light than usual. "I *know*," said the voice, "for I sat to him: I am the arch-angel Gabriel." "Oho!" I answered, "you are, are you: I must have better assurance than that of a wandering voice; you may be an evil spirit—there are such in the land." "You shall have good assurance," said the voice, "can an evil spirit do this?" I looked whence the voice came, and was then aware of a shining shape, with bright wings, who diffused much light. As I looked, the shape dilated more and more: he waved his hands; the roof of my study opened; he ascended into heaven; he stood in the sun, and beckoning to me, moved the universe. An angel of evil could not have *done that*—it was the arch-angel Gabriel.' The painter marvelled much at this wild story; but he caught from Blake's looks, as he related it, that rapt poetic expression which has rendered his portrait one of the finest of the English school."

Extract from: *Revue Britannique* . . . *Paris* . . . 1833. (See no. 411.)

Pp. 183-186. Les deux plus célèbres habitans de l'hôpital de Bethlem, sont l'incendiaire Martin, frère aîné du peintre Martin, et Blake surnommé le *Voyant*. Lorsque j'eus passé en revue et soumis à mon examen toute cette populace de criminels et d'insensés, je me fis conduire à la cellule de Blake. C'était un homme grand et pâle, parlant bien, vraiment éloquent; dans toutes les annales de la démonologie, rien n'est plus extraordinaire que les visions de Blake.

Il n'était pas victime d'une simple hallucination, il croyait fermement, profondément à la réalité de ses visions ; il conversait avec Michel-Ange, il causait avec Moïse, il dînait avec Sémiramis ; rien de charlatanique chez lui : il était convaincu. Le passé lui ouvrait ses portes ténébreuses ; le monde des ombres accourait chez lui ; tout ce qui avait été grand, étonnant, célèbre, venait poset devant Blake.

Cet homme s'était constitué le peintre des Spectres ; devant lui, sur la table, des crayons et des pinceaux se trouvaient toujours placés, et lui servaient à reproduire les physionomies et les attitudes de ses héros qu'il n'évoquait pas, disait-il, mais qui venaient le prier d'eux-mêmes de faire leurs portraits. J'ai compulsé de gros volumes, remplis de ces effigies parmi lesquelles j'ai remarqué le portrait du Diable et celui de sa mère. Quand j'entrai dans sa cellule, il dessinait une puce dont le spectre à ce qu'il prétendait, venait de lui apparaître.

Edouard III était un de ses habitués les plus assidus ; pour reconnaître cette condescendance du monarque, il avait fait à l'huile, son portrait, en trois séances. Je lui adressai des questions qui devaient l'étonner, mais auxquelles il répondit naïvement et sans aucun trouble. "Ces messieurs se font-ils annoncer ? lui demandai-je. Ont-ils soin de vous envoyer leur carte ?

—Non, mais je les reconnais dès qu'ils paraissent. Je ne m'attendais pas à voir Marc Antoine hier au soir, mais j'ai reconnu le Romain dès qu'il a mis le pied chez moi.

—A quelle heure vos illustres morts vous rendent-ils visite ?

—A une heure ; quelquefois leur visites sont longues, quelquefois courtes. J'ai vu ce pauvre Job avant-hier : il n'a voulu rester que deux minutes ; j'ai à peine eu le temps d'en faire une esquisse que j'ai ensuite copiée à l'eau forte . . . Mais chut . . . voici Richard III !

—Ou le voyer-vous ?

—En face de vous, de l'autre côté de la table. C'est sa première visite.

—Comment savez-vous son nom ?

—Mon esprit le reconnaît, mais je ne sais pas comment.

—Quelle est sa physionomie ?

—Rude, mais belle : je ne vois encore que son profil. Le voici de trois quarts ; ah ! maintenant il se tourne vers moi : il est terrible à contempler.

—Pouvez-vous le questionner ?

—Assurément, que voulez-vous que je lui demande ?

—S'il prétend justifier les meurtres qu'il a commis pendant sa vie ?

—Votre demande lui et déjà parvenue, nous conversons d'ame à ame, par intuition et par magnétisme. Nous n'avons pas besoin de paroles.

—Quelle est la réponse de Sa Majesté ?

—La voici, un peu plus longue qu'il ne me lá donnée : vous ne comprendriez pas le langage des esprits. Il vous dit que ce que vous appelez meutre et carnage n'est rien ; qu'en égorgeant quinze ou vingt mille hommes on ne leur fait aucun mal ; que la partie mortelle de leur être non seulement se conserve, mais passe dans un meilleur monde, et que l'homme assassiné qui adresserait des reproches à son assassin se rendrait coupable d'ingratitude, puisque ce dernier n'a fait que lui procurer un logement plus commode et une existence plus parfaite. Mais laissez-moi, il pose très bien maintenant, et si vous dites un mot il s'en ira."

Je quittai cet homme auquel on n'avait rien à reprocher et qui ne manquait pas de talent comme graveur et comme dessinateur.

Extracts from : Dibdin's *Reminiscences of a Literary Life. London.* 1836. (See no. 254.)

Pp. 784-789. "It was during the progress of working at my Decameron, that I received visits from two Artists of very different complexion and degrees of reputation: I mean Northcote and Blake. The former was the pupil and biographer of Reynolds—the latter . . . pupil of no Master, but a most extraordinary artist in his own particular element: although I believe he professed to have been a pupil of Flaxman and Fuseli—artists, as opposite in all respects as a chaste severity differs from a wild exuberance of style. . . . I soon found the amiable but illusory Blake far beyond my ken or sight. In an instant he in his 'third heaven'—flapped by the wings of seraphs, such as his own genius only could shape, and his own pencil embody. The immediate subject of our discussion—and for which indeed he professed to have in some measure visited me—was, 'the minor poems of Milton.' Never were such 'dreamings' poured forth as were poured forth by my original visitor:— his stature mean, his head big and round, his forehead broad and high, his eyes blue, large and lambent—such as my friend Mr. Phillips has represented him upon his imperishable canvas.* 'What think you, Mr. Blake, of Fuseli's Lycidas—asleep, beneath the opening eyelids of the morn?' 'I don't remember it.' 'Pray see it, and examine it carefully. It seems to me to be the pencil of poetry employed to give intelligence and expression to the pen of the poet'—or words to this effect were, I think, pronounced. I learnt afterwards that my Visitor had seen it—but thought it 'too tame'—tameness from Fuseli! I told Mr. Blake that our common friend, Mr. Masquerier, had induced me to purchase his 'Songs of Innocence,' and that I

* This portrait, which gives more elevation and dignity to the original than he should seem actually to have possessed, is nevertheless a most faithful and happy resemblance. And Schiavonetti's burin has done ample justice to the *pencil* of the painter. There is yet *another* "portrait of the man," as well worth the contemplation—and that is, the brief, but spirited, and most exceedingly interesting Biography of him by Allan Cunningham, Esq.

had no disposition to 'repent my bargain.' * This extraordinary man sometimes—but in good sooth very rarely—reached the sublime; but the sublime and the grotesque seemed, somehow or the other, to be for ever amalgamated in his imagination; and the choice or result was necessarily doubtful. Yet there are few books of which I love to turn over the leaves, more assiduously and carefully, than ' Young's Night Thoughts,' emblazoned by his truly original pencil.† When Blake entered the arena with *Stothard*, as a rival in depicting the *Dramatis Personæ* of Chaucer's Canterbury Tales, he seems to have absolutely lost his wits; his pencil was as inferior to that of the former, as his burin was to that of *Cromek*, who engraved Stothard's immortal picture.

* Mr. Cunningham has judiciously quoted one of these songs, among the prettiest, which shall find a place here—from my *own* copy of it thrown by in a portfolio some twenty years ago:

> " Passing down the valleys wild,
>   Piping songs of pleasant glee,
> On a cloud I saw a child,
>   And he laughing said to me," etc.

† In the original conformation of these "Reminiscences" I had intended to have devoted an entire chapter to the *Fine Arts*, and therein to have given Blake not more than his due. Under this impression, I wrote to my friend, Mr. D'Israeli, to furnish me with the loan of such materials of this master as I knew him to be in the possession of. His reply not only staggered me, but induced me to abandon nearly my whole intention in regard to Blake. It shall here tell its own tale, because I do not know any other pen which could tell that tale with greater felicity of diction.

> " *Bradenham House, Wycombe,*
> " 24 *July* 1835.
>
> " My dear friend,
>   " It is quite impossible to transmit to you the one hundred and sixty designs I possess of Blake's; and as impossible, if you had them, to convey every precise idea of such an infinite variety of these wondrous deliriums of his fine and wild creative imagination. Heaven, hell, and earth, and the depths below, are some of the scenes he seems alike to have tenanted; but the invisible world also busies his fancy; aereal beings which could only float in his visions, and unimaginable chimeras, such as you have never viewed, lie by the side of his sunshiny people. You see some innocent souls winding about blossoms—for others the massive sepulchre has opened, and the waters beneath give up their secrets. The finish, the extreme delicacy of his pencil, in his light gracile forms, marvellously contrast with the ideal figures of his mystic allegories; sometimes playful, as the loveliness of the arabesques of Raffaelle. Blake often breaks into the ' *terribil via* ' of *Michael Angelo*, and we start amid a world too horrified to dwell in. Not the least extraordinary fact of these designs is, their colouring, done by the artist's own hand, worked to his fancy; and the verses, which are often remarkable for their sweetness and their depth of feeling. I feel the imperfection of my general description. Such singular productions require a commentary.
>
> " Believe me, with regard,
> " Your sincere well wisher,
> " I. D'Israeli."

Extract from: *The Scottish Chiefs. By Miss Jane Porter. London.* [1841.]
(See no. 257.)

POSTSCRIPT TO APPENDIX, ADDED MAY 1841.

"The preceding note having been appended to the first edition of this work, at the time of its answering date; an extraordinary circumstance which occurred a few years afterwards, regarding certain portraitures of Sir William Wallace and Robert Bruce, the author of these pages is tempted to repeat now, as being a something strange and romantic story. The original relater of it was Mr. Blake, a young painter of remarkable talents; but which were, at times, carried away into wild fancies; a mirage of waking dreams, which he gravely asserted, on describing them, were real visions from the departed world. Soon after the publication of the 'Scottish Chiefs,' his ardent nature had deeply interested him in their fate; but most particularly in that of Wallace; of whose unjust doom he was often in the habit of speaking to a friend of the author of the book, and with a force of language, and indignation at the fact, as if the noble victim's death had been only an event of yesterday.

"In one of my friend's calls on the young painter, he found him in an almost breathless ecstasy, which he explained to him, by telling him that he had just achieved two sketches—one of Sir William Wallace, the other of his enemy, Edward the First! —Both chiefs having actually appeared to him successively, and had successively stood, at his earnest request, to allow him to make a hasty sketch of their forms.

"While he related this, he placed a small canvas, of the common portrait size, on his easel, before my friend; on which was drawn, in a bold and admirable manner, the head of a young warrior in the prime of his days: as Wallace is described to have been, even at the time in which he was cut off. There was neither helmet, nor any covering on his head, excepting the rich golden-tinted light-hair, that waved high and loosely from off his broad and very elevated forehead. The face was, nearly a front view, remarkably handsome—open in its expression, and full of an ardent, generous courage: the blue eye being bright and expanded, and the lips of a noble contour, seemed cheering his devoted followers to deeds of glory. All was gallant sunshine over that fine countenance, which, while you looked on it, might almost induce you to believe the reality of the vision. Also, the high bearing of its corresponding neck and chest. The first was entirely bare; and the latter simply discovered a low breastplate of plain workmanship, half covered by his plaid, broached on the shoulder. This was all which was even outlined in this mysterious portrait. For the painter told my friend, that having turned to dip his pencil for a further touch, when he looked up again, the vision was gone!—While my friend was contemplating this extraordinary portrait, its enraptured artist had described its origin, in this wise:—
'He was sitting, meditating, as he had often done, on the heroic actions and hard

fate of the Scottish hero, when, like a flash of lightning, a noble form stood before him; which he instantly knew, by a something within himself, to be Sir William Wallace. He felt it was a spiritual appearance; which might vanish away as instantly as it came; and, transported at the sight, he besought the hero to remain a few moments till he might sketch him. The warrior Scot, in this vision, seemed as true to his historical mental picture, as his noble shade was to the manly bearing of his recorded person; for, with his accustomed courtesy, he smiled on the young painter;—and the sketch was outlined, with a tint or two besides. But, while eagerly proceeding, the artist bent his head once too often, to replenish his pencil; and turning again, to pursue the noble contour, the spirit of the "stalworth knight" had withdrawn from mortal ken. But (Blake proceeded to say), it had not left a vacancy! Edward the First stood in its place; armed from head to foot, in a close and superb suit of mail; but with the visor of his helmet open!'

"The artist, it appears, had as little difficulty in recognising the royal hero; as, when his heart, as well as his eyes, bowing before the august figure just departed, told him it was the Caledonian patriot he beheld. His English loyalty, however, made him rise before the royal apparition. Nevertheless, he saluted the monarch with the same earnest privilege of enthusiastic genius, which had dictated his request to the Scottish chief; and he asked the stern-looking, but majestic warrior-king of England, to allow him to make a corresponding sketch. This too, was accorded. And he had arrived at about the same point, as in the former portrait, when the British hero also disappeared;—and Blake was left—not so disappointed at not having accomplished all he wished, as enraptured at having been permitted to behold two such extraordinary characters; and to have thus far, identified their personal presence to himself; and to the world, to all posterity! For such was his own conviction. The vast expense of life's energies, wrought in this young man, by the over-active exercise of his talents; and the burning enthusiasm, which almost ever over-stimulated their action; swiftly consumed his constitution; and not very long after the painting of these two visionary portraits, he died of a rapid decline—my friend purchased them both; and subsequently showed them to me; recounting the little history, I have just repeated. And, I confess, I looked upon them with no small pleasure; for each bore a strong resemblance to the pictures my mind had before imbibed of both heroes, from all the historical descriptions I had ever heard, or read. There is, however, a roughly-visaged old head, that I have often seen, in rude oil-painting, and in equally rude engraving, which is pretended to be the portrait of Sir William Wallace. But it does not in any one respect, answer to the historical, or traditionary accounts of the knight's person; excepting that it has part of a coat-of-mail on its breast, and the usual tartan plaid, which marks a Scottish warrior of any age. But it has two contradictions to attested facts, which completely disprove its authenticity as a likeness of that hero. It is the head of a weather-beaten, and evidently thick-set elderly man, beyond fifty years of age. Whereas, Wallace was hardly more than thirty, when he died on the scaffold. His figure too, was eminently tall and well-proportioned; and his hair was noted for being 'yellow like gold.' While, on the reverse, the beard, rough eye-brows, and scant locks of the pretended old portrait of the hero, are dark—almost amounting to black. That it may be a picture of some distinguished personage of the name of Wallace, is very likely; from the great respect in which it is even now held in this country—(and particularly by sea-men; who have been known to keep the print hung up in the cabin of their little vessels, by way of a talisman against storms, or enemies!)—therefore, I see not why the real original of the memorial in question, may not have been some celebrated naval defender of the Scottish sea, or shore, of the family of William Wallace; but of a later period than himself; as the costume of the portrait, evidently appears of a more modern date.—(1841.)"

Extract from: *Life of Thomas Stothard R.A. By Mrs. Bray. London.* 1851. (See no. 263.)

Pp. 20-21. "In the early times of which I am now speaking, Stothard would occasionally spend a few days with his friends in sailing up the Medway, landing and sketching as they pleased. In one of these excursions he was accompanied by his old friend Mr. Ogleby, and Blake, that amiable, eccentric, and greatly gifted artist, who produced so many works indicative of a high order of genius, and sometimes no less of an unsound mind. Whilst the trio were one day engaged with the pencil on shore, they were suddenly surprised by the appearance of some soldiers, who very unceremoniously made them prisoners, under the suspicion of their being spies for the French government; as their country was then at war with France. In vain did they plead that they were only there sketching for their own amusement; it was insisted upon that they could be doing nothing less than surveying for purposes inimical to the safety of Old England. Their provisions were brought on shore, and a tent was formed for them of their sails, suspended over the boat-hook and oars, placed as uprights in the ground. There they were detained, with a sentinel placed over them, until intelligence could be received from certain members of the Royal Academy, to whom they appealed, to certify they were really peaceable subjects of his Majesty King George, and not spies for France. Stothard made a very spirited pen and ink drawing of this scene, whilst under detention. On their liberation, they spent a merry hour with the commanding officer, to whom the artist remarked, that an opportunity had been given him for making a sketch he had not anticipated; whilst Ogleby declared that once being taken prisoner was quite enough for him; he would go out no more on such perilous expeditions."

Extract from: *The Athenæum, Dec.* 1863. *Stothard and Blake. By Robert T. Stothard.* (See no. 420.)

An account of Blake's relations with Stothard and Cromek by Stothard's son:

"I cannot admit Mr. Gilchrist's assertion that there was any apparent ill-will between my father and Blake; for on one occasion I was sent to Blake with a message from my father, when I found him living in a court off the Strand, and met him on the stairs, saying to me 'he had a battle with the devil below to obtain the coals,' which seemed to me to indicate madness.

"Cromek was at that time very frequently at my father's, either for the purpose of getting him to touch a proof for him, or on other matters of which I then knew not the exact nature. I have heard it stated by my father that Cromek got Blake to make for him a series of drawings from Blair's 'Grave'; Cromek found, and explained to my father, that he had etched one of the subjects but so indifferently and so carelessly [see Cumberland's 'Thoughts on Outline' as an instance in that particular branch of his (Blake's) carelessness as an engraver] that he employed Schrovenetti [*sic*] to engrave them. Cromek's success by their sale induced him to speculate further, and he employed my father (who had no time for going about and seeing what other artists were employed upon or engaged in, and therefore his seeing Blake's design of the 'Pilgrimage to Canterbury' is doubtful) to paint that picture for him soon after he had completed the Burleigh staircase commission for the Marquis of Exeter. Whether Cromek had seen it or not dates will prove : this of which I am speaking was in 1804-5. Cromek was daily with my father, living then as he was opposite nearly, at 64, and my father at 28, Newman Street.

"What I think proper to state, and as it may not be uninteresting to those who are lovers of Art (for I was commissioned to write my father's Life) I shall begin, as will be seen in it, by stating that Cromek agreed to give my father for a painting from Chaucer 100 l, or 100 guineas, as that author was a favourite with him, so much so that he could often relate stories from him. They determined on the 'Pilgrimage to Canterbury,' for there had been a little vignette of the same subject engraved for him, I think, before. In 1805 or 1806 the painting was shown to the public at Cromek's house . . ."

APPENDIX VI

THE PORTRAITS OF WILLIAM AND CATHERINE BLAKE

[The following catalogue of the portraits of William Blake has been compiled in the belief that it will be found useful by students of his life. There can be few other poets or artists of whom so interesting a series of portraits has survived. In all probability the present list is not absolutely complete, but it contains several which have not been noticed before, notably those by Flaxman, Barry, Harlow, and Ensom. Reproductions of several are given in the present work, and they have been chosen from among those which are little known or have not been reproduced anywhere else. Two engravings with which I am not acquainted have been mentioned by other writers, namely, a portrait inscribed " del A. L. Dick Sc" (Grolier Cat., no. 148), and another engraved by Schiavonetti after J. Jackson, R.A. (Nat. Gal. Cat., p. 65); but as these may merely have been made after the well-known painting by Phillips I have not included them here. Nor have I included portraits such as the composite drawing given by E. J. Ellis in his edition of the *Poetical Works* (see no. 170). At the end I have added a list of four portraits of Mrs. Blake, the first of which has not been recorded before.]

PORTRAITS OF WILLIAM BLAKE

Life-mask

1 Life-mask of Blake's head, 30 cm. high, cast in plaster by J. Deville, the phrenologist, in 1823, age 66.

The original cast, dated 1823, was in the Linnell collection, with which it was sold at Christie's on March 15, 1918 (lot 171, Martin, 42 gns.).
A replica, or copy, was in the possession of the late Sir William Blake Richmond, R.A. (Nat. Gal. Cat., no. 105). The cast is usually described as having been made when Blake was " about fifty," but the date on the original shows that actually it was done when he was in his sixty-sixth year.

Reproductions:
    i. Ellis and Yeats, vol. II, 1893. Profile.
    ii. Perugini's *Selections from Blake's Works*, 1901. Three-quarter face.
    iii. Russell, *Letters*, 1906. Full face.
    iv. Ellis, *The Real Blake*, 1907. Four views.

Oil Paintings

2 Painting in oils, 88 × 68 cm., by Thomas Phillips, R.A., 1807, age 50.

Seated figure, half-length, three-quarters face to right, holding a pencil in the right hand.
Now in the National Portrait Gallery.

Engraved copies:
    i. On copper by L. Schiavonetti. Frontispiece to Blair's *Grave*, 1808 (see no. 81).
    ii. On steel by W. C. Edwards. In Cunningham's *Lives of the Painters*, 1830 (see no. 249).

Reproductions from Phillips's painting or from Schiavonetti's engraving are too numerous to specify.

3   Painting in oils by Thomas Phillips, R.A., 1807, age 50.

Head and shoulders, three-quarters face to right. A finished oil sketch for no. 2.

Exhibited at the Burlington Club in 1876, being then the property of J. R. P. Kirby. Later acquired by H. Buxton Forman, for whom it was engraved on steel by W. B. Scott. Present owner not known.

Engraved copy: Engraving on steel, 19 × 14 cm., by W. B. Scott. Done in 1881 for H. Buxton Forman. One hundred impressions were taken, 25 remarque proofs and 75 ordinary proofs, on India paper. The plate was used again as frontis-piece to *Literary Anecdotes of the Nineteenth Century*, 1895 (see no. 319).

Painting in miniature

4   Miniature on ivory, 12.5 × 10 cm., by John Linnell, 1827, age 70.

Head and shoulders in profile to the right.

Exhibited at the Tate Gallery in 1913 (Nat. Gal. Cat., no. 111; Manchester Cat., no. 170). Sold with the Linnell collection at Christie's on March 15, 1918 (no. 170, Carfax, 70 gns.). Now in the possession of Mr. T. H. Riches.

Engraved copy: By T. H. Jeens. In Gilchrist's *Life*, 1863 and 1880, vol. 1 (see nos. 270 and 285).

Reproductions:
> The original miniature in Story's *William Blake*, 1893 (see no. 312).
> The engraving by Jeens in Gilchrist's *Life*, 1907 (no. 345).

Drawings and Studies

5   Pencil sketch of Blake as a young man, 15 × 10 cm., by his wife, Catherine, 1785, age 28.

Profile looking to the right, with flame-like hair.

Given by Mrs. Blake to a friend who sold it about 1886 to Daniels, print-seller, Mortimer Street. It was acquired by Mr. Herbert P. Horne, and is now in the collection of Mr. Edward Marsh, C.M.G. Exhibited at the Tate Gallery in 1913 (Nat. Gal. Cat., no. 104; Manchester Cat., no. 169A).

Reproductions:
> i. In Ellis and Yeats, vol. III, 1893.
> ii. In the present work.

6 Outline drawing in pencil, 13.5 × 11.5 cm., by James Barry, R.A., about 1790 (?), age 33.

>   Three-quarter length, seated with legs crossed showing an indication of knee breeches. The right elbow rests on a table ; the hand hangs down and holds a pencil. The left hand rests on the knee. Not quite full face, hair long and thrown back from the forehead. Date unknown, but probably about 1790. The drawing was badly creased and fragile, so that mounting was necessary. It was inscribed below : " Portrait of Blake by James Barry," but this came away in mounting. The outlines, which were very faint, were carefully pencilled over by John Fullwood, R.B.A., about 1903.
>   Now in the possession of Mr. E. J. Shaw of Walsall.
>   The drawing has not been reproduced.
>   There is also a drawing of Barry by Blake (see no. 687).

7 Pencil drawing, 13 × 11 cm., by John Flaxman, about 1803, age 46.

>   Head and shoulders, full face.
>   In a sketchbook containing a series of 34 studies by Flaxman of his contemporaries. Sold at Hodgson's, Jan. 25, 1905 (lot 372, Quaritch). Offered in one of Quaritch's catalogues in 1910 for 5 guineas. Bought by the late Charles Fairfax Murray, and given by him some time afterwards to the Fitzwilliam Museum, Cambridge.
>
>   *Reproduction* : In the present work.

8 Pencil drawing, about 12 × 10 cm., by John Flaxman, R.A., about 1803, age 46.

>   Profile, looking to the left.
>   Inserted in the volume containing Blake's designs for Gray's *Poems* (see no. 8).
>   The property of the Duke of Hamilton.
>   The drawing has not been reproduced.

9 Pencil drawing touched with ink, 10 × 10 cm., by Thomas Phillips, R.A., 1807, age 50.

>   A study for no. 2 above.
>   Exhibited at the Grolier Club in 1905 (Grolier Cat., no. 140).
>   The drawing has not been reproduced.

10   Pencil sketch, 8 × 8 cm., by himself, about 1810, age 53.

    Head in profile looking to the left. Sketched by Blake on p. 67 of the *Rossetti MS.* (see no. 5). The property of Mr. W. A. White.

    Reproduction: In the present work.

11   Drawing in black crayon, 21.5 × 17 cm., by George Harlow, about 1810 (?), age 53.

    Half-length figure, nearly full face. The hair is thrown back and hangs low down on the neck. The left hand holds a sheet of paper. On the back of the drawing is inscribed: " From Mr Fuseli's sale. William Blake, drawn from life by G. Harlow."
    Now in the possession of Mr. E. J. Shaw of Walsall.
    The drawing has not been reproduced.

12   Pen and ink drawing by William Ensom, 1815, age 58.

    This drawing is recorded in the D.N.B. (see no. 293), but it is not known to me and has not been reproduced as far as I am aware.

13   Pencil drawing, 18.5 × 14.5 cm., by John Linnell, 1820, age 63.

    Head and shoulders, three-quarters face looking downwards to the right; eyes closed. Inscribed at the bottom: " Portrait of Wm Blake 1820. J. L. fec^t."
    Exhibited at the Tate Gallery in 1913 (Nat. Gal. Cat., no. 106; Manchester Cat., no. 175). Sold with the Linnell collection at Christie's, March 15, 1918 (in lot 169, Carfax, 85 gns.). Now in the possession of Mr. T. H. Riches.

    Reproduction: In the present work.

14   Pencil study, 12.5 × 9 cm., by John Linnell, about 1820, age 63.

    A slight sketch of Blake's head in profile, looking to the right. Marked at the top: " Mr Blake," and signed " J. L." at the bottom.
    Exhibited at the Tate Gallery in 1913 (Nat. Gal. Cat., no. 107, i; Manchester Cat., no. 173, i). Sold with the Linnell collection at Christie's in the same lot as the preceding. Now in the possession of Mr. T. H. Riches.

    Reproduction: Story's *Life of Linnell*, 1892, vol. 1, p. 243 (see no. 306).

15 Pencil studies, 12.5 × 9.5 cm., by John Linnell, about 1820, age 63.

Two studies of Blake's head, one above the other, in profile, looking to the right. Also a study of his right eye and eyebrow. Marked "Mr. Blake," and signed "J. L." at the bottom.

Exhibited at the Tate Gallery in 1913 (Nat. Gal. Cat., no. 107, ii; Manchester Cat., no. 173, ii). Sold with the Linnell collection at Christie's in the same lot as the two preceding. Now in the possession of Mr. T. H. Riches.

These studies have not been reproduced.

16 Pencil sketch, 10 × 12 cm., by John Linnell, 1821, age 64.

Half-length, seated full-face at a table with folded arms. Inscribed at the bottom: "Mr. Blake Sep^t 12 1821. J. L. fec^t."

Exhibited at the Tate Gallery in 1913 (Nat. Gal. Cat., no. 108; Manchester Cat., no. 172A). Sold with the Linnell collection at Christie's in the same lot as the three preceding. Now in the possession of Mr. T. H. Riches.

This sketch has not been reproduced.

17 Pencil sketch, 11 × 17 cm., of Blake and Varley arguing, 1821.

Half-length figures seated at a table. Varley on the right talks with animated gestures; Blake, seen in profile on the left, leans back listening. The figures are marked respectively "Mr. Blake," and "Mr. Varley." At the left-hand bottom corner is written "Cirencester Place," and at the right, "J. L. Sep^t 1821."

Exhibited at the Tate Gallery in 1913 (Nat. Gal. Cat., no. 109; Manchester Cat., no. 172). Sold with the Linnell collection at Christie's in the same lot as the four preceding. Now in the possession of Mr. T. H. Riches.

Reproductions:
    i. In Story's *Life of Linnell*, 1893, vol. 1, p. 162 (much reduced; see no. 306).
    ii. In the present work (full size).

18 Pencil drawing, 18 × 11.5 cm., by John Linnell, about 1825, age 68.

Half-length figure, seen three-quarters face to the right, with his hands clasped in front, and wearing a tall broad-brimmed hat. Hampstead Heath in the background. Inscribed at the bottom: "Wm Blake at Hampstead. J. L. fec^t.", and on the back of the drawing Linnell has written: " Mr. Blake. On the Hill before our cottage at Hampstead, c. 1825, I guess."

Exhibited at the Tate Gallery in 1913 (Nat. Gal. Cat., no. 110; Manchester Cat., no. 174). Sold with the Linnell collection at Christie's in the same lot with the five preceding. Now in the possession of Mr. T. H. Riches.

> *Reproductions*:
>   i. In Story's *Life of Linnell*, 1893, vol. 1, p. 230 (reduced; see no. 306).
>   ii. In the present work (full size).

19 Drawing in brush and pencil, 11 × 7 cm., by Frederick Tatham, 1827, age 70.

Head in profile to the right. Side by side to the right is a profile of Blake as a young man derived from no. 5. Inscribed below: " Portraits of William Blake." Bound up with the MS. of Tatham's *Life* (see no. 339). Now in the possession of General Archibald Stirling.

> *Reproductions*:
>   i. Ellis and Yeats, vol. 1, 1893.
>   ii. Richter's *William Blake*, 1906 (see no. 343).
>   iii. de Selincourt's *William Blake*, 1909 (see no. 359).

20 Pen and ink sketch, 16.5 × 11.5 cm., by John Linnell, 1827, age 70.

Head and shoulders, in profile to the right. Signed: " J. Linnell fec." This is the first sketch for Linnell's miniature, no. 3 above.

Exhibited at the Grolier Club in 1905 (Grolier Cat., no. 141).

This sketch has not been reproduced.

21 Pen and ink sketch, 7 × 5 cm., by Frederick Tatham, done from memory in 1860.

Head in profile looking to the left. Sketched from memory by Tatham for Alexander Gilchrist at 6 Great Cheyne-row in 1860. It is probably based on Blake's profile of himself in the *Rossetti MS.* (see sketch no. 9 above) which it closely resembles.

> *Reproduction*: H. H. Gilchrist's *Anne Gilchrist*, 1887, p. 131 (see no. 294).

PORTRAITS OF CATHERINE BLAKE

1   Pen and ink sketch, 6.5 × 5 cm., by William Blake, about 1785 (?).

    Head and shoulders in profile. Curls hang over the forehead and down the neck. Round the sketch are rough notes of flying figures, groups, and other suggestions for compositions. Now in the possession of Mr. E. J. Shaw of Walsall.

    The sketch has not been reproduced.

2   Sketch, 8 × 6 cm., by William Blake, about 1793.

    Pencil drawing of Mrs. Blake's head, three-quarter face, looking to the right. Contained in the *Rossetti MS.* (see no. 5). The subject is represented as a young-looking woman, and the sketch must therefore belong to the earlier period at which Blake was using the book.

    Reproduction: In Gilchrist's *Life*, 1880, vol. 1, facing p. 375.

3   Pencil drawing, 25.5 × 20.5 cm., by William Blake, about 1802 (?).

    Half-length figure, seated, wearing a cap and looking down at her hands which are on her lap. Inscribed by Blake at the right-hand lower corner: "Catherine," and in another writing: "Mrs Blake, Drawn by Blake." Drawn on the back of a leaf from Hayley's *Ballads*, 1802.

    Exhibited at the Burlington Club in 1876 (item 110 in the catalogue), being then the property of Mrs. Gilchrist. Exhibited again at the Tate Gallery in 1913 (Nat. Gal. Cat., no. 112; Manchester Cat., no. 171). Now in the possession of Miss A. G. E. Carthew, London.

    Reproduction: In Gilchrist's *Life*, 1880, vol. 1, p. 361.

4 Pencil drawing, 9 × 9 cm., by George Richmond after a drawing by Frederick Tatham, about 1830.

Head and shoulders, almost full face, wearing a cap. The subject has the appearance of age. Bound up with the MS. of Tatham's *Life* (see no. 339). Now in the possession of General Archibald Stirling.

Reproductions :
  i. In Gilchrist's *Life*, 1880, vol. 1, p. 412.
  ii. In Gilchrist's *Life*, 1907, facing p. 386.

THE END

INDEX

[The numbers in the Index refer to the pages.]

INDEX

ERRATA

P. 10, l. 3 from bottom, and p. 23, l. 7.   *For* " Mrs. Mathews " *read*
" Mrs. Mathew."

P. 59, l. 4.   *For* " MDCCXLIX " *read* " MDCCXLIV."

P. 84, l. 10 from bottom.   *For* " Mr. K. A. Esdaile " *read* " Mrs. K. A.
Esdaile."

P. 212, l. 11 from bottom.   *For* " Phillips " *read* " Philips."

P. 404, l. 3.   *For* " Carey " *read* " Cary."

LONDON : CHARLES WHITTINGHAM AND GRIGGS, LTD.
CHISWICK PRESS, TOOKS COURT, CHANCERY LANE.